DICTIONARY

⊰⟐ OF THE ⟐⊱

AMERICAN WEST

OVER 5,000 TERMS
AND EXPRESSIONS FROM
AARIGAA! TO ZOPILOTE

WIN BLEVINS

SASQUATCH BOOKS
SEATTLE

This book is offered

in honor

of the sacred pipe.

Printed in the United States of America
Distributed in Canada by Raincoast Books, Ltd.
07 06 05 04 03 02 01   6 5 4 3 2 1

Cover design: Karen Schober
Interior design and composition: Kate Basart
Copy editing: Kris Fulsaas

Library of Congress Cataloging in Publication Data
Blevins, Winfred.
        Dictionary of the American West : over 5000 terms and expressions from Aarigaa! to Zopilote / Win Blevins.—2nd ed., expanded and rev.
        p.   cm
Includes bibliographical references .
ISBN 1-57061-304-4
English language—Dialects—West (U.S.)—Dictionaries. 2. Popular culture—West (U.S.)—Dictionaries. 3. Americanisms—West (U.S.)—Dictionaries. 4. West (U.S.)—Dictionaries. I. Title.
PE2970.W4 B5 2001
427'.978'03—dc21   2001040063

SASQUATCH BOOKS / 615 Second Avenue / Seattle, Washington 98104
(206)467-4300 / www.SasquatchBooks.com / books@SasquatchBooks.com

Contents

Acknowledgments

Aside from my assistant, Ruth Valsing, my primary aide in writing this book has been Ernie Bulow of Gallup, New Mexico, a master of many subjects. My first consultant on Indian peoples has been the Honorable Clyde M. Hall of Fort Hall, Idaho, man of medicine. My constant telephone advisors were novelist Richard Wheeler and historian Dale Walker. Thanks, Ernie, Clyde, Richard, and Dale.

I have depended principally on the following writers and Westerners in the areas of specialty indicated: the late Fred Bean, Spanish; Lenore Carroll, frontier women; Whit Clayton, Mormons; Robert Conley, Cherokees; John Byrne Cooke, Spanish; Fred Crane, cowboys, and rodeo; Murphy Fox, mountain men and Indians; the late Francis Fugate, food; Michael and Kathleen Gear, Indians; Dick James, Mormons and mountain men; Joe Marshall, Lakotas; W. C. Jameson, land forms, Texas, Spanish; Judi A. Myers, Wyoming; Howard Rides-at-the-Door, Blackfeet; Shelley Ritthaler, ranching; Sam Weller, Mormons.

I have also depended on Josi Arando, Patricia Boda, Rob Bosworth, Katie Breeze, Irene Brown, Frank Caplette, Jenna Caplette, Don Coldsmith, Max Cordova, Frank Craighead, Bill Cunningham, David Dary, Paula Dimmler, Raymond Dorr, Katie Duffy, Loren Estleman, Max Evans, Rush Fish, Kathy Gaudry, Lewis Graft, Bill Gulick, Linda Hasselstrom, Charlotte Hinger, Douglas Hirt, Dick House, Terry Johnston, John Joerschke, Elmer Kelton, Fred Kingwill, William Kittredge, Reginald and Gladys Laubin (both now across the big divide), Marcia Landreth, Preston Lewis, Tex Little, Mel Marshall, Gary McCarthy, Doris Meredith, Marlys Millhiser, Candy Moulton, Larry Names, Loren Nauman, Joan Nay, Jim Overstreet, Jane Pattie, Joseph Porter, Louis Price, Bryon Price, Richard Rattenberg, Dusty Richards, Jerry and Cena Richeson, Joyce Roach, Jory Sherman, Chris Shutz, Marc Simmons, Virginia Squier, Gary Svee, Claude Tabor, Verland Taylor, Claudia Thompson, Jim Bob Tinsley, Jenna Williams, Bryan Woolley, and Nellie Yost.

I acknowledge gratefully also the help of hundreds of Westerners who've talked to me about language over the years. It's been an education.

The Western Writers of America, both the organization and the individual members, have provided essential cheer and support.

My assistant, Ruth Valsing, went above and beyond the call of duty. Without her dedication, this book would not have been completed.

My most special thanks goes to my wife, Meredith, who makes life good, and my family. With little interest in the subject, they cheerfully put up with endless hours of my talk about good language and bad, which should earn them canonization.

Author's Note for the Second Edition

This book is an expanded and revised edition of the original, published in 1993. I have included Alaska, have increased the number terms relating to the Pacific Coast states generally, and have sought out new terms of contemporary American Indian English. Hundreds of main entries have also been rewritten.

I hope readers find the book useful, and have fun reading it.

—Win Blevins, Canyonlands, May 2001

Introduction

Dictionary of the American West was conceived while listening to writers gripe. Some years ago, a group of writers at a convention of the Western Writers of America fell to talking about how our editors didn't understand Western words. The funniest and most appalling story was about an editor who knew *buckskins* is a word for Davy Crockett deerskin clothes but didn't know it's a color of horse. So she wrote in the margin of a manuscript, "I know buckskins get old and stiff and smelly, but I'll be damned if I'll believe they can whinny or canter."

Like other minorities in this country, Westerners speak a language that has arisen in their particular circumstances to suit their special needs and ways of seeing things. As with black English or the lingo of, say, lobster men or truck drivers, it's only half familiar to other Americans. So when millions of tourists appear each summer, they get confused. (If they're told to walk along the *bench* to the *coulee* and follow the coulee to the *divide*, they may even get seriously lost.) Readers of the vast literature about the West need help. I well remember feeling bewildered when I first came to the West thirty-five years ago, and feeling still more bewildered when I began to explore Indian cultures and the culture of my own ancestors, the Cherokees. The purpose of this book is to mark the trail clearly.

For me the dictionary became a passion. Words enabled me to grasp the mind-set of the people who used them. The many words for irrigation ditches and the men who oversee them brought me a feeling for this lifeline of people that allows them to grow their beans and melons and at the same time connects them to the river. The speech of the mountain men—*Wagh, hoss, mind your hair now!*—took me into their dangerous and intoxicating world. Indian people's ways of talking took me home to their ways of thinking. The tumult of words for cowboy gear led me to understand the complexity of that under-appreciated job, as well as the cowboy's pride in his equipment. Altogether I made intimate acquaintance with the West, and came to see more deeply and clearly this place and these peoples, those still living and those gone over, of my heart's circle. So the least personal kind of book, a dictionary, became very personal.

From the beginning I've known that the West has been thoroughly misrepresented. Misrepresented by the newspaper reporters who sensationalized it, by the artists who romanticized it, by the Wild West shows that turned it into caricature. It's been elevated (or lowered) to myth by Zane Grey, Max Brand, Louis L'Amour, and the other novelists. Reinvented by grand movie directors like John Ford, Howard Hawks, and Sam Peckinpah. Turned now into a joke of an icon by drugstore cowboys and the likes of Marlboro and Busch Beer.

Sometimes I want to grab people and say, But if you'd only look at the *real* West!

Adventure and daring? The mountain men top all for that. Heroism and villainy? How about the Donner party? Tragedy? Observe the Lakotas and Cheyennes fighting the U.S. military for their very existence. Nor is all this fascinating stuff historic. Getting to know today's deserts, less forbidding as they are—the curious plants, the odd critters, the wondrous land forms—has been a great experience for me. Everything strange, wonderful, inspiring, amazing, outlandish, romantic, extravagant, fascinating is in the real West, both yesterday and today. The myth is puny beside it.

Human cultures, I've discovered, reveal themselves intimately in their language. To carry some of that insight to the reader, I've gone well beyond listing mere denotations of words to tell the lore, the stories, the human meanings behind them, even to suggest the way of seeing the world they sprang from. For me that has been an act of devotion.

Along the way, naturally, I got to know previous dictionaries and glossaries of Western words. They represent love and intelligence and honorable labor, and I am grateful to the writers of each of them. I'm aware of a profound indebtedness to them.

Yet I also discovered that, until recently, previous dictionaries of the West often didn't get it right. They were Anglo-centric, Texas-centric, male-centric, and cowboy-centric. Mostly they left out women, Indians (particularly contemporary Indian people), Hispanics, blacks, French-Canadians, mountain men, half-breeds, emigrants, missionaries, Mormons, and everyone else who didn't cut a big figure in the myth or was somehow inconvenient. Horses played a bigger role in those books than all these disenfranchised people put together.

One of my big goals here is to put back what has been left out—that is, to restore some of the full richness of the history of the West. I was astonished to find that older Western dictionaries did not include such words relating to Indians as *Sun Dance*, *sand painting*, *kachina*, *vision quest*, *sweat lodge*, *medicine pipe*, and the like. Or such words relating to Mormons as *ward*, *stake*, *plural marriage*, and *sealing*. Or for fur men such words as *voyageur*, *plew*, *free trapper*, and *bourgeois*. Much less terms of contemporary Red English like *forty-niner song*, *schmoehawk*, *snag*, *Jine*. To redress these lapses I have delved into the stories of cavalry wives, warriors, medicine men and women, polygamists, explorers, people of color, and so on. I've chosen as collaborators many of these very people—Western women, Mormons, members of the Shoshone, Crow, Blackfeet, Lakota, Navajo, and Cherokee tribes, mountain-man hobbyists, and others who can fill in the conspicuous blanks.

The notion of the West in this book, then, is newly large and inclusive. Inclusive not only of the many kinds of Westerners and their jobs and activities, but also of time and place. The French-Canadian fur men who explored most of the West play a part here. So do Hispanics of both yesterday and today. So do all contemporary Westerners, who are still remaking the language every day. Despite the limitations of space inevitable in any publishing venture, I've tried to cast a wide loop.

It is my hope that in these pages all kinds of Westerners may live in honor.

The author and editors of a book like this have to make many specific choices about what to include and what to leave out. Some of my inclinations I've noted above—chiefly to put some emphasis on the words of and about Westerners most often left out of previous lexicons.

After some years of work I realized that I had unconsciously developed a central standard for what would be included in the dictionary—what the general reader would want and expect in a dictionary of the West. If I think a reader would be sharply disappointed not to find a word given full treatment here, I've given it. Thus some words appear that are not even Westernisms, like *stagecoach:* that conveyance became a central part of the myth of the West, and it gets its due here. Sometimes this same policy led me to attend to matters that don't have particular personal interest for me. The reader's legitimate expectations govern all.

I have also emphasized some job categories more than others—cowboys, mountain men, sheepherders, and Indian traders have drawn more attention than loggers, miners, fishermen, and oil-rig men. This is because the first group is indigenous to the West, and their new lingo was worked out on the home ground here; if *hackamore* is now used in the Midwest and East, it was imported from the West. Loggers, miners, fishermen, and oil workers, though, brought many of their methods and much of their language from the East or from Europe—loggers from Maine and the North Woods, miners from Cornwall and Wales, fishermen from New England, and oilmen from Pennsylvania. It also seems to me that cowboying is central to the West in the American imagination, while logging, mining, fishing, and oil drilling are less so. At the same time I have striven to give full attention to the terms associated with mining that are native to Westerners—*forty-niner*, for instance, and *hangtown fry*, *Washoe zephyr*, *overthrust belt*, and the like, and paid considerable attention to terms that though born on foreign soil became Western.

Readers may notice an apparent imbalance of main entries in favor of the Southwest: there's a compelling reason for this. New words or usages come into the language very substantially from foreign languages, and the Southwest had and has a very different experience with its speakers of other languages than has been experienced elsewhere. While in the Rockies, the Great Plains, the Intermountain West, and the Pacific Northwest such speakers were mainly French, Russian, and Indian, in the Southwest they were Indian and Hispanic.

In the Southwest these peoples have prospered in numbers, impact, and in the attention they draw from Euro-American culture. The influence of Hispanics on mainstream America grows every day, more and more words of Mexican Spanish come into use by folks who don't speak Spanish, and Anglo acquaintance with these words keeps rising.

Something similar can be said for the Southwest's Indian peoples. The Pueblo people increase in numbers steadily and the Navajos spectacularly; their art and culture attract more and more admiration, more and more tourists.

In other areas of the West this isn't true. The French and Russian influences continue to diminish, and the Indian peoples are not drawing comparable attention.

Similar inclinations have governed my inclusion and exclusion of Indian tribes. Since there are more than five hundred tribes, including them all was out of the question. So I've tried to include those I think the reader wants most to know something about, those with an impact on history or current affairs. That means not only looking into the progression of settlement of the West and the history of the Indian Wars, but also into current controversies over fishing rights and endangered species.

In addition, in this new edition I've made a special effort with terms coming from the Pacific Coast and Alaska. Redwoods, great salmon rivers, tundra, and arctic landscapes paint a story not told elsewhere in the West. And from northern California to the Bering Straits the Russians had their influence, still visible in the architecture, still with us in words like *piva* (home brew) and *nushnik* (outhouse). As the land alters, changing the ways needed to exist on it, and people live different cultures, the language changes.

The last reason for including a certain word is simply that it's interesting to me.

WESTERN AMERICAN ENGLISH: A BABEL

Listen for a moment to an old trapper in the 1840s. Though he was French-Canadian, he lived in what was then Mexico, now probably New Mexico. He had Mexican wives, and children. Being crudely fluent in English, French, and Spanish, he made a fine stew of all three:

> *Voyez-vous* dat I vas nevare tan pauvre as dis time; mais before I vas siempre avec plenty café, plenty sucre; mais now, God dam, I not

go à Santa Fé, God dam, and mountain men dey come aquí from autre côté, drink all my café. Sacré enfant de Gârce, nevare I vas tan pauvre as dis time, God dam. I not care comer meat, ni frijole, ni corn, mais widout café I no live.

Nor was this all. Such a fellow likely had found a Crow wife, or a Shoshone woman along the way, and learned some of those languages conjugally. He might have been to the Pacific Northwest and so had acquired some of its Chinook trade jargon. He was acquainted with Indian Pidgin English, a patois worked out by Indians, white men, and their translators. Doubtless he had a smattering of other Indian languages. Surely he was competent in the sign language. And from all these genes came that marvelous mongrel American Western English.

Because these many sources give Western language much of its spice and richness, I've tried to represent them generously here. The test has been simple in theory and difficult in application: when a word from another language has gotten into English, I've included it—because it's no longer foreign. Most of these words have come from Mexican Spanish, though some came into use from French, Russian, and Indian languages, the Chinook jargon, or other sources. Some of these words are so common that we don't even think of them as foreign-born—*pronto*, for instance, or *savvy, plaza, mesa*. Others retain their Hispanic flavor in our minds but are recognized by all: "*Si, si, amigo*" is heard from playful children on school yards in Ohio. *Cerveza* is on the lips of barflies in Montana. *Tortilla* is in grocery stores and on the menus of fast and fine restaurants, *bienvenidos* is on the public-address system in Kmarts, *avenida* and *embarcadero* are on street signs in northern California. (Some Spanish words are also included because they were in common usage in the nineteenth century, even if they're no longer current.) The best rule of thumb, in my mind, is whether Americans who don't speak Spanish (as I don't) know the word.

I've used a similar guide for pronunciation and spelling, to give an idea of how those of us who don't speak Spanish say the word, how we spell it. This means that both pronunciation and spelling are anglicized (and most accent marks omitted). This is a legitimate part of the way a language adopts a new word. When speaking French, we correctly call France's great city pah-REE; when speaking English, we properly say PAIR-is.

A large part of the vitality of English comes from its eagerness to adopt words from other languages, in the process usually changing the pronunciation, meaning, or usage (though sometimes not). Thus they become English words.

INDIAN-ENGLISH PIDGIN: On first contact, people with different languages often create a pidgin language, a form of simplified speech that allows them to communicate in rudimentary ways. From the start, the Indian peoples of this continent and the European newcomers improvised just such a form of speech. The Indian-English pidgin soon developed words that allowed them to trade and communicate basic desires, for instance, words like *big medicine, big water, big talk.* (In *American Talk* J. L. Dillard says this pidgin was influenced by a pidgin the black slaves had developed for the same purpose. See especially the first chapter for an informative discussion of Indian-English pidgin.) In time, with lots of Indians using it, whites learning it, and translators adopting it, Indian-English pidgin became a kind of language of its own.

In this form it went far, carried across the continent, for instance, by explorers and mountain men. So the word *moccasin*, which we lazily think of as "Indian," first adopted by whites from Algonquian languages, was then dispersed far and wide, and eventually became the term of most Indian people for that footwear. The pidgin was even used by Indians of different languages to talk with each other. Thus it gained a certain legitimacy, but it is not an Indian language. It is a subspecies of English born of Indian-white contact.

As a result words like *winter* (for year), *moon* (for month), and *buffalo soldier* (for a black soldier) would make no sense in a dictionary of, say, the Dakota or Shoshone language. But they make excellent sense here.

RED ENGLISH: With the pidgin left in the past, Indian peoples have developed an English of their own. Separated by their native languages, they joined together to form collectively a variant of the dominant language. Like black English, it reflects the worldview of those who speak it, demonstrates their culture, and is possessed of a nifty vitality. Though I cannot describe it definitively, here are some notes toward a definition.

First, let's observe that it does not include most words from the contact language, words that Native people find archaic and often laughable; neither does it include many historic terms (*winter* for *year*, *moon* for *month*, *wohaw* for *cow*, *goddam* for *white man*). Red English is the way Indian people talk right now.

On the simplest level, Red English is a manner of pronunciation. Many Indian people say "init" for "isn't it," for instance, and "Indin" for "Indian." (Here we need a caution that the alternative pronunciations of a sublanguage are not incorrect but simply different.) Most Indians raised on a reservation have developed distinctive ways of saying some words.

More significantly, they develop distinctive rhythms for entire sentences and conversations. Most Americans have some idea of the rhythm of black street jive. Likewise, Red English has a spoken rhythm that distinguishes it from standard American speech. Its pace is deliberate, generally, sometimes sauntering. The voices are quiet, the language modest and understated. Its beauties are subtle and modulated, not flamboyant and attention-getting.

One important characteristic of Red English is its way of not speaking too specifically of personal feelings and other highly personal matters. The style has a certain indirection, offering an indication of what is felt without naming it outright and intruding on yourself or others. Indicating without quite saying, skirting near a feeling and assuming your audience knows and understands—all these ways are typical of Red English.

Often this Red English makes itself different by giving familiar English words a different meaning. *Grandfather*, for instance, among Indian peoples is likely to have a much broader reference than to your parents' fathers—it means the Deity, the great powers that be; it also may mean ancestors; it means not only your father's father but that man's brothers as well. Terms of Red English for family members in general have a broader meaning than in standard English; *brother* and *sister* are likely to include what the dominant culture calls *cousin*. The word *family* itself includes far more, because the family itself feels different to Native peoples. They don't think of nuclear and extended families; to them it's all one, close-knit, all-embracing family.

Indianizing is what they call the process of giving a standard word a distinctly Native meaning. The Cherokee-Huron poet Allison Hedge Coke, for instance, writes that the cops treated her *somehow*, using that term in a way that might not be understood by an Anglo audience but is well understood by her contemporaries. It's her way of saying, "I don't need to label this, you know what I mean." *Somehow* is now a widespread Indianizing word.

Sometimes the process of Indianizing is unconscious or barely noticed, as with *grandfather*. Sometimes it happens spontaneously. Sometimes a deliberate choice is made to tweak a word into new shape. All that is part of the process of Indianizing.

Red English also chooses to use some words differently from the way the Euro-American culture does in order to reflect a different attitude, like showing more respect, or having a bit of fun with something. Most Indian people don't use the word *squaw* because it feels derogatory. They use *preliterate* instead of *illiterate*. When a well-known Indian speaker on history jokes that he's "an Indin on the reservation, an Injun in the nearby town, an Indian all over the state, and a Native American in Washington, D.C.," he's playing both with pronunciation differences and different word preferences.

Red English has many special words that don't exist in the wider culture, terms that reflect the Indian worldview, art, customs, and so on. Some of these are historic, some new. *Sun Dance, vision quest, sweat lodge, sing, ledger art, tipi, quillwork*—these have been handed down for generations. Many of the terms related to the peyote religion (*crossfire, road man*) were born in the twentieth century. *Red power, apple* (red outside but white inside), *Uncle Tomahawk, schmoehawk* (an Anglo who makes money by representing himself as an Indian), and *buckskin curtain* sprang out of the new political consciousness of the last three decades. *Eye dazzler, forty-niner song, fancy dancer,* and *old pawn* are modern terms that speak of art. *Rez, rez rat, rezzed out, commod bod* (a body made fat by government-issued commodities), and *IHS teeth* (reflecting unkindly on the dentistry provided by the Indian Health Service) are contemporary responses to reservation life. Sometimes the terms display a fine self-deprecating humor.

A subtle characteristic of Red English is its oblique thought patterns. Speakers seem to circle toward thoughts instead of moving in sharp, straight lines. They surround ideas. They name them not in organized shapes of logic but in clusters of suggestion and association. Instead of giving advice, for instance, a Native will often tell a story with a moral. This kind of thought has a beauty very different from the rigors of the discursive English writing taught in colleges.

Two centuries ago British scholars looked down on American culture in general. "Who reads an American book?" they mocked, and sneered at American English in particular, calling it full of "wigwam words." Now let us embrace wigwam words, and celebrate them.

RACIST VERSUS RESPECTFUL LANGUAGE

In writing this dictionary, I've spent a lot of time with the offensive names Americans of various ethnic groups call each other. In the process I've come to have some opinions about how we can speak of each other, and to each other, respectfully.

Let us grant that America has a nasty history of ethnic name-calling, and grant as well that the language is still with us, and that some people continue to use it with relish. In the West it has meant mostly ugly epithets for Indian people and Hispanics, who in turn have their unpleasant epithets for their tormentors. By all standards of human dignity, and courtesy toward other human beings, we need to throw out this language and speak to each other decently.

Some white Americans, though, have almost become tongue-tied. In fear of offending someone, they grow obsequious. They say to themselves or to each other, "Is *Indian* a bad word? Probably *Native American* is safer. What about *squaw*? If it's even questionable, let's not touch it. Do we call people of Mexican descent *Mexican-American? Hispanic? Latino?* Or *Chicano*?" Other people, eager to promote guilt, enjoy the uncertainty and even fawning this fear causes.

All Americans need to be able to talk comfortably to each other and about each other. Maybe it will help to look at the last two paragraphs and ask, Who is "we," anyway? The real Americans, as opposed to . . . exactly who? For some of us a strange, new day has already arrived. As a descendant of Irishmen, Welshmen, and Indians, I am on three sides of the name-calling. Am I entitled to call three sides "we"? Or all sides "they"? As bloodlines get further mixed, these questions will get more and more odd. Can we learn to stop the we-they thinking?

Let's move forward to the cases most important to the West. Just what is respectful language to Indian people and to Hispanics and what's not? We will quickly see that good intentions do not lead us easily to good language.

Take the confusion about *Native American* and *Indian.* From the 1970s, when the term rushed into fashion, until recently, *Native American* was de rigueur and *Indian* outdated. That seems to be changing, and for interesting reasons.

First, *Native American* has never had the support of Indian people in the way the media assumed. Many traditional people didn't care for it. It never was used nearly as commonly on reservations as *Indian.* The American Indian Movement (AIM) didn't support it. Activist Russell Means opposed it. The leading Native newspaper *Lakota Times* stated its preference for *American Indian.*

Various people have observed that *Native American* is a misnomer. Everyone born here is native. Historically, Native Americanism was a nineteenth-century political movement aimed at sweeping everyone who wasn't white and Protestant off these shores. Who wants to be associated with that?

And besides, if *Indian* was a Euro name for Native people, so is *Native American.*

As for *Indian,* it wasn't quite the ridiculous term people said. Columbus didn't think he had arrived in India when he called local people Indians—he thought he'd come to the East Indies. India wasn't called by that name at the time anyway, but was known as Hindustan. And today Indian people are used to the term *Indian,* and daily use it about themselves. Many have developed a sense of humor about it. They say, Sure glad Columbus wasn't looking for Turkey. Or the Virgin Islands.

What name do Native people prefer? They're almost unanimous—the name of the tribe: Ute, Fox, Cree, or whatever.

What about a name for all Indians as a group? They have no such term in their languages. Among English words about them, the momentum now seems to be shifting back from *Native American* to *American Indian.*

Now we must check out the strange case of the folk etymology. Somehow—and the paths must be very curious—legends arise about the origins of words and seize people's emotions, like the story that Columbus named the Indians of this continent after the Indians of the subcontinent of Asia. These folk etymologies are only venial sins, but in some ways they bedevil the language ethnic groups use toward each other. Note how this works in these three similar cases.

THE CASE OF ESKIMO: A decade or so ago the term *Eskimo* lost favor to *Inuit* as the name of the peoples of the Arctic. The reason, we were told, was that *Eskimo* meant "eater of raw flesh," and so was demeaning. (Those of us who like sashimi wonder why being called an eater of raw flesh is insulting anyway.) The editors at hundreds of newspapers and publishing houses, and the anchors of news shows, got rid of the term faster than an out-of-date hair style.

Two difficulties: *Eskimo* does not mean "eater of raw flesh," and no one seems to know how that notion got started. Also, the Eskimos of Alaska don't like *Inuit*—they want to be called *Eskimos*.

To make things trickier, according to Russell Tabbert's excellent *Dictionary of Alaskan English*, the Arctic people of Canada, Greenland, and Siberia prefer *Inuit*, but those in Alaska prefer *Eskimo*. The only way out of this dilemma seems to me to be courtesy: use the name the people in front of you, or the people you're speaking of, prefer. Thus Alaskan Eskimos should be *Eskimos* once more, and that is the usage I've usually chosen in this dictionary.

THE CASE OF SQUAW: For about a century Westerners have known that Indian people take the word *squaw* as offensive. About a generation ago a story about this word gained currency—that it was originally a dirty word for female genitalia. Though the origin of this story is mysterious, the assault on *squaw* grew furious. Several states have considered legislation banning it from place names; some states passed such legislation.

There's just one problem: the folk etymology is again false. *Squaw* is a reputable word or word-part meaning "female" in the Algonquian languages of the Northeast. *Squasachem*, for instance, means "female chief." American colonists heard it, understood it, and used it correctly, without offense. (Thanks to the Abenaki scholar Margaret Bruchac for good work on this subject.)

Does this mean the word is inoffensive? Not at all. *Squaw* was borne west with other words of Indian-English pidgin by frontiersmen and settlers who applied it to Indian women of other tribes. These tribes saw it simply as a white-man's word. They recognized that much of the time it was used in a demeaning way, as in "dirty squaw," "drunk squaw," "squaw whore." They took offense, and rightly so. In much of the West, Indian women view it as one of the most derogatory of sexist and racist words.

At the same time, others do not. Navajos, by far the majority population where I live, speak freely and easily of "going to the squaw dance," an important ceremony also known as the enemy way.

Though the story about *squaw* being a nasty reference to female reproductive parts is false, in much of the West *squaw* is still a fighting word, and that's enough reason to avoid it.

THE CASE OF THE ANASAZI: Here is a last instance of folk etymologies leading us astray: We are now asked by agencies of the federal government to call the ancient peoples of the Four Corners by the name *Ancient Puebloans*. Reason: They say *Anasazi* means "ancient enemies" in Navajo. Yet my Navajo friends say the word simply means "the old ones." Therefore I've stayed with the term people are more accustomed to, *Anasazi*.

Though the most common words for people of Mexican-American descent are not bedeviled by folk etymologies, they are problematic. Literally, *Hispanic* is inaccurate, since it doesn't mean "Mexican, Latin, or Mexican American" but something much broader—according to *Webster's*, "relating to the people, culture, or speech of Spain, Spain and Portugal, or Latin America." *Mexican* isn't accurate either; neither is *Latino*; *Chicano* is outdated; *Mexican-American* is accurate but unloved.

Americans of Mexican ancestry in the Southwest generally now seem to prefer *Hispanic*; in California the style is now *Latino*. Some people see *Hispanic* as denying Indio blood, and wish instead to acknowledge it.

In this book I've gone with *Hispanic*, the preference of the majority, except in reference to restaurants and food. I couldn't bring myself to write *Hispanic restaurant*.

Altogether, how *can* we come around to using acceptable language to each other?

In my judgment, as a member of a culture of many colors, I feel that we should acknowledge our unfortunate history around words, and then chuckle about it, laughter being a far healthier response than the alternatives. As we move closer to respect for self and others, let's drop the guilt and the guilt inducement. Leave behind the anger, resentment, and fear, forget the eagerness to please. Let's see human beings everywhere. Then it's simple: Respect all, and speak to all with respect. When the heart is good, that will be enough.

DICTIONARY

⊰ OF THE ⊱

AMERICAN WEST

A

À LA COMANCHE A description of a rider hanging over the side of his horse; from the style of the Comanches in warfare.

AARIGAA! In Alaska, an exclamation that means "good," "fine." From the **INUPIAQ** language.

AARONIC The lower priesthood of the Church of Jesus Christ of the **LATTER-DAY SAINTS**. For boys twelve to eighteen and new converts, these priests assist the bishop and act as teachers and deacons. (See also **MELCHIZEDEK**.)

ABALONE An edible mollusc of coastal California, much sought for its delicate taste. It takes verb form, as in signs warning "no abaloning" (or "abaloneing") or "I've abaloned."

ABOARD On horseback.

ABOVE MY BEND Beyond my capabilities; same as, *above my huckleberry.*

ABOVE SNAKES Above ground, meaning still alive.

ABRA In the Southwest, especially Texas, a narrow valley, a defile between close hills; a break in a **MESA**.

ABRAZO To say hello or goodbye by embracing someone with both arms and giving a pat on the back, a custom still existing in the Southwest today, especially among Hispanics. Borrowed from Spanish.

ACCESS ROAD Among loggers, a road built into remote areas of commercial timber for access for cutting and hauling. Such roads also give access to firefighters, hikers, hunters, packers, and other recreational users. They are viewed as a benefit by some, as destruction by others.

ACE HIGH A **POKER** hand that has an ace but no pair or better combination to bet on. The expression also may simply refer to anything top-notch or first-rate. When William Foster-Harris says in *The Look of the Old West,* "The Spencer . . . was also ace high in the early West, a real frontier gun," he means it was a humdinger, the cat's meow.

> COMBINATIONS: *Aces back to back* is an ideal situation; from when a player's first two cards are aces, one face up and one face down. *Ace in the hole* and *ace up your sleeve* mean "any hidden advantage." These expressions come from stud poker. A gun in a shoulder holster or other hideout might be a figurative ace in the hole.

ACEQUIA (uh-SAY-kee-uh) (1) In the Southwest, an irrigation ditch. The main ditch is known as an *acequia madre*. Borrowed from Spanish, it is frequently Americanized to *sakey*, also spelled *saykee*. (2) In New Mexico, an acequia is an association of landowners that manages a ditch. The shareholders are called *parciantes* and can number from a few to over a hundred; their allotment of water (which varies according to water flow and the location of their land) is called a *sucro* (a share) or a *pión* (a New Mexican variant of *peón*). (See also **MAYORDOMO**.)

ACION (ah-see-OHN) In the Mexican–American border country, a stirrup-leather. (See also **STIRRUP**.)

ACOMA The People of the White Rock and their Pueblo. Acoma, sitting on a mesa about an hour's drive west of Albuquerque, New Mexico, was visited by Coronado in 1540 and is said to date to the eleventh century. The people of Acoma are now known for their pottery. (See also **PUEBLO**.)

ACORN CALF An undersized **CALF**, often sickly; a runt; a **CULL**.

ACROSS LOTS In the quickest, shortest way; via shortcuts.

ACTIONABLE FIRE Any forest fire that requires suppression, according to current policy of a national park or national forest. In many places policy does not allow the suppression of fires caused naturally.

ADDED MONEY In **RODEO**, the money provided by the rodeo committee. Together with the entry fees, it makes up the prize money.

ADIOS (ah-dee-OHS) Good-bye, a farewell, as is *vaya con Dios* ("go with God"). Borrowed from Spanish.

ADIT A passage, roughly horizontal, used to enter and drain a mine.

ADOBE A brick made of earth or clay and straw and dried in the sun; a clay suitable for making adobe bricks; the buildings that are made of the bricks. Usually the bricks are formed in wooden molds, built into thick walls, and plastered over. Adobes are common in the Southwest, especially in churches, public buildings, and homes that date from the Mexican or Spanish colonial periods, many of them handsome and of historic value. Use of adobe brick dates at least to ancient Egypt. Sometimes, as in the phrase *adobe dollar*, the word connotes an object of little value. Borrowed from Spanish.

The French in Missouri in the early eighteenth century used a building material of clay and straw, similar to adobe, called *bousillage*.

ADOBE-WALLED Executed; put up against an adobe wall and shot. Watts says that the expression probably arose during the 1870s, when Texas and Mexican cowboys stole cattle back and forth across the border, and some Texans who got caught were 'dobe-walled. (See also **DRY-GULCH**.)

AFOOT Without a horse. In the West, this meant that you had fallen into misfortune, had gone broke, or were lame-brained. You couldn't cover enough ground to get to food and water. You couldn't get out of the weather. You were vulnerable to wild critters. Cattle wouldn't respect you, and neither would other men. So to be afoot was to be in sad shape.

AGAVE (ah-GAH-vay) A succulent Southwestern plant (*Agave* sp.) with evergreen leaves arranged in a rosette on the ground; a common species is the *century* *plant*. Each leaf ends in a sharp spine; century plants bloom once and then die. They are used to make alcoholic drinks, soaps, and fibers; Indians use them as food. Borrowed from Spanish. (See also MAGUEY, MESCAL.)

A-GOING AND A-COMING Thoroughly, all the way, utterly. A man who beat another man at cards a-goin' and a-comin', or a-comin' and a-goin', had given him a whomping.

AGUA Water or rain. Borrowed from Spanish. COMBINATIONS: *agua caliente* (hot water); *agua dulce* (literally sweet water—potable water); *agua miel* (the juice of the MAGUEY before PULQUE, MESCAL, and TEQUILA are made from it).

AGUARDIENTE Booze, especially fiery booze. Originally it meant a brandy made in El Paso, but the meaning widened to include almost any kind of spirits. The MOUNTAIN MEN loved the aguardiente they got at Taos and Santa Fe in the 1820s, '30s, and '40s. Smith says that it is primarily a product of the MAGUEY, as are PULQUE, MESCAL, and TEQUILA, and makes those who imbibe it amorous. Borrowed from Spanish, it is an elision of *agua ardiente* (fiery water). It has been spelled in such creative variations as *awardenty* and *aquardiente*. (See also FIREWATER.)

AHKIO In Alaska, a light sled for freight.

AHO! "Thank you." An expression of the CROW language, it has become pan-tribal. Usually it offers thanks to the spirits and is said at the end of prayers and in association with rituals and ceremonies, sometimes like "amen." At POWWOWS and RENDEZVOUS, it may be a rousing affirmation, something like "Amen, brother!"

AI Artificial insemination, impregnating a cow with a "straw" of semen; usually done to obtain sperm from a high-quality bull that the rancher could not ordinarily afford. A *gomer bull* is an infertile bull used to bring the cows into heat so they will be ready to be inseminated.

AIM To intend, as in "I aim to lick that stupid, stubby-legged, red-eyed son of a she-cat."

AIM The American Indian Movement, an organization founded in 1968; one of various organizations formed in the last several decades to increase RED POWER. At first an urban movement, it spread to the RESERVATIONS, especially those of the SIOUX and other peoples on the Northern Plains most dispossessed. AIM activists once took over the BUREAU OF INDIAN AFFAIRS office in Washington, D.C., and in 1973 AIM members joined some OGLALA in what is known to many Indians as the second Battle of Wounded Knee. A SHOSHONE man of medicine said, "[AIM] takes the role of shock troops because the federal government and American people don't listen, and Indians are second-class citizens in their own country."

The opinion of its effectiveness in Indian country in the 1970s was divided, and some Indians and Anglos derisively called it AsshoGhosles in Moccasins. All the same, many of the changes sought by the organization have become policy of the Bureau of Indian Affairs and tribal councils.

AIR THE LUNGS A cowboy term meaning to cuss. Cowboys used to be notorious for their profane and scatological vocabulary, which they barely managed to suppress in front of women. Now the cussing has generally achieved gender equality.

AIR THE PAUNCH To throw up after drinking too much. Cowboy talk.

AIR-SEASONED Said of timber that has been seasoned in the air rather than in a kiln.

AIRTIGHTS Canned food. The cowboys of the days of the open range did have some canned food, mostly peas, peaches, meat, and milk. Tinned food was mass produced after the Civil War and became common in the West in the late 1800s.

AJO (AH-hoh) A common name for the desert lily *(Hesperocallis undulata)* of the Southwest; properly the name of the Southwestern garlic plant. Borrowed from the Spanish word for garlic.

ALAMO As a common noun, it means cottonwood tree. The Franciscan mission in San Antonio that became known as the cradle of Texas liberty was named for this ubiquitous Western tree. It is now used mostly as a Southwestern proper name. Borrowed from Spanish (where it means "poplar").

ALASKAN HUSKY In Alaska, any sled dog, especially a Siberian husky or a malamute. Originally derives from a denigrating name for Eskimos. Similar formations are *Alaskan high kick* (or one-foot high kick, an Eskimo kicking game), *Alaska tea* (made from the evergreen *Ledum*), *Alaska time* (maybe early, maybe late, depending on the weather), *Alaska trade* (of compliment for compliment); for animals—*Alaskan husky, Alaskan jay, Alaska king crab* (also called a *spider crab*), *Alaskan mackerel* (also called a *kelp fish*), *Alaskan malamute, Alaska pollock, Alaska robin, Alaskan turkey (salmon)*; for plants—*Alaska cotton, Alaska pine.*

ALBARDON A packsaddle similar to the **APAREJO**. Borrowed from Spanish.

ALBINO A color of horse, white with blue eyes. (For the many colors of horses, see also **BUCKSKIN**.)

ALBONDIGA A ball of meat or fish. It is common on menus in the Southwest. Borrowed from Spanish.

ALCALDE The mayor or justice of the peace of a Hispanic community; also called a *regidor*. The alcalde's territory was known as an *alcaldia*. Borrowed from Spanish (where it means "mayor").

AL-CAN Nickname for Alaska Highway; stands for Alaska-Canada Highway.

ALEUT A Native group of the Aleutian Islands, Shumagin Islands, and part of the Alaska Peninsula.

ALFALFA A leguminous plant (*Medicago sativa*) with purple flowers grown throughout the irrigated West for hay. Both the word and the plant came to the West from Mexico. An *alfalfa cube* is a **CAKE** of pressed alfalfa used to feed cows during the winter. *Alfaloofee*, in Wyoming, is a comical name for alfalfa.

ALFILARIA The common pin grass (*Ergodium cicutarium*) of the Plains; also spelled *alfileria* and *alfilerilla*, and sometimes Americanized to *fileree* or *filaree*. Borrowed from Spanish.

ALFORJA (al-FOR-ha) A saddlebag for a packhorse; a box of rawhide or canvas (perhaps even wood) carried on a packsaddle. Borrowed from Spanish.

ALICE ANN In the Southwest, a sorrel horse. According to Smith, it's a corruption of *alazan*, which is Spanish for sorrel. (See also **BUCKSKIN**.)

ALKALI (1) A powdery, white mineral that salts the ground in many low places in the West, particularly **SINKS**. It inhabits Western water, whitening the ground where water has risen to the surface and gone back down. It also spoils drinking water and gave many early Westerners the intestinal affliction (*turistas*) known as *being alkalied*. One Western meaning of alkali is a country with alkaline soil.

(2) A fellow who's been in the country for a long time. He is said to be alkalied, that is, accustomed to the country. Often he's an old fellow but not necessarily so—any experienced man qualifies. The cattleman in Stewart Edward White's *Arizona Nights* said about the Westerner's attachment to the land, "An old 'alkali' is never happy anywhere else." Also known as a *grissel heel, longhorn,* or *sourdough*.

(3) As a verb, blinded by booze.

COMBINATIONS: *alkali desert, alkali dust, alkali flat* (a plain ruined by alkali, often an undrained, barren, hostile desert), *alkali grass* (which grows in alkaline soil), *alkali heath* (a plant), *alkali pan* (a shallow depression filled with alkali), *alkali sink* (a spot that doesn't drain), *alkali spot* (an area of gumbolike alkaline soil), *alkali spring, alkali water*.

ALL HANDS AND THE COOK Everybody; the entire outfit, all the cowboys and right on down to the cook.

ALL MY RELATIVES A translation of *mitakuye oyasin*, a **DAKOTA** phrase frequently repeated during the **SWEAT LODGE** and other ceremonies, prayers, and rituals. Literally it means "all my relatives" or "we are all related." According to **LAKOTA** shaman Wallace Black Elk, it acknowledges the speaker's "personal relatedness to everything that exists."

ALODIK In Alaska, fried bread served as a sweet. (See also **FRY BREAD**.)

ALTA CALIFORNIA Literally, upper California; what became the state of California in the United States, as opposed to lower (Baja) California, which remains part of Mexico.

AMA In the Southwest, the mistress of a house. Borrowed from Spanish.

AMBULANCE On the frontier, a light, canvas-topped army wagon for carrying personnel, wounded or healthy; might mean almost any government wagon for transporting people. Also called a *prairie wagon*, it had no necessary association with hospitals or medical care.

AMIGO Friend; ubiquitous in the Southwest. Borrowed from Spanish.

AMOLE (uh-MOLE-ay) A YUCCA plant, especially the bulb, used to make soap. Borrowed from Spanish, which borrowed it from Nahuatl.

AMONG THE WILLOWS (1) On the lam, on the run, running from the law. (2) When said of a couple, making love.

ANASAZI The most widely used terms for the PUEBLO people who inhabited the Four Corners country of Colorado, New Mexico, Arizona, and Utah until seven centuries ago and are the ancestors of the modern Pueblo people. The Anasazi left CLIFF DWELLINGS, such as those at Mesa Verde, that are today the eloquent voice of their sojourn in the CANYON COUNTRY. They developed pottery, an economy based on agriculture, and an elaborate ceremonial religion. Near the end of the thirteenth century, they left their large pueblos, perhaps because of drought or pressure from enemies, and started afresh in the Rio Grande Valley and in the country of the ZUNI and HOPI peoples. (See also HOHOKAM.)

The term has come under fire recently on the grounds that it is a NAVAJO word meaning "ancient enemies," and *Puebloan ancestors* has gained favor in some quarters. But Navajo-speaking authorities say *Anasazi* simply means "the ancient ones" in their language.

ANDALE (AHN-duh-lay) Get going, get a move on. Southwestern cowboys say this to cows on a TRAIL DRIVE a lot. Borrowed from the imperative form of the Spanish verb *andar* (which means "to walk").

ANGAKOK The ESKIMO term for a shaman.

ANGEL An innocent at a horse auction, likely to buy unsound horses.

ANGLE IRON The metal triangle the cook raised a ruckus on to get all hands to dinner.

ANGLO In the Southwest, anyone not of Indian or Hispanic blood; a white person, especially a white Euro-American; "black Anglo," though, is not nonsense. New Mexico declares its public pride in being a state of three cultures, Indian, Hispanic, and Anglo.

Even beyond the ubiquitous *paleface*, the Indians had and have many words for white people. Various **PLAINS INDIANS** knew them as *goddams* (doubtless from their incessant cussing). The **DAKOTAS** know them as *wasicun* ("the fat-takers"). The **CROW** term for a white person is *baaschiile* ("person with yellow eyes"). To the **ARIKARA** they were "people with yellow hides." The **KIOWA** knew the whites as *bedalpago* ("hairy mouths"), referring to their mustaches (many Indians found facial hair objectionable). Eskimos (or Inuits) called them *people with big eyebrows*. *Big knife* and *long knife* distinguished Americans from the French, English, and pre-Revolutionary settlers. An early **NAVAJO** term for white men was *those who fight with their penises*, because they were always woman-hungry. The Mohawk called the Scotch *kentahere*, because their flat hats reminded the Indians of buffalo droppings. Some Indians knew the German and Dutch as *yah yah ulgeh* ("the ones who say *ja, ja* all the time"). Southwest Indians called Anglos *tata*, said to be a term of respect. *Long beard* was used. The Iroquois named the white man "he who makes axes," in their language *asseroni*, which some Indians may want to re-adopt satirically today.

ANGORAS Chaps made from goat hide, with the hair on and showing (in fact, showing off); **WOOLLIES**. (See also **CHAPS**.)

ANIMAL A bull of the domestic bovine variety. It seems that, unlike modern folk, Americans of the nineteenth century found any mention of sex in female company indelicate. So, yes, they even substituted *animal* and *cow* for *bull* and stooped to euphemisms like *duke, toro,* and *bovine*.

ANIMAL DAMAGE CONTROL (ADC) The federal agency in charge of eradicating predators, $30 million was spent annually (as of the early 1990s) on destroying predators that threaten (or are perceived as threatening) crops or livestock. Individual ranchers contact the ADC, which then removes (by trapping, aerial shooting, or, less commonly, poisoning) the offending animals, usually **COYOTES**. (See also **GOVERNMENT TRAPPER**.)

ANIMAL GUIDE Among Indian peoples, a spirit helper in the form of an animal that protects or guides the supplicant. To find an animal guide is one object of the **VISION QUEST**. A person with the hawk for his animal guide might say (if he spoke of it at all), "The hawk is my medicine."

ANIMAL UNIT Forest Service bureaucratese for a critter that eats a standard amount while grazing on public land. A cow with an unweaned calf equals 1 cow unit or pair. The Forest Service fellows have also come up with an animal-unit conversion factor, by which a bull is 1.25 cow unit, an elk 0.7, a weaned calf 0.6, and so on. Different areas of the West support markedly different numbers of animal units. On the Plains of South Dakota, rancher and writer Linda Hasselstrom figures ten to forty acres of grass, plus hay and **CAKE**, are required to feed 1 cow unit for a year.

ANNUITY A yearly issue of food staples, to an American Indian tribe, usually on the basis of a treaty and in return for grants of land or other valuables. The history of annuities is a sad one. Often the amount that got to the people was diminished from the amount shipped, filched by various hands along the way; often annuities were brutally late, so that people went hungry; sometimes annuities were suspended as punishment. The suffering was considerable. (See also **COMMODITIES**.)

Some funny stories are told about the issues. The **NAVAJOS,** it is said, were issued pinto beans and coffee beans at Fort Sumner, during their internment after the Long Walk. Quickly they learned that Mexicans were a lot smarter than Americans—no matter how long you boiled those American beans, they never got edible.

ANQUERA A piece of leather at the back of the **CANTLE** of a **STOCK SADDLE,** often used for riding double, sometimes mostly for looks. Borrowed from Spanish.

ANTELOPE The common name for what is formally the *pronghorn* or *prongbuck;* also known popularly as a *goat.* The moniker *antelope* dates at least to Lewis and Clark, who commented on its "wonderful fleetness." On the Northern Plains, this graceful animal has made a huge comeback in numbers. In the 1920s, fewer than 100,000 lived in Wyoming; now Wyoming people joke that the state is well off as long as the goats outnumber the people.

COMBINATIONS: *antelope brush* (a Western shrub), *antelope ground squirrel* (a chipmunk), *antelope dance* (a ceremony of the Hopi), *antelope jackrabbit,* and *antelope goat* (the Rocky Mountain goat).

ANTI-GODLIN In a sideways, crooked, or roundabout way. *Whomper-jawed* has about the same meaning.

APACHE A tribe of the Southwest celebrated for ferocious raiding of its Hispanic, Indian, and Anglo neighbors. The name probably stems from the Zuni word *ápachu,* meaning "enemy"; they call themselves *Diné,* the People (their kinsmen the Navajo use the same term for themselves, and most tribes call themselves the People). The Pueblo Indians called them the *Querechos.*

The six principal Apache groups (moving roughly southwestward along their traditional lands from southwestern Kansas to central Arizona) were the Jicarillas, the *Kiowa,* the Lipans, the Mescaleros, the *Chiricahuas,* and the largest group, the Western Apaches, also called the Coyotero. Some were purely hunter-gatherers, some raised crops as well, and those on the Southern Plains had a buffalo-hunting culture.

The Chiricahua and Western Apaches, who lived in historic times in western New Mexico and east-central Arizona (which was known as Apacheria), became the best known because they fought the Apache Wars until subdued by American armies under Nelson Miles and George Crook. They became known for a remarkable aptitude for surviving and thriving under the extreme conditions of the desert and for resistance to white encroachment.

The Chiricahuas, the last holdouts under Geronimo, Mangas Coloradas, and Cochise, were considerably dispersed and now live at Fort Sill, Oklahoma, and on the Mescalero Reservation in New Mexico. The Coyoteros live on the San Carlos and Fort Apache Reservations near their historic territory in Arizona. The Mescaleros have their own reservation in New Mexico, as do the Jicarillas. The Kiowa-Apaches, once buffalo hunters, live in western Oklahoma. The Lipans, once the terror of Texas, are said to be culturally extinct.

APACHE PLUME A shrub (*Fallugia paradoxa*) of the Southwest, so named because its feathery clusters of seeds reminded someone of an Apache war bonnet; also called *poñil*.

APAREJO (ah-pa-RAY-ho) A Mexican packsaddle that fit the back of a pack mule like an opened, upside-down book. Traditionally, it rested on a **JERGA** (saddle cloth), which lay on a **SALEA** (sheepskin), and was secured very tightly by a wide grass band so that heavy loads could be borne without chafing. Borrowed from Spanish, where it means riding gear.

APISHAMORE (uh-PEESH-uh-mohr) A saddle blanket of the **MOUNTAIN MEN** and later Westerners, preferably made from soft buffalo-calf skin and often used as the rider's bed at night. From **OJIBWAY**.

APPALOOSA A horse bred by the **NEZ PERCÉ**, distinctively marked on the rump and back with dark spots and known for its excellence as a saddle horse from at least the time of Lewis and Clark. Some lexicographers suggest that the name comes from the Palouse River, where **MOUNTAIN MEN** may first have seen the horse. Variant spellings include *Palouse, Pelouse, apaloochy*, and *appalousy*. (See also **BUCKSKIN**.)

APPLE (1) An Indian who's red on the outside but white on the inside; the Indian equivalent of what blacks call an Oreo or Uncle Tom; same as Uncle Tomahawk. (2) What you're not supposed to grab when a horse acts up—the saddle horn. South Dakota writer Linda Hasselstrom jokes that some folks accuse other riders' saddle horns of featuring tooth marks.

APPLE-HORN A style of saddle with a horn that looks like an apple rather than like a disc, like some early Mexican-influenced saddles; a popular saddle with Texans in the trail-drive period after the Civil War.

APPOLA A word imported by the **MOUNTAIN MEN** from their French-Canadian comrades and meaning "a method of broiling meat on a stick kabob-style, with fat and lean strips alternated"; also the stick itself. Sometimes spelled *apola*.

APRON STRAPS Straps on the skirt of a saddle used to hold slicker, bedroll, and other gear.

APRON-FACED A description of a horse with a white forehead and face.

Arapaho and Shoshone Indians in front of J. K. Moore's store in Wyoming, 1883.
[COURTESY OF AMERICAN HERITAGE CENTER, UNIVERSITY OF WYOMING.]

ARANCEL In the Southwest, a tariff or import duty; also spelled *aransel*. Borrowed from Spanish.

ARAPAHO A Great Plains tribe of the Algonquian family with a buffalo-hunting culture. When first contacted frequently by whites, the Arapaho lived on the Plains of eastern Colorado and southeastern Wyoming. Earlier they had permanent villages and raised crops near the Great Lakes. On the high Plains, they allied themselves closely with **CHEYENNES** and were a force in the 1860s wars on the Central Plains and the fighting in Powder River country in 1865–66. They fought alongside the **DAKOTA** (Sioux) and Cheyenne in the climactic Indian wars of 1876–77. Today the southern Arapaho live in Oklahoma and the northern on the Wind River Reservation in Wyoming.

ARBUCKLE'S (1) Arbuckle Brothers **COFFEE,** a brand so common in the West that it became a generic term for coffee, just as Levi's has become for jeans, Winchester for rifle, and Stetson for hat. It was the word for coffee at **NAVAJO** trading posts until World War II. "During the late nineteenth and early twentieth centuries," according to historian Francis Fugate, "the Navajos drank prodigious amounts of coffee, strong and black, boiled with sugar in the pot. They would have nothing but Arbuckle's Ariosa. They would ask the Indian agent for *Hosteen Cohay*—which when translated literally from the Navajo language means 'Mr. Coffee.'"

The cowboy likes his coffee strong. One Wyoming hand said in the 1980s that the trick to making coffee is that "it don't take as much water as you think it do."

Other names for coffee are *black water, bellywash, black jack, brown gargle, cafecito, Indian coffee,* and *jamoka.*

(2) A hand so green the boss must have sent away and gotten him with the trading stamps that come with Arbuckle's.

ARCH A huge span of sandstone created by erosion; a sandstone fin eroded out. Arches are commonly found in the canyonlands of southeastern Utah, especially in Arches National Park. Delicate Arch, a natural model for the gateway arch in St. Louis, is surely one of the grandest sights on this Earth.

ARCTIC A warm boot that repels water, often lined with fur; also called an *Arctic boot* or *overshoe*. COMBINATIONS: *Arctic Slope, Arctic haze, Arctic trout, Arctic wine* (straight whiskey).

ARENA DIRECTOR The director of a RODEO, the person who assures that all goes according to Hoyle as much as it can with unruly stock and more unruly cowboys. He works for the producer or STOCK CONTRACTOR, or one of these people may act as the arena director.

ARGONAUT A California gold rush (1848–1849) fortune seeker. The original Argonauts, ancient Greeks, searched for the golden fleece with Jason.

ARIKARA A Native tribe that lived in earth lodges on the upper Missouri River; an offshoot of the Pawnee. These Indians, commonly known to early Westerners as Rees or Ricarees, had a Caddoan language and lived like their upriver neighbors the MANDANS in a half-sedentary (rather than nomadic) style. In the earliest years of FUR-TRADE travel up the Missouri, they posed an obstacle to upriver movement but were stilled by military intervention and disease. They were moved to Fort Clark and then to the Fort Berthold Reservation, where they merged culturally with the MANDANS and HIDATSA.

ARIZONA NIGHTINGALE A burro, known with ironic humor for its raucous song. (See also COLORADO MOCKINGBIRD.)

ARIZONA STRIP The common name for the huge chunk of Arizona desert bounded by the Grand Canyon on the east and south and the Nevada and Utah state lines on the west and north. It is wild and then some. A few folks do some herding there. The splendid writer Edward Abbey's mythical home, Wolf Hole, was there. Before the Strip got littered with a number of roads and bridges, it had little law—the nearest authority was on the other side of the Grand Canyon. That's why the Mormon polygamists founded the settlement of Short Creek there, now known as Colorado City.

ARIZONA TENOR A fellow who coughed from tuberculosis—such victims came to the desert for the sake of the dry air.

ARKANSAS TOOTHPICK A humorous name for a wicked kind of knife, dagger-style, with a long, tapering blade, designed for both hand-to-hand fighting and throwing; second in frontier popularity only to the BOWIE KNIFE; sometimes called a *frog stabber*.

ARKIE A logger's nickname for a worker from Arkansas. Like *Hoosier* and *Okie,* it is both an indication of home state and a disparagement.

ARMITAS Half **CHAPS**, or **CHINKS**; a leather apron protecting a rider's legs (as far as his boot tops) against nuisances like brush and the rubbing of the rope. Jo Mora, in *Trail Dust and Saddle Leather*, says they're good in hot weather and light brush. They were popular with **VAQUEROS** and are still popular with **BUCKAROOS** but not cowboys of the Texas or Northern Plains style. Also known as *armas* or *chigaderos*.

ARRASTRE A primitive mill for pulverizing silver and gold ore. Usually a huge stone was dragged around and around on a stone bed by a **BURRO**. Also spelled *arrastra* and *rastra*, and also called a drag mill. Borrowed from Spanish (where it means "mining mill").

ARRIERO A Southwesternism for muleteer. Also called a *mulero*. Both terms are borrowed from Spanish.

ARROYO A narrow gully with steep dirt walls and a flat floor that is a creek or rivulet when it's wet, but usually is dry. Arroyos are bad places to camp in—flash floods turn them into melees in no time—and they're good places to get a car bogged in the sand. Also called a *wash*, or *dry wash (arroyo seco)*. The West has lots of terms for topographical features that are similar but not identical—**BARRANCA, COULEE, GULCH,** *gully, ditch, ravine*. Borrowed from Spanish (where it means stream).

ARTILLERY A lightly mocking term for the firearms a man is carrying, especially his handguns.

ASI A cold-weather wattle-and-daub house of the **CHEROKEE** people.

ASPEN A broad-leaved tree *(Populus tremuloides)* with a straight white trunk. It is common at higher elevations in the West, reproduces by runners, and is dependent on fire for healthy regeneration. When small, it is valuable winter browse for ungulates, and when full grown, it makes a smokeless, ashless fire, important in Indian country. Also called *quakie, quaker,* and *quaking aspen.* As David Lavender says in *One Man's West,*

> The tiniest breath of air will twist the light-colored undersides of the leaves about until the whole tree seems to dance and twinkle.
>
> The Utes have a legend about these delicious groves. In olden days, they say, the aspens were the proudest of trees. When the Great Spirit visited the Earth and all other things shivered with anticipation, the aspens remained stiff and unbending. The Spirit cursed them and ordered that henceforth they should tremble whenever an eye was turned upon them.

ASSAY In mining, to evaluate or hold precious-metal values, as in "That sample assays a hundred bucks a ton." The noun form is not an Americanism.

COMBINATIONS: *assay balance* (a scale used in assaying), *assay master* (the head assayer), *assay office* (the agency that performs assays), *assay stamp* (the mark of the assay office), *assay value* (the calculated value of gold or silver in an ore sample, as determined by assay).

ASSESSMENT WORK The effort required by the federal government to be done each year on an unpatented **MINING CLAIM**. If it isn't done, or at least filed, the claimant loses whatever rights he has. In the last few decades, many unpatented claims have really been vacation spots, with a few explosives employed annually to keep up appearances.

ASSINIBOIN Originally a large **GREAT PLAINS** tribe living in northern Montana and across the border in Canada. They had a buffalo-hunting culture and were particularly known as traders. They were consistently friendly to whites and associated closely with the Americans at Fort Union. Ravaged by smallpox and other diseases, they eventually joined the **ATSINA** and **DAKOTA** (Sioux) on the Fort Peck and Fort Belknap Reservations in Montana, where they live today.

ASSOCIATION SADDLE Though a bronc saddle is made to give the rider an advantage in trying to stay on a bronco, this saddle sanctioned by the Professional Rodeo Cowboys Association "gives the hoss all the best of it" by removing whatever a rider might anchor himself to. For this reason, it is required for contest riding at **RODEOS**. Also called a *committee saddle* and a *contest saddle*.

ASTORIAN A fur man associated with Astoria, Oregon; a member of a party sent out by John Jacob Astor's Pacific Fur Company in 1810 (by sea) or 1811 (by land) to found a **FUR-TRADING** post at the mouth of the Columbia River. Though ambitious as a financial enterprise and an affirmation of American sovereignty, it was short-lived as an American post. The main contributions the Astorians made were the explorations of the unknown West and their discoveries of good beaver country.

ATAJO (uh-TAH-ho) In the Southwest, a pack-mule caravan. Borrowed from Spanish. British Lieutenant George Frederick Ruxton, traveling in the West in the mid-1840s, described them in *Life in the Far West:*

> The atajos, numbering from fifty to two hundred mules, travel a daily distance—jornada—of twelve or fifteen miles, each mule carrying a pack weighing from two to four hundred pounds. To a large atajo eight or ten muleteers are attached, and the dexterity and quickness with which they will saddle and pack an atajo of a hundred mules is surprising. The animals being driven to the spot, the lasso whirls round the head of the muleteer and falls over the head of a particular mule. The tapojos is placed over the eyes, the heavy aparejo adjusted, and the pack secured, in three minutes.

ATIGI One Alaskan name for a parka.

ATOLE (uh-TOH-lay) Cornmeal; gruel or porridge made from corn; a weak corn soup popular among the poor of the Southwest and Mexico. Lieutenant Ruxton, that intrepid British traveler of the 1840s, found it "an insipid compound," but then he found little in New Mexico he liked. The term comes from Nahuatl by way of Mexican Spanish.

ATSINA This Native tribe, commonly known as the Gros Ventre of the Prairie and sometimes confused with the Gros Ventre of the Missouri (the **HIDATSA**), maintained a buffalo-hunting culture in northern Montana and Canada. An offshoot of the Arapaho, they allied themselves so closely with the **BLACKFEET** that the **MOUNTAIN MEN** sometimes regarded them as the same tribe. Like the Blackfeet, they were hostile to American (though not British) encroachment. In 1873 they joined the Assiniboin on the Fort Belknap Reservation in Montana.

AUTO CAMP A place for "automobilists" to camp, especially in the 1920s in Yellowstone National Park. Cars were permitted into the park in 1916, to the eternal regret of those who love wilderness.

AUX ALIMENTS DU PAYS The expression of a **FUR TRADER** or trapper meaning "to live off the land"; literally, "from the food of the land."

AVALANCHE LILY The dogtooth violet of the Pacific Northwest. Appears near the snow line.

AVALANCHE TRANSCEIVER A radio device that transmits and receives. Used by skiers, skiers, snowmobilers, snowshoers, and other winter travelers in mountain terrain. If an avalanche buries a victim, the transceiver automatically sends a signal to be received by other members of the party, intended to lead rapidly to the victim's location. COMBINATIONS: *avalanche shovel, avalanche probe.*

AVANYU Among **PUEBLO** people, a water serpent, feathered water serpent, or horned water serpent; appears often on pottery. The plumed serpent Quetzalcoatl is a major figure in the mythology of Mexico and Central America.

AVOCADO Properly the avocado pear, a buttery tropical fruit, especially popular in the Southwest in salads and **GUACAMOLE** and with Mexican food. The word comes from Nahuatl via Spanish.

AYORAMA An **ESKIMO-ALEUT** expression meaning "Life is like that" or "It can't be helped."

AZOTEA (ah-so-TAY-uh) The flat roof of an adobe house. Borrowed from Spanish.

BABICHE (bah-BEESH) A thong of skin, especially eel or reindeer skin, often woven into mesh for **SNOWSHOES**. A French-Canadian term.

BABY BEEF A calf under a year old that will be raised for market.

BACH (BATCH) To bachelor it; for men to keep house without women's help. Sometimes spelled *batch.*

BACK EAST The reverse of out West. With some folks, it had the implication of "back in civilization"; with others, it had the implication of "back where everything is messed up."

BACK STRAP The tenderloin, the strips of meat on either side of the backbone of a game animal, known as fine eating.

BACK TO THE BLANKET Where an Indian goes when he "reverts" to his old, "uncivilized" ways. For instance, he might leave off his pants in favor of a **BREECHCLOTH**, pass up indoor plumbing, and fail to show up at his job. Once only derogatory, the phrase now may describe an Indian returning to his roots and trying to keep his culture alive, generally seen as praiseworthy.

BACKBURN A fire set so that it eats up the fuel of a larger, advancing fire and thus starves the big fire; or a fire set to change the direction of the convective heat created by the big fire; or both. In verb form, to set such a fire. Also called a *backfire.*

BACKED UP TO A FREE AIR HOSE To be pregnant, according to *Ten Thousand Goddam Cattle* by Katie Lee, an old Western hand.

BACK-HANDED TRADE A horse trade that was reversed. Usually anything extra thrown in with the horse was not returned with the horse; that is, if you gave cash along with a horse, you lost the cash in a trade that was reversed. Also called a *back trade.*

BACKTRACK To track backward, the way someone came; a fellow who does this is a *backtracker.* The *back track* is the back trail.

BAD MEDICINE (1) The less complicated white-man meaning is: a man who is bad medicine is dangerous, an **HOMBRE** not to be fooled with. (2) The Indian meaning is subtler: A man or woman with bad medicine has spirits set against him, something akin to a hex on him, or is out of tune with the spiritual world. The situation bodes ill and needs to be remedied, usually by ritual or a specific healing ceremony. (See **MEDICINE**.) Consider also what it means when a person's medicine is good.

BADGER HOLE A person's cabin, his home.

BADLANDS What the French called *mauvaises terres pour traverser*—bad country to travel through; in Spanish, MALPAIS. It was first applied to a big area of South Dakota that is eroded, barren, gullied, and full of strange rock formations; by extension, all such regions all over the West, except that volcanic wastes are more likely to be called malpais. Badlands are likely to be populated by *badlanders*. Sometimes the word appears as *badland*.

BADMAN A tough guy; a rowdy, a ruffian, a gunman, a killer; a *bandido*, CABRON, holdup man, long rider, outlaw, ROAD AGENT, and all their snaky kin. According to Barrère and Leland's *Dictionary of Slang, Jargon and Cant*, "This [term] has a special meaning in the West, where it indicates a heartless cruel murderer. Rowdies and bullies in their boasting often describe themselves as 'hard bad men from Bitter Creek.'"

The badman is ultimately the black hat, the fellow Jack Palance portrayed with such vividness in the film version of *Shane*, and then he is a force for evil, in the mythology of the West, to be defeated. But a bit of him is also in the hero, and that is one of the great tensions in the myth: You have to be a little bit bad to be good, to be effective, to get the job done.

BAIDARKA Russian name for a skin boat also known as an *Aleut kayak*.

BAILE (BY-lay) In the Southwest, a Hispanic dance or dance hall; not a particular dance but the entire festivity. Borrowed from Spanish.

BAIT (1) A trap lure for a wolf or other game animal. "To make a good bait a buffalo was killed and cut open on the back, and into the meat blood and entrails three vials of strychnine—three-eights of an ounce—were stirred," explained James Willard Schultz in his classic of life among the Blackfeet, *My Life as an Indian*. Hunters still set baits for bears. (2) In forestry, any offering of food or other necessities to draw animals to an area, whether to improve hunting or for other purposes.

BAKING STONE Among PUEBLO people, a flat slab over a fire to bake bread on; among California Indians, a shaped piece of soapstone.

BALD-FACED Said of a horse or cow with a white blaze on its face. (See also BUCKSKIN.) In Wyoming, colloquially known as a *bolly-faced* cow. A *bald-faced shirt* is a white dress shirt or BOILED SHIRT.

BALING WIRE Wire you fix anything with. Used to tie bales of hay (*bale* is an Americanism but not a Westernism), it is recycled to fix fences and any sort of machinery, from pickups to combines. Its second function is getting under the hooves of horses and cows at the very times they can be tripped. Ranchers everywhere pick up loose baling wire and wad it up to keep critters from getting tangled in it. Today, more and more, twine is being used in place of wire.

BALKY The natural temperament of horses and mules—contrary enough to do anything but what the rider wants; the same as *cold-shouldered*.

BALL (1) What a flint or percussion muzzle-loading rifle or pistol shoots, as opposed to a elliptical bullet. Not a Westernism but an essential element in the whites' taking of the West. The load for a muzzle-loader is **BLACK POWDER**, cloth patch, and ball, put down the barrel in that order. (2) Sometimes it meant a shoot-out—the *commencement of the ball* was the first shot.

BALLOON What a logger calls his pack or bedroll. Also known as *gear* or a **BINDLE**.

BALSA In the Southwest, a raft of bound reeds or bulrushes, especially **TULES**.

BAND A herd of critters, whether horses, buffalo, elk, or sheep. As a verb it means to "group the critters together." A *band wagon* was the wagon of a peddler carrying miscellaneous goods for cowboys.

BANDANNA In the old days, a cowboy wore his bandanna for the same reason he wore his pants, to be decent and acceptable in society. It might be any color, though red was the most common, and made of silk, cotton, or linen. He folded it into a triangle and tied it around his neck with the knot at the back. It might be used for anything the cowhand could imagine. Jo Mora listed "a few" uses in *Trail Dust and Saddle Leather*: as a filter for the dust that moving cattle make, a sling, a water filter, a tourniquet, a towel, a bronc blind, a pigging string, an ear muff, and a pad for a hot handle. And as the shoot-'em-up movies have told us endlessly, it made a good mask for a fellow **ON THE PROD**. Also called a *wipe*.

BANDBOX A conceited dandy given to big words and showing off his knowledge. "'I'd rather have mud on my carpet than that bandbox in any of my chairs,'" said Owen Wister's Mrs. Starr about the polysyllabic soldier Augustus Albumblatt.

BANDIDO (ban-DEE-doh) A bandit; often a Mexican bandit. Borrowed from Spanish.

BANDOLIER A strap over the shoulder that from the 1890s forward held a soldier's extra cartridges; sometimes a ceremonial strap. Also spelled *bandoleer*.

BANG JUICE A chemical that gives a big bang. Among miners, a word for nitroglycerin. Among loggers, a word for dynamite. (See also **POWDER**.)

BANGTAIL See **BROOMTAIL**.

BANK NOTE (1) Currency issued by individual state banks (during the Civil War) and widely distrusted in the West. (2) Metaphorically, anything useful as money—the German physician Frederick Adolphus Wislizenus called beaver skins bank notes.

BANNACK A kind of bread common among the **METIS**, and among whites and Indians on the Northern Plains from the reservation period (beginning in the 1860s) forward. You mix flour, white ashes, and water and cook it in a skillet; when you don't have a skillet, you wrap it around a stick, barber-pole style, and hold it over a flame. Also spelled *bannock*.

BANNOCK A Native tribe that lived and lives in southeastern Idaho. The original name, Ba-nah-qui, mispronounced by trappers as Bannock, means "water I live by." An offshoot of the northern **PAIUTE**, Bannocks have been closely associated with the **SHOSHONES** for centuries. During the period of emigration, they were known for their predations on the Oregon and California Trails. In 1868 they moved to the Fort Hall Reservation in their historic territory in Idaho, but erupted into rebellion once more, led by Chief Buffalo Horn in the Bannock War of 1878. Now they are mostly intermixed with the Shoshone at Fort Hall.

BAR In the design of a brand, a flat line, such as the B–B, called "B bar B."

BAR DOG A bartender.

BAR MINING The washing of gold from river bars (bar diggings), either during low water or by deflecting the water.

BARABARA A community house of the Aleutian Islands, made of a rectangular pit and sod-covered roof.

BARBED MESQUITE Mesquite grass (*Bouteloua* sp.), a valued winter forage in West Texas.

BARBER'S CHAIR In logging, a vertical slab, like the back of a chair, left on a stump by not-quite-successful felling.

BARBOQUEJO (bar-bo-KAY-ho) (1) A Southwestern term for the chin strap for a cowboy hat. Borrowed from Spanish. (2) The chin-strap of a halter. (3) Smith says it originally meant a bandage on the chin of a corpse awaiting burial.

BARBWIRE The wire that won the West. This kind of wire, patented (in the form that became dominant) by Joseph F. Glidden, featured strands of wire twisted in various ways to hold barbs that would keep livestock off. It was essential to fencing the **GREAT PLAINS**, which have almost no wood to use for fencing. In fact, it did away with almost all the rail, hedge, board, and earth fences; it turned the open range into a lot of private pastures; it made raising purebred stock possible because ranchers could keep the common herd bulls away from their cows; it made farming possible because livestock could be kept away from crops; it ended the era of the cattle drives and the great **ROUNDUPS**.

Some ranchers liked the old-time ways and hated the damned fences, which they associated with farming, not ranching. They put men after the wire with wire cutters. Range wars threatened or even erupted, and legislatures had to protect the fences with laws.

In the 1880s, when barbwire sprouted up all over the West, a cowboy's fencing tool became his most important weapon. An old West was unmade and a new one made.

It's fun to fantasize about what the buffalo would have done to it, and how they will trample it if they make the comeback they deserve.

Also spelled *barbed wire* and even *bobwire*, the latter perhaps a Southerner's soft way of saying it.

BAREBACK RIDING One of the standard events of a **RODEO**. The rider must stay on the horse equipped only with *bareback rigging*, a leather strap with a suitcase-like handle that is cinched around the horse's belly.

BAREFOOTED Said of an unshod horse. Indian horses went unshod (except for rawhide shoes, sometimes), but where the white folks went, a blacksmith was sure to follow. A variant is *barefoot*.

BARK MARK In logging, a sign on a log's bark that indicates ownership. The stamp brand on the end of the log did the same but was hard to see in the water.

BARKING AT A KNOT A cowman's way of referring to the impossible. Adams says it's like trying to scratch your ear with your elbow.

BARRACKS 13 According to Smith, the military guardhouse. When his unlucky number came up, that's where a soldier put in some time.

BARRANCA A ravine, a gully; also called a *quebrada*. Borrowed from Spanish. (See also **ARROYO, COULEE**.)

BARREL CACTUS Any of several cylindrical cactuses (*Ferocactus acanrodes* or *Echinocactus* sp.). They can be as high as twelve feet but usually range from two to five feet. Used by travelers as an emergency source of moisture, they are also known as *devil's head*, *Turk's Head*, *hedgehog*, *cottontop*, and *vizniga*.

BARREL-JACKET PUNISHMENT A form of discipline that exhibits army humor. According to Teresa Griffin Vielé in *Following the Drum*, at one frontier post "it consisted of an old flour barrel with a hole cut for his head to pass through, and a pair of holes for his arms. This was a reward for a chronic tendency to 'spree,' which somewhat interfered with the strict performance of his military duties." (See also **WOODEN OVERCOAT**.)

BARREL STOVE A fifty-five-gallon barrel rigged as a wood stove for heating and sometimes for cooking; common in Alaska and the northern Rockies. Also called a *Yukon stove*.

BARRIER A rope that bars the way out of the chute for a roper or bulldogger in a **RODEO**. The barrier is released at the same time the flag is dropped, and the flag starts the time count. To break the barrier is to violate the starting line, which adds a penalty of ten seconds to the contestant's time.

BARRIO An urban ghetto inhabited by Southwestern Hispanics, and usually afflicted with poverty, unemployment, and the attendant problems. Originally, a political subsection of a community.

BASKET MAKER An Indian of an early period of habitation of the Southwest, in the first 500 years A.D. Their culture preceded extensive use of pottery there.

BASQUE BARBEQUE A lamb barbeque; a barbeque where the eaters are Basques, who are often sheepmen.

BASTOS The skirt of a saddle. Sometimes spelled *bastas*. Stewart Edward White noted in *Arizona Nights* that a bull would have gored the rider's horse but for his leather bastos. Borrowed from Spanish (where it means "saddle-pad").

BAT WINGS See CHAPS.

BATAMOTE (bat-uh-MOH-tay) The seep-willow tree of the Southwest. It is also called *aguamote, guatamote,* and *water wally,* which seems charming. Borrowed from Spanish.

BATEA (buh-TAY-uh) A rough wooden bowl used to wash gold. Smith says it is still used in out-of-the-way Mexican mining operations. Borrowed from Spanish (where it means "pan").

BAYETA (1) A long-wearing wool yarn, used by the **NAVAJO** to make bayeta blankets. (2) The cloth made from that yarn. Also appears as *bayjeta* and *vayeta.* Borrowed from Spanish (where it means "flannel").

BAYO In Mexican Spanish, a dun, brown, or sorrel horse with dark mane and tail and a dorsal stripe. In *The Mustangs,* J. Frank Dobie lists *bayo azafranado* (saffron), *bayo blanco* (pale dun), *bayo cebruno* (smoky), *bayo coyote* (what Anglos know as a coyote dun), *bayo naranjado* (orange), and *bayo tigre* (like a **ZEBRA DUN**). (For horse colors see also **BUCKSKIN**.)

BAYOU SALADO See PARK.

B-BOARD A review board of the army in the post—Civil War period that examined the records of officers with questionable ratings and sometimes removed them from the service, according to Smith. Because these boards cleaned out poor officers, they were often called *benzine boards.*

BEAD (1) For Indians all over North America, the most common item of personal decoration. Beads were made (before white contact) of shell, stone, bone, wood, teeth, claws, seeds, bird beaks, clay, and other materials, and were of many shapes, including tubular. After white contact, glass beads became a hugely popular item in the Indian trade. They came mainly from Venice, which was famous for beads traded all over the world, and from Bohemia and Holland, and were made in many colors, sizes, and decorative styles. Some of the distinctive beads during the

Beadwork on a belt of wampum, ca, 1890.
[COURTESY OF NATIONAL ARCHIVES (106 IM-18A).]

period of the Western Indian trade were the sky-blue *chief bead*, the *cornaline d'Aleppo*, the *Russian blue*, the *greasy yellow*, and the *Cheyenne red*. They came in such sizes as *seed bead* (small), *pony bead* (larger), and multicolored beads that might be as large as a joint of a thumb. Such large beads were worn strung on necklaces; seed beads were used for coverage of substantial areas; and pony beads were used for outlines.

Among the **PLAINS INDIANS**, *beadwork* was done by the women (and **ERDACHES**), mostly in geometric patterns until floral beadwork was introduced from the Indians of the Canadian woodlands. Items that were beaded included clothing and pieces of personal adornment.

Beading is still an important practice among Indians of the West and continues to change according to new ideas, fashions, techniques, and materials, like all elements of the cultures. Though the term is not a Westernism, it is essential to an acquaintance with Western Indians.

(2) A rifle's front sight, which is the source of the expression *to draw a bead on* someone or something, meaning "to put your sight on it."

BEAN-EATER A jocular but derogatory term for a Hispanic.

BEAN MASTER The cook, the prima donna of the Dutch oven. See **COOKIE** for his various sobriquets. A *beanery* is a restaurant, especially a low-class establishment that relies on beans a lot. (See also **GREASE JOINT**.)

BEAR DOCTOR Among some California Indians, a **MEDICINE MAN** whose **ANIMAL GUIDE** is a bear.

BEAR GRASS Not a grass but a member of the lily family. In the Northwest, it is the common name for a tall, grasslike plant with a conspicuous white flower (*Xerophyllum tenax*). In the desert Southwest, sotol (*Dasyliron* sp.) and members of the genus *Nolina* (bearing a resemblance to yuccas) are all called bear grass.

BEAR SIGN On the range, doughnuts. The cook who made good ones was beloved, which might mean he was cussed only gently.

BEAR TRAP (1) A severe horse bit. (2) A style of saddle. (3) In a river, a movable dam.

BEARBERRY A low evergreen plant (*Arctostaphylos uva-ursi*), which has a red berry larger than a currant and is a favorite food of moose. It is also called *larb* or **KIN-NIKINNICK**, an ingredient in the smoking mixture that goes by the same name.

BEAR-CLAW NECKLACE Among Indian peoples, a neck decoration made of the claws of the grizzly bear, symbolizing (someone's) triumph over the bear and the courage that took. Still sought by collectors. A trader in southeastern Utah is reported to have let her fingernails grow very long, cut them off, strung them on a thong, and offered them in a case as a bear-claw necklace. (Let the tourist beware.)

BEAR'S ASS! A common oath of **MORMON** country for reasons no one seems to know. Mormons of the early Deseret period, like other frontier people, were prone to scatological talk.

BEARD The pointed seed head of some western grasses that can get stuck in the cattle's soft tissues and cause infections or even blindness.

BEAT THE REPORT For a soldier, to goldbrick, to malinger, to shirk his duty, especially by pretending to be sick.

BEAVER (1) The semi-aquatic, soft-furred animal that originally lured the French, English, Spanish, Russians, Mexicans, and Americans to the Western Plains, mountains, and deserts of the United States; the source of Western wealth, the trappers' bonanza, and a creature mythical for its industriousness and wiliness.

The beaver had a treasure human beings sought avidly, a soft underfur (*muffon*) that made perfect felt for hats. Since this fur was valuable, it became the staple of the **FUR TRADE** and stirred Indians and **MOUNTAIN MEN** to trap the beaver ceaselessly. They also valued the poor fellow for his tail, which was a delicacy when boiled. All this desirability might have been the critter's undoing, some people say, except that in the 1830s beaver hats whimsically went out of fashion, and silk came marching in. The beaver is alive and well and living throughout the modern West.

(2) A word for the felt hat that was made from the underfur of the critter, both the civilized man's dress hat and the wide-brimmed topper of the outdoorsman. (Thus, when the Scots baronet William Drummond Stewart described mountain man Bill Williams as wearing a beaver with a hole in it, we need not try to imagine a fifty-pound castor curled on his head.) Beaver is still an important source of felt for Western hats.

(3) The common term a **MOUNTAIN MAN** used for himself and his **COM-PAÑERO** (companion). Other terms include **CHILD**, **HOSS**, and **NIGGER** (a word without racial implications in this case).

(4) A word for money, because beaver pelts were a universally accepted medium of exchange. "Whose beaver you earnin'?" was asking "Who's your employer?"

BED GROUND Where the cattle or sheep lie down for the night to sleep. On **TRAIL DRIVES**, the hands would then take turns riding in a circle around the cows, singing and whistling to keep them settled down. The bed ground was chosen by the trail boss or the cook, either of whom would ride ahead and find a good spot. Getting the herd to lie down is called *bedding down* or, less commonly, *fathering the herd*.

To *bed out* is to bivouac, to sleep out, usually without a tent, as cowboys did on trail drives and roundups. They used a *bed wagon*, which on trail drives hauled along the hands' bedding, **WAR BAGS**, and other essential items. It was also known as the *hoodlum wagon*. Small outfits didn't have a bed wagon but carried this stuff in the **CHUCK WAGON**. The cowboy slept in a bedroll (also called *bedding roll* or just *roll*), usually consisting of a tarpaulin, blankets, and a **SUGAN** (comforter).

Among cowboys, a critter that's been busted hard enough to make it lie still is called *bedded*, and to *bed him down* means to "kill someone." (See also **DRY-GULCH**.)

BEDROCK (1) The solid rock that alluvial gold rests on. (2) Figuratively, the bottom, the fundamental, the essential. (3) Fine, excellent, first-rate. In *The Virginian*, Owen Wister writes, "That play is bedrock, ma'am!" (4) To *get down to bedrock* is to go past the small talk and get down to essentials. (5) To *bedrock a horse* is to ride it down, break its spirit.

BEEF (1) To convert a cow into meat for the pot. Since it was usually someone else's cow in the open-range days, it was said of many a rancher that he never tasted his own beef except when in somebody else's camp. (2) To complain. (3) An ox; a steer, especially one more than four years old.

COMBINATIONS: *beef book* (the account of the ranch's cattle; the *tally book*), *beef roundup* (the fall roundup in which the cattlemen cut the herd, that is, separated out the animals ready to ship to market, also known as the *butt* or *steer cut*), *beef drive* (driving beef to the shipping point), *beef biscuit* (a biscuit of beef and bread made in Texas, or canned beef), *beef tea* (something completely unappetizing, water befouled by cows).

BEEF ISSUE The distribution of beeves to Indians on a reservation on *issue day*; also called a *cattle issue*. It was often followed by a mock buffalo hunt, the Indians killing their meat in "sporting" fashion.

The treaty between the federal government and an Indian tribe requiring a beef issue was called a *beef treaty*. Such agreements notoriously were violated Indian agents so consistently stole rations allotted to Indians by treaty that *agent* became a way of saying *thief*. Indians often rebelled against going to a reservation because it meant virtual starvation.

Drawing rations at the agency on issue day. Indians form a line while officers' wives and issuing agent stand in center with sacks of flour at Camp Supply, Indian Territory, ca. 1871.
[COURTESY OF NATIONAL ARCHIVES.]

BEEF PLUMB TO THE HOCK A description of a person who's big and fat (perhaps two ax handles across the beam).

BEEFALO Like CATTALO, a cross of the buffalo and the beef cow, according to Webster's five-eighths beef and three-eighths bison; various mixtures have been tried. Usually ranchers who crossbreed cows with buffalo are seeking more meat on the frame and so more profit, but the American supermarkets and meat buyers have traditionally resisted the result.

BEEFSTEAK To ride a horse in a way that galls its back. Light riders don't do this.

BEET VACATION A distinctive privilege of school children in sugar beet areas, who got out of school for the harvesting.

BEGGING DANCE A ceremony of some tribes of the Northern Plains intended to encourage people of means to give to those who are in need.

BELDUQUE (bell-DOO-kay) In the Southwest, a big sheath knife; also spelled *berduque* and *verduque*. Borrowed from Spanish.

BELL (1) A belled sheep, used as a marker. Sheepherders bell about ten sheep in every thousand as a way of keeping track of them. (2) Sometimes a jocular term for a rattler's rattles, as in "bells on his tail." A rattler was also called a *belled snake*.

In the army, *bell sharp* was an expression that described a trained mule. The experienced mules responded to bell commands. The new mules, not yet bell sharp, had their tails shaved for recognition and thus were called **SHAVETAILS**.

A *belled mare* (or *bell*) was a mule or horse that led the others in a bunch; sometimes for greater visibility, a white mare was chosen.

BELLY BUSTER A Texas word for the pole used to shut wire gates, because of what happens if you let it slip. Also called a *jaw buster*.

BELLY GUN A short-barreled pistol stuck naked into the waistband of your pants instead of holstered.

BELLY UP (1) To go belly up is to die. (2) Most Westerners have been known to belly up to a bar, bring up a stool, and have a drink.

To *belly through the brush* is to be on the dodge, trying to stay ahead of the law; a *belly rope* is a roper's loop that ends up around a critter's belly instead of its neck, a comical error.

BELLY WASH Weak coffee; according to loggers, weak coffee is *soda pop*.

BELLYCHEATER An army cook. Also known as *bellyrobber*.

BELLYFUL OF BEDSPRINGS A horse that's a good bucker.

BENCH A flat stretch of land, usually above a river and below hills, often irrigable. It is a venerable Westernism, dating to the journals of the Lewis and Clark Expedition.

BEND To slowly change the direction in which **CATTLE** are moving; especially, to turn a stampede.

BEND AN ELBOW To drink booze. When someone is drunk, he's *on a bender* and *paints the town red*. (See **ROOSTERED**.)

BENZINERY A low-grade drinking place. Cheap whiskey was sometimes called *benzine*.

BERDACHE An Indian male who dressed and lived entirely as a woman, fulfilling that cultural role within the tribe; sometimes called in Indian languages a "would-be woman" and sometimes thought of as a third sex. Common among the tribes of the Americas, these men-women had social and religious powers: They might be givers of sacred names; first to strike the **SUN-DANCE** pole; leaders of scalp dances; good luck to war parties; visionaries and predictors of the future; matchmakers; excellent artisans in beadwork, quillwork, hide-tanning, and making clothing; creators and singers of songs. Understood as following a vision by most Indians, they were not tolerated by whites. They persist even today, discreetly. Among the Sauk and Fox, they were known as the *I-coo-coo-a*; Chippewa, the *Agokwa*; Cheyenne, the *he-man-eh*; Sioux, the *winkte*; Crow, the *ba'te*; Shoshone, the *teni-wiaph*; Navajo, the *nadle*. From French.

BERINGIA The Bering Land Bridge, a wide piece of land between Alaska and Siberia exposed during the Ice Age between ten thousand and fifteen thousand years ago; believed to have offered passage for migration of people and animals from Asia to North America, or the reverse.

BETWEEN A ROCK AND A HARD PLACE Between two unsatisfactory alternatives. *Between hay and grass* means that time of year between winter and spring when the hay has run out and the grass isn't yet up for the stock to feed on.

BIBLE (1) What a waddy (cowboy) called his cigarette papers. (2) *Bible Two* was the fugitive list of the Texas Rangers. Rangers read it more often than the real Bible; it was also called the *black book*.

BIBLE-PUNCHER A preacher. (See also **BLACK ROBE**.)

BICYCLE To scratch a bucking horse with your spurs, in a pedaling motion; usually seen in **CONTEST RIDES** in **RODEOS** to encourage the horse to bust loose like a tornado. (See also **RAKE**.)

BIDDY What a sheepherder calls an old ewe.

BIENVENIDO Welcome. So common in the Southwest today you can hear it on the public-address systems in discount stores announcing the latest shoppers' specials. Borrowed from Spanish.

BIG In American Red English, big doesn't necessarily mean big physically but special or powerful. *Big day*, for instance, means Sunday, and *big canoe* a sailing ship.
　　COMBINATIONS: Mathews gives these other *big* compounds without defining them, but some of the meanings are clear from usage: *big chief* (important

leader), *big dog* (horse), *big hearts, big lodge* (fort), *big gun* (cannon), *big medicine* (special spiritual power), *big river, big speak, big talk* (council), *big village, big waters* (ocean).

In Anglo usage, *big* adds emphasis in the following combinations: Among loggers, *big bull* and *big savage* (names for the boss or general superintendent; see also SUPREME BEING), *big hole* (a logging truck's lowest gear), *big sticks* (the woods).

Among cowboys, *big boss* (the owner of the herd, the owner of the cow outfit; sometimes he's known as the *big augur* or simply *augur*), the *big house* (the main ranch house), *big jaw* (a disease of cattle also known as lump or lumpy jaw), *big jump* (death), *take the big jump* (to die; see also CASH IN YOUR CHIPS); *big loop* (the noose of a rustler), *big windy* (a yarn, a tall tale), *big antelope* (a SLOW ELK, a euphemism for meat from another man's cow).

A *big casino* is an idea or asset you imagine will be a BONANZA. *Big ditch* is an irrigation system's main ditch, in the Southwest sometimes known as *madre acequia*.

BIG FIFTY A .50-caliber Sharps rifle used by professionals for buffalo hunting. It was the buffalo hunter's business tool, sixteen pounds unloaded, with three-quarter-inch, 120-grain, black-powder cartridges for differing ranges.

BIG KNIFE A Red English name for white Americans other than the French and English. (See also ANGLO, LONG KNIFE.)

BIG MUDDY The Missouri River, traditionally said to come from an Indian name, *Pekitanoui*, meaning muddy water.

BIG TIMBER A big grove of cottonwood trees on the northern bank of the Arkansas River in Colorado, used by the southern CHEYENNE as a favored camping place and a fording place for the river. William Bent built his New Fort there, downstream from the site of Bent's Old Fort, now a National Historic Site.

BIGFOOT See SASQUATCH.

BIGHORN The Rocky Mountain sheep, commonly known as the bighorn sheep. They are distinguished by their huge horns, which curl tightly on the sides of their heads and are bigger around at the base than a man's biceps. Legendary for their surefootedness, bighorns live in the high, rocky places, not the forests; there is also an endangered desert variety. They are something of a rare sight: Even the noted hunter and outdoorsman Teddy Roosevelt, when he visited Yellowstone National Park as president, stopped shaving and ran lathered to see bighorns at Tower Junction. Lieutenant George Frederick Ruxton, a British traveler in the West during the 1840s, reports in *Life in the Far West* that "the hunters assert that, in descending the precipitous sides of the mountains, the sheep frequently leap from the height of twenty or thirty feet, invariably alighting on their horns, and thereby saving their bones from certain dislocation." This tale demonstrates that Westerners got an early start in STUFFING DUDES.

BILAGANNA NAVAJO term for white man; also spelled *billakona*. Smith says it is simply the result of the Navajo attempt to pronounce the word *Americano*. Tony Hillerman, through his mystery novels set in Navajo country, is making this word commonplace.

BILER (BEE-ler) Slang for a snowmobiler. Bilers are sometimes disliked by the other principal winter cavorters in the mountains, cross-country skiers, and vice versa; the skiers complain about the noise and smell of the snow machines, and the bilers complain about being complained about. Yellowstone and Grand Teton National Parks in 2000 announced the banning of snowmobiles from those parks. In remote parts of Alaska and the Rocky Mountains, snowmobiles offer the only workable winter transportation.

BILL SHOW A Wild West show, like Pawnee Bill's or Buffalo Bill's. A cowboy full of tricks and show was a *Bill-show* cowboy.

BILLIKEN In Alaska, a wooden doll probably carved by an ESKIMO, making a souvenir or good-luck charm. Not originally Eskimo or Alaskan but a product of Missouri.

BILLY HELL A hell of a lot of hell; what you raise when you're really raising cain.

BINDLE STIFF (1) A Western hobo. (2) In logging, a logger with a bindle (a bedroll, a BALLOON). STIFF often means "working man."

BIRD CAGE A twentieth-century name for CHUCK-A-LUCK, a gambling game that uses a metal cage in the shape of an hourglass.

BIRD CALL A wind instrument of Southwestern Indians made of two pieces of concave shard bound together with YUCCA fibers.

BIRLING Log rolling, or log birling; turning a log underfoot as it floats, which loggers known as *river drivers* did as both work and sport. They were called *birlers* and held *birling matches*.

BISCUIT Another word for the saddle HORN, which is also called an APPLE, DINNER PLATE, and *pig*.

BISCUIT-SHOOTER A waitress; a *cookie pusher*. Also one of the many terms for cook, as is *biscuit-roller*. (See also COOKIE.)

BISHOP The spiritual leader of a WARD of the Church of Jesus Christ of the LATTER-DAY SAINTS. He is a lay minister and receives no compensation, so normally holds a job in the community.

BIT (1) Originally an eighth of a Spanish or Spanish Colonial dollar (thus *two bits, four bits, six bits* as common ways of expressing monetary value); later a Spanish coin worth twelve and one-half cents. A *short bit* was a dime; a *long bit* was twelve and one-half cents. A *bit house* was a saloon that charged one bit (or two, or another number of bits) for drinks, cigars, and so on. If you asked for change, says William Foster-Harris in *The Look of the Old West*, they threw you out.

(2) The metal bar in a horse's mouth to which the reins are attached. There are many types in the West. The two most common kinds are the *snaffle bit* and the *curb bit*. The curb bit has a port (upward curve or extension) and sometimes a roller in the mouthpiece, and uses metal extensions to increase the pull of the rein by leverage. The snaffle is jointed in the middle of the mouthpiece and uses no leverage, so is less severe. A *bat bit* has a straight mouthpiece, neither jointed nor curved upward. The *bit chain* fastens a rein to the ring on each end of the bit (to prevent the horse from biting the rein). Bits

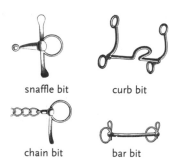

snaffle bit   curb bit

chain bit   bar bit

Horse bits.
[From *Moseman's Illustrated Guide for Purchasers of Horse Furnishing Goods*, ca. 1892.]

are also mounted with silver and otherwise made decorative. Indians used bits of rawhide. (See also **SPADE BIT**.)

BITCH (1) A primitive lamp made by sticking a rag into a cup of grease and lighting it. (See also **HAPPY JACK**.) (2) A sling beneath a wagon for firewood; also called a *cuna* or a *caboose*. (See also **COONEY**.)

BITE THE DUST To be thrown from a horse. Every cowboy gets "throwed." Range wisdom has it that "there ain't no horse that can't be rode, ain't no man that can't be throwed." When you do get throwed, you're said to have **DIRTIED YOUR SHIRT,** *eaten dirt without stooping, chased a cloud, chewed (or eaten or tasted) gravel, eaten grass, gone forked end up, gone grass hunting, gone picking daisies, gone up to fork a cloud, gotten busted, gotten dumped, gotten dusted, gotten flung away, gotten grassed, gotten piled, gotten spilled, gotten spread-eagled, kissed the ground, landed on your sombrero, lost your hat and gotten off to look for it, lost your horse, met your shadow on the ground, picked daisies, sunned your moccasins, taken a fart-knocker, taken a squatter's right,* or *taken up a homestead.*

    Bite the dust also meant "to hit the dust with your face from any cause," such as a blow or a bullet. The climax of a formulaic Western tale comes when the villain bites the dust. To *bite the ground* is to get killed. (See also **CASH IN YOUR CHIPS**.)

    To *bite off more than you can chew* is to take on a job you can't handle; from the notion of biting off a bigger piece of plug tobacco than your mouth can deal with.

BIZCOCHITOS Thick, crisp cookies flavored with anise. Borrowed from Spanish.

BLAB A board fastened to a calf's nose that hangs down and keeps the critter from nursing but permits it to graze; thus is it weaned. Sometimes called a *butterboard weaner* or, in full, a *blab board.*

BLACK BLIZZARD An expression of the **GREAT PLAINS** for a terrible dust storm. COMBINATIONS: *dust blizzard, ground blizzard* (a storm of snow blowing up from the ground). *Blizzard-choked* is an expression for cattle pushed into a draw, a fence, or the like by a blizzard.

BLACK MIKE What loggers call stew.

BLACK POWDER See DuPONT.

BLACK ROAD In DAKOTA tradition, a way of living that is full of conflict, danger, and difficulty; it runs east and west. The RED ROAD, by contrast, is peaceful and fulfilling. (For more information, read *The Good Red Road* by Kenneth Lincoln and Al Logan Slagle.)

BLACK ROBE A priest, especially a Jesuit; a term the Indians of the Plains and mountains used in their languages and tried on white folks in the English; a frontierism not peculiar to the West. A *black-robe woman* is a nun. The most famous of these Jesuit proselytizers was Pierre Jean De Smet, whom the Western Indians admired.

Other Westernisms for priests and preachers: *bible-puncher, converter, cura, gospel-sharp, sin buster, sin twister,* and *sky pilot.*

BLACKBALLED OUTFIT In the days of the open range, a ranch prohibited from sending a REP (a representative looking for his outfit's strays) to the main ROUNDUP. Outfits were blackballed when folks thought they were rustling or helping RUSTLERS.

BLACKFEET A Native tribe of Algonquian origin that became a buffalo-hunting culture living in the nineteenth century in the country around the Missouri and Saskatchewan Rivers. Consisting of the Bloods, the PIEGANS, and the SIKSIKA, the Blackfeet were fiercely proud and aggressive, making war on Indians and whites alike and being especially intolerant of American trappers and traders. The Gros Ventres were closely associated with these tribes, but were detached ARAPAHO. The Blackfeet tribe was reduced by smallpox in the late 1830s. After the Baker massacre of Piegans in 1870, many Blackfeet went to Canada. Their U.S. reservation is now in northwestern Montana. Though some dictionaries say otherwise, the Blackfeet say that their tribal name has no form that looks singular in English—it's correct to say "one Blackfeet"—and it seems only courteous to adopt the usage they prefer.

BLACK-FOOTED FERRET A Western weasel on the verge of extinction. Scientists reintroduced this creature into the wild in 1991.

BLACKJACK (1) The wagering card game *vingt et un,* or twenty-one, imported from France. The goal for the player is to get a total of points (face cards counting ten, aces eleven or one, numbered cards their face value) closer to twenty-one than the dealer gets; if any player or the dealer goes over twenty-one, he is *busted.* Principal blackjack terms include *bust, drag down, hard seventeen, hit me, soft seventeen, twenty-one,* and *vingt-et-un.*

(2) A small, flexible, leather club with a weighted head. (The verb form, to blackjack a fellow, is not a Westernism.) (3) In logging, coffee (which is also called *blackstrap*). (4) In mining, a dark kind of zinc blend.

BLACKJACK STEER An undernourished steer from timber country.

BLACKLEG (1) A disease that primarily afflicts yearling calves, causing fever and gaseous swelling. Infectious, it can kill within a day or two. (2) Lieutenant George Frederick Ruxton tells us in *Life in the Far West* that scurvy was called blackleg in Missouri in the 1840s.

BLACKSNAKE A whip of plaited leather used by **BULLWHACKERS** and other handlers of draft animals.

BLADDER DART Among **ESKIMO** people, a harpoon with a seal bladder inflated and used as a marker (because it floats to the surface) when sea hunting.

BLADDER FESTIVAL A ceremony of renewal of **ESKIMO** people, lasting five days. The name comes from the bladders of sea mammals, which are inflated, painted, and hung in the ceremonial house.

BLANKET INDIAN An Indian who holds to the traditional ways of his culture; a "wild, uncivilized" Indian; now archaic. (See also **BACK TO THE BLANKET, HAT INDIAN**.)

BLANKET TOSS Among Alaskan Natives, a game at festivals, tossing a person up and down over and over on a blanket.

BLAZE (1) A shallow cutting away of a tree's bark to mark it, usually to indicate a trail. Trails in the West are still blazed in this way. The verb form means to make such a cut and, by extension, to create a new trail. (2) A white stripe on a horse's face. Such a horse is called a *blaze-face* or *blaze-faced*. (See also **BUCKSKIN**.)

BLAZER A bluff, a lie, a trick, a deception. To *run a blazer* is to try to deceive someone.
    One narrator of Stewart Edward White's *Arizona Nights* runs a blazer with his life at stake. Coming out of his mine shaft, he finds some **CHIRICAHUA** Apaches waiting for him with bloody thoughts. Luckily, the blasts he has set below start going off. When the third and last one blows, he yells that a fourth is coming. "It was just a cold, raw blazer," he admits, "and if it didn't go through I could see me as an Apache parlour ornament. But it did. Those Chiricahuas give one yell and skipped."

BLAZING STAR A **STAMPEDE** of animals, especially pack animals, not as a herd but bursting in every direction at once. A wonderfully expressive Westernism.

BLIND (1) An eye-covering for a horse; also called a *blinder*. See also **SLIDING LEATHER BLIND**. (2) A fine levied on a soldier by a court martial; according to Smith, a blind cost a soldier his pay but not his freedom. (3) As an adjective, it means something concealed, not seen, as in the title of Ralph Beer's good novel of Montana ranching, *The Blind Corral*. A *blind canyon* is a **BOX CANYON**. A *blind trap* is a disguised corral for catching wild horses or cattle. Brush, branches, or camouflaged poles wing the corral, forming a chute, and the hunters of wild horses or wild cattle chase the animals into the trap.

BLIND STAGGERS A disease affecting the brains of horses, causing them to stagger. One source says it is caused by selenium poisoning. Originally an Americanism, not a Westernism, but now common mostly in the West.

BLM See BUREAU OF LAND MANAGEMENT.

BLOAT The distention of the gut of a cow caused by trapped gas. Bloat, caused by malfunctions of the digestive system or drastic changes in diet, can be relieved by applications of mineral oil, by massage (both of which move the gas through the digestive tract), or by inserting a tube down the animal's throat (to discharge the gas out the mouth).

BLOCKER LOOP An oversize roping loop named for Texas cowman John Blocker, or possibly his brother Ab, and said to descend ultimately from the VAQUEROS. Sometimes said to be the most versatile of all roping throws, the Blocker, or *Johnnie Blocker*, may be thrown mounted or on foot and used to catch the head, forefeet, or heels. Thrown from the right shoulder with a leftward twist of the hand so that the loop sails left, it delivers, according to W. F. French, "a bigger opening at the right place and at the right angle."

BLOND SWEDE A logger's expression for an elderly man.

BLOOD BAY A bay horse (brown or reddish brown with black mane and tail) of especially dark red. (For horse colors, see BUCKSKIN.)

BLOSSOM In mining, a kind of quartz colored by oxides that promises lead. Also known as *blossom rock*.

BLOT A BRAND To make a brand unrecognizable. A *blotched brand* is one that has been blotted.

BLOW (1) To leave, to clear out of the country. (2) To arrive, to blow in with the tumbleweeds. (3) To take a rest, a breather, as in "let's let the horses blow" or in the noun form, *take a blow*. (4) To lose a STIRRUP, which, like pride, often goeth before a fall. In RODEO, blowing a stirrup disqualifies the rider. (5) Among loggers, to head to town to celebrate.

BLOW OUT HIS LAMP To kill a man. (See also DRY-GULCH.)

BLOW THE WHISTLE Among contemporary Plains Indians, to participate in the SUN DANCE; also, to *use the whistle*. Perhaps so named because of the use of eagle-bone whistles by dancers. Historically some warriors were given the right in visions or through membership in a warrior society to blow the whistle while making a war charge.

BLOWDOWN A group of trees felled by a high wind, or an area of such trees. A blowdown can be hard for a hiker to get through and worse for a rider. (See also **DOWN TIMBER**.)

BLOWOUT (1) A party, a celebration, a fancy social event. In Santa Fe, General Benjamin Grierson "attended a number of 'blowouts,' at which the people were fashionably dressed and the ladies' gowns were described in the local press." (William H. and Shirley A. Leckie, *Unlikely Heroes: General Benjamin H. Grierson and His Family*.) (2) An explosion in a mine. (3) In mining, a big outcrop with a smaller vein underneath. (4) In dry country, a place where the loose sand has blown away, creating a dip and killing the surrounding grass.

BLUE NORTHER See **NORTHER**.

BLUE PELT A summer beaver pelt, thin and dry, not worth a cent.

BLUE-CHIP Of great value. According to linguist J. L. Dillard in *All-American English*, though this term is now mostly applied to stocks and securities, it originated in poker, where the most valuable chips are blue.

BLUECOAT A term of Plains Indians for U.S. soldiers. Cavalrymen were **YELLOW LEGS**, from the yellow stripe on their pants.

BLUE-SKY (1) To chew the dog, to visit, to pass the time of day. It may be an expression mostly of the Northern Plains. (2) As a modifier, something fantastical, as "he gave me a blue-sky figure."

BLUESTEM A native grass (*Andropogon* sp.) common in the West and valued as forage. Big bluestem (*Andropogon fucatus*) grows up to twelve feet high and is a major grass of the tall-grass prairie; *little bluestem* (*A. scoparius*) is a bunch grass that is three to five feet tall.

BLUFF From the mid-1840s and for several decades thereafter, bluff was a common name for **POKER**. A bluff is one of the key ploys of a good poker player, or even a bad one. When you bluff, you raise the bet with a feigned confidence that you hope will convince the other players that you hold better cards than you do; then they may drop out *(toss in their hands)*, leaving the pot to your weak hand. You can run a bluff better if you have the luck to get a couple of good cards dealt face up. Of course, the ploy may not work. Western writer Bret Harte put the eternal question this way: "But what if he sees that little bluff and calls ye?" Thus the expression to *call your bluff*.

BOARDING SCHOOL As it has to do with American Indians, a school where Indian children were (and sometimes are) brought for training in the Anglo culture. The best known was the Carlisle Indian School in Pennsylvania. Boarding schools were principal elements of the U.S. government policy of assimilation. Though many Indians wanted education, they also often regarded it as "killing the Indian to save the child." To this end, Indians at various times were even forbidden to speak their native languages at these schools.

Children were often taken by force, and separated from their families for the first time in their lives. Since Indian family members were almost never apart, this separation was a great source of pain; Indian children too often committed suicide at boarding schools. The schools were often church-sponsored, and priests unfortunately often proved to be pederasts.

BOARDINGHOUSE MAN A word for a cook among loggers. (See also **HASHER**.)

BOAR'S NEST What a logger calls a lumber camp and what a cowboy calls a line camp. (See also **LINE RIDER**.)

BOBTAIL (1) A discharge from the army that offered no character reference; not quite so black a mark as the *blue ticket*. (2) The *bobtail watch* was the first watch of night during a **TRAIL DRIVE**. (3) Modern cowboys use bobtail to mean short—a *bobtail cow* is one with a short tail and a *bobtail crew* is one short of enough cowboys to get the job done properly.

BODEGA A store that sells wine or liquor. Borrowed from Spanish.

BOG HOLE Boggy ground or quicksand; by extension, anything tricky, hard to figure, likely to snare you in a way you don't want.

BOG ITS HEAD For a **BRONC** to lower its head to jump, thus a good time for the rider to check his balance and try to explain to himself what he's doing on the **HURRICANE DECK**.

BOG RIDER A cowboy who rides along bogs and marshes to find *bogged* cows and pull them out. In the spring in Texas, cows flee to the bogs for relief from the heel flies.

BOG THEM IN For a rodeo rider to fail to *bicycle*, to scratch his horse with his spurs; also called *bog time in*.

BOGGY-TOP A Texas expression for open-faced pie, pie without a top crust.

BOIL OVER For a horse to *blow up*, go crazy and start to **BUCK**.

BOILED SHIRT A starched shirt, a shirt with a stiff front. Also known as a *biled shirt*, a custom of dress disliked on the frontier. Sometimes called (amusingly) a *fried shirt*. Mark Twain remarked in *Roughing It*, "The miners [of California] had a particular malignant animosity toward what they called a 'biled shirt,' doubtless associating it with snobbishness, or 'upper-class' ways of life in general."

BOILER One of a logger's names for the cook. (See **HASHER**.)

BOILERMAKER AND HIS HELPER A cowboy's name for a whiskey with a beer chaser.

BOIS D'ARC (BOH-dark) Literally, "bow wood"; the wood of the Osage orange, used to make bows. It's also grown as a hedge on the Eastern Plains. From French.

BOIS DE VACHE Cow chips, or buffalo manure (later, cow manure), used as a fuel; Americanized to *bodewash*. Making fires with **BUFFALO CHIPS** was a necessity on the Plains because trees were few and far between. From French (in which it means literally "wood of the cow").

BOLO TIE Strictly a modern form of the man's necktie—Webster's shows the word's first usage in 1964. It is a length of cord, often braided or woven, usually in the Southwest. It is often clasped with something ornamental, like a fine piece of blossom turquoise, a nice piece of jewelry from ZUNI or HOPI, or some beadwork or QUILLWORK, and is one of the small sartorial indulgences of the conventional Western male. Occasionally spelled *bola*.

BOLOGNA BULL A bull whose meat will bring a low price and may be used to make baloney (bologna sausage).

BONANZA (1) A lucky find of a valuable mineral deposit. (2) The deposit itself. (3) To be *in bonanza* is to be producing at a handsome rate. Sometimes a bonanza is, as Maurice Weseen called it in *A Dictionary of American Slang*, "a hole in the ground owned by a champion liar."

BONE HUNTER A person who hunted buffalo bones on the Plains, where the *buffalo runners* (buffalo hunters) and coyotes had left them. Fertilizer plants bought the bones. Surely these fine beasts being chopped into fertilizer is a symbol of the magnificent brought to naught. Bone hunters were also called *bone pilgrims*. (See also BORRASCA.)

BONEYARD A cemetery, *boot hill,* or *bone orchard*, whether for people or critters. In cowboy talk, *bone-seasoned* meant experienced.

BOOGER DANCE A ceremony of CHEROKEE Indians in which they ridicule the behavior of enemies, including whites. Dancers wear grotesque *booger masks. Booger* is reported to be a version of *bogey*.

BOOGERED Buffaloed; intimidated. Max Evans, in his classic comic novel *The Rounders*, has one cowboy admit of Old Fooler, the meanest critter ever to be bridled, "This horse had me slightly boogered." That's classic, leg-pulling Western understatement. *Boogered up* is a cowboy term for "crippled."

BOOGIE BOARD Among surfers, a short, rigid-foam board held under the upper part of the body for body-surfing.

BOOK COUNT The number of cows the *tally book* says there are. In the days of the open range, big cow outfits were often bought and sold by absentee owners by their book count, which was sometimes a BLUE-SKY tally.

BOOKS WON'T FREEZE In the cattle country of the NORTHERN PLAINS, an ironic expression assuring cattlemen that their investments were safe. Some hard winters froze a lot of cattle there, especially the winter of 1887, and some Eastern and British investors got hurt. But the great herds were often sold by the number of animals on the books (BOOK COUNT), not actual count, and no books froze to death. The tale is that the remark originated with Luke Murrin, a saloon keeper who used it to cheer up his Wyoming cattlemen customers.

BOOM (1) A rush of water used to wash out deposits of gold (also called a *boom flume*); similarly, a rush of water in a river.

(2) In logging, a barrier of logs or timbers that impounds floating logs in a river; also, the logs thus held back. It is also used as a verb meaning "to form a boom." COMBINATIONS: *boom gather* (a worker who collects logs in booms), *boom house* (where the boom workers live), *boom man* (a worker who floats logs downstream), *boom master* or *boom tender* (the supervisor of a boom), *boom rat* (a worker who rafts logs in a boom), *boom stick* or *boom log* (a log fastened to other logs to make a boom), *boom-stick cutter* (a worker who makes boom sticks).

(3) A rush of business activity, often caused in the West by the coming of a railroad, the discovery of valuable minerals, the arrival of trail herds, and the like. Over most of the West, of course, this was often followed by a bust. Wyoming has a classic boom-and-bust economy. The fur trappers came in the 1820s and left when the market dropped. The 1840s saw thousands of emigrants in wagons; 1868 brought a gold rush to South Pass; the 1880s a boom of cattle-raising. The next century brought oil and gas booms. In the 1970s the exploitation of the **OVER-THRUST BELT** set **SEISMIC CREWS** and drilling crews to work all over the state. Yet busts followed every boom. Even in the 1980s the towns of Lander and Evanston suffered depressions when mineral exploitation ceased, and Jeffrey City and Hannah dwindled to nearly nothing.

BOOMER A **SOONER**, a fellow who started his land rush before the legal date; also, a man who was a booster for settling lands, especially Indian lands, before it became legal. The expression came into currency in the mid-1880s, just before the whites made several grabs of Indian Territory of the legal-but-not-right variety.

BOOSHWAY Among American beaver men, a field leader, the fellow who set procedure and discipline on the trail; often one of the backers. Nowadays, among **BUCKSKINNERS** (**MOUNTAIN-MAN** hobbyists), the booshway is the man who organizes camp at **RENDEZVOUS** and sets and enforces rules. Also spelled *bushway*. An Americanization of the French **BOURGEOIS**.

BOOSTER A shill for a gambler, a decoy, a **CAPPER**.

BOOT YARD A cemetery, especially for those who died with their boots on; also called a **BONEYARD**, *bone orchard, pave patch, still yard,* and, in the twentieth century, *boot hill.*

BOOTBLACK COWPUNCHER An old-time cattleman's expression for an Easterner who got into the cow business for what he hoped would be the profits.

BOOTJACK A device for removal of a cowboy boot. It has a flat part to hold down with one foot and a forked part to stick the heel of the other boot into. Sometimes the forks are designed in the shape of horns or, jokingly, a woman's legs. A boot is difficult to get off with hands alone any time, and after a few drinks is nigh impossible.

BOOTLEG (1) To sell whiskey illegally. A native Western word, it originally meant to smuggle whiskey to the Indians in violation of law in a flat bottle that fit in the leg of a boot. Later it came to mean selling anything illegally. The fellow who does that is a *bootlegger*. (2) Among miners, an explosive charge that doesn't break the rock.

BOOZE BLIND Very drunk; so drunk he couldn't hit the ground with his hat in three throws; so drunk he could see critters that weren't there; so drunk he thought he could sing. Also known as *gypped,* **ALKALIED, ROOSTERED,** *a walking whiskey vat.* (For the many words for booze, see also **FIREWATER**.)

BORAX LAKE A lake with lots of borates (compounds of boric acid); a salt or **ALKALI** lake.

BORDER SHIFT A tricky maneuver to get a loaded gun into your shooting hand. If one hand got short of ammunition, you threw the loaded gun into the other one.

BORRACHO A border word for being drunk, or a drunkard. Borrowed from Spanish.

BORRASCA A mine that's poor or worthless; the opposite of *bobabza* or **BONANZA**. Borrowed from Spanish.

BORROW PIT In the West, the ditch on each side of a road, where earth was "borrowed" to form the roadbed. Also called a *borrow ditch, barrow pit,* and, in Texas, *bar ditch.*

BOSAL The noseband of a **HACKAMORE**, usually about finger-thick and braided from rawhide. It does for a hackamore what a bit does for the bridle. A *bosal brand* is a **BRAND** burned where the bosal goes, on the nose. From the Spanish *bozal* (meaning "muzzle"), a spelling that also occurs in American English.

BOSQUE Forest or woods, used widely in the Southwest. Also occurs in an Americanized version, *bosky.* The place of imprisonment of the **NAVAJOS** at Bosque Redondo in the mid-1860s has been called the first American concentration camp (see **LONG WALK**.) From Spanish.

BOSS (1) What you sometimes call a cow—"Hiy, boss, get, boss." (2) The hump on the back of a buffalo's neck. The *boss rib* is a cut of meat from the boss, and a delicacy. It was eaten roasted by the **MOUNTAIN MEN** and boiled by later whites. (3) Among loggers, the supervisor of the tree-felling crew is the *boss faller. Boss-simple* describes a fellow intimidated by his boss.

BOSSLOPER An independent **FUR TRADER**. Common among those hobbyists who re-create the **MOUNTAIN-MAN** lifestyle, known as **BUCKSKINNERS**. Also spelled *bushloper.* An Americanization of the Dutch *boschloper*, it is the usual form of the word today.

BOSTON A **CHINOOK** word for an American, as opposed to a Briton. Thus we are told by Sheldon Jackson that certain Indians "have patriotic ideas, are proud to call themselves 'Boston Siwashes,'" that is, Indians of the United States. The term arose because the first U.S. ships to touch the Northwest coast came from Boston.

BOTTOM Endurance, especially of a horse. A **CAYUSE** with bottom can go all day and then some. The same can be said of some men.

BOUDIN (BOO-da, with the second syllable approximately as the *a* in *corral* and nasalized) A delicacy made from buffalo intestine, much loved by the **PLAINS INDIANS** and by the **MOUNTAIN MEN**, who learned of it from the Indians. Modern Louisiana has a dish of the same name. From French (in which it means "blood pudding"). James Willard Schultz, who spent his entire adult life among the Blackfeet, described its preparation in *My Life as an Indian:*

> [He brought to the lodge] a few feet of a certain entrail which is always streaked or covered with soft, snowy white fat. This Nät-ah'-ki [his Blackfeet wife] washed thoroughly and then stuffed with finely-chopped tenderloin, and stuffed it in such a manner that the inside of the entrail became the outside, and consequently the rich fat was encased with the meat. Both ends of the case were then securely tied, and the long sausage-like thing placed on the coals to roast, the cook constantly turning and moving it around to prevent it burning. After about twenty minutes on the coals, it was dropped into a pot of boiling water for five or ten minutes more, and was then ready to serve. In my estimation, and in that of all who have tried it, this method of cooking meat is the best of all.

BOUNCE (1) To turn animals from the direction of their movement. (See also **BEND**.) (2) To startle deer from cover. (3) Rarely, to jump a mineral claim.

BOUNCER The strapping fellow who collected the late rents in a board-inghouse.

BOUNTY HUNTER A man who killed to collect bounties for animals, Indians, and men on the lam. Montanans hunted wolves for bounties; Mexicans hunted **APACHES**; altogether too many people carried on wars of extermination against other critters for money.

Bounty—Bill Redmond's winter haul from the Upper Gros Ventre River, Wyoming. [COURTESY OF TETON COUNTY HISTORICL SOCIETY.]

Mathews shows 100 pounds being offered during colonial times for Indian scalps, and fifteen and twenty cents in the nineteenth century for gopher and wolf pelts.

BOUNTY JUMPER A man who enlisted in the army, collected his bounty for signing up, and lit out for other parts.

BOURGEOIS Among French-Canadians, the head of a **FUR-TRADING** party, and usually a fancy fellow with fine clothes who slept in a tent while his **VOYAGEURS** slept under the canoes. The second in command in the party was called the *little bourgeois*. (See also **BOOSHWAY**.)

BOVINE In *Ten Thousand Goddam Cattle*, Katie Lee says cowboys used this word for a cow that's gentle, not feisty, the opposite of **SNORTY**. Range cowboys call cattle owned by farmers "bovines," meant in a derogatory way.

BOW An arch supporting the cover of a **PRAIRIE SCHOONER** or other Plains-crossing wagon.

BOW DRILL Among some Indian peoples, a wooden stick and bow string used to start a fire. The drill point was set against soft wood and a bow string twisted around it. Then the fire-maker drew the bow back and forth. As the stick rotated rapidly, the friction made the soft wood smolder. Native peoples used hand drills of grass, bristles, quills, stone, wood, and bone, and even a pump drill.

BOWIE KNIFE This famous piece of cutlery was created by Arkansas blacksmith James Black in about 1830. A remarkable metalsmith, Black was especially skilled at hardening and tempering steel. James Bowie, a noted knife-fighter, ordered a certain knife from Black, who made for him instead

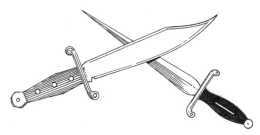

Arkansas toothpick beneath a Bowie knife.
[Drawing by E. L. Reedstrom.]

what became the first Bowie knife. It rose into legend when Bowie died fighting at the **ALAMO**. Lengths of Bowie knives varied on the frontier, twelve or fourteen inches being common, and they featured a cutting edge of more than two inches on top as well as the dozen inches on the bottom. Also called a *Kansas neck blister*.

BOX CANYON A canyon with just one reasonable way in and out; a **BLIND** canyon, and so the obstacle of many a hero of pulp fiction, and the comeuppance of many a villain.

BOX FIT An ideal fit for a pistol in a holster—form-fitted enough to allow the wearer a quick draw but snug enough to prevent the gun from bouncing out when he was riding.

BOX UP THE DOUGH Among loggers, to cook.

BOX-AND-STRIP BUILDING A traditional, pioneer-style ranch building in Texas, with outer walls of one-by-twelves nailed vertically on a two-by-four frame, the joins covered with one-by-fours, and featuring a broad front porch.

BOYSENBERRY A berry developed in California by Rudolph Boysen from the blackberry, raspberry, and loganberry.

BRACE To fix a card game, especially **FARO**. COMBINATIONS: *brace box* (a dishonest faro box), *brace faro* (a game in which the cards are secretly stacked), *brace game* (a fixed game), *brace gambler* (a cheater).

BRACEROS A Mexican agricultural worker who entered the western United States legally between 1942 and 1963 as a result of the Braceros treaty. Adapted from the Spanish *brazos* (meaning one who works with his arms, a manual laborer).

BRAHMA Cattle imported to the United States from India and popular in the Southwest, where they stand up to the elements well. They are sometimes called *Brahmins*.

BRAINS What loggers call a representative of the main office.

BRAKE STICK A lever that helped the stagecoach driver apply the brakes with considerable force.

BRANCH In a bar, water. A Wyoming bartender said she could nearly get by with knowing how to make only one drink, Canadian Club and water, invariably ordered as "CC and branch." In Texas it would probably be "bourbon and branch." This usage comes from Southerners' calling a creek a branch, a custom that hitchhiked westward.

BRAND (1) The brand, along with the **EARMARK**, is the sign of ownership of stock. It is burned into the hide with a hot **BRANDING IRON** for permanence. Brands are registered with the state or with a *cattlemen's association* to prevent duplication, and *brand books* are issued to show ownership.

4	Four Lazy F	◇L	Diamond L
RꙄ	R Lazy S	Ɛ	EW
⋈	Lazy Y Three	V/	Flying V Slash
J	Rafter J	ꓤ	Walking B
(Y	Crescent Lazy Y	JY	JY Quarter Circle

Some examples of Wyoming brands.

Interpreting brands takes some knowledge and experience. They are read from left to right and from the outside in; there are conventions, like translating wings as "flying," letters turned on their sides as "lazy," those with little legs as "walking," and those written in cursive style as "running." (See illustration on preceding page.) A brand that isn't clear is called a *puzzle brand,* and one that is over-elaborate (as Mexican brands were often thought to be) was a *fool brand* or a *map of Mexico.*

Brands have different names depending on their design. A *barbed brand* is a cattle brand with horn-like projections; a *bench brand* is a cattle brand sitting on a horizontal stroke with two legs; a *boxed brand* is one enclosed in a box; a *connected brand* is one with the figures running together; a *county brand* was used in the early days of Texas and represented a county; a *forked brand* is one with a V-shape sticking out of any letter or figure; a *rafter brand* has a roof drawn above it; a *rocking brand* is above a quarter circle (like a rocking chair's runners); a *tumbling brand* is one that leans sideways; a *swinging brand* is one hanging from a crescent.

(2) A cow or herd of cows of a brand. Andy Adams in *The Log of a Cowboy* says, for instance, "I must have inspection papers before I can move a brand out of the county in which it is bred."

(3) To *start a brand* was to start a cow outfit and, by extension, to get married and raise a family.

COMBINATIONS: *brand artist* (a fellow with a nice touch with a branding iron, sometimes a **RUSTLER**); *brand blotter, brand blotcher,* or *brand burner* (a rustler who mutilated brands so they couldn't be read); *brand book* (a cattle association's record of brands, which established ownership of the brand); *bosal brand* (a brand on a horse's nose where the **BOSAL** would go); *fast brand* (a brand deep enough to stay); *jaw brand* (a small brand on the jaw of a horse); *range brand* (to brand calves where they are found instead of at a roundup); *set brand* (a brand made with a **STAMP IRON**); *slow brand* (a brand not registered with the cattlemen's association, a rustler's brand).

(See also **BRANDING, BRAND INSPECTOR, HAIR BRAND, ROAD BRAND.**)

BRAND INSPECTOR A man hired to check brands on cows to prevent theft. In modern Wyoming, for instance, each county has at least one brand inspector, and cattlemen are not permitted to transport cattle out of their home counties without a paper from the brand inspector. Also called a *cattle inspector.*

BRANDING Burning the brand into the hides of newborn calves or other new stock. Branding is done in the spring, when the calves are new and small. In the old style, the cow-calf pairs were rounded up and the calves roped, branded (usually on the left hip), and **EARMARKED** and the males castrated (**CUT**). Stewart Edward White gives a picturesque description of the traditional way of branding in *Arizona Nights:*

> Homer leaned forward and threw [his rope]. . . . Immediately, and
> without waiting to ascertain the result of the manoeuvre, the horse

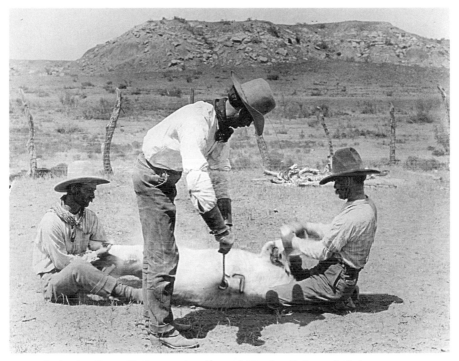

Cowboys branding a calf with a stamp iron. The men holding the calf's feet are the flankers.
[Photograph by Erwin E. Smith; courtesy of Amon Carter Museum.]

turned and began methodically . . . to walk toward the branding fire. Homer wrapped the rope twice or thrice about the horn. . . . Nobody paid any attention to the calf.

The latter had been caught by two hind legs. As the rope tightened, he was suddenly upset, and before he could realize that something disagreeable was happening, he was sliding majestically along on his belly. Behind him followed his anxious mother, her head swinging from side to side.

Near the fire the horse stopped. The two "bull-doggers" immediately pounced upon the victim. It was promptly flopped over on its right side. One knelt on its head and twisted back its foreleg in a sort of hammerlock; the other seized one hind foot, pressed his boot heel against the other hind leg close to the body, and sat down behind the animal. Thus the calf was unable to struggle. . . . Then one or the other threw off the rope . . .

"Hot iron!" yelled one of the bull-doggers.

"Marker!" yelled the other. Immediately two men ran forward. The brander pressed the iron smoothly against the flank. A smoke and the smell of scorching hair arose. Perhaps the calf blatted a little as the heat scorched. In a brief moment it was over.

When the calf had been earmarked and castrated (the latter unmentioned by White), "The calf sprang up, was appropriated and smelled over by his worried mother, and the two departed into the herd to talk it over."

What White described was the *Texas method,* using one mounted roper; in what is called the *Mexican* or *California method*, two mounted ropers fell the calf and hold it with their ropes during branding. These ropers are called the *catch hands*.

These days branding hasn't changed much. Calves may be trapped by a CALF TABLE instead of a rope, and they usually get a vaccination along with their other treatments; but they're still castrated and burned with a hot iron. Some ranchers, however, use liquid nitrogen to "freeze" a brand.

COMBINATIONS: The *branding chute* is a narrowing chute that ends in a calf table that clamps the steer tight for branding; the *branding corral* is a pen where branding is done; *branding season* is the time for branding calves, not long after they're born in the spring. The *branding crew* is the men and women who do the branding. On family outfits these days, the branding crew will be made up of hands from several ranches and will move from ranch to ranch, generally on consecutive weekends. The *branding fire* is a fire for heating BRANDING IRONS. Now a branding heater fueled by propane is often used in lieu of open fires, and some outfits have electric branding irons.

BRANDING IRON The tool used to burn on a brand. The STAMP IRON was a long-handled iron that branded in one application. DOTTING IRONS, common in Texas in the 1830s, stuck it on one piece at a time, one iron for a half circle, another for a straight bar, and so on. The RUNNING IRON has no stamp at the end but just a little curl, a fishhook, a circle—any round shape. With this the BRAND ARTIST sketches in the design freehand. In some states the running iron is illegal, in part because RUSTLERS like it. A pothook or a CINCH RING could also be used as a running iron.

The irons are made of any scrap iron the blacksmith can work with and average two to three feet long, the longer the better, to keep the end of the handle from getting too hot. Sometimes they have a wooden handle. To apply the stamp just right requires a nice touch. The hand must know when the iron is just hot enough. A red-hot one will scorch cruelly, spoil the brand, and leave a wound that may get infected. A cold iron will not get through the hair to the hide.

BRASADA Brush country, especially the impenetrable brush country of Texas and most especially the barbarous brush country of southwest Texas, between the Nueces and Rio Grande Rivers, where stubborn steers like to hide and even BRUSH-POPPERS hate to ride after them. A *brasadero* is a man or critter of the brasada. A *brasada measure* is the length a man can stretch out his arms, and is used to measure a REATA. Borrowed from the Spanish *bruzada*.

BRAVE A term of white folks for an Indian warrior; any Indian adult male. Usually pejorative and now outdated even more than is the use of "Negro" for blacks. *Brave-maker* means "booze."

BRAVO A nickname for the Rio Grande, which was also called the Del Norte. From the Mexican name for the Rio Grande, Rio Bravo del Norte.

BREA (BRAY-ah) Tar, pitch, especially for use on roofs or as seaming material in the Southwest. Borrowed from Spanish.

BREACHY A way of describing a cow that has a way of finding her way through fences to where she isn't supposed to be.

BREAD WALLET A person's stomach.

BREADROOT See PRAIRIE TURNIP.

BREAK A HORSE To train a horse, usually to saddle-riding, sometimes to the bridle or harness. Trained horses in the West are not "broken" but "broke"— "broken" would mean ruined. A horse may be broke to different degrees, from *green-broke* to *cavvy-broke* to *halter-broke* to *lady-broke* to *family-broke* (gentled enough for everyone in the family). He may also just have had "the kinks taken out of him," which means he's been ridden once, is a little bit used to the saddle, doesn't know how to neck-rein, and needs a rider who knows more than he does and is more willful.

A cowboy at work breaking a horse.
[PHOTOGRAPH BY ERWIN E. SMITH; COURTESY OF AMON CARTER MUSEUM.]

The two traditional ways of breaking horses in the West are by HACKAMORE and by BIT, which were done where the trainers had learned the ways of Mexican VAQUEROS or Texas cowpokes, respectively. No doubt each has its virtues, and each certainly has its partisans, who sometimes have their hackles up. David Lavender, in *One Man's West*, recalls how breaking was done before his time:

> In earlier days a horse was seldom touched until it was three or four years old. Then a young rider would decide to take the kinks out of it. In a swirl of dust, squeals, and flashing hoofs the colt would be roped, thrown, blindfolded, and saddled. While one man "eared the critter down"—twisted its ears to make it stand still—the rider would mount, reach forward, and slip off the blindfold. Now the horse could see where it jumped, and jump it did, exploding as far and as high as it could go.

> Cowboys who had reached the weary age of thirty regarded this procedure with jaundiced eyes. There you sit, beaten mercilessly between the hard cantle and the hard pommel of the saddle. If you are pitched off the ground is waiting like a club. Or perhaps the horse falls on top of you, snapping a leg or collarbone. Even if you become adept at sticking, your innards simply cannot stand that pounding many times; as the cowboys say, "It makes an old man out of a young one right quick."

> It doesn't do a horse much good either, often leaving the animal sullen, wind-broken, or treacherous. When ranches had more horses than they could use a spoiled colt wasn't so much of a loss. But now that cattlemen have to utilize fully each acre of grass the horseherds have diminished in size. Every animal must be productive, and more care is shown in their breaking. They are eased through their training and cajoled not to buck, instead of the other way around—all of which suits the older hands right to the ground.

These terms relate to broke horses and their training: *bridle-wise*, said of a horse trained to neck-rein, *cold-jawed* (hard-mouthed), DEAD-MOUTHED or HARD-MOUTHED (unresponsive to the BIT), *head-shy* (leery of the bridle), *halter puller* (in the habit of pulling back on the halter rope), *halter-shy*, *neck-reiner* (broke to respond to the rein against its neck), *one-man horse*, *owlhead* (an untrainable horse), *raw one* (an unbroke horse), *smooth-mouthed* (an old horse), *sour-mouthed* (a horse that fights the bit), SHAVETAIL (a broke horse, the opposite of a BROOM-TAIL), *tender-mouthed* (sensitive to the bit), *unroostered* (just broken in).

Breaking horses is also called *busting broncs, peeling bones,* and *making shavetails.*

Breaking age is the age when Western horses are broke to ride, usually three to four years. *Breaking patter* is the soft, comforting talk to a bronc, and a *breaking pen* is a small corral used to break horses, usually with a snubbing post in the middle. To *break in two* is how a horse feels to the rider when he bucks—head going one way and hind end another.

BREAK YOUR PICK Among miners, to get fired or to quit.

BREAKOVER In fire-fighting, a term for where a fire crosses over a line or barrier meant to control it. Also called a *slopover*.

BREAKS Rough country, terrain interrupted by gullies and the like—thus the breaks of the Missouri River, cut-up country near that river in northern Montana. Also spelled *brakes*.

BREAKUP Spring thaw, especially in Alaska. From the cracking up of the ice on the rivers. In winter these frozen rivers are sometimes used as roads, so breakup may make Alaskans even more isolated than winter did. A *breakup boot* is rubber footwear worn during the thaw to keep the feet dry. See also **FREEZEUP, ICE POOL**.

BREAST PLATE A large ornament, usually of metal or **HAIR PIPES**, worn on the chest by Indians, half-breeds, or (rarely) Anglos influenced by them.

BREAST-COLLAR See **MARTINGALE**.

BREECHCLOTH A strip of cloth worn by a man, usually an **INDIAN, HALF-BREED**, or sometimes a **MOUNTAIN MAN**, as a loin-cloth. It might be short and plain, for work, or long and elaborately quilled or beaded, for show. It was often complemented by leggings. Also called a *breechclout* or, rarely, *breeching*.

BREED See **HALF-BREED**.

BREEDING RANGE An area used for putting the herd bull with the cows.

BRIDAL CHAMBER Among miners, the far end of the narrow tunnel where the work is being moved forward. (Sexual humor, from the idea of new penetration.)

BRIGHAM (1) In Arizona, gravy or sop. (2) Ephedra, also known as *Brigham tea, Mormon tea, Brigham weed, desert tea,* and by other names. Ephedra is a low, wiry bush from which Brigham Young, at least in legend, brewed what was deemed a healthy tea. The "Words of Wisdom" of the **MORMONS** prohibit black tea and other drinks with caffeine. (3) A Mormon toast. Lift your glass and cry "Brigham!"

BRIGHAMITE An adherent of the **MORMON** leader Brigham Young; sometimes it was meant in contradistinction to a **JOSEPHITE**, one whose allegiance was to Joseph Smith but not Brigham Young.

BRINDLE Said of a cow with stripes or spots of different colors; **BROCKLED**.

BRING UP THE DRAGS (1) To ride at the back of the herd. (See also **FLANK, SWING, POINT**.)

BRISTLECONE PINE A short, often nearly prostrate pine (*Pinus aristata*) that grows on exposed ridge tops and dry slopes, especially on the mountains in the Great Basin. They are among the oldest living plants in the world; a group near Bishop, California, has trees that are more than 4,600 years old.

BROADAX BRIGADE A logger's word for a crew of TIE HACKS, men who cut railroad ties with heavy axes.

BROADHORN (1) A flatboat, so called because of the tin horn such boats used. (2) A TEXAS LONGHORN.

BROCKLED When said of a cow, BRINDLED, bearing spots of various colors.

BRONC BUSTER A hand who rides the ROUGH STRING, the unbroke horses. In the old days, he rode them once and called them broke, or at least broke enough to put into some cowboy's STRING. Often he wore a *bronc belt* to support the back and stomach muscles.

It was a crazy, man-destroying job, but one young bucks often liked the challenge of. In his wonderful novel *The Rounders*, Max Evans opines that a bronc rider is "a cowboy with his brains kicked out." He's also called *bronc breaker, bronc scratcher, bronc snapper, bronc squeezer, bullbat, buster, contract buster, flesh rider, gentler,* HAZER, *horse breaker, jinete, mansador, peeler,* and *rough-string rider.*

A *bronc fighter* is a cowboy who spoils the horse instead of breaking it. A *bronc stomper* is what the old-time cowboys called a man who could ride the ROUGH STRING. (See also BREAK A HORSE.)

BRONC SADDLE A saddle for breaking horses or riding horses with bronco temperaments. It has undercut and back-bulged FORKS and a heavily dished CANTLE.

BRONC SPUR A spur whose shank turns in toward the horse, to make scratching the bronco easier.

BRONC STALL A horse stall small enough to keep a wild horse from kicking or biting.

BRONCO (1) Strictly, a wild horse, a mustang; later, an unbroke horse. Jo Mora in *Trail Dust and Saddle Leather* gives the traditional view that "when a horse has been broken he positively ceases to be a bronco." Less strictly, though, a hard-to-handle horse; sometimes just a synonym for *cow pony*. Also spelled *broncho* and frequently shortened to *bronc*. Borrowed from Spanish (where it means "wild, untamed"). (See also BREAK A HORSE.)

(2) The term is sometimes applied to wild or rebellious people—thus Joseph Porter in *Paper Medicine Man* speaks of "bronco Apaches," and the *Westerners' Brand Book* tells us that a man who makes mistakes isn't necessarily "all bronco."

BROOMTAIL A wild mare; sometimes any wild horse; sometimes an unbroke mare or horse. Such a critter is called broomtail as opposed to SHAVETAIL because hands on the Northern Plains pulled hair out of the tails of wild horses (to shorten the tail) when they were broke so that they could tell the broke from the unbroke horses at a distance. Also called a *broomie*. Other terms for wild horses are *bangtail, fantail, fuzz-tail, mesteño* (mustang), *mustang,* and *pestle-tail*. Most of these have the implication of a horse with a bushy tail.

BRUJO In the Southwest, a sorcerer, or in the feminine form *bruja*, a witch. Borrowed from Spanish.

BRUSH (1) A little (or not so little) fight, as in "We had a brush with the Blackfeet." (2) The backwoods. (See also **BRASADA**.) A *brush arbor* is an improvised shelter with a brush roof to keep the sun off. (See also **RAMADA**, **SHADE HOUSE**.)

BRUSH MONKEY In California, an unskilled laborer who does menial jobs on a logging outfit.

BRUSH POPPER A cowboy who works the **BRASADA**, the brush country of Texas; also, a horse accustomed to working brush.

Breaking brush is hairy work, best left to riders who think they are some hombres. The cattle pick the densest thickets to hide in, and the popper has to move through fast while the brush tears at his skin and clothing. As a result, the brush popper uses nothing on his person or his saddle that snags easily. He has a hard-earned reputation for toughness. He rides a *brush horse* and uses a *brush hook* to slash the brush. A *brush roper* uses a shorter rope and a smaller loop than the cowboy who works the plains, and takes less space to swing it. Also called a *brasadero, brush buster, brush hand, brush thumper, brush whacker,* and *limb skinner*.

A *brush roundup* is a cattle drive in the brush, usually the Texas brush country. The cattle are called *brush snakes, brush splitters,* or *brush steers*. The cattle lie low, so the riders move slowly and try to move them out, often at night. A cow that's hiding in the brush is *brushed-up*.

BUCK NOUNS: (1) A deerskin. (2) A dollar, perhaps deriving from *deerskin*, for deerskins were sometimes used as money. (3) A male Indian, usually with a pejorative implication; in extension of the meaning of male animals such as deer and sheep. (4) Any male human being, as in "I was just a young buck then." (5) In **POKER**, a pocket knife passed around to show who is the dealer (perhaps so called because the knives often had handles of buckhorn) and the source of the expression *pass the buck*.

Pertaining to saddles and staying in them, a *bucking roll* is a pad, blanket, or even a coat rolled and tied to the **FORK** of a saddle to give a **BRONCO** rider something to wedge himself against. It may be manufactured but is often improvised. A *bucking rim* is a projection on a saddle's **CANTLE**, and a *bucking rein* is a single rope on the **HACKAMORE** that helps a rider stay on a bucking horse.

The *bucking strap* is a tight strap around the critter's flank that irritates it, causing harder bucking. It's not the same as a *buck strap*, a leather loop attached to the fork of a saddle as a handhold for a rider who's trying to stay on a horse that's bucking. Top riders sneer at such an aid, and it's barred at **RODEOS**.

VERB USAGES: (1) What a horse (or bull) does to try to unseat its rider—what Texans call *pitching*. Adams gives a lot of expressions for bucking, many of them wonderfully expressive: *arching his back, blowing the plug, blowing up,* **BOGGING**

HIS HEAD, *boiling over, breaking in two, bucking on a dime, bucking straight away, bucking the saddle, buck-jumping, casueyiug, cat-backing, chinning the moon, circling buck, coming apart,* **COMING UNDONE,** *coming unglued,* **CRAWFISHING, CROW-HOPPING,** *double shuffling, fall-backing, fence-cornering, fence-worming, folding up, frog walking, goating, hauling hell out of its shuck, hopping for mama, jackknifing, kettling, kicking the lid off, laying a rail fence, moaning, pinwheeling, pitching fence-cornered, pump handling, pussy-backing, rainbowing, rearing back, sheep-jumping, shooting his back, slatting his sails, straight bucking, sticking his bill in the ground, sunfishing, swapping ends, swallowing his head, taking you to church, throwing the pack, turning a wildcat, turning through himself, unloading, unwinding, walking beaming, warping his backbone, whing-dinging, wind-milling, wrinkling his spine.* (2) To carry or tote something heavy, like hay bales or water. (3) To contend against something, for instance, snow, as in "We had to buck deep drifts."

In **RODEO,** to *buck straight away* is for a horse to buck in long jumps straight ahead, instead of twisting and turning every which way. Such a horse is easier for some cowboys to stay on, harder for others. *Bucking on a dime* describes a horse that bucks in one place. *Buck the saddle* is what an unbroke horse is likely to do when the empty saddle is first put on its back.

BUCK AGUE A hunter's nervous excitement when taking aim at a deer or other game animal. Also called *buck fever.*

BUCK AND RAIL A style of fence in the parts of the West with rocky ground and plenty of trees. The bucks, made of poles crossed like an X, support the horizontal rails.

BUCK NUN A hermit; a cloistered male.

BUCK OUT A cowboy term for dying. If you *bucked out in smoke,* you went in a gunfight. (See also **CASH IN YOUR CHIPS.**)

BUCK THE TIGER To play **FARO.** The gambler's faro box and cloth had various pictures of tigers. A faro player was sometimes called a *bucker,* and gambling, particularly playing faro or **MONTE,** was sometimes called *bucking.*

BUCK WOOD Among loggers, to saw trees. **FALLERS** fell the trees, and buckers saw them into lengths.

BUCKAROO A cowboy, especially a hand of the **GREAT BASIN** of northern Nevada, northern California, eastern Oregon, and western Idaho. According to Jim Bramlett in *Ride for the High Points,* the type of horsemanship seen on these ranges goes back directly to the horse-training techniques perfected by the **CALIFORNIOS** in the 1700s and 1800s. The Californio style of horse jewelry—silver spurs, **BITS,** and conchos—and other Californio-styled horse gear are used by buckaroos today, although this equipment is modified for more strength. These cowboys sometimes wear lace-up boots with *toe spiders* (pieces of leather riveted onto the boots).

The Californio influence has led hands of other styles to use the word *buckaroo* with a hint of mockery. Said the Pinedale, Wyoming, *Roundup* in 1988, "This is a Nevada/Oregon term for the profession [of being a cowhand] and, around these parts, has a slightly childish ring to it."

A *buckaroo saddle* is a kind of saddle often preferred by buckaroos, developed from the Californio saddle. It has narrow FORKS (to keep the legs closer together), bucking rolls, and a high CANTLE and is DOUBLE-RIGGED.

The word has such variants as *buckhara, bukkarer, buccaroo, buckaree,* and *buckayro.* May be an Americanization of the Spanish VAQUERO.

BUCKBOARD A passenger wagon with a floor of springy boards that provide a certain cushion against the bumps of the road and usually with springs under the seats. It might be drawn by one or two horses and rigged for two or four passengers. Also called a *buck wagon.* The *buckboard driver* is what old-time ranch folks called the *mail carrier,* who came by buckboard, but seldom came.

BUCKET HUNTER What a cowboy calls a calf that drinks not from a cow but from a bucket.

BUCKET MAN A rustler's derisive name for a cowboy.

BUCKET OF BLOOD A rough saloon. The name came from a notorious drinking place in Havre, Montana, owned by Shorty Young, and it spread to similar dives.

BUCKLE BUNNY A rodeo groupie. "Buckle" refers to the oversize buckles awarded to event winners. A popular Western joke is that the difference between a cowboy and a cowman is that the cowboy's buckle covers his belly.

BUCKSHOT A shotgun load with large balls, as opposed to bird shot. It was designed for shooting large game like deer, but since it spread and wrought havoc at close range, it was the choice of stagecoach guards and law officers concerned about defending against groups of men.

BUCKSHOT LAND Soil that's poor, clayey.

BUCKSKIN From the original meaning, "the hide of a buck deer," have come several meanings particular to the frontier or the West: (1) Clothing made from such skin, a complete outfit of which was generally called *buckskins.* From colonial times, American frontiersmen imitated Indians by wearing buckskin. (2) The color of buckskin. (3) A popular horse color is buckskin (tan), and the horse was referred to as a buckskin. The old cow pony was of every color and marking: ALBINO, APPALOOSA, bay, BAYO, bayo coyote, black, BLOOD BAY, brown (brown with mane and tail of the same color), blue, blue roan, buckskin, buttermilk (palomino), CALICO, California sorrel, chestnut, CLAY BANK, CREMELLO, coyote dun, dapple, dapple gray, FLEA-BITTEN gray, GATEADO, gray, GRULLA or GRULLO, Indian red, iron, iron gray, line-backed, liver chestnut, MORO, PAINT, PALOMINO, piebald, PINTO, pinto-overo, SABINO, skew-bald, SORREL, strawberry roan, TOBIANO, white, zebraed, ZEBRA DUN.

Color didn't really mean anything—training and temperament were all—but most hands wanted mounts of solid color. Spotted ponies were supposed to be Indian horses, thus of low breeding. (See also **MUSTANG**.)

BUCKSKIN CURTAIN A creative recent coinage meaning the obstacles that separate Indian America from the dominant culture, as the Iron Curtain once separated Eastern from Western Europe.

BUCKSKINNER A hobbyist who re-creates the lifestyle and physical culture of the **MOUNTAIN MAN**, including going to **RENDEZVOUS**, living in **TIPIS** or other period shelter, wearing authentic clothing, shooting **MUZZLE-LOADERS**, and so on.

BUENAVENTURA The name of a river that Americans of the early period of Western exploration believed ran west from the Rockies into San Francisco Bay. It turned out to be mythical. Before anyone knew that, the **MOUNTAIN MAN** Jedediah Smith and others spent a lot of time and blood looking for it.

BUENO "Good." Also, during the days of the open range, a cow that was a good find because its brand wasn't in the brand book and you could slip it by a brand inspector. Borrowed from Spanish.

BUFFALO (1) The Westerner's name for the bison, a magnificent creature standing as tall as a tall man and weighing up to a ton. Basically a creature of the Great Plains, the buffalo's range extended east to the woodlands of Canada and the United States. The term comes from a misinterpretation by the early Spanish explorers; they called the animal *bufalo*, the name for the wild ox of Africa and India.

The Indians hunted the buffalo from the earliest days, at first by driving them over cliffs, later on foot with the bow and arrow, and in historic times on horseback with bow or gun. For them the beast was a source of meat, clothing, shelter, bedding, weapons, and other utensils, and it became a focus of Indian religion, the skull and

A buffalo bull.
[DRAWING BY E. L. REEDSTROM.]

other parts often being used for **MEDICINE**. Following the buffalo made the **PLAINS INDIANS** nomadic. From the 1840s, white immigrants found the buffalo an excellent supply of meat. (See also **CIBOLERO**.) From 1870 to 1883, though, professional buffalo hunters (known as **BUFFALO RUNNERS**) destroyed the great herds for the sake of supplying Eastern markets with hides and bone. Probably more than 40 million were killed. Their demise opened the vast grasslands to cattle and cattlemen. Now private and governmental programs of breeding and preservation have brought the animal back to modest numbers. The ghost dancers believed the buffalo will one day come back. We can hope so.

(2) Also used as a verb, meaning to confuse, cheat, or intimidate someone, in use since the 1870s. From a similar sense comes the MOUNTAIN MAN expression *buffalo-witted*, meaning dim-witted.

COMBINATIONS: *buffalo coat* (a winter coat made from a buffalo robe), *buffalo crossing* (a place where buffalo ford a river), *buffalo dance* (a ceremony preparing Plains Indians for a buffalo hunt), *buffalo horse* (a horse used by the Indians for running down buffalo, also known as a *buffalo runner*), *buffalo ground* (where the buffalo roam), *buffalo lick* (where buffalo licked salt), *buffalo pound* (an area where buffalo gathered in the winter), *buffalo range* (the area where buffalo grazed), *buffalo run* (a trail made by buffalo), *buffalo running* (hunting buffalo on horseback), *buffalo tea* (the fouled water left in buffalo wallows), *buffalo trace* (a trail made by buffalo), *buffalo wallow* (a hollow in the ground where buffalo rolled and scratched themselves, often serving as a catchment basin for rainwater), *buffalo whopper* (a hand who chased buffalo off the cattle range), *buffalo wood* (buffalo chips), and *buffalo wolf* (another name for the gray wolf, *Canis occidentalis*, which preyed on buffalo).

PLANTS: *buffalo burr* (*Solanum rostratum*—a short, drought resistant annual with sharp spines), *buffalo berry* (a shrub—*Sheperdia canadensis*—with an edible but bitter red berry).

BUFFALO CHIP The dried pie of buffalo manure, called by the French BOIS DE VACHE, literally "wood of the cow." It was the universal firewood of the treeless plains. Says Jo Mora in *Trail Dust and Saddle Leather*, "It made a good hot fire in dry weather, though when too wet it did not burn so readily, all of which scarcely added to the sweet temper or the efficiency of the cook." It's also called euphemistically *babcock coal, prairie chip, prairie coal, prairie fuel, prairie pancake,* and *prairie wood.*

BUFFALO GRASS A species of grama grass (*Buchloe dactyloides*) common on the arid Great Plains; short and not inviting in appearance, but the principal sustenance of the buffalo. On the Northern Plains, says David Dary in *Cowboy Culture*, "because of the dry climate and the high protein content of the slender blades, buffalo grass cured into a dry feed that stayed palatable and nutritious all winter long." (See also PRAIRIE.)

BUFFALO ROBE The hide of the buffalo prepared for use with the hair left on. The Indians used the robes as blankets, wraps, and surfaces for painting records of important matters, like battles or visions, or keeping the WINTER

A Dodge City, Kansas, buffalo hide yard in 1878—40,000 buffalo hides are pictured.

COUNT. The robe of the WHITE BUFFALO, which was sacred, was painstakingly prepared and offered to the sun.

Preparation of the robes, done mostly by women, was meticulous. Says David Dary in *Entrepreneurs of the Old West*, "Most tribes on the Northern Plains fastened the edges of a raw or green hide to pole frames, using rawhide thongs, much like an old-fashioned quilting frame made of four stout poles tied together at right angles." The women scraped the hide "clean of the last pieces of flesh. They then sprinkled the hide with water and smeared it with buffalo brains and grease. After the hide dried in the sun, the Indian women would rub it [for several days] with a sinew cord until it was soft and pliable."

Later, Anglos used buffalo robes as carriage and sleigh robes and similar warm coverings, and this demand helped nearly exterminate the great beast. According to white Indian James Willard Schultz, a particularly thick, glossy, silky buffalo robe was called a *beaver robe*.

BUFFALO RUNNER (1) A buffalo hunter—the term is deceptive in that these professionals did not hunt buffalo by running them on horseback, the traditional sporting method, which Bernard De Voto in *Across the Wide Missouri* describes as "what seems to have been the finest of all sports on the continent, perhaps the finest sport hunters have enjoyed anywhere. . . . What gave the hunt an emotion equivalent to ecstasy was the excitement, the speed, the thundering noise, the awe-inspiring bulk of the huge animal in motion, the fury of its death, and the implicit danger of the chase."

The professional sought not excitement but dollars, thus killing large numbers from fixed positions. A buffalo hunter "never called himself a buffalo hunter—that was the mark of a tenderfoot," says David Dary in *Entrepreneurs of the Old West.*

The runners called the animals *buffs* or *bufflers* and were afflicted by *buffalo mange* (lice). They often resorted to drinking *buffalo cider* (the contents of the buffalo's stomach) or *buffalo tea* (the foul water left behind in buffalo wallows). They used a *buffalo gun*, one that could drop a one-ton animal with a single blow; it delivered a big piece of lead catapulted by enough powder to fly at high velocity. A popular one was the BIG FIFTY, made by Sharps, a .50-caliber rifle with varying sizes of cartridges. This gun was so powerful that it wiped out tens of millions of buffalo in a dozen or so years, and satisfied the bloodlust and greed of even the buffalo runners.

Buffalo-hunting crews had their own pecking order. At the top was the runner (hunter), who made the shot. Second came the *buffalo skinner*, a fellow with a nice touch and a very sharp knife. They were followed much later by *bone hunters*, or pilgrims, who gathered the bones for fertilizer.

(2) A horse used, especially by an Indian, to hunt buffalo.

BUFFALO SKULL The dried, bleached skull of the buffalo, painted ceremonially, often used by Plains Indians in ceremonies. See also BUFFALO.

BUFFALO SOLDIER An Indian pidgin English name for a black soldier, probably from the texture of the soldier's hair. In the post–Civil War period, two black regiments of cavalry and two of infantry went to the Indian Wars. Black enlisted men and noncommissioned officers fought under white commissioned officers and rendered yeoman service, especially in the APACHE wars. One soldier wrote, "The officers say the negroes [sic] make good soldiers and fight like fiends. . . . The Indians call them 'buffalo soldiers,' because their woolly heads are so much like the matted cushion that is between the horns of the buffalo."

BUFORD Among RODEO cowboys, a calf or steer that puts up little resistance to being thrown or tied.

BUGGED UP Dressed up.

BUGGER To spook; to jump in fright. A cow that got buggered could cause a STAMPEDE.

BUGGY BOSS A lightly mocking name for an Eastern ranch-owner who inspected his ranch from a buggy because he didn't ride well enough to do it from horseback. The modern equivalent is a *windshield farmer*.

BUGLE A piercing combination of cries, song, and grunts made by male ELK as part of their fall mating ritual; the noise is intended to let the other bulls know where their territories are.

BUILD A LOOP To shake out the noose of your rope for a throw.

BULL (1) The male of the cow, buffalo, elk, and moose species. (2) By implication, a big version of something, anything. (3) Among loggers, an ox. (4) As a verb, what a cow does when she's in heat—puts her front legs on the hind end of a bull or even another cow.

COMBINATIONS AMONG LOGGERS: *bull block* (a huge pulley block for SKY-LINE LOGGING), *bull bucker* (the leader of the crew that bucks the fallen trees), *bull chin* (the big chain that hauls logs uphill), *bull cook* (in the old days of logging, the man who fed the oxen and, more recently, the fellow who takes care of the odd chores in a logging camp), *bull donkey* (a name for a big donkey engine), *bull of the woods* (the foreman of a logging camp or the winner of a contest in which loggers fight to see who can stay up on a big log the longest), *bullpen* (a bunkhouse), *bullpen boy* (the fellow who took care of it), *bull wheels* (enormous wooden wheels).

AMONG COWBOYS: *bull hides* (heavy CHAPS, cut from the thick skin of beef bulls), *bull pen* (a corral for bulls), *bullbat* (another name for a BRONC BUSTER), *bulling steers* or *bullers* (castrated beeves that still have some sexual odor and so draw other steers, which makes them nuisances on the trail), *bull nurse* (what cowboys called the hand picked to accompany the cattle on their train ride to the stockyard), *bullpuncher* (another name for a COWPUNCHER.)

Bull thrower is an occasional word of a MOUNTAIN MAN for his rifle, meaning "killer of buffalo bulls."

BULL BOAT A boat made of buffalo hides stretched on a willow frame. It was a favorite of the MOUNTAIN MAN because it had little draft and could be jerry-built almost anywhere in beaver country. In Stewart Edward White's novel *The Long Rifle*, the veteran trapper Joe Crane taught newcomer Andy Burnett how to build one:

> Joe stuck upright in the ground a circle of light willow poles, bent the ends over toward a common center, and tied them together to form a great inverted basket twelve or fourteen feet long. This he covered with the buffalo skins sewed together. Underneath he built a slow fire. As the skins warmed he assiduously rubbed a mixture of buffalo tallow and resin into the seams, which cooled as hard as the dried hide itself. Then he and Andy, working on opposite sides, carefully pulled up the willows from the earth, turned the thing over, cut off the projecting ends, bound on a rough gunwale of willow.

> "Thar she be!" said Joe. "That's a bull boat."

You steered it with poles. One built by the mountain man Nathaniel Wyeth was made from three bull skins, was eighteen feet long and five and a half feet wide, and was pointed at both ends. The vehicle was indispensable in the FUR TRADE because it could haul a big load of furs down the West's shallow streams.

BULL DURHAM The celebrated smoke of the cowboy, sold as loose tobacco in a little muslin sack with a famous picture of the bull. Starting at the end of the Civil War, Bull Durham came from Durham's Station, North Carolina. Competing brands were Sitting Bull, Pride of Durham, Duke of Durham, Ridgewood, Navy Tobacco, Navy Plug, Starr Navy, and others. In the Old West, a man carried the makings and rolled his own. Smoking *tailor-mades*, also called *ready-mades*, was looked down on.

BULL PEN A large, empty space in early reservation trading rooms, often with a wood-burning stove. The Anglo trader was often alone, so a high wooden counter kept the Indians from direct access to the stock on the shelves. Common practice was for the Indian to bargain for a single item at a time, taking as long as he liked to seal the deal. Traders often provided free tobacco or other treats during the process.

Also sometimes a term for a mountain **HOLE** or **PARK**.

BULL PRICK Not a natural bovine insemination conduit, but a hard-rock miner's drill.

BULL SNAKE A non-poisonous snake valued because it chases away rattlesnakes. Also called a *blow snake*, *gopher snake*, or *glossy snake*.

BULL TRAIN A string of **PRAIRIE SCHOONERS** drawn by oxen and under a single command. For some reason, Westerners often give oxen, which are castrated, the name "bulls," whose reason for being is that they aren't. James

A bull train—oxen transporting supplies in the Arizona Territory, 1883.
[Courtesy of National Archives (111-SC-89099).]

Willard Schultz described a trader's train on the Plains of Montana in the 1870s: "Berry's train now consisted of four eight-yoke teams, drawing twelve wagons in all, loaded with fifty thousand pounds of provisions, alcohol, whisky, and trade goods. There were four bull-whackers, a night-herder who drove the 'cavayard'—extra bulls and some saddle horses—a cook, three men who were to build the cabins and help with the trade, with Berry and his wife, and I." Also known as a *bull outfit*, a *bull team*, a *bull wagon*, and a *grass train*.

The *bull-wagon boss* or *(master)* was the chief of a bull train. (See also **BULL-WHACKER**.)

BULL WHIP A whip of braided rawhide, tapering from a stout wooden stock to a popper at the end, used by **BULLWHACKERS** and **MULESKINNERS** to control their animals. Legends have grown up about the skill of these men with this tool. Not originally a Westernism.

BULLDOG (1) To wrestle a steer; to throw it by hand. The black cowboy Bill Pickett is said to have been the first man to do it, partly by inflicting his teeth on the steer's nose. Generally, the bulldogger rides alongside the critter's left side, drops onto it, reaches over the neck, grabs its nose or some loose neck skin, grips the left horn with his left hand, and with a quick twist brings down man and beast. Bulldogging is a **RODEO** stunt, since there's little occasion for it in ranch work. A *bulldogger* is a rodeo competitor who specializes in bulldogging.

(2) A bulldog is also a short **TAPADERO** (stirrup cover), generally of one piece and often lined with sheepskin; it is stitched together under the foot and snugged all the way back to the heel.

COMBINATIONS: *Bull riding* (a rodeo event in which the cowboy indeed rides a bull bareback, an endeavor for neither the faint of heart nor sane of mind); the riders used to hold on to a *bull rigging* (a **SURCINGLE** with handholds built into it), but now use only a *bull rope* (a loose rope, which the rider wraps around his hand; the rules permit contestants to hold on with only the wrapped hand, not touching the rope, the bull, or himself with the free hand). *Bull tailing* (a popular game of early Southwestern Hispanics was like bulldogging in that a bull was thrown down—"busted"—hard, but the **VAQUEROS** did it by grabbing the tail and riding forward and to the side); *bull-running* (another game of the Californio ranchers, in which riders played bulls with lances and then chased, caught, and tailed them).

BULLET (1) A gold nugget. (2) A frontier guessing game adopted from the Indians, like thimblerig, the pea-under-the-shell game. (3) In **POKER**, an ace.

BULLROARER A ceremonial noisemaker of Southwestern Indians. Made of the sternum of a big animal, or of wood, it is whirled around the head by a cord and makes a whirring or moaning sound. It is associated with wind, thunder, and lightning. Also called a *rhombus*, a *whizzer*, and a *lightning stick*.

BULLWHACKER The driver of a **BULL TRAIN**; he used a **BULL WHIP**. These freighters, among the legendary characters of the emigrant period of the West, were called *bullskinners*, *bull pushers*, and *bull punchers*. (See also **MULESKINNER**.)

BUM CALF An orphan calf; a **DOGIE**; often has the implication of a runt. Also, *bum lamb*, an *orphan lamb*, a *bummer*, and a *buttermilk*. To *bum a lamb* is to remove it from its mother. A *bum steer* is a bad deal, mistaken advice, or a lie.

BUMS ON THE PLUSH The marvelous expression of loggers for the idle rich.

BUNCH To herd cattle, horses, sheep, and so on into a group. The *bunch ground* is where the animals gather during a roundup, and a *bunch quitter* is one that won't stay with the herd.

BUNCH GRASS Any of a number of Western grasses that grow in tufts; a way of describing a kind of growth rather than a single species. A *bunch grasser* is a horse that lives on bunch grass or a person who lives in foothills.

BUNK A timber on a logger's sled that supports the logs. Also a verb, to put a log on a bunk.

BUNKHOUSE Sleeping and living quarters for cowhands, miners, or loggers; sometimes the word carries the implication of being temporary. Historian David Dary offers these other words for such living quarters: *doghouse*, *shack*, *dump*, *ram pasture*, **DICE HOUSE**, *dive*.

BUNKIE Bunkmate. The term was first used by soldiers during the Plains Indian wars, where it also meant "blanket-mate under the open sky," and it may simply have meant "buddy, pal." Also spelled *bunkey*.

BUNKO A swindler. Also a gambling game played with dice or cards; perhaps derivative of the Spanish *banca*, also spelled *bunco*. The verb form, to *bunko someone*, and the compounds (*bunko artist*, *bunko game*, *bunko joint*, and so on) are not Westernisms. The general meaning, any "confidence game," came later.

BUNNY BOOT In Alaska, a very warm boot of felt or insulated rubber, especially one issued by the U.S. military. The rubber version is also called a *vapor-barrier boot*.

BUREAU OF INDIAN AFFAIRS (BIA) This bureau of the federal government was formed in 1824 under the Department of War (and that tells a tale) to administer U.S. policy toward the Indians. In 1849 it was switched to the Department of the Interior, where it has remained. Almost from its inception, the bureau has been notorious for its inefficiency and graft, and it was responsible for much suffering among the Indians and for much resentment. In the 1970s and '80s the BIA changed to a policy of hiring Indians almost exclusively and turned over many of its functions to the tribes, but from the Indian point of view, further improvement is needed. For instance, some call for the establishment of the BIA as a cabinet department. (Others call jocularly for each tribe to form a Bureau of Caucasian Affairs.)

BUREAU OF LAND MANAGEMENT (BLM) This Department of the Interior agency is the result of the combination in 1946 of the Federal Grazing Service and the General Land Office. It manages 270 million acres of public lands in the West (mostly unforested) and 520 million acres of mineral rights, basically everything left over after establishing tracts of the Forest Service, Defense Department, Indian tribal lands, and Park Service. Most uses of this land are consumptive and include grazing and mineral exploitation and development; some scenic areas are set aside for recreational use; maybe it's unfortunate that none are set aside specifically for replenishing the spirit.

BUREAU OF RECLAMATION The government department that builds dams and manages waterways in the West, also known as Bu Rec. Established by the Newlands Act of 1902, it was intended to aid farmers stricken by droughts and to improve on the ineffective job that states and private enterprise were doing. Through irrigation the efforts of the bureau made it possible to farm in areas like the High Plains, southern Arizona, and most of California; the large dams also made urban development in the West possible. In theory, some projects are paid for by user fees, but most dams end up being heavily subsidized by the federal government. For a history of water use and the bureau in the West, see Marc Reisner's *Cadillac Desert*.

BURGLAR A horse with a hidden defect. A horse trader who isn't on the up and up may have several such horses, say E. R. Jackman and R. A. Long in *The Oregon Desert*, and will avoid guaranteeing the questionable aspect. The burned buyer later brings the horse back for whatever small satisfaction he can get, and the trader sells the same bad horse over and over.

The term *horse-trader* does not imply generosity, honesty, or openness; it generally suggests a shrewd, tight-lipped, cunning businessman. It is well accepted in much of the United States that what the buyer doesn't discover about the horse is his problem—no refunds. There are hundreds of tricks to cover up specific defects of a horse—usually to hide lameness.

BURN CATTLE A cowman's occasional word for **BRANDING**; also called *burning rawhide*. To *burn them and boot them* is to brand calves and turn them loose.

BURN POWDER To shoot a gun.

BURN THE BREEZE To ride fast; also known as to *burn the prairie, burn the earth,* and *burn the wind*.

BURRITO A Mexican-American-style food, generally some combination of refried beans, cheese, green **CHILES**, and meat wrapped hot in a flour **TORTILLA**. As peddled by America's fast-food industry, it has become a hugely popular snack, and in the United States the word no longer means a small donkey.

BURRO A donkey. Texas used to have wild herds of them. Some Western deserts still have wild burros, and the Bureau of Land Management sees them as a problem. Borrowed from Spanish. Also known as an **ARIZONA NIGHTIN-GALE,** *desert canary, Colorado mockingbird, mountain canary, Rocky Mountain canary,* and *Washoe canary.*

BURRO MILK Cowboy talk for nonsense.

BURROWING OWL A small prairie owl that lives in **PRAIRIE-DOG** burrows and is found mostly in the West.

BUSCADERO First, a tough, gun-totin' lawman; later, any tough who carried a gun. Borrowed from the Spanish *buscador* (meaning "to hunt or search"). Also known as a *pistolero.* A *buscadero belt* is a broad belt for two guns, one on either side, and a *buscadero holster* is a holster inserted in a wide cartridge belt, both used chiefly in Hollywood.

BUSH Among Alaskans, the backcountry, the wilds.

BUSH BOY A **NAVAJO**-country term, used mostly by Anglos, for a Navajo who is very much unassimilated into white culture and modern ways. Typically a bush boy might be a **LONG HAIR** (man with hair uncut, in the traditional style), live on the far western side of the reservation or in the canyons on the south side of the San Juan River, speak no language but Navajo, and get the necessities of life in traditional ways.

BUSHELING Among loggers, paying by piecework for felling and **BUCKING.** Loggers also called it *by the inch* or *mile* or *bushel.*

BUSHWHACK (1) For modern hikers and climbers, to walk (or sometimes crawl or slither) through rough, overgrown country without benefit of trail. It is not anyone's favorite activity but may be a necessity for getting where you want to go. (2) Its older meaning, to ambush, usually had the implication of a cowardly attack. (3) In obsolete usage, to force a keelboat upstream against a swift current by pulling on bushes and trees along the bank.

BUSINESS RIDING Hooking your spurs into the horse's cinch when it bucks; thus the rider "makes it his 'business' to stay on—if possible."

BUST (1) To **BREAK A** horse. (2) To throw a steer or other critter down hard. The right way to do it is to rope it by the head, flick the rope around its far side and bottom, ride off at an angle, and so bring it down. Also called *fairgrounding* or *tripping* him, it is sometimes a **RODEO** event. (3) In **BLACKJACK,** to go over twenty-one points and thus lose.

BUSTED FLUSH A flush (a **POKER** hand with five cards of the same suit) that's short one card or more. Since it's a worthless hand, the phrase by extension means anything that's ruined.

BUSTHEAD One of many Westernisms for whiskey. (See also **FIREWATER.**) It has the implication of low quality.

BUSTLE A ceremonial decoration, usually made of feathers, worn on the backside by Indians at dances. Sometimes a shield is worn as a bustle.

BUTCHER At BRANDING, the fellow who cuts EARMARKS and puts identifying marks on the wattle or DEWLAP.

BUTT LOG In logging, the section of tree nearest the stump; the biggest log. Also *butt cut.*

BUTTE A steep hill or rocky formation that stands off by itself; if broader and flat-topped, it would be called a MESA.

BUTTER CLAM In the Pacific Northwest, an edible clam also known as a *Washington clam* and a *money shell.*

BUTTON (1) A cowboy's affectionate word for a boy. Other cowboy names for children are *doorknob, hen wrangler, pistol, weaner, whistle, yearling,* and *younker.* (2) A braided knot of leather or rawhide on tack.

BUTTON BLANKET In the Pacific Northwest, a blanket decorated by Indians with mother-of-pearl buttons in animal shapes.

BUY CHIPS In POKER, to get ready to come into a game; by extension, to put yourself into other situations, such as disputes, without an invitation.

BUZZ SAW A spur with a rough rowel that has sharp points.

BUZZARD (1) A turkey vulture; the high-flying scavenger of the West. The Western writer Edward Abbey wrote often that his ambition was to return in his next incarnation as a buzzard. (2) An unflattering epithet for a man, usually an old man.

    COMBINATIONS: *buzzard bait* (a worthless horse, fit only to become carrion, or for that matter, a worthless man), *buzzard-head* (cowboy talk for a useless or mean horse), *buzzard wings* (a wide pair of CHAPS; same as *bat wings*).

BUZZWORM A rattlesnake.

⇥C⇤

CABALLERO (kah-bah-YAIR-oh) A horseman; a gentleman.

CABALLO (kah-BYE-oh) is a *hoss, cayuse, mount,* stock horse, and so on; this version is likely to appear lightly or mockingly. Borrowed from Spanish.

CABANA (kuh-BA-nuh or kuh-BAN-yuh) Originally, a small, crudely made cabin; now a beach or pool shelter. Borrowed from Spanish.

CABESTRO (1) A halter made of horsehair rope. (2) A horsehair ROPE. (3) A person who can be led around by the nose.

CABIN FEVER The depression or irritability people get when penned up in a cabin during a long winter. It has been known to lead to quarrels, fights, divorces, insanity, and even murder.

CABOODLE All of it, the whole lot, as in "the whole kit and caboodle." According to the linguist J. L. Dillard, it's from Indian pidgin English.

CABREE A PRONGHORN, an ANTELOPE. Variants are *cabri, cabery,* and *cabril.* From Canadian French.

CABRON (kuh-BROHN) (1) A cuckold. (2) A scurrilous outlaw. Owen Wister said it is, along with *chiva,* one of the two worst insults a Mexican can offer. Borrowed from Spanish (where it means "single male goat").

CACHE (CASH) Among MOUNTAIN MEN, a hole in the ground where furs and other valuables were hidden for safekeeping; also took verb form—"Let's cache these hides." Now in Alaska, a small storage shed, usually raised off the ground to keep animals such as bears out. From the French, meaning "hiding place."

CACIQUE (kuh-SEEK; kuh-SEE-kay) Among Southwestern Indians, a ruler, a chief. Borrowed from Spanish.

CACKLEBERRIES What a logger called eggs. (See also HEN FRUIT, *States eggs* under STATES.)

CACTUS In reference to a wide variety of desert plants, the word is not a Westernism. But it can also mean the desert country itself. COMBINATIONS: *cactus boomer* (longhorns), *cactus candy* (made by boiling the pulp with sugar), *cactus forest, cactus mouse, cactus rat, cactus woodpecker* (the Gila woodpecker), *cactus wren.*

CAGER What a miner called the attendant of a cage (shaft elevator). One of his duties was to put the cars on the cages at landings.

CAHOOTS To be partners with a fellow was to be in cahoots with him or to be *thrown in* with him. A verb form existed that appears to have disappeared—to *cahoot with him.* Perhaps from the French *cahute,* meaning cabin or hut.

CAKE A supplementary feed made of cottonseed and other grains compressed into pellets. These days it comes in fifty-pound sacks or loose by the pickup load. The *cake wagon* is the wagon that carries the cake to the cattle for feeding. Called *cottonseed cake, cotton cake,* or, historically, *caddy.*

CALABASA (1) A calabash, a gourd. Borrowed from both French and Spanish. (2) A Mexican-American-style squash dish made from the calabasa. Stewart Edward White has some starving Anglos offered calabasa by a poor Mexican girl in *Arizona Nights.*

CALABOOSE A jail. Borrowed from the Spanish *calabozo.*

CALF Calves have a rich bunch of names that allow the cattlemen to say just what sort of calves they are: ACORN CALF (a runt), BUFORD (a small, weak calf that's easily thrown), BUM CALF or *buttermilk* (an orphan), CHURNDASH CALF

Cars coming out of a shaft, attended by cagers. Comstock Mine, Virginia City, Nevada, 1868.
[PHOTOGRAPH BY O'SULLIVAN, COURTESY OF NATIONAL ARCHIVES.]

(one that runs around a lot), *deacon* (a runt), dogie (a motherless, half-starved calf), *free martin* (a sterile heifer born twin to a male), *full ear* (one that isn't earmarked), *green calf* (one with some size but no meat), *hairy Dick* (an unbranded calf), LEPPY (an orphan), LONG YEARLING (a calf nearer two years old than one), OREJANO (a calf without an earmark), *poddy* (a big-bellied, half-starved orphan), *pussy calf* (fat and heavy), SANCHO (a dogie), *short yearling* (a calf that is a year old), SLEEPER (a calf a rustler has earmarked but not branded), SLICK (an unbranded calf), *spike weaner* (a calf being weaned via a circle of spikes on its nose), WEANER (a calf of weaning age), *wind-belly* (an orphan with a distended belly), *yearling.* The season's newborn calves are the *calf crop.*

COMBINATIONS: *calf around* (cowboy talk for loafing), *calfy* (a cow that looks like she's about to calve), *calf rope* (among Texas ranchers, once an equivalent to saying "Uncle"—surrendering, quitting, admitting defeat), *calf roundup* (spring roundup, for the purpose of branding calves), *calf wagon* (a wagon for carrying calves born on trail drives; before the calf wagon—also called a *blatting cart* or *blatting wagon*—came into use, such calves were sold, given away, or killed).

CALF FRIES Deep-fried calf testicles. See MOUNTAIN OYSTERS.

CALF PULLER A winching device used to help pull a calf out of a cow having difficulty giving birth. They range from simple chains to pullers with hydraulic jacks.

CALF ROPING One of the five standard events of any Professional Rodeo Cowboys Association RODEO. The contestant rides after a calf, ropes it, runs to it, and ties three of its legs together as fast as he can. A *calf horse* is the horse trained to back away from the roped calf and keep a taut line. This event sprang from a genuine ranching skill, roping and tying calves for BRANDING.

CALF TABLE A small chute used to hold calves tight for BRANDING. The calf is pushed into the chute, then the chute is turned into a horizontal position—thus the term "table." It's sometimes called a *calf cradle*.

CALF-LEGS A description of a horse with short legs.

CALICHE (kuh-LEE-chuh; kuh-LEE-chee) In the Southwest, a crust of calcium carbonate on top of the soil, or near the surface; it also refers to hard clay soil. Borrowed from Spanish (where it means "flakes of lime").

CALICO (1) A spotted horse or cow. (2) A woman (though not originally a Westernism, common on the range). (3) To go courting (also not originally a Westernism). *Calico fever* is cowboy love-sickness.

CALICO QUEEN One of the many terms for a prostitute. The Westerner is fecund with names of things that interest him, so he has or had many expressions for the woman for sale: *ceiling expert, chippy, crib girl, Cyprian, dance-hall girl, frail denizen, frail sister,* **GIRL OF THE LINE,** *girl of the night, horizontal worker, hurdy-gurdy girl, inmate of a house of ill fame, margarita, nymph du pave, nymph du prairie, painted cat, soiled dove, sport, sporting woman, woman of evil name and fame.* In the 1870s and '80s, newspaper editors needed to talk about such matters, and propriety led to creativity.

CALIENTE (kah-lee-EN-tay) Hot, as in water, salsa, or the weather. Borrowed from Spanish.

CALIFORNIA BANK NOTE A hide used as currency (in Mexican California).

OTHER CALIFORNIA COMBINATIONS: *California battalion* (the Americans in Mexican California who protested against Mexican administration in 1846); *California beer* (a homemade brew, sometimes alcoholic, usually not); *California bet* (a bet considered foolish in the dice game bank craps); *California Bible* or *California prayer book* (a deck of cards); *California blackjack* (a bet in blackjack considered foolish); *California blanket* (hobo lingo for newspaper used as bedding); *California buckskin* (baling wire); *California collar* (a hangman's noose); *California C-note* (a joking term for a ten-dollar bill, a C-note being a hundred-dollar bill); *California fourteens* (dishonest dice with two fives on one and two deuces on the other, seven being a winning throw); *California house* (an outhouse); *California lantern* (a portable light made of a bottomless glass bottle with a candle inside, so the flame is shielded from wind); *California pants* (heavy, double-weave wool pants, said to be comfortable on long horseback rides); *California room* (a sun room with large windows); *California sight* (a back sight on a rifle notched to help the shooter judge elevation); *California skirt* (a round-skirted stock saddle); *California sock, moccasin,* or *overshoe* (a makeshift sock of cloth); *California twist* (a rope throw with one overhead twist and without whirling).

ANIMALS: *California condor* (the immense vulture of central and southern California; long an endangered species and the inspiration of many efforts to aid its survival), *California goose, California gray* (whale), *California hare, California horse, California jay* (like the bluejay of the East but witout a crest), *California lion, California mustang, California nuthatch* (like the white-breasted nuthatch), *California pony, California peacock, California quail, California redworm, California salmon, California sardine, California sicklebill, California sorrel, California stingray, California trout, California vulture, California widgeon, California woodpecker* (known for boring holes in redwoods and filling them with acorns), *California yellowtail.*

PLANTS: *California fan palm* (the native palm of the state, *Washingtonia filifera*), *California bay, California bee plant, California bluebell, California blue oak, California buckthorn, California coffeeberry, California coffee tree, California grass, California holly, California laurel, California lilac, California live oak, California maple, California nutmeg, California olive, California pitcher plant, California poplar, California poppy, California rose, California sidesaddle flower, California sunflower, California white pine.*

CALIFORNIA TRAIL A route emigrants used to cross overland to California, especially the **FORTY-NINERS**. Though it had variations, the route most often used left the **OREGON TRAIL** at Soda Springs, Idaho, followed the Humboldt River to its **SINK**, struck westward, ascended the Sierra along the Truckee River, and crossed the range via Emigrant Gap. Most notorious of all groups to use the trail was the Donner party.

CALIFORNICATE In states near California, a common expression (even a bumper sticker) is, "Don't Californicate Oregon" (or Idaho, Arizona, or any state). It means, "Don't turn our state into California." The humorous implication of the "fornicate" part is, of course, "Don't screw us up."

CALIFORNIO In the nineteenth century, a person born in California and of Mexican ancestry.

CALL (1) A **POKER** player's demand that the other players still in the hand show their cards; in the verb form, to make that demand. The alternatives to calling would be to *raise* (to increase the stakes) or to *fold* (to give up). This sense of call can be extended to metaphorical use, to call a person about anything, to challenge him to put up or shut up.

(2) A bugle call, the effective measurement of time on an army post. At sunrise comes *reveille*, at about nine o'clock *guard-mount*, and then, says Martha Summerhayes in *Vanished Arizona*, "various drill calls, and *recalls*, and sick-call and the beautiful stable-call for the cavalry . . . the thrilling fire-call and the startling assembly, or *call-to-arms*, when every soldier jumps for his rifle and every officer buckles on his sword, and a woman's heart stands still."

CALL A BRAND To give words to the symbols of a **BRAND**, which can look arcane to the uninitiated.

CALL THE PLAY In a gun fight, a suggestion that your adversary start the action by going for his gun. This is probably more common on the sound stage than it was in dusty streets.

CALZONERAS (kahl-so-NAIR-uhs) Pants popular among Hispanics of the Southwest in the nineteenth century, split on the outside from the knee down and decorated fancily along the split. Borrowed from Spanish.

CAMAI In Alaska, "hello."

CAMAS (1) A plant (*Camissa esculenta*) with an edible bulb, an important food of Indians of the northwest United States and Canada. The early Oregon settlers ate it so much they got nicknamed *camas-eaters*. It is sometimes confused with a poisonous plant, *Zigadenus elegans*—hence the term **DEATH CAMAS**. (2) An area with camas. Also spelled *commas* and *kamas*. From **CHINOOK**.

The bread made from the root was called *camas bread* or *passhico*.

COMBINATIONS: *camas field* or *meadow* (flat, plain, prairie, ground), *camas pocket gopher*, *camas pouched rat*.

CAMINO REAL (kuh-MEE-noh ray-AHL) In the Southwest, a main highway or principal route. It is sometimes used as a proper noun, as in the name of the old road from Mexico City to Santa Fe. Borrowed from Spanish (where it means royal road).

CAMOTE (kah-MOH-tuh) A sweet potato eaten by the **PAPAGO** Indians. A Southwestern term borrowed from Spanish.

CAMP INSPECTOR A fellow who looks like a logger but is really a drifter, wandering from camp to camp to try the hospitality.

CAMP ROBBER The Rocky Mountain jay, a plump gray and black fellow that loves to feed on scraps from camps. Watts says "lone prospectors were said to be superstitious about them and would offer them no harm."

CAMP RUSTLER In **SHEEPHERDING**, a man who looked after the gear and moved the sheep camp while the herder was with the sheep; also called a *campero, camp mover, camp jerker,* or *camp tender*.

CAMPESINO (kahm-puh-SEE-noh) Pertaining to peasants, rural. Borrowed from Spanish.

CAMPO SANTO A cemetery. Borrowed from Spanish (where it means "sacred ground").

CAMPOODY A hut of the **PAIUTE** Indians; a village of these huts; by extension, sometimes an Anglo's cabin.

CANDLEFISH An edible fish of the Pacific Northwest, so oily it can be burned as a candle or, with a stick, made into a torch. Vital to the **TLINGIT**; traded extensively with interior tribes via **GREASE TRAILS**. Also called *eulachon, ooligan,* and **HOOLIGAN**.

CANDY SIDE Among loggers, a well-equipped crew, not a **HAYWIRE** outfit.

CANDY WAGON Especially in the Pacific Northwest, a crew bus, light truck, or similar vehicle used to carry food to men working in the woods, or to transport the men themselves.

CANELO A cinnamon-colored horse; a red roan. (See also **BUCKSKIN** for horse colors.)

CANNED COW What a cowboy calls canned milk.

CANNER A useless horse whose final address is Oscar Mayer; an animal fit only to be sent to the canning factory. Other terms for poor (objectionable or defective) horses: *buzzard bait, buzzard head* (a mean horse), *chicken horse* (a canner), *churn-head* (a dumb, stubborn horse), *crockhead* (a dumb horse), *croppy* (an outlaw), **CROWBAIT**, *jughead* or *knothead* (a dumb horse), *killer* or *man killer, nag, notch in his tail* (a horse that has killed a man), *oily bronc* (a mean horse), **OUTLAW** (a mean, uncontrollable horse), *plug, salado* (a **WIND-BROKE** horse), *salty bronc* (a mean horse), *skate, snide, snake-eyed* (a mean horse), *wassup* (an outlaw), *whistler* (a wind-broke horse), *widow-maker* (an outlaw).

CANT DOG A **PEAVEY,** a long wooden lever used by loggers to drive logs.

CANT HOOK A tool similar to a **CANT DOG** but smaller and without a spike on the end.

CAN'T-BE-RODE HORSE An outlaw; a horse that's hard to ride. A pungent old Western saying is "Ain't no horse that can't be rode, ain't no man that can't be throwed."

CAN'T-HOOK CATTLE A cowboy expression for cows without horns.

CANTEEN The post exchange on a military base. Into the 1880s this place was known as the **SUTLER'S** store. Renamed the Post Co-operative store in February 1889, it was popularly known as the canteen, and later as the PX.

CANTINA (1) In the Southwest, a tavern, usually Mexican-style. (2) A leather box packed by a mule. (3) In the Pony Express, the pockets of the **MOCHILA** that actually held the mail. Borrowed from Spanish.

CANTLE The back of the **STOCK SADDLE** seat, which is raised. Its back is called a *cantle drop.* To *cantle-board* is to ride loosely, so you bump the cantle, or to scratch the horse with your spurs all the way back to the cantle.

CANYON A gorge; a steep-sided valley. It was originally a Southwestern term. To canyon means for a stream to go into a canyon; variant expressions are *canyon up* and *canyon out.* From the Spanish *cañon.*

CANYON COUNTRY The country of southern Utah and northern Arizona, with adjacent portions of Colorado and New Mexico. With its **SLICKROCK** canyons ultimately shaped by the mighty gorges of the Colorado River and its tributaries, it is the home of the mule deer, antelope, bighorn sheep, mountain lion, lizard, rattlesnake, and even a few people. It is the strangest, least pretty, most beautiful, most god-forsaken, most god-blessed land the Great Mystery has yet created.

CAP ROCK (1) An erosion-resistant rock that tops mesas, buttes, and small rock formations. (2) In mining, barren rock presumed to lie on top of ore.

CAP-AND-BALL Describes a weapon fired by **PERCUSSION** cap. These muzzle-loading guns were common in the West in the heyday of the open ranges, even after metal cartridges had been introduced. It cost money to buy a new gun, or to convert your old one, and the cartridges were expensive.

A *cap pouch* was the leather pouch carried on the belts of soldiers of the era of the Indian wars for storing percussion caps. To *snap a cap* was to fire a gun, particularly with a percussion cap. These caps were also known as *caplocks*.

Cap-and-ball layout was cowboy talk for a ranch that wasn't up to date and hard-working.

CAPITAN Chief, head man, captain. The boss of a sheep-shearing crew is called a capitan. He generally owns the equipment and contracts with the owner. The shearers work for the capitan rather than the rancher. Borrowed from Spanish. The form *capitaine* is borrowed from French.

CAPONERA (kah-poh-NAIR uh) A herd of geldings. Borrowed from the Spanish *capón* (meaning a castrated animal).

CAPORAL (ka-puh-RAL, with an *a* like *corral*) Foreman (or assistant foreman), manager, or boss on a sheep or cattle ranch, usually with the implication that he was a Mexican. Most common in Texas. Borrowed from Spanish.

CAPOTE (kuh-POHT) The usual winter coat of the fur men, made from a blanket that is hooded and closed with a belt or sometimes double-breasted and buttoned. Early spellings like *cappo* and *capot* suggest that the *t* may once have been silent. Also called a *blanket coat*.

CAPPER A shill for a gambler. Thus the Abilene, Kansas, *Chronicle* in 1871 celebrated the departure of many "prostitutes, 'pimps,' gamblers, and 'cappers.'"

CARACARA In the Southwest, a vulturelike hawk. Borrowed from Spanish.

CARAJO! (kah-RAH-hoh) (1) A Mexican's exclamation, ejaculation, or eruption of vehement feeling, like the French-Canadian's *sacré bleu*. In Spanish, it means, in Mathew's euphemism, "the virile member." (2) The sort of fellow who would use such language; for instance, a **MULESKINNER** or ox driver. (3) The stem of the **CENTURY PLANT**, visually reminiscent of a "virile member." (4) As a verb, to cry out "Carajo!" Writes Lewis Garrard in *Wah-To-Yah and the Taos Trail*, he "*sacre*-ed in French, *carajo*-ed in Spanish-Mexican." Sometimes spelled *caraho*.

CARAVANSERAI A fancy name for a hotel, fashionable in the West during the nineteenth century. Also spelled *caravansary*.

CARBINE A light, short rifle for use by horsemen. During the Indian-fighting days in the West, U.S. cavalrymen used **SHARPS**, Spencer, and Springfield carbines. Not originally a Westernism.

CARCAJOU (kar-kuh-JOO) The wolverine. In the lore of Canadian fur men and many Western Indians, the wolverine was legendary for its ferocity. Originally a French-Canadian word.

CARCEL (KAR-suhl) A jail. Borrowed from Spanish.

CARD MECHANIC A cheat at cards; a person who manipulates cards to his own advantage. A team of such fellows was called a *card mob*. Other such terms include: *bottom dealer, bottom-card mechanic, broad pitcher* (or *tosser*), *card-sharp, gut puller, hearse driver, heel, leg, mechanic, monte dealer* (or *tosser* or *thrower*), *monte sharp, saddle-blanket gambler, second dealer, square decker, tinhorn.*

CARELESS WITH HIS BRANDING IRON Said of a known or suspected **RUSTLER**, who finds ways to get his brand on calves that aren't his, even in the twenty-first century.

CARGADOR (kar-guh-DOHR) (1) A fellow (usually a Mexican, sometimes an Indian) who packs loads on his back; used by traders in the old days and by the army. Borrowed from Spanish. (2) The freighter who seconds the pack master of a mule train. *Carga*, which was also used in the old Southwest, means load.

CARNE (KAR-nay) (1) In the Southwest, meat. *Carne asada* is on the menu of many Mexican-American restaurants. Borrowed from Spanish. *Carne seca* is, literally, dried meat: beef **JERKY**. (2) Short for **CHILI** *con carne*.

CARNOTITE Uranium-bearing ore or rock. (See **YELLOWCAKE** and **MOOSE PASTURE**.) This was the stuff of the money-colored dreams that caused the uranium boom in **CANYON COUNTRY** in the 1950s. In more elemental times, the Indians used it to make war paint.

CARRERA DEL GALLO (kuh-RAIR-uh de GUY-oh) A rough **VAQUERO** game. Roosters were buried up to their necks in the ground. Riders galloped down on them, leaned out of the saddle, and tried to jerk the bird out of the ground by the neck. Usually the birds got decapitated. Anglos called the game *chicken pull*. The Old South had a similar game, gander-pulling, played with geese tied to a pole or tree. From Spanish (where it literally means "run of the roosters").

CARRETA (kuh-RAY-tuh) A two-wheeled Mexican oxcart. It had wheels made of one solid piece or (more often, according to Smith) of two pieces joined at the hub, and without rims. The hubs were infamous for their squeaking, which could be heard for miles. Borrowed from Spanish. A *carretela* was a carriage, and a *carretero* was a cart driver.

CARRYING THE BALLOON Among loggers, hunting for work. The logger called his bedroll a *balloon*.

CARTWHEEL (1) A big coin, usually a silver dollar. (2) A long-pointed **ROWEL**.

CARTRIDGE BOX A leather pouch worn on the waist belt or shoulder belt of soldiers of the era of the Plains Indian wars for carrying the cartridges for their rifles (usually Springfields) or carbines. A *cartridge belt* was a belt worn around the waist, which had multiple loops for holding metallic cartridges.

CARVING SCALLOPS ON HIS GUN Making notches on the handle of your pistol to indicate a slaying; more popular in movies than the real world.

CASA House, used frequently by Anglos in the Southwest. *Casa grande*, literally "big house," in the old days usually was the main ranch house, where the owner lived. Today "Mi casa es su casa" ("My house is your house") is the epitome of Southwestern hospitality. Borrowed from Spanish.

CASCARA SAGRADA (kahs-KAH-ruh sah-GRAH-duh) The buckthorn (*Rhamnus purshianus*) of the Pacific Coast. The Indians used the buckthorn bark as a laxative. Borrowed from Spanish (where it means "sacred bark").

CASE OF SLOW What was wrong with the loser in a gun battle.

CASED WOLF A name for the COYOTE, whose pelt, instead of being split, was peeled from the body and dried on a frame, that is, cased.

CASH IN HIS SIX-SHOOTER What an outlaw was said to do when he used his pistol to withdraw money from a bank.

CASH IN YOUR CHIPS Also *cash in your checks* or just plain *cash in*. (1) To quit a game of POKER or FARO, at which time the player trades his chips for money. (2) Figuratively, to die. Thus *American Humorist* in 1888 asks, "Do you and each of you solemnly swear that you will . . . cling to each other through life till death calls upon you to cash in your earthly checks?"

Western language has a cornucopia of expressions for dying. You may *ride an old paint with your face to the West*, *hang up your saddle* (or *sack your saddle*), *cross the great divide*, *go to the last roundup*, and *go south*. If you die, your friends will *send your saddle home in a feed sack*. CHEYENNES *go to the Milky Way*, BLACKFEET *go to the sandhills*, and LAKOTAS *go beyond the pines*. Anglos also *pass in their chips* (or *checks*), *go belly up*, *take the big jump*, *bite the dust* (or *ground*), *buck out*, *finish their circles*, *land in a shallow grave*, *get a halo gratis*, *get sawdust in their beards*, *go over the jump*, *go over the range*, *go up*, *go up in smoke*, *have no-breakfast-forever*, *ride the long trail*, *shake hands with St. Peter*, *turn their toes to the daisies*, and so on. MOUNTAIN MEN *come*, *lose their hair*, *go under*, or *go beaver*.

CASTOR (1) Castoreum, a substance from a beaver's perineal glands that is the main ingredient of the bait for a beaver trap. It was dried, then mixed with alcohol, cinnamon, nutmeg, and cloves, all to attract the wily beaver. The MOUNTAIN MAN also called this MEDICINE and carried it in a stoppered horn slung on his shoulder. (2) A PLEW, or beaver skin. (3) A synonym for BEAVER.

CASUEYING (kuh-SOO-ying) A Texas term for the bucking (or in Texas, *pitching*) of a horse.

CAT WAGON A cowboy's name for a wagon carrying prostitutes. (See CALICO QUEEN.)

CATALOG WOMAN A cowboy's name for a wife a fellow got from an agency that served such needs; a mail-order bride.

CATAMARAN Among loggers, a raft used to raise sunken logs with windlass and grapple.

CATCH AS CATCH CAN However you can get it done. The expression comes from a calf-roping contest in which the roper is allowed to throw the rope any old way as long as he snags a calf and holds it.

CATCH COLT A colt that sprang from an unplanned mounting; sometimes used to describe an illegitimate child.

CATCH DOG A dog trained to corner and hold wild cattle. Such animals were used in the early days in south-central Texas when wild cattle were common. J. Frank Dobie says some of these animals were even able to pick MAVERICKS out of branded cattle and to throw them to the ground and keep them down until a man came. The spotted Catahoula leopard dog from Louisiana is one of the more important breeds. Sometimes spelled *ketch dog*.

Any rope with a noose for catching critters is a *catch rope*. In fancy you might hope to *catch a filly* (human variety). When drunk (ALKALIED), you may try to *catch the devil*. Often spelled *ketch rope*.

CATGUT What a cowboy sometimes calls a rawhide rope.

CATLINITE See PIPESTONE.

CATTALO A cross of the BUFFALO and the beef cow; also spelled *catalo*. (See also BEEFALO.)

CATTLE See COW. COMBINATIONS: *cattle broker, cattle country* (any big area of land good for grazing cattle, particularly the grasslands of the Great Plains), *cattle feeder* (owner of a FEED LOT), CATTLE INSPECTOR, CATTLEMAN, *cattle puncher* (COW-PUNCHER), *cattle queen* (a woman cattle baron), *cattle ring, cattle thief* (a RUSTLER).

CATTLE ASSOCIATION An organization for the promotion of the rights of cattlemen. (See also STOCK GROWERS' ASSOCIATION.)

CATTLE BARON A man who had a cattle empire, especially in the days of the open range; also known as *cattle king, cattle czar*, or *livestock king*.

CATTLE BUYER A man (or, recently and rarely, a woman) who makes a living by being a sharp judge of cow flesh, usually for a FEED LOT owner. He makes his living buying and selling *feeder cattle*. A *packer buyer* does the same for a meat packing plant.

CATTLE DETECTIVE Usually an employee of a cattlemen's association who is charged with catching RUSTLERS; sometimes a polite term for a hired gun representing big ranching interests against settlers; also called a *livestock detective*.

Tom Horn was a cattle detective for the Wyoming Cattlemen's Association, and much feared. He was hanged in 1901 for killing Willie Nickell. Modern detectives for organizations such as the Texas and Southwestern Cattle Raisers Association are highly respected professionals.

CATTLE GRUBS Heel fly larvae that live under the hides of cattle and horses.

CATTLE GUARD A set of rails, either real or painted, across a road in cow country; cows will not walk across them; sometimes called a *cattle gap*. According to the Pinedale, Wyoming, *Roundup*, a local resident "told a story at the library [one] night about some friends of hers who thought that cattle guards are actually people. 'Well, you have sheepherders, don't you?' they asked. 'You must have cattle guards.'" A good Western joke about tourists is the tale of one who asked, "What color uniforms do the cattle guards wear?"

CATTLE INSPECTOR See **BRAND INSPECTOR**.

CATTLE ISSUE See **BEEF ISSUE**.

CATTLE POOR Said of a man who owns lots of cattle when cows are cheap and cash is scarce; the equivalent of *land poor*. An old Wyoming joke goes, "What would you do if you had a million dollars?—Buy a cow outfit and run it until I went broke." The joke is out of date. A million would buy only a teensy-weensy cow outfit these days.

CATTLE RING A conspiracy of powerful men and interests to tie up cattle range, available water, and so on. Thus the Santa Fe *Western New Mexican* wrote in 1885, "Rev. Sligh's Interpreter asserts the existence of a cattle ring in New Mexico whose motto is, 'the man with the water hole must go.'" An infamous example was the Santa Fe Ring, whose purpose was to promote a land grab by the financial powers behind the Maxwell Land Grant Company—it succeeded.

CATTLE TRAIL The route of a **TRAIL DRIVE**. Cow trails were everywhere in the West, but the ones popularly thought of first are the trails north from Texas, where the great drives of the 1860s, '70s, and '80s were made. Best-known were the Goodnight-Loving Trail, the Chisholm Trail, the Shawnee (or Sedalia) Trail, and the Western Cattle or Dodge City Trail. The Southern Trail led from Texas to California. The Spanish Trail was actually

Tom Horn, livestock detective and hired gun for Wyoming cattle ranchers in the early 1900s.
[COURTESY OF AMERICAN HERITAGE CENTER, UNIVERSITY OF WYOMING.]

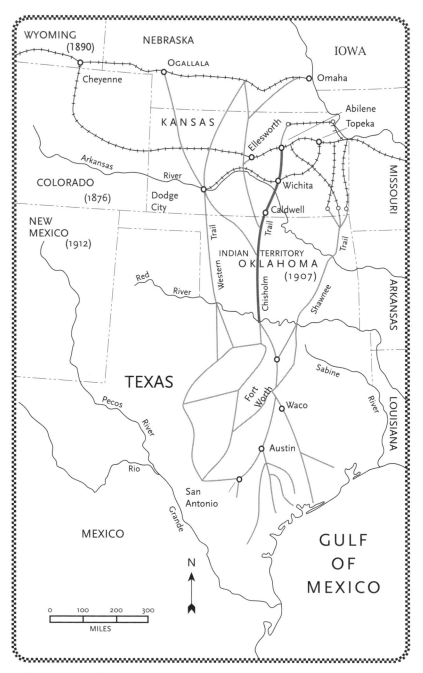

Texas cattle trails, 1870s. [MAP BY WENDY BAYLOR.]

two, one leading from Texas to New Orleans (the Old Beef Trail) and the other to California. The Chisholm and the Western led to the cow towns of Kansas, where the railroad provided cheap transportation to the East for beef, and these gave birth to some of the best Western lore and myth. The Western Cattle Trail later extended north to the grasslands of Wyoming and Montana.

The trail drive is a legendary cowboy activity, celebrated in movies like *Red River* and novels like Larry McMurtry's *Lonesome Dove*. It was a considerable enterprise, headed by a trail boss, with riders for the **POINT**, **SWING**, **FLANK**, and **DRAG** positions (perhaps a dozen drivers for a herd of, say, 3,000), strings of horses and wranglers to take care of them, and a cook with at least one chuck wagon. The major dangers were stampedes, the crossing of rivers, and sometimes people who wanted to steal the trail herd. In some years of the big drives from Texas to the Kansas railheads during the 1870s, on trails like the Chisholm and the Western, more than half a million cows went north.

CATTLEMAN Not a cowboy but the owner-operator of a cattle ranch. It matters not whether it's a *rawhide outfit* (dinky ranch) or a spread the size of the XIT (a Texas Panhandle ranch once three million acres in size), whether it's a **COW-CALF OPERATION** or a breeding ranch—if he owns it and runs it, he's a cattleman. These days, in the case of the large outfits, the fellows who own them and the fellows who run them are often different people. In that case, a real cattleman would probably see the manager as the cattleman and use the word for the owner only out of politeness. And in the case of certain outlanders, especially those who live on the other side of big oceans, he probably couldn't manage the politeness.

A frequent joke is that the difference between a cowboy and a cattleman is that the cowboy's buckle covers his belly. (Not vice versa.)

CATWALK A narrow walkway above a shipping chute, where a cowboy stands to push cattle onto rail cars. Also a narrow walk on a steamboat.

CAUTION Among miners, a posted notice indicating ownership and probably warning that any claim-jumper will be shot on sight.

CAVVY The cowboy's version of *cavallard* (the Anglo version of the Spanish *caballada*, "herd of horses"). The term is used mostly on the Northern Plains and in the Northwest, referring to the saddle horses kept by a ranch other than the unbroke horses and the ones saddled at the moment. Also known as a **REMUDA**. In the open-range days, ranches kept large horse herds, and each cowboy was assigned a **STRING** out of them. A *cavvy man* was the **WRANGLER**, the *remudero*.

These two words have as many variants as a new heiress has cousins—*cavyard, caviard, cavalyard, cavvie yard, cavayado, caviya,* and *cavvy yard;* in **BUCKAROO** country, where Oregon, Idaho, Nevada, and California come together, it's usually *cavviata*.

Cavvy-broke is broke enough to be in the cavvy, which means barely broke.

CAYAC A young buffalo bull forced away from the herd by the older bulls and not allowed near the cows. From a Louisiana French word meaning roughneck.

CAYUSE An Indian tribe of the Walla Walla country in Oregon and Washington, closely associated with the Walla Walla, **NEZ PERCÉ**, and Umatilla. When emigration became heavy on the Oregon Trail, the Cayuse traded horses with the emigrants, giving rise to the name *cayuse horse*. Diseases brought by the Anglos decimated the tribe, and in 1847 they rose against the Whitman mission near Fort Walla Walla. Getting what they thought was revenge for poisonings by Dr. Marcus Whitman, they killed him, his wife, Narcissa, and others there. They were punished militarily in return by the white settlers. Subsequently, most of the Cayuse integrated into neighboring tribes and now live on the Umatilla Reservation in Oregon.

CAYUSE (1) Horse, especially a wild horse of the Northwest; or a horse of the **CAYUSE** Indians of Oregon Territory. The term once meant any wild horse, and then any horse, but it retained some overtone of condescension: A cayuse was thought wild, native, nondescript, runty, ill-mannered, and unreliable, not a creature of breeding like the horses brought out from what was then known as the United States (often called by Indians and early Westerners *American horses*). (2) A cold wind from the east, opposite of a **CHINOOK**. Spelling variants include *kiuse* and even *skyuse*.

CEDAR BRAKE Rough country covered with cedar, those stunted, shaggy, twisted trees all over the West that are really junipers. Though it's also spelled *cedar break*, most authorities seem to prefer *brake*, as in canebrake. A cow that ranges out in the brakes is called a *cedar braker*.

CELERITY WAGON A mud wagon, or light stagecoach, used by the Butterfield Stagecoach Line, developed particularly for the rough and mountainous sections of roads. The **CONCORD** coach was heavier. Also called a *celerity coach* or simply a *celerity*.

CELESTIAL HEATHEN The Chinese, because an old name for China was the Celestial Empire; not originally a Westernism but common in the West. A Chinese was also likely to be called *John Chinaman*.

CELL THEORY A new theory of range management, also known as "holistic resource management." Under this system, cattle are moved from one small division (cell) of a pasture to another every few days, encouraging the cover grasses and discouraging the undesirable weeds. Developed by Allan Savory and sometimes called *intensive grazing*.

CENTER-FIRE RIG The saddle with a single **CINCH** hung from the center of the tree (wooden framework). (See also **SINGLE-RIG**.)

> COMBINATIONS: *Center-fire* (a cartridge with the ignition powder in the center instead of in the rim), *center-firing* (in **FIRE-FIGHTING**, a method of controlling

a fire by setting fires in the middle, creating a strong in-draft, and thus drawing the perimeter fire toward the middle).

CERVEZA (sehr-VAY-suh) Beer. Borrowed from Spanish. It's now commonplace in English, especially in the Southwest.

CHAIN (1) To drag a chain between two tractors over sagebrush rangeland. This practice is supposed to improve the range for cattle but usually results in erosion, an increase of weed species, and destruction of Indian artifacts. (See also **RAIL**.)

(2) Among loggers, a measurement of length, sixty-six feet.

CHAIN HOBBLE A length of chain, just a couple of feet, attached to one leg of a horse at one end and left to dangle at the other end. As a method of hobbling, it's hurtful and dangerous.

CHALCHUITE (CHAL-choo-it) A kind of New Mexican turquoise; the green chalchuite is particularly prized. An adaptation from Spanish.

CHALUPA (chuh-LOO-puh) In the Southwest, a deep-fried **TORTILLA** or other bread (usually made of *masa*) spread with any combination of beans, meat, and salsa. Borrowed from Spanish.

CHAMISO (chuh-MEE-soh) A shrub (*Adenostoma fasciulatum*) of the semi-arid areas of the Southwest; also spelled *chamise, chamizal;* sometimes known as *greasewood*. Borrowed from Spanish. The *chamise lily* is California's redwood lily or *chaparral lily* (*Allium rubescens*). The Indians used the bulbs for food.

CHAPARRAL (sha-puh-RAl, the *a* as in *corral*) (1) At first, chaparral meant scrub oak, then a thicket of scrub oak, then a thicket of mesquite, vines, and any sort of shrubbery all tangled together. Now it means brush so thick as to be nearly impenetrable. Longhorns used to love to hide in it and make the **BRUSH POPPERS** work like hell to get them out. (2) By extension, it means a patch of chaparral or a plain covered with chaparral. From the Spanish *chapparo* (oak).

COMBINATIONS: *chaparral berry* (the **BUFFALO BERRY**), *chaparral bird or cock* (the **ROAD RUNNER**), *chaparral deer, chaparral fox* (a wily person), *chaparral lily* (chamise lily), *chaparral pea, chaparral tea.*

CHAPARRO (shah-PAHR-roh) The evergreen oak of Texas, and elsewhere in the Southwest. Borrowed from Spanish.

CHAPO A stocky, short-coupled horse; sometimes called a *chupo.*

CHAPS (SHAPS, the *a* as in corral, traditionally a soft *sh*, not a hard one as in Chap Stick) Leggings—leather overalls—the cowboy wears to protect his legs when he's thrown from a horse or when the horse falls on him, pushes him against a fence or another animal, does its damnedest to bite him, or most particularly bolts him through brush, cactus, or chaparral; also used for warmth or for protection against rain or snow. One of the cowboy's essential pieces of equipment.

It's short for *chaparreras*, which in turn derives from **CHAPARRAL,** one evil that chaps ward off.

It is said that chaps come from the **VAQUEROS;** a brief glance at early paintings will inform anyone that they also descend from the **MOUNTAIN MEN,** who copied them from the Plains Indians. No one rode the mountains, Plains, or deserts long without discovering the need for some hide covering on the legs.

They can be made from the skin of any handy beast, the most common being calf, bull, sheep, goat, and deer. They come in lots of styles. *Bat wings* (also called *buzzard wings*), perhaps the most popular, sport wide wings on the side and a snap or buckle in back. *Bull hides* are made of the thick hide of a bull. **SHOTGUNS** (also called *stovepipe chaps*) wrap all the way around, like pants, and are straight and narrow as the barrels of a side-by-side—these are the usual chaps of the Northern Plains. **ANGORAS,** the fancy-looking ones with the curly white hair left on, are from angora goats; they're also called **WOOLLIES.** (All chaps with the hair left on are called *hair pants*.) *Cheyenne leg* is a Wyoming style of chaps, cut away on the under side of the thigh and loose below the knee.

Parade chaps are ones strictly for show, maybe for the grand entry parade at a rodeo. *Pinto chaps* are ones with the hair on, and spotted because hair of another color is sewn on top. A *chap guard* juts out from a spur shank to keep the chaps from hanging up on the rowel. *Chap strings* hold the chaps together across the hips. A *chapping* is the beating of a cowboy with a pair of chaps.

CHAQUETA (chah-KAY-tuh) A sturdy jacket, made of leather or cloth, that protects a rider against **CHAPARRAL;** most common in the border country of west Texas. A Southwestern adaptation from Spanish.

CHARCO In the Southwest, a pool of standing water. Borrowed from Spanish (where it means "puddle").

CHARLIE TAYLOR A stand-in for butter made of syrup or sorghum mixed with fat. Probably used in the early range period, when eggs and dairy products were scarce, or on trail drives, where they were scarcer yet. According to historian Francis Fugate, "not . . . a compliment to Charlie Taylor, whoever he may have been."

CHARRO Among contemporary Southwestern Hispanics, the term often refers to the Mexican riders who compete on the Mexican **RODEO** circuit, a separate circuit, quite active in Southern California.

CHAW TOBACCO An expression for chewing tobacco first recorded on the Kentucky frontier. Frontier brands were Star Navy, Navy, Day's Work, and Brown Mule. Contemporary brands include Beechnut, Lancaster, Levi Garrett, Swisher Sweet, and R. J. Gold in pouches and Red Man, Skoal, Copenhagen, Hawkins, and Kodiac in the little round tins that wear circles in the pockets of shirts and jeans.

CHEATGRASS Downy brome (*Bromus* sp.), a grass that was introduced from central Asia in the late 1800s. It has taken over much of the sagebrush grasslands, replacing the native wheatgrasses. Its sharp seeds lodge in animals' throats. It is often called simply *cheat*, or occasionally *rescue grass*, since it is one of the first grasses to **GREEN UP** in the spring.

CHEECHAKO (chee-CHAH-koh) A tenderfoot. From **CHINOOK**; also spelled *checaco* and *cheechalko*.

CHEEK To pull a horse's head around toward you by the cheek strap. A rider does this when mounting to keep the horse from bolting forward, or at least to force its motion into the rider to make swinging up easy. Often done when getting on an unfamiliar horse.

CHELKONA A ceremony of the **PAPAGO** Indians for rain-making and fertility.

CHEROKEE One of the **FIVE CIVILIZED TRIBES**, along with the **CREEK**, **CHOCKTAW**, **CHICKASAW**, and Seminole. In the seventeenth century, early in the period of white settlement, the Cherokee lived in the southern Appalachians. Soon reached by white traders, the tribe acquired guns, plows, livestock, strong drink, smallpox, and other accouterments of "civilization." They fought on the British side against the French, then warred with the Carolinas, 1759–61, in what was known as the Cherokee War, and then fought on the British side during the Revolution.

In the 1820s they became literate (via an eighty-six-syllable phonetic alphabet created by the Cherokee scholar Sequoyah), started a weekly newspaper, adopted a constitution modeled on that of the United States, and made large advances in agriculture. The state of Georgia then became determined to have them removed to the West. After various legal battles with the state and federal governments, most of the Cherokee were forcibly removed in stages to what became Indian Territory. The final march of 16,000 Cherokees along what was called the **TRAIL OF TEARS** in 1838–1839 killed about 4,000 people. Now the larger part of Cherokees live in Oklahoma, with Talequah as their capital; those who stayed in the East live in North Carolina.

The *Cherokee outlet* is a bar of land some fifty-seven miles wide in northern Oklahoma, given to the Cherokees in 1828 to provide access from their lands (in what would become Indian Territory) to good buffalo-hunting grounds. It is sometimes confused with the *Cherokee Strip*, a narrow strip (about three miles wide) of the Cherokee outlet in what is now Kansas.

CHEW IT FINER A way of asking the speaker to say something again in simpler terms.

CHEW THE DOG To visit, talk, pass the time of day.

CHEYENNE A nomadic, buffalo-hunting Algonquian tribe of the Northern and Central Plains, well known for its terrible conflicts with U.S. armed forces.

The name Cheyenne was the **DAKOTA** name for the tribe; it meant "red talkers" or "people of a different speech." They call themselves Tsistsistas, meaning "the People." The tribe had a crop-raising culture around the western Great Lakes until the eighteenth century but, because of pressure from the Dakotas, moved onto the Great Plains. There they became allied with the **ARAPAHOS** and **LAKOTAS,** roaming in the Powder River country and the area of the North Platte River, following the buffalo, and living in a sacred way, guided by their great medicine objects, the Four Sacred Arrows and the Buffalo Hat.

In the 1830s a tragedy befell them when they lost the Sacred Arrows to their enemies the **PAWNEE,** and several decades later a horn of the Buffalo Hat was broken, another calamity. They regard these two events as a source of the troubles that followed. From the mid-1830s, some Cheyennes elected to hunt near Bent's Fort on the Arkansas River in eastern Colorado, so the tribe was divided into northern and southern circles.

Though the Cheyennes were uneasy about white encroachment along the Oregon Trail and toward the Denver gold fields, the conflagration started only when John Chivington led the 3rd Colorado Volunteers in a massacre of Black Kettle's village at Sand Creek in 1864, killing hundreds of Indians. Several years of war followed in the territory between the Arkansas and Yellowstone Rivers, with the Cheyennes, Lakotas, and Arapahos chasing whites out of the Powder River country. Then George Armstrong Custer perpetrated another massacre along the Washita River in 1868, killing hundreds more, and the Southern Cheyennes settled on a reservation in Indian Territory (in what is now Oklahoma).

The Northern Cheyennes kept fighting and, with the Lakotas and Arapahos, inflicted a resounding defeat on Custer at Little Big Horn in 1876. After the Dull Knife Battle in 1876, they were brought in, starving, and sent to the southern reservation. In 1878 several hundred of them made a defiant break for home, the Powder River country. They eluded and outfought troops for months to get there and eventually were given the reservation they demanded.

Today the Southern Cheyennes live in Oklahoma, and the Northern Cheyennes live on the reservation along the Tongue River in Montana.

CHIA (CHEE-uh) A Southwestern desert plant (*Salvia columbine*) of the mint family whose seeds the Indians used to make a drink. Borrowed from Spanish.

CHICA An affectionate term for a girl or very young woman, often one's sweetheart; for a small girl, the diminutive form is *chiquita.* Borrowed from Spanish.

CHICANO A Mexican-American. It has activist political connotations, and many Americans of Mexican descent prefer to speak of themselves as Latinos, Hispanics, Mexicans, or Mexican-Americans; at any rate, Chicano now seems to be out of favor. The preferred term seems to be *Latino* in California and

Hispanic in the rest of the Southwest (see the Introduction to this book). From the Nahuatl word *Mexica,* which the Aztecs used to refer to themselves; hispanicized to *Mexicano*; the later form of the word—*Xicano* or Chicano—first appeared in 1848.

CHICKASAW (1) One of the **FIVE CIVILIZED TRIBES,** with the **CHEROKEE,** Seminoles, **CREEK,** and **CHOCTAW.** The Chickasaws originally lived in Mississippi and Tennessee, an area reached early by traders. The Chickasaws then adopted various elements of the white lifestyle, thus being "civilized." In the 1820s, however, they were forced to move west to Indian Territory. They allied themselves with the Confederacy in the Civil War. Today they live in eastern Oklahoma.

(2) Short for the Chickasaw horse, a calico beast noted for toughness and longevity.

CHICKEN (1) Short for **PRAIRIE CHICKEN.** (2) A boy or young man, especially a soldier or sailor, who is a particular friend of an older man. Homosexual feelings are surely implied, though not all users may have been aware of them. Mathews shows this meaning as Western and dates it 1888.

COMBINATIONS: *Chicken fixings* (high-quality food, not common stuff, and, by extension, anything fancy or top drawer, whether in food or dress); *chicken horse* (a runty horse killed for dog or chicken feed); *chicken saddle* (a particularly small one).

CHICKEN RANCH A brothel.

CHICO (CHEE-koh) (1) A Mexican-American term for greasewood. (2) Also a fond name for little boys or a friend, used occasionally in the Southwest. Borrowed from Spanish. *Chica* is the feminine version, sometimes an equivalent of "dear" or "sweetheart."

CHIDDY **NAVAJO** term for pickup truck, sometimes thought to be derived from the short form of Chevrolet, Chevy.

CHIEF BLANKET A blanket worn at ceremonies or for dress-up occasions, with a special design of triangles that become diamonds as the blanket is wrapped around the wearer. The custom began among the **NAVAJOS** and became pan-Indian.

CHIEFS' COAT In the **FUR TRADE,** a military-style coat for giving or trading to Indian leaders.

CHIGADEROS Half **CHAPS.** (See **ARMITAS.**)

CHIHUAHUA (chee-WAH-wah) (1) A large state in northern Mexico. (2) A tiny Mexican breed of dog. (3) A large **ROWEL** on a **SPUR,** a type usually worn in the old days by Southwestern Hispanics. (4) A freighting wagon (called in full a *Chihuahua cart*) with two solid wheels, and smaller than a **CARRETA.** (5) Any town near a frontier military establishment with saloons and other dens of iniquity where soldiers could spend their pay. (6) An exclamation of surprise. Borrowed from Spanish.

The *Chihuahuan Desert* lies mostly in Mexico, although there are small portions in southern New Mexico and southwestern Texas.

CHIKAMAN In the Pacific Northwest, an expression (from the **NOOTKA**) for cash money.

CHILCHIPIN (chil-chuh-PEEN) A Southwestern chile used to make Tabasco sauce. Borrowed from Spanish.

CHILD The common way a **MOUNTAIN MAN** referred to himself and his companion: "This child" (or this **BEAVER**, *hoss,* **COON**, **NIGGER**), he would say, meaning himself, "is goin' to make 'em come," meaning "kill beaver." Or the mountain man might say, "That child is some," a way of expressing respect. Thus did the mountain man refer to himself or a companion figuratively. The tireless traveler Lieutenant George Frederick Ruxton wrote in *Life in the Far West* in 1849 using excellent trapper talk, "This child has felt like going West for many a month, being half froze for buffalo meat and mountain doin's."

CHILE (CHI-lee; CHEE-lay) (1) What newcomers to the Southwest call a hot pepper—chile the vegetable and not **CHILI** the stew. It comes in many varieties, from mild to hot, and is served in forms *verde* or *colorado,* that is, green or red (vine-ripened). Though for a couple of centuries it was primarily associated with the food of poor Southwestern Hispanics, in the last two decades Americans generally have come to recognize the fine New Mexican cuisine based on the chile. (2) A sauce made from chiles, generally poured over diced meat. It is piquant and delectable.

Borrowed from Spanish, the word comes originally from the Nahuatl word *quachille.* The plural of chile is *chiles,* and the plural of chili is *chilis.* Though some authorities list *chilies* as a plural, it confuses the two and thus defies sense.

CHILENO A ring **BIT**.

CHILI (1) Strictly, a stew made with meat and red **CHILES** or chili powder. Chili gourmets generally insist that it contain neither beans nor any form of tomatoes: they hold big contests to determine the most delectable. (2) A stew made with chili powder, beans, and tomato; it may be *con carne* (with meat) or not. Some variety of this is what you'll get, in either restaurants or grocery stores, if you ask for chili outside the Southwest. (3) Short for *chili-eater,* a pejorative name for a Mexican.

Chili chaser is a Southwestern name for a border patrolman.

CHILKAT BLANKET A blanket woven from mountain-goat hair and dog hair by Tsimshian and **TLINGIT**, peoples of the Northwest.

CHIMICHANGA A deep-fried **BURRITO**; now a popular menu item in Mexican restaurants.

Chinese fishing camp.
[Courtesy of National Archives (22-FA-145).]

CHIMNEY ROCK A tall, slender formation of rock, often sandstone, from a couple of dozen to several hundred feet high; it sticks up from the ground like a house chimney or the barrel of a six-shooter pointed to the sky. Hundreds of thousands of emigrants noted "the" chimney rock on the **OREGON TRAIL**, a spire on the north bank of the Platte River a day's travel (by prairie schooner) east of Scottsbluff in Nebraska. It was a sign that the traveler was leaving the prairies and passing into a new kind of country, the real West.

CHINA PUMP A sort of pump used for extracting **TAILINGS**, improvised by Western gold miners. (See also **CHINAMAN'S CHANCE**.)

CHINAMAN'S CHANCE A poor chance. During the California gold rush, the Chinese were permitted to work only **TAILINGS** or played-out claims for gold, so they had a poor chance of striking **PAY DIRT**.

CHINATOWN The section of town, or outside of town, where the Chinese lived in cities of the early West; the only place they were permitted to live. *Chinese laundry* and *Chinese wheel* (a variety of fireworks) also appear to be Westernisms.

CHINDI A **NAVAJO** term for spirit, ghost, evil spirit. Traditional Navajos fear chindis and avoid the dead, belongings of the deceased, burial sites, and all else associated with the dead.

CHINK (1) A small chunk of wood used for filling the space between logs in a log cabin. (2) To chink is to fill those spaces with anything—sticks, mud, whatever. (3) A rude name for a Chinese person. This usage may be Western or British in origin. (See also **CELESTIAL HEATHEN**.) (4) Shortened form of **CHINKADEROS**.

CHINKADEROS Short **CHAPS**; usually shortened to "chinks." (See also **ARMITAS**.)

Chinook (1) A trade jargon used by Indians of the Northwest Coast, based on the Chinookan language but simplified. (2) A Chinookan-speaking Indian tribe originally located on the north side of the Columbia River as far upstream as Gray's Bay. Bands currently live at Chinook, Washington; Oakland, Oregon; Klamath, Oregon; and on the Shoalwater Reservation, which is shared with other tribes. One group spells the name *Tchinouk*. (3) A language family of dialects spoken by various tribes of the Northwest Pacific coast.

chinook (1) A blessed phenomenon in the northern regions of the West—a warm, dry wind that sometimes moves in from the west, usually suddenly, raising the air temperature sharply. It will often melt the snow away even in the middle of winter. (2) *To chinook* is for such a wind to blow. (3) A variety of **salmon**.

chip Short for **buffalo chip** or *cow chip*, the common fuel of the Great Plains. A *chip sack* was a bag for carrying the chips, and a *chipper* was a rancher so poor he burned cow chips at home.

chip in In **poker**, to *ante up*, to put a chip into the pot; by extension, to put money into anything, to join in any enterprise.

Chippewa See **Ojibway**.

chiquito (chuh-KEE-toh) Little one; used fondly for children or any little creature. Borrowed from Spanish.

Chiricahua (chi-ri-KAH-wah) (1) A branch of the **Apache** tribe that lived in western New Mexico. (2) A wild turkey. From the Apache language.

chiseler On the Northern Plains, a **prairie dog** or ground squirrel.

chispa (CHEES-puh) A small nugget of gold. Borrowed from Spanish (where it means spark or flake).

chiv A California term for a Southerner; short for "chivalry."

chivarras (CHEE-var-uhs) Another word for **chaps** or leggings, usually made from goatskin. Borrowed from Spanish (where it means "young goat").

Choctaw One of the **Five Civilized Tribes**. The Choctaw lived in western Alabama and Mississippi, adopting many elements of white lifestyle from an early date, especially agriculture and a legal code. In the early 1830s, they were forcibly removed to Indian Territory. Today they remain principally in southeastern Oklahoma. A *Choctaw's mile* is a short distance. *Choc* is what loggers called a beer made by the Choctaw.

choke the horn and claw the leather What a rider does when he's desperately trying to stay on a horse that's moving straight, sideways, 'round and 'round, or up and down too damn fast. It's supposed to be a mark against pride to grab the saddle horn any time, and in a **rodeo**, it will disqualify the rider. Many riders these days seem to have more common sense than pride (or are just not used to horses that act up anymore) and *grab leather* often enough.

One of my favorite woman ranchers, however, denies loudly her late husband's allegations that her saddle horn has tooth marks.

Also called to *choke* or *grab the apple; reach for the apple; pull* or *hunt leather; grab the nubbin, leather,* or *post; shake hands with Grandma; sound the horn; squeeze the biscuit; squeeze lizzie.*

CHOKECHERRY A shrub (*Prunus melanocarpa*) found in much of the West that bears wild cherries. The Navajo make a purple dye from the bark and roots, and Anglos make jelly from the berries.

CHOKEDAMP In mining, gas that suffocates miners.

CHOKER (1) In logging, a short steel cable with a loop at one end and a hook at the other, used for looping around logs. A *choker setter* is the fellow who puts the choker on, and a *choker hole* is a hole that is dug under the log to place the choker. *Choker hole* is also a logger's word for cheese.

CHOLLA (CHOY-yuh) A Southwestern cactus (*Opuntia* sp.) that grows in weird, twisty shapes and has soft, clingy spines that are meaner than your mother-in-law's tongue. Some of the varieties are *deer bush, jumping cholla, teddy bear, pencil,* and *staghorn.* Borrowed from Spanish (where it means "head").

CHONGO Among Hispanic women, a style of hair worn in a bun. The same term is applied to the old **PUEBLO** and **NAVAJO** styles, for both men and women, of tightly binding long hair behind the head with white cloth.

Also a steer with a droopy horn, and the drooping horn.

CHOP SUEY A surprising but genuine Americanism and probably a Westernism. Chop suey (meaning "odds and ends" or "hash" in Cantonese) is reportedly unknown in China, and Herbert Asbury in *The Gangs of New York* says it was "invented by an American dishwasher in a San Francisco restaurant." It is generally a mixture of vegetables, bean sprouts, and meat. A *chop suey joint,* naturally, is a Chinese restaurant.

CHORE BOY A fellow in a lumber camp or on a ranch who helps the cook or does other chores, such as cleaning the bunkhouse.

CHOUSE To handle cattle roughly and stir them up. David Dary in *Cowboy Culture* quotes old-time Texas rancher Hiram Craig on the subject: "The roundup boss would let no one ride through the herd and 'chouse,' or unnecessarily disturb them; these fellows found guilty of such misconduct were called 'loco'ed.' Oft times it was known for the roundup boss to put him out of the herd and cut his cattle for him." Also spelled *chowse.* (See also **GIN**.)

CHOW Food; **CHUCK**. The word evidently was borrowed from the Chinese in California. Along with the other great preoccupations of Westerners, such as sex, booze, and death, food has gotten a lot of names: *chicken fixings* (fancy food), *chuck, chuckaway,* **DOINGS, FIXINGS, FLUFF DUFFS** (fancy food again), *kow-kow,* **MUCKAMUCK,** *soft grub* (fancy food once more).

COMBINATIONS: *chow line, chow time.*

CHRISTMAS A logger's term for payday.

CHUBASCO (choo-BAHS-koh) A severe southerly rain and wind storm that originates in the northern Gulf of California. Borrowed from Spanish.

CHUCK (1) What the cowboy calls food, grub, **CHOW**; also mealtime. It comes from *chuck wagon*. To *chuck it in* is to feed like a trencherman. Since the old-time Westerner's imagination was fired by the important things in his life, such as whiskey, eating, death, and sex, he had lots of words for food. For his oversize breakfast he might have **HEN FRUIT** (eggs), *hen-fruit stir* with *long sweetenin'* (pancakes with molasses), *chuck wagon chicken* (fried bacon), *sow bosom* (salt pork), and **BEAR SIGN** (doughnuts). For dinner (which he ate about noon) he might consume **CALF FRIES** (the testicles of newly castrated calves), *Mexican strawberries* (beans), and **HUCKYDUMMY** (biscuits with raisins). And for supper—**SON-OF-A-BITCH STEW** (a stew of sweetbreads, tripe, brains, kidneys, and other parts of a freshly killed calf), **POOCH** (tomatoes, bread, and sugar), and **BOGGY-TOP** (pie without crust on the top). All of it, naturally, washed down with **ARBUCKLE'S** (coffee). He also had names for food in general: *chicken fixings* (fancy food), **CHOW**, *chuckaway*, **DOINGS**, **FIXINGS**, *fluff duffs* (fancy food again), *kow kow*, **MUCKAMUCK**, *soft grub* (fancy food once more).

    COMBINATIONS: *chuck tender* (a camp cook or his helper), *chuck eater* (a greenhorn learning to cowboy, but only effective at doing away with the chuck), *chuck away* (the cookie's cry for chow time), *chuck house* (where the food was prepared on a ranch or in a mining camp), and *chuckline riders* or *grub liners* (unemployed cowboys who would go from ranch to ranch, spend a night or two, and get a few free meals).

    (2) In **CHINOOK** jargon, stream or water. (See also **SALMON CHUCK**.)

CHUCK WAGON The mobile cookhouse of the range, used for both **TRAIL DRIVES** and **ROUNDUPS**. Charles Goodnight, first cattleman in the Texas Panhandle, the inventor of **GOODNIGHTING** and pioneer of the Goodnight-Loving Trail, is said to have been the fellow to come up with the chuck wagon. Earlier cowboys carried supplies on pack animals or, on long drives, in carts or wagons. In 1866, according to J. Everts Haley's biography of the rancher, Goodnight had a wagon rebuilt and considerably

Chuck wagon.
[DRAWING BY E. L. REEDSTROM.]

strengthened, and then on the back of the wagon devised the first *chuck box*, a combination work table and storage box for food staples and utensils for cooking and eating, plus medicines. The box had a lid on a hinge that let out to make a table for cooks to work on. Later chuck wagons carried a little grain for their draft animals, a water barrel, a tool box, a JOCKEY BOX, big pots and skillets, a shovel, an ax, and some dishpans.

By custom the cowboys stored their bedding in the wagon bed. Underneath the chuck wagon was slung a COONEY, which was used to carry cow chips for COOKIE to use for fuel or wood if he was lucky enough to come on any. Naturally the chuck wagon became the social center of the roundup and trail drive, where the fellows ate, got their coffee, smoked their cigarettes, told their lies, sang their songs, and had their fun.

Also called a *growler*, a *camp wagon*, or simply *the wagon*. In this century the chuck wagon can even be a truck—thus the expression *chuck truck*.

CHUCK-A-LUCK A gambling game played preferably with three dice. Not originally a Westernism. The game is of British origin and became immensely popular in the West. Also called *chucker-luck* and BIRD CAGE.

CHUCKLE-HEADED Evidently addle-brained (muddle-headed, confused). In *Arizona Nights*, one of Stewart Edward White's narrators says he walked into a trap "chuckle-headed as a prairie dog."

CHUCKWALLA A big Southwestern lizard, used by Indian people of the low deserts for food.

CHUG To SPUR a horse forward.

CHUNKED In the Southwest, impudent.

CHUPADERO (choo-puh-DAY-roh) The Spanish name for the cattle tick, sometimes used in the Southwest.

CHURN-HEAD A cowboy name for a dumb, stubborn horse; CROCKHEAD. (See also CANNER.)

CHURN-TWISTER A cowboy name for a farmer. (See also GRANGER.)

CHURRO (CHOO-roh) A coarse-wooled sheep introduced from Mexico to the Navajo and the Indians of the pueblos. Also a Mexican-style confection of deep-fried bread and sugar, shaped like a wand. Borrowed from Spanish.

CHUTE (1) A passage between fences or rails, sometimes narrowing, in which horses or cattle may be held for chute BRANDING or through which they may be driven into a corral, onto CALF TABLES, into RODEO arenas, onto trucks or railroad cars, and so on. (2) In logging, a slide for moving timber. (3) In mining, a shaft for moving ore.

In rodeo lingo, a *chute-crazy horse* is one that acts up in the chute. This horse is also called a *chute fighter*. His opposite is a horse that gets *chute freeze*, that balks in a chute and won't move at all.

CIBOLA (SEE-boh-luh) (1) The region of the **SEVEN CITIES** of Cibola, which proved to be the **ZUNI** pueblos and not the source of fabulous riches that the Spanish explorers were looking for. (2) Originally, not capitalized, the Spanish word for **BUFFALO**, sometimes used in the Southwest

CIBOLERO A Mexican or Norteño **BUFFALO** hunter. This fellow hunted the bison for its meat, not its hide, and did not participate in the mass slaughter of the herds starting about 1870. Still, in the 1840s ciboleros numbered about 1,600 and, along with the big hunts of the **METIS** at the same time, helped to start the buffalo on its decline.

CIENAGA (see-EN-uh-guh) A Southwestern term for a marshy area, often because of a spring or seep on a slope. Borrowed from Spanish.

CIGARITO (see-guh-REE-toh; sih-guh-REE-toh) In the Southwest, a small cigar or cigarette. Borrowed from Spanish.

CILANTRO Coriander, an herb popular in Southwestern cuisine; also called *Chinese parsley*. Adopted from Spanish.

CIMARRON (see-muh-ROHN; sih-muh-RON) (1) The **BIGHORN** sheep. (2) A loner, whether critter or human. Borrowed from the Spanish *cimarrón* (where it means "wild and unruly").

CINCH (1) A **GIRTH** for a saddle, often made of braided horsehair, canvas, leather, or cordage. Made up of the belly band and the **LATIGO**, the cinch passes under a horse's or mule's belly to hold the saddle or pack on the animal's back. In Texas, it is usually called a *girth*; also sometimes called a **SOBRECINCHA** or *cincha*. (See also **SURCINGLE**.) (2) To secure the saddle on the horse's back, to *cinch up*.

(3) A card game also known as Double Pedro or High Five, a popular Northwestern partnership game. It is a variation of the game known as all fours or high, low jack.

COMBINATIONS: A *cinch hook* is a hook on a **ROWEL** (or a **SPUR**) that can be hooked into the cinch to prevent you from being thrown, and a *cinch ring* is the ring at the end of the cinch.

CINCH BINDER A bucking horse that rears up on its hind legs and falls over backward. (See also **STOCK HORSE**.)

CINCO DE MAYO The celebration of a Mexican victory over the French in 1862, celebrated not only throughout Mexico but in the southwestern United States as well.

CIRCLE BUCK A way of describing a horse's bucking when it does it in a nice circle, usually thirty or forty feet across.

CIRCLE RIDING At a ROUNDUP, some cowboys would ride in a circle around a big area, pushing the cattle from the perimeter toward the center. A hand at this duty is called a *circle rider*, and the horse he rides is a *circle horse*.

CITIZEN BAND A group of Indians who wanted to give up their tribal identity to become U.S. citizens. Also called a *citizen party*.

CLAIM (1) An assertion of ownership or right of use on public land, especially mineral rights, patented or unpatented. (2) A piece of land covered by such a claim. In the old days, claims had to be *proved up* (see also PROVE), those not worked for more than a week were considered abandoned. (3) To make such a claim.

CLAN ANIMAL Among Indians, the totem or protector animal of a clan.

CLAPPER Among Pacific Northwest Indians, a rhythm instrument made from a split stick; makes a clapping noise when waved.

CLAWHAMMER COAT A fancy coat with tails, usually an object of derision in the West.

CLAY BANK (1) A yellow-dun color. (2) A yellow-dun or brownish-gray horse. (See also BUCKSKIN for many horse colors.)

CLEAN UP (1) In mining, to get the mineral that has value out of the gravel and rock in the sluices or the mill. A clean-up is also called a *clearing*. (2) Among cowboys, to *clean up* a herd is to CUT (separate) all the cows of your brand out of a herd.

COMBINATIONS: To *clean his plow* is to give a fellow a beating. A *clean setter* is a rider who doesn't *show daylight* (let light show between buttocks and saddle). To *clean out a town* is as an 1882 Wichita newspaper describes it: "The average cowboy is a bad man to handle. Armed to the teeth, well mounted, and full of their favorite beverage, the cowboys will dash through the principal streets of a town yelling like Comanches. This they call 'cleaning out a town.'"

In logging, *clean-boled* describes timber that is free of branches.

CLEAR-CUT In logging, the felling of all the salable trees in a given area in one cutting; the opposite—selecting only specific trees to fell—is called SELECT CUTTING. Clear-cutting is a controversial practice in many Western forests today.

CLEAR-FOOTED Said of a horse that is surefooted—one that doesn't stumble, put his feet in prairie-dog holes, and the like. (See also STOCK HORSE.)

CLIFF DWELLING A house, or usually a group of houses, of the ANASAZI (or Ancient Puebloans), such as those everywhere in the Four Corners, for instance at Mesa Verde in Colorado and Canyon de Chelly in Arizona. They were built all over the Southwest in places where steep dirt slope met vertical stone, or in cavernlike overhangs in the cliff. Such dwellings were easy to defend because they could be approached only up the steep slopes from below. Food was grown on top of the mesa above or on the floor of the canyon, and water was gotten from springs or creeks. Many such dwellings are extravagantly beautiful. Also called, rarely, a *cliff city*.

CLIMAX FOREST The term of a forest ranger or a logger for a plant community that is the culmination of vegetation for a given spot. This community usually endures a relatively long time, and when it burns, decays, or is cut, the cycle starts over. A ranger offers this description of how a climax forest of Douglas fir such as might be found in central Idaho comes into being: After a major burn come grasses, herbs, and shrubs; then sunlight-tolerant trees, such as the ponderosa and other pines; then, under the canopy of shade provided by the pines, shade-tolerant trees like the Douglas fir. When Doug fir gets big, it wants sun, and so tops out. It will then maintain that state for hundreds of years before decaying or burning, so the cycle can start again.

CLIP A BRAND To cut away a critter's hair, grown long during the winter, to get a good look at the brand.

CLIP HIS HORNS To render someone harmless.

CLOSE TO THE BELLY In **POKER**, cautious play, without bluffs. Also known as *close to the vest*.

CLOUD HUNTER A cowboy's word for a horse that likes to rear. (See also **STOCK HORSE**.)

COARSE GOLD Among miners, gold in big grains, as opposed to dust.

COASTER (1) A longhorn of the Texas coast. (See also **TEXAS LONGHORN**.) (2) A little wagon in a freight outfit, attached to the end; a small wagon for hauling food and gear; a **SHEEPHERDER'S** wagon. Also called a *cooster* or *kooster*.

COBBLER A sweet drink made of fruit juice, ice, and wine or whiskey. Also called more specifically a *sherry cobbler* or a *whiskey cobbler*.

COCINERO (koh-see-NAY-roh) A cook; usually a camp cook. When female, a *cocinera*. Also a *coosie, coosy, cosi, cusi, cusie*, and so on. Borrowed from Spanish. (See also **COOKIE**.)

COCK-A-DOODLE-DOO A cowboy's word for a ranch foreman.

COCKTAIL On a **TRAIL DRIVE**, the last watch of the night; the first was called **BOBTAIL**. Also called *cocktail guard* or *cocktail relief*. Modern cowboys call a *cocktail crew* one that has lots of help, the opposite of a *bobtail crew*.

CODE TALKER An American soldier who was Indian and used an encoded form of his native language to radio information, orders, etc. on the battlefield. The best known of these were the **NAVAJO** code talkers of World War II. (Mattel put out a Navajo action figure in tribute to them, and a feature film is now being made about Navajo code talkers.) The **CHOCTAW** served this function in

World Wars I and II, the **COMANCHES** in World War II. These codes went unbroken.

COEUR D'ALENE The Skitswish Indians, a Salish tribe that historically lived near Coeur d'Alene Lake in northern Idaho, where their present reservation is. Not nomadic, they were generally friendly to whites and receptive to traders. They are also known as *Pointed Hearts* or *Hearts of Awls*. Coeur d'Alene translates to "awl-heart" from the French and is said by one authority to have been one chief's expression for the size of a trader's heart. Probably he meant the point of the awl.

COFFEE COOLER (1) In the nineteenth century, an Indian who would agree to anything for a cup of coffee; a **HANG-AROUND-THE-FORT INDIAN**. (See also **ARBUCKLE'S**.) (2) Anyone who lazes around instead of facing up to his duty. Perhaps this sense of the term comes, as Smith suggests, from the observation that such fellows give their coffee plenty of time to cool before they down it and head out.

COHAB A term of a gentile (non-Mormon) for a **MORMON** engaged in **PLURAL MARRIAGE**. Same as a **POLYG**, and just as derogatory. A canyon near Utah's Capitol Reef National Monument is named Cohab Canyon. Cohabs continue to be shunned socially and sometimes even prosecuted legally today, when most Americans pride themselves on religious tolerance. Owen Allred, leader of the Apostolic United Brethren, a Mormon group that practices plural marriage, comments ironically, "They say it's all right for a man to live in a commune down in Taos with a dozen women, unmarried, and make love to all them and then go off and leave the mothers and children. But it's not all right for a man to marry more than one woman and support them, and the children."

COJINILLO (koh-hee-NEE-yoh) A Southwestern expression for a pocket of a saddle or small case attached to a saddle for carrying small objects; a favorite place for a bottle. Borrowed from Spanish, it's the diminutive form of *cojín*, "saddle pad."

COJONES (koh-HOH-nays) Testicles; by implication, courage. Borrowed from Spanish.

COLACHE (koh-LAH-chay) Boiled pumpkin or squash, a dish of the **CALIFORNIO** period. Borrowed from Spanish.

COLD BRAND A brand that burns just the hair, not the hide, and so will grow over. Also called a **HAIR BRAND**. Rustlers apply such brands out of dishonesty, others out of ineptitude. The expression is used both as a noun and a verb.

COLD-MEAT WAGON Cowboy term for a hearse.

COLEAR (koh-lee-AR) In the Southwest, to **TAIL** an animal, a method of throwing cows off their feet, literally by their tails, used by the **VAQUEROS** from horseback. Borrowed from Spanish.

COLEMANITE The most common source of American borax, named after W. T. Coleman, who led one of the San Francisco vigilance committees.

COLONEL In the West (as in the South and New England), this is a title of courtesy and respect, without military implications. Or maybe it's really a matter of height and girth: Briton James Robertson wrote in *A Few Months in America*, published in 1855, "in the South and West nearly all tall men are called generals, stout men judges, and men of middling proportions captains or colonels!"

COLONIST (1) In the West, generally, simply a word for a settler. A *colonist car* was a railroad car intended to transport such settlers. (See also **EMIGRANT**.) (2) In Texas, an American settler who came to the country before Texas was admitted to the Union. (3) In Kansas, an abolitionist who came to the state in 1854–58 to participate in the struggle over slavery.

COLOR Prospector talk for a sign of the presence of gold, either in the **PAN** or in dirt. It's color that makes the miner keep working.

COLORADO MOCKINGBIRD A BURRO.

COLORADO PLATEAU A vast region of high mountains, deep canyons, and rimrock desert over the Four Corners area, where Arizona, Colorado, New Mexico, and Utah meet. The presence of twenty-five parks testifies to the grandeur of the scenery. The plateau is defined, in both soul and body, by the Colorado River, which splits it from the northeast to the southwest, where it creates the Grand Canyon. The deserts are very arid, averaging about six inches of rainfall annually.

Historically, the region was home to indigenous peoples with remarkable civilizations, including the **ANASAZI**. Now it is sparsely populated with reservations, ranches, and small towns but much visited, and the locus of many controversies over dams, mining, and other exploitation. In the 1950s "uranium on the cranium" was the economic slogan; the same decade saw the flooding of Glen Canyon to create the huge reservoir called Lake Powell, still loved and loathed.

COLT A pistol made by Samuel Colt. The Colt revolving **SIX-SHOOTER** became the West's most popular pistol. Its common name was *dragoon*. Patented in 1836, it was adopted by the Texas Rangers, carried west by many forty-niners, and bought by the government in large quantities during the Civil War, especially the Navy (.36) and the Army (.44). It was a **CAP-AND-BALL** weapon until 1873, when Colt introduced a metallic cartridge. In this form, known variously as the *Peacemaker*, the *Single Action Army*, and the *Frontier*, it became *the* handgun of the West, outselling competitors like **REMINGTON** and **SMITH & WESSON** as Winchester dominated the market for rifles, Levi's the market for jeans, and Stetson the market for hats.

COLUMBIA SALMON The **CHINOOK SALMON**. ANIMALS: *Columbia jay, Columbia owl, Columbia short-tailed grouse, Columbia River turkey* (a salmon), *Columbia River smelt* (the **CANDLEFISH**), *Columbia River tyee.* PLANTS: *Columbia pine* (the Douglas fir), *Columbia poplar, Columbia red berry, Columbia spruce* (the Sitka spruce).

COMANCHE A Shoshonean tribe of Indians known among whites principally for their qualities as horsemen and warriors.

Separating from the **SHOSHONES** of historic times on the Northern Plains, the Comanches lived in the seventeenth century in what would become eastern Colorado. Then they acquired the horse, followed the buffalo nomadically, and began to develop their reputation as superb riders and the scourge of all other Indians and whites on the Southern Plains.

The Comanches drove the **APACHES** from most of Texas and warred relentlessly on the Spanish colonists there. *Comancheria* is the area of the Central and Southern Great Plains claimed by the Comanches, 400 miles wide and 600 miles from north to south. In order to trade, though, they excepted the New Mexicans from their raids and welcomed American traders to the country. A *comanchero* was a trader (usually Mexican) with the Comanches.

For more than a century, while Texas was Spanish, then Mexican, then independent, and finally part of the United States, its history was written in white and Comanche blood. Settlers there and in northern Mexico learned to dread the *Comanche moon*, the full moon of August or September when the Comanches most liked to raid, and the *Comanche yell*, their blood-curdling war cry. Because Comanches were so fierce, their name became synonymous among whites with bestiality. On the other hand, it was a high compliment to say that a fellow rode like a Comanche.

In the 1830s and 1840s, smallpox and cholera devastated the tribe, and in 1853 it made a treaty with the United States. In the 1870s, due to the destruction of the huge buffalo herds of the Southern Plains, the Comanches were brought onto reservations in Indian Territory (in Oklahoma); these reservations in turn were ended early in the twentieth century when the U.S. government allocated 160 acres to each Comanche.

From 1879, led by Quanah Parker, the Comanches adopted the peyote religion from the Yaquis of Mexico, and it has evolved into the **NATIVE AMERICAN CHURCH**.

Also spelled *Camanche* and *Cumanche*.

COMB To get a horse to buck by **SPURRING** it. To *comb someone's hair* is to whack him on the head with a pistol barrel.

COME To die. To *make 'em come* means to kill 'em, an expression of the **MOUNTAIN MAN** applied equally to beaver, Indians, and other critters—"this child made 'em come." (See also **CASH IN YOUR CHIPS** for many expressions about dying.)

COME OFF THE RIMROCK Katie Lee says in *Ten Thousand Goddam Cattle* that it means to back away from sensitive conversational territory and get easy and friendly again. (See also **RIMROCK**.)

COME UNDONE To go crazy, to act wild. A half-broke horse may see something scary and come undone, leaving the careless rider on the ground and undone.

COME-ALONG (1) A halter that hurts a horse when it doesn't follow and relaxes when it does. (2) A portable winch used by modern cowboys and other workers to get their pickups unstuck and to get other heavy moving jobs done.

COMMITTEE SADDLE A saddle acceptable for **RODEO** competition; an **ASSOCIATION SADDLE**; also called a *contest saddle*.

COMMODITIES Foodstuffs issued by the U.S. government to Indian peoples and other poor folks. In early reservation times (about 1870–1900), Indians would bring their wagons once a month to collect rice, flour, beef, beans, and the like. Often they disliked or misunderstood the food. Not knowing what to do with white flour, they painted their faces with it, or dumped it on the ground and used the sacks for dresses. Some thought the rice was dried maggots. When some noticed the blue stamps on the meat, having seen tattoos, they thought the white people were making Indians into cannibals, feeding them dead whites.

In modern times Indians have picked up their commodities issues, such food as white flour, honey, cornmeal, oatmeal, macaroni, and canned meats, from warehouses any time during the month. The quality of the food has been notoriously bad, and the resulting diet bad. This gave rise to two irresistible terms: *com bod* (or *commod bod*), the lousy body shape you get from eating too many commodities; and *commodity fart*. Very recently, the quality of food is said to have improved, even to include fresh fruit.

COMMON DOINGS Plain, ordinary, no-pretense food; the opposite of *chicken fixings* (see also **CHICKEN**). In 1838 in *The Far West*, Edmund Flagg wrote, "'Well, stranger, what'll ye take, wheat bread and chicken fixens, or corn-bread and common doins?'" (See also **CHOW, CHUCK**.)

COMPADRE (kahm-PAH-dray) Originally what a Hispanic father and godfather called each other; literally, "co-father." In the U.S. Southwest, it has come to mean partner, buddy. *Comadre* is the female equivalent. Borrowed from Spanish.

COMPAÑERO (kahm-pah-NYAY-roh) Partner, companion. Borrowed from Spanish. The feminine form, *compañera*, appears seldom to occur in the United States.

COMSTOCK LODE The rich silver and gold claim at Virginia City, Nevada, named after one of its partners (who was not the discoverer), Henry T. P. Comstock. Thus compounds like *Comstocker, Comstock boom, Comstock slang, Comstock king*. Not to be confused with *comstockery* or *comstockism*, the sort of rabid censorship of supposed indecencies advocated by Anthony Comstock (1844–1915).

CONCHO (KAHN-choh) Disk-shaped silver ornaments that typically decorate belts, **CHAPS, LEGGINGS, SPURS**, bridles, and so on. Anglos, Southwestern Hispanics, and Indians (especially **NAVAJOS**) all wear them. They can also be made of brass or leather. Saddle conchos, called *string conchos*, come in sets of eight. From the Spanish word *concha*, meaning shell.

CONCORD The word for stagecoach just as Colt was the word for pistol and Stetson the word for hat. It was named for Concord, New Hampshire, where from 1827 forward Abbott, Downing and Company made what were regarded as the best coaches. The coaches used thoroughbraces for shock absorption for the first time. Known for their elegance, these coaches were built mostly by hand of steel, brass, and white ash, weighed more than a ton, and sold for more than $1,250. Up to nine passengers sat in three rows of seats inside, and more sat on the top. *Boots* in front and back held luggage. Driver and shotgun guard sat on top. The coach might be drawn by four, six, or eight horses. Sometimes called a *Pitchin' Betsy* because of its rocking motion.

COMBINATIONS: *Concord buggy, Concord hack, Concord spring wagon, Concord stage.*

CONDUCTA (kuhn-DOOK-tuh) A Southwestern term for a caravan, convoy, or escorted party, often with the implication of something valuable being transported. Borrowed from Spanish.

CONESTOGA A big freighting wagon of the early West made in Conestoga Valley, Pennsylvania. It was a behemoth—more than two dozen feet long, nearly a dozen high, and weighing the better part of two tons—and was borne on big wheels (even bigger in back than in front) with iron tires. Ideally, Conestoga wagons were pulled by three pairs of Conestoga horses, big draft beasts, by oxen, or by ten mules. The Conestoga was sturdy and built to move a lot of freight and so was popular for heavy hauls on the Great Plains. Those big horses typically lugged it twelve to eighteen miles a day. It had a boat-shaped body, deeper in the middle than at either end, so the contents would not spill out the end when it was going uphill or downhill, and a hooped canvas covering. Also known as a *Pennsylvania wagon* or *ark,* it was nicknamed **PRAIRIE SCHOONER** because of its shiplike profile, a *Pitt schooner* because it was often manufactured in Pittsburgh, and a *scoop wagon* because of its scoop-shaped bed. It came to be the wagon of choice on the Santa Fe Trail. Studebaker made wagons of the same type but slightly lighter for the Plains crossing. Later Plains freighters came to prefer wagons less bulky.

CONFIDENCE MAN A swindler. Now often shortened to *con man.*

CONGÉ (kaw-JAY) A license or licensee for **FUR-TRADING** under the French. Borrowed from French.

CONSUMPTIVE USE In governmentese, use of resources (wood, water, or minerals) that reduces the supply: logging, irrigation, or mining. Nonconsumptive use, such as boating, hiking, and camping does not remove the resource.

CONTEST RIDE A **RODEO** term for a legal ride on a bucking horse. A legal saddle is a *contest saddle.*

CONTRACT BUSTER A BRONC BUSTER who makes a deal to break a certain number of horses for a certain price.

CONTRARY Among the Plains Indians, either a man who carried a thunder or contrary bow daily (and the responsibilities that went with it) or a man or woman who belonged to a contrary society. In *The Cheyenne Indians*, George Bird Grinnell has described these two sorts of contraries:

> The members of the society were people who feared thunder, and from time to time they held a ceremony and made an offering to thunder. During this ceremony they did things backwards, like backing into and out of the lodge, sitting not on their bottoms but their backs, doing the opposite of what was told them, etc. The people enjoyed this silliness, but the ceremony had a serious purpose, to protect the people against thunder.

> The individual contrary also did things backwards and also feared thunder, which had warned him in a dream. But his status as a contrary dominated his life every day. He carried the thunder or contrary bow, a lance that might be touched by no one but him and was used to strike coup. He sat and lay not on hides and beds but on the bare ground. He lived off to one side of the camp and seldom spoke to people. He was a war leader and under some circumstances was forbidden to retreat. Altogether, being this sort of contrary was both an honor and a heavy responsibility. A man bought the lance and the status from another contrary and could not give up his station until another person who had dreamed the thunder dream bought it from him.

CONVERTER A cowboy name for a preacher. (See also BLACK ROBE.)

COOK MUTTON To set fire to a sheep range, an occasional tactic of cattlemen during RANGE WARS.

COOKIE The range cook. In *Western Words*, Ramon Adams wrote this hymn to him:

> If ever there was an uncrowned king, it was the old-time range cook. He had to be good to qualify as a wagon cook because he had to be both versatile and resourceful. He was the most important individual in camp, and even the boss paid him homage. He was conscious of his autocratic powers, and his crankiness is still traditional.

> The present-day range cook follows this tradition. He can absolutely be depended upon to have three hot meals a day, rain or shine, cold or hot, that are good to eat and in sufficient quantity that, no matter how much company drops in, there will be plenty to go round. Through necessity his equipment is limited; yet this does not seem to hinder his speed. On one day he may be trying to cook in the rain with a scant supply of wet wood; on another he may have difficulty keeping the wind from scattering his

fire, blowing the heat away from his pots or sand into his food, and yet he works without discouragement. The outfit must be fed on time. . . .

Though the boys kid him and cuss his crankiness, they certainly will not concede this privilege to an outsider. If he is clean, they will tolerate the poor quality of his bread.

Almost any cook likes to talk, and while the boys eat, he squats against the rear wheel of the wagon and entertains himself and them by discussing everything from the weather and women to politics and poker. If he is a good cook, the boys do not interrupt him.

Some authorities say that hands chose the outfits they hired on with by the quality of the cook. If you were already signed on and the cook was bad, says Jo Mora in *Trail Dust and Saddle Leather*, you still had an option. You could kill the son of a bitch. Then you had to cook yourself. Your compañeros might agree to treat your rash act as justifiable homicide, but they would never let you step around the responsibility that came with it. The boys have to eat, don't they?

Though range cooks ran the gamut for type, a few generalizations apply: Most of them were older men, some retired from the hard business of cowboying. Most were Anglos, but you'd also find many a "Portugee," Negro, and "furriner" among them. And of course they were equally likely to be crackerjack cooks (though never culinary *artistes*) or lead-biscuit klutzes. For a lively history of this range archetype, see Adams's *Come and Get It: The Story of the Cowboy Cook*.

The cow-camp cook's name was also spelled *cookee*, but since the historic cook probably neither read nor wrote, he couldn't tell you which was right and didn't give a damn. Some of the nicknames for cookie: BEAN-MASTER, BELLY CHEATER, *belly robber, biscuit roller*, BISCUIT-SHOOTER, COCINERO, *cook's louse* (a cook's helper), *coosie, dinero, dough-belly* (and -BOXER, *puncher, roller,* or *wrangler*), *greasy belly, grub spoiler, grubworm, gut robber, hash slinger, kitchen mechanic, old woman* or *old lady, pothooks, pot rustler, rustler,* SALLIE, *sheffi, sop and taters,* SOURDOUGH.

The logger uses some of these sobriquets and has a roster of others (see also HASHER).

COOLER The jail; the CALABOOSE.

COON Along with BEAVER, CHILD, hoss, and NIGGER, one of the MOUNTAIN MAN's quiver-full of terms for himself and his COMPAÑEROS. It's likely an extension of the habit frontiersmen of Kentucky and surrounding regions had of calling themselves and each other *coon* and *old coon*.

COONCAN A gambling card game of the Southwest. It derived from a Spanish game called *con quien?* and was named rummy by the English.

COONEY In the days of the open range, a cowhide slung under a CHUCK WAGON, primarily as storage for buffalo chips, cow chips, and firewood but also for anything else that needed carrying. The front legs of the hide were fastened to the front axle, the back ones to the rear axle, and the sides nailed to the wagon sides. For some reason this device has an abundance of names—**BITCH**, caboose, cradle, and *'possum belly*, plus the alternate spellings *coonie* and *cuna*. From the Spanish *cuna* (cradle).

COON-FOOTED A descriptive term for a horse whose rear feet aren't straight. (See also **HORSE**.)

COOTIE CAGE A logger's word for a bunk.

COPPERS Beaten copper plaques that were symbols of wealth among Northwest Coast tribes.

CORDELLE (1) The rope men used to pull keelboats upstream. (2) The verb form means to heave a boat upstream with a cordelle. A *cordeller* was a fellow who did the heaving. In the early days of travel on the Missouri, before the coming of the steamboat, **KEELBOATS** were poled and cordelled upriver, and that could be brutal, back-breaking work, grunting along the shore or through the shallows.

CORDGRASS A native grass (*Spartina pectinata*) of the tall-grass prairie that grows six to ten feet tall and prefers wet areas. Its leaves are lined with minute barbs, earning it the nickname *ripgut*, but it makes good cattle forage and hay.

CORDILLERA (kohr-dee-YAIR-uh) A mountain range. Borrowed from Spanish.

CORDUROY (1) Logs (often split logs) laid across soft or wet spots in a road to make them passable for wagons. (2) A road that's been corduroyed. It's also known as a *hickety-crickety* or *hunker-chunker*. The Al-Can Highway was being corduroyed as late as the 1940s.

CORN Maize, aside from being a food staple for whites, Hispanics, and Indians alike, was and is a symbol of fertility to some tribes. Corn (*Zea mays*) is indigenous to the western hemisphere, where many species and varieties have been developed by Natives over the centuries. The Navajo use corn pollen ceremonially. Some tribes hold corn dances, or **GREEN CORN DANCES**. Indian peoples use the cobs to burn, as stoppers, scrubbers, playthings, etc. They use the husks to wrap food for cooking (such as tamales), to make dolls, to make cordage, etc. Pueblo people and Hispanics, especially, grind it into *cornmeal* to eat.

CORN FREIGHT The freight of a *mule train* as opposed to a **BULL TRAIN**. Oxen (which, paradoxically, pulled a bull train) lived off the country by eating grass but moved slower. **SKINNERS** probably argued about mules versus oxen much as modern folk argue about foreign cars versus domestic makes, with some feeling.

CORONA A word for the pad put beneath a saddle or an **APAREJO**; often fancy and usually saddle-shaped. Borrowed from Spanish (where it means "crown").

CORRAL A pen for livestock. Most Western corrals are built of posts and planks or poles to withstand the pounding sometimes given by horses and cattle, but they may be constructed of anything, from ropes (thus the term *rope corral*) to

A circular log corral in Teton County, Wyoming.
[COURTESY OF TETON COUNTY HISTORICAL SOCIETY.]

wagons to adobe. They're usually round, so that the critters can't crowd themselves into corners and get hurt. (2) In verb form, it means to get critters penned up. (3) Freighters also corralled wagons at night: They circled their wagons and fastened them tightly to each other with the yokes and chains, as a defense against marauders. (4) By extension, it means to get hold of or control of anything. "She was slow in corrallin' our idea on account of her bein' no English scholar," wrote Owen Wister. Borrowed from Spanish.

CORRAL BOSS The fellow responsible for a dude ranch's mounts and for matching horse to dude. Also known as *corral pup.*

CORREGIDOR (koh-REDG-uh-dohr) In the Southwest, a magistrate of a Hispanic town. Borrowed from Spanish.

CORRIDA (kohr-REE-duh) A Southwestern term for a ranch's crew, the men who hunt down the cattle. The *corrida comida* is a large noonday meal of several courses. Borrowed from Spanish.

CORRIDO A Southwestern term for a ballad, as in "El Corrido de Gregorio Cortez." Corridos were often written to narrate local legends, love stories, or historical events. They are an important part of the oral tradition of the transborder region.

COTEAU (kuh-TOH) A high MESA; a DIVIDE. Borrowed from French.

COTTONWOOD The tree (*Populus fremontii*) that, with the willow, is the trademark tree of the arid West. A water hog, it grows along the banks of rivers, creeks, and, in modern times, irrigation ditches. On the treeless plains, it thus marks water for the thirsty traveler and no doubt for the cow, antelope, and elk as well. The bark of the sweet cottonwood was an important source of feed for the horses of Indians, **MOUNTAIN MEN,** and other early Westerners. It provides shade for many a ranch house that would otherwise bake in the sun, and a barrier against wind. It got its name from the downy stuff it broadcasts every spring.

COMBINATIONS: To *have the cottonwood on someone* (rare) is to have the advantage on him. A *cottonwood blossom* is a hanged man, especially one hanged from a tree. (See also **STRING PARTY.**)

COULEE (KOO-lee) A ravine, with or without a stream. Mostly a term of the **NORTHERN PLAINS** and mountains, it derives from the French *couler* (to flow). Also spelled *coolie, cooley, couley,* and *coulie.* (See also **ARROYO, GULLY.**)

COUNT OUT What a herd is said to do when the tally promised matches the tally delivered. In *Log of a Cowboy,* Andy Adams writes, "just so the herd don't count out shy on the day of delivery."

COUNTERBRAND (1) A new brand put on the other side of a cow or horse, invalidating the original brand, which may be burned over; a **VENT BRAND;** a **SALE BRAND.** (2) In verb form, to make such a brand. Or, if you fouled up the first brand, you might immediately counterbrand the animal yourself. The idea was to do it legally and have it understood that you weren't a *brand artist* **(RUSTLER).**

COUNTRY ROCK In hard-rock mining, the mass of rock alongside a lode, vein, or dike (not a variety of popular music).

COUNTRY WIFE An Indian woman married, according to the custom of the country, to an Anglo fur man. Many traders and trappers had both city families and country families—sometimes a family in each of several different tribes.

COUNTY HOTEL A jocular name of loggers for the county jail.

COUP An honor a **PLAINS INDIAN** might gain by a deed of valor. Indian warfare was a dashing sport on horseback with a high purpose. The main object was, acting alone, to do something that showed bravery. The essence of courage was to touch an enemy, alive or dead, with your hand or something held in your hand, like a *coup stick.* Touching, you would cry out that you'd

Beaver Dick Leigh, his second wife, Susan Tadpole, and their three children.
[COURTESY OF TETON COUNTY HISTORICAL SOCIETY.]

vanquished a foe so your comrades would take notice and be able to act as witnesses. Honor was also gained by making the second, third, and fourth touches on an enemy, killing an enemy, scalping an enemy, rescuing a comrade, receiving a wound, and stealing an enemy's horse, but these were secondary.

After a battle, the warriors would congregate and claim their coups and act as witnesses for one another. A unwitnessed coup was no coup. Back in camp, each man recited in a ceremonial way what he had done, and others testified to it. *Counting coup* entitled a man to wear an eagle feather in his hair, and the feather's position showed the degree of honor. Throughout his life, on appropriate public occasions, a warrior would count coup (recite his war deeds), which were public knowledge. His status in the tribe depended on the number and quality of his coups. An Indian warrior without coups had no standing, couldn't speak up in council, couldn't even give his child a name—he was disenfranchised.

The acquisition of stature via coups explains much of the Plains Indian's longing to fight other Indians even after he had accepted being confined to a reservation. He needed to be recognized as a man by the community.

As for the Anglo custom of killing at a distance, even from behind cover, with guns, without looking your enemy in the eye, the Plains Indians didn't understand it—what was the point?

The term derives from the French *coup* (meaning "blow").

COUREUR DE BOIS (koo-RUR de BWAH) A French-Canadian **FUR TRADER** who operated independently. The big companies proceeded legally on the basis of their **CONGÉS**, but coureurs de bois ignored the regulations, roamed the wilds in small groups, and sought the furs. In many ways, sojourning among the red men, they became as much red as white, learning Indian languages, taking Indian wives and having Indian children, adopting Indian customs, and altogether becoming men who stood in the circle of the people. They were the first men to penetrate some of the remote regions of North America. And always they brought back the **PLEWS** (beaver pelts)—and sold them to whatever buyer they pleased. See Peter C. Newman's *Caesars of the Wilderness* for an excellent picture of the Canadian fur trade. Borrowed from Canadian French.

COURTING FLUTE A simple flute used by young men of the Plains and Woodlands Indians to woo young women. It was usually made of cedar or box elder and appropriately carved. The song a young man played might have been composed for him by a **BERDACHE**, a man-woman skilled in such matters; some of those songs were reputed to be irresistible; on hearing them, their object would come forth and go anywhere with the young man, entranced by him. Also called a *love flute*.

COUSIN JACK Among miners, a Cornishman, many of whom were miners in the West. His wife was a *Cousin Jenny*. Sometimes Cousin Jack meant a Welshman, and his wife was *Cousin Anne.* Americans sought expertise in underground mining operations from Cornishmen because they had generations of experience in the tin mines of the old country. Welshmen also had valuable experience in smelting techniques. A *Cousin Jack lantern* was a miner's lamp made from a tin can and a candle.

COVENA A Papago bluebell. The **PAPAGO** and **PIMA** Indians used its root for food.

COVER YOUR DOG For the roundup boss to get all the cattle in a particular region gathered up.

COVERED WAGON A generic word, perhaps more common now than during covered-wagon days, for the wagons Anglos used to haul emigrants and freight across the Plains. (See also **CONESTOGA.**)

COW (1) The female bovine, but also any bovine, regardless of sex; a herd of cattle of both sexes and every size is spoken of as "them cows." (2) The female of the buffalo, elk, and moose species. (3) A purse or kitty. (4) According to Mathews, a log raft with a log cabin on it.

COMBINATIONS: *cow alfalfa* (a weed that grows in Utah), *cow boss* (the man in charge of the roundup or the cattle part of a big outfit), *cow business, cow bunny* (a cattleman's sweetheart), *cow call, cow camp* (cowboy camp), *cow chip* (dried dung), *cow crowd* (a bunch of cowboys), *cow critter* (any bovine, even bulls), *cow dog* (a canine trained to handle cattle), *cow country, cow driver* (a man who trails cows, particularly on a long trail drive), *cow fever* (the fervent desire to go into the cattle business), *cow hunt* (an early Texas roundup of wild cows), *cow game* (the cattle business), *cow geography* (a map of cow country), *cowgirl, cowhide,* **COW HORSE,** *cow grease* (butter), *cow juice* (milk), *cow outfit* (cattle ranch), *cow pie* (dung), *cow paper* (a promissory note with cows as the security), *cow rigging* (a cowboy's work clothes), *cow salve* (butter), *cow skinner* (a winter storm so severe that ranchers are left with only cow skins), *cow thief, cow trail, cow waddy* (a cowboy), *cow whistle* (the whistle on a train to keep cows off the tracks), *cow wood* (dried dung), *cowology* (the science of raising cows). (See also **COW-CALF OPERATION, COW TOWN.**)

COW HORSE A horse that knows at least something about working cattle, may have some *cow sense* (that instinctive understanding of cows and how stupid and mean and perverse they are), may even have some skill at cutting or roping, has perhaps only a moderate prejudice against human beings, and is only run-of-the-mill dangerous. Generally called by this name with affection and a touch of suspicion. Sometimes they're called *cow ponies.*

Westerners have scores of terms for saddle horses (not to mention draft horses, pack horses, and wild horses). Some of the general ones are *bronco, cayuse, cow pony, cuitan* (an Indian pony), *dilsey* (a saddle mare), *hay baler, hay burner, jennet* (a small Spanish mare), *mockey* (wild mare), *montura* (saddle mare), *Navvy* (a Navajo pony), *pony, pinto, rocking-chair horse* (one with an easy gait), *range horse* (one untouched by man except for branding), *ridge runner* (wild stallion), *ridgling* (a stud with testicles not descended), *saddler* (an easy-gaited horse), *stud* (a stallion), and *show horse* (a quarter horse). (See also **STOCK HORSE, MUSTANG, CUTTING HORSE**.)

COW TOWN The end of the trail; a trail town; the railhead the cowboys finally got to at the end of one of the great trail drives; especially the Kansas destination of any of the principal trails north from Texas. During the days of the great drives, these towns had a few respectable people and facilities and a cornucopia of places that would spoil a Texas cowboy's sobriety, celibacy, and solvency in about that order. (Naturally, he got ruint with joyous abandon.) Cow towns often got to be cow towns because they wanted to be—they wooed the drivers of the great herds—and later turned into decent places to live because their citizens couldn't stand the booze peddlers, gamblers, whores (see also **CALICO QUEEN**), crooks, and killers who preyed on the cowboys, and so gave them the boot.

Later, when the days of the great trail drives had passed, *cow town* meant simply a commercial center in cow country, like Miles City, Montana, or Fort Worth, Texas.

COWBOY This most American of terms, at least American in mythology, got its start in medieval Ireland as the word for the boys (literally) who tended cattle. During the American Revolution it meant, of all things, a Tory. But we know it, properly, as the best-worn of all the handles for the men of the American West of the nineteenth century who rode the range and did the hard, down to earth jobs required to raise cows. They're still doing them.

The best known of these fellows rode during the heyday of the cowboy, the twenty or thirty years following the Civil War. He rode, he roped, he branded. He doctored. He nursed. He trailed or, later, fixed fence. (Building and fixing fences were the bane of his existence, partly because he had to do them on foot.) On the Northern Plains, he fed—every winter morning and evening, no exceptions. Depending on his personality, he smelled the air (and the dust and alkali) and felt the motion of his mount, and looked about and thanked

Cowboy.
[DRAWING BY E. L. REEDSTROM.]

God for letting him be where he was; if he was of sour disposition, he cussed his horse, cussed the country, cussed his employer, and cussed God for sentencing him to . . . everything he resented.

Cowboys are hard to generalize about. The cowboy's main fault, from the modern point of view, is that he is likely to have narrow horizons: He keeps his books in the outhouse, and he doesn't use them there for reading matter. He likes food from fried chicken to chicken-fried steak and isn't interested in experimentation. Coors Light is his choice over any wine, California or French. In the old days, his musical likes didn't go beyond fiddles and guitars (pronounced GIH-tars), these days not beyond country twanging. He's likely to have prejudices, and if you're an Indian or a Mexican or a black, or simply a woman, you may not like some of them. (Still, there are thousands of cowboys this doesn't apply to.)

This fellow works prodigiously. He takes care of cows as though they were children, and he doesn't knock off just because the clock says it's quitting time. He can fix almost anything mechanical. He's decent, and then some. He has a strong sense of justice and will travel many a mile to set things right.

Most important, you can depend on him. For instance, it's a most basic Western courtesy to leave gates as you find them: open if they were open, closed if they were closed—they're keeping cows in or out. In *The Solace of Open Spaces*, Gretel Ehrlich tells of a Wyoming cowboy who cut his foot off by accident. On the way to town for medical help, he stopped his pickup, hobbled painfully to the gate and opened it, and then got out to close it again after he went through. Otherwise, he said, "What would they a thunk?"

If he's on your side, the cowboy will stick. For most of them, the old expression will do: He's a good man to ride the river with.

The cowboy has gone by more names than you can count, and "cowboy" wasn't one of them at first. The Texas fellow was first a VAQUERO (and that didn't suggest he was Hispanic). Later, after the Civil War, the term "cowboy" came into widespread use. In the Great Basin, though, he was more likely to be a *buckaroo*, which also implied somewhat different techniques and gear. He has also gone by *cowpoke* (or just *poke), cowprod(der)*, COWPUNCHER (or just *puncher*), *dabster hand*, GUNNYSACKER (to sheepmen), HAND (*cowhand* or *top hand*), *heel squatter, leather pounder*, RANAHAN (or *ranny*), *saddle slicker, saddle stiff, saddle warmer, trail hand*, WADDY, WRANGLER, and of course *you son of a bitch*. If he's called a *cowboy of the Pecos*, he's been *alkalied* in the rough country drained by the Pecos River, which even lizards avoid, and is the toughest kind of rawhide. In the twentieth century, a new distinction became necessary—*ranching cowboy* means a working hand, as opposed to a *rodeo cowboy*, a performer.

The word *cowboy* suggests a person who puts action ahead of thought: A speeder is said to be *cowboying around*, and Ronald Reagan was called the cowboy president. The word is often used as a verb, too, as in "I been cowboying over on the Picketwire," or in *cowboy up*, to prove yourself as a hand. It is also the basis of combinations like *cowboy hat* (some Westerners prefer *stockman's hat*), **COWBOY BOOT,** cowboy song, cowboy movie, and so on. A horse that's *cowboy broke* is a horse nobody but a real hand could ride, the opposite of *lady-broke.*

COWBOY BOOT The cowboy boot is an essential part of the West. I quote Ramon Adams's definition of "boot" in *Western Words:*

> The cowman's footwear. The cowboy's boots are generally the most expensive part of his rigging, and he wants them high-heeled, thin-soled, and made of good leather. The tops are made of lightweight, high-grade leather, and all the stitching on them is not merely for decoration but serves the purpose of stiffening them and keeping them from wrinkling too much at the ankles where they touch the stirrups. . . .
>
> The boots are handmade to order. The cowman has no use for hand-me-down, shop-made footgear, and no respect for a cowhand who will wear them, holding to the opinion that ordinary shoes are made for furrow-flattened feet and are not intended for stirrup work. The high heels keep the cowman's foot from slipping through the stirrup and hanging, they let him dig in when he is roping on foot, and they give him a sure footing in all other work on the ground. Too, the high heel is a tradition, a mark of distinction, the sign that the one wearing it is a riding man, and a riding man has always held himself above the man on foot.
>
> A cowhand wants the toes of his boots more or less pointed to make it easier to pick up a stirrup on a wheeling horse. He wants a thin sole so that he has the feel of the stirrup. He wants the vamp soft and light and the tops wide and loose to allow the air to circulate and prevent sweating.
>
> When a man is seen wearing old boots so frazzled he can't strike a match on 'em without burnin' his feet, he is considered worthless and without pride.

(2) A rack on a stagecoach that holds mail and baggage. (3) A horseshoe calked at both heel and toe. (4) The scabbard of a saddle gun. (5) Rawhide coverings on **HONDAS** or other leather loops to prevent wear. (6) Between two horse traders, whatever extra value (cash or other valuables) a man trades along with the horse to make the deal even.

COWBOY CHANGE Cartridges used as equivalents of gold and silver coins.

COWBOY COCKTAIL Whiskey neat (straight).

COWBOY COFFEE The brew you make on the range, strong enough to float a horseshoe. You use a pot that's been making coffee for months or years without ever being washed—well seasoned. You keep part of the old grounds and add some new ones and some water (and "it don't take as much water as you think it do"). You boil it, add cold water to settle the grounds, and pour. Also called *Indian coffee;* for other names for coffee, see also **ARBUCKLE'S**.)

COW-CALF OPERATION A kind of cow outfit. The owner has cows and at least one bull (or these days, artificial insemination) and therefore calves. He or she sells the calves to feed lots and keeps the cows for next spring's bunch.

COWED OUT An expression of campers for potential camping sites ruined by cattle.

COWHIDE (1) The skin of a cow. (2) Boots or whips made of cowhide. (3) To flail a man with such a whip. Such beatings were said to be wicked—an early reference says that a lawyer cut a fellow's jacket to ribbons with a cowhide. Cow*skin* is also used in this sense.

COWICHAN SWEATER A sweater with lots of lanolin in the wool, worn against rainy weather by British Columbians. Developed by the Cowichan Indians, a Salishan-speaking tribe of Vancouver Island and the lower Fraser River in British Columbia.

COWISH An Oregon herb valued by Northwest Indians for its edible roots and known to whites since the Lewis and Clark Expedition. Also spelled *couse, cowas,* and *cows.*

COWPEN HERD A small herd of cows; probably a herd so little it could be gotten into a single corral.

COWPEN SPANISH Tex-Mex talk; the Spanish that Texas hands learned from the Mexican VAQUEROS.

COWPUNCHER (1) Now another word for a cowboy. Originally, during the days the railroads were making hay by hauling cows on the hoof from the Plains to the cities of the Midwest and East, it meant either: (2) A fellow who helped push the cattle onto rail cars by poking them with a long stick, or (3) a fellow who used a prod to keep the cows standing during the journey, so they wouldn't get trampled. Sometimes both. Maybe *cowpoke* and *cowprod(der)* meant the same, too. David Lavender in *One Man's West* says that movies and magazines first confused cowpunchers with cowboys, and for decades, real cowboys thought the term degrading.

COYDOG What comes when a coyote and dog get together, male and female. South Dakota rancher and writer Linda Hasselstrom says it's common in her country and that coydogs can be very large. Also called a *coyote dog.*

COYOTE (usually pronounced KIY-yoht by Westerners rather than kiy-YOH-tee; the Spanish pronunciation is coy-YOH-tay) (1) The prairie wolf, the barking wolf, the prairie lawyer, the song dog, the trickster of Western myth, the irrepressible populater of our plains and mountains. (2) A man who skulks like a coyote. (3) A squatter. (4) An Indian or *breed.* (5) A Dakotan. (6) A person who guides illegal aliens across the American-Mexican border.

The word has other meanings in verb form. (1) In mining, to run small drifts, dig little holes coyote fashion. (2) To VAMOOSE, to clear out. (3) To drift around, as in "I was coyoting around the upper Yellowstone country." (4) To *out-coyote* a man is to outsmart him at his own game.

Among Indians, the coyote is important in myth, and many-faced. He is a creator but a trickster, mankind's principal helper but a fool; he is victim and villain, savior and cheat. In some myths, he is like Prometheus, the bringer of fire. In CROW mythology, coyote created the Earth and the two-legged, four-legged, winged, rooted, and other tribes that inhabit it. In lots of stories, he is sly, devious. In PUEBLO myth, he is often the scapegoat, the one who gets tricked or fooled. Always, though, he endures.

Anglos have not liked him so well. While they admire his singing, they don't like his tendency to kill livestock. Though many government specialists insist that *Canis latrans* feeds mainly on small animals like rabbits and mice and attacks domestic critters rarely, most sheepmen spit and say quietly, "Bullshit!" As a result, most states in the West have their government trappers, whose job is to wage ceaseless war on the coyote.

Historian David Lavender, himself raised on a Colorado ranch, argues (along with other authorities) that coyotes save lots of grass for the stockman by getting rid of foraging insects and rodents, and so do more good than harm. He admits, "It is whistling in the wind to say so, however. Most ranchers remain adamant in their determination to exterminate 'every one of the danged varmits that walks.'"

Yet Anglos do feel a sly love for this creature. Listen to our cowboy songs. Read J. Frank Dobie's *The Voice of the Coyote* or Max Evans's fine little novel *One-Eyed Sky*. Watch the cartoon co-starring the roadrunner and Wile E. Coyote.

And, by God, the coyote is a survivor. Many of the animals that appear to define the Old West, such as the buffalo and the wolf, exist only marginally these days. The coyote has prospered. We fence the pastures, and he uses the grass along the fences for cover. We build our cities, and he thrives in the foothills, foraging from our leavings. He originally ranged from the Mississippi to the Pacific Coast and from down in Mexico nearly to the Arctic. He's still mostly there and has been expanding his range eastward.

His name, from the Nahuatl *coyotl*, has been spelled creatively—*kiote* most often as a variant, also *cayota, cuiota,* and so on. He's sometimes nicknamed Otie by cowboys.

COMBINATIONS IN MINING: *coyote gold* (very fine gold dust), *coyote hole* (a digging in a river bank that is neither wet nor dry, but in between), *coyote diggings* (small diggings, especially small drift tunnels, often run down and not productive), *coyote placer* or *coyote shaft* (a small shaft dug into the hillside).

The early days of settlement in the West, when homesteaders and others lived in DUGOUTS (also known as *coyote houses*) were referred to as *coyote days*. A *coyote well* is a desert water hole, especially if it's hard to find. A *coyote dun* is a dun-colored horse with a dorsal stripe.

PLANTS: *coyote tobacco*, a name Indians of Mexico and the Southwest gave to tobacco smoked for sacred purposes; *coyote melon (Cucurbita palmata)*, a Southwestern gourd said fit to be eaten only by coyotes, and *coyote thistle*, the *Eryngium* of California.

To *coyote around the rim* is to hint, to talk around the edges of a subject.

CRACK SHOT A first-rate shot, a center shot; the man who can make such a shot.

CRACK-A-LOO A gambling game. Players pitched coins against the ceiling, and the coin that came to rest nearest a crack in the floor won. Also called *crack-loo*.

CRADLE (1) In mining, a rocker, like a child's cradle, used to wash gold-bearing earth. (2) In verb form, to do that washing. (3) Another word for **COONEY**, the hide slung under a wagon for carrying cow chips. Also called a *cradle rocker*.

CRADLEBOARD The leather, pouchlike home of an Indian infant, with a board for a back. Though in pictures the mother is usually carrying her child in the cradleboard high on her back, she was just as likely to hang the board from a lodgepole or from the pommel of her saddle or to prop it against a tree. The cradleboard had and has a front of soft, tanned skin, usually beaded. Originally, before being enclosed in the cradleboard, the child would be wrapped in a blanket, with some soft material like the inner bark of the cedar stuffed in to absorb his or her soiling.

Two Apache babies in the cradleboards. [COURTESY OF NATIONAL ARCHIVES (111-SC-87304).]

CRAPS A gambling game with dice that descends from the older game called *hazard*. You win if you begin by rolling seven or eleven or by matching a point. If you start with craps (two, three, or twelve), you lose. Playing craps is called *shooting craps*. COMBINATIONS: *crap board, crap game, crap house, crap roller, crap shooter, crap-shooting, crap table*.

PRINCIPAL CRAPS TERMS: *bones* (dice), *fade, fimps, ivories* (dice), *no-dice, snake-eyes* or *bird eyes, viggerish*. The points a player can establish and chants as he rolls the dice are *bird nuts* (double aces); *two rows of rabbit turds* (double threes); *little Dick, little Joe, little Joe from Baltimore*, or *Kokomo* (four); *fever dice, little Phoebe, feebee*, or just *Phoebe* (five); *sixie from Dixie, Johnny Hicks, Sister Hicks, oh so sick* (six); *eighter (Ada) from Decatur, Ada Ross the stable hoss*, or *Ada Ross on a fartin' hoss* (eight); *niner from Carolina* or *Caroline nine* (nine); *big Dick* or *big Joe from Boston* (ten). Seven and eleven cannot be points and are called, respectively, *little natural* and *big natural*. Two and twelve are *craps*, and to throw them is to *crap out*, losing your bet and your turn at the dice.

CRAWFISH (1) To back out, to creep out backward; especially appropriate when applied to politicians. (2) When said of a horse, it's more violent: It means it's bucking backward. Hence, of a man or horse, *crawfisher*.

CRAWL (1) To creep up on quarry, a usage that surprisingly appears to occur first in the West. (2) To manage to stay on a horse.

CREASE To shoot a wild horse in the neck in an effort to stun it so you can capture it. Usually the shot killed the horse, which in the view of early Westerners was no catastrophe. Also, to stun a man with a bullet (to his head, not his neck).

CREEK A Native tribe originally living in what became Georgia and Alabama; properly known as the Muskogee; one of the **FIVE CIVILIZED TRIBES**. During the eighteenth century, because of an improved economy (based on methods and trade goods acquired from the white man) and assimilation with other Indian peoples, the Creeks were the dominant tribe in the Old Southwest. Staying independent, they leaned toward the British side against the Spanish, who were in Florida, and sided with the British in the American Revolution as well. In time they began to feel pressure on their lands from the governments of the United States and the state of Georgia. Some Creeks fought Andrew Jackson in the Creek War in 1813 and were defeated, and the tribe was forced to cede lands.

In 1834–35 the Creeks were forced to migrate to what would become Indian Territory (in Oklahoma), with many dying on the way. There they formed a compact with the **CHEROKEE**, **CHOCTAW**, and **CHICKASAW**, tribes against the buffalo-hunting tribes of the Plains.

Because the Creek split and took both sides in the Civil War, they were again forced to cede land to the United States. In the first years of the twentieth century, the Five Civilized Tribes made an effort to create a separate state, but in the end Congress merged their lands with Oklahoma and admitted that territory to the union as a state in 1907.

CREEK DIGGINGS In mining, shallow mining for gold beside a creek.

CREEK ROBBING In the Pacific Northwest, setting nets illegally at the mouths of streams to catch salmon that are returning to their spawning ground. A person who does this is a *creek robber* or *creek poacher*. See also **FISH PIRATE**.

CREEP FEED A pellet feed, usually used for calves. (See also **CAKE**.)

CREMELLO (cray-MAY-oh) An albino horse with white coat, pink skin, and china-blue eyes. (See also **BUCKSKIN**.)

CREOLE A person of mixed European and Native blood. In the Southwest, a Creole is a person of Spanish and Indian heritage; in Louisiana, French and Native, or sometimes a Native-born black; in Alaska, Russian and Native. In a contrasting meaning, in Louisiana, sometimes a white person descended from European colonists.

CREOSOTE BUSH The ubiquitous shrub (*Larrea divaricata*) of much of the Southwestern desert country, with a yellow blossom, an oily leaf, and a bit of a stink. Also called *greasewood* and, by Southwestern Hispanics, *hedionilla*. Some Anglos used to say it relieves rheumatism.

CRESTED WHEATGRASS An exotic grass (*Agropyron cristatum*) introduced for forage in the late nineteenth century. It does well in arid areas and is a good forage in the spring, not as good later. Generally called simply *crested*. *Western wheatgrass* (*Agropyron smithii*), largely displaced by **CHEATGRASS**, is also called *bluestem wheatgrass*.

CREVICE A miner's term for trying to pry gold out of cracks in rock with a knife.

CRIB (1) A saloon, gambling den, or whorehouse—usually all three in one high-living, hellacious combination. A *crib girl* was a whore (see also **CALICO QUEEN** for many names for these frail denizens). (2) In mining, the timber lining a shaft.

CRIBBER A horse that sucks air into its stomach while placing its front top teeth on a bar of wood. This can cause colic, which is often fatal. This nervous habit is contagious in a barn; a cribber is to be avoided. Also called a *stump sucker*. (See also **STOCK HORSE**.)

CRICKET A roller on a horse's **BIT**. With it, the mount can make a kind of music for man and beast.

CRICKSAND Quicksand. A wonderful blending of *crick*, the frequent Western pronunciation of *creek*, with the original term *quicksand*.

CRIMP A bend in a playing card put there by a cheat; a name for the cheat, who is also called a *crimper* and a *crimp artist*.

CROCKHEAD One of the cowboy's many terms for a stupid, stubborn, no-good horse. (See also **CANNER**.)

CROP TREE In logging, a tree in a stand chosen to grow to maturity, when it will be harvested as lumber.

CROP-EARED (1) A way of describing a critter whose ears have been cropped by nature, as by frostbite. (2) A horse with ears that have been deliberately cropped to show that he's a can't-be-rode critter is called *croppy*.

CROSS A HERD To force a herd of horses or cattle across a stream. You yell, wave your hat, jump up and down, and hope.

CROSS DRAW The pulling of a pistol from the off-side of the body. It is holstered butt forward for this purpose. Also called *border draw* since it was popular in the Texas-Mexico border country.

CROSS FOX In Alaska, a red fox during a color phase in which it has a dorsal stripe and cross stripe.

CROSSBRANDER (1) A cattle thief, a brand blotter. (2) In the verb form, to crossbrand, it means for a seller to rebrand, or **COUNTERBRAND**, on the shoulder as evidence that he's surrendered his claim.

CROSSBUCK SADDLE A wooden packsaddle that looks like a small sawhorse. Also called a *sawbuck saddle* and *crosstree saddle*.

CROSS-FIRE (1) For a horse to bump a forefoot against its opposite hind foot when it walks. (2) One of the two branches of the **NATIVE AMERICAN CHURCH**, the one with more Christian elements in the ceremonies; the other is the *half-moon*, which stresses traditional Indian elements. The *fireplace* is the peyote ceremony of the church.

CROSS-HOBBLE To tie one front foot of a horse to the back one on the opposite side to prevent it from kicking.

CROTCH Among loggers, a small sled made from the fork of a tree and used to skid logs, hauled by horses. Also known as a *dray*, **GO-DEVIL**, and *lizard*.

CROW A Siouan tribe of **PLAINS INDIANS** with a buffalo-hunting culture. Their name is also rendered in English as *Absaroka* (pronounced ab-SAHR-kuh, not ab-suh-ROH-kuh, as Charlton Heston said it in the movie *The Mountain Men*, plus dialectical variants like ab-SAHR-kee). It means not "crow" but "children of the big-beaked bird," usually considered the mountain raven, which is often mistaken for the crow. Like their neighbors the **LAKOTAS**, **CHEYENNES**, and **BLACKFEET**, they based their physical culture on the buffalo, until the extinction of the great herds, and their religion on the buffalo and the **SUN DANCE**.

The Crow split off from the **HIDATSA** in prehistoric times and came to live on the southern tributaries of the Yellowstone River, in what now is eastern Wyoming and southeastern Montana. Though they made few alliances with neighboring tribes and were particular enemies of the Blackfeet, **SHOSHONES**, and Lakotas, they welcomed the **MOUNTAIN MEN**, their first substantial contacts among the whites, and traded willingly. During the period of the Plains Indian wars (1860s and '70s, by which time they were divided into the Mountain and River Crow), they furnished the U.S. Army with scouts to fight against their traditional enemies.

In 1868 they accepted confinement to a reservation in their traditional country in south-central Montana, where they live today, beside the Big Horn River and the Custer battlefield.

CROW BAIT A worthless horse. (See also **CANNER**.)

CROW HOP Stiff-legged bucking by a horse. It's not a serious effort to get rid of a rider.

CROWDING PEN A small, strong **CORRAL** where you hold cattle tightly, to do work such as loading into a truck, sorting, or **BRANDING**.

CROWN In fire-fighting, for a fire to soar into the tops of the trees.

CROWN DANCE A religious ceremony of the **APACHE**. Also known as the *mountain spirit dance*, it is done to ward off evil spirits or sometimes as a puberty rite for young girls.

CRUISE To explore forest country for stands of timber worth harvesting. The loggers who did this were called *cruisers, timber cruisers,* or *land-lookers,* and they wore high-laced boots called *cruisers.*

CRUMB What a soldier or logger (and sometimes a cowboy) called a louse. So a logger called his bedroll a *crumb roll,* and a cowboy called it a *crumb incubator.* Getting rid of your body lice was called *crumbing up.* Among loggers, the fellow who cleaned the bunkhouse was the *crummie.* (See also **PANTS RATS**.)

CRUPPER A band of leather attached to a saddle or **APAREJO** and passed beneath the horse's tail to keep the saddle from sliding forward. A crupper made in two sections is called a *panel crupper.*

CRUSH PEN A narrow branding **CHUTE**.

CUESTA (KWAY-stuh) A steep, narrow ridge, a **HOGBACK**. Borrowed from Spanish (where it means slope).

CUFF A leather gauntlet or wrist guard worn by some cowboys. Some authorities say it was useful to prevent rope burns; some say it wasn't practical but was for show.

CUFFY A frontier nickname for a bear. Also spelled *cuff* and *cuffee.*

CUIDADO! (kwee-DAH-doh) "Look out!" Or, more accurately for the Western vernacular, "Watch your ass!" Borrowed from Spanish.

CUI-UI A fish of northern Nevada, historically used as food by local Indians.

CULL (1) In the cattle business, an animal rejected from the herd. Ranchers usually cull cows that no longer yield calves every year. Sometimes called *cut-backs.* (2) In logging, a tree, log, or lumber to be rejected. (3) In verb form, to do the cutting out.

CULTURAL RESOURCES In governmentese, the remains of sites and implements used by humans in either historic or prehistoric times. The task of Cultural Resource Management (CRM) is assessing, protecting, and preserving the cultural resources on public lands.

CULTUS Worthless, useless. Thus Owen Wister wrote, "He can't bile water without burnin' it. . . . He's jest kultus, he is." A *cultus potlatch* is a present, a gift. (See also **POTLATCH**.) Also spelled *kultus.* From the **CHINOOK** trade language.

CUP (1) A groove in the teeth of a horse that gives away its age. (2) In logging, a notch in a stump or the base of a tree made to hold a chemical.

CUPID'S CRAMP The ache a cowboy feels when he's in love. Sometimes takes the form *cupid's cramps.*

CURA An old Southwesternism for a priest. (See **BLACK ROBE** for similar names.)

CURANDERO (koo-rahn-DAIR-oh) In the Southwest, a healer; a **MEDICINE MAN**; sometimes carries the implication of quackery. Borrowed from Spanish.

CURB BIT One of the favorite bits of Western riders, one with an upward curve (called a *port)* in the middle; a popular curb bit was called a *grazing bit.* The *curb strap* runs from the bit underneath the horse's chin. (See also **BIT, SNAFFLE BIT, SPADE BIT.**)

CURED GRASS Grass that has matured where it grew, uncut. In the West it's an important source of nutrition for cows in the winter.

CURL HIM UP One expression of Westerners for killing someone. (See also **DRY-GULCH.**)

CURLY WOLF A mean fellow; a tough guy; maybe a bit of a bastard. Watts says it's a rough-and-tumble compliment.

CURRY HIM OUT To rake a horse with your **SPURS**. To *curry the kinks out* is an expression for **BREAKING A** horse.

CUSS WORD A profane word. The convention of not using these words in front of women, naturally, is a fountainhead of Western verbal creativity. Though *cuss* (in both the noun and verb forms) appears not to be a Westernism, the first use of *cuss word* I've seen is in Mark Twain's *Roughing It* (1872).

CUSTER HAT A version of the **KOSSUTH HAT** with both sides pinned up. But what General George Armstrong Custer often wore was the *planter's hat,* a leftover of the pre–Civil War South.

CUSTOM-MADES A term for a cowboy's **BOOTS** when they're not store-bought but made to order. The old insistence on custom-mades is waning.

CUT A word with a **PARFLECHE**-full of Western meanings. (1) To *cut a herd* is to divide it into groups. (2) To separate a particular cow or a group of cattle from a larger group. This maneuver is best done on a **CUTTING HORSE**. It is a tricky matter, and these days the skill may be exhibited at a *cutting competition.* Cutting-horse riders say the horse does the work: Without guidance, it sees how to force the cow the way it wants the critter to go and does the dodging and darting. It is worth noting that unless the rider anticipates the horse's moves and leans with it, he ends up in the dust himself.

COMBINATIONS: Cowboys at a big **ROUNDUP** would make both a *calf cut,* grouping the cow-calf pairs in one bunch, and a *steer cut* (or *beef cut*), separating out the steers that are to go to market, for each ranch. *Cutting double-barreled* is to use two cowboys to cut a herd at once; a *cut herd* is a bunch of cows separated from the main herd; a *cutting gate* is a swinging gate that forces cattle into one pen or another.

(3) To castrate a steer, so he'll put on weight instead of burning off pounds chasing heifers, changing his attitude "from ass to grass," as Westerners say. It's usually done at branding with a sharp knife. (4) To *cut down* is to level a

pistol at a man, as in "I cut down on him with both hands." (5) To *make the final cut*, jocularly, is to get thumbs up at the Last Judgment.

COMBINATIONS: *cut a trail* or *cut for sign* (to come on a trail and identify it by signs), *cut a rusty* (cowboy talk meaning to do your best), *cut her loose* (what the RODEO cowboy says when he's ready for the gate to be opened), *cut him some slack* (give him a break), *cut straw and molasses* (a cowboy's description of food he doesn't like), *cut plug* (a piece of tobacco cut from a plug of tobacco), *cut the bed* (what a cowboy called sharing his bed), *cut the beef* (to separate the market-ready animals), *cut the deck deeper* (to explain more fully, to "come again"), *cut the dust* (to take a drink, preferably alcoholic), *cut over* (said of land that has been logged).

CUT YOUR WOLF LOOSE To go on a bender, to do something outrageous, to raise some hell while stimulated by strong drink. (See ROOSTERED for expressions for drunkenness.) Adams's example is riding a horse into a saloon. He tells of a bartender who received a complaint from an Eastern customer about the horses in the saloon. The bartender answered that the Easterner had a lot of nerve coming in on foot.

CUTBANK An overhanging bank on a stream, on the outside of a bend where the water has undercut the bank. Also spelled *cut-bank* and *cut bank*.

CUTTHROAT (1) The object of the Rocky Mountain fly fisherman's affections, the native brook trout, distinguished by a pair of orange slashes on its throat. (2) A SHOSHONE name for a LAKOTA (Teton Sioux) Indian, because the sign language for the Sioux is a slash of the hand across the throat. The two tribes were long-term enemies.

CUTTING HORSE A horse skilled at cutting cows out of a herd. They're also called *carvers* and *carving horses, choppers, chopping horses, sorting horses, whittlers*, and *cut horses*. The rider points the horse toward the cow and calf to be cut out and lets the animal take over. A cutting horse is a source of pride to its rider and to the whole outfit. Nowadays the tradition is kept alive in the *cutting competition*, a contest for cutting horses and their riders. It's judged by how efficiently the rider can cut out a cow critter from a herd in three minutes. Stewart Edward White describes the precision work of a cutting horse called Little G:

> The cow and her calf turned in toward the centre of the herd. A touch of
> the reins guided the pony. At once he comprehended. From that time on
> he needed no further directions. Cautiously, patiently, with great skill,
> he forced the cow through the press toward the edge of the herd. . . .
> When the cow turned back, Little G somehow happened always in her
> way. Before she knew it she was at the outer edge of the herd. There she
> found herself . . . facing the open plain. I felt Little G's muscles tighten
> beneath me. The moment for action had come. Before the cow had a
> chance to dodge among her companions the pony was upon her like a

thunderbolt. She broke in alarm, trying to avoid desperately the rush. There ensued an exciting contest of dodgings, turnings, and doublings. Wherever she turned Little G was before her. Some of his evolutions were marvellous. All I had to do was to sit my saddle, and apply just that final touch of judgment denied even the wisest of the lower animals. . . . At last the cow, convinced of the uselessness of further effort to return, broke away on a long lumbering run to the open plain. There she was held by men forming the new herd, called a cut herd.

D

D RING A metal ring on a saddle, used to attach the cinch or a martingale. It may be flat on one side (like a D) or completely round.

DAB To toss, as in "Just dab your rope on."

DAKOTA A large, powerful Native tribe commonly known as the Sioux that became celebrated because of their fierce resistance to white encroachment on the Northern Plains. Dakota leaders like Crazy Horse, Red Cloud, and Sitting Bull and events like the Little Bighorn battle and the Wounded Knee massacre have become legendary in Anglo and Native cultures.

Dakota is a word in their Siouan language meaning "alliance of friends." The language has two other dialectical forms, Nakota and **LAKOTA**; the latter may now be the word they most commonly use to refer to themselves. Historically, they also called themselves the Seven Council Fires. The word *Sioux* is a French version of their Ojibway foes, meaning "adder" or "enemy." Historically they lived near the western Great Lakes but, because of pressure from the Ojibway, gradually migrated further and further onto the Plains, as far west as modern Wyoming.

The Dakota divided themselves into seven tribes: Mdewakanton, Sisseton, Wahpekute, and Wahpeton (these four known to whites as the Santee); Yankton and Yanktonai (these two known to whites as the Yankton); and Teton. The Santee were Minnesota farmers, the Yankton a semi-agricultural culture in the eastern Dakotas, and the Teton (much the largest group) a nomadic, buffalo-hunting culture in the Dakotas and Wyoming. The Teton Sioux themselves comprised seven tribes—the Blackfoot (not to be confused with the **BLACKFEET**), Brulé, Hunkpapa, Miniconjou, Oglala, Sans Arc, and Two Kettle. These were the best-known Dakota combatants of the Indian wars of the 1860s and '70s.

Their religion is centered around the VISION QUEST, the SUN DANCE, and other ceremonies seeking blessings from the spiritual power they see in nature, and emphasizes an individual gaining of rightness with that divine spirit.

The Teton Lakota fought against the U.S. government, especially about the Bozeman Trail and use of the Black Hills, during the middle and late 1860s. After an 1868 treaty, many accepted reservation life; others continued to fight. They inflicted defeats on troops led by George Crook and then George Custer in the spring and summer of 1876, but during the following winter they suffered severely from lack of food. Many surrendered the following summer; others stayed in Canada until 1881. The government ended the GHOST DANCE fervor in 1890 with a slaughter of unarmed men, women, and children at Wounded Knee Creek.

Since that time the Dakota have lived principally on reservations in South Dakota; other reservations are in North Dakota and Nebraska. They have suffered under government policies that suppressed their culture, their religion, even their language. In their terms, the sacred hoop was broken.

In the 1970s and '80s, a new consciousness of Indian rights has helped them to reassert their customs and values. In 1973 some occupied the village at Wounded Knee for two months against opposition from the Federal Bureau of Investigation, and brought international attention to their circumstances. Now the Dakota are fighting to regain the Black Hills.

COMBINATIONS: *Dakota sandstone*, a common rock formation in the Black Hills and on the eastern slope of the Rockies; *Dakota Territory* (formed in 1861 with Yankton as its capital and continuing until the admission of North Dakota and South Dakota to the union in 1889), *Dakota turnip* (the PRAIRIE TURNIP).

DALL SHEEP A mountain sheep primarily of Alaska and the Yukon, much sought by those who hunt for trophies. See also BIGHORN.

DALLES (DALZ, with the *a* as in corral) The name of a tribe of CHINOOKAN Indians living on the east side of the Columbia River near The Dalles, Oregon, near the falls. *Dalle* was a word of the VOYAGEURS for rapids in a river, and they also named Eastern rapids the Dalles. A variant of this word is *dells*.

DALLY When roping, to wrap the rope around the saddle HORN, then use the saddle horn as a kind of snubbing post to bring the cow short when it hits the end of the rope. The end of the rope you dally, the one opposite the noose, is called the *home end*. Since the critter is trying to get away, the turn around the horn must be taken quickly and with care not to get the fingers or especially the thumb caught between rope and horn. A cow going hard away from a planted roping horse generates considerable force, and careless placement of fingers has cost many a cowboy a digit.

The technique was invented by the VAQUEROS of New Spain. After years of tying the rope to the cinch or the tail of the horse, they developed this use of

Dall sheep in Alaska.
[Courtesy Alaska Department of Fish & Game.]

the saddle horn. The word is an Anglo version of the vaquero term for it, *dar la vuelta* (to take a twist or turn around something), or in the form of a command as it would have been used in a pinch, *dale vuelta*. The cowboy simply shortened it to dally. Sometimes he tried to keep the Spanish *vuelta* and said *dally* (or *dolly*) *welter* or *dally welta*.

Some Texas cowboys, known as TIE-HARD-AND-FAST MEN, instead of dallying tie the rope hard to the saddle horn. They generally work with a shorter catch rope, thirty to forty feet, as opposed to the forty- to eighty-foot REATA of the dally man. And the tie-hard-and-fast men generally stick to shorter throws.

You can cause some excitement by stirring hands of each technique to argue about which is better. Dallying has the advantage of not subjecting horse, saddle, rope, and cow to a severe jerk when the critter hits the end of the rope, because the rope slips a bit on the horn. But it's harder on fingers, and Texas saddles are DOUBLE RIGGED (equipped with two cinches) to take the jolt of the hard tie. Another disadvantage of tying hard and fast is that you can't let go of what you've roped. There are stories of cowboys having the saddle ripped straight off the horse by a big bull. In *Trail Dust and Saddle Leather*, old hand Jo Mora opines:

I'm not saying one system is better than the other. . . . It just depends on what the job is that's got to be done. The hard and fast for rough and ready speed; the dally for the artist. In flat, open country the former is tops; but take it in the rough hills with lots of trees and patches of chaparral, the long reata and the dally system, in the hands of an expert, are unbeatable.

COMBINATIONS: A fellow who advises you to *dally your tongue* is telling you to shut up. A *dally man* is a cowboy who uses dallies instead of tying hard and fast. People joke that if a hand is missing a thumb, you know he's a dally man.

DANCE Among Indians, a term for a religious ritual. It is not simply a dance (a series of rhythmic, patterned movements), nor is it primarily a social event, like an Anglo dance. Such rituals as the SUN DANCE of the PLAINS INDIANS or the SNAKE DANCE of the HOPI, for instance, are likely to be religious observances that last a week or more. Though these observances at times involve a measured, stately form of dancing to drums, singing, and other music-making, this part is merely the part of the ceremony most accessible to the rest of the tribe and to the public. The ceremonies involve much more (prayer, sacrifice, meditation, ritual, and so on) and are imbued with high religious purpose. Such dances include the *antelope dance*, CROWN DANCE, GREEN CORN DANCE, and *dog dance*. (See also SING, the NAVAJO name for similar ceremonies.)

Indians also dance for substantially social purposes (though seldom entirely without religious connotations) and even hold dance competitions these days. Some dancers (both Indian and Anglo) travel from POWWOW to powwow competing for substantial prizes.

DANGLER A pear-shaped metal ornament hanging from a SPUR. Also called a *jinglebob*.

DANIEL BOONE A derisive term of a cattleman of the open-range days for a long-haired Anglo who dressed the part of a scout or BADMAN.

DASHBOARDS A cowboy's mocking name for someone else's big feet. Historically, cowboys have taken pride in their small feet.

DATURA In the Southwest a poisonous weed (*Datura meteloides*) of the nightshade family, commonly called JIMSON WEED or *stinkweed*. It is a hallucinogen and is used ceremonially; some tribes of California Indians had a cult that centered around it.

DAUNSY A cowboy word for downcast, depressed.

DAY HERD (1) The herd left after the cow-CALF pairs have been cut out for branding. (2) As a verb, it means to watch the cattle by day.

DAY HOLE Among miners, a level of a mine that connects with the surface.

DAY MONEY The prize money paid for one day's go-round at a **RODEO**. Many rodeos have a go-round of each event on Friday and again on Saturday, with day money paid each time, and then a final go-round of the competitors with the best averages for the big prize on Sunday. A *day-money horse* is one that *bucks* well enough to get a rider a decent score but not well enough either to help him win or to land him in the dust.

DAYLIGHTING Letting daylight show between your bottom and the saddle. It's poor riding technique.

DAY'S DROP Among sheepherders, the number of sheep born (*dropped*) in one day.

DE NADA (day NAH-duh) A Southwestern expression meaning "It's nothing," often used in response to thanks for a favor or kindness. Borrowed from Spanish.

DEACON SEAT The characteristic piece of furniture of a logging camp, a bench-like seat made of a log split in half.

DEAD MAN (1) On the range, a support for a fence post, usually a heavy object such as a rock or a piece of wood, buried and wired to the fence as an anchor. (2) In logging, a spar or log sunk into the ground and used as an anchor for lines.

DEAD MAN'S HAND In **POKER**, a hand with a pair of aces and a pair of eights. By tradition Wild Bill Hickok was holding this hand when he was shot dead by Jack McCall; the linguist J. L. Dillard thinks the tradition dubious. Some sources also say the hand has two jacks, not aces, and two eights.

DEADFALL (1) A low-class den of drink and gambling. (2) In logging, a dead tree that has fallen down, or an area covered with such trees.

DEADLINE A line some man or critter is not supposed to cross, sometimes on penalty of bodily harm. Cattlemen set down deadlines for sheep. In Kansas during the days of the big **TRAIL DRIVES**, the deadline prohibited Texas cattle from coming into the eastern part of the state because they were thought to bear **TEXAS FEVER**. The sheriff's deadline in Texas for a while was the Nueces River—no lawman was supposed to cross it. In mining, deadlines warned workers away from dangerous workings.

DEAD-MOUTHED A way of describing a horse that's insensitive to the **BIT**. (See also **HARD-MOUTHED**.)

DEADWOOD An advantage—to *have the deadwood on* someone might be to have the drop on him.

DEAL FROM THE BOTTOM OF THE DECK In **POKER**, to deal a player the bottom card instead of the one he is due, the top one. By extension, to cheat or take unjustified advantage in any situation.

DEAL ME IN In **POKER**, a request to be included as a player in a hand. By extension, to ask or agree to be part of anything. *Deal me out* means the opposite.

DEARBORN A light carriage, usually covered and curtained, named for General Henry Dearborn. Common in the East and used on the **SANTA FE** and **OREGON TRAILS**.

DEATH CAMAS A variety of the lily family (*Zigadenus elegans*) that is poisonous to stock and people. Also called *poison camas*. (See also **CAMAS**.)

DEATH SONG Among **PLAINS INDIANS**, a warrior's song given to him by a spirit helper to prepare the singer appropriately for death. It is what a warrior wishes to intone as the last words of his life, a call for strength to do whatever is necessary and to accept what comes. It is not a traditional or communal song but unique to the singer.

DECOY BRAND A brand put out of easy sight; used to trick **RUSTLERS**.

DEHORN Among cowmen, to take the horns off cows or (more often) calves. In the old days, the horns were sawed off. Now the operation is usually done at branding, when the horns are just nubs, with a tool called a scoop. The wound is then treated to create coagulation and prevent infection and flies. Cattle with horns are a nuisance to each other and to the people who work with them.

DEL NORTE (del NOHR-tay) A name for the Rio Grande until the mid-nineteenth century. From the Mexican name for the river, Rio Grande del Norte. The Rio Grande was also called the *Rio Bravo*.

DELAWARE The Algonquian Indians who lived in New Jersey and adjacent areas before white contact and called themselves Lenni-Lenape ("real men"). Displaced early in the colonial period without much resistance, they moved gradually to what is now Ohio. In the latter half of the eighteenth century there, they joined the Shawnee in raids against American frontier settlements. Defeated, they dispersed widely. Some went to a reservation in Kansas, and some joined the whites in Rocky Mountain beaver-trapping. They became in Bernard De Voto's words in *Across the Wide Missouri* "the only Indians the mountain men ever thought of as companions in their trade." Many eventually became citizens of the **CHEROKEE** Nation in Oklahoma and still live there.

DEMOCRAT PASTURE A grazing area that was mostly unfenced but was bounded by rimrock or other natural barriers.

DEN A frontier verb meaning to track a bear to its den. Animals (and sometimes people) were said to *den up*, to hibernate, to stay in their dens for the winter.

DENTALIUM The shell of a Pacific Northwest shellfish, often used by many Indian peoples as decoration, especially when combined with beads. Also called a *money shell*, from its onetime use as currency.

DENVER OMELET An omelet with ham, onions, and green pepper, sometimes served as a sandwich. *Denver mud* was a patent medicine consisting of cloth-wrapped mud as a poultice.

DEPOUILLE (day-POO-yuh) A thick layer of fat on the back of the **BUFFALO**, valued by Indians and **MOUNTAIN MEN** as food. Also called *depuis* and *depuyer*. From the French *dépouillé*.

DERRINGER The common percussion hideout pistol of the antebellum frontier, named after its inventor, Henry Deringer (with one *r*). Small, single-shot, and often of large caliber, it was effective at short range. **REMINGTON** made a particularly popular model. Occasionally the word was used as a verb—"he got derringered."

DESERET (1) The state of Deseret, the name of the utopia founded in the desert by the **MORMONS**. As mapped by Brigham Young and his advisors, Deseret included what is now Utah, most of Nevada and Arizona, and parts of California, Idaho, Oregon, New Mexico, and Wyoming. The Territory of Utah, the official Deseret established by Congress, was smaller but was larger than the modern state. (2) A word coined in the *Book of Mormon* meaning "honeybee." The Utah state symbol, the beehive, comes from the word. To Mormons, the honeybee symbolizes the spirit of cooperative industriousness. (3) A Mormon name for Salt Lake City.

The *Deseret alphabet* was a set of characters invented by Mormon George D. Watt in hope of helping the **LATTER-DAY SAINTS** establish a new written language.

DESERT CANARY A jocular name for a **BURRO**.

DESERT RAT A human denizen of the desert, especially a **PROSPECTOR** who wanders the desert.

DESERT VARNISH A black glaze or patina on desert rock, formed from manganese and iron oxide, usually appearing where water streaks the rock.

DEVIL'S BACKBONE A name given to various spiny ridges (**HOGBACKS**) all over the West.

DEVIL'S CORKSCREW A name of local cowmen for *Daimonelix*, a large, spiral fossil of the Badlands, South Dakota.

DEVIL'S KITCHEN The name given to a variety of hot and unpleasant rocky areas in **CANYON COUNTRY**. Similar to **HELL'S HALF ACRE**.

DEVIL'S SLIDE A name describing gullies that are bordered by parallel fins of sedimentary rock.

DEW CLOTH The inner liner of a **TIPI**.

DEWLAP To cut the loose skin on the underside of a calf's neck (also called a dewlap), done for the same reason you brand it or crop its ears, to make a mark of ownership. The cut skin is left to hang in a distinctive way. (See also **JUG HANDLE, VARRUGA, WATTLE**.)

DIAMONDBACK A rattlesnake (*Crotalus atrox*) with diamond-shaped markings on its back. Common in the Southwest and known for its deadliness, this is the second-largest rattler, sometimes reaching seven feet in length. (See also SIDEWINDER.)

DICE HOUSE What a cowboy sometimes called the BUNKHOUSE. He also called it a *dive, doghouse, ram pasture,* and *shack.*

DICHO (DEE-choh) A Southwestern term for a saying, proverb, or epigram. Borrowed from Spanish.

DIE ON THEIR BACKS What sheep sometimes do when they turn turtle. The critters have a hard time getting right side up again, especially when they're heavy with wool, so the sheepherders must put them back on their feet.

DIE-UP The deaths of substantial numbers of cattle from cold, disease, starvation, and so on. In Texas, die-ups brought on what was called the *skinning season,* a period of cutting the skins off dead cattle and selling them. Some of the most famous die-ups occurred in the winter of 1886-87 on the Northern Plains. Some ranchers were said to be able to walk across their entire ranches on the carcasses of their cattle.

DIFFERENTIAL GRASSHOPPER A big, particularly destructive grasshopper (*Melanoplus differentialis*), found from the Plains to the Pacific Coast.

DIGGER An Anglo name for an Indian of the Southwest, Great Basin, or Pacific Coast who lived on roots and other vegetables he gathered. Usually Diggers wore few clothes and lived in brush dwellings. Most of these Indians were SHOSHONES or PAIUTES. Though the name may first have been a translation of the name of a Paiute tribe of southwestern Utah, it quickly became an epithet of Anglo contempt. They were also called *Shuckers* or *Root-eaters.* A *digger ounce* is a lead weight that came to more than an ounce, sometimes much more. It got its name because it was often used to cheat Digger Indians when weighing the gold they brought in.

DIGGER (1) A cowboy's name for his SPURS. (2) A *stove-up* (crippled) horse.

DIGGING STICK Among many Indian peoples, a sharpened stick used to make holes for planting seeds, and by women to dig up roots.

DIGGINGS An area of PLACER mining. People spoke, for instance, of the diggings at Virginia City, Montana, or at Last Chance Gulch.

DILLY ROAD A miner's name for the mine railroad.

DILSEY A mare used as a saddle horse. In the older West, mares were not commonly ridden.

DIME NOVEL A short piece of adventure fiction published in the latter half of the nineteenth century, usually set in the West or on the frontier and written with stereotypical characters and formulaic plots.

Erastus Beadle brought out the first series of dime novels starting in 1860, and some were hugely successful with the mass audience. Typical dime-novel characters were Deadwood Dick and Hurricane Nell. Buffalo Bill and Calamity Jane were actual Westerners used as characters in these adventure stories. Perhaps the best-known dime novelist was Edward Z. C. Judson, who wrote under the pen name Ned Buntline.

The term came to be used as a way of describing an improbable heroic fantasy—*dime-novel hero, dime-novel Indian, dime-novel rescue.* It also yielded the forms *dime novelist, dime-novelism, dime-novelish,* and even *dime-novelty.* There were also *half-dime novels,* which sold for a nickel. Not a Westernism but an Eastern term for a pseudo-Western product.

DINAH One of the names of miners and loggers for dynamite. They also call it *dine.* (See also **POWDER**.)

DINEH See **NAVAJO**.

DINERO (dee-NAIR-oh) A Southwestern term for money, often used flippantly. Borrowed from Spanish.

DINGUS A thingamajig; something you can't think of the name of. This borrowing from Dutch seems first to have appeared in the West in the 1870s.

DINK What **RODEO** cowboys call a person or a horse for the steer-wrestling or roping events that isn't well trained, doesn't give a good performance.

DINNER PLATE What American cowboys called the broad, flat **HORN** of the old Spanish saddle.

DIP (1) On the range, an insecticide for ridding stock of ticks and lice. You swim the livestock through a deep vat (the *dipping vat*) containing the insecticide. (2) A cowboy word for pudding, also a sauce made with sugar and flour.

DIRT The substance a **FORTY-NINER** hoped would make his fortune. He spoke of *rich dirt, poor dirt, pay dirt,* and so on. This use of the word then spread to other Western diggings. A name for **PLACER** mining was *dirt washing.*

DIRTY YOUR SHIRT To get thrown from your horse. (For other such expressions, see **BITE THE DUST**.)

DISCOVERY The location of a valuable mineral on a claim. Discovery is required under mining law for valid title. The first locator of a mineral is entitled to what is called the *discovery claim.* The General Mining Act of 1872 established the right of discovery. By getting the rewards of their discovery, ordinary people were sometimes able to accumulate fortunes. From a **PLACER** discovery claim, other claims are numbered up or down the stream from the first. On a lode claim, the opening the first locator makes is called the *discovery shaft* or *tunnel.*

DISH The seat of a saddle, which is referred to as either *deep-dished* or *shallow-dished,* depending on the depth of the seat below the **FORK** and **CANTLE**.

DISH-WHEELED A way of describing a man or beast that's knock-kneed.

DITCH COMPANY (1) Now a company that brings water to ranchers for irrigation via ditches. (2) In the latter half of the nineteenth century, a company that sold water to miners for their sluices.

COMBINATIONS: A *ditch rider* is the man who patrols the irrigation system, checking the condition of the ditches and perhaps turning the water into laterals. The fellow in charge of the fair distribution of the water is sometimes called the *ditch boss.*

DITTY A cowboy's word for a gadget or contrivance new to him; it's like the word DINGUS.

DIVIDE The point of separation between watersheds, where water flows one way or the other. A divide is usually formed by ridges on hills or mountains. It may be conspicuous or imperceptible. Those who traveled the Oregon Trail couldn't tell where they passed from Atlantic to Pacific waters on so major a divide as South Pass, which is on the Continental Divide.

Divides were crucial to explorers and other early travelers: In an unmarked land, watercourses and divides were guideposts. Later, divides helped ranchers define their ranges. And from the time of the MOUNTAIN MAN to today, "Go over the divide," meaning "cross from one watershed to another," has been a staple of Western direction-giving.

COMBINATIONS: Sometimes a divide was called a *dividing ground.* To *cross the great divide* (sometimes just to *cross the divide*) means "to die." (See also CASH IN YOUR CHIPS for other expressions about death and dying.)

DIXIE Now the southwest corner of Utah, around St. George, a country with magnificent RIMROCK scenery and, since it's warm, a fruit-growing center. The early LATTER-DAY SAINTS also attempted to establish a cotton and silk industry there. Originally Dixie was larger, extending into Mormon Arizona.

DOCTOR C. C. What a logger called the doctor who came to his camp. The initials stood for *compound cathartic.* (See also SAWBONES .)

DODGER Among loggers, a worker who takes the DOGS out of logs.

DOFUNNY Doodad, trinket, such as an open-range cowboy might carry in his WAR BAG (sack for personal belongings).

DOG (1) Short for PRAIRIE DOG. (2) A logger's term for a spike that was pointed at one end, bent in the middle, and had an eye at the other end, used to grab logs. In full, *log dog.* In this sense it's also used as a verb—to *dog a log,* to grab or hold it. (3) Short for BULLDOG, to wrestle a steer to the ground.

COMBINATIONS: *dog hole* (saloon), *dog loop* (a small noose for roping calves), *dog travois* (one pulled by dogs), *dog pole* (an element of that travois), *dog warp* (a rope with a hook used to break up log jams), and as a verb, to *dog warp* a log jam.

DOG ROBBER Historically, a striker, an orderly, a soldier acting as attendant or servant to an officer. Strikers ate in the officers' mess. Smith says the term came into being because they were jokingly said to be cheating the dogs of the officers' leftovers.

DOG SOLDIER A member of an important **WARRIOR SOCIETY** of the **CHEYENNE** or other Plains tribes. These warriors were charged with keeping order when the entire tribe was hunting, moving camp, or the like, and with protecting the rear in tribal flights from enemies. They were known for their group discipline and fierceness. Because of the determination of some Cheyenne dog soldiers, whites in the latter half of the nineteenth century misunderstood the term to mean rebellious, outcast, or especially savage warriors. The people selected to enforce the camp rules at modern **BUCKSKINNERS' RENDEZVOUS** are also called dog soldiers.

DOG-FALL To throw a **STEER** down with its feet underneath it, instead of getting it all the way off its feet.

DOGHOUSE (1) An extra-wide **STIRRUP** of bent wood, mostly of the early period on the range. Adams says they had enough wood in them to make a doghouse. (2) One of the cowboy's words for a bunkhouse. (See also **DICE HOUSE**.) (3) The room on an oil rig for a **SEISMIC CREW** where all the controls are kept.

DOGIE (DOUGH-gee, with a hard g) An orphan calf, usually runty, usually unbranded; sometimes simply any calf. On **TRAIL DRIVES**, dogies weren't strong enough to keep up well and so were a nuisance. A dogie was also called a **BUM CALF** and a *buttermilk*. The dogie has entered Western mythology as an occasion of sentiment and pathos. One of the most famous cowboy songs, "Git Along, Little Dogies," is addressed to him:

> *Oh, you'll be soup for Uncle Sam's Injuns;*
> *It's, "beef, heap beef," hear them say.*
> *Git along, git along little dogies,*
> *You're going to be beef steers by and by.*
> *Whoopee, ti yi yo, git along little dogies.*
> *It's your misfortune and none of my own.*
> *Whoopee, ti yi yo, git along little dogies.*
> *For you know Wyomin' will be your new home!*

Since the word was variously spelled in the early days (*doughie, dogy, doge, dogey*), lots of folks both ordinary and academic have speculated widely about its origin. Some note that starved calves have swollen bellies and so were sometimes called *dough-guts*, which could have become *dogie*. Linguist J. L. Dillard in *All-American English* says *dogie* may have come from the Creole *dogi-man*, meaning "short man," or from *doga*, a term Owen Wister heard in the West and recorded as meaning any "trifling stock."

By extension came *dogie lamb*. Later *dogie* came to be applied to anything unlikely to survive, often meant in a jocular way, as in "this dogie enterprise." It also became a verb, *dogied* (orphaned). And a *dogie man* was a farmer or rancher who took in dogies to raise.

DOGSLED A light, over-snow vehicle pulled by dogs, consisting of a basket on runners, a railing, a stanchion, a OUIJA BOARD, and a GEE POLE. (For the freighting model, see YUKON SLED.) The dogs are known individually as SLED DOGS or *mush dogs*, collectively as a *dog team*. To travel by dogsled is to MUSH ON.

DOGTOWN GRASS A variety of prairie grass (*Aristida*) also known as *needle grass* and *red threeawn*. It has sharp bristles that work into wool, and even skin, and so is dangerous to sheep.

DOGWOOD A cowboy word for sagebrush.

DOINGS (1) Food, as in *buffalo doin's*, *common doin's*, or *chicken doin's*. Along with the other great preoccupations of Westerners such as sex, booze, and death, food got a lot of names: *chicken fixings* (fancy food), *chow, chuck, chuckaway, fixings, fluff duffs* (fancy food again), *kow kow, muckamuck, soft grub* (fancy food once more). (2) Any particular activity, from a Taos dance to a RENDEZVOUS to a good Indian fight, any of which may be *fine doin's*.

DOLL BABY A small, whittled-out, wooden peg used to spin MECATES (horse hair lead ropes or reins).

DOLLY (1) A variant of DALLY, a turn or two of the rope taken around the saddle horn to make an anchor to bring whatever critter you've roped to a sudden stop. (2) In logging, a wheeled platform used to move logs.

DOLLY VARDEN A spotted trout of Alaska, the Pacific Northwest, and the Rockies. Called after the colorfully dressed character of the same name in Dickens's *Barnaby Rudge*. Also known as *arctic trout, salmon trout*, and other names. The *golden fin* or *golden trout* is a kind of Dolly Varden found in California and Alaska. See also CUTTHROAT, RAINBOW TROUT.

DOME Any landscape feature that looks like an upside-down bowl; as a technical geological term, a symmetrical upfold in which the rock layers dip downward in all directions. Teapot Dome, near Casper, Wyoming, was the downfall of the Harding administration, when federal oil reserves there were secretly leased in the early 1920s.

DON This title used for Spanish nobility, once commonly inserted before Christian names in the Southwest as an indication of respect, became a common noun in English meaning "upperclass Mexican." Thus early California history may be called *the days of the dons* and Mexico *the land of the dons*. Borrowed from Spanish.

DONKEY A portable engine used in cable logging. See also BURRO.

DOODLEBUG A divining rod, a device used to locate (or pretend to locate) valuable deposits of oil, water, or ore. Hence *doodlebug artist, doodlebugger,* and *doodlebuggery.*

DOOR KNOB A small boy, a kid. (See also **BUTTON**.)

DOPE (1) To treat or doctor almost anything, animate or inanimate. Cowmen doped calves, and sheepmen doped sheep. Drivers doped (greased) stagecoach wheels. Early-day skiers even doped the bottoms of their skis. (2) As a noun, the word meant any preparation that you administered—medicine, opium, sawdust in dynamite, or pitch for the bottoms of shoes.

DORMIDERA (dohr-mee-DAIR-uh) The California poppy (*Eschscholzia californica*). It was also called the *copa de oro* (cup of gold). This name, from Spanish, means "sleeper" and comes from the fact that this poppy unfolds only in sunlight.

DOTTING IRON A primitive **BRANDING IRON**. The cowhand burned on the entire brand in one effort with a **STAMP IRON**, but he had to make several applications with a dotting iron. It had half circles of two different sizes and a bar. By combining these, you could make a lot of brands. (See also **BRAND, RUNNING IRON**.)

DOUBLE EAGLE A twenty-dollar gold piece. It gave way to the term *double sawbuck,* a twenty-dollar bill.

DOUBLE OUT (1) To hitch more teams to a wagon to pull it out of the muck. (2) To put grass onto mud to make a way to pull a mired wagon out.

DOUBLE RIG A saddle cinched twice, front and back, the way **TIE-HARD-AND-FAST MEN** like it because of the stability it gives the saddle. It's also called *double-barreled, double fire,* and *double cinched.* (See also **SINGLE RIG**.)

DOUBLE SHUFFLE An abrupt change in the rhythm of a horse that's bucking.

DOUBLE-WINTERED An old expression for cows kept on good northern grass for two winters to get them prime.

DOUGH BOXER A name of both cowboys and loggers for a camp cook. They also called the cook a *doughbelly, dough puncher,* a *dough roller,* and a *dough wrangler.* (For many cowboy names for cooks, see **COOKIE**.)

DOUGHBOY A U.S. infantryman. The origin of this term is unknown, but some suggestions have to do with the American West. Libby Custer said the spherical buttons on Civil War infantry uniforms were called doughboys because they were shaped like the doughboys (doughnuts) of sailors. In time the name passed naturally to the soldiers themselves, she says. Mathews speculates that Hispanics in the Southwest applied *'dobe* (adobe) to U.S. soldiers for unknown reasons, and it converted to doughboy. Smith tells a charming story about American soldiers storming the Bishop's Palace in Monterrey during the Mexican War. They seized flour and rice and, since they were starved for a hot meal, made biscuits. The results were half-done and doughy, so they jokingly called each other doughboys.

DOUGHERTY WAGON A passenger wagon, called an *ambulance* in army parlance. No one seems to know who Dougherty was or how he gave his name to this conveyance. Also spelled *Doherty* and also called a *Dougherty ambulance*.

DOUGHGOD To the cowboy, a biscuit; to the logger bread.

DOUGLAS FIR Named after the Scottish botanist David Douglas, it is the great lumberman's tree (*Pseudotsuga douglasii*) of the Rocky Mountains, the Northwest, and Alaska. Also known as the *red fir, Oregon pine, Douglas pine,* and *Douglas spruce.* Now Douglas fir is so common as lumber for houses in the West that carpenters sometimes refer to framing up a house as *firring up.*

Other important western firs are *red fir, subalpine fir, Pacific silver fir,* and *white fir.*

DOWN BELOW Or simply *below.* An Alaskan way of referring to the **LOWER 48** states.

DOWN IN YOUR BOOTS A cowboy expression for afraid or cowardly.

DOWN TIMBER Trees that are no longer standing. In some places in the West, down timber can extend for many square miles and make travel impossible. The terms *down log* and *down tree* are applied to individual trees either blown or cut down.

DOWN TO YOUR LAST CHIP Broke, busted, cleaned out, financially embarrassed. Also known as *down to the blanket.*

DOWNER A cow that for some reason is too weak to stand, whether because of a hard winter or a hard ride in a cattle car. You have to *tail up* such critters (grab them by the tail and force them up). An animal on the floor of a cattle car is also called a *down steer.*

DOWNWINDER A person who lived downwind of a nuclear site for atomic testing in the 1950s and 1960s, when nuclear weapons were being tested aboveground. Downwinders in Utah of the Nevada site and in Washington of the Hanford site were exposed to high levels of radiation, resulting in claims of increased cancers.

DRAG (1) The back end of a trail herd, which is also called the **TAIL.** The drag position (called *at drag,* or *eating* or *swallowing drag dust*) is no fun for the hands assigned to ride it—they have to make the sick and the stragglers keep up, chase the breakaways, and suffer the dust. They're likely to use cow calls and noisemakers for the job. Since it's unpleasant, green hands usually get assigned to ride drag. The other positions for riders with a trail herd are **FLANK** (on the side almost halfway forward), **SWING** (on the side most of the way forward), and **POINT** (at the front). The cowboys at drag are called *drag riders* or *drag drivers.* (2) A cow that's dragging, falling behind.

(3) The trail and spoor left by a snake. (4) A log or other weight roped to a horse's leg as a hobble. This kind of hobbling is called *logging.*

DRAW (1) A gully, a ravine. (2) A form of **POKER** (or *bluff*, a nineteenth century name for poker) that permits the player to discard some cards and be dealt others. In full, *draw poker* (or *draw bluff*). (3) In poker, the deal that follows the discard. (4) The motion of pulling a pistol, as in, "He beat me to the draw." Some gunmen's Western draws were the **CROSS DRAW**, hip draw, and **SHOULDER DRAW**. (5) As a verb, to pull out a pistol. (6) Also as a verb, in poker or other card games, to take new cards after discarding.

    COMBINATIONS: *draw a bead on* someone (to aim a weapon at someone, the front sight of a gun often being a bead), *draw dead* (for a **RODEO** contestant to draw a bad horse or steer, a critter he can't win any money with because the horse won't buck or the steer won't run), *draw to an inside straight* (in poker, to draw a card hoping to get the single number within a sequence to make five in a row; figuratively the phrase has come to mean taking a long chance).

DRAY A log sled, a sled used to reduce the friction in skidding logs because one end was on the sled. COMBINATIONS: *dray-haul* (to convey logs in that manner), *dray in* (to haul logs from the forest to the landing or skidway).

DREAM BOOK What some cowboys once called a pack of cigarette papers.

DREAM CATCHER Among Indian peoples and Anglo souvenir-seekers, a hoop (often made of willow) with a web inside (usually made of artificial sinew) with a hole in the middle. The story is that if you hang it near your bed, the web will catch the bad dreams and let the good ones through. Often decorated with feathers, beads, etc.

DREAMER CULT A religious group of Columbia River tribes from about 1850. Followers of the Indian prophet Smohalla, they resisted white ways, opposing moves to the reservation, agriculture, and white religion. Yet they incorporated portions of Mormon and Catholic dogma, using trances and revelations; Smohalla claimed to have risen from the dead. This movement had some impact on Nez Percé Chief Joseph's decision to resist white encroachment. Adherents were sometimes called *Smohalla Indians*.

DRENCH SHEEP To worm sheep by squirting medicine down their throats.

DRESSED UP LIKE A SORE TOE Dressed up in a fancy way. It appears to imply that the decked-out fellow feels embarrassingly conspicuous.

DRIFT (1) Of cattle, to wander as a herd in some direction, usually in front of a cold wind or a snow storm. When they drifted in the days before fenced grazing lands, they sometimes got far off their range or came against a *drift fence* and stood and froze to death. Cattle also drifted to better grass or water. In this sense the word was also used as a noun—"the season's drift." (2) For a cowboy to move cattle (his own outfit's or a neighbor's) slowly and gently, as though they were meandering that way of their own will. (3) For a man to wander, go slowly, almost aimlessly—"I 'spect I'll drift down there sooner or later."

(4) Among miners, a horizontal tunnel, usually following a vein off a main shaft. By contrast, a crosscut intersects a vein.

COMBINATIONS: *drift cattle* (cattle that have drifted), *drift fence* (a fence to prevent cattle from drifting far—a barrier, not an enclosure), *drift smoke* (fire smoke drifted from where it started and now without its billow). *On the drift,* though, when said of a mine shaft, means crooked.

DRIVE (1) For cowboys, to herd cattle from one place to another. It may be a TRAIL DRIVE, a ROUNDUP, or a drive of cattle to a different range, depending on context. On a trail drive, cowboys often drove cows a long way, even from Texas to Kansas or on to Wyoming and Montana. At a roundup (or *gather* or *cowhunt*), they drove them out of the far reaches of their range to a central spot where they could be *branded* (in the spring) or *cut* (separated) for shipment to market (in the fall). Now cattle are driven mostly to move them from one range to another, as from summer range to winter pasture or from deeded land to national forest and the like.

(2) To *drive logs* was to float them downstream from the forest to the sawmill or the shipping point. Log drives were dangerous—they led to log jams—and required expert handling by log drivers *(birlers)*. Now this transportation is entirely by logging truck. To *drive the river* also meant to drive logs down the river. Water high enough to drive logs was called *driving pitch.*

(3) In stagecoaching, a drive was the distance coach and driver usually traveled before being changed, about sixty miles. (4) A drive was also a V-shaped trap to chase animals into, and (5) the group action of chasing animals (such as rabbits or others regarded as pests) from an area and killing them.

The word is commonly both noun and verb—the cattle drive, and to drive cattle; the log drive, and to drive logs. (See TRAIL.)

DRIVING PIKE A tool of a *log driver,* with a wooden shaft, a sharp point, and a hook. (See also DRIVE.)

DROOP-EYED A way of describing a calf with cut eyelid muscles. Cattle thieves cut them to keep the calf from seeing its mother and following her.

DROP (1) The advantage in a shooting situation. To *get the drop on someone* means to get your gun pointed at him before he can do the same to you. Now it has been extended to mean any kind of advantage. Mathews implies that the phrase may come from military positioning: Artillery on elevated ground literally has the drop on lower targets. (2) The top, front part of a pair of *drop-front* trousers.

DROP BAND A herd of ewes about to lamb (*drop* or give birth to their lambs). They're tended by a *drop-band herder.*

DROP GAP A place in a barbwire fence where a rider can let himself through.

DROP STIRRUP A strap that hangs below the stirrup to give a short rider (once usually a woman) a leg up.

DROP YOUR ROPE ON A HEIFER Figuratively, to marry.

DROUTHY (usually pronounced to rhyme with *mouthy*) (1) A way of describing calves suffering from drought, arid country, or grass needing rain. (2) Also, unhappy visitors to Kansas when that state was dry—short of booze, not water. Sometimes Easterners or others eager to be proper correct the spelling to *droughty,* and the pronunciation to match.

DRUGSTORE COWBOY A fellow who's got the name but not the game; a person who acts and dresses like a cowboy but doesn't have the skills of a hand. Also called a *phildoodle.*

DRUM (1) To solicit (*drum up*) orders, to make sales. The fellow who traveled soliciting trade in the West after the Civil War was called a *drummer,* and as a greenhorn he was the object of a lot of fun. (2) Among contemporary Indians, a drum is not only a rhythm instrument but a group of singers in traditional Indian style, a band of musicians that makes music for **POWWOWS**; short for *drum group.* In 1990, for instance, the group Red Bull was a popular drum on the powwow circuit. (3) For a grouse to make a reverberating noise with its wings.

DRUM ICE In Alaska and the Yukon, ice formed on a body of water that has subsequently receded, leaving a gap between the water and ice. The ice resounds underfoot and perhaps will break under weight. Also called (more commonly in Canada) *shell ice.*

DRY A thirst for booze, as in "Hosses, this child's got to wet his dry." New Englanders had long used this word as an adjective in this sense, according to linguist J. L. Dillard, but the **MOUNTAIN MAN** exhibited a little creativity by making it into a noun.

DRY COW (1) A cow that didn't bear a calf this year and so isn't giving milk. According to South Dakota writer and rancher Linda Hasselstrom, these cows gain weight fast and are inclined to be troublesome. Because they don't support another critter, they have too much energy left over. A cow that's dry one year may live to see another season. If she's dry again, she'll surely be a *cull,* one of the cows taken to the sale ring. Also known as an *open heifer* or *dry stuff* (a lactating cow is called *wet stuff*).

(2) The term is also applied to ewes, and a group of such ewes is called a *dry band.*

DRY DIGGINGS A **PLACER**-mining operation away from water. When water wasn't available to wash the dirt, miners dry-washed with cloths, with a dry-washing machine (a device for sifting dirt for gold with air currents), or used a crude pulverizer called an **ARRASTRE**.

DRY DRIVE A cattle drive across a piece of country that has no water. A *dry camp* is a camp made without water. The terms are also used as verbs, to *dry-drive,* to *dry-camp.*

DRY FARMING Farming without irrigation. The dry farmer uses water stored in the soil. By plowing deeply, breaking up the soil, using dust mulches, and growing appropriate crops, he is sometimes able to farm successfully west of the 100th meridian, one traditional line of demarcation of the arid West. A *dry-lander* is a person who farms in the arid part of the West, using either irrigation or dry farming.

DRY PAINTING A ritual of **NAVAJO, PUEBLO,** and sometimes **APACHE** and California Indians. Dry painting, though valued as art by Anglos, is to Indians not aesthetic but religious. As part of a ritual, each one is destroyed at completion of the ceremony. Designs are not created by the makers but prescribed by tradition.

The paintings are made on the floor of a **HOGAN** or **KIVA,** sometimes on a piece of buckskin, or outdoors. The materials—sands of different colors, powdered minerals, charcoal, pollen, cornmeal, leaves, and flowers—are gathered in a ritualistic way. These are spread on a base layer of sand by assistants working under the direction of a *singer,* a man of **MEDICINE.** The ceremonies often last for many days and are centered on the recitation of the chants that restore harmony to the natural and spiritual worlds.

A Navajo making a dry (or sand) painting.
[DRAWING BY E. L. REEDSTROM.]

Principally through the efforts of singer Tl'ah Hastiin (Hosteen Klah), many reproductions of dry paintings and other elements of Navajo life are preserved in Santa Fe's Museum of Navajo Ceremonial Art. Dry paintings are also called *sand paintings.*

DRY STORM A rainstorm that brings negligible rain to the ground, commonplace on the High Plains and deserts. You can see rain falling from the clouds and coming to nothing halfway down. A dry storm can also be a sandstorm.

DRY UP Among contemporary **PLAINS INDIANS,** to make the sacrificial fasting of the **SUN DANCE,** including going without water.

DRY WASH In the Southwest, a wash; an *arroyo,* especially an *arroyo seco*; a dry, flat-bottomed gully with steep walls created by occasional runoff. These washes can flood suddenly and violently.

DRY-GULCH To ambush someone, especially by hiding near a road in a gully or gulch and shooting him in the back as he rides by. It was regarded as the method of a coward. Other Western expressions for killing people are **ADOBE**

WALL *him, bed him down,* **BUSHWHACK** *him, curl him up, do him,* **KICK HIM INTO A FUNERAL PROCESSION,** *make wolf meat of him, Pecos him, put a window in his skull, salivate him, sarve him up brown,* **SAVE HIM, STRAP HIM ON HIS HORSE WITH HIS TOES DOWN,** and *wipe him out.*

DUBBER A Native instrument for scraping fat and flesh off a buffalo or elk skin; also called a *hide scraper.* The handle was usually made of bone or elk antler, and the business end (shaped like an adze) was iron (or flint or obsidian). The word has a verb form—to *dub* (to scrape a buffalo hide).

DUDE A person from the East who vacations on a ranch. The word may still carry some of the original implication of a greenhorn, a person who doesn't know his way around a ranch, a horse, or a cow. It sometimes suggests a person decked out in city clothes or in a fancy way. (One authority traces it back to the British use of the word a century ago, when it meant "fop.") Now, though, dude is generally offered as a term of genial welcome, and the owners of guest ranches don't really mind if you call them dude ranches. (Dude ranches are also known among cowboys as *wild willow* or *willie west.*)

In most of the West fifty or a hundred years ago, dudes came to a ranch for the entire summer and spent some serious time learning to ride and even participating in the cow-punching. This life is wonderfully depicted in Strothers Burt's book set in Jackson Hole, *Diary of a Dude Wrangler.* Today, most dudes come for a week or two for a pack trip, a float trip, or some trail rides. Some dude ranches are even becoming (heaven help us!) spas and diet centers. And dudes come not only from the East but from all over the world.

JY Dude and Cattle Ranch, Jackson Hole, Wyoming.

COMBINATIONS: The word *dude* has lots of offspring—not only *dude ranch* and *dude rancher* but *dude puncher* and *dude wrangler* (cowhands who take care of dudes instead of cows and horses, respectively). A female dude is either a *dudess* or a *dudine.* A dude you're taking pity on is a *dudie.* Dudes exude a quality known as *dudeness, dudism,* or *dudery;* besides, they're *dudish.* They live in *dudedom,* which is not only any spot on the map outside the West but a place in their minds. Unfortunately, dudes are occasionally susceptible to the blandishments of *dudolos* (the word plays on *gigolo*). A *dude horse* is so gentle it will permit dudes to sit on it and will even let their children play around its legs. *Dude chaps* (or any other gear or clothing) means a fancy-looking item that would embarrass any self-respecting hand.

You can find out a lot about dudes by seeing the fine movie *City Slickers* (1991).

DUEÑO (DWAYN-yoh) A Southwestern term for a proprietor of a store, ranch, or other enterprise. The feminine form, *dueña*, meaning "chaperone," is rare in the West. Borrowed from Spanish.

DUFF The bed of half-decayed matter found on the floor of forests and made of leaves, cones, needles, and bark. When dry, it burns easily.

DUGOUT (1) An Anglo dwelling dug out of the side of a hill or, like a basement, into flat ground. Those built into hillsides were usually finished with a log-framed door and a log roof, the roof topped with sod. The ones in flat ground often had sod walls above the ground. Most people who lived or visited in them seem to have agreed that dugouts were unpleasant places, earning the name "half-human." They were frequently used by Mormons, especially in central Utah, and by keepers of stage stations who feared Indian attack. (2) Among cowmen, a shallow hole with sloping sides dug down to water level so cattle can water. (3) A canoe made by hollowing out a big log. Not originally a Westernism in this meaning.

DUGWAY (1) Now a road scraped out of a steep hillside. (2) During the heyday of the great **TRAIL DRIVES**, it meant a cut (called a *cutting*) in the bank of a river to let cattle and wagons get to the stream and out of it on the other side. (Western rivers often have vertical, or undercut, banks.) (3) Among **MORMONS**, in the days of their emigrations, it meant a "rut dug deeply in the slope." According to David Lavender in *One Man's West*, "the inside wheels of the wagons fitted into this slot so snugly that the vehicle could not fall out—maybe."

DULCE (DOOL-say) (1) In the Southwest, a sweet, a dessert, especially a candied fruit or similar confection. *Pan dulce* is a sweet bread or roll. (2) Southwestern Anglos have extended the word to mean "sweetheart." Borrowed from Spanish (where it means "sweet"). The Americanization *dulcie* also occurs.

DUN A tan horse with black mane, tail, and socks and often with a dorsal stripe. (See **BUCKSKIN** for horse colors.)

DUPONT A brand name that became the common word among **MOUNTAIN MEN** for **BLACK POWDER**, as Stetson and Winchester became common for hat and rifle. The manufacturer, E. I. Du Pont de Nemours and Company, was founded in 1802. The predecessor of modern smokeless gunpowder, black powder was made from saltpeter, charcoal, and sulfur, then caked and rolled into grains—fine for pistols, coarser for rifles. All guns were fired with black powder until the 1890s. Before cartridges, the shooter measured the powder into his weapon for each shot (though the measuring was often imprecise, especially when done on a galloping horse).

Here's damp powder and no way to dry it was an expression of the MOUNTAIN MEN for a bad fix. Wet powder, of course, wouldn't ignite. Hobbyists are still shooting black powder today for fun and even hunting with it—the shooting has a spirit that's said to be addictive. (See also POWDER.)

DURHAM (1) A breed of cows also called *shorthorns* in the West. They were imported to interbreed with Texas longhorns and other cattle on the Northern Plains in the 1870s and 1880s, until Herefords became more commonly used for that purpose. (2) Short for BULL DURHAM.

DUST (1) As a noun, short for gold dust. As a verb, (2) to get gone, to leave in a hurry. In this meaning, it appears as to *dust along*, to *get up and dust*, to *dust for*, and to *dust out*. (3) To move around quickly or in a spry way. (4) To cover a cow with powdered insecticide. (5) To fan a horse with your hat.

COMBINATIONS: *dust bag* (a sack for gold dust), *dust blizzard, dust cutter* (a glass of whiskey after a dusty ride), *dust mulch* (a layer of dust used in dry farming to prevent evaporation), *dust pneumonia* (a lung ailment of people and livestock, usually in dust bowls, that comes from breathing air full of dust), *dust the trail* (to travel), *have dust* (to get into a fight), *eat dust* (to get outraced by someone), *be out for the dust* (to have money as a motive). (See also DUST BOWL, DUST DEVIL.)

DUST BOWL A piece of country often afflicted with drought and dust storms, bringing grief to farmers. The Dust Bowl is a region of the South-Central Plains in Texas, Oklahoma, Kansas, Colorado, and New Mexico, where drought and dust storms ruined a lot of farmers in the 1930s.

Dust devil passing over Midland, Texas, February 20, 1894.
[COURTESY OF NATIONAL ARCHIVES (27-S-2).]

DUST DEVIL A little whirlwind of dust or sand, such as can be seen anywhere on the Plains and in the deserts. Also called *wind devil, dancing devil, Idaho brain storm, remolino* (Spanish meaning whirlwind), and *sand auger*. Some Native people say a dust devil is a spirit moving around.

DUSTER (1) A light overcoat, especially one made of linen, used to keep dust off. Now (but not originally) associated mostly with the West. (2) A **DUST STORM** or sand storm. (3) A *dry hole*, a hole drilled for oil that is unproductive.

DUTCH OVEN A heavy, three-legged, cast-iron pan with a lid that **COOKIE** was always using over open fires, especially to make sourdough biscuits. The pan sat directly on coals, and coals were heaped on top of it to cook the food from all directions. Dutch ovens were used by pioneers and cowboys alike because of their versatility, being useful as an oven, a stew pot, and a frying pan. Named Dutch for either the Pennsylvania Dutch or the Dutch peddlers, it is still used today, particularly by packers and outfitters.

DUTCHMAN In the West this term was not limited to the Pennsylvania Dutch (German and Swiss immigrants to Pennsylvania, from the anglicized pronunciation of the German word for "German," *Deutsch*). It meant any European or, depending on the speaker, any European who didn't speak English and wasn't a Frenchman, Italian, or Spaniard. Such a fellow was often addressed as *Dutch* or *Dutchy*.

DYNO A miner's word for the fellow who handles the explosives. Also called a *powder man* or *powder monkey*.

E

EAGLE BILL A **TAPADERO** (leather toe fender worn on the stirrups). Perhaps so called because it looks like the beak of an eagle.

EAGLE BONE WHISTLE A musical instrument made from the hollow wing bone of an eagle. Used during ceremonies like the **SUN DANCE** by Plains Indians, it makes a piercing, haunting sound. Ceremonial *eagle-wing fans* were (and are) made from thirty-seven feathers of the immature golden eagle (preferably the larger feathers of the female). These fans are used in dancing, in healing (to gather and disperse smoke), and in various other ceremonies, including the *sweat lodge* and *peyote meetings*.

EAGLE FEATHER The feathers and other parts of the golden eagle, and to some extent the bald eagle, were prized by most Western Indians for their **MEDICINE**, the qualities of spirit associated with the birds, especially swiftness, courage, and prowess in hunting and war.

Bald eagles feasting on salmon.
[COURTESY OF ALASKA DEPARTMENT OF FISH & GAME.]

Single eagle feathers, tied to headdresses, shields, and coup sticks, were symbols of **COUPS**. Entire eagles were skinned and used as **MEDICINE BUN-DLES.** Heads and talons were mounted on ceremonial staffs and dance sticks. Talons were used in necklaces or shields. Headdresses were made from the skin and head. Large numbers of feathers were used together in war bonnets, bus-tles, and shields, to suggest the motion of the bird in flight; the fluffs on these were the eagle's downy breast feathers. Any part of an eagle awarded by a **MED-ICINE MAN** might become part of a medicine bundle. Whistles were made from the upper wing bone and used in war and in the **SUN DANCE**. Feathers of the gray (immature bald) eagle were also valued, especially for war bonnets, and gave protection against the wearer's being wounded. The full-length eagle-feather headdress is perhaps the best-known article of regalia of the Plains Indians.

Some Natives raised eagles (often tethered) and plucked the feathers. Plains Indians usually caught their eagles by baiting them to camouflaged pits and grabbing their legs as they fed. This eagle-catching was done only by older men given the power by established practitioners. The catchers prepared by *making medicine* and did not eat or drink in the pits. They then traded the feathers to other members of the tribe. Found feathers were not used unless caught before they hit the ground. If a feather is dropped at a **POWWOW**, the whole powwow may stop for a feather-pickup ceremony. Feathers from live eagles are particularly prized for their power.

Some tribes (including the **CHOCTAW** and **CHEROKEE**) held eagle or eagle-tail dances.

Many traditions associated with eagles are still alive or making a comeback. Eagles and their feathers are protected by federal regulation, but Native Americans can use them ceremonially.

EAR (1) The point of the uppermost cloth of a TIPI. The ears are held up by long poles and adjusted to control the venting of the smoke. (2) To *keep your ear to ground* is to listen for something; it came from the plainsman's practice of listening at the ground for far-off sounds.

EAR DOWN To twist or bite the ears of a horse to get him to stand still; said especially of broncos, when one cowboy ears down the horse while another saddles it for a first ride. Horses that have often been eared down and thus wary of having their ears touched are called *ear-soured*.

EAR HEAD A headstall (bridle) with a loop for one of the horse's ears but without *nose band*, *browband*, or *throat latch*; used only on well-broke horses.

EAR WEIGHT CONTEST An ESKIMO game in which contestants loop string through their ears, tie as much as seventeen pounds on, and see how far they can walk. At least one winner walked more than a thousand feet.

EARMARK A cut in the ear of a cow that is made at BRANDING and, like the brand, indicates ownership. Also called an *ear crop*. Used as both noun and verb.

Earmarks, not originally Western, became much elaborated in the West. Typical earmarks were the *barb*, *bit* (a nick in a cow's ear used as an earmark), *comet split* (looks like a comet), *crop* (cut straight off), *double over-bit*, *double under-bit*, *ear tag*, *fanned split*, *full split*, *grub* (entire ear removed), *hack*, *jingle bob*, *key split* (cut like a cotter key), *over split*, *over sharp*, *over hack*, *over slope*, *overbite*, *sawset*, *sawtooth*, *seven underbit*, *seven overbit*, *sharp*, *slope*, *slash*, *split*, *steeple-fork*, *swallow-fork*, *underbite*, *under sharp*, *under split*, *under slope*, *under hack*, *ear tag*, and *tattoo*.

These days earmarks have been replaced by ear tags. Americans often use the term metaphorically—as in "he's earmarked for stardom"—without being aware of the original meaning.

EARTH FIRST!ER An adherent (since the organization does not have members) of the environmental activist group Earth First! Inspired by Edward Abbey's novel *The Monkey*

seven under bite   seven over bite

swallow fork   split

over bit   under bit

under slope   over slope

Like brands, earmarks are a means of identifying livestock.

Wrench Gang, Earth First! is known for its strong and controversial positions and for the kind of direct action known as ECOTAGE.

EARTH LODGE Some Indians of the Eastern Plains, such as ARIKARA, MANDANS, and PAWNEES, lived in earthen dwellings. They made these lodges with frames of posts and beams covered with branches and mud or sod. The lodges had central firepits and smoke holes.

EASY KEEPER A horse that thrives on any feed.

EASY ON THE TRIGGER Short-tempered; ready to explode.

EATING IRONS Cowboy talk for silverware.

ECOTAGE Since the 1970s, sabotage for the sake of the environment, sometimes with humor. The good writer Edward Abbey, for instance, liked to say, "If God hadn't meant me to put sugar in the gas tank of that bulldozer, he wouldn't have left it there." However, ecotage can be dangerous to people who make their living on the land. (See also EARTH FIRST!ER, SAB-CAT.)

EIGHTY-NINER A person who participated in the Oklahoma land rush of 1889— 50,000 to 60,000 white people are said to have flooded into the newly opened lands in INDIAN TERRITORY on the day of April 22 alone.

EJIDO (ay-HFE-doh) In the Southwestern border country, the village common. Borrowed from Spanish.

EL DORADO (el doh-RAH-doh) (1) Wherever in the West the adventurer imagines he will find his fortune, usually in gold; especially, a place where gold has been discovered and, especially, California after the strike at Sutter's Mill. By implication the fortune is a will-o'-the-wisp.

(2) A Spanish term that means literally "the gilded man." Originally it was applied to a sixteenth-century chieftain of Colombia, who, according to legend, had his body oiled and then sprinkled with gold dust.

ELDER In the MORMON Church, an office of the MELCHIZEDEK priesthood. Only men may be elders. Male missionaries are called elders; female missionaries are called *sisters.* The general authorities of the church are commonly addressed as Elder (Smith, Jones, etc.).

ELK This is the wapiti *(Cervus elaphus)*, a large member of the deer family, royalty in the American panorama of wildlife. Its cousins are the red deer of Europe and Asia, but not what Europeans call an elk, which is a moose. The bull weighs up to a thousand pounds, and is crowned by immense antlers with five to seven points.

Originally, the elk was distributed throughout North America, except for in the South and the Great Basin. Now the Rocky Mountain elk ranges through the Rockies in the United States and Canada, the Roosevelt inhabits rain forests from California to the Kodiak Islands, the Manitoba elk lives in Manitoba and Saskatchewan, and the tule elk inhabits parts of interior California.

For Indian peoples and early settlers, the elk was an important source of food, implements, and clothing—the teeth were and are valued as ornaments. Now even a sighting is a fine memory. To go to the Great Yellowstone region in the autumn and listen at night to the bulls bugle their cries of love to the cows is a glimpse of heaven.

ELK TOOTH A canine tooth or tusk of the elk (wapiti), frequently used by **PLAINS INDIAN** people for decoration on women's clothing.

EMBARCADERO (em-bar-kuh-DAIR-oh) A wharf or port; frequently used in California place names. Borrowed from Spanish.

EMIGRANT An American who left the East or South to settle on the frontier, especially the frontier that was not part of the United States in the first half of the nineteenth century; most especially, one who went to Texas before its statehood, one seeking a new life in Oregon Territory, a Mormon who went to **DESERET** (Utah Territory), or a California gold-rusher. Sometimes spelled *immigrant*.

COMBINATIONS: *emigrant agent* (a person employed by a railway or land company to promote emigration to the West), *emigrant aid society* or *company* (an organization devoted to bringing antislavery settlers to the West, especially to Kansas), *emigrant cattle* (cattle not native to the country and by implication perhaps not hardy), *emigrant car* (a railway car set aside for transporting emigrants, usually at special rates), *emigrant gravy* (butter), *emigrant rate* (a special rate established by railroads wanting to populate the West to support their own operations—for instance, in 1869, $40 instead of the regular $75 from Omaha to California), *emigrant road* or *route* (a trail established by use for the passage of emigrants in wagon trains, especially the Oregon Trail), *emigrant train* (either a group of emigrants, wagons, and livestock making its way west or a railroad train carrying emigrants), *emigrant wagon* (a **PRAIRIE SCHOONER,** a wagon carrying emigrants and their belongings west).

EMPRESARIO (em-pruh-SAHR-yoh) A colonizer of Texas during its days under Mexican sovereignty. The government of Mexico gave these empresarios large grants of land in return for bringing in settlers. An individual settler was granted 4,428 acres (a *sitio*), which he could purchase from the Mexican government for a nominal fee. Borrowed from Spanish (where it means "manager" or "contractor").

ENCHILADA (en-chi-LAH-duh; en-chee-LAH-duh) A **TORTILLA** with meat, beans, and chiles (or some combination of these) rolled inside; tortillas stacked and covered with meat and chile sauce. Borrowed from Spanish. The *whole enchilada* is contemporary slang meaning the whole thing, the *big enchilada* is the *head honcho*, the boss.

ENCINA (en-SEE-nuh) In the Southwest, especially California, the live (evergreen) oak, in contrast to the deciduous oak, which in American Spanish is called a **ROBLE.** Common in place names, it also occurs in the form *encino*. Borrowed from Spanish. An *encinal* is a grove of these oaks. (See also **LIVE OAK.**)

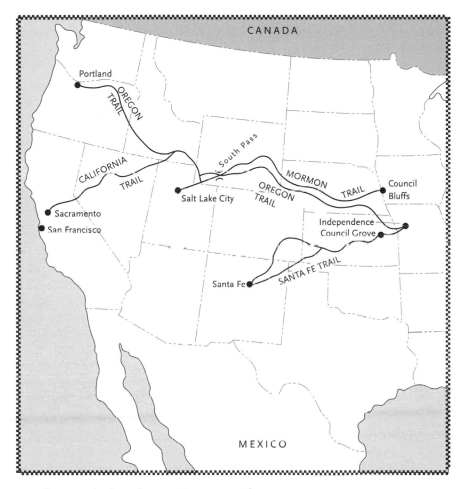

Emigrant trails, 1840s. [MAP BY WENDY BAYLOR.]

END TOWN A town sprung up at the temporary end of the tracks of a rail line, especially the Union Pacific line west of Omaha. (See also **HELL ON WHEELS.**)

ENDOWMENT A course in understanding the **MORMON** religion, undertaken by the devout. On the recommendation of the *bishop* and stake officials, seekers participate in a service of instruction in which they pledge to keep the commandments of virtue, charity, and tolerance, and to serve their fellow man according to the teachings of Christ. To complete it is to receive your *endowments,* given in a ceremony in a **LATTER-DAY SAINTS** temple. Before the temples were built, this ceremony took place in an *endowment house.*

ENEMY One of the miner's names for the *shift boss*. Also called a *gaffer* or a *shifter*.

ENGAGÉ (ahn-gah-ZHAY) A French-Canadian trapper or canoe man who paddled wilderness streams to conduct the **FUR TRADE**. The engagé was a trapper hired for wages, in contrast to a **FREE TRAPPER**, who was on his own. (See also **VOYAGEUR**.)

EPHRAIM A **MOUNTAIN-MAN** nickname for the grizzly bear, especially in the form *old Ephraim*.

ERMATINGER MONEY Currency issued in Oregon Territory in the 1840s and 1850s by the Hudson's Bay Company; named after Francis Ermatinger, one of the company's traders.

ESKIMO The Arctic and sub-Arctic indigenous peoples of eastern Siberia, Alaska and Canada, and Greenland; also their language, Eskimo-Aleut. Another name for them, now in favor, is **INUIT**; though Canadian, Greenland, and Siberian indigenous peoples are said to prefer the term *Inuit*, those in Alaska usually do not. They are distinct from American Indians, as indicated by blood typing and other features. In their icy world, Eskimos eat flesh almost entirely, depending in summer on caribou, and hunting walrus, whales, seals, and fish in **KAYAKS** and **UMIAKS**. They have an animistic spiritual practice (see **ANGAKOK**). Transportation, traditionally by **DOGSLED**, is now by snowmobile. They live in winter in **IGLOOS** (usually of wood and sod rather than snow blocks) and historically in summer in hide tents. Though hunting was their traditional occupation, many Alaskan Eskimos now work in the mining or oil industries.

The widely circulated report that the word *Eskimo* means "eater of raw flesh," which contributed to the choice of *Inuit* in its place, is false.

ESKIMO ICE CREAM An ice cream–like **ESKIMO** dish made of snow, fat or tallow, and berries. COMBINATIONS: *Eskimo doughnut* (bread fried in seal oil), *Eskimo kiss* (a nose rub), *Eskimo yo-yo* (a toy made of two balls of fur on a string, and the game played with them). ANIMALS: *Eskimo curlew, Eskimo duck, Eskimo brant.* PLANTS: *Eskimo potato* (corms, roots, or tubers from any one of three plants), *Eskimo rhubarb* (wild rhubarb).

ESPOSA (es-POH-suh) In the Southwest, an occasional word for wife; *esposo*, "husband," is rarely used. Borrowed from Spanish.

ESTANCIA (es-TAHN-shuh) In the Southwest, a ranch, especially a big ranch. Borrowed from Spanish.

ESTANCO (es-TAN-koh) In the Southwest, a government trading post or store. Borrowed from Spanish.

ESTUFA (es-TOO-fuh) (1) Among **PUEBLO** Indians, a big, circular, above-ground ceremonial room with a sacred fire, for men. Similar to a **KIVA**. (2) A stove or oven; an **HORNO**. Borrowed from Spanish (where it means "heater" or "fire").

EUCHRED Outwitted. From the card game euchre, which, though not originally Western, was commonly played in the West.

EXCUSE ME, MA'AM Cowboy talk for a bump in the road.

EXODUSTER Originally a black who joined in the African-American migration to Kansas and other points West in the late 1870s; later a **DUST BOWL** refugee.

EYE DAZZLER A **NAVAJO** blanket, made with commercial yarns, starting in the 1890s. It features a busy triangle pattern and bright colors.

EYEBALL In early Texas, to cut off the upper eyelids of cows to keep them from going into the brush, where their eyes would easily get scratched. *Eye openers* were little sticks used to prop the eyes open, for the same reason. But an *eye-baller* was a meddler.

F

FACE-LICKING A good time, with people extra friendly, as at a reunion.

FACTORY (1) A combination **INDIAN AGENCY** and **FUR-TRADING** house of the type established and operated by the U.S. government on the frontier from 1796 to 1822 with licensed agents appointed by Congress. Common trade goods were firearms, lead and powder, axes, traps, blankets, cloth, sewing materials, clothing, jewelry, kitchen utensils, food (such as salt, sugar, and coffee), tobacco, pipes, and wampum (beads used as money or ornaments). The system was not intended to make a profit but to help pay for the operation of the posts and the maintenance of armed forces on the frontier, and to make the Indians dependent on the white man, and thus more agreeable to white settlement. The main Canadian posts were also called factories. The principal officer of a fur-trading company at a trading post was called the *factor*. The head of a big post like the Hudson's Bay Company's Fort Vancouver was called the *chief factor*.

(2) After the Civil War, a factory was a Texas business specializing in hides, tallow, and salted beef.

FADED MIDGET A small, dusty-looking rattlesnake of eastern Utah, western Colorado, and southwest Wyoming.

FAG In cowboy talk, to get out fast.

FALLBACK A backward fall by a bucking horse. Trying to stand on its hind legs, it tumbles onto its back. Also called a *rearback*.

FALLEN HIDE The hide of a cow that dies naturally. The custom of the Texas range was that this hide belonged to the finder.

FALLER A logger who fells trees. Loggers often say he *falls* them. He's also called a *feller* and a *sawyer*. Fallers worked in pairs.

FALSE FRONT A building with a front facade sticking above and to the sides of the principal structure; also, the facade itself. Often in early Western settlements, the false front hid a tent rather than a building.

FAN (1) To shoot a revolver by holding it in one hand with the trigger held down, and with the other palm knocking back the hammer and letting it spring forward repeatedly. A method of shooting often used in movies and in practice but seldom by experienced men in a serious scrape. Also known as *flip-cocking*. (See also **THUMB THE HAMMER**.) (2) To wave your hat while riding a bucking horse.

FANCY DANCER An Indian dancer who competes at **POWWOWS** in an elaborate, very physical, improvisational dance. Showy costumes, athletic display, and creativity are highly valued. Some Indians and Indian families are able to make a living competing on the powwow circuit.

FANDANGO A Hispanic dance in triple time. Used by **MOUNTAIN MEN** and later most Americans to mean any Hispanic dance or, by extension, any get-together of a crowd, even for a fight. It also had a verb form—to *fandango someone,* to throw a celebration for him.

FANTAIL A wild horse with an ungroomed tail; the opposite of a **SHAVETAIL**. (See also **BROOMTAIL**.)

FARO A gambling game played with cards and popular in the West of the nineteenth century. In faro, the players bet on the order in which the cards will be turned over by the dealer. The cards were kept in a dealing box with wires like an abacus on top to keep track of the play. (Since this box usually had a tiger painted on it, playing faro was called *bucking the tiger*.) The players could bet on any card either to win or lose (a bet to lose was *coppered,* that is, marked with a Chinese coin or similar marker). The dealer turned the cards over in turns of two from top to bottom, from the first (*soda*) card to the last (*hock*)—thus the expression *from soda to hock*. Both soda and hock were dead cards. The name is said to come from the French word for "pharaoh."

Principal faro terms are *behind the six* (the money drawer, usually behind the six in the layout); *blaze; brace; cage; call the turn* or *call it both ways; case; casekeeper; case cart; copper the heel, the odds, the deal,* or *the pile; cross colors; cutter; faro bank; layout; one side against the other; paroli* (an Italian term meaning "a bet of your original stake plus everything you've won"); *play the bank; play the evens; short faro; single out; sleeper; snap* (an improvised game of faro); *Spanish* **MONTE**; *strippers; sure-thing bet; tell box, sand tell box,* or *snake tell box; twist the tiger*.

FEATHER DUSTER An occasional Anglo expression (no doubt mocking) for an **INDIAN**. (See also **SIWASH**.)

A faro game in the Orient Saloon at Bisbee, Arizona, ca. 1900.
[PHOTOGRAPH BY C. S. FLY; COURTESY OF NATIONAL ARCHIVES (111-SC-93344).]

FEATHERED OUT Cowboy talk for dressed up. Same as *decked out in full war paint*.

FEED BAG (1) A MORRAL (nose bag), a sack with oats or other feed that fits over a horse's head. (2) A restaurant. Restaurants were also called *beaneries, grub houses,* and *swallow-and-get-out troughs*.

FEED OFF YOUR RANGE To be nosey, to inquire inappropriately into another person's affairs.

FENCE-CORNERING Bucking in a zigzag pattern, as certain fences run. Also called *fence-worming*. (See also BUCK.)

FENCE-CRAWLER A horse or cow that has a way of getting through a pasture or corral fence. Also called a *fence-breaker*.

FENCE-CUTTER A man who cut fences during the Western wars over enclosing the open range. Usually big cow outfits fenced public land and the small ranchers or farmers cut the fences, but sometimes it was the other way around. Fence-cutting often was the start of big trouble.

FENCE-LIFTER A gully washer, a goose drowner, a heavy rain.

FENCING TOOL The modern cowboy's ever-needed tool, a combination cutter, hammer, and pliers. It's the size of a big pair of pliers. Also called *fencing pliers*. (See also WIRECUTTERS.)

A *fence stretcher* is a tool that stretches the BARB WIRE tight before the cowboy staples it.

FENDER On a saddle, a leather shield between the rider's leg and the horse. Also called a **ROSADERO.**

FIADOR A light rope used with a **HACKAMORE,** usually of hair but sometimes of rawhide or cotton. It ties to the **BOSAL** and acts as a throat–latch, holding the hackamore in place. A common corruption of this term is **THEODORE.**

FIDDLE An occasional word for a horse's head.

FIERRO (fee-EHR-roh) In the Southwest in the nineteenth century, a buying **BRAND,** the brand the new owner of livestock applied. When he sold animals, he put on a **VENTA,** a **SALE BRAND.** Literally, a fierro is a **BRANDING IRON.** Borrowed from Spanish.

FIESTA In the Southwest, a celebration, a festivity with a Hispanic accent. Borrowed from Spanish.

FIFTY-FOUR FORTY The latitude many Americans of the 1840s insisted on as the permanent boundary between U.S. and British possessions between the Rocky Mountains and Puget Sound. Their slogan was "fifty-four forty or fight!"

FIGHT THE BIT For a horse to toss his head when reined; for a person to act impatient, unruly.

FIGHTING WAGES Cowboy pay when there were rustlers to be rousted or range wars to be fought. Except when fighting wages were paid, cowboy earnings were low.

FILL A BLANKET To roll a cigarette. To *fill your hand* is to draw your gun.

FILLY A young female, not only of the equine but the human species.

FINNER In the Pacific Northwest and Alaska, fish swimming near the surface. When commercial fisherman see the fins, they suspect a school (especially of salmon) below, and set to.

Commercial fishing boat in Alaska.
[COURTESY OF ALASKA DEPARTMENT OF FISH & GAME.]

FIRE BOAT In Indian contact English, a steamboat; also called a *fire canoe.* A *fire box* was a stagecoach escorted by soldiers.

FIRE BREAK A strip of earth several yards wide cleared to keep fire from spreading. Sometimes called a *fire guard* or *fire land*.

COMBINATIONS: *fire boss* (the boss on a large fire-suppression effort); *fire finder* (a device used by spotters to locate forest fires); *fire lane* (a strip of ground bared of trees and vegetation, similar in appearance to a hiking trail, made to prevent the fire from spreading); *fire sector* (a section of fire control line under the command of a *sector boss*); *fire tower* (a forest watch tower used to spot fires); *escaped fire* (a **PRESCRIBED FIRE** that is burning out of specified conditions). A fire that is deliberately set for ecological reasons is a **PRESCRIBED BURN** and a **WILD FIRE** is an out-of-control forest fire.

Among miners, the *fire boss* is an official who inspects the mine for gas each morning. He posts his findings on a blackboard called the *fireboard*.

FIRE ESCAPE Among cowboys, a preacher. (See also **BLACK ROBE**.)

FIRE MAN Among many Indian people, the person who tends the fire that heats the rocks outside a **SWEAT LODGE**.

FIRE OUT A BRAND To change it to show a new owner.

FIRE STEEL A piece of steel bent by a blacksmith into a D-shape to fit around the fingers for striking against flint to create sparks for starting a fire; thus the expression *flint and steel*. When the steel struck the flint, sparks fell onto char cloth, a prepared linen, and began to glow. Blowing and the adding of tinder soon gave forth a flame and thence a fire. Not originally a Westernism.

FIREWATER An Indian pidgin English term for booze. (See this book's Introduction for a discussion of Red English.) In the Indian trade, it was often pure alcohol cut with the water of the closest creek and seasoned with tobacco, red chiles, and whatever else pleased the fancy of the trader—according to report, even snake heads. The term came from a custom developed by Indians trading with the Canadian fur men. The Indians, knowing that the alcohol was customarily diluted, would spit the first mouthful of booze on the fire. If it flamed, they'd trade for it; if it put some of the fire out, they wouldn't.

Booze (along with death, sex, food, and other central preoccupations) appears to have set the Westerner's imagination aflame. Other names for it include **AGUARDIENTE**, *base burner*, **BOILERMAKER AND HIS HELPER**, *brave maker*, *Brigham Young cocktail*, *bug juice*, *bumblebee whiskey*, *cactus juice*, *choc*, *coffin varnish*, *conversation fluid*, *corn*, **COWBOY COCKTAIL**, *dehorn*, *drunk water*, **DUST CUTTER**, *dynamite*, *forty rod*, *fool's water* (a term of Red English), *gut warmer*, *honeydew*, *hooch*, **INDIAN WHISKEY**, **IRRIGATION**, *jag*, *jig juice*, *joy-water*, *Kansas sheep dip*, *lamp oil*, **LEOPARD SWEAT**, **LIGHTNING**, *lightning flash*, **MESCAL**, *mountain dew*, *neck oil*, *nose paint*, *Pass brandy*, *Pass whiskey*, *pine top*, *pop skull*, *prairie dew*, *red disturbance*, *redeye* (and *hundred-yard redeye*), *red ink*, *rookus juice*, *salteur liquor*, *scamper juice*, *scorpion Bible*, *sheepherder's delight*, *shinny*, **SNAKE-HEAD WHISKEY**, *snake poison*, *stagger soup*, *station drink*, *strong water*, *strychnine*, *sudden death*, *tanglefoot*, *Taos lightning*, *tarantula juice*, **TISWIN**, *tongue oil*, *tonsil* *paint, tonsil varnish, tornado juice, trade whiskey,* **VALLEY TAN,** *white mule,* and *wild mare's milk.* (See also **ROOSTERED.**)

FIRST LAUGH CEREMONY Among the **NAVAJOS,** a child is born as a social creature when he or she laughs for the first time. Whoever made the child laugh sponsors a celebration.

FIRST RATTLE OUT OF THE BOX Cowboy talk for quick.

FISH What a cowboy called the yellow slicker he always kept (and still keeps) tied behind his saddle, so named because the trademark was a fish. Aside from keeping the water off, it served to cover his bedroll (sometimes called a *slicker roll*), to wrap gear in for a river crossing, to cover a pack, and even to wave at stampeding cattle.

FISH BURNER Alaskan slang for a **SLED DOG.** Similarly, in the Northwest, a Japanese-made motorcycle is a *rice-burner.*

FISH PIRATE In Alaska, a person who steals salmon from the corral traps in rivers. Such a person may be a competitor who sees a good opportunity, or a full-time thief. Also called a *salmon pirate, trap pirate,* and *trap robber.*

FISH WHEEL In the Pacific Northwest, primarily Alaska, a device for catching salmon, in either commercial or subsistence fishing, popular for at least a century. A large wheel mounted on a raft (commonly fifteen to twenty feet across, sometimes a good deal larger) is driven by the river's current. Baskets mounted on the wheel scoop up salmon and drop them onto a slide, which courses them to a box, sometimes a box with water in it that allows the return of illegal fish to the water. Reportedly also called a *salmon wheel.*

FIVE BEANS IN THE WHEEL Cowboy talk for five cartridges in the cylinder of the **SIX-SHOOTER,** with the hammer on the empty chamber. Cowboys usually carried their hand guns this way for safety.

FIVE CIVILIZED TRIBES An Anglo term for the **CHEROKEE, CHICKASAW, CHOCTAW, CREEK,** and Seminoles, because these tribes, in the view of the whites, took up "civilized" ways readily. The confederacy was established formally in 1843, with an intertribal code of law. Despite their being "civilized," these tribes were removed from the southeastern states to Indian Territory by carrot and stick, mostly stick. They confederated partly to form a united front against the "wild" tribes of the Plains.

Since the tribes had black slaves, many of them sided with the Confederacy during the Civil War, and in retribution the federal government reduced their lands. Later, as a result of the work of the Dawes Commission, talks at the Sequoyah Convention, and laws passed by Congress, the members of the Five Civilized Tribes became citizens of the United States and their lands part of the new state of Oklahoma, admitted to the Union in 1907.

FIX FOR HIGH-RIDING To get ready to **VAMOOSE** quick, or to do something that will necessitate vamoosing quick. Other expressions with similar meaning are *flying your kite* and *jump a lot of dust*.

FIXINGS (1) Among **MOUNTAIN MEN, POSSIBLES** (essential personal gear). (2) Also, food to prepare for dinner, material needed to make something, camp gear, the makings for a cigarette, and any equipment or supplies you wanted it to mean, sometimes with the implication of something extra or fancy. (See also **CHOW**.)

Along with the other great preoccupations of Westerners such as sex, booze, and death, food got a lot of names: *chicken fixings* (fancy food), *chuck, chuckaway, doings, fluff duffs* (fancy food again), *kow kow, muckamuck, soft grub* (fancy food once more).

FLAG (1) To flag **ANTELOPE** was and is to decoy them close by waving a red bandanna or similar object in the air. Insatiably curious, antelope often come to a flag. (2) Among sheepherders, to set out white flags or lanterns to keep coyotes away.

COMBINATIONS: Among loggers, *flag's up* was the call to eat. They called dinner *flaggings*. In **RODEO**, the *flagman* is the man who signals the start or end of the timing for a competitor.

FLANDREAU INDIAN One of a group of Santee **DAKOTA** who separated from the tribe, became Christian, and lived at Flandreau, Dakota Territory. Dr. Charles Eastman, the Dakota physician, was a Flandreau Indian.

FLANK A riding position alongside a herd on a **TRAIL DRIVE**—it's on each side most of the way to the rear. A man in this position is called a *flank rider*. The other positions (from front to back) are **POINT, SWING,** and **DRAG**.

At branding, *flankers* are men who work in pairs to throw and hold calves. When the roper has heeled and dragged the calf, one flanker grabs the calf's tail, the other the rope, and they jerk in opposite directions at the same moment. Down goes the calf. Then they hold the calf's legs and keep it down while others brand, earmark, vaccinate, and (if a bull calf) castrate it. This sort of flanking can also be done by a single man: he reaches across the calf, grabs the loose skin under the brisket, and jerks the beast off its feet—that is commonly called *wrestling calves*.

FLANK RIGGING In rodeo **BRONC RIDING**, the *back cinch* (also called the *scratcher cinch*), which adds incentive to the horse's bucking.

FLAPBOARD A board at the back of a **CHUCK WAGON** that was let down on hinges to make a table.

FLARE In the oil patch, burning off oil from a well to let the workers know something is happening.

FLASH RIDER Cowboy talk for a **BRONC-BUSTER** (or *peeler, fighter, squeezer,* or *twister*); a fellow who makes **SHAVETAILS**.

FLASHARITY Cowboy talk for fancy riding clothes, those that are too **FOFARROW** or **FUMADIDDLE**—fancy.

FLAT BOAT The first principal vehicle of westward migration down the Ohio River. The thirty- or forty-foot-long boat was built cheaply, with heavy timbers and a kind of house on the deck. When you reached your destination, you probably took it apart and built your house from it, because it wouldn't go upstream. That's why it was succeeded by the **KEELBOAT,** which would go both upstream and downstream and was a principal instrument of expansion up the Mississippi and Missouri Rivers. Also called a *broadhorn.*

FLAT HEAD Among loggers, a lawyer. Spirited dislike for lawyers is old in the West—*son-of-a-bitch stew* and *district attorney stew* are synonymous.

FLATHEAD INDIANS A Salish Native tribe who have been living in western Montana since the early 1800s. Their culture was like that of the buffalo-hunting tribes to the east. Though some Northwestern Indians did, the Flatheads did not flatten their heads; the name has several possible origins, including the sign-language expression for them (two hands on the side of the head) and the fact that the heads of the slaves among them were flattened. They were also called the *Cat Indians.* The Flatheads were notably friendly to whites during the period of westward expansion and responded enthusiastically to the Catholic missionaries who came among them. Today they live in their home country on the Flathead Reservation in northwestern Montana.

FLEA TRAP Cowboy talk for a bedroll. Later a sleeping bag was a *flea bag.*

FLEA-BITTEN A cowboy's description of a white horse with freckles.

FLEECE (1) A **MOUNTAIN-MAN** term for the flesh along the hump, ribs, and spine of the buffalo. (See also **DEPOUILLE**.) (2) The inner lining of a saddle, usually made of fleecy hair or a similar product.

FLOAT GOLD (1) Gold in the form of flakes and dust washed down from the hills; the gold obtained by **PLACER** mining. Also called *floated gold* or simply *float.* (2) Gold that floated away—escaped—in the mining process.

FLOAT STICK A stick the beaver trapper attached to his trap. If the beaver swam away with the trap, the stick showed where it was. This stick was the source of one of the best-known expressions of the **MOUNTAIN MAN,** "He don't **KNOW WHAT WAY THE STICK FLOATS**."

FLOATER A person banished from a Native tribe for a serious offense, such as killing another member of the tribe. Some **PLAINS INDIANS** still float people by action of the tribal council; the law they use to do it may be called a *floater clause.*

FLOATHOUSE In Alaska and British Columbia, a house constructed on a raft. Sometimes complete with flower gardens, they're floated from spot to spot until they find a home on terra firma. Not a houseboat, which is more water-worthy.

FLOATING OUTFIT A group of cowboys, usually half a dozen men and a cook, riding the winter range to brand calves missed at the **ROUNDUP** and to keep cows from drifting. Their **CHUCK WAGON** was called a *floating wagon.*

FLOUR GOLD Gold in very fine particles, ground fine as flour. Also called *flour dust.*

FLUFF DUFFS Hotel food, fancy food: the food women cooked back at the ranch to show the hands they weren't at the **CHUCK WAGON**. Along with the other great preoccupations of Westerners such as sex, booze, and death, food got a lot of names: *chicken fixings* (fancy food), *chuck, chuckaway, doings* (fancy food again), *kow kow, muckamuck, soft grub* (fancy food once more).

FLUME A wooden channel that brought water to a **PLACER** operation.

FLUTE CEREMONY A summer ceremony of the **HOPIS**, sponsored by two flute societies, to bring rain; alternates yearly with the **SNAKE DANCE**.

FLY A sheet used to keep water off, especially at the back of a **CHUCK WAGON** to protect the cook.

FOFARROW Among the **MOUNTAIN MEN**, trinkets, gaudy clothing, and similar show-offy stuff. Thus Lieutenant George Frederick Ruxton in *Life in the Far West* has one of his trappers complain, "First I had a Blackfoot—the darnedest slut as ever cried for fofarrow. . . . There warn't enough scarlet cloth nor beads, nor vermillion in Sublette's packs for [her]."

The word also took an adjective form—thus a woman might be described as *too fofarrow*. Adapted from the Spanish *fanfarrón* (meaning "braggart"), with perhaps some influence from the French *trom frou frou*, and spelled variously.

FOG To move along fast, make dust, get along pronto, especially on horseback.

FOLLOW THE TONGUE What a freighter did with his wagons. At night he would spot the North Star and point the tongue of the lead wagon to it as a guide to help or determine the right direction for the morning's travel.

FOLSOM MAN A prehistoric people (about 8000 BC) of the east side of the Rockies, discovered through the finding of *Folsom points* (arrowheads) in New Mexico in 1928.

FONDA In the Southwest, a restaurant or an inn. Borrowed from Spanish.

FOOL HEN A common name (originally from the **MOUNTAIN MEN**) for the **SAGE GROUSE**. The bird sits so still (for whatever reason) that men can get close enough to fell it with a stick, stone, or whip.

FOOL'S GOLD Iron pyrite, which looks like gold. By extension, any sucker's notion of riches.

FOOT-AND-WALKER LINE A term for a stage line that made its passengers get out and walk—or push—across hard places in the road or up steep hills.

FOREFOOT To rope a horse by the forefeet. If you throw badly and catch only one foot, you're likely to break the leg. Also called *mangana*. (See also **ROPE**.)

FOREST SERVICE The agency of the Department of Agriculture that administers public lands. The Forest Reserve Act of 1891 protected significant forested reserves on public land, not to prevent their exploitation but to provide for their conservation and wise use for the greatest number of people in the long run. Under the Department of Agriculture, the U.S. Forest Service manages this land to promote *multiple use*—timber, water, grazing, wildlife, mineral development, wilderness, recreation, and other uses. The principal goal is not preservation.

FORGE For a shoed (shod) horse to hit its back hoofs against its front ones when running. It's a bad habit and makes a sound like the ring of hammer on anvil. To do this is also called *to anvil*.

FORK (1) A tributary of a river. Thus the Lewis Fork, the original name of the Snake River, and Henry's Fork, its main tributary. Some Westerners have so forgotten the meaning of this word that state highway signs sometimes give streams redundant names like Henry's Fork River. (2) The front of a **SADDLE TREE**, below the horn. (3) In verb form, to mount up. Sometimes it's a command—*fork your horse* meaning get mounted and ride. To *fork a horse* is also known as to *hairpin a horse*.

FORKED END UP Where a rider may end up if he's thrown—on his head. Thus a man who speaks of being *still forked end down* means he's OK.

FORKED TONGUE To *speak with forked tongue* (a term of Indian pidgin English) is to lie; now usually used with a sense of archaism.

FORT UP To barricade yourself; to take a position defensible against attack, especially Indian attack. **EMIGRANTS** forted up by driving their wagons into a circle. **MOUNTAIN MEN** sometimes killed their horses and forted up behind the bodies.

FORTY YEARS' GATHERING What a cowboy calls his personal gear—sometimes it's a *thirty years' gathering*. A logger calls his a *fifty years' gathering*.

FORTY-NINER (1) A California gold rusher in 1849. A *fifty-niner* is a Colorado Front Range gold rusher; a *sixty-niner* is a Montana gold rusher; and a *seventy-niner* is a Leadville, Colorado, gold rusher. (See also **EIGHTY-NINER**.) (2) A person who advocated the forty-ninth parallel as the final boundary between U.S. and British territory in the Northwest. (See also **FIFTY-FOUR FORTY**.)

FORTY-NINER SONG Now a song sung by Indian people, often at powwows or in camp after the powwow, but also on cross-country auto rides, in protests, etc.; also called a forty-nine song. Usually they're songs of looking for love, finding love, or having been jilted; often I've-got-the-blues songs, sometimes political songs, distinctly from the point of view of Indian people. One forty-niner song, for instance, speaks of having the "muscatel relocation blues" and "lemon-vodka, big-city Injun woes." A person who participates in forty-niner singing is a **FORTY-NINER** and is said to be *forty-ninering.*

Ethnomusicologist Ed Wapp of the Institute of American Indian Arts explains the complex and interesting history of these songs. They came originally from ceremonies of the Kiowas, Comanches, and Cheyennes on the Southern Plains during the nineteenth century. These peoples performed songs and dances to prepare for war expeditions. Such a ceremony came to be known humorously as a *forty-nine,* named in a circuitous way after the prostitutes of the California gold rush. Through the Indian boarding school experience, other Indians learned these songs and put different words to them, or invented words for songs that used vocables only. In this new form they became very popular and spread to most tribes. The war ceremonies are still enacted and are still called *forty-nine,* or by Kiowas simply *the nine.*

FORTY-ROD Booze. (See **FIREWATER** for the many colorful names for liquor.)

FOUR CORNERS The place where Utah, Colorado, New Mexico, and Arizona all meet. The surrounding area is called Four Corners country; roughly the same as the **COLORADO PLATEAU.**

FOUR DIRECTIONS The Red English term for the four main directions of the compass; also called the *four winds.* The four directions are integral to the religions of many Indians—pipes are ritually offered to the sky, the Earth, and the four directions. The directions appear often in **PLAINS INDIAN** art in *four-directions wheels,* circles of quillwork or beadwork. They also have colors and themes associated with them: east is red, home of the eagle, the sun, the dawn, the new day, and birth; south is yellow, where you are coming from, fruition; west is often black, home of the thunder beings, and of middle age; north is white, home of the white giant, and of old age. The colors associated with sky and Earth are often blue and green, respectively. The contemporary **MEDICINE MAN** Wallace Black Elk says, "The 'power of the Four Winds' is the power over space."

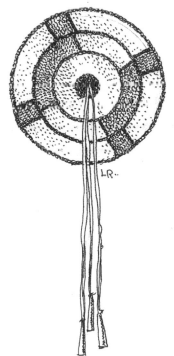

A four-directions, or four winds, wheel.
[DRAWING BY E. L. REEDSTROM.]

FOUR-FLUSHER A trickster, a bluffer. It comes from **POKER**—you bluff that you have a flush when you have only four cards of the suit instead of the required five.

FRAGGLE In Texas, to rob.

FRAIDY HOLE Where you go to get away from a tornado; a **STORM CELLAR** or cave.

FREAK What a cowboy calls a man who is reluctant to work or is a complainer.

FREDDY Contemporary slang for an employee of the U.S. Forest Service; it has a derogatory connotation when used by **EARTH FIRST!ERS** and some other environmentalists.

FREE GRASS The public range; open range; the paradise for cattlemen that was the original **GREAT PLAINS**. The intrusion of private ownership and fences forced some of the most fundamental changes of the nineteenth-century West. It also led to range wars. The big cattle companies needed their free grass and did their damnedest to keep farmers and small ranchers out. If a fellow owned the land right around the water source, he could control the range for many square miles around. An advocate of cowmen running critters on the public grass was called a *free-ranger*.

COMBINATIONS: *free lunch* (the custom, apparently started in California in the early 1850s, of taverns providing free food at noon to those buying drinks); *free trader* (an independent fur trader, rather than a trapper, not outfitted by one of the large fur companies). (See also **FREE TRAPPER**.)

FREE TRAPPER A beaver man who trapped on his own instead of working for one of the fur companies. He was usually a French-Canadian or American who had begun in the trade as an employee, acquired his skills, and gone independent. Some still had to get outfitted by the big companies and so were obliged to sell their **PLEWS** (beaver skins) to their creditors; others were completely free. Their opposite number was the **ENGAGÉ** (hireling).

Free trappers sometimes worked in small groups of co-equals but often traveled with the large company brigades, where their savvy made them welcome. They were the zenith of one line of development of the North American frontiersman, celebrated by writers such as Washington Irving. Many also became nearly as Indian as white, with Native wives, children, languages, and customs, and these *squaw men* suffered notably with the flooding of whites into the West.

FREEZE-OUT A winner-take-all variety of **POKER**. Each player stayed until broke, the last man getting everything.

FREEZE-UP In Alaska, the annual blockage of creeks and rivers (and sometimes harbors) by ice. It makes the waters unnavigable for watercraft, but changes them into roads for snowmobiles. See also **BREAKUP, ICE ROAD**.

FREIGHT TRAIN A caravan of **PRAIRIE SCHOONERS** or other wagons, often ten to twenty, enough to provide defense against whatever Indian opposition might come. The crew was a captain and several lieutenants (or in the Hispanic world a *caporal* and several *capitans*), a **WRANGLER**, a **NIGHTHAWK**, the drivers (**MULESKINNERS** for a *mule train*, **BULLWHACKERS** for a *bull train*) and swampers, who were men-of-all duties.

Trains moved mornings and evenings, and nooned through the worst heat of the day. A bull train, one drawn by oxen, would average twelve miles a day on a fair trail, a train drawn by mules half that much again. Oxen were slower but surer and could carry more freight because they thrived on grass alone. Mules were faster but delivered less load and needed corn.

Also called a *freight outfit*. (See also **JACKASS MAIL**.)

FREIGHT YOUR CROP To get liquored up and kick up your heels; to go on a bender. (See **ROOSTERED** for many colorful expressions for getting drunk.

FREMONT CULTURE The customs, implements, etc., of an Indian people who lived in west-central Utah, around what is now Capitol Reef National Park, for nearly a millennium from 400 A.D.; perhaps an offshoot of the **ANASAZI** culture.

FREMONTIA Another name for **GREASEWOOD**, named after the Western explorer John C. Frémont. A variety of cottonwood tree, hollygrape, herb, pine tree, and pine squirrel are also named after him.

FRENCHMAN In the West, usually not a Gaul but a French-Canadian of mixed blood. The term was common among **MOUNTAIN MEN** and probably did not reflect the scorn for other cultures characteristic of many later Westerners.

The French-Canadians (sometimes called *Franco-Canadians*) preceded the Americans in the Western beaver trade, explored much of the country, learned the Native peoples, and developed many of the ways. They brought many words to the mountain man's vocabulary, including **APPOLA**, **BOIS D'ARC**, **BOUDINS**, **CARCAJOU**, **COULEE**, **ENGAGÉ**, **HIVERNANT**, **MANGEUR DE LARD**, **PARFLECHE**, **PLEW**, and **VOYAGEUR**.

FRENO (FRAY-noh) Either the whole bridle or just the **BIT**. Borrowed from Spanish.

FRESNO A buck scraper; a scoop used to move earth to build a dam. Drawn by horses, it looked roughly like a wheelbarrow without a wheel. It was known for its **STINGER** or *Johnson bar*, which smarted like hell when it kicked. It took its name from the Fresno Agricultural Works in Fresno, California.

FRIED CHICKEN Cowboy talk for bacon that's breaded and fried.

FRIENDLY An Indian who wasn't a **HOSTILE**. Sometimes it meant an Indian like the **LAKOTA** leader Red Cloud or the **SHOSHONE** chief Washakie, men who decided with independence and integrity on a road of peace and even accommodation with the white man. Sometimes it meant an Indian who was fighting on the white side temporarily to get back at hereditary enemies. Often it meant a **HANG-AROUND-THE-FORT** Indian, who was unfaithful to his own traditions, not walking his good **RED ROAD**. And the words have morphed into odd meanings. Today the Hopi who favor the tribal government and traditional leadership call one another friendlies and hostiles.

FRIJOL (free-HOHL), **FRIJOLES** (free-HOH-lees) A bean. When pinto beans are boiled and then mashed and fried with lard, they are *refried beans* (frijoles), a favorite of Southwestern Hispanics and known to Anglos primarily through Mexican restaurants. In Texas, they are sometimes called redundantly *frijole beans*. Borrowed from Spanish. (For the names cowboys called beans, see **WHISTLEBERRY**.)

FROG WALK A form of mild bucking in short hops, not likely to throw a rider. (See also **BUCK**.)

FROG-EYE PUDDING Cowboy talk for tapioca pudding.

FROM WHO LAID THE CHUNK A way of describing something terrifically well done. Adams cites the example *he burned the breeze from who laid the chunk*, meaning "He rode very fast."

FRONT-DOOR PUNCHER Cowboy talk for a cow**PUNCHER** who spends all his time in town.

FRONTIERSMAN A man knowledgeable in the outdoor ways of the Western wilds (surprisingly, apparently not of the East or the Middle Border).

COMBINATIONS: *Frontier Colt* (a model of Colt revolver popular in the Far West after 1873), *frontier day(s)* (a celebration of the ways of the Old West, usually annual; one of the best known is held in Cheyenne, Wyoming, each July), *frontierism* (an expression or custom of the frontier, often by implication crude or barbarous).

FROZE To yearn for something, to have a powerful itch for it. Thus hungry **MOUNTAIN MEN** spoke of being *froze for meat*. It rarely or never occurs in the form *freeze*.

FRUIT TRAMP A migrant worker who follows the harvest from orchard to orchard, usually paid by the day or unit; often a Mexican. Woody Guthrie wrote a fine protest song about them, "Deportee," a tale of a plane of fruit workers that crashed, and the newspaper did not even give the names of those killed, but merely referred to them as deportees.

FRY BREAD A deep-fried puffy bread usually associated with Indians. Originating in the Southwestern tribes, it has become pan-tribal. Also called *fried bread*.

FRYING SIZE A cowboy's description of a kid or a small man.

FULL HOUSE A very good **POKER** hand consisting of three cards of one kind and two of another. By extension, any good situation.

FULL SIXTEEN HANDS HIGH A way of describing a cowman of integrity and ability. The phrase comes from the conventional way of measuring the height of a horse, the number of hand-spans from the ground to the withers—sixteen would be big.

FULL WAR PAINT Cowboy talk for dressed up, as to go to church; *feathered-out*.

FULL-STAMPED SADDLE A saddle whose leather is stamped with designs. Aside from looking fancy, this stamping gives a rider's legs something to get friction against. Its opposite is called a *slick saddle*.

FUMADIDDLE A way of describing something fancy, frilly, unnecessarily extravagant, something *faradiddle*, something **FOFARROW**.

FUR TRADE The commerce in the skins of animals, which was a key impetus in the exploration and colonization of North America. The main object of the hunt was beaver, which was used to make felt, which in turn was made into hats. At various times other animals' skins were important in the trade, especially buffalo, deer, and sea otter.

The search for beaver began in the early seventeenth century by the French in what later became Canada, and led directly to the exploration of that country all the way to the Pacific and Arctic Oceans. In the United States it was a motivating force for westward exploration, and the **MOUNTAIN MEN** roamed over most of the Far West before emigration or settlement were dreamed of. Russian ships plied the trade in otter skins along the Northwest Pacific Coast starting in the middle of the eighteenth century.

In both Canada and the United States the quest for furs dominated relations with the Indians, and set patterns for later Indian-Anglo relations. Principal fur-trading companies were the Hudson's Bay Company, the North West Company, John Jacob Astor's American Fur Company, and the Rocky Mountain Fur Company. The heyday of the fur trade was 1820–1840.

When the silk hat became popular in the 1830s, the price of beaver fell sharply. Then buffalo became the center of the trade, leading in the 1880s to the near-obliteration of that animal.

Many Western terms spring from the fur trade—see **BEAVER, ENGAGÉ, FREE TRAPPER, HIVERNANT, PARTISAN, PLEW,** and **VOYAGEUR** for starters.

FUSIL (foo-SEE) A muzzle-loading musket of the type the Hudson's Bay Company and Northwest Fur Company traded to the Indians; a *trade musket*. Also called a *fuzee* and a *fuke*. It generally was not a weapon of high quality. Borrowed from French.

FUSTE (FUHS-tee) In the Southwest, a Mexican saddle or a saddle tree with cloth thrown over it. Borrowed from Spanish.

FUZZ-TAIL A wild horse; a *mustang*; an unbroke range horse with a bushy tail. (If it was broke, it would be a **SHAVETAIL**.) Also called a *fuzzy*, and to *run fuzzies* was to catch wild horses.

⤐G⤐

G.T.T. See **GONE TO TEXAS.**

GABACHO (gah-BAH-cho) An epithet for Anglos used by Southwestern Hispanics, usually disparagingly. Their word for a Spaniard is *gachupin*. See also **GRINGO.** Adapted from Spanish (where it originally meant "French-like" or "foreigner").

GAFF (1) To **SPUR** a horse. (2) Among loggers, the metal point on a pike pole.
   Gaffer, among miners, means the shift boss. Among loggers, it indicates the general superintendent. (See also **SUPREME BEING** for more logging terms for bosses.)

GAGE D'AMOUR (gahj dah-MOOR) A hide pouch that hung around the neck of a **VOYAGEUR** or **MOUNTAIN MAN** and held a small clay pipe. According to the 1840s British adventurer Lieutenant George Frederick Ruxton in *Life in the Far West*, it was usually "a triumph of squaw workmanship, in shape of a heart, garnished with beads and porcupine quills." Originally simply any token of love given a fur man by an Indian woman, it came to mean the most common of such items, the hide pouch.

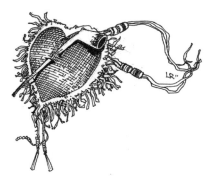

Trapper's gage d'amour.
[DRAWING BY E. L. REEDSTROM.]

GAIN Among miners, an amount of gold or silver mined.

GALENA The main ore for lead. This word was usually used in the West to mean the lead in bullets. Thus when the **MOUNTAIN MAN** spoke of needing *DuPont and galena*, he meant powder and lead (and he probably formed his own balls from a bar of lead). When the frontiersman spoke of a *galena pill* (or *blue pill*), he meant a bullet: "One Galena pill is no dose for me—come on with a whole lead mine."

GALL BITTERS A drink popular among **MOUNTAIN MEN.** The recipe of plainsman Rufus Sage: one pint water with one-quarter gill buffalo gall. Sage describes it as "a wholesome and exhilarating drink" and a sure cure for dyspepsia. Also known as *prairie bitters.*

GAL-LEG A **SPUR** with a shank shaped like a woman's leg, at least in the eye of a cowboy who hasn't been to town in a while.

GALLETA (gah-YAY-tuh) A Southwestern grass (genus *Hilaria*) popular as graze for livestock. Borrowed from Spanish.

GALLOPING GOOSE A decrepit or makeshift unit of rolling stock (such as a freight car) on a railroad.

GALOOT A fellow, especially one who's a bit of a character.

GAMBUSINO (gahm-boo-SEE-noh) A gold prospector, a small-time miner, even a fellow who pilfers gold. Borrowed from Spanish.

GAME OF THE ARROW A game George Catlin found the **MANDAN** Indians playing in the 1830s. The object was to get the most arrows in the air at once. The term is an English translation of an Indian (probably Mandan) phrase. The game is still played among the **CROW** in a somewhat different form.

GANADERO (gah-nah-DAIR-oh) A Southwestern term for a cattleman. Borrowed from Spanish.

GANADO RED (gah-NAH-doh red) A bright red color produced by an aniline dye. Named for Ganado, Arizona, it was the first non-vegetable dye used by the **NAVAJO** weavers.

GANCHO A shepherd's crook or a hook made of metal. Borrowed from Spanish.

GANT UP To get gaunt, thin, skeletal-looking; said especially of **LIVESTOCK**. Such critters were said to be *ganted* or *ganted down*.

GAPER In card games, a tiny mirror the dealer holds, to sneak a look at the cards.

GARBAGE CAN What a logger called a *Bunyan camp*, one with miserable living accommodations.

GARMENT A white undergarment worn by **MORMONS** that symbolizes purity and modesty. It is worn by members who have received an *endowment*.

GATE HORSE A rider posted at a corral gate to count cows, to keep them in or out, or for any other reason.

GATEADO (gah-tay-AH-doh) A dun-colored horse striped like a cat, much like a zebra dun. Borrowed from Spanish. (See also **BUCKSKIN**.)

GATHER As a noun, the cattle that have been rounded up.

GAUNTLET A cowboy's glove, generally sewn of **BUCKSKIN**, fringed, and embroidered with handsome designs, especially (in Texas) with a star. Gauntlets are also sometimes decorated with beadwork.

Gauntlets with lone star.
[DRAWING BY E. L. REEDSTROM.]

GAZOOK A gawky, awkward person.

GEE POLE In Alaska, a long pole on the right side of a dogsled, which the driver uses to steer. Perhaps from the command *gee* to a horse, meaning "right."

GEED UP Crippled, banged up, out of action.

GENTE DE RAZON (HEN-tay day rah-SOHN or duh rah-SOHN) In the Hispanic Southwest, a term meaning people of quality, educated people, members of the upper class. It distinguished the so-called higher class from the poor, the Indians, and others thought to be less civilized. Sometimes used in the short form alone, *gente*. Borrowed from Spanish (where it means, literally, "people of reason").

GENTILE Among **MORMONS**, any non-Mormon. In various groups it consistently means "not one of us." Shakers used it to mean non-Shakers; Jews use it to mean non-Jews.

GENTLE To **BREAK A HORSE**, especially to train it gradually and with its cooperation, not quickly and roughly, as cow ponies used to be broke. Horse trainers are sometimes called *gentlers*. Other horses are also called *gentlers* when they are necked (tied by the neck) to wilder horses in an effort to teach the wilder ones some manners.

GENUINE JIMMY What a logger called a camp doctor, perhaps a corruption of Quinine Jimmy. (See **SAWBONES** for other names for doctors.)

GEODUCK (GWEE-duhk) The giant clam found on the entire Pacific Coast, eaten first by Native peoples and now by all. It gives the forms *geoducker* and *geoduckling*. Said to be a **NISQUALLY** word.

GET HER MADE For a logger to accumulate enough of a stake to move on.

GET THERE WITH BOTH FEET To succeed in a big way. Thus a gambling fellow "got there with both feet at the starting, and was eight hundred ahead once, but he played it off at monte."

GETAWAY MONEY The cash a rodeo cowboy has at the end of one **RODEO**. He hopes it's enough to buy gas, sandwiches, and beer until the next rodeo in the next town.

GETTER A **COYOTE** trap that's now illegal. The coyote pulls on a scented wick and cyanide is injected into its mouth; often other animals are poisoned by it.

GHOST BEAD A bead of cedar sold by **NAVAJOS** and other Southwestern Indians today.

GHOST CORD A **STRING** tied by a **BRONC BUSTER** around a horse's lower jaw and tongue and used to punish him for bucking. Also called a *twitch*. Not regarded by Westerners as good horse-training technique.

GHOST DANCE A ceremony of the Indians of the **GREAT PLAINS** and **GREAT BASIN**. Although it is now mostly associated with the **PAIUTE** prophet Wovoka (Jack Wilson) and the cataclysmic events among the **LAKOTAS** in 1890, it

Arapaho Indians doing the ghost dance, ca. 1900.
[DRAWING BY MARY IRVIN WRIGHT; COURTESY OF NATIONAL ARCHIVES (111-SC-87767).]

existed among Shoshonean peoples from a much earlier date in a form called *naraya*. Tradition says it was given to the people by **COYOTE** to keep away sickness and harmful events. New impetus was given to the ghost dance by the visions of the Paiute Wovoka during an eclipse of the sun on January 1, 1889. In his vision, Wovoka was given songs and a dance that would make white people disappear and bring Native peoples back to their former high estate. Perhaps it is better translated as *Spirit Dance*.

This religion spread quickly to the **PLAINS INDIANS**. The Lakota adopted it in 1890 and added a new revelation, a *ghost shirt* thought to protect the wearer from danger, even from bullets. The ghost dance excitement on the **SIOUX** reservations alarmed many white people and led indirectly to the massacre at Wounded Knee in December 1890. The ghost dance ceremony was held as recently as 1974 and 1975 on the Rosebud and Fort Hall Reservations, respectively. The naraya was revived by the **SHOSHONES** in the 1990s.

COMBINATIONS: *ghost dancer, ghost dancing.*

GHOST TOWN A town that is abandoned, or nearly abandoned. Evidently it's strictly a modern term. It is generally a mining town, widowed when the ore (or rumor of ore) played out. People also use the terms *ghost cabin, ghost camp,* and *ghost city.*

GIG (1) To **SPUR** a horse. (2) To swindle.

GILA MONSTER (HEE-luh) The only poisonous lizard (*Heloderma suspectum*) in the United States. This dweller of the Southwestern deserts stands a hand-span high and a foot and a half or more long. It is nocturnal and shy, colored pink, beige, and black. It takes its name from the Gila River in Arizona and New Mexico, whose valley it haunts.

GIMLET To ride a horse so badly that you make its back sore.

GIN To disturb cows, to make them move around unnecessarily, which burns the fat off them. Cattlemen will grumble at foolish hands who gin cows around. Similar to **CHOUSE**.

GIRAFFE A car used in a mine to hoist ore up inclines, "absurdly called so," says Charles H. Shinn's *The Story of the Mine*, "because the hind wheels are very large and the front ones low, so as to keep the car level."

GIRL OF THE LINE One of the many Western words for a prostitute. These women were called girls (or ladies) of the line because they did their business in tents lined up in *cow towns,* mining camps, railroad camps, and the like. (For many other names for prostitutes, see **CALICO QUEEN**.)

GIRTH The Texas word for the **CINCH** of a saddle.

GIVEAWAY A tradition in many Indian tribes, from the **GREAT PLAINS** to the Southwest to the Pacific Northwest, of giving away material goods during ceremonies (from naming ceremonies to funerals) as a gesture of generosity. Families of those holding or participating in ceremonies make gifts at large to tribal members. In many tribes, generosity is held to be a cardinal virtue. Today, for instance, a **CROW** couple getting married is likely, instead of receiving gifts as an Anglo couple would, to make gifts to all who attend the wedding. The Pacific Northwest form of the giveaway is the **POTLATCH**.

GLORY HOLE In mining, an open pit, especially a funnel-like hole around a shaft entrance. Also a spot rich in ore, or an abandoned stope.

GO UNDER To die. First an expression of the **MOUNTAIN MEN**. Says the linguist J. L. Dillard in *American Talk*, "The sign language . . . expresses 'die' by moving one hand from above the other to below it. The mountain man's *go under* is clearly a verbalization of this sign."

Go over the range also means to die. *Go wolfing* is a term of early Western traders meaning to leave a body on the Plains for the wolves. (For many other Western expressions for dying, see **CASH IN YOUR CHIPS**.)

GOAT (1) **ANTELOPE**, a pronghorn. This usage is common both historically and today. (2) Sometimes a **BIGHORN** sheep. (3) For a horse to buck halfheartedly.

GOATHEAD The puncture vine *(Tribulus cistoides),* which offers to the foot or paw a particularly nasty sticker. Chiefly Southwestern.

GODDAM (1) An Indian term for a white man (and for once really an Indian term, not a translator's word), naturally based on the white's frequent expression.

(See **ANGLO** for many Native terms for white people.) (2) An Indian's term for a freighting wagon, an unceasing object of Anglo cursing.

GO-DEVIL (1) A logging sled. (2) A wire from bank to stream, along which a bucket was pulled, hauling water.

GOLD The word *gold* yielded lots of Western combinations. Tools used in gold-mining: *gold borer* (an auger), *gold canoe* (a **CRADLE**), *gold* (or *gold-mining*) *dredge*, *gold monkey* or *goldometer* (a locating rod), *gold pan*, *gold rocker* (a cradle), *gold separator*, *gold sluice*, *gold washer* (a cradle), *gold weight*.

OTHER MINING TERMS: *gold blossom* (gold-bearing rock detached from the vein), *gold camp*, *gold digger* (a **PLACER** miner), *gold digging*, *gold dirt* (pay dirt), *gold excitement*, *gold fever* (or *gold colic*, the acute desire to find gold), *gold hunter* (*gold hunt* and *gold-hunting*), *gold mania*, *gold nugget*, *gold panning* (see also **PAN**), *gold rush* (and *gold rusher*), *gold seeker*, *gold strike*.

MISCELLANEOUS COMBINATIONS: *gold brick* (before it became a swindle and a way of avoiding work, it was a real brick of gold, a form in which gold was transported), *gold coast* (on the Pacific shore, a coastal area of northern California and southern Oregon), *goldfish* (a soldier's term for canned salmon served commonly in army messes in the Southwest), *Gold Mountain* (the name Chinese immigrants gave to California), and the *gold spike* (a railroad spike driven at Promontory Point, Utah, on May 11, 1869, to symbolize completion of the first transcontinental railroad).

GOLD DUST Gold in fine particles, as commonly found in **PLACER** mining (panning and the like). Dust became an important medium of exchange in the second half of the nineteenth century, when Westerners were sharply suspicious of paper money (Confederate paper having proved worthless). This term was not originally an Americanism.

Gold dust gave rise to two combinations: *gold dust scales* (used for weighing the dust accurately) and *gold dust exchange* (where you traded dust for money).

GOLDEN BIBLE *The Book of Mormon*, which **MORMONS** believe was given to Joseph Smith inscribed on golden plates.

GOME A **PAPAGO** Indian game somewhat like soccer, and the name of the ball used, according to Smith. The ball was wooden and baseball-sized; it was not kicked but thrown with the tops of the feet.

GONE BEAVER Originally a **MOUNTAIN-MAN** term meaning "trapped," "dead"— what a beaver was when it put its paw in a trap. Later it also referred to a man who got sick, fell in love, or otherwise got lost or done for. Similar expressions are *gone coon*, *gone gander*, *gone goose*, *gone gosling*, *gone nigger*, and *gone sucker*. Of these, **COON** and **NIGGER** were mountain-man usages.

GONE OVER THE RANGE Cowboy talk for death. *Gone up* was an occasional term for being killed; one source reports it as Denver slang, short for *gone up a tree*, that is, hanged. (For other terms for dying, see CASH IN YOUR CHIPS; for terms for getting hanged, see STRING PARTY.)

GONE SOUTH An expression of Red English, especially CHEYENNE, for those who have died and are traveling the Milky or Spirit Way. BLACKFEET say *gone to the sand hills*, LAKOTAS *gone over the pines*.

GONE TO TEXAS This sign hung on the doors of Yankee and Southern folks who decided they could do better with a fresh start. It was particularly a way of kissing lawmen and creditors goodbye. At first the expression was literal, later figurative. Often abbreviated G.T.T.

GOOD INDIAN Sometimes this meant a so-called decent redskin, one friendly to whites; sometimes it meant simply a good fellow; most often, in the Old West, it meant a dead Indian. When the Penateka-Comanche chief Toswai referred to himself as a good Indian, Little Phil (General Phillip Sheridan) said, "The only good Indians I ever saw were dead," which over time became "the only good Indian is a dead Indian," which is about as offensive as remarks get.

GOOD SCALD Cowboy talk for a good job. To *scald* is to dip the pig in boiling water (to remove the hair) when slaughtering hogs.

GOOD STICK A successful mounting or successful breeding session.

GOODNIGHTING An operation on the scrotums of bulls to help them on TRAIL DRIVES. Cattleman Charles Goodnight noticed bulls' testicles getting banged around on long drives; sometimes the testicles would swell, and the animal would have to be CUT (castrated); sometimes it died. So Goodnight started cutting off the scrotum and sewing the testicles up tight against the body. This procedure worked well, seemed not to impair the bulls' breeding ability, and was soon adopted widely. It's seldom used today because it can sometimes cause sterility.

GOOSE PEN In California and the Pacific Northwest, a hole in a redwood or redwood stump created by fire, and sometimes used for storage. The tale is that a California packer corralled his thirty-three mules in a goose pen in the 1870s.

GOOSEY A way of describing a horse or a man that's jumpy, nervous, unpredictable. As a verb, to *put the spurs to* a horse.

COMBINATIONS: *goose moon* (an occasional Red English term for the month when the Canada geese come back from the south, heralding spring); *gooseneck* (a hairpin curve in a river so severe that the stream bends back on itself, as in the goosenecks of the San Juan River near Mexican Hat, Utah; also a SPUR with a shank shaped like a goose's neck and head); *gooseology* (the philosophy of people who were "sound on the goose"—in favor of slavery—during the struggles about slavery in Kansas; why the goose was pro-slavery is unexplained).

GOPHER A burrowing rodent of the genera *Geomys*, *Thomomys*, or *Citellus*, ubiquitous on the prairies (there are so many in Minnesota that it's known as the Gopher

State); not the same as a **PRAIRIE DOG**. The burrows gophers make were and are dangerous to horses and so to riders. By extension, a gopher may be any man who digs; for instance, a miner, or a logger who makes holes under logs for the choker. In verb form, to make exploratory diggings for gold on a small scale. The result is a *gopher drift, gopher hole,* or *coyote hole.* A *gopher hole* also means a **DUGOUT** (half-underground house) of the sort early settlers lived in.

GO-ROUND A round in a **RODEO**, one sequence in which all competitors get an opportunity to compete in one event, such as *saddle bronc.* The winner of each go-round gets some **DAY MONEY** (prize money for winning that day's event). Often rodeos hold one go-round in each event each day, and on the last day match the top hands in the final go-rounds.

GORPER Contemporary slang for a certain kind of backpacker or other back-country goer, usually urban or with urban attitudes and with a romantic view of the wilderness and back-to-nature values. The teasing term comes from *gorp,* a trail food of mixed nuts and fruits (originally, Good Old Raisins and Peanuts) popular among such folk. They're also called *hanky-heads* or *granolas.*

GOSPEL SHARP A preacher. The term is based (wonderfully) on the similarity to *cardsharp.* Also *gospel shark.* (See **BLACK ROBE** for other names for preachers.)

GOTCH EAR A droopy ear on a cow, caused by ticks that weaken the cartilage. Also takes the form *gotched.*

GOUCH HOOK The pothook **COOKIE** uses to handle heavy lids.

GOURD DANCE A summer ceremony of the **KIOWA** Indians, including various rituals. Once suppressed by the government, it was brought back in the 1950s.

GOVERNMENT JOB What a logger called personal work done on company time.

GOVERNMENT TRAPPER A hunter who works for the federal government, usually for **ANIMAL DAMAGE CONTROL** in the Department of Agriculture. His duty is to reduce predators, mostly **COYOTES**.

GRACIAS (GRAH-see-uhs) Thank you. Borrowed from Spanish, of course, and now common even beyond the Southwest.

GRAIN To scrape a beaver (or other) hide clear of flesh, fat, or hair. The **MOUN-TAIN MEN** accomplished this task with a graining block, which the 1840s adventurer Lieutenant George Frederick Ruxton described in *Life in the Far West* as "a log of wood with the bark stripped perfectly smooth, which is planted obliquely in the ground." After graining, the hides were stretched and dried, often on hoops made of willow branches.

GRAMA Short for *grama grass,* any of the species *Bouteloua* common in the West. These grasses are noted for their nutritional value. Explorers and overland pioneers were often surprised to find that grama seems as nutritious when dry and brown in the winter as when green in the spring and summer. Also spelled *gramma*; not the same as *gama grass*, which grows from eastern Texas eastward. From Spanish.

GRANDE (GRAHN-day) Big, grand, great. From Spanish, and ubiquitous in Southwestern place names (for example, Rio Grande).

GRANDFATHER, GRANDMOTHER Among most American Indians, these terms bear a wider meaning than in Anglo culture. Generally, Indians have far more than four grandparents, because the brothers and sisters of their grandparents are also addressed as Grandfather and Grandmother. Also, the great powers—such as the four directions, the Earth, the sky, and the great mystery—are likely to be addressed in prayer as Grandfather and Grandmother. Grandfather is a term of many Indians for the deity, often seen as embodied in the sun. Says the contemporary Lakota shaman Wallace Black Elk, Grandfather is "the male aspect of the Creator personified by wisdom, the sky, light, etc., [the Lakota call him] *Tunkashila*," grandfather. Thus Nicholas Black Elk begins his well-known prayer in *Black Elk Speaks*: "Hey-a-a-hey! Grandfather, Great Spirit, once more behold me on earth and lean to hear my feeble voice." Also, among many Indians, a term of respect for any older man. Sometimes, in Red English, Grandfather meant the president of the United States. The healing stone of the Lakota is called the grandfather stone.

Grandmother is also a term of Indians for the deity. Wallace Black Elk calls Grandmother "the female aspect of the Creator personified by knowledge, the Earth, birth, etc." Also, among many Indians, a term of respect for any older woman. Sometimes, in Red English, Grandmother meant Victoria, Queen of England.

GRANGER What the cattleman called a farmer. The National Grange, the origin of the word, was founded in 1867 and was strongest in the upper Mississippi valley. The word *granger* was more common on the northern prairies and Plains than in the Southwest, where *nester* was more usual. In the days of the open range, farmers were often unwelcome intruders. For cowboy words for farmers, see **NESTER**.

COMBINATIONS: *granger agitation, granger laws, granger legislature, granger movement, granger party,* and the like. *Grangerism* meant the philosophy of the farmers' movement.

GRAPE STAKE Especially in California, redwood split rather than sawn and used to support grape vines, or placed vertically for fences.

GRAPEVINE Short for *grapevine telegraph*, the mysterious way news appeared to get around on the frontier. Native equivalents are *moccasin telegraph, mukluk wireless,* and *seagull wireless.*

GRASS The word inspires a couple of fine colloquial expressions: *As long as grass grows and water flows* was a phrase in treaties made with Indians, meaning "forever"— this land will be yours as long as the grass grows and water flows; "forever" came pretty quick. To *get grassed* means to get thrown off a horse. (See also **DIRTY YOUR SHIRT**.) *Grass-bellied* means "bloated, big-bellied"; in *Lin McLean*, Owen Wister used *grass-bellied with spot cash* to mean flush with money.

GRASS FAT A cow fattened on grass alone, without supplements; such a cow is called a *grasser*. (Once, having to eat beef from such a critter was regarded as a sign of poverty. Now it's fashionable for its leanness.)

GRASS FREIGHT Goods freighted across the Plains in wagons pulled by oxen, not mules. It was so called because oxen *(bull teams)* would feed on grass along the way. Mules had to have corn hauled along. Goods hauled by mules (called *corn freight*) got there faster but cost more.

GRASS QUESTION The issue of grazing rights, an inflammatory issue in the days (approximately the 1880s) of the closing of the open range.

GRASS ROOTS The soil just under the surface of the ground, where some optimistic miners predicted *grassroots bonanzas*.

GRASS ROPE Originally a rope made from **BEAR GRASS**, later a rope made from *sisal, manila hemp,* or any fiber except cotton.

Like the use of the double-rigged versus single-rigged saddle, dallying versus tying hard and fast, the grass rope versus the rawhide **REATA** provides never-ending contention among cowboys. It also used to be a sign of where a hand got his cowboying education. Good Texas hands, Stewart Edward White reminds us in *Arizona Nights*, were "addicted to the grass-rope, the double cinch, and the ox-bow stirrup." Buckaroos and Californios went for the **REATA** and single-rig. (See also **LARIAT**.)

GRASS STAGGERS The illness a horse or cow got from eating **LOCOWEED**.

GRASSHOPPER (1) In Western steamboating, to pole a boat over a sandbar or shoal area with spars. Also called *walking a boat* (over a sandbar). (2) Short for *grasshopper plow*, which was adapted for breaking up the tough sod of the Plains.

GRAVEL IN HIS GIZZARD A way to describe a brave man.

GRAVEYARD OF THE PACIFIC The mouth of the Columbia River, because it was and is hazardous to ships. The bar at the mouth is a particularly dangerous obstacle.

GRAVEYARD SHIFT In **TRAIL-DRIVING**, the watch on the herd from midnight to two o'clock in the morning. Also known as the *graveyard stretch*. *Graveyard stew* was a range term for milk toast.

GRAVY RUN In **RODEO**, a fortunate draw of critter, such as a horse that's a good bucker, making it easier to win.

GRAZING PERMIT Permission from a federal agency (primarily the U.S. Forest Service or the **BUREAU OF LAND MANAGEMENT**, but sometimes the National Park Service, U.S. Fish and Wildlife, or even the Department of

Defense) for a stockman to raise cows, sheep, or horses on government lands. Such permits usually last for ten years and are dependent on certain provisions, such as limiting the number of animals and the amount of time in a given area, maintaining fences, and developing water sources. Most sizable ranches in the West have grazing permits, since they have insufficient land to grow hay and graze cattle in the summer. Permits, also known as *grazing allotments*, are theoretically available to anyone, but in practice existing allotments are continued, and the permits are "sold" with a ranch, although the permit is always the property of the U.S. government. Grazing on public land is a bone of contention between the environmental and agriculture communities; a rallying cry for environmentalists was "Cattle free by '93." (See also **ANIMAL UNIT**.)

GREASE JOINT A cowboy term for a restaurant, which he also calls a *beanery*, **FEEDBAG**, *grub house*, **NOSE BAG**, or *eat-and-get-out trough*.

To *grease the skids* was what loggers did to make the logs move more easily down the **SKID ROAD** (the path or road from the forest to the loading point). Now, by figurative extension, what anyone may do to facilitate any deed.

GREASE TRAIL Paths by which the **TLINGIT** traded *hooligan grease* with Interior tribes.

GREASER Now a derogatory Anglo name for any person of Mexican descent. The term dates at least to 1836 in Texas. In historic usage, it appears to have meant not just any Hispanic but a male of the lower classes. Yet there are also references to *greaser girls*. Some uses may indicate that the term wasn't always demeaning. Two army wives, Teresa Vielé and Libby Custer, appear to use it relatively innocently. Vielé wrote of Texas in the 1850s in *Following the Drum*: "One Mexican girl, as she milked her goats, talked and smiled most coquettishly, the while showing her beautiful eyes and teeth to great advantage to a 'greaser,' who evidently appreciated her charms! His slouched sombrero and enormous black moustache, with traces in his dress of the picturesque garb of Spain, produced an exceedingly artistic effect."

The etymology of *greaser* is uncertain. One folk version: Their big carts (*carretas*) had wooden wheels on wooden axles, and they squealed like the devil. A Mexican would walk alongside and constantly grease the axle, thus he was a greaser, a job suited only for a flunky. On the other hand, Lieutenant George Frederick Ruxton, who traveled in Mexico and New Mexico in the 1840s, in *Life in the Far West* traces the term to the Mexican-Spanish *pelado*, meaning "peasant" or "ill-bred person."

Greaser also came to mean "the Mexican-Spanish language." The cowboy was also likely to call Hispanics **BEAN-EATERS**, *chilis, chili-eaters, Mexicanos, never-sweats, oilers, pelados, pepper guts, shucks, spicks, sun-grinners,* and (when the Mexicans were cowboys) **VAQUEROS**. Most of these names have been spoken in the past in a spirit of denigration, a spirit that needs to die. Some derogatory terms of Hispanics for white folks are GABACHO and GRINGO.

COMBINATIONS: *Greaser madhouse* was what cowboys termed Mexican brands, which were elaborate, and were also known as *maps of Mexico*. New Mexico was occasionally called, derisively, *Greaserdom*.

GREASEWOOD A name for various resinous shrubs, especially of the goosefoot family *(Sarcobatus vermiculatus)*, abundant in the arid parts of the West. Also called *toroso*. (See also CREOSOTE BUSH.)

GREASY SACK OUTFIT A small *cow outfit* (cattle ranch). The name got started because little outfits had their cowhands carry their food to roundup in sacks tied behind the cantle. Outings by such riders became known as *greasy sack rides*.

GREAT BASIN The interior West, the central part of the continent between the Rockies and Sierra Nevada; more strictly, those areas of eastern California, Nevada, southeastern Oregon, and western Utah that do not drain to the sea—the rivers end in *sinks* (dry lakes) and marshes.

The Great Basin Desert is one of the four desert types in the United States. It's characterized by cold winters, high elevations, *basin-and-range* topography (alternating north-south mountains and valleys), and annual rainfall of four to ten inches. Sagebrush, shadscale, rabbit brush, and winter fat are the dominant plants; there are no cactus except the smaller species of prickly pears. It is far from the classic idea of desert.

The Great Basin had Indian cultures distinct from those in the surrounding regions. The Indians were primarily what the whites called DIGGERS: SHOSHONES and PAIUTES who maintained a non-horse culture and subsisted primarily on roots and other vegetables that they gathered.

GREAT DIVIDE The boundary of life and death. To *cross the great divide* is to die. *Divide* here is a metaphoric extension of the word for a ridge that separates two watersheds. (For many other Western expressions for dying, see CASH IN YOUR CHIPS.)

GREAT PLAINS The steppes of the American West, the region between the prairies and the Rocky Mountains from the provinces of Canada to Texas. Generally considered to start at about the 100th meridian, they are defined principally by aridity: If there's enough moisture for farming, it isn't the Great Plains. Anglos at first didn't appreciate this area, calling it the Great American Desert, the name given by Major Stephen H. Long after his 1820 exploring expedition to the Rocky Mountains; for decades afterward, Americans thought of the Plains as a barren wasteland, untillable and useless. Promotion by the states, territories, and railroads eventually changed this idea. Despite setbacks because of periodic droughts, irrigation and dry farming have turned the Great American Desert into a huge producer of beef and wheat. Ian Frazier celebrated the area in *Great Plains* (1989).

Less strictly, the term sometimes includes the prairies as far east as the Mississippi River Valley.

GREAT SPIRIT Indian contact English for the chief deity, also called *grandfather* and the *great mystery*, with or without capitals. In this usage, *great* meant "grand" or "important," as in *great white father* for the president of the United States, *great water* for the ocean, and *great medicine* for a big mystery or impressive machine.

Because Great Spirit was a term of Indians speaking a sort of English to white men or of translators rendering Indian languages to white men, it is not to be trusted as reflecting anything genuinely Indian in philosophy or religion. From Indian attempts to convey something of their religion to sympathetic ears came this great spirit, who also goes by the name *Manitou*. *Great spirit* necessarily implied a simple monotheism only to Christians eager to hear that and nothing more.

George Bird Grinnell, for instance, in his seminal study *The Cheyenne Indians*, writes: "The Cheyennes say there is a principal god who lives up above—Heammawihio—and that there is also a god living under the ground—*Ahk tun o' wihio*. Both are beneficent and they possess like powers. Four powerful spirits dwell at the four points of the compass. In smoking, the first smokes are offered to these six powers." Though other Indian religions often identify a creator, they also commonly identify two principal deities, or the creator is not central—or there is no creator figure.

GREAT WHITE FATHER A term of the Red English contact language (primarily of translators) for the leader of the white people, the president of the United States. Despite the implication, Indian people did not generally think of him as playing the role of a father, so the term was to some extent self-deluding.

GREEN CORN DANCE A major summer ceremony of the **CHEROKEE**, **CREEK**, Seminole, and other tribes originating in the South. Held when the corn is ripe, it brings renewal in many forms, and forgiveness. It lasts up to eight days and is a time of renewal of the spirit and making new possessions such as clothes. Also called the *green corn ceremony, feast,* or *festival.*

GREEN RIVER KNIFE The knife of the beaver men, according to Lieutenant George Frederick Ruxton in *Life in the Far West* (1848) and much popular history since. Some people have thought the knife was named after that beaver haven of the **MOUNTAIN MEN**, the Green River, one of the great streams of the West, or that it was manufactured at Green River, Wyoming (half a century before that town existed). Recent research indicates that the knife of the heyday of the Rocky Mountain beaver trade, 1820–1840, was a knife made by John Wilson and that the Green River knife, manufactured at the Green River works of

John Russell on the Green River in Massachusetts, came to the mountains only after the heyday of the **FUR TRADE**. Other manufacturers stamped their blades "Green River" to exploit the popularity of the Russell knife, which was of high quality. The initials GR on a British trade knife of the 1820s actually stood for Georgius Rex, king of England.

COMBINATIONS: *Up to the Green River* became an expression of the 1840s meaning "to the hilt" (in the sense of all the way), because that's where Green River was stamped on the blade. To *go up Green River* was to die.

GREEN UP What the grass does in the spring. Also used as a noun, as in *come greenup*, meaning "come spring."

GREEN-BROKE A way of describing a horse that's only had the kinks taken out of it, that is, has been ridden only once or twice and so is apt to be hard to control. (See also **BREAK A HORSE**.)

GREENER A fellow who doesn't know his way around the West yet; a *green hand*, a *greenhorn*, a *juniper*, a **GUNSEL**, a **PILGRIM**, a **TENDERFOOT**, what was known during the time of the **MOUNTAIN MEN** as a **MANGEUR DE LARD** (**PORK-EATER**), the opposite of an **ALKALI** or **SOURDOUGH**. The word also took the form *greeny*.

Greeners have been the source of a lot of fun among Westerners. To *string a greener* means to play a trick on one, such as putting a snake in his bedroll.

GRINDELIA A range shrub named after the Russian botanist David Hieronymus Grindel. One plant of the *Grindelia* genus, curlycup gumweed, is used in the treatment of swelling caused by poison oak or poison ivy.

GRINGO A derogatory word of Southwestern Hispanics for an Anglo, a stranger, someone who doesn't speak Spanish; the reverse angle of **GREASER**. Various folk etymologies for the word have been offered—short for "greens go home" during the Mexican War (Americans had green uniforms) and a shortening of "Green Grow the Lilacs" (a favorite American song during the same war). However, a form of the word originated in Spain in the late eighteenth century. In Malaga, the word *griego* (Greek) referred to people speaking Spanish with a foreign accent; the word may have been transformed into *gringo*. The etymology remains uncertain.

GRIZZLY BEAR The great American bear, huge, quick, immensely strong, dangerous, and damned hard to kill. Teddy Roosevelt argued that this magnificent creature, and not the bald eagle, should have been the national emblem of America.

Even its scientific name *(Ursus arctos horribilis)* strikes fear; some of its common names are *old* **EPHRAIM**, *Old Caleb*, **SILVERTIP**, *white bear, yellow bear*, and just plain *griz*. The species used to inhabit North America from Alaska to Mexico. The version that still roams Wyoming, Montana, and Idaho can run

Grizzly bear fishing in Alaska.
[Courtesy of Alaska Department of Fish & Game.]

as much as 1,000 pounds; the coastal Canadian and Alaskan grizzlies, called *brown bears* and other names, go half again that big. The fur is often tipped with silver (grizzled), and the back is humped. The critter feeds largely on vegetation and carrion, and also kills for meat.

Indians of the Plains and mountains respected the bear hugely—those with the courage to fight and kill a bear wore its claws in a necklace.

Among the first whites into the country, the MOUNTAIN MEN, the bear quickly became legend. One of the great tales of the West is how trapper Hugh Glass fought a grizzly in 1823, was left for dead by his companions in South Dakota, crawled a couple of hundred miles eastward to the nearest fort, and walked west to the Rocky Mountains to take revenge on the men who abandoned him, but in the end forgave them. John G. Neihardt and Frederick Manfred have written splendid books, respectively *The Song of Hugh Glass* and *Lord Grizzly*, from the Hugh Glass tale.

Nineteenth-century adventurer Lieutenant George Frederick Ruxton expressed in *Ruxton of the Rockies* the admiration of whites and Indians for the bear:

> The grizzly bear is the fiercest of the *ferae naturae* of the mountains. His great strength and wonderful tenacity of life render an encounter with him anything but desirable, and therefore it is a rule with the Indians and white hunters never to attack him unless backed by a strong party. Although, like every other wild animal, he usually flees from man, yet at certain seasons, when maddened by love or hunger, he not infrequently

charges at first sight of a foe, when, unless killed dead, a hug at close quarters is anything but a pleasant embrace, his strong hooked claws stripping the flesh from bones as easily as a cook peels an onion.

Those who go into the backcountry in Wyoming, Idaho, Montana, and Alaska are still plenty wary of grizzlies. Sightings are frequent. And many summers, someone who's insufficiently careful is injured or killed by a griz. Unfortunately, the National Park Service and Forest Service have had difficulty finding a way to let the bears live free and still keep people safe.

Grizzlies are also **CHAPS** made of a griz skin with the hair left on. *Grizzly* was once a Western lager. In mining, a grizzly was a screen in a sluice that caught the larger rocks. The grizzly bear was a dance craze about 1910, preceding the turkey trot. And the *grizzly bear cactus* is a prickly pear *(Opuntia erinacea)*.

GROS VENTRE OF THE PRAIRIE See **ATSINA**.

GROUND APPLE What a logger called rocks in the section he was cutting.

GROUND FIRE In forestry, a fire that burns the combustible material on and in the soil layer, along with small vegetation. A fire in the tops of the trees is called a *crown* fire.

GROUND HOG (1) A logger's name for a **TIE HACK** who camped away from the main camp. (2) What miners called a truck that pushed cars up a grade.

GROUND MONEY Among **RODEO** cowboys, money split equally among all competitors in an event because no one qualified and thus no one won.

GROUND-HITCHED A way of describing a horse standing as though hitched, even though the reins are just dropped to the ground. Many Western horses are trained to stand this way, and many a rider has had to walk back because he thought his horse was so trained. Also called *ground-tied*.

GROWN STUFF Fully grown cattle (as opposed to calves and yearlings).

GRUB An **EARMARK** that consisted of cutting off the whole ear of the critter. Grub, as in food, is not a Westernism but slang dating from mid-seventeenth-century Britain.

COMBINATIONS: *grub cache* (stored food); in forestry, *grub felling* (felling by cutting the roots, which also is called *grubbing out* or *stubbing out*); *grub house* (restaurant); *grubliner, grub rider,* or *grubline rider* (an out-of-work cowboy riding from ranch to ranch looking for free meals; also called a *chuckline rider*); *grub loco* (for a critter to nose at loco weed and try to eat it; critters who grubbed loco were called *grubbers*); *grub pile* (among cowboys, stored food, a meal, and a call to dinner); *grub slinger, grub spoiler,* or *grubworm* (cook; see also **COOKIE**); *grub wages* (pay just enough to eat on); *grub wagon* (**CHUCK WAGON**, a wagon carrying food and cooking utensils for cowboys).

GRUBSTAKE The supplies needed by a prospector to go on a search for valuable minerals. The supplier took the risk of perhaps losing his money and shared in any **DISCOVERY**. He was known as a *grubstaker*, and so was the prospector he staked. The deed of putting up the supplies was called *grubstaking*.

GRULLO (GROO-yoh; GROO-yuh) A horse the slate-blue color of the sandhill crane. This crane, which inhabits Western marshes, is called in Spanish a *grulla*, and the word for the horse of this color is also spelled *grulla* (and *gruya* and *gruyo*). The horse has a dark mane, tail, and socks and often has zebra stripes or a dorsal stripe. When the color is grayish, the horse is also called a *mouse dun*. It has a reputation for hardiness. (See **BUCKSKIN** for other horse colors.)

GRUNION In California, a silversides, a small smelt. During *grunion runs,* the fish come onto the beaches to spawn, and fishermen pick them up by hand.

GRUNT What a logger called pork.

G-STRING A nineteenth-century name for a breechcloth.

GUACAMOLE (gwah-kah-MOH-lee; gwah-kah-MOH-lay) A sauce of mashed avocado and perhaps spices. This Southwestern term, borrowed from Spanish, has now spread throughout the United States.

GUACO (GWAH-koh) The Rocky Mountain bee plant *(Cleome serrulata)*. Its juice is used by **PUEBLO** peoples to make a black pigment for decorating pottery. Borrowed from Spanish.

GUAGE (GWAH-heh) A Southwestern term for a gourd used for drinking, mentioned by both Josiah Gregg and Lieutenant George Frederick Ruxton in the 1840s. Borrowed from Mexican Spanish (which got it from Nahuatl).

GUAPA (GWAH-puh; WAH-puh) In the Southwest, a way of describing a woman who is both beautiful and sexy. The masculine equivalent, which appears occasionally, is *guapo*. Borrowed from Spanish.

GUAYACAN (gwah-yuh-KAHN) A shrub or small tree of West Texas *(Porlieria angustifolia* or *Guiacum angustifolium)*, used to heal various illnesses. Borrowed from Spanish.

GUAYAVE (gwa-YAH-vuh) A bread made by some **PUEBLO** Indians from corn. It looked like a hornet's nest. Borrowed from Spanish.

GUAYULE (wy-OO-lee) A Southwestern shrub *(Parthenium argentatum)* that yields rubber. In the 1970s and 1980s, University of California scientists (Berkeley) experimented with using guayule, which grows wild over much of the Southwest, as a potential commercial source of rubber. The word came to Mexican Spanish from Nahuatl. Another plant of the Southwest producing an inferior rubber is *pingue*.

GUERRILLERO (gayr-ruh-YAIR-oh) A Southwestern term for a guerrilla, probably from the Mexican War for Independence, and by implication a raider or even a **BUSHWHACKER**. Borrowed from Spanish.

GUEST RANCH A euphemism for a **DUDE** ranch, now used everywhere.

GUIA (GEE-uh, with a hard g) A written permit allowing merchandise into Mexico; once used to admit American goods into that country on the Santa Fe Trail. Borrowed from Spanish.

GUISADO (wee-SAH-doh) A Southwestern term for a meat and vegetable stew, a Southwestern version of *pot au feu*. Borrowed from Spanish.

GULCH A ravine; a deep, steep-sided gully, with or without a stream at the bottom. The term was especially applied to areas of gold diggings, as in Alder Gulch (Virginia City, Montana) and Last Chance Gulch (Helena, Montana).

    MINING COMBINATIONS: *gulch claim, gulch diggings, gulch gold, gulch mine* (or *miner* or *mining*), *gulch washings*.

    To *be gulched* was to be trapped in a gulch, as sheep might be. To *gulch* was to mine in a gulch. If you hauled wood down the gulch, you said you *gulched it down*.

GULLET The hole on a saddle just below the horn, often used when carrying the saddle by hand.

GULLYWASHER A very heavy rain, one powerful enough to clean out the gullies or dig new ones. Also known as a *goose drowner*.

GUM PLANT A range shrub of the genus **GRINDELIA**. Used to treat bronchial afflictions and poison ivy.

GUM ROCKER In a sluicing operation, a split, hollowed log below the *sluice box* and *splint basket* that received the gravel. (See also **PLACER**.)

GUMBO A soil (primarily of the Northern Plains) that gets gummy and sticky when wet and can make roads impassable. According to Sinclair Lewis in *Free Air*, it is "mud mixed with tar, fly-paper, fish glue, and well-chewed, chocolate-covered caramels. When cattle get into gumbo, the farmers send for the stump-dynamite and try blasting."

GUN Traditionally in the West, a pistol, not a rifle.

    COMBINATIONS: *Gun battle* and *gunplay*, as far as the evidence shows, are strictly modern terms for a *gunfight* (which first appeared in the very late 1800s and means "a shooting affray"). (*Gunfighter* appeared about the same time, *gunfighting* a generation later.) Evidence does not appear to confirm a distinction sometimes made between *gunfighter* and *gunman*, that the first is a good fellow, the second a **BADMAN**; the first use of

Left: Colt cartridge; right: Remington percussion.
[DRAWING BY E. L. REEDSTROM.]

gunman is in 1903—in a New York newspaper. *Gun hand,* meaning the hand you shoot a pistol with, is from about the same date. *Gun toter* (a man who carries a gun) and *gun-toting* come from the 1920s. *Gunslinger* is another word for *gun fighter.*

One authentically old term is *gunsman,* which was used on the frontier of the Revolutionary period but was probably not restricted to the use of pistols. Other Old West terms for a gunfighter were **SHOOTIST**, *gunny,* and *gun shark.*

The *gunman's sidewalk* is said to have been the middle of the street, for visibility. *Gun-shy* was cowboy talk for cowardly. *Guns on the table* is a way of describing something fair, aboveboard. *Gun wadding* was cowboy talk for white bread. *Gun cap* is another name for a *percussion cap.*

Gunfighter.
[DRAWING BY E. L. REEDSTROM.]

The verb forms to *gun, gun after,* and *gun for* are not especially Western.

Other Western names for a gunfighter are **BUSCADERO**, *leather slapper, pistolero, pronto bug,* **QUICK-DRAW ARTIST**, *short-trigger man,* and *tie-down man.*

GUNNING STICK In logging, a pair of sticks attached to a tree to control the direction of its fall.

GUNNYSACKER What sheepmen sometimes called cowboys who attacked sheep herds with gunnysacks over their heads.

GUNSEL A **GREENER**, greenhorn, **PILGRIM**, **TENDERFOOT**; a newcomer, a fellow who doesn't know what's what in the West yet. Adams says that the word was invented at a California **RODEO** in 1938 by John Bowman to poke fun at a dude.

GUSANO The worm in the bottle of mescal, which reportedly concentrates the alcohol in its body. It's macho to eat it after draining the bottle. From Spanish.

GUSSUK Among Native people in Alaska, a white man, especially a Russian.

GUT HAMMER A logger's term for the triangle the cook dings to call dinner.

GUT TWISTER A horse that bucks well.

GYP **ALKALINE** water, brackish water not fit for drinking. A well of such water is called a *gyp well.* Getting sick from drinking it is called *getting gypped* (but *gypped* also means "drunk"). Bad water is called *gyppy.*

GYPO A small logging contractor; in full, *gypo outfit* or *gypo contractor.* The term was originally uncomplimentary. Also spelled *gyppo.*

H

HACIENDA (ah-see-EN-duh; hah-see-EN-duh) In the Southwest, a big ranch, especially one owned by a Hispanic; the main house on the ranch. Its owner is called a *hacendado*. Hacienda now often refers to secluded Spanish-style houses that may even be in town, the implication being that the home was there before civilization intruded. Borrowed from Spanish.

HACKAMORE A halter with reins (*mecate*) and a noseband (**BOSAL**) instead of a **BIT**, used for breaking horses and riding. It is a cowboy adaptation of the Spanish *jaquima* ("headstall"), which sounds similar.

The **VAQUEROS** (especially in Spanish California) developed the old method of breaking horses with a hackamore, a method sometimes still used. It takes lots of time but is said to yield sweet-mouthed mounts. They use the hackamore alone for some months, then get the horse used to a bit without reins, and eventually graduate to a spade bit. A colt thus trained is called a *hackamore colt*.

Hackamore.
[DRAWING BY E. L. REEDSTROM.]

HAIR A euphemism for **SCALP**, especially among **MOUNTAIN MEN**. Taking scalps was called *lifting* or *raising hair*. "Hang onto your hair" was a favored mountain-man farewell. If the **BLACKFEET** went out *hunting hair*, they were seeking scalps, that is, at war. Sometimes *hair-lifter* was a joking name for an Indian.

HAIR BRAND A brand applied lightly (or through a wet blanket) so that it burns only the hair and not the hide. **RUSTLERS** put on hair brands so they could rebrand the animal after the hair grew back. *Trail brands* were sometimes hair brands. When grown back, such brands are said to be *haired over*.

HAIR IN THE BUTTER Cowboy talk for a delicate spot.

HAIR OF THE BEAR A **MOUNTAIN-MAN** expression for bulldog courage, and a high compliment.

HAIR OFF THE DOG A way of describing a person who's experienced.

HAIR PIPE A long, tubular **BEAD**, tapered at both ends, made of various materials, used especially in the making of chokers and breastplates.

HAIR ROPE A light rope made from hair taken from the tails of horses, too light for throwing but often used as a **MECATE**.

HALF-BREED A person with parents of different races, usually a white father and Native mother. Though many Indians accepted half-breeds generously, some did not and do not. Whites usually treated them as Indians and often said that half-breeds combined the worst elements of both races. The term originated on the Eastern, not Western, frontier. Also called a *half-and-half.* (See also METIS, MESTIZO, RED RIVER METIS.)

In the nineteenth century, these people were usually the children of traders or trappers and Indian women. Often they continued as traders, living among Native people, speaking the language, not quite either red or white. Their descendants are still frequently on reservations, mostly accepted as Indian people, but often the object of prejudice from full-bloods.

COMBINATIONS: *half-breed bit* (a bridle BIT with a small curb and an uncovered roller), *half-breed legging* (a legging covering only the calf, popular among MOUNTAIN MEN and often decorated with BEADS,) *half-breed scrip* (a certificate given to a half-breed in return for his land, entitling him to other lands).

HAME-HEADED What a cowboy sometimes calls a stupid horse, which he also calls a JUGHEAD and an OWLHEAD. (See also CANNER .)

HAND (1) Another term for a cowboy; short for *cowhand.* By modern extension, a worker at anything. It is usually complimentary. As the Pinedale, Wyoming, *Roundup* noted in 1988, "If some(one) calls you a real hand, you know you are doing a good job no matter what it is you are doing." Historically, *top hand* got to be a recognized rank. In Texas in the 1890s, says David Dary in *Cowboy Culture,* "first-class" hands got $35 a month, "top hands" $40 to $45. (See also BUCKAROO, COWBOY, RANAHAN, VAQUERO, WADDY.)

(2) A way of measuring a horse's height, a hand being the span of four fingers. (See also FULL SIXTEEN HANDS HIGH.) Mustangs are generally thirteen hand, other breeds larger.

HAND GAME A hugely popular gambling game of many Native peoples (and not only Western tribes) played in teams. Also called the *stick dice game, stick poker,* and *Indian poker.* The Scots baronet William Drummond Stewart described it in his novel *Edward Warren:*

> [Players were] seated in a circle. . . . A small piece of carved bone, often taken from the body of a fox, was held by the gambler, who joining his closed fists together one above the other, could thus pass it into either, he then separated them and threw his arms wide apart, singing and jerking his body up and down, and again bringing his hands together, and changing or pretending to change the bone, the gamblers choosing only when the hands were held wide apart. If the guess is right, the guesser pulls away his pile with that of the bone holder, previously arranged beside it. If inclined, a new bet is made.

Mormon pioneers heading west with handcarts.
[PAINTING BY WILLIAM HENRY JACKSON; COURTESY OF UTAH HISTORICAL SOCIETY.]

Now the **NAVAJOS** play a similar guessing game called the *shoe game*. Players group themselves into opposing sides, and behind a blanket a piece of **YUCCA** is hidden in one of four shoes. Then the other side must divine which shoe, less by shrewdness than inner knowing. Chants raise a great spirit of enthusiasm, and large amounts of money are wagered.

HANDCART COMPANY A name given to groups of **MORMONS** who emigrated to Utah in the 1850s and '60s, toting their belongings in hand-pulled carts. They sometimes suffered terrible hardships and gained heroic status in Mormon history. Some non-Mormons also crossed the Great Plains with handcarts; for instance, some gold rushers to Denver in 1859. The word also takes the form *handcarter*.

HAND-TREMBLING A traditional method of divination and diagnosis of illness among the Navajos. The man of **MEDICINE** makes offerings, sings songs, and, while singing, divines the nature of illness through the shaking of the hands. He is then able to recommend a particular healing ceremony and someone to perform it. See also **STAR-GAZING, SING**.

HANG To catch trout with the bare hand. The technique is to ease one hand under the fish, gently stroke toward the gills, grab it in the gill region, and throw it onto the bank.

HANG TEN Among surfers, to get all ten toes hanging off the front edge of the surf board, an acrobatic feat.

HANG-AROUND-THE-FORT INDIAN An Indian who spent most of his time around a trading post; by implication, he or she had abandoned some traditional ways and might have descended to drunkenness, prostitution, begging, or the like.

HANGTOWN FRY A dish of the northern California mining camps, eggs scrambled with oysters. Hangtown was an early name for Placerville, California. The concoction resulted, reportedly, from a flush miner's demanding the best and most expensive meal available. Because eggs and oysters were the most expensive foods in camp, the restaurant combined them.

HAPPY HUNTING GROUND An Anglo phrase for the presumed Indian version of heaven; often jocular. The idea of an afterlife is not a major part of most Native world views. By extension, any ideal situation, such as a treasure trove of rare books for a bibliophile.

HAPPY JACK Cowboy talk for a lamp made of a tin can and a candle. (Compare BITCH.)

HARD CHINK Hard money, minted coins, the most common money of the West, where paper currency was distrusted.

HARD GOODS Among the NAVAJOS, a term taken to mean coins, jewelry, and other durable objects of accepted value.

HARD-MOUTHED A way of describing a horse with a mouth unresponsive to the bit.

HARD-ROCK STIFF A miner who works the big rock formations underground. Also called a *hard-rock man, rocker, quartz miner, quartz reefer.*

HARD-WINTERED Run down, in poor circumstances, as though after a hard winter.

HARVEY HOUSE Any of a chain of restaurants built by Fred Harvey to serve meals to customers on the rail lines. They are remembered in the literature for good food and good-looking waitresses. A former railway mail clerk, Harvey opened his first eatery at Topeka, Kansas, on the Atchison, Topeka, and Santa Fe line in 1875. Later his son Ford expanded the line to include hotels and railway dining-car service.

HASHER One of a logger's names for a cook, whom he also calls a BOILER, DOUGH BOXER, *dough puncher, dough roller, dough wrangler, grease ball, grease burner, gut burglar, gut robber, hash burner, hash slinger* (which also means a waitress in a *hashery*), *kitchen mechanic, lizard scorcher, mess boiler, mess moll* (if a woman), *mulligan mixer, pot walloper, sizzler, star chief, stew builder,* and *stomach robber.*

HASSAYAMPER From Hassayampa River in Arizona came a legend and a character. The gold rush on the river gave rise to the myth that whoever drank its waters, especially when drunk, would become a liar. Thus old-time Arizonans, when bragging or yarning, were called Hassayampers.

HASTA LA VISTA (AHS-tuh lah VEES-tuh; HAHS-tuh lah VEES-tuh) So long; see you later. In the Southwest, a common Hispanic-flavored substitute for goodbye. *Hasta luego* has the same meaning. Borrowed from Spanish.

HAT INDIAN An Anglo term for an Indian who favored what was thought of as progress. His stance was suggested by his wearing an uncreased government-issue hat (a **RESERVATION HAT**.) A **BLANKET INDIAN** favored the traditional ways.

HAT RACK A name for a cow that's tick-ridden and a bag of bones, or a wide-horned cow, as in "look for that speckled cow with the hat rack."

HATCHET PIPE Among many Native peoples, an implement that was both smoking pipe and tomahawk. Also called a *pipe tomahawk*, it was made by the English for the Indian trade. This device, also called a *tomahawk pipe*, dated from colonial times and symbolized both war and peace. When you sank the blade into the ground, you were left with the pipe, the symbol of peace—thus the phrase *bury the hatchet* as a synonym for "making peace."

HATCHETMAN A Chinese gangster, especially in San Francisco's Chinatown; also called a *highbinder*.

HAUL IN YOUR HORNS To back off, back down. Another way of saying it is *haul in your neck*.

HAUL OUT To get going (the opposite of *haul up*).

HAUL ROAD In Alaska, a primitive road for freighting goods into a location, or logs out.

HAVASUPAI A Yuman-speaking Indian tribe whose name means the Blue or Green Water people. An agricultural people who also hunt and gather, they live primarily along the Colorado River, especially in the Grand Canyon. Living in isolation, they now make much of their living from tourism.

HAWKEN A muzzle-loading percussion rifle made by St. Louis gunsmiths Jacob or Samuel Hawken from the 1820s until the Civil War. Though most Hawkens probably got to the mountains relatively late in the heyday of the **FUR TRADE** (1820–1840), they are celebrated in the literature as the **MOUNTAIN-MAN** rifle. The Hawken brothers adapted these rifles (known as *Plains* or *mountain rifles*) from the **LONG RIFLE** for horseback travel in the West—they were heavy, sturdy, either full stock or half stock, usually *percussion* rather than flintlock, with an octagonal barrel.

Some other makers of Plains rifles carried by the mountain men were Dickert, Gill, **HENRY**, Leman, Mills, and Tryon.

HAY BURNER (1) A horse, which is also called a *hay baler*. (2) Also, a stove rigged to burn hay.

HAY HAND A man hired for haying season. Also called a *hay slayer, hay waddy, alfalfa desperado,* and other teasing terms.

HAYWIRE Messed-up, crazy; from the cow-country practice of twisting up loose wire before throwing it on the ground. A *haywire outfit* is a poorly run ranch or a logging outfit with poor equipment, which must by implication be kept together with haywire.

HAZE (1) To move cows; for instance, out of a corral. (2) To ride alongside a **BRONC** and keep it from running into obstructions while the bronc buster is trying to break it. (3) In **RODEO**, to ride alongside a steer and keep it going straight so the **BULLDOGGER** has a chance at it. The rider who does the last two jobs is called a *hazer.*

To *haze the talk* is to lead the subject in a certain direction.

HBC See **HUDSON'S BAY COMPANY**.

HEAD FOR THE SETTING SUN What a wanted man did when the law got close.

HEAD-AND-TAIL STRING A string of pack animals *tailed up* (their halter ropes tied to the tail of the animal in front).

HEADDRESS Among Indian peoples, a head garment worn in war, for ceremonies, or on dress-up occasions. The most familiar is the full-length, eagle-feather **WAR BONNET** of the **PLAINS INDIANS**, but there were many others, including the **ROACH** (also associated with Plains Indians), the **TABLITA** of the **PUEBLO** peoples, the wooden slat headdress worn by **APACHES**, etc. They were often made of the skin, horns, feathers, or entire carcasses of animals, and in those materials **MEDICINE** was (and is) believed to reside.

HEADER (1) The **TEAM ROPER** whose job is to throw a rope over the steer's head (the other team member is the *heeler*). **COMBINATIONS**: *head and heel* (a team-roping event in **RODEO**, the steer being roped by the head and heels against time), and *head catch* (a rope throw onto an animal's head or neck rather than its feet).

(2) Especially in California, the reaper that cuts the heads off grain, leaving the straw. The grain is then transferred to a *header barge* (or *bed, box,* or *wagon*).

HEADGATE In ranching, the main gate on an irrigation ditch. (Sometimes spelled as two words.)

HEADRIGHT In the Republic of Texas (1830s and '40s), a land grant to every man over twenty-one. Similar in purpose to the Homestead and other land acts, but it required only surveying, not residency on the land (see also **HOMESTEAD**.) It also means the right of Indians to their tribal lands and oil or mineral royalties.

HEAP A lot, very much, in the Red English contact language (or translator English). Thus *heap hungry, heap scared, heap mad*. A *walk-a-heap* might be an infantryman.

HEAR THE OWL HOOT To kick up your heels with the help of whiskey; to have lots of colorful experiences. (See also **ROOSTERED**.)

HEART-AND-HAND WOMAN A wife gotten from a matrimonial agency, especially from the publication put out by one such agency, *The Heart and Hand*.

HEAT YOUR AXLES In cowboy talk, to run fast.

HEATHEN CHINEE A mocking term for a Chinese person that appears to have come from a line in Bret Harte's poem "Plain Language from Truthful James," and used jokingly through the West.

HEEL (1) To rope cows by the hind feet (which isn't done to horses); also called to *hind foot*. (2) To *heel yourself* or to *be heeled* is to get a gun, to be armed. Owen Wister reports that Doc Holliday warned Ike Clanton, "Heel yourself and stay that way."

A *heeler* is a roper who catches the steer by its hind feet. In **RODEO**, he works as a part of a team with a **HEADER** against time. In a *heeling catch*, the loop is thrown so that the critter runs into the rope, and it is then jerked tight. It was and is commonly used on ranches to catch calves for branding and, according to David Dary in *Cowboy Culture*, was even used by California vaqueros to rope grizzly bears. Other principal roping catches are the *pitch, slip, backhand slip, fore-footing, Hoolihan, and Blocker*. (See also **BLOCKER LOOP**.)

A *heeler* is also an Australian shepherd, a dog that works cows by nipping at their heels. *Heel squatter* is a name for a cowboy who can get comfortable squatting on his heels. A *heel band* is the part of a **SPUR** that goes around the heel of a boot.

A *heel fly* is a tiny fly that lays its eggs just above cows' hoofs on the back side and drives them crazy. *Heel flies* is sometimes a name for Texas rangers, who made themselves a nuisance with persistence. *Heel-fly time* is spring.

HEIFER BRAND A handkerchief on a man's arm at a dance, signifying that he's prepared to take the role of a woman and accept male dancing partners.

HELL AROUND To raise hell, to pursue a wild lifestyle.

HELL ON WHEELS (1) A big, temporary town that kept moving westward with the construction of the Union Pacific Railroad; it was carried on freight cars to the end of the track. These towns consisted of one huge tent and lots of smaller tents and shacks, together housing places for drinking, gambling, dancing, and whoring, and sleeping as many as 3,000 residents. Also called **END TOWNS**, *end-of-line towns, hurrah places*, and *towns with the hair on*.

(2) A name for a horse that's hard to keep from bucking.

Cheyenne, Wyoming, was the terminus of the Union Pacific Railroad for a season.
[COURTESY OF AMERICAN HERITAGE CENTER, UNIVERSITY OF WYOMING.]

HELL'S HALF ACRE (1) A low dive. Also called a *hell.* (2) A rough piece of country. Many places in the West have carried this as a place name, including (temporarily) Yellowstone National Park's Middle Geyser Basin and the lava-flow wilds of Craters of the Moon National Monument in Idaho.

People could be described as *hell bent for breakfast* or *hell for leather* (quick, lickety-split); *hell in his neck* (stubborn); *hell west* or *hell west and crooked* (cockeyed); and *hell with the hide off* (strictly trouble).

HEMP (1) Cowboy talk for a rope. (2) In verb form, to hang (someone). *Hemp fever* was a morbidly jocular term for a hanging; *hemp party* was a group of vigilantes or a lynch mob, depending on your point of view, and a *hemp necktie* was the rope they did the deed with. (See also **STRING PARTY**.)

HEN FRUIT A logger's name for eggs (as *States fruit* meant "eggs from the United States"). *Hen-fruit stir,* among cowboys, meant "pancakes" (which were also called *splatter dabs*). The *hen wrangler* was the chore boy.

HENRY The first practical, repeating, breechloading rifle, .44-caliber, developed by Benjamin Tyler Henry in 1860 and made by the New Haven Arms Company. The Henry was the forerunner of the **WINCHESTER**, for New Haven Arms reorganized as the Winchester Repeating Arms Company.

HEN-SKIN A feather-stuffed comforter.

HERCULES POWDER A miner's explosive charge, primarily nitrate of soda.

HERD COMBINATIONS: *herd boss, herd guard, herd law, herd ground* (a herd's range, or where it was bedded down). *On herd* meant on duty watching the cows; to *keep cows under herd* meant to keep them in a group; to *ride herd on cattle* meant to watch them and keep them under control; to *be the whole herd* was to be a person of importance. A *herder* was either a sheepherder or a foreman of a Chinese railroad gang.

HERD-BROKE A way of describing a bunch of cows used to moving as a herd and so not requiring such hard riding.

HERE'S HOW A frontier toast meaning to your health. Derived from the Red English salutation "How!" A toast among Mormons was *Brigham!*

HEREFORD The most common breed of Western range cattle today, red with white faces. Originally Herefords were imported from Herefordshire, England, in the 1880s to improve the Texas longhorns.

Also a cowman's jocular name for the white shirt he wears when dressed up in a suit.

HERMIT WARBLER The yellow warbler of the West, especially the Sierra Nevada, with a yellow head, black throat, and white breast.

HEYOKA The sacred clown or **CONTRARY** of the **LAKOTA**.

HIAQUA (hih-AHK-wuh, with a short *i* like the one in *city*) Among Indians of the Pacific Northwest, shells and strings of shells used as money. Adapted from **CHINOOK** jargon.

HICKORY A strong, durable cloth (thus *hickory shirt, hickory trousers*).

HIDALGO (hee-DAHL-goh; ee-DAHL-goh) In the Southwest, a Hispanic landowner, usually an aristocrat. Borrowed from Spanish.

HIDATSA A tribe with an agricultural economy that lived along the Missouri River in the Dakotas. Also known as the Minataree, the Gros Ventre of the Missouri, and the River Crows, they had a culture similar to their neighbors the **MANDANS** and spoke a Siouan language. (The Indians known to whites as the **CROWS** were a group that broke off from the Hidatsa.) Reduced by disease and warfare with the **DAKOTAS**, the Hidatsa joined with the Mandans and **ARIKARAS** to form the Fort Berthold Reservation, where descendants of the three tribes live today.

HIDE DROGHER In nineteenth-century California, a vessel that plied the coast transporting cow hides; a man who worked on such a vessel.

HIDE HUNTER (1) In the 1870s and 1880s, a professional buffalo hunter. Also known as a **BUFFALO RUNNER**. These men killed the animals for their hides alone. (2) More broadly, any person who hunted animals for their hides. A *hide buyer* was a person who bought buffalo or cow hides. A *hide camp* was a camp of buffalo hunters.

HIDE RICK A stack of buffalo hides waiting to be sold. In old pictures, these stacks are often the size of a house.

HIDE RUSTLER A man who killed another's cow for its hide; also called a *hide thief*. The skin of a dead cow in early American Texas belonged to the finder. *A hide with a stovepipe hole* was a cowhide with the brand cut out, as a canvas tent may have a hole cut out for a stovepipe.

HIDE-AND-TALLOW FACTORY A pen where cattle were slaughtered for their hides and fat alone.

HIDEOUT A shoulder or hip pocket holster. A *hideout gun* was a small, concealed pistol.

HIGH COMBINATIONS: *high lonesome* (a big drunk), *high lope* (a fast lope on a horse, a gallop), *high roller* or *high poler* (a bucking horse that jumps high), *high-headed* (a way of describing a horse that holds its head too high, blocking the cowboy's view), *hightail it* (to make tracks fast, to move fast, from the way scared cows run with their tails up), *high-line rider* (an outlaw, a man obliged to keep to the high country), *high-grass constable* (a country lawman).

HIGH GRADE A way of describing rich ore. A *high-grader* is both a fellow who works rich ore and a fellow who steals it, which is called *high-grading*.

HIGH HEEL Among cowboys, to walk.

HIGH PLAINS The part of the Great Plains that mediates between the Plains and the mountains. It is characteristically higher, more broken, steeper; marked by RIMROCK, BUTTES, MESAS, and other steep formations; drier even than the Plains and even less suited to farming; treeless and subject to high winds; characterized by ALKALINE soil. The western half of Nebraska is Plains, for instance, and the eastern half of Wyoming High Plains. This country is best suited to growing ANTELOPE, which in Wyoming are doing well.

HIGH RIGGER Among loggers in the Pacific Northwest, the workman who rigs, and often tops and limbs, spar trees. Similar to *high climber*.

HIGH-BALL OUTFIT Among loggers, a top, hard-working outfit.

HIGH-CENTERED Stuck on the center of a TWO-TRACK in your car or truck. The differential hangs in the dirt and edges the rear wheels off the ground.

HIGHFALUTIN Fancy, pretentious.

HIKE In Alaska, the sled-dog command that replaced MUSH—"Let's go."

HILLBILLY COWBOY A hand on an outfit that works far from civilization.

HIP SHOT A shot with a GUN from the hip, so not aimed but only pointed; used strictly at close range.

HIPPODROME STAND See ROMAN RIDING.

HIS LEG IS TIED UP A way of describing someone who's at a disadvantage. The expression comes from the custom of tying up the legs of broncs to shoe them.

HISHI (HEE-shee) Strands of disc-shaped BEADS, usually made from shell or turquoise. In modern times much-praised hishi comes from Santo Domingo Pueblo.

HIT THE TRAIL To get going. (Anyone ever notice how many words and expressions the West has for "Let's get the hell out of here"?)

Hit the breeze has the same meaning, probably with more suggestion of hurry; *hit the flats* and *hit the sod* say the same.

HITCHES In the West, knots are called hitches, and they're *throwed*, not tied. The *diamond* (or *Kit Carson* or *pack hitch*) is favored by packers for its dependability. When throwed right, it makes a diamond shape on top of the load. Other hitches are the *basket hitch* (used for a load likely to slip), *half-diamond, pole hitch, prospector's* (or *crosstree* or *sheepherder's*) *hitch, one-man hitch, S hitch, sling hitch, squaw hitch,* and *W hitch.*

HITCHING RACK A pole to hitch your horse to; also called a *hitch rack,* a *hitch* (or *hitching*) *rail, hitching bar, hitching pole,* and *hitching post.* Not necessarily Western, but most common in the West.

HIVE OFF To leave, hit the trail.

HIVERNANT (EE-vair-naw; HEE-vair-naw) An experienced beaver trapper or trader; a man who has spent winters in the wilderness. In the late eighteenth century, the hivernants of the Northwest Company in Montreal formed an exclusive club, the Beaver Club. French-Canadian term for, literally, a "winterer." Also occurs in the form *hivernanno.* (See also COUREUR DE BOIS, MOUNTAIN MAN, VOYAGEUR.)

HOBBLE Western types of hobbles, some of them nice improvisations, are the CHAIN HOBBLE, *clogs,* CROSS-HOBBLE, *crow* (or *Scotch*) *hobble, double hobble, running W,* and SIDELINE.

HOBBLE YOUR LIP Advice to shut up.

HOBBLED STIRRUPS Stirrups tied beneath the horse. They make it easier for the rider to keep his seat during bucking but are regarded by skilled riders as not only unnecessary but dangerous. In the early part of the twentieth century, women RODEO riders competed in the saddle bronc competition with hobbled stirrups.

HOBBLE-TONGUED A way of describing a stutterer.

HODDENTIN The sacred meal of the APACHES; the pollen of the tule (bulrush).

HOE DIG The dance the cowboy sometimes called a hoedown. He also used the verb to *hoe it down* (Easterners *hoed it off.*) Joseph McCoy, a mover and shaker in Abilene, Kansas, during its cowtown years, described this colorful phenomenon:

A more odd, not to say comical sight, is not often seen than the dancing cow-boy. With the front of his sombrero lifted at an angle of fully forty-five degrees, his huge spurs jingling at every step or notion; his revolvers flapping up and down like a retreating sheep's tail, his eyes lit up with excitement, liquor and lust, he plunges in and "hoes it down" at a terrible rate, in the most approved yet awkward country style; often swing "his partner" clear off of the floor for an entire circle, then "balance all" with an occasional demoniacal yell, near akin to the war whoop of the savage Indian.

HOG DOLLAR In northern California, a silver dollar.

HOG RANCH An establishment pretending to be a ranch but actually supplying whiskey and whores to soldiers. In the late 1870s, the Hayes administration prohibited liquor sales at Western military posts. The soldiers responded by going to the nearest hog ranch for satisfaction.

HOG WALLOW A depression in a **PRAIRIE** or on a plain, of a type frequently found in Texas; the grass found in such depressions (and now elsewhere) is called *hog-wallow mesquite*.

HOGAN The **NAVAJO** word for "lodge." It takes male and female forms, respectively conical and domed. Traditionally, the female form is one octagonal room, made of horizontal cedar logs caulked with mud and with the entrance facing east. The roof is a dome with a smoke hole. These small houses are still common on the reservation.

Navajo hogan, 1889.
[Photograph by F. A. Ames; courtesy of National Archives (106-FAA-54).]

When someone dies in a hogan, a hole is made in a wall to let the *chindi* (spirit) out, and Navajos will not enter that dwelling again; if one is forced to enter, he will purify himself ceremonially later.

HOGBACK (1) A steep, narrow ridge that arcs back to earth. (2) Sometimes also a horse that's the opposite of a swayback.

HOGLEG A **REVOLVER**; originally a Bisley single-action **COLT**; later, any big pistol.

HOG-TIE To tie a cow so that it's helpless, as for **BRANDING**. The two hind legs and one front one are pulled together and tied with half-hitches. A special soft rope about three feet long is used—it's called a *pigging string, hogging string,* or *hogging rope.* Sometimes this job was called *hogging down.*

HOHOKAM The **PIMA** word meaning "the vanished people," those who left the pueblo ruins along the Gila River and may be the ancestors of the modern **PIMA** and **PUEBLO** people. They lived in that region from about 100 B.C. to 1450 A.D., and developed irrigation techniques and techniques of etching metal. In Mormon belief, these people were the **LAMANITES**.

HOJA (OH-hah) In the Southwest, a corn shock used as cigarette paper. Borrowed from Spanish (where it means "leaf").

HOLDUP (1) An armed robbery, especially of a train or stagecoach. (2) A robber, also called a *holdup man.* (3) A rider who stationed himself at a junction to keep a trail herd headed in the right direction.

HOLE A mountain **PARK**; open meadows surrounded by mountains, such as Jackson Hole, Wyoming; Brown's Hole, on the Utah-Colorado-Wyoming border, and Pierre's Hole, Idaho. Some of the most beautiful places in the West are holes, yet the term is falling into disuse.

HOLE CARD An unrevealed weapon or advantage. The term comes from stud **POKER**, where the first card, or two cards, are dealt face down, and said to be *in the hole.*

HOLE UP To take refuge in a shelter or hiding place.

The Hole in the Rock trail where Utah pioneers hauled their wagons down to the Colorado River.
[Courtesy Utah Historical Society]

Hole-in-the-Wall, where Butch Cassidy (George LeRoy Parker) and the Sundance Kid (Harry Longbaugh) made their hideout.
[COURTESY OF AMERICAN HERITAGE CENTER, UNIVERSITY OF WYOMING.]

HOLE-IN-THE-ROCK A remarkable piece of wagon road cut by **MORMON** pioneers down the cliffs on the west side of the Colorado River near the mouth of the Escalante River, in what is still some of the wildest country in the United States. The pioneers cut the road in 1880 so they could establish a colony on the San Juan River in southeastern Utah.

HOLE-IN-THE-WALL A notorious hideout for outlaws in Wyoming's Powder River country. It was used by the Wild Bunch, led by George LeRoy Parker, better known as Butch Cassidy.

HOLIDAY Among loggers, an unwooded area in the timber.

HOLLER CALF-ROPE To throw in the towel; to cry uncle; to say "I've had enough, I quit."

HOMBRE (AHM-bray; OHM-bray) Especially in the Southwest, man. Sometimes it implies a rough fellow, a tough; but often it means a real man, a stand-up guy (see Elmore Leonard's fine novel *Hombre*). Borrowed from Spanish.

 COMBINATIONS: *hombre bueno* (an arbitrator), *hombre del campo* (a skilled outdoorsman), *hombre viejo* (literally "old man"; the *Cereus schotti*, the old man cactus of New Mexico and Arizona), *seldom hombre* (an unusual man; John Russell, the hero of *Hombre*, is both a real hombre and a seldom hombre).

HOME EVENING A contemporary Mormon term for one evening in the week set aside for religious study, planning of family activities, or the like.

HOMESTAKE A stake that's enough to get a person home, usually back to the States.

HOMESTEAD The principal sense of homestead, as a tract of public land given rather than sold to settlers, follows the Homestead Act of 1862. It was the result of a land reform movement to prevent speculators from buying up land in hopes of making a high profit and creating "speculators' deserts" that actual settlers couldn't use, except at daunting prices. It provided that citizens might claim up to 160 acres (or at some times and in some places up to 640 acres) in exchange for living on the land and making certain improvements. By combining the Timber Culture Act of 1873 (another 160 acres, 40 of which needed to be planted in trees), preemption (the right to live on and then file for 160 acres at $1.25 an acre), and the Desert Lands Act of 1877 (640 acres could be obtained for a small fee and the proof of irrigation), 1,120 acres could be obtained altogether. Homesteading thus became a major factor in the settling of the West. The rate of failure was high, however, for much of the land was difficult to farm, too small to irrigate or ranch, or too large to farm conventionally. Not long after the Homestead Act came the term *homesteader* (which usually carried the implication of "farmer") and use of *homestead* as a verb.

Because homesteaders were small operators, big-spread cowboys looked at them with the impatience they felt for other farmers and **NESTERS**, calling them *homesuckers*.

COMBINATIONS: *homestead exemption law* (in most states, a law exempting homesteads from attachment or sale for debt), *homestead act* (or *bill* or *law*), *homestead claim, homestead entry, homestead grant, homestead right, homestead settlement* (or *settler*).

HONDA (HON-doo; HON-duh) An eyelet at the end of a cowboy's **LARIAT** or rope for making a noose. In a lariat, the honda was usually braided in. On a rope it was simply a slip knot. It could also be made of horn or metal. Borrowed from Spanish *hondón* (eyelet).

HONEST INJUN Anglo slang meaning "No kidding?" or "Really?"

HONEST PITCHER Cowboy talk for a horse that starts bucking right when mounted, instead of waiting for a bad time.

HONEY MESQUITE A common mesquite of the Southwest (*Prosopis juliflora*), also known as *algarroba*.

HONKY-TONK A dance hall, saloon, or other place of low amusements. Thus towns at the ends of **CATTLE TRAILS** were called *honky-tonk towns*.

HOOCH Booze, especially illicit, home-distilled booze. The word probably comes from the name of the name of the Hoochinoo people of Admiralty Island, Alaska, who were well known for the product of their illegal stills. (One source claims that it comes from the Tlingit word for "grizzly bear fort.")

HOODEN A cabin for cowboys to sleep in.

HOODLUM WAGON The *bed wagon* on a **TRAIL DRIVE**, often called simply a hoodlum. It carried bedding and other supplies not in the **CHUCK WAGON**. Its driver, usually the fellow who watched the horses at night, was called the *hood*.

HOODOO (1) A fantastical rock formation. "Hoodoo" is an Americanization of *voodoo* and implies a place of weird doings. Yellowstone National Park has a Hoodoo Basin and the Hoodoo Mountains. (2) Another name for a **RUSTLER**. (3) In southwestern Colorado, a hoodoo was a small hut or a cave converted into a hut. (4) A *hoodoo stick* was a divining rod for ore instead of water.

HOOEY The last half-hitch in the process of **HOG-TYING**.

HOOF IT To walk, usually not a preference among cowboys.

HOOFED LOCUST Cowboy talk for sheep, because of their supposed destructiveness to the range.

HOOKY BOBBING Mostly in the Pacific Northwest and Alaska, catching a ride by holding onto the rear bumper of a moving vehicle and being pulled along on your boots.

HOOLIGAN WAGON On a **TRAIL DRIVE**, a wagon carrying fuel and water.

HOOLIHAN (1) A quiet, no-fuss rope throw for catching horses in a crowded corral—one quick whirl, a flat noose, and a head catch. A hoolihan loop is also called a *herd loop*. (2) A method of **BULLDOGGING**. When the rider leaps onto the steer, instead of twisting its head, he uses the force of his weight to knock it down. This technique is prohibited at **RODEOS**. (3) Hoolihaning is raising hell, painting the town red. The origin of the term is unknown. Sometimes spelled *hooley-ann*.

HOOP DANCE Originally a ceremony of Indian peoples of the western Great Lakes, with one or two hoops. Now a showy dance at **POWWOWS**—the dancer uses more than a dozen (sometimes many more) hoops at once, and makes them into the shapes of animals, etc. The hoop is a central metaphor for some Indian cultures, its circularity representing the wholeness and continuity of the people. When Black Elk feared that his people were destroyed, he said, "The hoop is broken."

HOOP-AND-STICK GAME A game played by Indians all over the continent, of such importance that the **CHEYENNES** name a month after it. It's played in many ways. The Cheyennes roll hoops with rawhide mesh in the center and try to make little lances stick in the mesh. When they succeed, they capture the hoop and throw it at their opponents.

HOOPLA An interjection of a stage driver to his horses. Perhaps the sense of "an excited outcry" came from this usage.

HOOSEGOW A jail. Adapted from the Spanish word *juzgado* (courthouse).

HOOSIER Among loggers, a beginning logger. The term started when a lot of inexperienced Indianans were recruited as lumbermen in the Pacific Northwest.

Hoosier belt is cowboy talk for farm country. To *hoosier up* was to conspire against someone or malign him.

HOOTER A hoot owl or an outhouse.

HOOT-OWL HOLLOW Cowboy talk for some very remote dwelling place .

HOPI A **PUEBLO** people of high **MESAS** in northeastern Arizona. They speak a Uto-Aztecan language and traditionally were farmers and hunter-gatherers. They have occupied some of their present villages for seven centuries and more, and one of these, Walpi or Oraibi, may be the oldest continually inhabited set-

Clifton Arizona Jail, built in 1881.
[COURTESY OF NATIONAL ARCHIVES (111-SC-89496).]

tlement in the United States. Their name means "the peaceful people." *Moqui*, an adaptation of the **ZUNI** word for them, has been used since 1790.

The Hopi have a rich religious and ceremonial life centered around dances held at traditional seasons, including the famous **SNAKE DANCE**. Their **KACHINAS**, carved to teach the children the names and characteristics of the various spirits, are widely collected as art objects. The Hopi are also known for their weaving, pottery, baskets, and silversmithing.

They are now engaged in a struggle with their **NAVAJO** neighbors for control of lands and mineral rights. Though the two tribes are historic enemies, for a century, Navajos have lived on land allotted to the Hopi. A U.S. government effort to get each tribe onto its own lands has caused controversy and has resulted in the forced removal of many Navajos from Hopi lands. Rights to coal, and the right of the Peabody company to mine it, are part of the issue.

HORN On a stock saddle, a leather-covered protuberance meant for help with roping (and not for the rider to hang onto). A cowboy dallies his rope around the horn when he's roped a calf, or he ties the near end of his throwing rope there. Some Mexican horns were big and flat (some Americans mockingly called them dinner plates). American cowboys and saddle-makers reshaped the Mexican horn to suit their own inclinations. (See also **DALLY**.)

To *horn people out* was to drive them off; to *horn a prospect* was to sell dubious mining stocks; an over-aggressive person was said to be *horning the brush*; and to *have your horns sawed off* was to have the starch taken out of you.

COMBINATIONS: *horn string* (used to tie a coiled rope to the saddle horn), *horned toad* (one of several lizards, especially of the Southwest), and a *horn-tossing mood* (an angry feeling).

HORN SPOON A tool made from a cow horn and used to assay crushed rock; often called simply a horn. The process was called *horning a prospect* or *assaying with a spoon.*

HORNO (OHR-noh) The outdoor, earthen oven of the Hispanic Southwest. Borrowed from Spanish.

HORNSWOGGLE The wriggling motions of a cow to get rid of a rope; in later usage, to deceive.

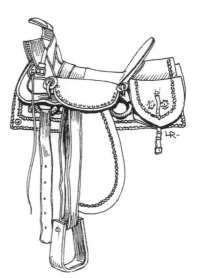

The front projection, the horn, is supposed to be for roping, not holding on to. [DRAWING BY E. L. REEDSTROM.]

HORSE See the specific type of animal, such as **BUCKSKIN, CANNER, COW HORSE, CUTTING HORSE, MUSTANG, SHAVETAIL,** and **STOCK HORSE.**

COMBINATIONS: *horse apple* (a horse turd; sometimes it means the fruit of the *bois d'arc,* which horses eat), *horse breaker* (a professional horse trainer; see also **BREAK A HORSE**), *horsehocky* (horse manure), *horsehair rope* (a braided rope, preferably from mane hair), *horse heaven* (a place in Cayuse country where horses formerly roamed), *to be horsing* (when said of a mare, to be in the breeding period), *horse jewelry* (metal ornaments on tack), *horse man* (a horse breeder), *horse opera* (a Western movie, and by implication, grade B), *horse ranch* (a horse-breeding outfit), *horse restaurant* (in California, a livery stable), *horse sense* (good, practical sense such as a cowpony has), *horse smoke* (among the **OSAGES,** a ceremonial pipe-smoking that promises the gift of a horse), *horse thief's special* (rice pudding), *horse fighter* (a **BRONC BUSTER**), *horse Indian* (a Plains Indian with a nomadic culture), *horseback outfit* (a mounted crew), *horseback work* (a cowboy's work), *horse pestler* or *horse rustler* (a wrangler).

HORSE CLAM The Coho clam, found along the entire American Pacific Coast.

HOSPITAL CATTLE Cows weak from the winter.

HOSTEEN A Navajo title of respect for a man, usually an older man; also used as a common noun to indicate a Navajo man, as in, "Is that hosteen tall?" The spelling *hastin* is now making headway.

The journalist and historian Francis Fugate pointed out that the Navajos of the trading post days called **ARBUCKLE'S** coffee *Hosteen Cohay*, which translates literally to "Mr. Coffee."

HOSTILE An unfriendly Indian, as opposed to an Indian on one's own side or a reservation Indian. An Indian perceived to be on the warpath, inimical to white interests. The term is sometimes used today in reference to a person who wants little to do with Anglos. See also **FRIENDLY**.

Since military units in the West often had Indians as guides or comrades in arms, they spoke of the enemy as hostiles. In official eyes, sometimes it meant any Indian who was off the reservation.

HOT IRON! The brander's holler when his branding iron gets too cool—the iron must be hot or you get a **HAIR BRAND** (one that burns the hair but not the hide). Branding irons right out of the fire were called *hot stuff*.

HOT ROCK A biscuit. *Sinker* and *sourdough bullet* were other names for biscuits. The terms show the inclination of the minds of Westerners to work in homely and colorful metaphors.

HOT ROLL A cowboy's bedroll and belongings, tied up and ready.

HOT SHOT An electrical charge that makes a horse buck; used in **RODEO**.

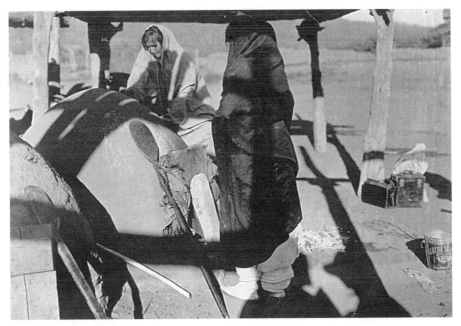

Taos women baking bread in an outside oven, an horno.
[Photograph by H. T. Cory; courtesy of National Archives (77-N-PU-106).]

HOT-FOOT To burn a calf's hoof to keep it from following its mother, a nasty trick played by some rustlers.

HOT-SPOTTING Among firefighters, stopping the spread of a fire where it's moving fast or in an especially dangerous way. This is usually of high priority.

HOTDOGGER Among surfers, one who shows off on his board for the benefit of watchers, especially girls on the beach. Now also used in other "extreme" sports, such as snowboarding.

HOUND EARS AND WHIRLUPS A range dessert, sourdough balls with a sugar-and-spice sauce.

HOUNDS Rowdies of the gold-rush days in San Francisco.

HOW! A salutation perhaps from Red English, usually accompanied by a raised, open right hand to show the absence of a weapon. A **LAKOTA** greeting is *"Hau, Kola?"* meaning roughly, "How are you, friend?"

HOZHONI (hoh-ZHOH-nee) The Navajo ideal of harmony with the world, oneness with all existence. *Hozhoniji* is a blessing rite welcoming a new infant into the family.

HUA! (WAH!) A command of a Santa Fe Trail trader to his draft animals meaning "Get going!" From the Spanish exclamation *Gua!*

HUARACHE (wah-RAH-chay) In the Southwest, an open-toed sandal of Hispanics and Indians. Borrowed from Spanish.

HUCKYDUMMY Cowboy talk for biscuits with raisins.

HUDSON'S BAY COMPANY A mammoth British trading enterprise often known by its initials. Since HBC was first in the West and liked to assert its seniority and preeminence, some Americans called it "Here Before Christ." The American trappers did not like it, as they did not like John Bull generally. See **FUR TRADE**.

HUECO TANKS (WAY-koh) Water holes in rock whose rainwater sometimes provided salvation for travelers, especially in Texas. From Spanish, where *hueco* means "empty." (See also **TANK, TINAJA**.)

HUERO (WAYR-roh) In the Southwest, a man with light or red hair and a fair complexion. Borrowed from Spanish.

HUG RAWHIDE To keep your seat stuck to the saddle during tough times.

HUISACHE (wee-SAH-chay) *Acacia farnesiana*, a shrub of the Mexican-American border country, known for its yellow flowers and sweet smell. Borrowed from Spanish.

HUMAN FRUIT A dead body hanging by a rope from a tree. Such a body was also said to have been *hung up to dry*. (See also **STRING PARTY**.)

HUMBOLDT HOUSE A kind of dugout built by Nevada miners into the side of a mountain. (The Humboldt is a principal Nevada river.)

HUMP RIB A prolongation of the vertebrae that support the hump of the buffalo and the meat on it. The **MOUNTAIN MEN** prized this meat.

HUMP YOURSELF (1) Get a move on. Also *hump your tail*. A *humper* is a thing that goes fast. (2) To *hump up*, for a horse, is to arch its back high, hoofs together.

HUNDRED AND SIXTY A quarter section of land, the primary amount claimable under the Homestead Act of 1862. Often used as a noun, as in the *west hundred and sixty*.

HUNG UP A way of describing a rider who has fallen out of his saddle, has a boot caught in a stirrup, and is in trouble.

HUNT In the **FUR TRADE**, the year's take of pelts. A *hunting boat* was a boat used by fur men. If you're caught where you shouldn't be, you say you're *hunting a horse* or *hunting strays*. A sheepherder who's gone a little loco is said to be *hunting water* and should be **SENT FOR SUPPLIES**.

Hydraulic gold mining town near Virginia City, Montana, 1871.
[Photograph by William Henry Jackson; courtesy of National Archives (57-HS-62).]

HUNT DIRT (1) To fall off a horse. Also *hunt grass.* (For similar terms, see **BITE THE DUST.**) (2) To *hunt leather* is to hold onto the saddle horn.

HUNTER SPIDER A name for a tarantula.

HURDY-GURDY (1) A dance hall or similar establishment with prostitutes, sometimes called a *hurdy* for short. Thus *hurdy-gurdy girls, hurdy-gurdy house, hurdy-gurdy saloon,* etc. The name perhaps came from the musical instrument of the same name, which was similar to a barrel organ. (2) Among miners, a water wheel such as might be used to run a stamp mill.

HURRICANE DECK The saddle of a bucking horse; a nicely descriptive term.

HUSKY Originally, a word for an **ESKIMO,** then for the dogs bred especially to pull **DOGSLEDS.** The *malamute* was also developed as a sled dog.

HYDRAULICKING Among miners, using water under high pressure to wash down gold-bearing earth. The pressure was directed by *hydraulic giants,* or *chiefs,* with nozzles. Thus *hydraulic diggings, hydraulic mining* (and **miner),** *hydraulic hose, hydraulic nozzle, hydraulic washing.*

HYDROPHOBIA SKUNK The spotted skunk *(Spilogale gracilis)* of the Southwest, whose bite is believed to bring madness.

HYMN Cowboy talk for a song he sings to the cows. As shown in Guy Logsdon's book *The Whorehouse Bells Are Ringing and Other Songs Cowboys Sing,* the words were often decidedly unacceptable in church.

I

ICE BRIDGE In Alaska, a bridge of ice over a winter stream, made by dousing the already frozen snow with water. See also **ICE ROAD.**

ICE CELLAR In Alaska, a freezer created outdoors by making a pit in the frozen ground.

ICE FOG In interior urban areas of Alaska, a fog of ice crystals formed when very cold air freezes moisture made by motor vehicle exhaust.

ICE POOL A pool of money created by those who bet on the spring day the ice on the river will break up. See also **BREAKUP.**

ICE ROAD In Alaska in the winter, a road kept solid by watering, creating layers of ice.

ICE THE RUNNERS In Alaska, the practice of putting water on the runners of a **DOGSLED** so that it freezes and thus reduces friction.

ICE WORM In Alaska, originally a tall-tale creature made popular by the works of Robert Service. Later, ice worms proved to be real—worms that live near the surface of glaciers.

ICTAS In the **CHINOOK** trade jargon, merchandise, trade goods.

IGLOO An **ESKIMO** house, from the Eskimo word for *dwelling*. Not ordinarily a dome-shaped structure made of snow blocks. Most often it is a semi-under-ground, rectangular house with walls of wood or whalebone and a sod roof; now they usually have wood stoves, wood floors, and doors made of wood. (This is often known, redundantly, as a *sod igloo*.) Snow houses are temporary, for when people are away from home and need quick shelter.

IN A BIND Among loggers, to be stuck in a hard place. It comes from the notion of having your saw bound by the weight of a log.

INCENSE CEDAR On the Pacific Coast, a large conifer (*Libocedrus decurrens*) also called *red cedar, white cedar,* or *post cedar,* known for its good-smelling sap.

INCOMPLETE ACT OF WORSHIP A euphemism for an act of *coitus interruptus* and, according to Shirley Leckie, the editor of the correspondence of army wife Alice Kirk Grierson, "the most common form of birth control in the nineteenth century."

INDIAN The term *Indian,* because of Columbus's famous mistake in thinking he was contacting the people of the East Indies (not the people of India), is of uncertain acceptance these days. In political circles, speakers show their sophistication by saying Native American.

Indians themselves are more tolerant of the older term. They do joke about it: Some say they're glad Columbus wasn't looking for Turkey; others are glad he wasn't seeking the Virgin Islands. One well-known member of the Gros Ventre tribe likes to say he's an Indin [sic] on the reservation, an Injun in the nearby town, an Indian all over the state, and a Native American in Washington, D.C.

Though some Indian people (perhaps mostly those who are college-educated) prefer the usage Native American, many others (perhaps mostly traditional Indians) do not; most accept either term. Even more would like to be identified more specifically as **CHEROKEES, SHOSHONES, HOPIS,** and so on. *The Lakota Times,* a former newspaper of the **LAKOTAS,** wrote in the early 1990s that it was returning from Native American to Indian or American Indian.

Historically, *Indian* was sometimes short for something associated with Indians, such as *Indian corn* or an Indian language—"She was speaking Indian." It also meant temper, anger, as in "He had his Indian up."

Many Western terms have been formed from the word *Indian* (and contemporary speakers should be alert to the denigration in some of them):

ANIMALS: *Indian cattle* (one name for longhorns), *Indian devil* (the wolverine), *Indian pony* (a mustang, usually disparaged by Anglos).

PLANTS: *Indian breadroot* (**PRAIRIE TURNIP**), *Indian currant* (*Lonicera symphoricarpos,* or St. Peter's Wort), *Indian grass* (*Sorghastrum nutans,* a four- to eight-foot grass of the tallgrass prairie), *Indian medicine* (any of a number of plants used for healing), *Indian paint* (*Lichospermum canescens* or *Sanguinaria canadensis,* also called *puccoon root, red root,* and *blood root,* used by Indians to render a red body paint), *Indian paintbrush* (*Casileja linariaefolia*), *Indian pine* (*Pinus taeda;* the loblolly), *Indian potato* (one of several plants with edible roots), *Indian tobacco* (also called *Indian weed,* any one of a number of native tobacco plants). Many more plants begin with the word *Indian.*

FOOD: *Indian bread* (the fatty meat along the spine of the buffalo, much favored by Indians and **MOUNTAIN MEN,** evidently an equivalent of *fleece;* in colonial times, this meant bread made from meal made from Indian corn), *Indian coffee* (coffee made by whites by a second boiling of the grounds, thought to be good enough for Indians but looked down on by Anglos), *Indian taco* (ground beef, lettuce, tomato, and cheese on fry bread, now a popular food in restaurants on and near reservations).

GOVERNMENT: *Indian annuity* (an annual payment due from the federal government for cessions of lands, minerals, or rights to a group of Indians, often not paid or much reduced by middlemen), *Indian Bureau* (Bureau of Indian Affairs), *Indian service* (a person's service either in the Bureau of Indian Affairs, presumably to help the Indians, or in the U.S. Army against the Indians), *Indian police* (from 1878, a force of Indians organized on reservations to keep order among Indians, prevent traffic in liquor, and control the distribution of annuities, usually under the direction of a white Indian agent), *Indian right* (an Indian's, or group of Indians', entitlement to land), *Indian superintendent* (from 1824, the commissioner of the Bureau of Indian Affairs; previously, any official in charge of Indian trade), *Indian ring* (a group of politicians, contractors, and the like organized to rob Indians of the annuities sent them by the federal government), *Indian scout* (either a scout for the U.S. military who was Indian or an Anglo scout used against Indians).

PEOPLE: *Agency Indian* (an Indian who lived on a reservation, not a "wild" Indian), *church Indian* (a Christian Indian), *good Indian* (in the bad old joke, a dead Indian), *Indian countryman* (a white who chose to live among Indians; also called a *white Indian*), *Indian doctor* (a healer, sometimes Anglo, practicing traditional Indian medicine), *Indian lover* (a derogatory term applied to anybody who argued in favor of, supported, helped, or sympathized with Indians), *praying Indian* (an Indian who had switched to Christian prayers), *treaty Indian* (a member of a tribe "pacified" by a treaty with the United States), *whiskey Indian* (an Indian inclined to drunkenness), *white Indian* (either an Indian of a tribe noted for light skin, such as the **CHEROKEE** or **ZUNI,** or an Anglo living as an Indian).

PLACES: *Indian country, ground, land,* or *territory* (a land area in Indian control, which was a changeable matter; the military still uses this—as recently as the

Persian Gulf War—to mean any land under the control of the enemy); capitalized, *Indian Territory* (a region assigned to Indian nations for their own use in what is now the state of Oklahoma), *Indian frontier, border, boundary,* or *line* (the rough demarcation between white settlement and Indian country).

MISCELLANEOUS: *Indian broke* (a way of describing a horse trained to be mounted from the Indian side—the right side, which was customarily used by Indians), *Indian deading* (an old winter Indian camp where steamboat men found downed and limbed cottonwoods for fuel), *Indian file* (single file, as Indians are presumed to move through woods), *Indian goods* (trade goods—see FUR TRADE), *Indian list* (cowboy talk for a blacklist), *Indian mortar* (a natural depression in rock, used for grinding), *Indian poker* (an Indian version of the popular card game, usually played by women), *Indian post office* (a mound of rocks where Indians left messages), *Indian razor* (a pair of tweezers or a shell used as tweezers by Indians to pluck facial hair), *Indian shoe* (a horseshoe of rawhide dried onto the hoof), *Indian trace* or *road* (a trail worn by regular use by Indians), *Indian trade, Indian trail* (usually the trail made by a village of Indians, complete with scrapings left by lodgepole travois, not just the hoof prints of a war party), *Iron Indian* (the figurehead on a steamboat).

PHRASES: *Indian up* (to sneak up), *play* or *do the sober Indian* (to stay sober while others drink), *play Indian* (to show no emotion in your face, or for children to pretend to be Indians), *seeing Indians* (a disease now unidentifiable but also known as *blue, devils, man-with-the poker,* or *red-monkeys*).

(See also BUREAU OF INDIAN AFFAIRS, DANCE, INDIAN AGENT, INDIAN CHIEF, INDIAN TRADER, INDIAN WHISKEY, RESERVATION, SUN DANCE, TIPI, TRADE BLANKET, WELSH INDIAN, WICKIUP, and the names of principal tribes.)

INDIAN AGENT Since 1824, a functionary of the BUREAU OF INDIAN AFFAIRS, usually a person in charge of the administration of a reservation. Though some such agents were good people, in the nineteenth century many were notorious for stealing the provisions sent to the Indians by the federal government. The office of the agent was called the *Indian agency.* Now such agents, called superintendents, are Indians.

INDIAN CHIEF A leader of a band or tribe of Indians. This term often represents a misunderstanding by whites of leadership among Indians. There were leaders generally and leaders for war (or hunting, traveling, and so on) in particular; whites often mistook war leaders as overall leaders. In any case, leadership among Indians usually was more flexible than among whites, with individuals and families having more autonomy.

INDIAN SCOUT Historically, a Native hired as a scout or hunter for the U.S. Army. The U.S. Indian Scouts were established in 1866, recruiting especially CROWS and PAWNEES, historic enemies of the LAKOTA (Sioux). Scouting was also an important function within the **PLAINS** tribes. Scouts especially looked for the **BUFFALO** herds in advance of the big hunts. See also **SCOUT**.

INDIAN TERRITORY A country roughly equivalent to the present state of Oklahoma, set aside starting in 1834 as a home for eastern Indians thought to be "in the way of progress." The **FIVE CIVILIZED TRIBES** underwent a series of removals from 1830 to 1846. One **CHEROKEE** march to Indian Territory in 1838–1839 became notorious as the Trail of Tears (or Trail Where They Cried). From 1889 Indian Territory was opened to white settlement in a series of *runs* to claim "unused" land. In 1907 both red and white districts were admitted to the union as the state of Oklahoma. Indian Territory was the successor to an earlier term indicating the land of red people, *Indian country.*

INDIAN TRADER An Anglo or Hispanic who traded (or still trades) with Indians, either from a trading post or by going to their camps or villages. In the north, these traders were almost invariably fur traders, but in the Southwest, they traded for other goods.

Often traders came to know the Indians intimately and sympathetically, even marrying into a tribe. In *Entrepreneurs of the Old West,* David Dary writes that Navajo trader John Lorenzo Hubbell "became something of a teacher, helping the Indians understand the ways of the white man. He was also a trusted friend, translating and writing letters for the Indians, settling family quarrels, explaining government policy, and even helping them when they became ill."

INDIAN WHISKEY Alcohol for trade to Indians, weakened by water and strengthened with spices. Acknowledging its origin with early fur traders, trail hand Teddy Blue gives one recipe in *We Pointed Them North:*

> Take one barrel of Missouri River water and 2 galls. of alcohol. Then you add 2 ozs. of strychnine to make them crazy—because strychnine is the greatest stimulant in the world—and 3 plugs of tobacco to make them sick—because an Indian wouldn't figure it was whiskey unless it made him sick—5 bars of soap to give it a bead, and half of a pound of red pepper and then you put in some sagebrush and boil it until it's brown. Strain this into a barrel and you've got your Indian whiskey, that one bottle calls for a buffalo robe, and when an Indian got drunk it was two robes.

See also **FIREWATER**.

INDIO (IN-dee-oh) In the Southwest, Indian; becoming more and more common. Borrowed from Spanish.

INDIVIDUAL What a cowboy of the old days called the horse he owned personally, as opposed to those in the **STRING** provided by the ranch.

INIT A dialectical pronunciation by Indian people of "isn't it"; an example of a pronunciation in effect creating a new word.

INNER CIRCLE Among cowboys *riding circle* (riding a wide loop to gather cows for **ROUNDUP**), a short circle, usually assigned to a hand with a horse of uncertain quality.

INSIDE In Alaska, the interior, which is sparsely populated. *Outside* means out of Alaska. The *Inside Passage* is the waterway between the mainland and the offshore islands from Puget Sound to Glacier Bay; it is plied by ferries, the principal form of transportation in the area.

INSTREAM FLOW The prescribed level of water flow released from a dam. It's the subject of much quarreling between fishermen and wildlife advocates versus ranchers and other water users, who often have needs hard to reconcile.

INUIT A term for all the various **ESKIMO** people, from the coasts of Siberia to Greenland. This word was put forward because the word *Eskimo* was believed (mistakenly) to mean "raw-flesh-eaters" and thus to have pejorative overtones. Some Eskimo peoples in Alaska do not care for the name *Inuit*, which is politically preferred, and *Eskimo* still has wider acceptance in Alaska, while *Inuit* is preferred in other areas.

INVITATION STICK Among some Plains Indians, a small piece of wood carved and marked. When placed by a lodge, it could declare a desire to court a woman, or invite people to a feast or ceremony.

IPANEE In Alaska, a term from the **INUPIAQ** language meaning "traditional," "old-time," the way Native people did things before white folks came. Sometimes also means "old-timer."

IRISH BABY BUGGY What miners and loggers called a wheelbarrow.

IRISH LORD In Alaska, a sculpin, a fish all mouth, head, spines, and sharp points, and not good to eat.

IRON Short for a **BRANDING IRON** or slang for a revolver or a horseshoe. COMBI-NATIONS: *Iron burner* was a logger's term for a blacksmith. An *iron man* (or *iron tender*) is a hand who heats branding irons in a fire and produces a hot one at a brander's need. To *iron out a horse* (or iron the humps out) is to take the kinks out of it. To *iron the calf crop* is to **BRAND** it. But to *be ironed by a blacksmith* was to have your legs shackled.

IRON CHINK In Alaska, a machine for cleaning salmon, eliminating all but firm flesh in a whisker of time. The name has a nasty edge, referring with a pejorative nickname to the Chinese who formerly did this work by hand.

IRON HORSE A railroad. An Anglo term in half-jocular imitation of Red English.

IRRIGATION (1) Slang for alcoholic refreshment. (See also **FIREWATER**.) (2) Irrigation of crop lands is a particularly Western practice in the United States and has yielded the combinations *irrigation bill* (law), *irrigation district* (a group of ranchers on one irrigation system), *irrigation ditch, irrigation pump, irrigation rancher*, and so on.

ISSUE DAY See BEEF ISSUE.

IT IS ALL WHEAT A Utah expression meaning "it's on the square, it's OK."

IVORIES Cowboy talk for poker chips or a gambler's term for dice.

IVORY WORK Among ESKIMOS, the process of carving ivory, as well as the completed artifact. Walrus tusks, the teeth of sperm whales, and elephant tusks are used.

J

JACAL (hah-KAHL) In the Southwest, a mud hut, a shack of the Indians or Hispanics. It was generally made of upright poles covered with mud but might be anything from an APACHE brush shelter to a rude ADOBE house. A temporary shelter was a *jacalito*. Borrowed from Spanish. American spellings ranged from *hackel* to *hayrick*.

JACK MORMON Historically, a gentile sympathetic to Mormons. Now, an apostate Mormon.

JACK RABBIT A hare with long ears and long legs. There are several varieties in the West, including those called *blacktailed, white-tailed,* and *white-sided. Jack* is sometimes short for jack rabbit. See also JACKALOPE.

JACK SALMON In Alaska, a coho or king salmon, male, that returns to its spawning ground a year early (out of eagerness, one hopes).

JACKALOPE In Wyoming and Utah, a combination of a jackrabbit's body with an antelope's horn, created not by nature but a taxidermist. A popular souvenir.

JACKASS MAIL Mail hauled by teams of mules (sometimes called *jack trains*), especially on the stage lines of John Butterfield or James Birch. Mules were sometimes thought tougher than horses for the work of pulling stage coaches. It also meant slow, inefficient mail lines, which were apparently operated by jackasses—thus *jackass express.*

JACKET To cover a *bum* (motherless) *lamb* with the skin of a dead lamb. Going by smell, the mother of the dead lamb will then nurse the bum lamb.

JACKLEG An incompetent fellow, a shyster, as in "a jackleg lawyer."

JACKPOT (1) Originally, in POKER, a pot, especially one for a hand in which jacks or better are required to open. Later, money won on a single go at a slot machine, or any bonanza. (2) In RODEO, an event with no added money, with the winners getting only the entry fees. (3) Among COWBOYS, a confounding or messed-up situation, and among LOGGERS, a confusing pile of logs.

JAM THE BREEZE In cowboy talk, to go full steam ahead.

JAMOKA Coffee. (See also **ARBUCKLE'S**.)

JAVALINA (ha-vuh-LEE-nuh, with first *a* as in *corral;* hah-vah-LEE-nuh) The peccary *(Tayassu tacaju)* of the Southwest. A piglike animal, it lacks the tail and tusks of the Old World pigs. Also spelled *havalina*. Borrowed from Spanish.

JAW CRACKER As late as the 1930s, the traveling dentist. David Lavender described him in *One Man's West:*

> He went from town to town, dragging his shop in a trailer behind his automobile. Whenever he appeared, all the possessors of toothaches, recurrent headaches, neuralgia, rheumatism, lumbago, or morning stiffness flocked to see him. He jerked out their teeth . . . and sent them home to let their wounded gums shrink into shape. On his return trip he measured his now-hungry clients for plates, made the dentures in his home office, and shipped them out C.O.D.

JAWBONE (1) Talk, especially mere talk. It is also used as a verb—to *jawbone*. (2) To *buy something on jawbone* was to get it on credit. Some cowmen have lived on jawbone.

JAYHAWKER (1) A man who fought in the war in Kansas during the mid- and late 1850s over slavery. (2) A Kansas guerrilla during the Civil War, on the Union side. These jayhawkers fought *secesh* (pronounced suh-SESH, from *secessionist;* Confederate) sympathizers, especially Missourians. (3) A man who harassed the Texas cattlemen after the Civil War, claiming that the herds they brought north were infested with **TEXAS FEVER**. Texas trail driver Jim Daugherty wrote, "The jayhawkers were said to be soldiers mustered out of the Yankee army. They were nothing more than a bunch of cattle rustlers and were not interested about fever ticks coming into their country but used this just as a pretense to kill the men with the herds and steal the cattle or stampede the herds." (4) Any lawless person.

JEHU A sobriquet for a driver of a stagecoach.

JERGA (HAIR-guh) A twilled wool made by Mexicans and used for carpets, saddle blankets, and clothing. It was checked black and white. From Spanish.

JERKLINE A single line used as a rein by a **MULESKINNER** or other driver of teams. The line was attached to the bit of only the lead animal. One pull signaled a move to the left, two pulls right. Sometimes it was called a *jerkrein.*

COMBINATIONS: *jerkline express* (horse or mule team), *jerkline outfit* or *string* (a team of mules or horses so driven), *jerkline driver, jerkline freighter,* and the idiom *to have a hold on the jerkline* (to have a situation under control).

JERKY Meat preserved by drying. The **PLAINS INDIANS** jerked meat (primarily buffalo, but any red meat) by cutting it into strips and drying it on a rack of twigs head-high above a low fire for several days. The **CALIFORNIOS** added the trick of dipping it in brine first. Many similar methods have been employed. The crux of the process is not smoking but drying.

Jerky is the basis of PEMMICAN, the other principal Western form of pre-served meat. Since jerky will last for months without spoiling, it was commonly carried by Indians on journeys, by MOUNTAIN MEN, and by other Western travelers. Though what's sold in stores as jerky today isn't jerky, the real McCoy is still made in Western homes.

It's also called *jerk* and, by Southwestern Hispanics, *tasajo*. To *jerk meat* means "to make jerky." The word is an Americanized version of the Spanish term for jerked meat, *charqui*.

In Montana in the latter nineteenth century, *jerky* also meant a wagon without springs.

JESSE A scolding, a thrashing, a person's comeuppance. A fellow in a fight was sometimes encouraged, "Give him jesse!"

JIGGER To run a horse until it's overheated.

JIGGLE The usual, relaxed gait of a cow horse; to ride at that pace.

JIMSON WEED The common name for DATURA (*Datura meteloides*), which is hallu-cinogenic. Also called *stinkweed*.

JINE Contemporary Indian slang for the word INDIAN, perhaps with self-deprecating humor. A dialectical pronunciation that has become a new word—Indian, Injun, Jine. See the dicussion of Red English in this book's Introduction.

JINETE (hee-NAY-tay) A skilled rider; a BRONC BUSTER; a cavalryman. Borrowed from Spanish.

JINGLE To ROUND UP the horse herd, which is kept in a *jingle pasture* (fenced and near the cowboys' quarters) for quick access in the morning. Sometimes the wrangler is called the *jingler*.

JINGLE BOB (1) An EARMARK known for its ugliness. The ear was cut from tip to base, and the bottom half flapped loosely. It was the earmark of the herds of John Chisum, one of the protagonists of the Lincoln County War, and his crew was known as the *jingle bob outfit*. (2) The jingling danglers on a cowboy's SPURS.

JINGLE YOUR SPURS! Get a move on!

JINGLER In Alaska, a string of bells or bottlecaps, whose jingling is thought to make SLED DOGS move along. Historically, a WRANGLER.

JOB To joke, to poke fun, to play a practical joke.

JOB'S COMFORTER Cowboy talk for a boil.

JOCKEY BOX A box carried on a wagon for miscellaneous small articles. On a CHUCK WAGON, it held horseshoeing equipment, hobbles, and maybe extra ropes.

JOCLA (jo-KLAH) An earring, usually a rope of turquoise **HISHI** (disc-shaped beads) that dangles from the ear. An adaptation from **NAVAJO**.

JOHN CHINAMAN Cowboy talk for rice. Also, a Chinese person; formed as *John Donkey* and *John Q. Public* were. *John Henry* (a signature), *John Law* (any law officer), and *Johnny Navajo* are similar Western formations. According to Smith, so was *John Daisy,* an army word for a mule. Modern Navajo call the most traditional of their tribe *John.*

JOJOBA (hoh-HOH-buh) A Southwestern plant *(Simmondsia chinensis)*, also called *coffee-berry.* Valued by Indians as food, the seeds are now prized for the oil they yield, similar to the oil of the sperm whale.

JONES' PLACE A line camp; a privy; a saloon.

JORNADA (hor-NAH-dah) A day's journey; more often, a waterless stretch of country that can be crossed in a single day, or at least a single drive, and usually hard on men, horses, and cows. Some jornadas made a hell of a day. The Jornada del Muerto (Dead Man's Journey) on the Rio Grande in New Mexico (between San Cristobol and Rincon) was about eighty miles long. The Jornada del Diablo (Devil's Journey) was a piece of rough, dry land in **PAPAGO** country.

JOSEPHITE A **MORMON** follower of Joseph Smith III (founder of the Reorganized LDS Church) rather than Brigham Young. After the death of Joseph Smith, the Mormon Church chose Brigham Young as its head, and he led them to the Great Salt Lake. The Josephites split off and formed the Reorganized Church of Jesus Christ of the **LATTER DAY SAINTS**. Centered in Independence, Missouri, it is generally abbreviated RLDS Church to differentiate it from the LDS church.

JOSHUA TREE A strange tree *(Yucca brevifolia)* with twisting branches. Sometimes called the *yucca palm,* it is ubiquitous near Joshua Tree National Monument in California.

JOSS HOUSE A temple. From the Chinese-English word *joss* (meaning "god"). *Joss sticks* are incense.

JUDGE LYNCH Lynch law personified; a death sentence without appeal or delay.

JUG HANDLE A slit in the loose hide under a cow's throat, forming a loop resembling a jug handle. It's a sign of ownership like an **EARMARK** or a **BRAND**. (See also **DEWLAP, VARRUGA, WATTLE**.)

JUGHEAD A dumb horse, one that doesn't understand what its rider wants. A mule or a man may also be called a jughead. (For other words for flawed horses, see **CANNER**.)

JUICE A cowboy's verb meaning to "milk a cow."

JUMP To come upon a man or animal suddenly, catching it unawares, as in to *jump a deer out of brush.*

COMBINATIONS: To *jump a* (mining) *claim* means to take it illegally, by force or skullduggery. One who does so is a *claim-jumper*, and *claim jumping* is sometimes referred to euphemistically as *relocating a claim*. When the dealer cuts the cards for his own advantage, he's said to *jump the cut*. To *jump over the broomstick* is to get married. To *jump up a lot of dust* means to come or go (on a horse) in a hurry.

JUNIPER (1) Americans everywhere use this word to mean various conifers; in the West, its berries are used occasionally for seasonings. (The Western juniper tree is generally called a cedar, incorrectly.) (2) The distinctly Western meaning of juniper is a **GREENER** or **PILGRIM**, an innocent in the West. Thus the narrator in Owen Wister's "A Pilgrim at Gila" rattles up to a water stop in a stage and says, "I jumped out to see the man Mr. Mowry warned me was not an inexperienced juniper."

JUSTINS Cowboy boots. The name comes from a fine bootmaker, Joseph Justin, whose firm started on the Red River and is now in Fort Worth, Texas. Some people say Justin is to boots what Stetson is to hats and Levis is to jeans.

K

KABLUNA In the Yukon, historically, a white person. From the **ESKIMO** language, in which it literally means "person with big eyebrows."

KACHINA (kuh-CHEE-nuh) In the religion of the **HOPIS** and other **PUEBLO** peoples, a spirit, a demi-god; a masked dancer or a doll representing these spirits. Youths of both sexes are initiated into kachina societies, become dancers, and participate in the principal ceremonies.

The kachinas, said to winter in the San Francisco Peaks southwest of the Hopi Reservation near Flagstaff, Arizona, appear at various times of the year and in many shapes.

Kachina dolls, made of wood, feathers, and so on and brightly painted, were originally made for Hopi children but now are often made for Anglo collectors. Some Hopi carvers have made names for themselves as kachina artists.

Spelled variously (especially *katcina*), it comes from the **TEWA** language.

KALADOR In Alaska, an entry chamber of a house for taking off heavy boots, parkas, and other gear.

KAMIK In British Columbia and the Yukon, a hide boot, like a **MUKLUK**.

KANGAROO RAT A rodent of the Western deserts (genus *Dipodomys*). It survives without drinking any water, relying on the water that is a by-product of food metabolism and by water-conserving behavior (limiting activity to night, temporary periods of hibernation, concentrated urine, etc.).

KANSAS WESTERN COMBINATIONS: *Kansas banana* (the pawpaw), *Kansas brick* (a square of prairie sod used to build a **SODDY,** also called a *Nebraska brick*), *Kansas sheep dip* (both a treatment for scab in sheep and, later, one of the many cowboy terms for whiskey—for others, see **FIREWATER**), *Kansas stable* (a stable built of forked posts and poles and covered with sod and brush), *Kansas zephyr* (a devil of a wind), *Kansas City fish* (salt pork; sowbelly).

KAUK Walrus skin, with blubber, boiled and eaten. Used in Alaska and the Yukon.

KAYAK In Alaska, a completely enclosed boat of hide or canvas stretched over a light frame, made for one, two, or three paddlers, who each use a double paddle. When there are multiple paddlers, often called a *baidarka.* Now a recreational craft used all over the United States.

KAZUNOKO In Alaska, herring roe in the ovarian membrane, a delicacy to the Japanese, gaining popularity on the American West Coast.

Kachina.
[DRAWING BY E. L. REEDSTROM.]

KEELBOAT During the quarter century up to 1820, the keelboat was the primary mode of transportation for people and supplies from Pittsburgh west. Named for its heavy timber keel (the vessel was also called simply a *keel*). Fifty to eighty feet long, pointed at both ends, and light of draft, the keelboat was distinguished from the *broadhorn* or *flatboat* in that it could go upstream. The keelboat moved slowly by a combination of sailing, poling, **BUSHWHACKING** (pulling on bushes and trees), and towing by a rope that might be 1,000 feet long *(cordelling).* It could haul up to 300 barrels of freight. A trip to, say, St. Louis, was easy down the Ohio River and hellish going up the Mississippi.

The keelboat required a tough, strong bunch of men to crew it, usually six to ten per boat, plus a captain who acted as steersman. One such fellow, Mike Fink, became legendary as the half-horse, half-alligator king of the boatmen.

KEEP THE DOUBLE DOORS SWINGING To kick up your heels with the help of whiskey. The double doors were the saloon doors. (See ROOSTERED.)

KENO (KEE-noh) (1) A lottery-like gambling game, first known as lotto and first popular along the Mississippi River and now in Nevada. The globe that held the numbered balls was called a *keno goose*. (2) A cowboy exclamation meaning "everything's OK."

KENTUCKY BREAKFAST Stewart Edward White explains this one eloquently in *Arizona Nights:* "He staked me to a Kentucky breakfast. What's a Kentucky breakfast? Why, a Kentucky breakfast is a three-pound steak, a bottle of whisky and a setter dog. What's the dog for? Why, to eat the steak of course." Another source describes a Kentucky breakfast as three cocktails and a chaw of tobacco.

KERES A PUEBLO people of the upper Rio Grande in New Mexico. Keresan-speaking, they occupy the pueblos Acoma, Laguna, Cochiti, San Felipe, Santa Ana, Santa Domingo, and Zia.

KETOH (GAY-toh; KAY-toh) The leather bracelets mounted with silver once worn by NAVAJO men. They derived from the wrist guards once used to protect the bare arm of an archer from the twang of the bowstring. Navajos added heavy silver elements, often sandcast silver or rows of buttons, to the basic leather band. Also spelled *getoh*.

KETTLE For a horse to buck or pitch.

KICK OUT Among surfers, to exit a wave instead of riding it all the way. By extension, to leave any situation or place.

KICK THE FROST OUT To loosen up a horse; to get the kinks out. To *kick the lid off* is for a horse to start bucking like the devil. (For other similar expressions, see BUCK.)

KICK UP YOUR HEELS To indulge in vigorous play or celebration, often when drinking. (See also ROOSTERED.)

KICKED INTO A FUNERAL PROCESSION A way of describing a person done in by a kicking horse. (See also CASH IN YOUR CHIPS.)

KICKER Especially in Alaska, a small boat propelled by an outboard motor (also called a *kicker boat*), or its motor.

KIDNEY PLASTER A mocking cowboy name for an Eastern (hornless) saddle; also called a *kidney pad* and a POSTAGE STAMP.

KILLED POTTERY Among various Indians, especially in the Southwest, ceremonial pottery that has been broken, usually in conjunction with burial practices, or the ritual cleansing or ritual leaving of a house.

KILLPECKER GUARD A cowboy name for the night watch on a cow herd.

KINKY When said of cows or women, whimsical, unpredictable.

KINNIKINNICK (KIN-i-kuh-NIK) Among many Indians, smoking tobacco. It is a mixture of tobacco and other ingredients, especially dried sumac leaves and the inner bark of the willow or dogwood. Different tribes made different mixtures, sometimes with red osier and bearberry.

Since kinnikinnick was part of many religious gestures, from private prayers to public ceremonies, tobacco was an immensely important item in the Indian trade. Kinnikinnick was and is used for smoking or as a gift to the earth.

A **CREE** word adopted by other Indians, the **MOUNTAIN MEN**, and subsequently other Westerners, it is spelled variously. (See also **MEDICINE PIPE**.)

KIOWA A Uto-Aztecan tribe of Indians associated principally with the Southern Plains.

In the sixteenth century the Kiowa lived around the Three Forks of the Missouri River in Montana. They gradually moved through eastern Wyoming and Colorado to the Arkansas River. There they became horse Indians with a buffalo-hunting culture much like the cultures of the **NORTHERN PLAINS** and with a religion featuring the **SUN DANCE**. They allied themselves closely with the **COMANCHES** and fought with other Indians to the north and the whites to the south, primarily in Texas where, in 1864, they fought at the battle of Adobe Walls.

Following decimation by disease and defeat in the Red River War (1874–75), the Kiowa accepted reservation life peacefully. They were briefly involved in the **GHOST DANCE** in 1890, and like their Comanche friends, many adopted peyotism and the **NATIVE AMERICAN CHURCH**. The reservation period ended with allotment of private land to individual Kiowas.

KIP PILE A buffalo hunter's term for a pile of buffalo calf skins.

KIT FOX A small fox of the **GREAT PLAINS** (*Vulpes velox*) important in Indian mythology.

KITCHEN STRING The horses that haul the **CHUCK WAGON**, which was occasionally called the *kitchen wagon*. Packers called the mule that carries the kitchen gear the *kitchen mule*. The flank strap on a saddle is called a *kitchen strap*.

KIUATAN (KYOO-uh-tan) In the **CHINOOK** trade jargon, an Indian pony.

KIVA An underground ceremonial chamber of **PUEBLO** Indians. For men only, kivas are circular, are entered by a ladder, and are used for social, political, and religious gatherings. Similar to an **ESTUFA**.

KLONDIKE An 1897–1899 gold-rush area of the Yukon; named for the principal stream that drains the region; from the Han words *tron-diuck*, meaning "hammered water." *Klondikers* were inhabitants of the region, especially prospectors; soon they were given the name **SOURDOUGHS**. Newspapers and steamer lines inflated the news of the strike notably; because the climate was severe, sickness, injury, and death ran high among rushers.

KLOOTCHMAN In the Pacific Northwest, an Indian woman. Often derogatory. From **CHINOOK** jargon, it also appears in the short form *klooch.*

KNEE To cut a tendon in the lower leg of a wild cow or mustang. After this surgery, the critter no longer can run but can be driven slowly and can bear young.

KNIGHT OF THE RIBBONS A driver of a stagecoach; the ribbons are the reins.

KNOBHEAD A mule.

KNOTHEAD A brainless cowboy or a brainless horse; a **JUGHEAD**.

KNOW HOW TO DIE STANDING UP To be brave.

KNOW WHAT WAY THE STICK FLOATS To know which end is up, know your ass from a hole in the ground, know poor bull from fat cow—to know what's what. The stick here is the beaver trapper's **FLOAT STICK** which attaches to the trap. Some specialists think an experienced man would know that the stick floats downstream in the creek; others think he could read information from the exact way the stick was floating.

KOSHARE (koh-SHAR-ay) The deities associated with fertility and weather control among the Keresan **PUEBLO** peoples, and a secret society whose members play the clowns of their ceremonies. Easily recognized by their black-and-white stripes and horns, they dance between the more sober ceremonial dances and bring everyone delight.

KOSSUTH HAT One of the two styles of hats worn by the U.S. soldiers in the post-Civil War period. Named for the Hungarian patriot Lajos Kossuth, it was high-crowned, made of felt, and embroidered with insignia indicating the corps. Also called a *Jeff Davis hat.* (See also **CUSTER HAT**.)

KOW-KOW In Alaska, grub. From maritime jargon. Along with the other great pre-occupations of Westerners such as sex, booze, and death, food got a lot of names: *chicken fixings* (fancy food), *chow, chuck, chuckaway, doings, fixings, fluff duffs* (fancy food again), *muckamuck, soft grub* (fancy food once more).

KOWTOW To show deference in the Chinese manner, by touching the head to the ground. It has come to mean any obsequious behavior.

KULICH In Alaska, a fruit-nut bread introduced by the Russians for Easter, now widely popular.

KUNZITE A pear-shaped, pink and lilac stone found in San Diego County of California; also called a *California iris.*

KYACK A *pannier* (carrying sack for a packsaddle).

L

LACE YOUR TREE UP To saddle your horse. A fanciful expression from the notion of tying your saddle tree on.

LADIES OF THE LINE See **GIRL OF THE LINE**.

LADINO (luh-DEE-noh) A Southwestern word for a **COW** or other brute that's wily and ready to hurt you, especially a longhorn of the Texas brush country. A *ladina* is the lead mare in a herd of wild horses. In Spanish, it first indicated a person who was learned and educated in Latin, then a cunning person.

LADRON (luh-DROHN) A Southwestern term for a thief. Borrowed from Spanish.

LADY-BROKE A description of a horse so well trained that even a lady can ride it. The other end of the spectrum is *cavvy-broke*. (See also **BREAK A HORSE**.)

LAGUNA (luh-GOO-nuh) A pueblo and a tribe of Keresan people located about forty-five miles west of Albuquerque, New Mexico, near a pond, where a Spanish mission was established in 1699. (See also **PUEBLO**.)

LAGUNA (luh-GOO-nuh) A pond, lagoon or lake. Laguna Madre separates Padre Island from the mainland of Texas on the Gulf of Mexico. This word has become common in proper names of towns and real-estate developments in the Southwest, where if they have water, they brag about it. From Spanish; literally means "lagoon."

LAIR ROPE Among **PACKERS**, the rope you tie the pack cover on with. Called *lair* for short. To do that tying was called to *lair up*.

LAKOTA What the Indians known to Anglos as the Teton Sioux call themselves. One of three dialectical versions of the word—the others are **DAKOTA** and *Nakota*—it may now be replacing Dakota as the most accepted form among these Indians.

LALLYGAG To dawdle, to lie around. The word first appeared in print in Idaho and Iowa in the late 1860s, but its derivation is unknown. Also spelled *lollygag*.

LAMANITE (LAY-muhn-iyt) Among **MORMONS**, American Indians, whom they speak of as their Lamanite brothers. According to the *Book of Mormon*, they are descendants of the prophet Lehi, who with his wife, sons and daughters, and their families migrated to the new world in 600 **B.C.** Sons Laman and Lemuel were sullen, disobedient, and rebellious, and because of this they and their descendants were marked with dark skin. (See also **NEPHITE**.)

LAMBER (LAM-mer) On a sheep ranch, a man who takes care of ewes and the new lambs during lambing season—spring. Cowboys call sheepherders *lamb lickers*, an unflattering name derived from the way ewes lick their lambs.

LAME PEN A pasture for a ranch's crippled animals. Also called a *sick* or *hospital pen*.

211

The land grants given to railroad companies were one of the major factors in the settlement of the West. Arizona Territory, 1898.
[COURTESY OF NATIONAL ARCHIVES (92-F-79B).]

LAMPERS Inflammation of the mouth of a horse.

LAND The first cut in a hayfield—you mow out a land near a fence and then backcut, explains South Dakota writer and rancher Linda Hasselstrom. Some ranchers cut their lands far enough from the fences to leave cover for birds and other wildlife.

LAND GRAB The seizing of big tracts of public land, usually not honestly; one of the great Western crimes. The perpetrator is called a *land grabber* or *land pirate*. If he only steals one or two claims, he's called a *land jumper*. If he hooks and crooks something the size of a New England state, he's called a capitalist. For instance, the Maxwell Land Grant Company grabbed 1.5 million acres more than it was entitled to in New Mexico. A land grab was also called a *land gobble*; a group intent on stealing from the public in this way was a *grant ring*.

LAND GRANT An issuance of public land, usually to a school or a railroad, by the federal government. Twenty-four colleges and universities in Western states have been supported by the Land Grant Act of 1862, also known as the Morrill Act. These are called *land-grant colleges* or *universities*. The government also granted lands to railroads as incentives for development and settlement, thus making the remaining government lands appreciate in value. From 1862 forward, these grants inspired a great rush of railroad-building in the West, thus the term *land-grant railroad*. At first, the new railroads received ten sections of public land per mile of rail laid, later as much as forty sections. This policy resulted in huge land holdings by the railroads and considerable public resentment.

Homesteaders needed to file claims with the U.S. government. Attorneys and surveyors in front of their office in Okuluhoma Territory, 1894.
[COURTESY OF NATIONAL ARCHIVES.]

Land in the West always meant land available for settlement, land up for grabs. Many terms rose up around it. SOME COMBINATIONS: *land agent* (an official in charge of a government land office or a private land broker), *land boomer* (a promoter of the value of certain lands), *land booster* (a speculator in land), *land certificate* or *scrip* (an entitlement to a tract of land, often given by the government to soldiers), *land claim* (a legal claim to a tract of land, sometimes based on a Spanish or Mexican grant), *land commissioner* (the head of the General Land Office in Washington, D.C.), *land leaguer* (a member of a group of Kansas settlers on former Osage land who fought railroad claims to their land), *land opening* (an occasion of making public land available to be bought and settled), *land rush* (a hurry by the public to settle former public lands), *land scalper* (a man who staked a claim on good farmland on the Plains in hopes of selling it to a settler), *land state* (a state with land available for homesteading). (See also HOMESTEAD, EMPRESARIO, SCHOOL SECTION.)

LAND IN A SHALLOW GRAVE   To die or be killed, then buried unceremoniously, usually in the middle of nowhere, as on an emigrant crossing or a TRAIL DRIVE. (See also MAKE WOLF MEAT.)

LANING (LAYN-ing) For a rider to mistakenly approach a cow on the opposite side of the cow from another cowboy, creating a lane between the two riders. The correct procedure is to have the two cowboys on the same side of the cow.

LAP AND TAP What RODEO cowboys call a simultaneous start for the roper and the calf or steer, with no head start for the critter.

LAP BOARD A way to poison coyotes, wolves, and other predators. A board was drilled and larded with strychnine. When the critters lapped it up, they died. A relic of a Western hostility to wildlife that is not entirely past.

LAP ROBE A BUFFALO robe, hair on, used for warmth on carriage rides and the like. Though it could be of wool or other cloth or fur, in the nineteenth-century West it was usually buffalo.

LAPBALL In Alaska, a bat-and-ball game similar to baseball played by Natives.

LARIAT (LAYR-ree-uht; sometimes layr-ree-ET) Though this word first meant a picket rope, it came to mean the cowboy's *catch rope*, whether made of rawhide, horsehair, or fiber (HEMP, MAGUEY, even linen or cotton). The fiber ones are generally thirty to forty feet long; the ones braided from rawhide have the advantage of stretching when a critter hits the end, lessening the jolt to rider and mount. An Anglo adaption of the Spanish *la reata*, meaning "rope" (see REATA). At the end is a HONDA, which is like the loop that makes a slip knot work. Hands also call the rope a LASSO (or one of the variants of that word), a *lass rope*, or a STRING.

According to old hand Jo Mora in *Trail Dust and Saddle Leather*, the linen and cotton varieties are for show ropers more than stock work. *Reata* (a term favored in California) refers to the rawhide variety: making and handling reatas requires considerable craft. A rawhide lariat is also called a *skin string* to distinguish it from one of hair or fiber. Originally lariats were always rawhide. Says Mora:

> The laws of supply and demand and the matter of economy was what first gave the grass rope its popularity. Modern trends for more speed and less time for leisure, a laziness and more often an inability to braid their own gear, and the grass rope came into the picture to stay. A waddie could stump into the trading post or general merchandise emporium and buy him 30 or 40 feet of whale line from a big coil at a small cost and whenever he wanted it . . . I've used both rawhide and grass, and I've seen them used for many years, and to classify them broadly, I would say that the grass rope was the efficient tool of the rough and ready, "let's go" operator: and the reata that of the finished artist, a sensitive, elastic, vibrant gear.

The word *lariat* is sometimes used as verb meaning to *catch with a rope* or to *stake a horse out*.

LARIAT PIN A stake for picketing horses. Also called a *picket pin, stake pin,* or *hitch pin*.

LARIGO The saddle's CINCH ring; what the cinch is fixed to. Also called a *larigo ring*.

LARK BUNTING The state bird of Colorado (*Calamospiza melanocarys*). Also called the *prairie bobolink.*

LARKSPUR A blue-flowered plant (*Delphinium nelsoni*) of the buttercup family with sharply different associations for Anglo and Indian. Cattlemen call it poison because it can kill cows by stopping the heart and the breathing. The roots are especially dangerous, and the leaves when wet are thought virulent. To **NAVAJOS**, though, larkspur is a sacred plant and is used in ceremonies.

LARRUP To beat, to whip. Larruping as an adjective means "great," "big," "extra-big," or the like.

LASHER The fellow who used the whip on the **JERKLINE** team. As assistant to the driver, he also applied the brake.

LASSO (LASS-soh, with the *a* as in *corral;* sometimes lass-SOO) One name for the cowboy's *catch rope,* used primarily on the West Coast. It dates from the vaqueros of New Spain and, like a **LARIAT**, is mainly for roping cows and horses. Originally, like the first lariats, it was of braided rawhide. Also called a *lass rope.* Lasso also occurs as a verb, meaning to rope something. From Spanish or Portuguese, depending on which authority you believe.

LAST ROUNDUP One of the Westerner's many expressions for death. It even appears as a past participle—*last rounduped.* (See also **CASH IN YOUR CHIPS** for many expressions for death and dying.)

LATERAL In an irrigation system, the ditch leading out of the main ditch.

LATIGO The wide leather strap that goes through the **CINCH** ring and secures a stock saddle on a horse.

LATILLA (luh-TEE-yuh) Historically, slender wands of wood used in the roof system of a Mexican-American or **PUEBLO** building. These wands are laid across **VIGAS** in what is called *viga and latilla* construction, and are attractively exposed inside to form the ceiling. This style is now widespread through the Southwestern architecture of all peoples.

LATTER-DAY SAINT A **MORMON**; a member of the Church of Jesus Christ of the Latter-Day Saints. This church calls itself "latter-day" because it regards itself as a reestablishment of the church of Jesus Christ on Earth, which in its view was lost after the deaths of Christ's apostles.

The church was founded in 1830 by Joseph Smith in New York. Smith attempted to establish a spiritual center for the church in Missouri, then in Illinois. Under Brigham Young, the church did establish itself in what is now Utah.

The word also appears in adjective form, as in the phrase *Latter-Day Saint newspaper,* and occasionally in the form *Latter-Day Saintship.* Mormons often refer to themselves by the abbreviation LDS.

LAY (1) Among miners, a lease given by the owner of a claim to a person who proposes to work the claim for a percentage on shares rather than for wages. This lessee is called a *layman* or a *leaser*. (2) Another word for a cow outfit. Also called a *layout*. A ranch run with **BADMEN** for hands is called a *tough lay*. (3) A cowboy's bed.

COMBINATIONS: A *layout* can be a person's clothing and other personal gear or a group of people, as in "I never liked him nor anybody in his layout." A *lay-up* or *layover* was a halt in a trail drive or wagon journey. Expressions using lay: *lay a rail fence* (for a bucking horse to pitch in a zigzag direction, also called *fence-cornering*), *lay the dust* (to kick up your heels when inspired by whiskey or to settle the dust a little in a rainstorm), *lay the trip* (for a roper to *bust* a steer), to *lay them down* (a poker term meaning to quit; to die).

LAZY BOARD On a **CONESTOGA** wagon, a plank on the left side where the driver rode, instead of having a seat inside.

LEAD (LEED) In mining, a vein or lode; by extension, any good discovery, including someone to talk to.

LEAD CHUCKER (LED CHUCK-er) One of the names a cowboy called his **SIX-SHOOTER**. He also called it a *lead pusher*, and when he got shot he *got leaded*, *got lead poisoning*, or *leaned against a bullet going past*. To *swap lead* or *swing lead* is to have a gun fight.

LEAD STEER (LEED STEER) On a **TRAIL DRIVE**, the steer that gets out front and stays there. Cowmen saw stamina and even character in lead steers and gave them names and even affection. Some herds were led by a *lead ox*, which would be available for the task repeatedly, since steers were sold for meat each year. A *lead ox* was also an ox used for **NECKING**. That meant he would be tied neck to neck with a **SULLING** longhorn in the Texas brush country and would bring the brute by force to the main gathering place of the cow hunt or roundup.

The *lead mule*, in a pair of draft mules, was the left one, or in a team larger than a pair, the one at the head left. The *lead wagon*, in a freighting outfit, was the wagon the horses were hitched to, drawing several wagons. The *lead drive men* were the widest circle riders at roundup. These riders made the widest loop because they knew the ins and outs of the country.

LEAD THE PELICAN For a soldier to be under arrest. This is a comical expression of the 7th Cavalry, according to Libby Custer. The outfit had caught a pelican and was bringing it along at the rear of a column. Says Mrs. Custer, "as an officer or soldier is condemned to this ignominious position also, when deprived of his place with his company, it became the custom to describe arrest as 'leading the pelican.'"

LEAGUE In the Southwest, this term may describe either linear distance or an area—either miles or acres. The distance meant is probably about two and one-half miles, the area about 4,400 acres. An adaptation from Spanish, it was often used to denote the size of Spanish and Mexican land grants.

LEAKY MOUTH A way of describing someone who talks too much.

LEATHERROOT A plant (*Psoralea macrostachya*) valued by the Pomos and other California Indians for the toughness of its fiber.

LEATHERSTOCKING A name for a frontiersman who wore hide leggings, which is how James Fenimore Cooper's Natty Bumppo got his nickname. The term originated on the Eastern frontier (the first reference is from Cooper) and was carried West.

LEAVE HIM IN THE SOUP To leave someone in hot water, to abandon a companion in a fix. An expression first recorded in a Dakota Territory newspaper.

LEAVING CHEYENNE A sentimental cowboy expression for going away. It comes from the old cowboy song "Goodbye, Old Paint, I'm leaving Cheyenne." This song was traditionally the last tune at cowboy dances:

> My foot's in the stirrup,
> My pony can't stand;
> Goodbye, old paint,
> I'm a-leavin' Cheyenne.

Larry McMurtry put the sentiment perfectly in his novel of the same title: "The Cheyenne of this book is that part of the cowboy's day circle which is earliest and best: his blood's country and his heart's pastureland."

LECHUGUILLA (leh-choo-GEE-yuh) A name for several **AGAVES** of the Southwest, indicator plants of the Chihuahuan Desert. From Spanish. A pocket gopher that feeds on it is called the *lechuguilla pocket gopher*.

LEDGE In mining, the lode, the *lead*, the ore deposit. The *ledge rock* is the true bedrock.

LEDGER ART Pencil or crayon drawings on lined pages from a ledger, often obtained from a trader, usually during the reservation period of the late nineteenth century. **PLAINS INDIANS** during this time, oppressed by reservation conditions, sometimes even imprisoned, found a new outlet for their artistic urges in these Anglo materials, art coming out in every circumstance. The drawings were made by men, in the pictographic style.

LEFT SIDE The correct side for mounting a horse; also called the *near side*. The other side is the *off side* or *Indian side*, which is the wrong side (among Anglos) to get on a horse. To Anglos, *Indian way* often seemed to mean "wrong way."

LEG BAIL Flight from the law while on bail. To *take leg bail* was to skip, to *take a powder*. Likewise, to *show leg* was to run away.

LEG KNIFE A knife worn by a long hunter or **MOUNTAIN MAN** in a thong or strap that circled his legging like a garter. He also wore a *belt knife* and a *patch knife*.

LEGGING (1) Giving a cowboy a whipping with a pair of leggings or **CHAPS**. (2) An irksome way of separating sheep of different brands that have gotten mixed. You grab each one by the leg and pull it out of the bunch.

LEGGINGS The leg coverings of an **INDIAN, LONG HUNTER, MOUNTAIN MAN, COWBOY**, or other mounted Westerner. They cover the legs but not the groin region, where a breechcloth sufficed among Indians and among some whites; normally whites wore trousers under leggings. They are usually made of deerskin, which is lighter and easier to sew than elk, moose, and buffalo and more durable than antelope.

Among cowboys, they're generally called **SHOTGUN CHAPS**, but leggings were native sons of the movable frontier long before cowmen ever got to Texas and heard of *chaparral* or *chaparejos*, the words that are the source of **CHAPS**. The Kentucky long hunters of the 1770s adopted them from Indians or previous American frontiersmen and bequeathed them to the mountain men. Later they were a common style of chaps on the Northern Plains.

An abbreviated form is the *knee legging* (or *breed legging*), which ties below the knee of an Indian woman or white man and hangs to the top of the moccasin or boot. It was and is often made of blanket. East of the Mississippi, leggings worn by Indians were sometimes called *Indian boots*.

The word is sometimes spelled *leggin* without an apostrophe.

LEGITIMATE SMOKE In fire-fighting, smoke from any acceptable fire, as in permitted burning or machinery—useful to know when a spotter calls in a sighting of smoke.

LEMON SUGAR An instant form of lemonade at Southwestern military bases in the 1870s and 1880s, according to Smith, and so a precursor of modern convenience foods. It came in cans containing powdered sugar and a vial of lemon extract.

LEMONADE SUMAC One of several sumacs (*Rhus tribolata, R. integrifolia, Schmaltzia trilobata,* or *S. emoryi*) whose fruits are used to make a drink. They range over the entire West and are sometimes used as ornamental shrubs. Also called *lemita* and *lemonade berry*.

LENT One of the cowboy's words for a green hand. In adjective form, he was *lenty*. (See also **ARBUCKLE'S**.)

LEOPARD SWEAT **MORMON** homemade whiskey, also known as *Valley Tan*. (See also **FIREWATER**.)

LEPERO (LEH-puh-roh) A low, scurrilous Mexican. Borrowed from Spanish.

LEPPY An orphaned calf. (Also called a **DOGIE** and a **BUM CALF**.)

LEVEL In mining, a drift, a horizontal passage.

LEVER BIT A severe form of the **CURB BIT**, known to be able to inflict pain.

LEVI'S The most famous brand of blue jeans in the West, to jeans what Stetson is to hats, Winchester to rifles, Colt to pistols. Levi Strauss, a tailor, originally made this bibless overall in California in 1850, using canvas and riveting the seams and pockets with copper to make them withstand the hard uses Westerners give them.

LICK Short for SALT LICK.

LIFT HAIR An expression of MOUNTAIN MEN meaning to take scalps and by implication to kill people, though not all those scalped necessarily died.

LIGHT To get down off your horse. A cordial but succinct expression of Western hospitality to a rider was sometimes, "Light and set."

LIGHT A SHOCK To leave quickly. Since corn was the universal food and was carried in its shuck, there were shucks around the campfires. Leaving one fire to go to another, a fellow found himself abruptly in blackness and his eyes not adjusted. So he lit a shuck, which would burn only briefly, and took off.

LIGHT BURN In forest management, limited burning to reduce available fuels, which might otherwise make fires difficult to suppress and likely to cause great damage. A good deal of the controversy about Yellowstone National Park's management of its forest prior to the fires of 1988 centers on its decision to do no light burning.

LIGHT IN THE TIMBER Said of a horse light-boned in the cannon bones (lower legs). (See also STOCK HORSE.)

LIGHT RIDER A rider who sits in the saddle lightly and so does not need to redo the cinch often and doesn't chafe the horse's back with the saddle.

LIGHTNING Low-grade whiskey. Though the earliest reference to lightning in Mathews is 1858 in San Francisco, various authorities refer to *Taos lightning*, meaning the rough brew distilled in Taos at least a couple of decades earlier. It occurs not only in that expression but in *Jersey lightning, white lightning, flash lightning*, and *lightning whiskey*. (For many Western expressions for booze, see FIRE-WATER.)

LIKE A STEER, I CAN TRY A wry expression indicating the futility of effort. Steers are impotent because they're *cut* (castrated).

LIKE GETTING MONEY FROM HOME Easy and pleasant. Though this phrase sounds collegiate, notes linguist J. L. Dillard, it is Western—Owen Wister recorded it in 1893. British aristocrats sojourning in the West often depended on remittances from home, and so were known as REMITTANCE MEN.

LINCOLN SHINGLE Hard bread issued as rations by the army during the period of the Indian wars, according to Watts. The bread was about three inches square and evidently very hard—other nicknames were *sheet-iron cracker* and *teeth-duller*. Watts says it was also called a *Lincoln pie* and a *McClellan pie*. The use of Lincoln's and McClellan's names (George B. McClellan was a Union general in the Civil War) indicates that the bread was probably a leftover from the Civil War. Some soldiers must have thought it was a literal leftover.

LINE (1) The boundary of a range, marked or unmarked. Sometimes it divided cattle outfits, sometimes cattle from sheep. In some uses, it meant the boundary between Anglo country and Indian, thought of as the extreme limit of civilization. (2) Historically, the area of a mining camp where the prostitutes worked. Also called the *row*. (See also **GIRL OF THE LINE, LINE RIDER, SHEEP DEADLINE, SHERIFF'S DEADLINE**.) (3) A cowboy name for a **ROPE**. (4) A logger's name for a cable. (5) An expression for the route **SEISMIC CREWS** follow.

As a verb, it means to fetter a horse by tying its forefoot to its hind foot, instead of **HOBBLING** the forefeet together in the usual way. Also called *side-hobbling* and *side-lining*.

LINE BREEDING Breeding cows to make sure of descent from a particular family, particularly on the female side.

LINE RIDER A cowboy who rode the line and lived in a *line camp*. In the days before fences, big cow outfits used such riders to keep their own cows mostly on their side of the line (on their own range) and other outfits' cows on the other side. They also pulled cows out of bogs, doctored them, nursed them, and kept predators away. With the coming of fences, they became known as *fence riders*, and their job was keeping the fences in good repair.

Now a line rider, also called a *line cowboy*, is simply a man who lives in a line camp in a remote part of the ranch and does cowboying. Though cow outfits are not as gargantuan as they sometimes were in the early days, they're often split up into pieces, some of which may be far from the main house.

The *line shack*, *line cabin*, or *line house* is a small cabin where a cowboy lives when he's riding the line. The *line boss* is the rider in charge of a group of cowboys.

LINE YOUR FLUE In cowboy talk, to eat.

LINEBACK A horse or cow with a stripe down its back. On **TEXAS LONGHORNS**, this stripe is called a *lobo stripe*. (See also **BUCKSKIN**.)

LINK STRAP In the U.S. cavalry during the period of the Plains Indian wars, a thong hooked to a horse's ring bit and the throatlatch buckle. When a trooper dismounted to fight, he linked the strap to the ring bit of another horse; one man could hold eight horses, freeing his comrades to fight.

LITERARY A gathering devoted to literary culture, as in "We went to literary last night." Such meetings were held on the **CENTRAL PLAINS** from the turn of the twentieth century forward, almost always on winter evenings. People read literature aloud, recited poems, debated, read their own works, and the like. Like the Chautauquas elsewhere, such gatherings provided some intellectual stimulation and social life.

LITTLE GIANT In **PLACER** mining, a metal pipe that carries water and has a nozzle (called a *giant*) at the end. As the water pressure goes up, the nozzle gets smaller, controlling the flow.

LITTLE MARY What the cowboys on a **TRAIL DRIVE** called the fellow who drove the *blatting cart,* the vehicle for the newborn calves that couldn't keep up.

LITTLE OLD This combination of adjective, observed Owen Wister, was "applied to anything, e. g., a little old pony; hard to say what it means." Two qualities it does not indicate are small and aged. Usually it's just a fond diminutive.

LITTLE RED WAGON Among miners, a portable toilet.

LIVE DICTIONARY What some cowboys called a schoolmarm or any other woman with lots of words. In Elmer Kelton's splendid novel *The Good Old Boys,* the protagonist, Hewey, a good old cowboy, meets a live dictionary, falls for her, and in the end has to decide whether to settle down with her or keep on rolling.

LIVE OAK The common name of a variety of evergreen oaks that grow in California and the desert Southwest. The acorns and foliage are an important wildlife food source, and the hard wood was used by California pioneers to make splitting mauls and carriage parts. (See also **ENCINA**.)

LIVESTOCK See **STOCK**.

LIVING FIREBREAK In forestry, a strip of ground where flame-resistant vegetation is growing.

LIZARD-TAILED OUTLAW Katie Lee, author of *All My Rivers Are Gone,* says this is a bad guy who is "mean and scrawny and quick to get away."

LLANO (YAH-noh) A Southwestern expression for a steppe, a dry, treeless plain. A fabled one is the Llano Estacado (or Staked Plain) of New Mexico and Texas, inhabited by Indians called *llaneros.* Borrowed from Spanish.

LO A generic name for **INDIANS** that has now fallen into disuse. Example: "The Lo's are passing . . . rapidly from the face of the earth." Its source is Alexander Pope's *An Essay on Man:*

> Lo, the poor Indian! Whose untutor'd mind
> Sees God in clouds, or hears him in the wind.

That first phrase became a mocking watchword among Americans, who for more than a century after it was written (1733) suffered from what they regarded as the maraudings of the Native people. (For Anglo terms for Indians, see also **SIWASH**.)

A similar word, also lightly derisive was *Mr. John,* as in "I saw by the tracks that Mr. John had passed this way."

LOAD Among cowboys, a verb meaning to tell tall tales. Also, a cowboy used to describe a fellow with long hair as having a *load of hay on his skull.* Some cowboys still might.

LOADED FOR BEAR To be fully armed, prepared for trouble, with a full head of steam up, spoiling for a fight. It can be a metaphoric preparedness: An angry wife waiting for a late husband is often described as *loaded for bear*. The phrase comes from the choice of loads a hunter has with his rifle, the option of more or less powder or lead. A heavy load would be chosen for a creature as big as a bear.

LOADING CHUTE A fenced ramp for getting livestock onto trains in the days of the great **TRAIL DRIVES**, usually from pens called *loading corrals*. Now loading chutes are primarily for getting critters onto trucks.

LOADING JACK In logging, a rig for loading logs and trucks. It was originally a framework for hoisting logs out of the water; now it is a rig with a loading block for picking up logs from the ground. The logger who is doing the work is a *loader*.

LOBBY In a logging camp, where the workers wash up and wait for mealtime.

LOBO The gray wolf or timber wolf (*Canus lupus lycoon*); see **WOLF**.

LOBO STRIPE The stripe down the back of a **LINEBACK**, especially a **TEXAS LONGHORN**. It may be white, yellow, or brown.

LOCATE (1) To file a mining claim. Usually the phrase is to *locate a claim*. The person who does the locating is called a *locator*. The act of filing a mineral claim was called *location*. The area of the claim, which is traditionally marked with *location stakes*, was also called a *location*. Staking a claim was also called *pegging* it. (2) To file a claim to land, especially land with springs and streams, under the homestead law. (3) To put cows onto a new range.

LOCK HORNS To fight. As applied to human beings, it often means to come into confrontation, to argue, to engage in a struggle of wills. From the behavior of buffalo bulls, elk bulls, and other horned male beasts—they fight with their horns to achieve dominance and the right to mate with the cows.

LOCKED SPURS Spurs with the **ROWELS** tied so they won't move. Then, if the rider puts them into the cinch (called *screwing them down*), the spurs will hold him fast; if the rowels rolled, the spurs wouldn't hold him. In **RODEO**, it's illegal to lock your spurs.

LOCO As an adjective (the most common use), it means crazy and can be applied to man or beast. As a noun, it can mean **LOCOWEED**, the poisoning that comes on livestock that eat locoweed, or a preparation made from locoweed that affects human beings. The poisoning is sometimes called *locoism*. Also occurs as a verb—to *get locoed* (to get crazy) or to *let something loco you* (make you crazy). Borrowed from Spanish.

LOCOWEED Any of a number of plants widespread in the mountain West, especially of the genera *Astragalus* and *Oxytropis*, that make livestock act crazy when they eat them. It can be fatal to cattle.

LODE CLAIM In mining, a legal claim to gold or other mineral in a lode or vein. A **PLACER** claim entitles the miner to wash gold from sand or gravel.

LODGE A Native dwelling or meeting place, especially the **TIPI** of the **PLAINS INDIANS**; also, the family that lived in the tipi. Sometimes the word refers to permanent dwelling places of agricultural Indians, such as the earth lodges of the **ARIKARA**. Since the word *lodge* was often a way of saying "family," Westerners used it to express the number of families of Indians, as in "a village of twenty lodges."

A *lodge skirt* is the lower part of the covering of a lodge or tipi, which was often raised in the summer to let in cooling breezes.

LODGEPOLE (1) A variety of pine (*Pinus murrayana*) with a straight trunk that makes a good pole for **TIPIS** (lodges). This pine has cones that open in the heat of a forest fire; it played an important role in the Yellowstone fires of 1988. (2) A pole, usually cut from the trunk of a lodgepole pine, used by **PLAINS INDIANS** (and some Anglos) to hold up a tipi. The Dakota-style tipi, according to Reginald and Gladys Laubin's *The Indian Tipi*, requires seventeen poles trimmed and peeled and anywhere from twenty to thirty or more feet long for lodges of family-dwelling size. The poles were also used to transport each family's material goods—they made **TRAVOIS** when traveling. And the travois left what was called a *lodgepole trail*, a track dug into the earth by the dragging butts of the poles. (3) To lodgepole is to drub or thrash, from when an early trapper beat an Indian wife. Later the meaning extended to all beatings.

LOG To take the timber from an area and cut it into logs. Such an area is called *logged off* when it is completely cleared of trees, *logged over* when it is partially cleared.

LOG SLED A wooden platform on runners that supports one end of logs as they are skidded, reducing friction. Also called a *log sledge, bob,* **CROTCH,** *drag sled,* **DRAY, GO-DEVIL,** *joe-log, lizard, log boat, mudboat,* **SCOOT,** *sloop, stone boat, travoy,* and *wood boat.*

COMBINATIONS: *logging berth* (a logging camp), *logging berry* (a prune), *log* **BIRLING** or *riding* (rolling a log underfoot as it floats, done as work, as sport, and even in competition), *logging chance* (a patch of forest suitable for logging), *log drive* or *log run* (the movement of logs downriver), *log interest* (the companies with a commercial interest or stake in logging), *log road* (not only a road for logging but one made of logs, that is, a **CORDUROY ROAD**), *logging show* (a logging enterprise).

EQUIPMENT: *log measurer* (a tool for gauging the usable board feet in logs), *log rule* or *scale* (a table of the number of board feet in logs of different diameters and lengths), *log shoot* or *chute* (a chute made of split logs for skidding logs downhill), *log stamp* (a device for marking the number of board feet on logs), *log way* or *jack* (a chute or slide for logs), *logging wheels* (a pair of wheels usually about ten feet in diameter used to transport logs, which are slung beneath the axle), *log wrench* (a **CANT HOOK** or **PEAVEY**).

LOGGER Novelist and historian Bill Gulick says a logger is a man who shaves with a double-bitted ax, cuts his hair with a chain saw, and stirs his coffee with his thumb. They had many names for themselves in the West (not including *lumberjack*). Names for loggers, generally not designating specialized tasks: **ARKIE, BINDLE STIFF,** *brush ape, brush cat, brush rat, bush rat, gabezo, jack, log cutter, logman, long logger, lumberer, lumber rustler, lumber stiff, Paul, Paul Bunyan's boy, savage, shanty boy, shanty man,* **SLAVE,** *tame ape, timber beast, timberjack, timber savage, timber wolf, wood head, wood hick.*

Specialized loggers: *log cuffer* (a worker who **BIRLS** [rolls] logs), *log driver* (a worker who floats logs downriver), *log jockey* (a worker in **BOOMS**), *long logger* (a West Coast logger who works with log lengths of forty feet), *log maker* (a worker who cuts trees into log lengths), *log watch* (an expert river driver).

Logger's smallpox was the calk-shaped scars on a logger's body. They came from getting kicked by loggers' boots, which had calks (metal studs) on the soles.

Logging, aside from the large meaning of harvesting timber, is hobbling a horse by tying a light log to its leg. Such a weight is also known as a **DRAG.**

LOGGERING In **RODEO,** to come out of the chute grabbing the saddle **HORN,** an embarrassing lapse.

LOGGING CHAIN A levered chain grab hook used in loading logs. Also any heavy chain used in logging. which may be more strictly a *log chain*. Wyoming people say a logging chain makes the best wind gauge: When the chain gets horizontal, it's breezy. When links start breaking off, it's blowing.

LOMA A Southwestern term for a rise or low hill. Often used in place names; for instance, Loma Linda. Borrowed from Spanish.

LONE RANGER Cowboy lingo for an unmarried man. Compare *buck nun,* which means hermit, and *lone wolf,* which means a man who goes it alone. *Lone wolf* also occurs in verb form—he's *lone-wolfing* it.

LONE STAR Pertaining to Texas. The flag and seal of the Texas Republic used a single star. Thus *Lone Star banner, Lone Star flag, Lone Star rattler, Lone Star State, Lone Star Stater.* But some caution is required: The state flags of Louisiana and South Carolina are also Lone Star flags; so is the Cuban flag. Sometimes *lone star* is printed in lower case; sometimes the phrase *single star* substitutes for it.

LONG CHANCE A chance against long odds. Mathews records as its earliest citation Stewart Edward White's *Arizona Nights:* "He's plumb scared at the prospect of suffering anything, and would rather die right off than take long chances." Drawing to an inside straight is a long chance. So was homesteading on the Great Plains. A great many people went broke doing each.

LONG HAIR (1) An old-timer, a longtime resident of the West, an old **ALKALI,** a **LONGHORN.** In the early West, men wore their hair long, perhaps because of the lack of barbers. In *Arizona Nights,* in the early twentieth century, Stewart Edward White described one such fellow: "The old man was one of the typical 'long hairs.' He had come to the Gailuro Mountains in '69, and since '69 had remained in the Gailuro Mountains, spite man or devil."

(2) Near the **NAVAJO** reservation today, a long hair means a traditional male Navajo, usually but not always elderly. The uncut hair itself shows an inclination to follow tradition.

LONG RIDER An **OUTLAW**.

LONG ROPE A **RUSTLER**.

LONG SWEETENING Molasses, the most common sweetener in the West in the early days—sugar was scarce. It was also called *blackstrap, larrup, lick, long lick,* and *long-tailed sugar.* Sugar was called *short sweetening.*

LONG TOM In **PLACER** mining, an inclined trough for washing ores that bear gold. It is sometimes capitalized.

LONG TRAIL A Western expression for death. (For various expressions for dying, see **CASH IN YOUR CHIPS**.)

LONG WALK The forced removal, by New Mexican militiamen led by Kit Carson, of the **NAVAJO** people from their homeland around the **FOUR CORNERS** area to Fort Sumner in New Mexico. The militiamen were mostly Hispanics, **UTES**, and **PUEBLO** men, long-standing enemies of the Navajos. After four long years, Navajo leaders completed treaty negotiations, and the people returned to their own country between the Four Sacred Mountains in 1868. Still legendary as a cause of suffering and death.

LONG YEARLING A cow that's nearer two years old than one. Likewise, another year older is called a *long two.*

LONG-EAR A cow without an **EARMARK**, by implication an unbranded cow.

LONGHORN CATTLE See **TEXAS LONGHORNS**.

LONGTIME CALIFORIN' In the early twentieth century, what Chinese immigrants would tell immigration officials, to establish they had lived in California and were legal citizens.

LOOK AT A MULE'S TAIL In cowboy talk, to plow. Traditionally, cowboys despised work that couldn't be done on horseback.

LOOKING UP A LIMB What a hanged man is said to be doing. He's also said to be *looking through cottonwood leaves.* (See also **STRING PARTY**.)

LOOKOUT (1) A rider who goes out ahead of a herd of cattle to find *graze.* (2) At a gambling table, a house man who watches the play, particularly to guard against cheating. (3) A *fire-spotter.*

LOOLOO An eccentric hand in **POKER** that under local rules is a top hand. When three clubs and two diamonds was a looloo in Butte, Montana, one celebrated afternoon, it even beat the four aces held by a stranger to town. Probably it would not have beaten the same hand held by a local.

LOOP What a cowboy calls the noose of his **LASSO**. Sometimes he spins the loop before throwing it, but often he just uses a quick flip. But if people say a fellow swings a *wide loop,* they mean he's a rustler.

LOOSE LEADER In Alaska, a dog allowed to run ahead of the dog team, unharnessed, as an inspiration to greater effort.

LOOSE-HERD To herd cattle so that they're neither widely scattered nor tightly bunched, giving them room to graze. The opposite is *close-herd.*

LOPE A smooth, relaxed gait for a horse, faster than a trot and slower than a gallop: a canter. It is used not only as a noun but a verb, as in "We loped our horses across the meadow."

LOP-HORN A **COW** with a horn that points down.

LOSE YOUR HAIR To get scalped; to die. The expression was recorded by Lieutenant George Frederick Ruxton in the 1840s. (For various expressions for dying, see **CASH IN YOUR CHIPS**.)

LOSE YOUR HAT To get **BUCKED** off. A hand spotted on the ground near his horse is likely to say, "I lost my hat and got off to get it," an explanation that may cause some joshing. To *lose your horse* meant the same.

LOUSE CAGE What a logger calls both his hat and the bunkhouse.

LOWBUSH MOOSE In Alaska, a funny name for a hare.

LOWER 48 In Alaska, the rest of the United States except for Hawaii; also called *Lower 49.* Similar to **OUTSIDE**. (See also **INSIDE**.)

LOW-NECK CLOTHES A cowboy's Sunday-go-to-meeting clothes.

LOWRIDER In the Southwest a car customized, typically by young Mexican-American men, so that it sits low to the ground, or raises on the front end. Also, a man who has such a car, and a man who lives the style associated with it. These young men are also called *cholos or pachucos.*

LUBBER GRASSHOPPER The common name for three different kinds of grasshoppers, primarily desert dwellers, that are major pests in the **GREAT PLAINS**. One of them (*Brachystola magna*), a big clumsy creature, is also known as the "Clumsy Locust." New World grasshoppers are often called locusts because of their resemblance to the Biblical locusts, with their voracious appetites and dense swarms.

LUFTAK In Alaska, a hide boot fashioned from the pelt of a bearded seal, or the sole of such a boot. (See also **KAMIK, MUKLUK**.)

LUMBER To log a tract of timber. The worker who does this work is a *logger* (and see that entry for other terms for logging men).

LUMINARIA Among Norteños of New Mexico, a candle, these days in a sand-filled paper bag and stationed in long rows along walkways, especially for festivals. Also called *farolito.* From Spanish.

LUMP OIL Cowboy talk for kerosene or coal oil.

LUMP-JAW (1) Actinomycosis, an infection of cattle and sheep that causes tumors around the jaw. Also called *lumpy jaw, lumped jaw, big jaw,* and *wooden tongue.* (2) Swelling or infection of a horse's mouth.

LUNGER (LUNG-er with a hard g) A person who came to the West in hopes that the dry air would benefit his health.

LYNCH To punish an alleged criminal without due process of law. Though lynching usually meant hanging in the West, early in the period of Western settlement it often meant beating or tarring and feathering. Associated with *vigilance committees* (made up of **VIGILANTES**), lynching did not, in fact, originate in the West but was named after a lynch-law policy started by Captain William Lynch of Pittsylvania County, Virginia, during the Revolutionary War. *Lynch law* was the practice of punishing without a proper trial, a *lynch mob* was a gang hot to do some lynching, **JUDGE LYNCH** was summary justice, and a *lynching bee* was a hanging. For a while, even the modifier *lynchy* had some currency, as in, "The mob had a lynchy look." (See also **STRING PARTY**.)

M

MACHADA (muh-CHAH-duh) In the Southwest, a flock of billy goats. Borrowed from Spanish. (See also **CABRON**.)

MACHERO (muh-CHAIR-oh) In the Southwest of the nineteenth century, a lighter for cigarettes and cigars. Adapted from the Spanish *mechero* (which has the same meaning).

MACHETE (muh-SHEH-tee) A heavy knife used for chopping plant growth. Borrowed from Spanish.

MACHO Now usually an adjective with the derogatory meaning "ultra-masculine," it originally meant a number of things connoting masculinity, from a male mule to a male mescal plant to the hook of a hook and eye. It gives rise to the noun *machismo,* meaning "a code of masculine courage and virility." Borrowed from Spanish.

MACKINAW (1) A heavy blanket originally traded to Indians of the Great Lakes region. The name may derive from the strait of Mackinac, between Lake Michigan and Lake Huron, or the trading post situated there. (2) A scow-shaped boat used by **FUR TRADERS** around the Great Lakes and on the Missouri River, forty or more feet long and ten feet wide, controlled by a steersman and four oarsmen, with a very shallow draft, strictly for downstream travel. (3) A plaid coat made from a blanket and popular among woodsmen. (4) Variously a hat, shirt, or gun with the same name.

MADE WOLF MEAT A way of describing a person who was killed and his body left on the prairie. (See also **LANDED IN A SHALLOW GRAVE**.)

MADRONA Any of several shrubby evergreens (genus *Arbutus*). The Mexican madrona is common along the border. Sometimes the same as the **MANZANITA** or the **MOUNTAIN MAHOGANY**.

MAGPIE Cowboy talk for a Holstein cow.

MAGUEY (MAH-gay; muh-GAY) A common name of the **AGAVE**. The fibers of the maguey were used by Indians for weaving and by whites to make a slender rope more useful for roping tricks than for hard cow work. The maguey also yields liquors known as **MESCAL** and **PULQUE**. It's occasionally spelled McGay. Borrowed from Spanish.

MAHALA MATS In California and Oregon, a creeper (*Ceanothus prostratus*) with lavender blossoms. Also called *snow brush* and *squaw carpet*.

MAIL-ORDER COWBOY A **TENDERFOOT** decked out too fancily in what he hopes is cowboy clothing. This fellow used to be more elaborately described as a *mail-order catalog on foot*.

MAKAH A Wakashan-language Indian tribe of the state of Washington, with reservations in Clallam County. Recently the tribe has made news with its dispute with the federal government over whaling rights.

MAKE Several Western expressions use the word *make*: to *make a hand* (to become competent at cowboying), *make a port* (among old-time freighters, to find a camping place), *make hair bridles* (to spend time in jail, where cowboys passed the time by doing just that), *make medicine* (to hold a conference or do some conjuring), *make shavetail* (to break horses; see **SHAVETAIL**), *make the town smoky* (to shoot it up), *make tracks* or *make dust* (to hurry), *make a nine in your tail* (to clear out, **VAMOOSE**, get gone; from the shape a scared cow's tail makes when she takes off), *make a hat* (among loggers, to take up a collection).

MAKE MEAT (1) Among **MOUNTAIN MEN**, to kill animals for food, especially buffalo. (2) Also to make *jerky* (cut meat into thin slices and dry it for preservation).

MAKINGS Paper and tobacco for making a cigarette. Old-time cowboys seldom smoked "tailor-made" (manufactured) cigarettes, and to refuse a man the makings was considered an insult. The first citations for this term are Western.

MAL DE VACHE (MAHL duh VAHSH) The diarrhea common to early travelers on the Great Plains, thought to be caused by **ALKALI** water or by the change to an all-meat diet. Borrowed from French.

MALETA (muh-LAY-tuh) In the Southwest, a rawhide saddlebag. Borrowed from Spanish.

MALPAIS (MAL-pie, with the *a* as in *corral*) Lava-bed country; **BADLANDS**. Sometimes occurs in the form *mallapy* or the like. The original French means "bad country to travel through."

MAMELLE A rounded hill. Also occurs in the form *mammilla*. Borrowed from Canadian French (in which it means a woman's breast).

MAN AT THE POT! A cow-camp cry. If you went to the pot for coffee, the cry obligated you to fill everyone else's cup.

MAN FOR BREAKFAST A murder; a body in the streets at dawn. Said to have been commonplace in the early days of Virginia City, Nevada, Los Angeles, and Denver. (See also **DRY-GULCH**.)

MANADA (muh-NAH-duh) In the Southwest, a horse herd, especially a wild herd of breeding mares led by a single stallion; any herd of horses or cows. Borrowed from Spanish. (See also **CAVVY, REMUDA**.)

MANADERO (mah-nuh-DAIR-oh) The stud or herd stallion that claimed a band of wild mares. From Spanish.

MAÑANA (mahn-YAH-nuh) In the Southwest, "tomorrow, sometime later, whenever"— the indefinite future, considered in a leisurely way. Borrowed from Spanish (in which it means "tomorrow"). Mexico is sometimes called *mañana land.*

MANDAN A Siouan tribe of the Missouri River Valley, living near the Heart River in North Dakota at the time of white contact. The Mandan economy was based on both hunting and agriculture; they lived in earth lodges and were skilled makers of pottery. Their society was based closely on clans and on ceremonial religious practices.

When the Mandans were reduced in number by smallpox in the middle of the eighteenth century and were under pressure from the westwarding **DAKOTA**, they settled near the Knife River with the **HIDATSA**, who also had a semi-sedentary way of life. There they were visited and studied by various whites (including Lewis and Clark, the artist George Catlin, and Prince Maximilian), some of whom thought them the long-sought **WELSH INDIANS**.

In 1837 the Mandan were again ravaged by smallpox—their tribe was reduced from 1,600 to 125—and eventually were forced to merge with the Hidatsa and **ARIKARA** on the Fort Berthold Reservation in North Dakota.

Mandan corn is an upper Missouri River corn with white, blue, and yellow kernels.

MANGA (MAHN-guh) In the Southwest, a poncho, a cloak. Borrowed from Spanish.

MANGEUR DE LARD (mon-JUR duh LAHRD, with the first syllable nasalized) Among fur men, a beginner, a greenhorn. Originally a French-Canadian term of the **VOYAGEURS**, it means, literally, **PORK-EATER** and occasionally appears in that form. It comes from the custom of the French-Canadians' feeding canoemen pork in their corn mush on the river routes between Montreal and

Lake Superior. The canoemen of the further interior were skilled at living AUX ALIMENTS DU PAYS (off the land).

MANIFEST DESTINY The doctrine held by many Americans, especially in the nineteenth century, of the inevitable domination of North America by white people or by the United States. It swept the country during the 1840s, at the time of the U.S. expansion in the Southwest through the Mexican War and in the Northwest through treaty with Great Britain.

MANILA The most popular of the hemp cowboy ROPES, three-strand and tough.

MANO (MAH-noh) In the Southwest, a stone used to grind grain by hand on a *metate* (bed stone). Borrowed from Spanish (in which it means "hand").

MANSADOR (man-suh-DOHR) In the Southwest, a Hispanic horse-breaker, especially of the old style of training horses with **HACKAMORES**, once the preferred way in California. Borrowed from Spanish.

MANSO (MAHN-soh) A Christianized Indian; also called a *mansito*. Borrowed from Spanish.

MANTA (MAHN-tuh) In the Southwest, a pack cover of coarse cotton cloth; also the cloth itself or a big shawl made from it. Borrowed from Spanish. A *mantilla* is a woman's shawl.

Paiute woman using a mano and metate, 1872.
[PHOTOGRAPH BY JOHN K. HILLERS, COURTESY OF NATIONAL ARCHIVES (57-PE-7).]

MANTECA (man-TAY-kuh) In the Southwest, lard. Borrowed from Spanish.

MANZANITA (man-zuh-NEE-tuh) A bush of the genus *Arctostaphylos* that covers hill-sides in dry parts of the Southwest, sometimes growing more than head high. It has a gorgeous, smooth red bark. Also called **MOUNTAIN MAHOGANY** (as are madrone and other shrubs with reddish wood). In Spanish, it literally means "little apple," a reference to its fruit.

MARIACHI (mah-ree-AH-chee) In the Southwest, a band of strings and brasses that plays a characteristically gay and sentimental music, often in restaurants or on the streets. Borrowed from Spanish.

MARINE HIGHWAY The Inside Passage, the ocean waterways north from Seattle along the Alaska panhandle, plied by ferries of the Alaska Marine Highway System.

MARIPOSA LILY Especially in California, a tulip-like flower (genus *Calochortus*) also called *butterfly weed, Indian potato, sego lily,* and many other names. By the name *sego lily,* it's the state flower of Utah.

MARK To **EARMARK** and dock the tails of lambs. Among sheepherders, a *marker* is a black sheep used to help in counting. Among cowboys, it is a cow with readily recognizable natural markings.

MARMOT A cousin of the woodchuck that lives in the mountainous West and hibernates during the winter. Also called a *rockchuck, mountain badger, whistle pig,* or, by French-Canadians, **SIFFLEUR.**

MARTINGALE A piece of tack that keeps a horse from throwing its head up. A leather strap connected to the cinch passes between the forelegs and splits to end in two rings, which the reins pass through.

MASA Corn that has been treated with lye and finely ground into a flour. It is the main ingredient in corn tortillas and tamales, and is an essential component in Hispanic diets, as wheat is in Anglo diets. Adapted from Spanish (in which it means "dough").

MATANZA (muh-TAN-suh, with the second *a* as in *corral*) In Spanish California, the killing of cattle for hides and tallow; the place where such killing was done. Borrowed from Spanish.

MAUL OAK In California, an evergreen also known as the *canyon oak* or *Valparaiso oak.* Its wood is hard enough to make heads for mauls.

MAVERICK A **SLICK**; an unbranded calf. Since it didn't follow a cow and so was of undetermined ownership, a maverick was a wonderful target for folks who wanted to increase their herds more rapidly than nature intended. This led to the verb form of the word, to *maverick,* to brand mavericks, that is, appropriate them. Throwing your brand on mavericks was called *jacking mavericks.*

In the early West, mavericking was more or less accepted as a way to get a herd started. A little later, it was controlled—at roundups, mavericks were divided fairly—and freelancing maverickers were considered thieves. Jim Averill and Cattle Kate, for instance, were hanged (unjustly) for being *maverickers,* and central Wyoming fought the Johnson County War partly over mavericking.

Freelance maverickers were liable to end up where they didn't want to be. The cowboy artist Charlie Russell, in *Good Medicine,* reports that one hand "quit punchin' and went into the cow business for himself. His start was a couple o' cows and a work bull. Each cow had six to eight calves a year. People didn't say much till the bull got to havin' calves, and then they made it so disagreeable that

Charlie quit the business and is now makin' hosshair bridles," which was how cowboys passed the time in jail.

The term *maverick* is supposed to have gotten its start when a Texas lawyer named Samuel Maverick failed to brand his calves. Then the next owner of the herd started identifying every unbranded calf in the country with some phrase like "That's one of Maverick's" and so claimed it as his own. Also spelled *mavoric, mavorick,* and *mauvric.* By extension, a person of no family or faction, an independent, a loner, a misfit.

A *maverick brand* is an unrecorded brand. A rustler who killed cows to make their calves mavericks was said to be running a *maverick factory.*

MAYORDOMO (MY-or-DOH-moh) In the Southwest, the manager of a ranch or an irrigation system. The (irrigation) ditch manager supervises the cleaning of the ditch in the spring and the repair of the dams and gates, regulates the flow, and determines the amount of water each shareholder receives. Borrowed from Spanish. Stanley Crawford in *Mayordomo* writes:

> What good is it to be the *mayordomo* of the Acequia de la Jara? . . . A job nobody much wants. But nonetheless a job, one of the few that a small community can give, often reluctantly, to one of its members. . . . You become even more involved and entwined [with the community]. Next to blood relationships, which rule the valley, come water relationships.

McCLELLAN (1) A light saddle for cavalry use. It was designed by Civil War General George B. McClellan after a Hungarian saddle and used for nearly a century by the U.S. military beginning in the 1850s. It had an open slot from pommel to cantle. (2) A military cap in the West of the 1870s and 1880s.

McLEOD TOOL Among loggers, a combination hoe, rake, and cutting tool with a short handle.

MEAT BAG Trapper talk for the stomach. A *meat biscuit* was a concoction of what boils out of meat, combined with flour, invented by Gail Borden of the condensed milk company. *Meat in the pot* was cowboy slang for a rifle.

MECATE (muh-CAH-tay) A rope of horsehair (or sometimes **MAGUEY**) used as reins with a hackamore. It is very long (usually twenty-two feet) to make a long lead rope. The mecate is black and white, tied with a knot (in Spanish, *la mota*) just above the heel knot, and is valued by many horse breakers who prefer the hackamore style. The word is often corrupted to *McCarty.*

MEDICINE Red English term for the Indian concept of the power of the spirits. Medicine is the sway of the spiritual dimension of life, from the grand deities to the minor spirits and to great mysteries like sun, rain, and wind. Sometimes the word seems to mean "sacred" or "mysterious." Almost all Western Indians sought (and often still seek) medicine, the benevolent power of the spiritual in their lives.

Medicine can be made physical in *medicine objects* to which this power has been brought. Such an object can be natural, as in the *medicine rock* of the Gros Ventres or the *medicine wolf* (the COYOTE); it can be part of an animal kept for its power. It can also be man-made, such as a totem object that embodies or represents power.

A man of great medicine has strong contact with the powers, and so is likely to have strength and courage, understanding of both the apparent and the invisible worlds, harmony to live well and to survive dangerous situations, the power to heal illnesses of spiritual and physical causes, and so on.

Medicine sometimes also meant healing among the Indians, which was often done with herbs but never entirely dissociated from matters of spirit. To *make medicine* is to appeal to Spirit via prayer, ritual, or ceremony.

The word can be used in combinations with many words to mean an object or a process of power—thus *medicine arrow, medicine dance,* and so on. It is also used for objects associated with power, as in *medicine lodge* (sweat lodge), where power is sought. OTHER COMBINATIONS: *medicine bird* (the mourning dove), *medicine dream* (a dream bringing spirits and their power), *medicine drum* (a drum used for conjuring), *medicine hogan* (a NAVAJO hut used for conjuring), *medicine man* or *medicine woman* (a person who has contact with Spirit and who conjures), *medicine pole* (a pole hung with an object symbolizing supplication), *medicine smoke* (a process of sacred smoking), *medicine society* (a PUEBLO society organized for religious purpose), *medicine song* (a conjuring song).

The word was also used in contexts referring to objects associated with white culture, where the spiritual element is less clear, which could be because of misunderstanding by white interpreters or because sacredness and mystery are being attributed to these objects. Thus a *medicine buffalo* was an ox, a *medicine dog* a horse, a *medicine iron* a gun, and a *medicine talk* an important conference.

Certainly purely white meanings arose: A *medicine show* was an entertainment by whites in pseudo-Indian style. And *bad medicine* meant either bad luck or, when a way of describing a man, a dangerous hombre. To a trapper, medicine was bait to make the beaver come to the trap. It could also mean simply "information," as in "I have no medicine on that." (See also BAD MEDICINE.)

MEDICINE BAG A small hide bag worn by Indians and some other Westerners around the neck and containing medicine objects. The contents might be a bit of sage or sweetgrass, a claw or tooth of the person's animal guide—whatever his medicine might be.

MEDICINE BUNDLE The sacred collection of an individual Indian, clan, tribal group, or tribe, containing medicine objects of great importance—frequently hides, skulls, wings, pipes, and other venerated objects. When belonging to an individual, these objects are kept safe, wrapped in a hide, and used occasionally for contemplation. Usually clan and tribal bundles are assigned to a keeper

for stewardship, a great responsibility. Often they are opened
periodically or on great occasions, to singing, dancing, and
smoking of any pipe associated
with the bundle. These bundles
may be a veritable Ark of the
Covenant to a tribe. Also called a
MEDICINE BAG or *medicine pouch.*

MEDICINE MAN or **WOMAN**
Among Indian peoples, a man
wise in the ways of **MEDICINE**
(spiritual power). He conducts
ceremonies that bring spiritual
power to the people or to the
individuals in the ceremony. He
or she may also be a healer,
using spiritual power or herbs;
but *medicine* usually refers more
to spiritual than earthly power.

MEDICINE PIPE A pipe used by Indians
(and not only Western Indians) to conse-
crate deeds or invoke spirit power. It
consists of an L-shaped or T-shaped
bowl of catlinite (representing Earth)
and a wooden stem (representing all
that grows on Earth) and may be
enhanced by eagle feathers (representing the winged creatures of the
air) and ornamentation. Often
revered by **PLAINS INDIANS** as a
sacred object. See Black Elk's account
of the pipe's central place in Lakota
ceremonialism in Joseph Epes
Brown's *The Sacred Pipe.* The tomahawk
was sometimes combined with a pipe.
This device, called a *hatchet pipe* or *tomahawk pipe,* dating from colonial times
and symbolizing both war and peace,
was an English invention. (See
HATCHET PIPE.) Here is part of the blessing a
modern Lakota of medicine, Lame Deer, gave

*Little Big Mouth, a medicine man, seated in
front of his lodge near Fort Sill, Oklahoma, with
medicine bag visible behind the tent, 1870.*
[PHOTOGRAPH BY WILLIAM S. SOULE;
COURTESY OF NATIONAL ARCHIVES
(75-BAE-1448D).]

Medicine pipe and tobacco pouch.
[DRAWING BY E. L. REEDSTROM.]

to the pipe of a visiting Anglo, Kenneth Lincoln, as recounted in Lincoln's *The Good Red Road*:

> Lame Deer counseled us to sing with the spirits—and to hear the holy silence of the soul's rest, the life-stirring sounds of pulsing and breathing, gratitude and reverence, the return gifts to Wakan Tanka [the great mystery]. Humility, sacrifice, respect, kindliness—right listening and feeling to find others' needs—these were proper qualities and graces of a human life. He repeated his words in four different ways as a litany, tightening a circular path to a core of suffering and communion. Then he told us to consider how wide the bowl reached, to embrace all creation in a sacred hoop, offering the pipestem to ancient spirits in all directions.

Tomahawk pipe.
[Drawing by E. L. Reedstrom.]

MEDICINE WATER In Red English, either (1) whiskey or (2) a hot, sulfurous spring. The 1840s adventurer Lieutenant George Frederick Ruxton tells us in *Life in the Far West* that **MOUNTAIN MEN** also associated hot springs with spirit power:

> The American and Canadian trappers assert that the numerous springs which, under the head of Beer, Soda, Steamboat Springs, &c., abound in the Rocky Mountains, are the spots where his satanic majesty comes up from his kitchen to breathe the sweet fresh air, which must doubtless be refreshing to his worship after a few hours spent in superintending the culinary process going on below.

MEDICINE WHEEL A circle of stones with stone spokes made by Native peoples, thought to be reflections of astronomical views, and used ceremonially. The one in Wyoming's Big Horn Mountains is eighty feet across and has twenty-eight spokes. In the 1990s the federal government allowed the **PLAINS INDIAN** people who consider it sacred to perform ceremonies (such as the **VISION QUEST**) there once more.

MELCHIZEDEK (mel-CHIZ-uh-dek) The higher or greater priesthood of the Church of Jesus Christ of the **LATTER-DAY SAINTS**. These priests are able to represent Christ on Earth and perform rituals of healing the sick, baptizing, confirming, and carrying out patriarchal duties. (See also **AARONIC**.)

MENUDO (men-OO-doh) Tripe soup, a popular dish in Mexican–American restaurants. From Spanish.

MERC A term for the general store, still in Western use. Short for *mercantile.*

MERICAT A word of the Indians of southeastern Utah for an American; originally, any **ANGLO** who wasn't a Mormon.

MESA A rocky, flat-topped tableland, either standing isolated or an area between valleys. More common in the Southwest and somewhat like **COTEAU** and *plateau* in the north. Borrowed from Spanish (in which it means "table"). The diminutive form *mesilla* ("little tableland") used to occur in the Southwest.

MESCAL (1) Any plant of the genus **AGAVE**, such as the century plant. (2) The **PEYOTE** plant *(Lophophora williamsii).* The practice of taking peyote (mescal) to gain self-knowledge is called *mescalism;* it is a central rite of the **NATIVE AMERICAN CHURCH**. (3) A food made from the agave (**MAGUEY**) by Hispanics and Indians. Since the baked root of the mescal was an important food of the **APACHES** east of the Rio Grande, those Indians were and are called *Mescaleros.* (4) A clear liquor made from the maguey plant (see **TEQUILA**.) Mescal is variously spelled, especially as *mezcal.*

    COMBINATIONS: *mescal bean* (not a bean not of the mescal but one mixed with that drink for narcotic effect), *mescal bud* (the flowering stalk of the century plant), *mescal ceremony* (a ceremony of **PLAINS INDIANS** involving the drinking of mescal), *mescal rattle* (a gourd rattle used in the mescal ceremony), *mescal thread* (a fiber from the agave used by Indians).

MESCAL BUTTON The top of the **PEYOTE** cactus (or mescal button cactus) that, when dried and then ingested, causes hallucinations or (from the religious view) visions. Also called a *mescal head.* The use of peyote has been an important religious ceremony of some Southwestern and Plains Indians for a long time and is now central to the ceremonies of the **NATIVE AMERICAN CHURCH**.

MESQUITE (muhs-KEET) In the Southwest, a low-growing, thorny, shrublike tree *(Prosopis juliflora)* with a hard wood. Indians made a flour from the beans, and livestock eat its seeds. Mesquite is notorious for its thickets, which are called *mesquital,* **CHAPARRAL,** or *mogotes,* and make the brush country of Southwest Texas nearly impenetrable. The word is variously and creatively spelled. From the Spanish *mexquite* (which in turn comes from Nahuatl).

    COMBINATIONS: *mesquite bean* (used by Indians as food and also as the basis of a mildly alcoholic drink), *mesquite grass* (a good forage, of the genus *Boutaloua*), *mesquite meal* (made by grinding the bean), *mesquite root* (a good fuel in a barren country).

MESS BEEF A pickled or salted beef of early Texas. The *mess house* was the ranch cookhouse, the *mess room* the cowboys' dining room, and the *mess wagon* the **CHUCK WAGON** (which had a storage box called the *mess box*) or the freighting wagon carrying the provisions.

MESTIZO A person of mixed blood. (See also **METIS**.) From Spanish.

METATE (muh-TAH-tay) In the Southwest, the bed stone on which Indians did their grinding of food with a **MANO**.

METIS (MAY-tee) A half-breed, especially one from the settlements of the Red River of the North, whose people descend from the Canadian fur men (French, Scottish, and British) and Indian women. Originally a French-Canadian term. The French form *metif* also occurs; the people of the Turtle Mountain Reservation near the U.S.-Canadian border in North Dakota call themselves and their language *Mitchef.* In the Southwest the Spanish version, **MESTIZO**, is more common. (See also **RED RIVER METIS**.)

MEXICAN In the Southwest, (1) a *peso* or *adobe dollar;* (2) a variety of sheep. *Mex* is short for Mexican Spanish or, usually used with some disparagement, a Mexican person. As an adjective, it is short for anything Mexican. *Mexicano* is much like Mex, without the disparagement.

COMBINATIONS: *Mexican bit* (a horse's bit with a curb ring rather than curb chain), *Mexican iron* (rawhide), *Mexican oats* (nonsense), *Mexican packsaddle* (an **APAREJO**), *Mexican saddle* (a saddle with a particularly high pommel and cantle, wooden stirrups, and heavy skirts), *Mexican spur* (an ornamented spur with big rowels), *Mexican strawberry* (either a bean or a species of prickly pear said to be delicious), *Mexico piece* (a Spanish piece of eight found in Mexico).

MI CASA ES SU CASA In the Southwest, a genteel expression of hospitality to a home or business; borrowed from Spanish, in which the literal meaning is "my house is your house."

MICKANINNY An **ESKIMO** child; says Thomas Clark, the word came from nineteenth-century whaling men, perhaps adapted from *pickaninny.*

MICO (MY-koh) Among the **CREEK**, **CHICKASAW**, **CHOCTAW**, and Seminole (and other Indians of the Muskogee linguistic family), a chief. Also spelled *meiko.*

MIDDEN When pertaining to archaeological sites of ancients such as the **ANASAZI**, a refuse heap containing the detritus of habitation. Such areas are sought by those who dig for artifacts on private land. If human bones are found, however, as they often are, the digging becomes illegal. Burial sites are protected by the Native American Grave Protection Act.

MIGRA (mee-GRAH) A Hispanic nickname for the U.S. border patrol. Adapted from the Spanish word *inmigración* ("immigration").

MILAGRO (mih-LAH-groh) (1) Miracle or wonder, as in John Nichol's *The Milagro Beanfield War.* (2) Among the Indians and Mexicans of the Southwest, a black cross to which silver charms in the shape of parts of the body are nailed to promote health and healing. Borrowed from Spanish (where it means "miracle").

MILD CURE In the Pacific Northwest, preserving salmon by cooling it in a light brine before smoking.

MILK PITCHER Cowboy talk for a cow that is giving milk. She may live on a *milk ranch* (dairy farm).

MILK THE BUSHES or **BRUSH** In the Pacific Northwest, to pull a small craft upstream by heaving on the bushes.

MILL A circular motion that desperate cowboys hoped to get a **STAMPEDING** herd into so that it would run out of its fury going around and around. A mill in a river, though, called a *merry-go-round in high water,* was plenty dangerous to the beasts and the men who tried to break it up. The word also occurs as both a transitive and intransitive verb—cowboys try to *mill a herd,* and cows *mill.* Owen Wister described the way cowboys mill a herd:

> It seems that a mere nothing suffices to cause a herd [to] stampede. An old cow will snuff once, and the bunch starts off like lightning, as if this had been a prearranged signal. Then the two ways to stop them are, first, to have three or four men on one side continually turning them, keeping along with them and so bring them around behind the rest, thus making an ever contracting ring till the whole is a mass of animals pivoting on its center; or a man takes the lead (which is very dangerous, because one trip means death under the hoofs of the following cattle), and he rides ahead, turning on a wide circle and contracting till the rotary motion is produced.

When hands forced a horse herd to mill, it was called *rounding up.*

MILL RIDER A cowboy name for a ranch hand who tends windmills. Also called a *miller.*

MILPA (MIL-puh) In the Southwest, a cultivated field, especially a cornfield. Borrowed from Spanish.

MINATAREE See **HIDATSA**.

MIND YOUR HAIR A trapper's farewell meaning "take care" or "watch your ass." Literally, "Look out for your scalp lest an Indian get it."

MINER Western names for miners and men who work in mines (according to Adams) are *abajador* (supplier of tools), *banksman* (the man at the head of a shaft who handles the bucket), *butty* (a fellow miner), *cager* (a worker who attends the elevator), *company buster* (a surface worker), *doublejacker* (the fellow who swings the big hammer to separate rocks for blasting), *dyno* (an explosives handler), *gold digger* or *gold washer* (a **PLACER** miner), *hard-rock miner* or *rocker* (a miner who works underground in rock, as distinguished from a placer miner), *muckman* (any miner), *nipper* (tool flunky), *pithead man* (worker who unloads cages), *pitman* (lift and pump examiner), *powder hand* or *powder man* or *powder monkey* (explosives handler), *quartz miner* or *quartz reefer* (same as a hard-rock miner), *river sniper* (placer miner), *rust-eater* (ironworker), *shack* (mine guard), *short faker* or *short-stage man* or *staker* or *ten-day miner* (itinerant miner), *shovel stiff* (worker with a shovel), *sluicer* (sluice operator), *tar baby* (cable lubricator), *tool nipper* (tool distributor), *tributer* (man who takes the proceeds less royalty for wages), and *wife* (fellow worker). See also **COUSIN JACK** and **PROSPECTOR**.

MINERAL ENTRY Filing a mining **CLAIM** on public land for the mineral rights. *Mineral entry withdrawal* is the removal of public lands (usually those lands that are required for administrative sites or are highly valued by the public) available for mineral entry.

MINER'S FRIEND The safety lamp known as a Davy lamp.

MINER'S LETTUCE A low plant *(Montia perfoliata)* that was a favorite of the **FORTY-NINERS**. It is now cultivated in Europe as winter purslane.

MINING DISTRICT A Western mining area (a region of diggings defined by natural boundaries) of one or more mining camps organized for self-government before law and government arrived officially. These districts operated through what were called *miners' meetings,* and through *miners' courts* they enforced *miners' law,* which could be ad hoc, inflexible, and abrupt. In an attempt to minimize disputes, the *mining recorder* kept an official record of claims. (See also **CLAIM, PLACER, DISCOVERY**.)

MINUTEMAN One of a group organized by stockmen of the Southwest to fight lawlessness along the U.S.-Mexican border.

MISSION INDIAN In the Southwest, an Indian living near a Franciscan mission, under its influence, and presumably in the process of conversion to Christianity. The Franciscan policy was to make the Indians "civilized," largely by teaching them agriculture, before it attempted to make them Christian.

MISSION STIFF (1) A parson. (2) A man who went to a mission and acted as though he were getting religion in order to get a hot meal and a bed.

MISSIONARY (1) From nearly time of contact forward, Europeans sent missionaries to the Indian peoples of North America, with very mixed results. From the point of view of the Christians, this effort was generous, giving the Christian God to a benighted people; many Indians accepted this gift gladly, and continue to accept it; many also regarded it as cultural imperialism, and continue to view it that way.

In the West the principal early missionaries were Catholic—French Jesuits who evangelized in the French-Canadian fur trade areas, Spanish Franciscans in the Pueblo country, Jesuits and Franciscans in California (where Junipero Serra founded twenty-one missions), Jesuits on the Northern Plains and in the Pacific Northwest (most notably Jean De Smet). These priests acted not only as evangelists but as explorers, physicians, educators, linguists, vintners, cartographers, ethnographers, and so on. Policy on the whole was to respect Native cultures insofar as possible, far different from the impulse of most

Americans to make Indians into white men. Some of these missionaries, especially De Smet, commanded immense respect from Indians.

The dark side of the missionary effort, though, is also inescapable. Many priests were pederasts, a blot particularly on the record of the boarding schools. California priests accidentally introduced diseases for which the Indians had no immunity, and missions often reduced Indians nearly to slave status. (See BLACK ROBE.)

(2) In a traditional rite of passage in the MORMON church, college-age young people spend up to two years in missionary work. They are supported by their families, and it is a time not only of prayer and teaching but also of abstinence from worldly concerns such as current events, dating, and possessions.

MISSOURI An Algonquian word meaning either "big muddy" or "people of the big canoes." The Missouri Indians, who were living near the mouth of the river at the time of white contact in the seventeenth century, were Siouan. Never numerous, they were later removed to Oklahoma.

MIX A WALK A logger's expression for quitting the job.

MIXED HERD A cattle herd of both sexes and various ages, the easiest kind to manage.

MOCCASIN TELEGRAPH The word-of-mouth means of transmitting news and gossip through a sparsely populated country, especially among Indian peoples. It is often mysteriously fast and effective. In Alaska, known as the *mukluk wireless* or *mukluk telegraph,* and as the *seagull wireless.* The Anglo equivalent is the *grapevine,* short for *grapevine telegraph. Moccasin,* a shoe of soft hide without a heel usually associated with Indians, is a term from Algonquian languages in the East.

MOCHILA (moh-CHI-luh) A leather covering draped over a cinched-up SADDLE, sometimes containing (as for PONY EXPRESS riders) pockets for mail or other goods. Variously spelled; for instance, *machilla, mochiler, mochile.* Borrowed from Spanish (in which it means "knapsack"). Also called *corus* or *macheer.*

MOCHO An animal with a droopy horn, GOTCHED ear, or cut-off tail. Borrowed from Spanish (in which it means "mutilated").

MOCKEY A wild mare.

MOJAVE (1) A Yuman Indian tribe of the lower Colorado River, living around modern Needles, California, once known for its aggressiveness against whites. Their name has been given to various plants and animals of that region and to the desert itself.

(2) The Mojave Desert lies primarily in southern California and Nevada and includes Death Valley. A basin-and-range topography, it receives two to five inches of rain a year (Bagdad, California, in the eastern Mojave holds the record for the longest period without rainfall—767 days). The indicator species for the Mojave is the JOSHUA TREE, a yucca that has become tree-sized. Other dominant

plants are **CREOSOTE BUSH**, **CHOLLA**, and **YUCCA**. Oases and stream beds support **MESQUITE**, willows, and **CALIFORNIA FAN PALMS.**

MONEY FISH In Alaska, a salmon worth top dollar.

MONKEY WRENCHER A person who defends the environment by figuratively throwing a monkeywrench into (sabotaging) the efforts of developers, loggers, miners, drillers, and the like. Destroying bulldozers and spiking trees, for instance, are acts of monkey wrenching. The late Edward Abbey coined this term in his comic novel *The Monkey Wrench Gang,* and it has become ubiquitous. It takes a verb form, to *monkey wrench.* (See also **ECOTAGE**, **SAB-CAT.**)

MONTE A gambling card game imported from Spain, played with forty or forty-four cards. The players bet on whether the suit of the card turned up will match the suits of the two cards taken from the bottom and put face up. It is not the same as *three-card monte* or *pass monte.*

Principal monte terms are *bottom layout, broad pitcher, gate, monte bank* (table), *monte banker* (dealer, thrower, or tosser), *monte layout, monte sharp,* and *top layout.* Borrowed from Spanish.

MOON-EYED A way of describing a horse with glassy, white eyes and allegedly with poor night vision. (See also **STOCK HORSE.**)

MOONLIGHT THEM In cowboy talk, to night-herd cattle. To *moonshine* was to ride at night without chuck wagons for the sake of an early drive, or to drive cows at night.

MOOSE This is the largest member (genus *Alces*) of the deer family. Awkward in movement, humped, spindly-legged, wattled, misproportioned, lopsided of face, the moose seems to many people comically beautiful. In the continental United States, the bull may weigh as much as a saddle horse, and stand taller and (with antlers) wider. Bulls from Alaska, where everything seems to be bigger, are said to weigh as much as 1800 pounds. The palmate antlers may stretch to five or even six feet.

Moose inhabit the entire planet's northern boreal forests. They browse on twigs, leaves, and aquatic plants. Hide and flesh are important to red and white people alike. Author John McPhee reports in *Coming into the Country* that moose hunting is so universal in Alaska that "Got your moose yet?" is an equivalent of "hello."

Cow moose are notably aggressive when protecting a calf, and many old-time Westerners consider the moose on the whole more dangerous to human beings than the grizzly bear, which is more demonized. *Mooching Moose and Mumbling Men,* the recollections of Dubois, Wyoming, packer Joe Back, is full of funny stories about hostile moose.

MOOSE GOOSER In the Pacific Northwest, a comical name for the engine of a train running through country covered by deep snow, thus at risk of hitting a moose moving along the tracks to avoid the snow. A *moose hunter stall* is the unfortunate result of a pilot's flying low for good visibility, stalling, and having little time to pull out.

MOOSE PASTURE A miner's mocking term for country that looks pretty but is valueless as a source of minerals, as in, "He staked a lot of moose pasture."

MOQUI An older name (used particularly by Mormons) for the **HOPI** Indians. In some usages, it appears to mean any **PUEBLO** people. It is an adaptation of the **ZUNI** word for the Hopis. Also spelled *Moki.*

MORADA (moh-RAH-duh) Among Norteños, a chapter house where the members of the **PENITENTE** sect keep the implements for their passion ceremonies, conduct rites, and eat meals brought from the outside by the women. Adapted from Spanish (in which it means "dwelling").

MORMON A member of the Church of Jesus Christ of **LATTER-DAY SAINTS**; as an adjective, pertaining to that church, its members, or their culture. Mormon, in church doctrine, was a fourth-century prophet and author of the *Book of Mormon.* The name means "more good" or "great good." The religion and culture are sometimes spoken of (in usages often no longer current) collectively as *Mormonry.* Mormon country is called *Mormondom. Mormonism* is the polity and doctrine of Mormons. *Mormoness* is an obsolete word for a Mormon woman. A *Mormonite* was a Mormon. To *Mormonize* is to make someone or something Mormon-like.

RELIGIOUS COMBINATIONS: *Mormon Bible,* the *Book of Mormon* (once, for a gentile to *take a Davy on the Mormon Bible* meant to swear on a ludicrous object), *Mormon Church* or *LDS Church* (both common names for the Church of Jesus Christ of Latter-Day Saints), *Mormon City* (Salt Lake City, in a usage now obsolete).

OTHER MISCELLANEOUS COMBINATIONS: *Mormon blanket* (a quilt made from scraps of clothing), *Mormon buckskin* (cowboy talk for baling wire), *Mormon candy* (carrots), *Mormon derrick* (a crane-necked mast used to lift hay from a wagon to stack in a sling), *Mormon dip* (cowboy talk for milk gravy), *Mormon dog* (a can with pebbles, used to make a racket to control cows, in place of dogs), *Mormon poison* (coffee, because caffeine is a no-no), *Mormon rainstorm* (a sandstorm), *Mormon shirttail* (a short-tailed shirt), *Mormon tree* (the lombardy poplar), *Mormon weed* (velvetleaf).

Among the teasing names gentiles use for Mormons are *carrot eater, carrot snapper,* and *cricket stomper.* (See also **JACK MORMON**.)

MORMON BATTALION The company of soldiers sent by Brigham Young to the Mexican War.

OTHER HISTORICAL COMBINATIONS: *Mormon board* (a road scraper), *Mormon brake* (a log tied behind a wagon on a downhill slope to slow it down), *Mormon buggy* (a light spring wagon with a fringed top), *Mormon coin* (gold coin of Mormon mintage in circulation about 1860), *Mormon candy* or *currency* (carrots), *Mormon expedition* (the military expedition of the federal government against the Mormons in 1857–58), *Mormon iron* (rawhide), *Mormon road* (the old trail from Salt Lake to Los Angeles via Las Vegas, or other old Mormon routes), *Mormon Station* (the original name for Genoa, Nevada), *Mormon tangle* (the packer's knot called a *squaw hitch*), *Mormon wagon* (a light, strong version of the prairie schooner used by Plains-crossing Mormons to migrate to Salt Lake in 1847), *Mormon War* (either the conflict at Nauvoo, Illinois, that precipitated the Mormon migration to Deseret, or the difficulties of 1857–58; see *Mormon expedition* above).

MORMON BRIDGE A place where a dirt road crosses a wash and is paved through it. In the wash, water will flow (or stand) after a rain, turning the surface to impassable muck; therefore in Utah, in lieu of a real bridge, people paved only the bottom of the wash. The practice endured at least to the 1950s.

MORMON CRICKET A locust that plagued Mormons in the late 1840s, and again in the 1930s and 1990s; according to the *Los Angeles Times* in 1990, the creatures are as "big as a church mouse" and able to "snap a wooden matchstick in two with their jaws."

MORMON TEA A tea made by Mormons and gentiles from plants of the genus *Ephedra*; also called *canutillo*.

MORNING STAR CEREMONY A sacrificial ceremony of the Skidi **PAWNEES**. Historically, once a year a pubescent girl would be abducted from another tribe. On the summer solstice she was ritually painted, tied, and at the rising of the morning star made a human sacrifice by the priests. The Pawnees decided to stop this practice in 1817. It explains the enmity for the Pawnees held by, among others, the **LAKOTA**.

MORO A horse of bluish cast. (For horse colors generally, see **BUCKSKIN**.)

MORONI In **MORMON** belief, the son of Mormon, who hid the golden plates in the earth to be revealed later to Joseph Smith. A statue of Moroni is a common symbol of Mormonism and is found on some Mormon temples.

MORRAL (mohr-RAL) In the Southwest, especially Texas, a nosebag or **FEED BAG** carried on the saddle horn. By extension, to *put on the morral* (or *put on the nose bag*) became an expression for a human being to eat. Borrowed from Spanish.

MOSEY To go, to move along. There's debate about whether it means "to leave at an amble," "to sneak away," or "to go lickety-split," as well as debate about whether the word comes from the Spanish verb *vamos;* therefore, there is debate about whether the word is Western.

MOSSY HORN (1) A longhorn whose horns have wrinkled with age. (See also **TEXAS LONGHORN**.) (2) Sometimes an old, wrinkled cowman. Also occurs as *moss horn* and *moss back*.

MOTHER HUBBARD LOOP In a catch rope, an extra-big loop, also called a *washer woman*. A Mother Hubbard saddle was an old-style Texas saddle with leather housing that detached from the tree.

MOTHER LODE The principal part of an ore vein. By extension, the real thing, the big hit, the grand stuff of fantasy.

MOTHER UP For a calf to find its mother, its milk, its haven, its comfort. In the pain immediately after branding, calves bawl until they get mothered up. According to the Pinedale, Wyoming, *Roundup*, it is also cowboy talk for getting married.

MOTOR MUSHER In Alaska, a name (originally joking) for a snowmobiler.

MOTTE (MOT) In the Southwest, a grove of trees. Adapted from the Spanish *mata*.

MOUNT (1) A hand's string, the horses assigned to him from the **CAVVY**. Reportedly used on the Southern rather than the Northern Plains. (2) A single saddle horse.

MOUNT MONEY In **RODEO**, pay for a rider in an exhibition but not in competition.

MOUNTAIN MISCELLANEOUS COMBINATIONS: *Mountain Crow* (the Absaroka—**CROW** Indians—of the Big Horn Basin), *mountain dew* (**AGUARDIENTE**), *mountain fever* (an illness of uncertain origin that afflicted Mormons and others on the Oregon Trail with headache, fever, joint pain, delirium, and occasionally death), *mountain wagon* (any wagon adapted for mountain travel, usually through heavier rigging and stouter brakes). (See also **MOUNTAIN OYSTER, MOUNTAIN PRICE.**)

   ANIMALS: *mountain badger* (the hoary **MARMOT**), *mountain beaver* (a sewellel), *mountain boomer* (a steep-country cow, a red squirrel, a mountain lizard, or a sewellel), *mountain buffalo* (what early plainsmen called the buffalo of the Rocky Mountains, generally smaller than the buffalo of the Plains, even though it is the same species), *mountain canary* (a **BURRO**), *mountain goat* (*Oreamnos montanus,* of the high northern Rockies; not a true goat but a relative of the chamois, and a denizen of the high crags), *mountain jay* (the Canada jay), *mountain plover* (a bird that nests in a depression on the ground on the Plains).

   PLANTS: *mountain holly* (Oregon grape), **MOUNTAIN MAHOGANY** (any shrub of the genus *Cercocarpus* or, in the Southwest, a manzanita).

MOUNTAIN LION This powerful, graceful feline (*Felis concolor*) is also known on this continent as the *catamount, cougar, painter, panther,* and *puma*. It is a predator, fiercely territorial, and the most solitary of loners. Since the cat has been ruthlessly hunted as a killer of livestock, its numbers are now low and its habitat diminished within the United States to the West and Southwest. Originally, it ranged from Patagonia to central British Columbia, and was found in every state.

The mountain lion figured large in the pioneering history of this continent, and in its stories. *A Crockett Almanac* tells a delicious one about when a cat leapt at Davy from a tree. He thrust his arm down its throat, grabbed its tail, jerked it inside out, and suddenly the cat was leaping the other way!

MOUNTAIN MAHOGANY Any of several shrubby evergreens (genus *Cercocarpus*), common in the Southwest. This bush is many creatures in many places—sometimes the name is interchangeable with **MANZANITA**, sometimes with **MADRONA**.

MOUNTAIN MAN The beaver trapper of the Rocky Mountains from about 1810 to 1840; also the other men who ventured forth with the trapping brigades, if they had wilderness skills; later, any guide who knew the country. This fellow was first known as a *mountaineer* or *mountain trapper* (so called by Washington Irving and Francis Parkman), but in the 1840s Lieutenant George Frederick Ruxton nominated him a *mountain man*. He's now such an American legend he's been parodied in a series of Busch beer commercials.

The mountain man was one of a succession of different sorts of men who roamed, worked, and settled on the Plains and in the mountains and deserts in the nineteenth century—in the approximate order of the explorer, the trapper, the **EMIGRANT**, the **MINER**, and the **COWBOY** (plus the sorts not quite so large in myth, the freighter, the Indian fighter, lawman, **BADMAN**, gambler, and so on). They reflect nicely the succession of Anglo economies that dominated the West in a whirlwind of change—the beaver, the emigrant trade, gold and silver, and cattle.

Though they had a reputation for crudeness and bestiality, mountain men were in fact extraordinarily varied in class, race, education, and social background. Around one or two campfires at **RENDEZVOUS**, a visitor might have found a religious, educated Yankee (Jedediah Smith), an illiterate blacksmith (Jim Bridger), a smart black who'd lived with Indians (Edward Rose), an Irishman of some gentility (Tom Fitzpatrick), a Mexican trader (Manuel Alvarez), the son of a Missouri justice of the peace (Bill Sublette), a French-Canadian (Antoine Clement), the Iroquois John Grey, and, say, a couple of Delaware Indians. And mountain men were mostly on the way to becoming Indians, with the outlook, habits, cuisine, languages, and customs of red men, with red wives and children. The talk shows aptly the mountain man's wild mix of cultures. Here's Laforey, an old trapper, begging Ruxton for some coffee in *Life in the Far West*:

> "*Sacré enfant de Grâce,*" he would exclaim, mixing English, French, and Spanish into a puchero-like jumble, "*voyez-vous* dat I vas nevare tan pauvre as dis time; mais before I vas siempre avec plenty café, plenty sucre; mais now, God dam, I not go à Santa Fe, God dam, and mountain men dey come aqui from autre côté, drink all my café. Sacré enfant de Grâce, nevare I vas tan pauvre as dis time, God dam. I not care comer

meat, ni frijole, ni corn, mais widout café I no live. I hunt may be two, three day, may be one week, mais I eat nothin; mais sin café, enfant de Grâce, I no live, parceque me not sacré Espagnol, mais one Frenchman."

What mountain men had in common was daring, hardiness, a fierce yen for wilderness and adventure, ability to deal with Indians (mostly by joining them), and extraordinary wilderness survival skills.

No white lifestyle went the way of all flesh so quickly and completely as the mountain man's. The small reason was the decline of the price of beaver. The big one was that the mountain man's life was based on wildness, on remoteness from white civilization. The trapper was gone back to nature, gone Indian. That couldn't last.

In 1836 the first white woman reached Wyoming in the company of mountain men. In 1847 the Oregon Trail saw about 5,000 emigrants, guided by mountain men. In 1858 the gold rush to Denver began, followed immediately by a news-paper. In 1869 the golden spike was driven, and a pregnant woman could ride in comparative comfort all the way to San Francisco. She probably thought the few mountain men left were queer old ducks, colorful but repellent with their Indian wives, children, and ways. Worse than the Indians, really, because they had no excuse. From a cock of the walk to a smelly old relic in half a lifetime. (See also ENGAGÉ, FREE TRAPPER, MANGEUR DE LARD, PARTISAN, VOYAGEUR.)

MOUNTAIN OYSTER One of the small dollops clipped off the calf at branding and cooked up for dinner—yes, the testicle. Sometimes animals other than cows are so victimized, especially pigs and sheep. The *oyster fry* or *calf fry* (they're usually breaded and fried, like chicken) was traditional in the high days of the roundup a hundred years ago and is traditional today. Though they're a source of levity, mountain oysters are tasty. They're also called *prairie oysters* and *Rocky Mountain oysters.*

MOUNTAIN PRICE In the Rocky Mountain FUR TRADE period, the price for an item of manufactured goods in the West, usually at RENDEZVOUS or at a trading post. This was the price to a trapper, who would then either use it himself or trade or give it to an Indian. A mountain price might be many times what the trader paid for it back in the settlements, in light of difficulty of shipment, hardship, danger, and greed, and this system did its part to keep the trappers from getting rich.

At the first rendezvous in 1825, General William H. Ashley charged $1.50 a pound for coffee and sugar, $3 for tobacco, $2 for powder (which was truly essential), $2 each for knives, $5 to $6 for cloth, and $9 for three-point North West blankets. These prices should probably be multiplied by thirty or more to get modern equivalents. At the same time, Ashley was paying $3 a pound for beaver pelts.

MOUNTAIN SPIRIT DANCE A ceremony of the **APACHE** in which the masked, kilted dancers portray (or become) Mountain Spirits.

MOUSE NUT In Alaska, a root of cotton grass stored by small rodents; sometimes then collected and eaten by people.

MOUTH To examine a sheep's teeth to determine how old it is. A *solidmouth* is a mature sheep with all its teeth. A *spreadermouth* is a sheep just past its prime; its teeth are beginning to spread and will soon fall out.

MOVE SHEEP A euphemism for running sheep off (sometimes off a cliff) in a range war.

MOVER In the first half of the nineteenth century, an emigrant; later, a person who kept wandering from farm to farm, failing at each place and sometimes using up the resources there.

MOZO (MOH-soh) In the Southwest, an assistant, especially on a pack train; a youth; a servant. The feminine form, *moza*, also occurred. Borrowed from Spanish.

MUCHACHO (moo-CHAH-choh) In the Southwest, boy, kid; a term of familiarity and endearment, usually applied to a youngster or a servant. *Muchacha* is the feminine form. Borrowed from Spanish.

MUCK (1) In mining, dirt, gravel, and other earth to be moved away. (2) As a verb, to move the dirt and gravel. A *mucker* does the work. A *muckman* is either a miner or a long-handled shovel, which is also called a *muck stick*.

MUCKAMUCK In the Chinook jargon of the Pacific Northwest, food, **CHOW**, **CHUCK**. A *high-muck-a-muck* is a boss, a mogul, a rich man (a fellow who has plenty to eat); a derisive expression for a person of importance. Also spelled *muckety-muck*. (See also **KOW-KOW**.)

MUD WAGON A poor man's **CONCORD** coach, open-sided, light and low, more simply constructed.

MUDHEADS Ceremonial clowns of the **HOPI** (in that language, *Tachutku*) and **ZUNI** (in that language, *Koyemshi*). So called from the earth-colored masks they wear at dances.

MUDSHARK An Alaskan name for the burbot, an edible fish.

MUFFOON The soft underfur of the beaver that was used for felt hats.

MUGGER The **HEADER** of a wild-cow milking team.

MUJER (moo-HAIR) Border cowboy talk for a woman. Borrowed from Spanish (in which it means "woman" or "wife").

MUKLUK A hide boot made after the style of the boots of Alaska Natives; originally, the sealskin sole of such a boot. The *maklak*, a bearded seal, was valued as the source of the hide. *Mukluk wireless* (or *telegraph*) is the Alaska equivalent of the **MOCCASIN TELEGRAPH**.

MULE Mules were called *hardtails, knobheels,* and *mulas.* When white, they were *gambler's ghosts* and, when packing food, *long-eared chuck wagons.* Herds of mules were *muladas* or *mulattos.*

COMBINATIONS: *mule ear* (a floppy strap at the top of a boot to help with pulling it on), *mule train* (either a train of wagons pulled by mules or a pack train of mules).

MULE DEER The principal, long-eared, common game deer of the West, also called *black-tailed deer.*

MULESKINNER The driver of a mule team, or his whip. Known for short as a *skinner,* this fellow was celebrated for his stubbornness and creative profanity. When his draft animals were oxen, he was called a **BULL-WHACKER.** Mules were faster than oxen but had to be fed corn: oxen thrived on available grass. (See also **GRASS FREIGHT.**) A muleskinner was also called jocularly a *mule puncher* as well as a *mulero,* which meant either the driver of a mule team or an attendant to a pack train of mules. The form *mulewhacker* also occurred.

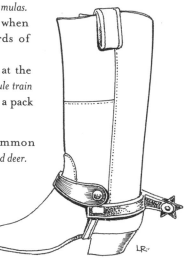

The straps used to pull the boot on are called mule ears.

[DRAWING BY E. L. REEDSTROM.]

MULEY A homeless cow, which is defenseless and keeps to itself. Muley cows have a bad reputation with cowboys as troublemakers. Sometimes a *mule deer* is called a muley, and one kind of small-brimmed, low-crowned dude hat was also a muley.

MULTIPLE USE The management of the resources of public lands (usually the national forests) in the way to "best meet the needs of the American people" and not necessarily realize the greatest dollar return. Calling multiple use *multiple abuse,* environmentalists often seek more emphasis on conservation of the resource and on recreational uses, and less on the economic uses such as grazing, logging, and mining.

MURPHY Murphy, Espenshied, and Studebaker were the principal freight wagons of the Plains after the **CONESTOGAS,** which they eventually replaced. Says David Dary in *Entrepreneurs of the Old West,* they were "made of the best timber, wide, tracked, strong and tight, high double box and heavy tired, and covered with heavy canvas over the bows." The Murphy, crafted by Joseph Murphy in St. Louis, was the most popular.

MUSH In Alaska, historically, a command to the dogs pulling a sled, meaning "Let's move." Now replaced by **HIKE.**

MUSHER In Alaska, a person who drives a **DOGSLED**, and generally keeps sled dogs. Also called a *dog musher* or *dog driver*.

MUSIC ROOTS Cowboy talk for sweet potatoes.

MUSKEG In Alaska, a bog of rotting plant matter and sphagnum.

MUSTANG A wild horse. From the Spanish *mesteño* (which has the same meaning). By extension, anything wild, free, unrefined. Mustang lore is rich in the West. The horse is the descendant of the Spanish horse, the continent's first modern equine, about thirteen hands high and short one vertebra, introduced in Mexico in 1621. By 1770 it had reached all the Native tribes, and it changed Indian life on the Plains.

It is small, of no breeding, often a mongrel, and it was the horse of the Indians. To some early Westerners, all this meant that it was to be despised. Others rooted for it as an underdog from the wrong side of the tracks. And before long the mustang developed a considerable reputation for toughness and general cowpony skills. (For much about the beast and attitudes toward it, see J. Frank Dobie's *The Mustangs*.)

For many people, the survival of the mustang symbolizes the survival of what's wild and precious in the West. The mustangs are still out there—in Nevada, Wyoming, and Montana, for instance. The federal government now has a program allowing people to adopt a wild horse.

COMBINATIONS: A *mustanger* (or *mustang runner* or *hunter*) was a fellow who caught wild horses to sell them, as Clark Gable and Montgomery Clift did in the fine movie *The Misfits*. *Mustanging*, as it was called, was usually done by *running* them into pens or traps. *Mustang cattle*, in Texas, were wild cattle. *Mustang court* was cowboy talk for a kangaroo court.

MUTUAL A nickname for Young Men's or Young Ladies' Mutual Improvement Association (MIA). It is an organization in the **MORMON** Church for youths twelve to eighteen, whose purpose is to teach the faith and provide social activities. The name has been changed in recent years to Young Men and Young Women.

MUZZLE On the northern cow ranges, a device that goes over a calf's muzzle and forces it to eat grass rather than suck. On other ranges, it's called a **BLAB**.

MUZZLE-LOADER Logger talk for a bunk you have to get into from the foot. The meaning that refers to firearms is not Western.

NAGOONBERRY The fruit of the dewberry, prized in Alaska for its taste.

NAJA (NAH-hah) A pendant on the bottom of a squash blossom in **NAVAJO** jewelry.

NAKED POSSESSOR In early American Texas, a person who held land by a long occupancy, though without title.

NAPA LEATHER Hides of sheep or goats tanned by a method created in Napa, California.

NATIONAL PARK SERVICE (NPS) Although this Department of Interior agency administers parks throughout the country, it had its genesis in the West. The first national park was Yellowstone, which was protected by Congress in 1872. The National Park Service was formed in 1916. The Park Service has two missions: "to conserve the scenery and the natural and historic objects and wildlife," and to provide for public use and enjoyment of these special areas. As everywhere in the West, conservation and public enjoyment are sometimes in conflict.

NATIVE AMERICAN A contemporary term meaning American Indian, often deemed appropriate (or politically correct) because it avoids the historic error of Columbus in giving an Asian name to Native peoples of this continent. (See also **INDIAN.**)

Though the good-hearted want to call minorities by the names they prefer, Native American is not necessarily the first choice. Many traditional Native people do not especially like it. **AIM** has not supported it. It has other associations that are hard to like (see below). Concerning the term *Native American,* Tim Giago, editor of *The Lakota Times,* the newspaper of the Great Sioux Nation, wrote on December 4, 1991:

> As the publisher of an Indian advocacy newspaper, the largest of its kind in America, we use American Indian, Indian or Native American, but we prefer to use the individual tribal affiliation when possible. For instance, if the subject of an article is Navajo we use that or Lakota, Ojibwa, Onondaga, etc.

> We are, more and more, pulling away from using Native American, because as so many phone calls and letters have pointed out to us, and correctly so, anyone born in America can refer to themselves as Native American.

> We realize the word "Indian" is a misnomer, but for generic purposes, we are often forced to use it when speaking of many different tribes. American Indian is also acceptable in Indian country.

The term *Native American* also has unfortunate associations historically. In the nineteenth century Native Americanism was prejudice against all Americans except native-born Protestants. The Native American Party of about 1840 promoted this intolerant view. It also meant a Hispanic born in America rather than Spain.

So to use tribal affiliation is the first choice, perhaps, and American Indian, Indian, Native, and Native American acceptable choices. (See the Introduction.)

NATIVE AMERICAN CHURCH The American Indian Christian church centered on the **PEYOTE** ritual. Thought by some to have been brought to the United States from the Yaqui in Mexico by Quanah Parker, it is still growing rapidly and is believed by its adherents to help contemporary Indians transcend the problems of living on reservations.

The central ceremony of the church, always held at night, preferably in a **TIPI**, is the eating of the peyote medicine as a sacrament. In the *half-moon* branch of the church, this ceremony is supervised by a priest known as the *road man*, because he advocates the good, **RED ROAD**. The other branch, called Cross-Fire, is more traditionally Christian.

According to an April 1990 Supreme Court decision, the religious use of the drug peyote is not protected by the Constitution. Many states and the federal government give the practice legal protection.

NATURAL BRIDGE A span of stone formed by erosion across a stream or a wash; it's similar to an **ARCH**. The **FOUR CORNERS** country has many, including the celebrated Rainbow Natural Bridge.

NAVAJO (NAH-vah-hoe) The most numerous contemporary tribe of U.S. Indians. They call themselves the Diné, meaning the people. The word *Navajo* is originally a Spanish form of a **PUEBLO** name for Navajo country; though it is sometimes spelled *Navaho*, the Navajos themselves usually use the Spanish spelling, with a *j*.

The Navajo have lived in Arizona, New Mexico, and southeastern Utah for more than four centuries and speak an Athapascan language. Their economy was and is based substantially on raising sheep and crops, and their social organization is strongly based on the family, extended family, and clan.

Inclined to raiding and territorial expansion, the Navajo were historically often in conflict with their Pueblo and other neighbors. They resisted white encroachment militarily after the U.S. acquisition of the Southwest from Mexico, and endured defeat during the Navajo War and subsequent interment at Bosque Redondo (once called the nation's first concentration camp). In 1868 they accepted the large reservation in the Four Corners country where they live today. Their population has increased in the last century.

Their religion (and the art that stems from it) is expressed in a series of chants that tell their mythic stories and bring living people into harmony with

A Navajo weaver spinning with a loom behind her.
[COURTESY OF NATIONAL ARCHIVES (75-N-NAV-T4).]

the natural and supernatural worlds. Some chants, such as the blessing way, mountain chant, and night chant, take days to perform. The Navajo sense of the world is vividly portrayed in the current mystery novels of Tony Hillerman.

The Navajo are known for the art they developed (sometimes adapting techniques from Pueblo peoples) to give voice to this understanding of the world. **NAVAJO RUGS** are especially prized by collectors. Silversmithing (often featuring turquoise) and **DRY PAINTING** (also known as *sand painting*) are also important Navajo arts.

COMBINATIONS: *Navajo agency, Navajo country, Navajo ruby, Navajo sandstone, Navajo silver.* (See also **CODE TALKER, HOGAN, HOSTEEN, PATHWAY, SING.**)

NAVAJO BLANKET A wool blanket or rug woven by a Navajo woman and known for tightness and beauty of design. The Navajos borrowed the loom technique, but not the designs, from the **PUEBLO** Indians. Using wool from their own sheep, Navajo women (for Navajo weavers are almost always women) wash, card, and spin it, and gather natural materials for dyes (or now use commercial dyes). Then, working from the bottom of the rug up, they weave the warp and the woof in a design of their own imagination. Even a small rug takes weeks to weave. Regional styles have developed in Navajoland, among them Two Grey Hills (the most valuable), Ganado, and Teec Nos Pos.

NAVVY Among early Anglos, a **NAVAJO** person; also, a Navajo pony.

NAVY (1) A nickname for a revolver made to U.S. Navy specifications, smaller than the army model and of lighter caliber. Colt made a popular one. Also called a *Navy six* (for **SIX-SHOOTER**). (2) Short for Navy plug, a brand of strong, dark chewing tobacco. (See also **CHAW TOBACCO** for other brands.)

NEBRASKA BRICK A facetious term for a sod square used to make a house; the **SODDY** itself. Also called a *Kansas Brick*.

NECK (1) To tie a critter you want to teach to lead to a trained critter by the neck, so that the two move together. (2) To wean a calf by tying it away from its mother.

To *neck rope* is to catch a calf or horse by the neck with your rope, as opposed, for instance, to forefooting it. To *neck rein*, when applied to a horse, means for it to turn by slight pressure of the reins against its neck, the usual way Western horses are broke. They turn in the direction away from the pressure.

NEPHITE In **MORMON** belief, a member of a vanished race of Israelites who flourished from about 600 **B.C.** to 400 **A.D.** in the Western Hemisphere. The prophet Lehi led his six sons and their followers to the New World from Jerusalem. Four of the sons (Nephi, Jacob, Joseph, and Samuel) were virtuous and light-skinned, and created an American light-skinned race; the remaining two (Laman and Lemuel) were dark-skinned and rebellious, and created a dark-skinned Indian race. (See also **LAMANITE.**)

The Three Nephites are legendary disciples, immortals who travel the Earth today dispensing blessings to those who need them. In occasional Mormon usage, simply a white person.

NESTER A derogatory cowboy term for a **HOMESTEADER**, farmer, squatter, or small rancher. Big cattlemen in the West regarded these small-timers as a plague, often because they fenced the land. Range wars like Wyoming's Johnson County War were conflicts between big cattlemen and nesters.

The word also has a verb form, to *nest*. Some sources suggest that the term came into being because the homesteads were bordered by brush used to keep critters away from first crops and so looked like bird nests. Other uncomplimentary names for the small farmer are *churn-twister, colonist, hay shaker, hoe-man, home sucker, hon-yocker, pumpkin-piler, plow-chaser,* **SODDY,** *sodbuster,* and *sand-lapper.*

NEZ PERCÉ (NEZZ PURS) A Shahaptian tribe, the Nez Percé were originally a salmon-fishing people on the Snake River, dwelling in pithouses. After they got the horse in the early eighteenth century, their culture changed. They bred and traded horses, producing the **APPALOOSA** breed. They began to cross the mountains to the Plains to hunt buffalo annually with their neighbors, the **FLATHEADS,** and came into conflict with the **BLACKFEET.** As they became more nomadic, they adopted features of the buffalo-hunting cultures, including the TIPI.

From first contact with whites, with the Lewis and Clark Expedition, the Nez Percé were friendly to whites, and they accepted missionaries in the 1830s. After the Nez Percé Reservation was established in Idaho in 1855, the U.S. government bought some of their land to accommodate a gold rush. Some Nez Percés never accepted this change, and it eventually led to the Nez Percé War of 1877. Under Chief Joseph, the Nez Percé fought the U. S. military so admirably that many whites called for better treatment for them. Now many Nez Percé live on the Nez Percé and Colville Reservations, both in their historic country.

Their French name has been the source of much confusion. Given them by traders (they called themselves the Nimipu), it means Pierced Nose; but the Nez Percés did not wear nose ornaments. And the Indians pronounce their name not in the French way but to rhyme with *fez purse*. This custom has in turn led to confusion when Anglo sophisticates see the name and pronounce it "NAY pair-SAY"; mountains and buildings get that name, and so on. Courtesy asks that Anglos pronounce the name as the people themselves do, at least for the tribe and perhaps for things named after the tribe. Despite the pronunciation, the tribe retains an acute accent over the final *e* in the name.

NICE KITTY Cowboy talk for a skunk.

NIGGER Among the MOUNTAIN MEN, simply another word for "fellow," whether white, black, or Indian. The white trappers often applied it to themselves—"This nigger means to make meat," and the like. Language changes, perhaps even with a word as unacceptable as this one: Linguist J. L. Dillard says the term *nigger* could be used without offense in American English until 1928; perhaps this was the intention in Mark Twain's *Huckleberry Finn* and Joseph Conrad's *Nigger of the Narcissus*.

Nigger (like *Indian*) was often applied on the frontier to anything seen as inferior or bad. Thus a *nigger brand* was a saddle sore; *nigger gin* was probably rough, home-brewed stuff.

OTHER COMBINATIONS: *nigger catcher* (a tab on a saddle for holding the latigo), *nigger day* (logger talk for Saturday), *nigger driver* (what loggers sometimes called the foreman), and *nigger-in-a-blanket* (a cowboy dessert, raisins in dough).

NIGHT HERD To ride around the cattle on the bed ground all night long to keep them settled and tranquil. The night herders on trail drives divided the night into two-hour watches. When working, each rider used an important horse in his string, the *night horse*, chosen for its night vision, surefootedness, and dependability. (Though never female, it was sometimes jokingly known as the *nightmare*.) In case of a stampede, the night horse had the rider's life in its hooves. Andy Adams described the normal routine of night-herding in *Log of a Cowboy*:

The guards ride in a circle about four rods outside the sleeping cattle, and by riding in opposite directions, make it impossible for any animal to make its escape without being noticed by the riders. The guards usually sing or whistle continuously, so that the sleeping herd may know that a friend and not an enemy is keeping vigil over their dreams. . . . The night horses soon learn their duty, and a rider may fall asleep or doze along in the saddle, but the horses will maintain their distance in their leisurely sentinel rounds.

And in the night herder's singing was the cradle of the one art of the West, the cowboy song.

NIGHTHAWK In the days of the open range, the *night wrangler*, the hand who watched the horses while others night-herded the cows; or the night wrangler for a caravan of wagons. This word was also sometimes used to mean **NIGHT HERDER.**

NISEI (NEE-say) A child of Japanese immigrants born in the United States. The Nisei of the 442nd Combat Team fought valiantly for the United States in Italy during World War II while many of their relatives were imprisoned in camps in the West. The term comes from Japanese, meaning second generation. *Isei* is the Japanese name for immigrant, the first generation. *Sansei* is the third generation.

NO BEANS IN THE WHEEL A way of describing a revolver that's unloaded and so leaves you defenseless.

NO MAN'S LAND A name for the panhandle of Oklahoma, a narrow strip of land between Colorado and Kansas on the north and Texas on the south. At one time, it belonged to no governmental administrative unit, thus the name. It is immediately west of the Cherokee Outlet (see under **CHEROKEE.**)

NO-BREAKFAST-FOREVER LIST A figurative list of the dead, especially those burned in prairie fires. (For more expressions pertaining to death, see **CASH IN YOUR CHIPS.**)

NOGAL (noh-GAHL) In the Southwest, a walnut tree. It can also be a hickory tree or, in Texas, a pecan. Borrowed from Spanish (in which it means "walnut").

NOONING Taking a midday stop on the trail. For Santa Fe Trail caravans, the break was often long enough for two meals to be served, both breakfast and dinner. Also called *nooning it.*

NOOTKA CYPRESS An evergreen (*Chamaecyparis nootkatensis*) of the Northwest Pacific Coast, valued for its hard wood. The *Nootka fir* is the Douglas fir.

NOOTKA HAT A fiber head covering woven by Nootka Indians. These people live on the west side of Vancouver Island.

NOPAL (noh-PAHL) The prickly pear **CACTUS** (*Opuntia* sp.) or its flat pads, which are used in Southwestern cooking. The fruit is also eaten. From Spanish.

NORTEÑOS Hispanics of northern New Mexico. Separated from the rest of Spanish colonial America, they developed in their own ways. The Spanish that is spoken in northern New Mexico is distinguished by archaisms that date back to the seventeenth century, and is rich in contractions and colloquialisms. William deBuys writes in *River of Traps:*

> Something happened in the soil of New Mexico. Isolated by broad deserts from their countrymen to the south, the *norteños* of New Mexico drew nourishment from the land in which they lived. People from other regions rarely appreciate that New Mexico was a frontier unlike any other in our national experience. While Virginia, Kentucky, or Missouri may have represented civilization's advancing edge for two or three generations, New Mexico remained a lonely and embattled frontier for three hundred years. It became *una patria,* a fatherland, in its own right.

NORTHER A freezing gale blowing from the north across Texas or other parts of the Southwest. Northers had and have a reputation for nastiness and can drive cows many a mile. Also called a *Texas norther.* A particularly bad one is a *blue norther,* one with rain is a *wet norther* and one without is a *dry norther*; a windy one is a *blue whistler*; also called a *blue blizzard, blue-tailed norther,* or *blue Texas norther.*

NORTHERN SPOTTED OWL In the Pacific Northwest, a small owl whose habitat is a large area of old-growth forest. This endangered species became the focus of much controversy when logging was stopped to protect that habitat. A difficulty is that the area required is large for such a small bird.

NOR'WESTER (1) Among **MOUNTAIN MEN**, a man of the Northwest Company, the onetime competitor of the Hudson's Bay Company for the furs of Canada and the American Northwest. The *Northwest blanket* and *Northwest gun* (or *fusee* or *fusil*), a smoothbore musket, were trade items of this fur company. (2) Also, a person of the Pacific Northwest or a tall tale of that country.

NOSE BAG (1) Cowboy talk for a restaurant (from the feeding of horses by nose bags). (2) Also a logger's term for a lunch bucket; a logging outfit that offered such lunches might have been derisively called a *nosebag show.*

NOTCHER A killer, a gunman (from their reported practice of notching their guns to keep count of their murders). A killer horse was said to have a *notch in his tail.*

NUBBING Cowboy talk for the saddle **HORN**.

NUSHNIK Alaskan term for an outhouse. Also spelled *nooshnik;* adapted from Russian.

NUT PINE Any of several nut-bearing pine trees of the Rocky Mountains or Southwest, such as *Pinus monophyllus.*

O

OBSIDIAN A black volcanic glass used by Indians for arrow and spear points. Found mainly from the Rockies west, it was a trade item to Eastern Indians.

OCEAN WATER A **NAVAJO** term for an improvised intoxicating beverage made by agitating hairspray with water, used by teenagers (and probably others) to get a cheap high. Also takes the short form *ocean*.

OCOTILLO (oh-koh-TEE-yoh) A cactuslike shrub of the Southwest (*Fouquieria splendends*) consisting of long, slender sticks that bear striking red flowers in the spring. It's also called *coachwhip cactus*. Borrowed from Spanish.

OFF HIS FEED Cowboy talk for someone who's looking poorly or feeling bad.

OFF THE RESERVATION When said of nineteenth-century Indians, literally off their assigned ground, with the implication that they were hunting, raiding, or otherwise acting up. By extension, a way of describing a person who's out of turn or out of bounds. A weak-minded person might have been called *off his mental reservation*.

OILER A slang name for a Mexican. Like **GREASER**, it was surely derogatory.

OJALA! (oh-hah-LAH) In the Southwest, an interjection of approval. Borrowed from Spanish (in which it means "I hope so").

OJIBWAY (oh-JIB-way; oh-jib-WAY) A large Algonquian tribe of the western Great Lakes region, also known as the Chippewa. In the Algonquian language both names refer to the puckered seam on their moccasins. They call themselves *Anishinabe*, "the first men."

Historically, they had a woodlands culture that was in many ways the ancestor of the **PLAINS INDIAN** culture: They lived in **TIPI**-like shelters, hunted and gathered (especially wild rice), and farmed. Central to their religion was the Midewiwin, Grand Medicine Society.

Contacted early by French fur traders, the Ojibway became important in the beaver trade, and major allies of the French against the British and the Americans. With the guns they traded for, this numerous and powerful tribe also drove the **DAKOTA** onto the **GREAT PLAINS**.

Now the Ojibway live on reservations in states along the Canadian border from Michigan to Montana and in two provinces of Canada.

OJO (OH-hoh) In the Southwest, a spring, especially a hot spring (*ojo caliente*). Borrowed from Spanish (in which it means "eye").

OKIE (1) A migratory worker from Oklahoma. John Steinbeck immortalized the plight of some of these people during the Great Depression in his novel *Grapes* *of Wrath.* Also any Oklahoman. (2) Among loggers, Okie was a derogatory term, implying an incompetent.

OKLAHOMA COMBINATIONS: *Oklahoma rain* (a sandstorm), *Oklahoma Run* (the Oklahoma land rush of 1889), an *Oklahoma* (a temporary shack during the Oklahoma Run), *Oklahoma fever* (the land hunger that brought people there).

OLD In the West as elsewhere, often a term of camaraderie or rank with no reference to age. Thus young **MOUNTAIN MEN** called each other *old* COON and *old hoss* in comradeship. The boss of a cow outfit was called *old man* while still in his twenties, and so on.

COMBINATIONS: Old **EPHRAIM** or Old Caleb (the grizzly bear), *old fruit* (in Texas slang, the genuine article, the real McCoy), Old **HICKORY** (a shirt of a dark blue checked material, common on the frontier prior to the Civil War), *Old Pills* (what loggers called the doctor), Old Reliable (cowboy talk for the Sharps rifle), *old settler* (any early settler, especially a **CHEROKEE** who settled in the West before 1819), *old sledge* (all-fours or seven-up), *old socks* (a logger's name for a buddy), *old woman* or *old lady* (the **COOKIE**, who was male).

OLD-GROWTH FOREST Forest with its natural cycles essentially undisturbed by logging, road-building, or clearing. Such forests are valued because they provide habitat for animals (such as the spotted owl) unable to adjust to conditions brought by intrusion, permit scientists to observe the workings of untouched natural systems, and for other reasons. (Some forests that have been cut selectively rather than clear-cut may still be considered old-growth.) The issue of whether to log such forest has been especially heated in the Pacific Northwest for more than two decades because the economies of Oregon and Washington depend heavily on logging. Also called *ancient forest* or *original forest.*

OLD IVORY In Alaska, so-called *fossil ivory,* tusks of walrus or other creatures valued by carvers for its yellow staining, due to aging. *New ivory* is seasoned but still white; *green ivory* is from newly killed animals and so is very white.

OLD MAN CACTUS In the Southwest, a cactus (*Cephalocereus senilis*) so called from its hanging white "hair."

OLD PAWN In the Indian trade of the Southwest, jewelry pawned by **NAVAJOS** or other Indians at the trading posts. Presumed either to be old or to be made for themselves, it is thought superior to the jewelry made for sale to traders or tourists. Many of the finest older pieces of traditional jewelry have passed from Navajo hands into private collections and museums.

OLLA (OY-yuh) In the Southwest, a water jar of earthenware or fiber. Women sometimes carried these jars with head straps. Borrowed from Spanish.

OMAHOG A jocular name for residents of Omaha, Nebraska.

ON THE DODGE On the run from the law. Similar expressions are to *belly through the bush, pull* (or *take*) *freight to the tules,* **GONE TO TEXAS,** *head for the sundown* (to be a *sundowner*), *look over your shoulder, on the high lope, on the scout* or *cuidado, stampede to the wild bunch, ride the coulees* or *the highlines,* and to *whip a tired pony out of Texas.*

ON THE PROD Full of piss and vinegar and looking for trouble. Said of both people and critters.

SIMILAR COMBINATIONS: *on the drift* (a way of describing a wandering cowboy), *on the peck* (similar to one the prod), *on the prairie* (a mountain-man expression for without charge, free), *on the skids* (doing badly, going downhill, as a log went along the **SKID ROAD**), *on tick* (on credit), *on the warpath* (fighting mad).

ONE-ARMED BANDIT A slot machine for gambling that has one lever.

ONE-HORSE OUTFIT A little ranch, a rawhide outfit, a **SHIRTTAIL RANCH**, a *two-by-four outfit.* By extension, *one-horse* describes anything small or inconsequential.

OOSIK In Alaska, a walrus penis bone, carved ornamentally; common as a souvenir.

OPEN RANGE Unfenced cattle country, uncontrolled and theoretically available to anyone. In practice, big ranchers often got title to the land that had water and let their cows wander freely over the public grassland, gaining a kind of de facto ownership. Thus fences brought the first big revolution in the Western cattle business, and the days of the open range became one of the great symbols of freedom lost.

In the days of the open range, *open-range branding* meant branding calves when and where you found them rather than at roundup. Since rustlers branded that way, it came to be regarded with disfavor.

OPEN-FACED COWS Cowboy talk for **HEREFORDS**, which have white faces.

OPERA Cowboy talk for a session of **BRONC-BUSTING** with spectators on the fences. The top rail was sometimes called the *opera house.*

OREGON COMBINATIONS: *Oregon jargon* (another name for **CHINOOK** jargon), *Oregon puddingfoot* (a horse bred from a draft animal and a riding horse, a type developed in Oregon, also called an *Oregon horse*), *Oregon question* (the issue of the border between U.S. and British territory in the Pacific Northwest, settled in 1846 by mutual acceptance of the 49th parallel), *Oregon short line* (a *fraid strap,* a strap on the fork of a saddle to help the rider stay on a bucking horse).

PLANTS: *Oregon grape* (*Mahonia aquifolium,* not a grape but an evergreen plant of the Northwest with an edible fruit that resembles grapes), *Oregon alder, Oregon ash, Oregon cedar.*

ANIMALS: *Oregon chickadee, Oregon elk, Oregon finch.*

OREGON TRAIL A major overland trail, used not by cattle, like the big north-south trails, but by westwarding emigrants and by freighters. In 1841 trails established by Indians and beaver men were consolidated into this trail, running more than 2,000 miles from the western edge of Missouri to the new settlements in Oregon's Willamette Valley. It followed the Platte River into Wyoming, then the Sweetwater River into South Pass, then crossed to the Snake River, and followed that to the Columbia River. The few way stations of the 1840s included Fort Laramie, Fort Bridger, and Fort Hall.

The largest migrations took place in the 1840s (including the Mormon migrations), and people and livestock kept using the trail for forty years. (See also **CALIFORNIA TRAIL,** which branched off the Oregon Trail toward California.)

The *Oregon country* was originally not the modern state of Oregon but the entire Pacific Northwest from California to Alaska between the mountains and the sea. This changed in 1846 with the acceptance of the 49th parallel as the U.S. border on the north and again in 1853 with the establishment of Washington Territory.

OREJANO (oh-ray-HAH-noh) A term of buckaroo country for a **SLICK,** a **MAVERICK,** a critter neither branded nor earmarked. In early Texas, it meant a wild (thus unmarked) cow. Borrowed from Spanish (in which it means "ear").

ORGAN-PIPE CACTUS In the Southwest, a tall cactus of many parallel cylinders, thus the name; found in the **SONORAN DESERT.** Also called **PITAHAYA.**

ORO (OH-roh) The Spanish word for gold, common in the names of places and businesses throughout the Southwest.

OSAGE (OH-sayj) The largest tribe of the Southern Siouan Indians. The word is a version of their name for themselves, which means "war people." Originally of the Atlantic seaboard, the Southern Siouan Indians (also including the Kansa, Omaha, Ponca, and Quapaw) lived, at the time of white contact in the seventeenth century, in Missouri, Kansas, and Illinois. They dwelt in permanent lodges (mostly of earth) but hunted buffalo. They warred with other Indians, particularly the **DAKOTA** tribes, but were generally friendly to whites and in the 1870s accepted removal to Indian Territory.

COMBINATIONS: *Osage hunting trail* (a trail between the Arkansas and Missouri Rivers made by the Osage), *Osage orange* (a tree, *Maclura pomifera,* of the country of the Osage, used by Indians to make bows and by Anglos as hedges), *Osage plum* (a wild, yellow plum known for its delicious taste).

OTERO (oh-TAIR-oh) Cowboy talk for a big **STEER.** From Spanish (in which it means hill).

OUIJA BOARD In Alaska, a small platform between dogs and sled where a musher stands and steers the sled by means of the **GEE POLE.** Also called a *gee board.*

OUTFIT (1) A ranch; a ranch crew. (2) An organization or crew rigged to do any job, like freighting or drilling. (3) Someone's personal gear. (4) A pickup truck, usually not just any pickup but one rigged to do a job, such as haul horses or hay. (5) Almost any collection of machinery or equipment—like *haying outfit, shearing outfit.* (6) Almost anything. In *Arizona Nights,* Stewart Edward White even calls a breed of chicken an outfit.

OUTLAW An uncontrollable horse, a man-killer; sometimes a cow that's half-wild. Horses spoiled in training or allowed to become unmanageable are often described as *outlawed.* (See also **STOCKHORSE**). The other familiar meaning—a lawless person, a fugitive from the law, a robber—long predates the West.

OUTRIDER A range rider; a cowboy who rode his employer's range far and yon to spot trouble. He was like a *line rider,* except that the area the line rider patrolled was the boundaries of the ranch only; the outrider went everywhere on the place. *Outridings* were inspection trips.

OUTSIDE MAN Among the **ALEUT**, a spirit who comes to get misbehaving children; a bogey man. He especially haunts his relatives, and may cause serious difficulties, even death.

OVER THE WILLOWS A cowboy description of a river in flood stage, because willows border most Plains and mountain streams. A river over the willows threw difficulty and danger in the face of a trail herd because the animals would resist going into the water, and likely not all would come out.

OVERGRAZED A way of describing rangeland damaged by too many cattle or sheep feeding for too long. Whether the federal government properly protects public land from overgrazing is a hot subject for debate in the West.

OVERLAND STAGE The system of mail transportation from St. Louis to San Francisco. Established in 1858 by John Butterfield, it was made obsolete by the completion of the transcontinental railroad in 1869. Its vehicle was the overland coach or stage. The stage lines carried passengers as well, at the rate of about fifteen cents a mile. The trip was a trial. (Those who want to know how great a trial are referred to Mark Twain's extravagant depiction in *Roughing It.*) *Overland stage* is also what contemporary Indians jokingly call the cross-country bus system.

The term *overland trade* meant mainly the trade on the Santa Fe Trail. Watts says *overland trout* may have been a fanciful **GREAT PLAINS** term for bacon.

OVERTHRUST BELT A region of the intermountain West (Wyoming, Utah, Colorado, and Idaho) discovered in the 1970s to be rich in deep deposits of petroleum and, as a result, much explored in the late 1970s and early 1980s.

OWL HOOT An **OUTLAW**. Thus the *owlhoot trail,* the outlaw's way of life. But to *hear the owl hoot* was to get a snootful or have lots of experiences—or both at the same time. To *hear the owl hoot* is an expression of Red English meaning to have a warning of bad things coming, such as a premonition of death.

OWLHEAD An untrainable, unridable horse. (See **CANNER** for other names of unfit horses.)

OX TRAIN A train of wagons pulled by oxen as opposed to one hauled by mules. Ox trains pulled what was called **GRASS FREIGHT** because oxen could work on grass alone, while mules required corn. Ox trains were more often called **BULL TRAINS**—paradoxically, since oxen are castrated.

OXBOW STIRRUP A big wooden stirrup bent like an ox yoke, which gave a similar name to an *oxbow bend* in a river. Sometimes called an *ox yoke*.

OZARK One name of the Quapaw, a Southern Siouan tribe of Missouri and Arkansas (see **OSAGE**). The French called these people *Aux Arcs* ("With Bows"), which the ungallic frontiersmen rendered as Ozarks.

P

PACIFIC RIM A region of common business and other interests, consisting of the countries touching the Pacific Ocean from western North America to China and Southeast Asia. COMBINATIONS: *Pacific seaboard, Pacific Northwest, Pacific salmon.*

PACK (1) To ride into remote country carrying your supplies on horseback. Originally, people packed everywhere the roads weren't good enough for wagons: Mountain men, miners, surveyors, the army, and others ventured into the wilderness by packing. Now it is mostly a **DUDE**'s entertainment and is called a *pack trip.* Hunters also often pack in. (2) To carry loads on the backs of pack animals. (3) To carry anything regularly: A sheriff packs a star, and a badman packs a gun; cows *pack irons* (brands) and loggers pack *balloons* (bedrolls). (4) A **MOUNTAIN MAN**'s word for a bundle of beaver hides, grained and ready for shipment to the States. The bundles are variously reported to have weighed either about 52 or about 100 pounds each. (See also **BEAVER, PLEW.**) (5) A **PACKER**'s word for the load on one side of an animal's back.

COMBINATIONS: *pack animal* (a horse, mule, or burro trained or accustomed to carrying loads), *pack cover* (a piece of heavy canvas used to keep the weather off loads), *pack dog* (a load-carrying dog, once commonly used by Indians), *pack hitch* (a diamond hitch, the most common lashing technique to keep loads where they belong), *pack-mule express* (a pack outfit serving as an express company), *pack outfit* (a firm that runs pack trips), *pack saddle* (a device that sits on the animal's back to lash loads onto; see also **APAREJO, SAWBUCK**), *pack trail* (one suitable for pack animals; also called a *pack way*), *pack train* (a string of such animals; if made of mules, it may be called a *mule train*), *"Pack up!* "(the instruction to get your pack animals loaded and ready to move).

A fine and funny book on packing is Joe Back's *Horses, Hitches, and Rocky Trails.*

PACK RAT The Rocky Mountain rodent also known as a *trade rat*. It ferrets small objects away from camps and hides them, and is said to leave worthless substitutes.

PACK THE MAIL In cowboy talk, to ride fast.

PACKER A man who loads the animals and delivers the loads where they're headed. Now he is almost entirely a man who guides dudes, fishermen, or hunters on pack trips. He's also called an *arriero, mozo* (when an assistant), and a *pack master* (when the boss). Some of the old-time packers were legendary. In *One Man's West,* David Lavender wrote of the ones who packed equipment and supplies to a mine near Ouray, Colorado, in the 1930s:

> Nothing stumped them. If some piece of freight came along which they couldn't get on one mule's back—and it had to be singularly heavy and ill-shaped to occasion this—they would sling it on poles hung between two mules. Unusually recalcitrant pieces of machinery were lashed to a flat sled and pulled up the narrow, twisting trail by a whole string of mules in tandem. In ingenuity, brawn, daring, and plain brute courage, in all the tricks of dealing with evil nature and rebellious livestock, the mountain packers have no peers.

PADDLE When said of a horse, to wing out with the forefeet when walking.

PADDLE WHEEL In the early West, a gambling game similar to roulette.

PADDLE-AND-ANVIL A method of finishing pottery, striking the coiled pot on the outside with a paddle while holding something round against the inside. *Paddling* is pressing a carved paddle against a pot to imprint designs on it.

PADRE (PAHD-ray) A Southwestern expression for a Catholic priest or monk. Borrowed from Spanish.

PAHA SAPA The LAKOTA name for their ancestral home, the Black Hills. Though the Hills were given to them in perpetuity by an 1868 treaty, a gold rush filled the Hills with white folks in 1874, and the land was lost to the Indians. The courts

An army packer ties barrels of flour on his mule, 1876.
[PHOTOGRAPH BY S. J. MORROW; COURTESY OF NATIONAL ARCHIVES (165-FF-2F-14).]

have ruled that the taking was illegal, and the parties are still negotiating for an acceptable remedy: the return of lands, payment, or both.

PAHO The prayer stick of the **HOPI** Indians, used in a supplicating way in ceremonies. A feather or some sacred meal may be attached, and the stick was often carved and painted. Also called *baho.*

PAIL A range verb meaning to milk a cow, an onerous task to a cowboy. Sometimes it means to water a cow from a pail.

PAINCOURT (PAN-koor) An eighteenth-century name for St. Louis. From the French, meaning literally "short of bread," it came from frequent scarcity of provisions in the town.

PAINT A spotted horse, white with large areas of either black, brown, or red. Now paint horses are registered and must be bred from quarter horses, thoroughbreds, or other paints. Historically, *paint* meant the same as **PINTO**, though some observers say *paint* was used more in the East and *pinto* in the West. These horses are often called *painted horses* or *painted ponies.* **APPALOOSAS**, which have small spots on the rump and back, are neither paints nor pintos. (See **BUCK-SKIN** for horse colors.)

　　Old-time cowhands liked paints for show but not for work, thinking that they lacked *bottom* (endurance). Since spotted horses in those days were Indian ponies, this may have reflected a prejudice against anything Indian.

PAINT DAUBER The man who paints the brand on sheep.

PAINT FOR WAR In cowboy talk, to get ready to fight. Based jocularly on the Indians' preparing for war by painting their bodies.

PAINT POT A *mud pot,* a boiling spring of mud. At Fountain Paint Pots in Yellowstone National Park, bubbling hot springs attack the rock, mix with the softened material, and create these wonderful oddities, which range from sorrel-colored to ochre. A *mud volcano* is a big paint pot.

PAINT YOUR TONSILS In cowboy talk, to drink whiskey. If you get drunk, you've *painted your nose.* (For many words for drunkenness, see **ROOSTERED.**)

PAINTBRUSH The Indian paintbrush *(Casileja linariaefolia),* a flower of the mountainous West that has somewhat the appearance of a paintbrush dipped in brilliant red, orange, or yellow paint. It is the state flower of Wyoming.

PAIR OF HEADLIGHTS Two eggs. Ordered with a string of flats for the engineer, says historian Francis Fugate, it asks for eggs with bacon.

PAIR OF OVERALLS Cowboy talk for two drinks. He wants them right quick for a good start.

PAIR UP For a cow and calf to get back together after branding; also known as **MOTHERING UP.**

PAISANO (pie-ZAHN-oh) (1) A Southwestern expression for a compatriot; a fellow countryman; a country man or peasant. When used by Anglos, it is sometimes derogatory. Borrowed from Spanish. (2) Another name for the **ROAD RUNNER.**

PAIUTE A Shoshonean people of the **GREAT BASIN** and California, also called *Pah-Utes, Pah-Yutas, Pah-Utches,* and the like. Whites often simply (and contemptuously) called them **DIGGERS.** Not using the horse, they subsisted by desert gathering and some hunting. They lived in brush shelters and wore little; they were skilled basket-makers. Divided into two groups, northern and southern, they now live on many small reservations in Oregon and Nevada.

PALAVER A parley; a long talk, such as a council between whites and Indians. Linguist J. L. Dillard says the term came into English from the Indian-English contact language, which got it from the maritime *lingua franca.*

PALEFACE White man. Perhaps a word of Indian-English pidgin, dating to the early nineteenth century. It may be mostly a term whites attribute to Indians jokingly. (See **ANGLO** for other Indian terms for white people.)

PALO ALTO (PAH-loh AHL-toh; PAH-loh AL-toh with the *a* as in *corral*) A slouch hat popular among California gold-rushers, resembling the later **STETSON** that was called Boss of the Plains. The Spanish translates as "high pole" or "tall tree"—*palo alto* was what the Spaniards named the California redwoods.

COMBINATIONS: *palo amarillo* (hollygrape and chamiso), *palo blanco* (the soapberry that yields berries that can be used for soap), *palo verde* (a green, leafless tree—also called *retama* or *lluvia de ora*—with spectacular yellow blossoms).

PALOMINO (pah-loh-MEE-noh) A golden horse with a cream-colored mane and tail (for many colors and markings of horses, see **BUCKSKIN**); a color of horse, not a breed. Borrowed from Spanish.

PALOUSE A grassland along the Snake River in western Idaho and eastern Washington, so named by the **VOYAGEURS** from their Canadian French word for grassland, *pelouse.* Anglos called the **NEZ PERCÉ** Indians of that region the Palouse (or Pelouse) Indians, and the horses they bred, Palouse horses (later **APPALOOSAS**). In that country a *palouser* is a homemade lantern (a candle in a can), a greenhorn, or a sunset.

PAN The gold-mining gear of the common man without money, a shallow vessel the shape of a big skillet but without a handle. He uses it to wash gravel, looking for yellow.

As a verb, *pan* means to wash gravel with a pan, to be engaged in the process of panning. Soil is said to *pan well* or *poorly.* It's also *panned out;* something that panned out succeeded. By figurative extension, even a person may be panned (checked out closely). (See also **PLACER**.)

COMBINATIONS: *pan amalgamation* (a process of separating gold and silver from ore in a panlike utensil, a *pan amalgamator* or *pan mill*), *pan charge* (what's in a pan amalgamator), *pan miner*, *pan tailings* (the residue from panning gold-bearing soil), *pan test* (a test made with a pan for gold in soil), *pan washing* or *working* (panning gold-bearing soil).

PANHANDLE A strip of land sticking out from a state or territory in the way that a handle sticks out from a pan. Though this term is not necessarily Western, it is associated with several Western states—the Alaska panhandle, Idaho panhandle, Oklahoma panhandle, and Texas panhandle. Residents of panhandles are called *panhandlers*. A panhandler is also someone who asks passersby for money or food.

Panning for gold near Virginia City, Montana, 1871.

[PHOTOGRAPH BY WILLIAM HENRY JACKSON; COURTESY OF NATIONAL ARCHIVES (57-HS-909).]

PAN-INDIANISM A movement among contemporary Indians to recognize common causes, beliefs, problems, and so on. Now Indians of many heritages are uniting to face the dominant Anglo culture and are presenting a common front to the U.S. government about Indian issues. Previously, historical animosities between tribes persisted (even having students from certain tribes at the same schools could cause serious difficulties), and the Indians worked together less in the political and cultural arenas.

Through pan-Indianism many terms, customs, and foods once associated with one tribe, or a few tribes, have spread throughout Indian culture—for instance, **FRY BREAD** and the bumper sticker it inspired: Fry Bread Power.

PANNIER (PAN-yer, the *a* as in *corral*) In packing, a container lashed onto a pack-saddle for carrying heavy loads. Bag panniers may be made of leather, cloth, or canvas. Box panniers are made of wood. The gear used on *pack trips* is largely carried in panniers. From the French *panier* ("basket").

PANOCHE (puh-NOH-chee) A Southwestern term for raw sugar or candy made of brown sugar. Adapted from the Spanish *panocha*, it's also spelled *panocha* and *penuche*.

PANSAJE (pahn-SAH-hay) A Texas term for a barbecue. Around the end of the nineteenth century, pansajes were for men only. Borrowed from Spanish.

PANTS RATS Cowboy talk for body lice, a nice bit of cowboy drollery. Also *seam squirrel*. A favorite Western painter, Charlie Russell, tells a funny story about them:

> It's one spring roundup, back in the early '80s. We're out on circle, an' me an' Pete's ridin' together. Mine's a center-fire saddle, and I drop back to straighten the blanket an' set it. I ain't but a few minutes behind him, but the next I see of Pete is on the bank of this creek, which didn't have no name then. He's off his hoss an' has stripped his shirt off. With one boulder on the ground an' another about the same size in his hand, he's poundin' the seams of his shirt. He's so busy he don't hear me when I ride up, and he's cussin' and swearin' to himself. I hear him mutter, "I'm damned if this don't get some of the big ones!"

Well, from this day on, this stream is known as Louse Creek.

PAPAGO A Piman Indian people of southern Arizona. Their name in their own language means Bean People, and their country is called *Papagueria*. Historically, they avoided conflict with the United States and allied themselves with non-Indians to fight the **APACHE**. They are known as expert desert-dwellers and fine basket-makers and have an agricultural economy. They now live in Arizona on the San Xavier Reservation, the Gila Bend Reservation, and the Papago Reservation proper, the second largest in the United States.

The Papago village Schuchuli, Arizona, was the first village to operate on electricity provided by a stand-alone system of photovoltaic power, in an experiment of the National Aeronautics and Space Administration starting in the late 1970s.

PAPER Marked cards used by dishonest gamblers. To *play the papers* meant to gamble.

PAPER BREAD A thin bread made from corn by the **HOPI** and **NAVAJOS**. Also called **PIKI**.

PAPER CARTRIDGE Ammunition for a muzzle-loading gun before the Civil War, **BLACK POWDER** behind a lead ball encased in heavy paper or linen for ramming down the barrel.

PAPER SON A ruse used by Chinese immigrants. A man with citizenship would claim that a younger man was his son so the fellow could be admitted to the United States.

PAPER WAGON A Red English word for a *stagecoach*, because stagecoaches carried the mail.

PAPOOSE A term of Indian-English pidgin (like **SQUAW**, originally Algonquian) for an infant or other small child. Not a Westernism but carried west by frontiersmen. Also spelled *pappouse*, *papouse*, and otherwise.

COMBINATIONS: *Papoose basket* was a Southwestern term for a basket or bassinet for infants. A *papoose board* was a **CRADLEBOARD.** *Papoose root* is *squaw root,* or *blue cohosh,* used by the Indians as a diuretic.

PARADA (puh-RAH-duh) A term of California and buckaroo country for a herd of cattle or sometimes a **CAVVY** (string of saddle horses). Borrowed from Spanish (in which it means "stopping place"). *Parada grounds* refers to a spot you pick for working cattle.

PARD Short for *partner*. Often a cowboy's pard was the fellow he was paired with daily on the range, but the word was used in other Western contexts as well.

PARFLECHE (PAR-flesh) (1) Among the **MOUNTAIN MEN** and the Indians of the Plains and mountains, **RAWHIDE;** a hide (usually buffalo) with the hair off. (2) The envelopes or boxes made by the Indians from this rawhide for storage, usually decorated with geometrical designs. (Other objects, such as shields and soles for moccasins, were also made of this rawhide.) (3) Among cowboys, it meant something similar, **WAR BAG** or portmanteau.

The term came to English from Canadian French, meaning to turn away *(parry)* an arrow *(flèche),* because of its ability to deflect arrows as a shield. It is not used in the Southwest.

PARK In the Rocky Mountains, a natural clearing, an area of open meadows surrounded by timber or mountains. Also called a **HOLE.** South Park is the celebrated Bayou Salado of the **MOUNTAIN MEN,** the region in Colorado around the head of the South Platte River, which the trappers loved for its abundant game and generally shining times. Brown's Park (or Brown's Hole) was first a trapper's meeting area, then a notorious hideout for outlaws. Yellowstone National Park is full of parks, open mountain meadows. Like the great canyons, the vistas of **SLICKROCK,** and the high peaks, parks are among the most beautiful places in the West.

PARKA A hooded coat for wear against cold weather. Of **ESKIMO-ALEUT** origin meaning "outer garment of skin," though parkas are now made of various clothing materials, including synthetics.

PARLOR CATTLE CAR A car on a train for cattle with a passage on one side for watering and feeding without unloading, apparently a great luxury. *Parlor* was applied to anything luxurious, fancy, or citified. Thus *parlor gun* (a derringer) and *parlor house* (not originally Western; a fancy whorehouse, in contrast with **CRIB**).

PAROLE A certificate given to Indian leaders by Lewis and Clark or other early U.S. government representatives, intended to establish the recipient as the legal head of his tribe. This practice of the government ignored customary Indian social organization and leadership.

PARTIDA (par-TEE-duh) Any group or band, especially a bunch of **CATTLE**; though the number is indefinite, the suggestion is of a lot. Borrowed from Spanish (in which it means "political party" or "faction").

PARTIDARIO (par-tee-DAH-ree-oh) A New Mexican sheepherder who sharecrops sheep. At the end of the season, he owes the owner a payment of wool and lambs, and often does not make enough money to do much more than cover his expenses.

PARTISAN (1) Among the **MOUNTAIN MEN**, the leader of a brigade of trappers. (See also **COUREUR DE BOIS**.) (2) The leader of an Indian war party. Borrowed from French, the word apparently came to English from the French-Canadian fur men.

PASEO (pah-SAY-oh) In the Southwest, a public walkway or boulevard; formerly meant a stroll or ride for pleasure. The similar *pasear* historically indicated a walk or trip, either as verb or noun. It could be as casual as "Let's pasear a little," but a California publication spoke in 1847 of a pasear back to the States.

PASS In gambling, to decline to bet. To *pass the buck*, in **POKER**, is to decline to deal. In the West, a player who did not care to deal passed on an object, frequently a buckhorn-handled knife, to the next player, as a sign that he was declining.

PASS In the Southwest, a kind of wine or brandy made in El Paso, known to Americans as Pass wine and Pass whiskey. From the Spanish *paso* (meaning "pass" or "ford").

PASTOR (PAH-stohr) A Southwestern term for a sheepherder, usually an Indian, Mexican, or Basque. Borrowed from Spanish, it's sometimes spelled *pastore*.

PAT HIM ON THE LIP Among loggers, to beat someone up, give him a thrashing.

PATCH LOGGING An approach to logging thought to improve on **CLEAR-CUTTING**. Instead of cutting large areas, the loggers cut in patches of 40 to 200 acres. These regenerate more quickly and pose less danger from fire and insect pests. Some environmentalists are concerned that patch logging doesn't leave sufficient wildlife corridors or stands of forest large enough to support some species of wildlife.

PATHWAY On **NAVAJO** baskets and rugs, a slender band of light color running from the center to the edge. It is a break in the pattern that allows the maker's spirit to escape. In full, the term is *weaver's pathway*.

PATIO (1) A courtyard within a building or connected to a building. Originally Southwestern (borrowed from Spanish), the term is now used throughout the United States. (2) In mining, a yard where ores were cleaned and sorted or where silver was amalgamated. This treatment of silver, chiefly Mexican, was called the *patio process*, or *cold amalgamation process*.

PATRIARCH In **MORMONISM**, a man (now usually elderly) of eminence, endowed with prestige and ordained to give blessings.

PATRON (pah-TROHN) (1) Among **VOYAGEURS** and other fur men, the master or steersman of a boat. In this usage, it is borrowed from Canadian French. (2) In the Southwest, first a *hacendado* (master of a hacienda) or other man of authority or wealth; now simply a boss. As applied to large landowners, the word originally was supposed to imply a benefactor to Indians and others living on his land. In this usage, the word is borrowed from Spanish.

PAUL PRY A cowboy's name for a meddler.

PAUNCHED In cowboy talk, shot in the stomach.

PAW AROUND FOR TURMOIL In cowboy talk, to look for trouble.

PAWNEE A confederacy of Caddoan Indian people who lived in the valley of the Platte River and had a lifestyle seasonally sedentary and nomadic. Most of the year they lived in earth lodges and farmed, but in the summer they lived in **TIPIS** and hunted buffalo. The name Pawnee (derived from the word *pariki*, meaning horn) is said to come from the hair-dressing style of the men—many twisted the forelock into the shape of a horn. The principal bands of this confederation were the Grand Pawnee, Loup (or Mohas, Skidi, or Wolf) Pawnee, and Republican Pawnee.

The Pawnees of the historic period were deeply religious and practiced human sacrifice until 1817. They carried on generations of enmity with most other tribes, especially the **DAKOTA, CHEYENNE,** and **ARAPAHO,** but mostly kept the peace with whites. In the 1850s, they settled on a reservation in eastern Nebraska and subsequently formed the Pawnee Battalion under Major Frank North (who had grown up among them) to protect the laborers of the Union Pacific Railroad from the Pawnees' historic enemies. In 1877 they were moved to Indian Territory (later the state of Oklahoma), where they remain.

COMBINATIONS: *Pawnee macaroni* (a favorite dish of the tribe, made from antelope entrails and fish worms), *Pawnee Rock* (a landmark of the Santa Fe Trail near the Arkansas River, where the Pawnees had battles with the **COMANCHE** and later with some Santa Fe traders), *Pawnee whistle* (a whistling sound Pawnees made to announce their arrival).

PAY DIRT Earth or gravel bearing minerals, especially gold, in economic quantities. The term *pay gravel* was also used among **PLACER** miners, and the terms *pay ore, pay rock, pay shoot, pay streak,* and *pay vein* were heard among hard-rock miners. To *hit* (or *strike*) *pay dirt* was to discover such earth or gravel and, by extension, to strike it rich or to succeed in a large way at anything.

PAY FOOT Twelve inches of lode. Also called a mining *foot.*

PEACEMAKER The most famous revolver of the West. Produced by **COLT** from 1873 on, it was known as the Single Action Army and the Frontier. Part of its usefulness was that (after a brief time as a .45-caliber weapon), it used the same .44-caliber ammunition as the Winchester 1873 model. (See also **SIX-SHOOTER.**)

PEAR BURNER Among cattlemen, a machine for scorching the sharp spines off PRICKLY PEAR cactus so cattle can eat it.

PEARL DIVER What loggers and cowboys called a dishwasher in a logging camp or in a restaurant.

PEAVEY A strong pole, about as long as a man is tall, used by loggers, especially in *log driving* (moving logs downriver). On one end, it has a metal socket, a curved steel hook, and a pike (this last distinguishing it from a CANT HOOK). Sometimes called a *peavey hook* or a *peavey log wrench*. The *peavy log* is the top log on a load.

PECHITA (pay-CHEE-tuh) In the Southwest, the MESQUITE bean, valued by the PAPAGO Indians as food and used as feed for livestock. In the Papago region of southern Arizona, *pechita* (or *béchete*) holes are common near sources of water; these depressions are used for grinding grains and nuts. Borrowed from Spanish.

PECKER NECK Cowboy talk for a horse trained for riding but not for working cows.

PECKER POLE What a logger called a small tree or sapling.

PECOS Literally, to shoot someone and throw the body into the Pecos River, which in the nineteenth century drained a lawless empire in West Texas and New Mexico. By extension, simply to kill a man. (See also DRY-GULCH.) A *Pecos swap* was a theft.

PECOS BILL Cowboy talk for a teller of WINDIES, a fellow who likes to STUFF DUDES. This fellow is also known as a *peddler of loads*. The legendary Pecos Bill was a Texan who was raised by coyotes, rode a mountain lion, and dug the Rio Grande by harnessing a twister. (See also YARN.)

PEDAL In Alaska, for the MUSHER to position himself on a rear runner and push with one foot to help the speed of the DOGSLED. Also called *pumping*.

PEDREGAL (pay-dray-GAHl) A rocky piece of country, especially a region of lava flow. Borrowed from Spanish.

PEELER (1) A BRONC BUSTER, a horse breaker. To *peel horses* was to break or train them or sometimes simply to stick with a critter that was bucking. On the frontier of the Eastern woodlands, a peeler had been a humdinger, an exceptional example of anything. Perhaps a man who could stick on green horses was thought a humdinger. (2) Among cowboys, especially in Texas, a man who skins cows, a STRIPPER. (3) A logger who takes the bark off redwood logs. He uses a *peeling bar* for the work.

PEEPSTONES A derogatory term of gentiles for the transparent stones of power that (in MORMON belief) Joseph Smith used when translating the golden plates inscribed with the *Book of Mormon*. They are properly called Urim and Thummin. Later, by extension, simply a magical stone.

PEEWEE A style of cowboy boot with short tops popular in the early part of the twentieth century.

PEG (1) To mark a mining claim with stakes. (2) For a **BULLDOGGER** to stick a steer's horn into the ground, which **RODEOS** don't permit.

PEG OUT Butt out; die away, become extinct. According to Joseph Porter's *Paper Medicine Man,* whites of the latter half of the nineteenth century expected the Indians "to give up their old ways and become civilized, or, as one newspaper bluntly put it, 'forever peg out.'"

PELADO (pay-LAH-doh) A Mexican who's ignorant and broke. The word (now uncommon) is an equivalent of **GREASER** and as contemptuous. Borrowed from Spanish.

PELON (pay-LOHN) Cowboy talk for a **MULEY**, a cow without horns. Borrowed from Spanish (in which it means "bald").

PEMBINA (pem-BEE-nuh) The highbush cranberry (a variety of *Viburnum americanum*) of North Dakota, whose fruit both Indians and whites use for food. French–Canadian fur traders built a succession of posts named Pembina on the Red River of the North, in the area of the present Pembina, North Dakota, and many **METIS** lived there; later, the American Fur Company and the federal government built posts there; still later, Pembina became a farming center. At one time, people campaigned for a separate territory called Pembina, to be formed from this part of northeastern Dakota Territory. The *Pembina cart* (or *buggy*) was a crudely constructed cart similar to the **RED RIVER CART.** Borrowed from French–Canadian, which was in turn based on Cree words.

PEMMICAN The universal preserved food of the Indians who lived on the buffalo, and later of the **MOUNTAIN MEN** and other frontiersmen who learned Indian ways. Pemmican was made from **BUFFALO** meat (though occasionally other red meat was used) that was jerked, pounded fine, mixed equally by weight with *marrow fat,* and stored in **PARFLECHES** or sewn into other skin sacks. Often dried berries were added, especially **CHOKECHERRIES** and **SERVICEBER-RIES.** Preserved in this way, pemmican lasted for several years.

Pemmican was the staple of Indian raiding parties and of all buffalo Indians during the winter. Summer pemmican was not pemmican made in the summer but made in the late winter or spring for the summer. It was reportedly a superb food and a good diet. The **VOYAGEURS** made a soup called *rub-baboo* by boiling pemmican in water and adding a little flour and sugar.

The Pemmican War was the struggle for dominance in the **FUR TRADE** from 1812 to 1821 between the Hudson's Bay Company and the Northwest Fur Company. Modern usages like *fruit pemmican* are a new ring on the original meaning—pemmican was almost entirely meat. (See also **JERKY.**)

PENITENTE (pen-uh-TEN-tay; pen-uh-TEN-tee) A member of a New Mexican Catholic sect that believes in the saving power of punishment and practices self-flagellation and even a form of crucifixion. Members scourge themselves with whips made from YUCCA fiber (*disciplinas*). Some become *Cristos* and carry their crosses and then are strapped to them in Good Friday ceremonies—some Cristos are said not to have survived this high, holy act. Though persecuted in the past, the sect persists today among some Norteños, and is back in the good graces of the Catholic Church on the condition of modifying its excesses. Also known as *Los Hermanos de Luz.* From Spanish.

PENNY ANTE A way of describing a POKER game in which the ante is limited to a penny. By extension, anything small, inconsequential.

PEON (pay-OWN; PEE-on) In the Southwest, a member of the Mexican laboring class. In the early and middle nineteenth century, a peon was literally a slave or a person held by debt to a landowner in a near-equivalent of slavery. From Spanish.

The word had verb forms, as in "Juan is peoned to the patron." Even Anglo cowboys spoke of hiring out as *peoning out.* The system whereby peasants were held in effective servitude by debt was called *peonage.*

PEOPLE OF THE NORTH Same as RED RIVER METIS.

PEPPER-AND-SALT ROPE A rope of alternating black and white hair.

PEPPERBELLY Texas cowboy talk for a Mexican who eats lots of CHILES. (See also GREASER, OILER, PELADO, which are other unfriendly appellations.)

PEPPERBOX A CAP-AND-BALL or metallic cartridge pistol of the mid-nineteenth century with five or six barrels that revolved to provide more than the one shot of the older pistol. This technology was later replaced by the revolver, in which the cylinder, not the barrels, turned. The pepperbox was also called a *coffee mill.* (For many Western words for a pistol, see SIX-SHOOTER.)

PERCUSSION A term for a firearm whose charge is set off by a percussion cap rather than a flint. Percussion (or *percussion-cap*) weapons succeeded the flintlock from the 1820s onward, and they preceded the breech loader. Metal cartridges incorporating percussion caps or priming compound put percussion caps out of business. A percussion cap (sometimes called a *primer*) was and is a small piece of copper containing a fulminate charge. The cap fits snugly upon the nipple. There the hammer strikes it, causing an explosion that sends a spark through the *touchhole* to the powder.

A *percussion lock* is a firing mechanism that uses percussion caps; also called a *caplock.*

PERMIT (1) A GRAZING PERMIT on public land. (2) A timecard used as a substitute for a union card by a logger.

Petroglyphs in Dinwoody Canyon, Wyoming.
[COURTESY OF AMERICAN HERITAGE SOCIETY, UNIVERSITY OF WYOMING.]

PERPETUAL EMIGRATION FUND Organized in September 1849 in Salt Lake City to aid **MORMONS** in need of secure transportation to the Salt Lake Valley. Donations of money, oxen, wagons, foodstuffs, and other goods were solicited from church members already in the valley and elsewhere. The means advanced for transportation was considered a loan, to be repaid as soon as possible after the travelers' arrival. The company was legally incorporated by the State of Deseret in 1851. When it was disbanded in 1887, it had assisted approximately 50,000 persons.

PERSUADER (1) A revolver. (See also **SIX-SHOOTER**.) (2) A **SPUR**. (3) A **BULL-WHIP**.

PESO (PAY-soh) The Mexican unit of currency, as the dollar is the basic U.S. monetary unit. The number of pesos needed to make a dollar has fluctuated widely. Now the word is often used in the Southwest as a jocular reference to any money. Borrowed from Spanish.

PETER OUT To give out, to get exhausted, as a vein of mineral might do and as people and animals do. Linguist J. L. Dillard says that this verb is a mining Westernism. Its derivation is unknown.

PETRIFIED FOREST An area where logs, stumps, and the like have become fossilized. Early Westerners were mystified and delighted by these places, such as the one in Yellowstone National Park, and they made up stories about them. Horses were said to tremble when they tried to nibble grass of rock. A hunter plunked off a bird's head, but it went on singing because it was stone. Jim Bridger jumped his horse over a huge chasm because even the law of gravity was petrified. And tale-tellers called the stone trees *putrefactions*, perhaps at first out of ignorance, later to have a little fun.

PETROGLYPH A prehistoric carving in rock, usually of gods, men, animals, or religious symbols. In the West, petroglyphs are often the remaining signs of ancient cliff-dwelling Indians (see also **ANASAZI**), and their meaning is much in dispute. A classic example of petroglyphs and *pictographs* (ancient painting on rock) is Newspaper Rock near Canyonlands National Park in Utah. (See also **PICTOGRAPH**.)

PETRUSKI In Alaska, a kind of wild parsley. Also spelled *petrushki*. From Russian.

PEYOTE (pay-OH-tee) A spineless **CACTUS** of the Southwest (especially *Lophophora williamsi*) that yields a hallucinogenic button, which is also known as *raiz diabolica* (literally, "devil root"). These *peyote buttons* (discs) were used as a door to religious visions by Southwestern Indians for centuries (or millennia) and now are the **MEDICINE** of the **NATIVE AMERICAN CHURCH**, eaten ceremonially to help meditation, prayers, and visions. This use of peyote is called *peyotism*; the skilled user is a *peyotero*. Adapted from the Aztec word *peyotl*, it is also spelled *payote* and *pellote*.

PICACHO (pee-KAH-choh, the *a* as in *corral*) In the Southwest, a summit, a peak; sometimes the name of a peak. Borrowed from Spanish.

PICARO (PEE-kuh-roh) In the Southwest, a vagabond, a rogue. Borrowed from Spanish.

PICAROON (pih-kuh-ROON) Among loggers, a pole with a curved hook and a pike, used in *log driving* to pull logs out of eddies and the like. Also called a *pick hand-spike* and a *pick pole*. A similar log-driving tool is the *pike pole*.

PICKED BRAND A cowboy practice of both legitimate and illegitimate purpose. The hair was picked off a **CALF**, using either pliers or a knife, into the shape of a brand, which looked, at a distance, like the calf had been properly branded. When the calf was old enough to separate from its mother, it was then rebranded by the rustler. *Picking a brand* also describes what was done to clarify a blotched or unclear brand; the hair was removed around the brand to make it more visible.

PICKER During shearing, the man who gathers and rolls the sheep fleeces in the shearing pen.

PICKET (1) To stake a horse so the critter can feed but not stray—to stake the horse out. This was and is done with a *picket pin*, which may be anything from a crude stick to a metal stake with a ring. From the pin to the halter runs a *picket rope*, preferably of thick, soft cotton. A *picket pin* may also be a *gopher*, so called because they stand straight and still. The phrase *cut your picket pin* meant "to leave."

(2) On the early Western frontier, a picket was a tree trunk set straight up in the ground to form a stockade or similar obstacle to Indian attack. The word was also used to mean the resulting stockade.

COMBINATIONS: *picket corral, picket fort, picket house, picket hut* and *picket shack* (used in the second half of the nineteenth century). Traders built a picket house on the Red River as late as 1875, setting the tree trunks into a ditch and filling in with dirt. The Picketwire is a river of southeastern Colorado, once called the Rio de las Animas Perdidas en Purgatorio. (That name is an anglicized pronunciation of the Spanish Purgatorio or the French Purgatoire.)

PICKUP A **RODEO** rider who helps a contestant off the critter he's been riding. The *pickup* (or *pickup man*) rides alongside and lets the cowboy get behind him. This is a considerable service because the cowboys are usually eager to get gone as soon as they've stayed on the number of seconds required. Pickups also help get the bucking critter away from riders on the ground and out of the arena.

PICTOGRAPH An ancient Native painting on a rock wall (or on hide, wood, shell, and other surfaces). Like **PETROGLYPHS**, pictographs usually show gods, men, animals, or religious symbols in a simple and stylized way. It is not a Westernism, and pictographs are not exclusive to the West, but they are one of its intriguing features.

PIE BUGGY A wagon sent to town for supplies. A *pie box* was a **CHUCK WAGON**, and a *pie wagon* was a trailer attached to this movable kitchen. To *have enough pie* was a California phrase for being done for.

PIEGAN (PAY-guhn; pee-GAN) A principal division of the **BLACKFEET** Indians, historically living in Montana and Alberta. The name comes from *Pikuni* ("poor robes"), their name for themselves. Confusingly, a clan of their longtime enemies the **CROWS** is named Piegan because they acted as Piegans supposedly do—they abandoned their comrades.

PIGGING STRING A six-foot thong of rawhide or horsehair (nowadays made of twisted nylon) used to **HOG-TIE** calves. Now it's mostly used in the **RODEO** event **CALF-ROPING**, where a cowboy ropes the runaway calf, throws it, and ties three feet together in as short a time as possible. Old-time cowboys seemed always to pack a bunch of pigging strings around in their pockets.

PIG'S VEST WITH BUTTONS Salt pork or sowbelly.

PIKE Among Californians of the second half of the nineteenth century, a mocking name for a certain kind of Missourian who emigrated to California, originally one who was from Pike County. A Pike was supposed to be lazy, disloyal, and otherwise worthless, if not a ruffian and a thief. This derogation later got applied to almost any newcomer to California. Also called a *Piker*. The term gives rise to *Pikedom, Pikish, Pike language,* and *Pike Countian.*

PIKE'S PEAKER An 1859 gold-rusher to the Pike's Peak, Colorado, area. Such folk had what was called *Peak fever* and adopted the motto "Peak or bust!" Also known as a *Peaker*.

PIKI (PEE-kee) A waferlike, multicolored cornbread of the **HOPI** Indians and **NAVAJOS**. It is baked on a *piki stone*, hewn by men and polished smooth by women. The stone is warmed by a fire built beneath it. Also called *paper bread*.

PILE DRIVER A name for a **BRONC** that bucks by going straight up and pounding down on all four legs at once, stiffly.

PILE THE ROPE INTO A CRITTER To rope an animal and throw it.

PILGRIM (1) A **GREENER**, a fellow new to the West. It may carry the implication of a person trying to catch on to the ways of the country more seriously than a *dude* or *greenhorn*. (2) A cow that hasn't wintered on the Plains, is new to the country, and by implication lacks toughness. Such cows were also called *barn-yard stock* and *States cattle*, that is, cattle from the United States proper. Though some sources say that *pilgrim* was applied to cows first and men later, the actual citations indicate it was the other way around. (3) Sometimes a horse that once was valuable but now has gotten too old.

PILLION A light woman's saddle; a pad behind a Hispanic man's saddle for a woman to ride on.

PILON (pee-LOHN) In the Rio Grande valley, something extra given by a merchant to a customer, like the *lagniappe* of Louisiana. Also spelled *pelon*. Borrowed from Spanish.

PILONCILLO (pee-lohn-SEE-yoh) In the Southwest, a cone of unrefined brown sugar. This treat was popular with Hispanics and pioneer Anglos. Borrowed from Spanish meaning "sugarloaf."

PIMA A Native people of the Sonoran Desert of southern Arizona and Sonora (a state of Mexico), a country called by the Spaniards Pimeria Alta (Upper Pimeria). The term *Pima* includes the tribes known as Pima, Sand Papago, and **PAPAGO**. Some were mainly hunter-gatherers, others farmers, all of them expert desert-dwellers. Historically, they avoided conflict with the United States and usually allied themselves with Anglos, Mexicans, and Hispanics to fight the **APACHE**. The Pima settled in Arizona on the Gila River Reservation, Ak Chin Reservation, and Salt River Reservation.

PIN GRASS A fine and common graze (*Erodium cicutarium*) of the Plains. Also called *pin clover* and **ALFILARIA**.

PINACATE (pin-uh-KAH-tee) A wingless beetle of the arid West. Derived from Nahuatl but borrowed directly from Spanish.

PINCH (1) All the gold dust the seller can pick up with a thumb and forefinger. A pinch was the coin of the realm in the California gold regions during the gold rush, and was about the smallest unit of exchange—a drink cost a pinch. (2) In mining, the narrowing of a vein. At that spot, which is also called a *cap,* the vein is said to be pinched. When it plays out entirely, it is said to be *pinched out* or *pinched down.*

PINCH CHUTE Cowboy talk for a branding chute.

PINE BEETLE Beetles of the genus *Dendroctonus* that burrow into the bark of pines such as ponderosa and lodgepole, ultimately killing the trees. The stand of dead trees then becomes a potential fire hazard.

PINE GROUSE The blue grouse of the Rocky Mountains *(Dengragapus obscurus).* Also called a *pine hen.*

PINEAPPLE CACTUS The Mojave fishhook cactus *(Echinocactus polyancistrus),* which bears beautiful pink and magenta blossoms.

PING-PONG In logger talk, to curry mules.

PINGUE In the Southwest, a perennial herb *(Hymenoxys floribunda)* that produces a kind of rubber. Also called *pinguay weed.*

PINHEAD A nickname for a telemark skier; also called *pinner.*

PINKERTON A detective of the Pinkerton agency, organized in Chicago in 1850 by Allan Pinkerton. Collectively, they were known (especially by striking workers who disliked them) as *Pinkertonians.* The company's policy of hiring private police was called *Pinkertonism* or *Pinkertonianism.*

PINOLE (pee-NOH-lay; pih-NOH-lee) A spicy flour of Southwestern Indians, usually flour from the **MESQUITE** bean mixed with parched corn meal and the whole spiced with cinnamon and sugar. Ground seeds or other ground beans are also used. Also spelled *pinol* and *pinola.* Tortillas are made from it, and it is also put into water to make a cooling drink. Borrowed from Spanish (which got it from Nahuatl).

PIÑON (PIN-yuhn) A pine tree of the Southwest *(Pinus parryana, P. edulis,* or *P. cembroides).* Along with the juniper, it is the characteristic tree of the **MESAS** of **CANYON COUNTRY.** Its nutlike seed was and is an important food for Indians, and its wood makes a fire with so pungently delicious a smell that it is one of the defining associations of the region. Borrowed from Spanish. Also spelled *pinyon* and occasionally *pinion.*

    COMBINATIONS: *piñon jay, piñon mouse, piñon pine.* The *piñonero* is the Clark's nut-cracker, a bird.

PINS Members of a secret society of **CHEROKEE** full-bloods formed ostensibly to perpetuate tribal traditions but actually to oppose slavery. Named the Keetoowah society by its members, it became known as the Pin Society because its insignia of crossed pins was worn by members on their hunting shirts and coats.

PINTAIL The sharp-tailed grouse *(Pedioecetes phasianellus).* (See also **PRAIRIE CHICKEN.**)

PINTO (1) A spotted horse; a piebald horse; a **PAINT**. Though the paint and pinto are now registered by different associations, old-time Westerners used the terms interchangeably. (2) The pinto bean, a variety of kidney bean. (See also **FRIJOL**.) Borrowed from Spanish (in which it means "spotted" or "speckled").

PINWHEEL (1) An unusual movement in a bucking horse: It flips forward and lands on its back. (2) Rolling a gun—the butt goes down, the muzzle up, and the gun is flipped and lands in the hand in firing position.

PIONEER To open new country as a pioneer. (The noun *pioneer* appears to be an Americanism, and the verb *pioneer* a Westernism.) Many Western communities have Pioneer Days, festivals commemorating the achievements of the pioneers. Utah, for instance, celebrates the 1847 arrival of the Mormons at Salt Lake each July 24, and Idaho celebrates England's withdrawal of its claim to the Oregon country each June 15. (See also **FRONTIERSMEN**.)

A *pioneer bucker* is a horse that constantly hunts new territory by bucking in figure eights or in circles.

PIPE (1) A pipe smoked ceremonially by Indians (see **MEDICINE PIPE**). (2) Among the **VOYAGEURS**, the distance paddled between rests for a smoke of the pipe, very approximately six miles. (3) In hydraulic mining, to wash away dirt with a stream of water.

PIPELINE (1) Among surfers, a wave whose crest forms a hollow tube in which the skilled and daring can ride. (2) The trans-Alaska pipeline transports oil from Prudhoe Bay to Valdez.

PIPESTONE The soft, red claystone found at Pipestone, Minnesota, and used by the **PLAINS INDIANS** (and other Indians) to carve pipe bowls. (See also **MEDICINE PIPE**.) The quarries of this stone, in the country of the **DAKOTA** Indians, were and are a kind of holy land—even enemy tribes could go there in safety to renew their supplies of pipestone. According to Indian stories, the stone is made from the blood of their ancestors or from the blood of the buffalo, and so is itself sacred. Now the area is Pipestone National Monument, and stone is still quarried by Indians for pipes. Pipestone is also known as *catlinite*, after the traveler, painter, and student of Indian ways George Catlin.

PIROOTING In the Southwest, meandering, fooling around.

PISKUN (PEES-koon) A **PLAINS INDIAN** trap for buffalo, shaped like a V and ending in a cliff. Many tribes ran buffalo off cliffs to make large kills. From the **BLACKFEET** language. Also spelled *pishkun*.

PISTOL (1) A green hand, an inexperienced cowboy. (2) A pocket flask of booze. Cowboys didn't call their handguns pistols—for that, see **SIX-SHOOTER**.

PITA (PIT-uh) (1) In the Southwest, a fiber the Indians used to make thread, cord, rope, and the like. It came mainly from the **AGAVE**. (2) The bag, box, net, or rope made from that fiber. Southwestern cowboys like LASSOS made of fiber. Borrowed from Spanish.

PITAHAYA (pee-tuh-HAH-yuh) In the Southwest, a name for the organ-pipe CACTUS, or other large, columnar cacti (*Lemaireocereus thurberi* and *Carnegiea gigantea*), including the SAGUARO. Borrowed from Spanish.

PITCH (1) When said of a horse in Texas, to buck. Thus Texas cowboys speak of breaking a horse as *taking the pitch out of it.* A horse that insists on bucking is called a *pitcher.* (For more words describing bucking, see BUCK.) (2) The gambling game known as all-fours or SEVEN-UP. (3) Among miners, a dip in a *lode.*

Pitching hay, before lots of modern machinery came along, was one of the arduous, never-ending jobs on any ranch—onto wagons, onto haystacks, and then back off. The hay hand was teasingly known as the *pitchfork gladiator* and other teasing names (see also RANCHER).

PITCH POST A fence post cut with sap still in it, to make it stand the weather better.

PITHOUSE Among Native peoples, a half-underground dwelling, built over a hole dug in the ground. Associated especially with the Indian peoples of the Columbia Plateau and the Southwest.

PITT SCHOONER See CONESTOGA, PRAIRIE SCHOONER.

PITTED A way of describing cows caught in holes, or forced into corners or draws or against fences in a blizzard. The beasts are absurdly good at getting into such spots and must be roped out or otherwise freed.

PIVA In Alaska, homebrew. Also sometimes spelled *pivo.* From Russian.

PLACER (1) A spot where gold is gotten by washing; a sand or gravel deposit bearing particles of gold. In such places, gold is gotten by methods using *dredges, pans, hydraulics,* and *sluices,* which utilize water and gravity. The term came from California gold-mining in 1842. (2) The word is also used as a verb—to *placer.*

Placer mining is based on a convenient fact of nature: Gold, originally locked into veins in hard rock and inaccessible without lots of money and equipment, gets washed away and ground into fine particles by rains and streams. In the sand and gravel, a common man can separate the gold out with water because gold is heavy and sinks. The great gold rushes of California, Idaho, Montana, and (to some extent) the Black Hills were placers, and ordinary people could afford to mine. Colorado booms and Nevada's Comstock Lode were based on mining veins.

COMBINATIONS: *placer camp* (a camp of placer miners), *placer claim* (a mining claim on a placer), *placer digging* (a location of placer mining), *placer district, field,* or *ground* (a region of placers), *placer dredge* (a dredge for placering), *placer gold* (gold in flakes and grains), *placer prospect* (a sign that placering would be productive). Many more are of obvious meaning: *placer bed, deposit, discovery, mine, miner, mining, operations, rush washer, working,* and so on.

PLAINS See **GREAT PLAINS.**

PLAINS INDIANS Those Native peoples who lived in historical times on the **GREAT PLAINS** and mostly had buffalo-hunting cultures. Before the reservation period (beginning about 1870) they were nomadic, got food by hunting and gathering rather than agriculture, lived mostly in **TIPIS**, and followed the buffalo. (See also **ARAPAHO, ARIKARA, ASSINIBOINE, BLACKFEET, CHEYENNE, COMANCHE CROW, COMANCHE, DAKOTA, GROS VENTURE, HIDATSA, KIOWA, MANDAN, MISSOURI, OMAHA, OSAGE, PAWNEE.**)

PLAINS RIFLE A muzzle-loading rifle that was shorter than the *long rifle*, with a half stock and usually a tapered barrel so the weight wasn't so far forward. Among the noted makers of Plains rifles were Jacob and Samuel **HAWKEN**, who worked in St. Louis from 1822 to 1861. Also called a *mountain rifle.*

PLAINS SADDLE A saddle that was on the scene by the middle of the 1870s. It was **DOUBLE-RIGGED**, had skirts lined with sheepskin, had a *Cheyenne roll,* and had a low, sturdy, leather-covered **HORN**. It was developed in part by two saddle-making brothers, John S. and Gilbert M. Collins, in Cheyenne, Omaha, Billings, and Great Falls. (See also **STOCK SADDLE.**)

PLANK HOUSE Among Indians of the Pacific Northwest, a large, rectangular dwelling for several families, made of planks hand-split from cedar, with a fire pit in the middle and sleeping platforms along the walls.

PLANTER In boating, a tree trunk with one end stuck in the riverbed, acting as a snag. (See also **SAWYER, SNAG, STRAINER.**)

PLAY A LONE HAND To act alone, either as a habit or on a particular occasion.

PLAY BOTH ENDS AGAINST THE MIDDLE In **FARO**, to fix the game by trimming the cards at either end of the deck.

PLAYA (PLY-yuh) (1) In the Southwest, a beach, a sandy strip on the ocean's shore. From Spanish. (2) Historically in the Southwest, a depression in the desert that holds water after rains.

PLAZA In the Southwest, a public square; historically, an open space of a mine or fort. Borrowed from Spanish.

PLEW The **MOUNTAIN MAN**'s term for the entire pelt of a **BEAVER**. The accepted derivation is that the French-Canadians called a choice pelt a *plus* (pronounced ploo), French for "more." Among the American trappers, it became the word for any beaver skin.

During the height of the Rocky Mountain **FUR TRADE**, ordinary beaver skins brought about $4 per pound on the open market, and a prime plew brought $6 or more. At one time, fur companies were competing hotly enough that they were paying $6 a plew for all hides, even those of kits. Prices always varied greatly: more for Great Lakes beaver, less for Southern hides, more for winter hides, less for summer (see also **BLUE PELT**), and so on. When prices fell in the mid-1830s,

Great Plains tribes. [MAP BY WENDY BAYLOR.]

many trappers left the trade and settled on the Pacific Coast. A few merely grumbled, "Give this child some 'bacca, if it's a plew a plug, and DuPont and Galena (powder and lead), and it's back to the mountains."

PLOWBOY What a rider is said to do when he holds a rein in each hand and pulls the horse's head around with one while laying the other on its neck.

PLUG (1) A rectangular bar of chewing tobacco. The tobacco was sometimes seasoned with such flavorings as licorice, molasses, sugar, fruit juices, and so on. (2) As a verb, to shoot something or someone.

PLUG IN In Alaska, an electrical outlet in a public area, business, or home for connecting block heaters on vehicles to electrical current, used in severe weather to keep the engine block from freezing.

PLUMB (1) As a modifier, completely or absolutely, as in to *hit the target plumb center* or to *be plumb loco*. (2) In Texas, as a verb, to *plumb a track* is to follow a faint trail.

PLUNDER Historically, a man's personal belongings, what he might keep in his **POSSIBLES SACK** or **WAR BAG**.

PLURAL MARRIAGE What the **MORMONS** called their practice of polygamy, which gentiles euphemistically called their "peculiar institution" and which was technically polygyny. "Not an indulgence but a divine command," says Wallace Stegner in *The Gathering of Zion*, "it had been revealed privately by Joseph [Smith] to his most confidential counselors, had been put into writing in 1843 . . . and had finally been publicly admitted in 1852, and printed in *Doctrine and Covenants*. Reports of this custom caused great animosity among gentiles toward Mormons during their days in Missouri and Illinois and during their pioneering days in Utah. John C. Frémont, campaigning for president in 1856, even called for the abolition of the great barbarisms of slavery and polygamy."

The Mormon reasoning was various: Polygamy was a practice of early Christians. It would prevent immorality. Since men often died under frontier hardships, it was a practical necessity. It would also create a larger population in anticipation of the second coming of Christ and provide bodies for righteous spirits wanting to come back to Earth. Mainly, though, it was God's revelation.

Plural marriage was not for everyone, but only for men of demonstrated spiritual and economic worthiness, with permission of the existing wife (or wives) and the permission of the Church. (Now some polygamous Mormon groups require that the husband be beyond the suspicion of mere lust.) Usually the men who were permitted plural wives were older and influential. Perhaps fewer than 10 percent of early Mormon men were in plural marriages.

In 1890, under federal pressure, church president Wilford Woodruff issued a manifesto forbidding further plural marriage. It did not deny divine sanction of the institution but merely changed church doctrine. Plural marriage did survive the Woodruff manifesto in remnants. Colonies in Mexico and Canada continued the practice. It is practiced today by splinter "fundamentalist" Mormon groups, such as the band at Colorado City on the Arizona-Utah border, and among the Apostolic United Brethren. Mormons engaged in plural marriage are summarily excommunicated, and the church treats its polygamous past as an embarrassment.

PLUTE What a logger called a rich man. Short for *plutocrat.*

POBLANO (poh-BLAH-noh) Short for *poblano hat,* a low-crowned, broad-brimmed **VAQUERO** hat worn from the eighteenth century forward. From Spanish.

POCKET Among miners, for a vein to expand into a pocket (cavity); the opposite of what it does when it **PINCHES**. Such a vein is said to be *pockety.*

COMBINATIONS: *pocket claim* (a mining claim where gold pockets), *pocket diggings* (a pocket gold-mining area), *pocket hunter* or *miner, pocket knife assayer* (a person who tests gold with a pocket knife).

POCO In the Southwest, little. Borrowed from Spanish.

COMBINATIONS: *poco a poco* (little by little), *poco frio* (a little bit cold), *poco malo* (a little sick), *poco pronto* (right now), *poco tiempo* (after a while).

POGAMOGGAN (pah-guh-MAH-guhn) A **PLAINS INDIAN** war club with a stone head. From an **OJIBWAY** word.

POGONIP A heavy fog that is filled with flying bits of snow, especially in the mountains of Nevada. It is dreaded and said to cause illnesses. The word is reported variously to be **PAIUTE** or **SHOSHONE**, and among the Shoshones to mean "white death."

POINT (1) The lead position for riders with a trail herd. The point riders, experienced hands, keep the herd headed the right way. The other riding positions are **SWING** (part way back along the sides), **FLANK** (most of the way back), and **DRAG** (at the rear, where the least experienced men ride). Point riders were also called *pointers, point men,* and *lead men.* Usually working in pairs, point riders for old-time **TRAIL DRIVES** had the most responsible and dangerous jobs on the team.

(2) In the **INDIAN TRADE**, a black mark woven into a blanket to indicate size. A three-point blanket is five by six feet, a four point is six by seven and a half feet. Every Indian knew that the points told the cost, typically one **PLEW** (beaver pelt) per point. (See also **TRADE BLANKET**.)

(3) A wooded projection of land, especially a bend in a river. This word is a contribution of the **VOYAGEURS**, who called it in French a *pointe.*

POKE A small sack or bag, especially one used to hold gold dust. Often the meaning is "the sack with the dust in it," as in, "They stole my poke."

POKER One of several card games in which a crucial skill is placing successive bets within a hand—*opening, calling,* and *raising.* Poker (the term comes from the French *poque,* which sounds similar and has the same meaning) came into this country through New Orleans, moved up the Mississippi, and spread all over the West. The two common forms are *five-card draw*, the most popular in the nineteenth century, and *five-card stud*, which deals four cards face up and the last face down.

Principal poker terms are ACE HIGH, *ace in the hole, aces up your sleeve, ante,* BLUFF, BUSTED FLUSH, *Calamity Jane* (queen of spades), *California prayer book,* CASH IN YOUR CHIPS, *chips,* CHIP IN, CLOSE TO THE BELLY (or *vest*), DEAD MAN'S HAND, *devil's bedposts* (four of clubs), *four flush* (and FOUR-FLUSHER), FULL HOUSE, GAPER, *ginny up the pasteboards,* JACKPOT, *lay down your character,* LOOLOO, *pack the deal* (to stack the cards dishonestly), *pass the buck, pat hand* (a hand good enough to bet on without drawing additional cards), SHINER, SHOWDOWN, SQUARE DEAL, STRIPPERS, SUNDAY SCHOOL, *sweeten the pot, there's a one-eyed man in the game* (a warning that someone is cheating), and YOU BET.

COMBINATIONS: *poker chip, poker face* (an expressionless face that reveals nothing), *poker clergy* and *poker sharp* (both meaning skilled players), *poker flat, joint,* or *room* (where the game is played).

POLLA (POY-yuh) In the Southwest, an attractive young woman. From the Spanish word for pullet, it is used like the American slang *chick.*

POLLO (POY-yoh) Literally, a chicken. Also, a client of a COYOTE, a person who smuggles illegal immigrants over the border from Mexico. From Spanish.

POLYG Gentile (non-Mormon) slang for a MORMON in a PLURAL MARRIAGE. Same as COHAB, and both are surely derogatory.

PONCHO (PAHN-choh) Originally a blanket with a slit in the middle so it could be pulled over the head as a cloak. Later, a similar cloak made of oiled cloth, rubber, or nylon. Borrowed from Spanish.

PONDEROSA The *bull pine* or *yellow pine* (Pinus ponderosa). This very large pine with a broad, open crown is a particularly valuable timber pine in the West and is widespread. It usually grows in the mountains in pure stands; the trees are far apart with little undergrowth. The thick reddish bark smells like vanilla.

PONY A MUSTANG; any horse. A *cowpony* is a STOCK HORSE accustomed to ranch work. A *pony beef* was a two-year-old bovine, ready to fatten for market.

PONY EXPRESS A fast mail service by horseback, especially the one that operated from Missouri to California from 1860 to 1862 and was made obsolete by the telegraph. It was also called the *pony post* and was manned by *pony riders,* who sometimes used a *pony-express mount* (a jumping mount from behind). Letters were required to have *pony stamps.*

POOCH Tomatoes stewed with bread and sugar.

POOR BULL Among MOUNTAIN MEN, a descriptive expression for a greenhorn's ignorance, from the idea that a greenhorn could not differentiate *poor bull from fat cow.* The phrase was shortened to simply *poor bull* and also meant poor doings, anything that was bad or unfortunate. Lieutenant George Frederick Ruxton, who traveled the mountain West in the 1840s, wrote in *Life in the Far West*, "the meat of the cow is infinitely preferable to that of the male buffalo. . . . From the end of June to September bull meat is rank and tough, and almost uneatable; while the cows are in perfection, and as fat as stall-fed oxen." The mountain men also said greenhorns don't KNOW WHAT WAY THE STICK FLOATS.

POOR DOE A word applied to tough deer meat, regardless of whether from a buck or doe.

POOR MAN'S DIGGINGS A gold field that could be easily worked, such as a PLACER field, not requiring significant capital. Also called a *poor man's mine* and *poor man's camp.*

POOR-WILL The Western version of the whippoorwill, with only two notes to its distinctive call instead of three.

POPPER The business end of the whip of a drover, freighter, or stage driver. It made the whip sound like a gun when it cracked.

POR FAVOR (pohr fah-VOHR) Please. Common among both Hispanics and Anglos in the Southwest. Borrowed from Spanish.

PORCH PERCHER What a cowboy called a loafer.

PORCUPINE GRASS A tall Western grass (*Stipa spartea*) known for sticking to socks and pant legs. A major plant of the mixed-grass prairie, it grows two to four feet high.

PORCUPINE QUILLWORK See QUILLWORK.

PORK-EATER A MOUNTAIN-MAN term for a greenhorn. A translation of the French-Canadian term MANGEUR DE LARD; another French-Canadain term for these fellows was *blanc-bec.*

PORT ORFORD CEDAR In the Pacific Northwest, an evergreen (*Chamaecyparis law- soniana*) named for Port Orford, Oregon, and commercially valuable. It's also called the *Port Orford cypress.*

POSADA (poh-SAH-duh) In the Southwest, a roadhouse, an inn. Borrowed from Spanish.

POSE A term of the VOYAGEURS for the distance they would carry goods on a portage before depositing them temporarily, resting, and going back for more. It was about a third of a mile and was also called a *pause.*

POSOLE (poh-SOH-lay; poh-SOH-lee) A mush of boiled corn and meat. Borrowed from Spanish (which got it from Nahuatl). Also spelled *pozole* and *pozzoli.*

POSSE In the narrow Western sense, a group of riders brought together by a law officer to track down an outlaw. In the larger sense, any group assembled for a common purpose, such as a search for a lost person. It comes from *posse comitatus,* meaning authority of the county.

POSSIBLES Belongings, accoutrements, especially camping gear. Primarily a term of the **MOUNTAIN MEN.** They carried their *possibles* in a *possible sack,* described by Lieutenant George Frederick Ruxton in *Life in the Far West* as a "wallet of dressed buffalo skin" for carrying "ammunition, a few pounds of tobacco, dressed deerskins for moccasins &c." It was a container in which you take anything you can possibly use and into which you stuff as much as you possibly can. Some cowboys later used the term *possible sack* but more often said **WAR BAG.** Borrowed from Spanish.

POSSUM (1) A crafty, dissembling, or cowardly person. (2) As a verb, to *possum* or *play possum,* to dissemble or pretend, as to counterfeit sickness. (3) A hide slung under the **CHUCK WAGON** to carry fuel for fires, which on the Plains sometimes meant wood but usually meant *cow chips* or **BUFFALO CHIPS**; in full, *possum belly.* In this usage, it was also called a **BITCH, CABOOSE, COONEY, CRADLE,** and *cuna.*

POST (1) To put up notice not to trespass, and especially not to hunt, on ranch property. The "first thing these new ranchers do when they buy a ranch is 'Post it,'" complains one Pinedale, Wyoming, resident. Posting sometimes causes resentment between ranchers and sportsmen because it prevents access, or convenient access, to public land. (2) As a noun, historically a frontier establishment, especially for trading. At the end of the eighteenth century, it began to supplant the earlier term *station.*

POSTAGE STAMP The cowboy's derisive name for what Easterners call a saddle. Cowboys don't see much use in a saddle that doesn't help you work cows. The Eastern saddle is also called a *chicken saddle, hogskin,* **KIDNEY PLASTER** or *pad, pumpkinseed saddle,* or a *pimple.*

POT (1) In **POKER,** the money in the middle when all bets are in. (2) What a logger called a **DONKEY ENGINE.**

POT SHOT An easy shot, perhaps from the notion of shooting for the pot, taking the sure shot with an eye to conserving ammunition, not as the sportsman shoots. *Pot* has a verb form: A man or critter that gets potted has been shot.

POTHOLE A shallow depression in the land that holds rainwater. Potholes can be lifesavers, particularly in **SLICKROCK** country. In Texas they're likely to become bog holes, a trap for cattle.

POTLATCH A word of the **CHINOOK** jargon for the giveaway ceremony of the tribes (principally the **TLINGIT, HAIDA, KWAKIUTL, TSIMSHIAN,** and **NOOTKA**) of the Alaska Panhandle, British Columbia, and the coastal region of Washington and Oregon. This was a central religious ceremony of these Indians; an individual who wanted to give a potlatch sometimes spent years in preparation, and it was accompanied by big feasts and other hospitable gestures. A marriage, the death of an important person, or even a minor life passage like the cutting of hair could occasion a potlatch; the main reason was often to affirm the status in the tribe of the giver. (See also GIVEAWAY.)

POTRERO (poh-TRAIR-oh) (1) In the Southwest, a pasture or meadow. (2) Less often, a WRANGLER of *potros* (colts). In both cases, borrowed from Spanish. (3) A narrow ridge between canyons.

POTRO (POH-troh) In the Southwest, a colt or filly, often with the implication that it is unbroke. Also called *potrillo* and borrowed from Spanish (where it means "colt" or "wild horse").

POUDERIE (POO-duh-ree) A VOYAGEUR term for a fine, powdery snow.

POUND LEATHER In cowboy talk, to ride fast.

POUR A contemporary Indian expression meaning to lead a SWEAT LODGE ceremony. The leader, who in a sacred manner is given the way to lead, pours water on the hot rocks during each round to make steam. The leader is likely to burn cedar, pray aloud, sing, and in all ways conduct the ceremony.

POVERTY GRASS One of several grasses (*Aristida dichotoma*) that grow in sandy soil where nothing else can.

POWDER (1) What loggers and miners call dynamite. The man who handles it is a *dyno, powder man,* or *powder monkey.* Other Westernisms for dynamite are BANG JUICE, DINE, DINAH, *grease, giant powder, noise, nifty powder, puff,* SHOT, SAWDUST, *stew,* and *vaseline.* (2) An answer to many a good skier's prayer—light, fluffy snow (because of low moisture content). Especially fine powder maybe called *champagne.*

POWDER HORN A container for black powder for a muzzle-loader, in the West often made from a buffalo horn, scraped thin and occasionally *scrimshawed.* In the days of the flintlock, two horns were generally carried, a small one for the fine powder used in priming and a big one for the coarser powder

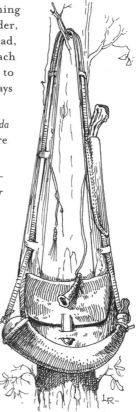

Powder horn and pouch.
[DRAWING BY E. L. REEDSTROM.]

used for the charge in the barrel. The shooter carried a charger, often made from the tip of an antler, that held the right amount of powder. Metal powder containers were called *powder flasks.* The advent of the **PERCUSSION CAP** made the small container obsolete, and the coming of the cartridge put both out of business. Barrels of powder at forts and the like were kept in buildings or cellars called *powder magazines.* (See also **DUPONT**.)

POWDER RIVER, LET 'ER BUCK A cowboy's battle cry, often derisive. The Powder River country is fabled as the home country of the **LAKOTA** and **CHEYENNE** peoples, and the locus of Struthers Burt's book *Powder River: Let 'Er Buck,* so it looms larger in the public imagination than it often does between its banks. After all, it's a Plains river. Adams gives this account of the origin of the expression, and says that it originally came from cowman E. J. Farlow of Lander, Wyoming:

> Some hands trailing cows to the railroad at Casper in the autumn of 1893 bedded down near the headwaters of Powder River, near the present Hiland, Wyoming, one night. They talked about crossing Powder River repeatedly the next morning, and spoke of getting their swimming horses. The next morning one cowboy, Missouri Bill Shultz, changed horses to get a good swimmer. Making their various crossings, they discovered that in the fall at that place, Powder River was just deep enough to wet a horse's hoof, and had barely enough energy to trickle from one hole to another.
>
> When they got to Casper, Missouri Bill toasted the hands like this: "Boys, come and have a drink on me. I've crossed Powder River." They had the drinks, then a few more and were getting pretty sociable.
>
> When Missouri Bill again ordered, he said to the boys, "Have another drink on me, I've swum Powder River," this time with a distinct emphasis on the words Powder River. "Yes, sir, by God, Powder River" with a little stronger emphasis. When the drinks were all set up he said, "Well, here's to Powder River, let 'er buck!"
>
> Soon he grew louder and was heard to say, "Powder River is coming upeeyeeeep!—Yes sir, Powder River is rising," and soon after with a yip and a yell, he pulls out his old six-gun and throwed a few shots through the ceiling and yelled, "Powder River is up, come an' have 'nother drink." Bang! Bang! "Yeow, I'm a wolf and it's my night to howl. Powder River is out of 'er banks. I'm wild and woolly and full o' fleas and never been curried below the knees!"
>
> Bill was loaded for bear, and that is the first time I ever heard the slogan, and from there it went around the world.

POWDER-BURNING CONTEST A gunfight. The cowboy characteristically makes light of mortal matters.

POWWOW (1) A conference of or with **INDIANS**. In verb form, to hold such a conference. (2) An act of conjuring, of making magic. In verb form, to conjure or make magic. (3) A social and religious event of contemporary Indians, coming together to feast, dance, trade, or socialize. In verb form, to participate in such an event. (4) Jokingly, any conference at all.

The term is originally Indian pidgin English but not Western—it is Algonquian and dates to the earliest colonial times. Now the third meaning is most prevalent—there is a *powwow circuit,* where Indians get together (along with interested Anglos) for a festival. Musicians and dancers travel to these get-togethers, many people wear their ceremonial best, and **DANCE** competitions are often held.

PRAIRIE A grassland, often with tall grasses and few trees. Adapted from the French word meaning "meadow." The prairies extend west from the Mississippi Valley to the Great Plains at about the 100th meridian. The key distinctions are that prairies are lower elevation than the Plains and get more rainfall. In the early West, little prairies were sometimes known by the French diminutive *prairillon.* (This was variously and creatively spelled—*peraira, papara, perara,* and so on.)

COMBINATIONS: *prairie belt* (a cartridge belt issued by the army in 1870), *prairie loo* (a game of counting sightings of game as you travel across the prairies, with the less common animals weighted to count more), *prairie telegraph* (the written messages that the pioneers left beside the wagon trails), *passed over the prairie* (a nineteenth-century euphemism for being raped by Indians).

PLANTS: *Prairie wool* (a cowboy term for *buffalo grass*), *prairie tomato* (a ground cherry).

ANIMALS: *Prairie beef* or *cattle* (buffalo), *prairie buffalo* (a French-Canadian name for a horned lizard of the prairies), *prairie eel* (a joking name for a rattlesnake), *prairie fox* (the kit fox), *prairie gopher* (a ground squirrel, genus *Citellus*), *prairie lawyer, tenor,* or *wolf* (all three mean "coyote"), *prairie rattlesnake* (one of several species of rattler that inhabit the prairies), *prairie rooter* or *shark* (a hog), *prairie runner* (an antelope).

FOOD: *Prairie butter* (a batter made from grease, flour, and water and used as a substitute for butter), *prairie dew* (a term for booze; see also **FIREWATER**), *prairie cocktail* (a salted and peppered raw egg drunk in booze or vinegar; also called a *prairie oyster*), *prairie oyster* (usually a mountain oyster: fried calf testicle; occasionally a *prairie cocktail*), *prairie strawberries* (a joking name for beans).

PRAIRIE CHICKEN One of several species of grouse of the Plains and mountains, the **SAGE GROUSE** (*Centrocercus urophasianus*), the *greater prairie chicken* (*Tympanuchus cupido*), the *lesser prairie chicken* (*Tympanuchus pallidicinctus,* a desert creature), and the *sharp-tailed grouse* (*Pedioecetes phasianellus*). Some of the creatures

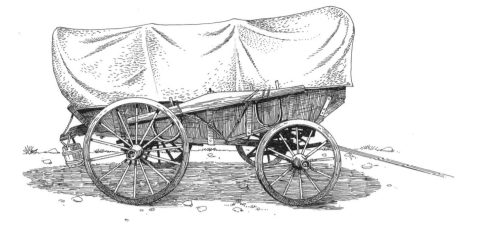

Prairie schooner.
[Drawing by E. L. Reedstrom.]

(perhaps all) were named **FOOL HENS** by the **MOUNTAIN MEN** because they stood still and let themselves be killed by a stone, stick, or whip.

PRAIRIE DOG A squirrel-like rodent (genus *Cynomys*) of the Plains and mountains that yips like a dog. Ranchers don't like them. Here's the South Dakota rancher and writer Linda Hasselstrom on the subject:

> They tend to live in ever-growing communities, digging a new hole for each new generation of pups, and may bear pups several times a year. Because they multiply quickly, and dig grass out by the roots, a prairie dog colony can kill hundreds of acres of grass in a summer. Ranchers deplore the amount of grass they eat almost as much as the large holes they leave, which are traps for horses and cattle to break legs in. Natural predators like coyotes can get a few, but when they retreat to their deep holes in rock-hard dry earth, very few animals bother them. Some ranchers used to kill prairie dogs with poison grain, but most such poisons act in a chain; that is, they kill not only the prairie dog but anything that feeds on it later: eagles, coyotes, owls.

COMBINATIONS: A *prairie-dog town* is a network of burrows dug by prairie dogs for their homes. It's also called a *prairie-dog village*. A *prairie-dog court* is a kangaroo court.

PRAIRIE FIRE A fire of the grasslands. Such fires were much feared by the inhabitants of the Plains and prairies because they swept all before them and destroyed everything, including the grass the cows fed on. Indian peoples frequently used fire for hunting and to improve the range. The native plants evolved to live with the cycle of fire (both natural and man-made) and are dying out in areas where fires are controlled. (See also **WILDFIRE**.)

PRAIRIE RATTLER See **SIDEWINDER**.

PRAIRIE SCHOONER A **CONESTOGA** wagon, or a smaller wagon developed from the large and cumbersome Conestoga, for Plains travel but still too clumsy for mountains and canyon country. Painted red and blue like the Conestoga, it got its name from the wagon's shiplike profile, and Libby Custer (wife of the general) says they "were well named, as the two ends of the wagon inclined upward, like the bow and stem of a fore-and-after." It was also called a *prairie clipper, a prairie ship,* and a *Pitt schooner* (because it was often manufactured in Pittsburgh).

The typical schooner was sixteen to eighteen feet long and four feet wide, and had wheels with iron tires and smaller in front than in back, wooden running gear that was vulnerable to drying and cracking, a hand brake, a front seat (often without springs), and a canvas top supported by bent hickory. The wagon usually carried less than a ton.

PRAIRIE TURNIP The prairie potato *(Psoralea esculenta).* The root of this wild vegetable was eaten either fresh or dried; it was a common item in the diet of the Northern **PLAINS INDIANS**. Also called *breadroot* (or *Indian breadroot*), *Indian turnip, ground apple,* and *Cree potato;* called *pomme blanche* by the **VOYAGEURS**.

PRAYER BOOK A cowboy's book of cigarette papers.

PRAYING COW A cow that's getting up. The critter rises hind end up and the cow momentarily looks like it's on its knees.

PRAZNIK In Alaska, a public holiday or religious feast with accents of the old Russian culture.

PREACHER On navigable waters in Alaska, a floating, uprooted tree that poses a hazard to boating. From the rising and falling motion of the tree, which was seen as resembling bowing. (See also **STRAINER**.)

PRESCRIBED BURN A controlled use of fire. The purposes may be to reduce fire hazard by preventing a buildup of unburned fuels, to increase forest productivity, to manage wildlife, to improve habitat, and so on. It's an attempt to re-create the natural cycle of fire in modern forests in a controlled way. Prescribed burning is controversial but increasingly recommended, especially after the big fires of 1988 in Yellowstone National Park.

PRESIDENCY In the **MORMON** Church, a council made up of a president and two counselors. The First Presidency is the highest body of this kind, the president being the executive head of the church.

PRESIDENTE (pre-zuh-DEN-tee; pre-zee-DEN-tay) In the Southwest, the leader of a town or the owner of a ranch. Borrowed from Spanish.

PRESIDENTIAL MEDAL A large, bronze medal issued by the U.S. mint at Philadelphia in the nineteenth century, showing the face of a president of the country on one side and a tomahawk, peace pipe, and the clasped hands of white and red men on the back. These medals were frequently given to Indians at treaty councils. Indians often prized them and kept them through generations. They also wore Indian peace medals of special issue. The Jefferson medal was still being made at the Denver mint in the 1980s. As with many governmental symbols, the friendship suggested was more an ideal than a reality.

This Jefferson medal was worn on a cord around an Indian's neck.
[COURTESY OF TETON COUNTY HISTORICAL SOCIETY]

PRESIDIO (pray-SEE-dee-oh; pruh-SIH-dee-oh) A fort, originally a Spanish garrison to protect a mission, and the area it administered. The best known, in San Francisco, has passed from military to civilian use and is now a local park. From Spanish.

PRICKLY PEAR A cactus of the genus *Opuntia*, and its pear shaped fruit, common on the Plains from Montana to Texas. Longhorns are said to have been able to eat it (thorns on) as a substitute for water. The fruit and cactus pads are a valued food in the Southwest. Often called the *pear cactus* and shortened to *pear*, especially when used as an adjective—"the pear region." Hispanics call the plant *nopal* and *tuna*—both from Spanish. *Pancake cactus, beavertail, blind prickly pear* (a spineless variety), and *Indian fig* are all kinds of prickly pears.

PRIESTHOOD OF THE BOW Among the **ZUNI** people, a warrior society in charge of war rituals. The leaders of this society and the **RAIN PRIESTHOOD** are usually important tribal leaders.

PROD POLE A stick to handle cows and keep them on their feet in cattle cars. These days a prod pole is often electric. Also called a *cattle prod*.

PRONGHORN The critter commonly known as an **ANTELOPE** (*Antilocapra americana*). Technically, it is not a member of that species but one unto itself.

PRONTO (PRON-toh) Right now; fast; quickly. Originally Southwestern, it is now used all over the United States. Borrowed from Spanish.

PROPHET The title of Joseph Smith, founder of the **MORMON** Church, and all his successors as head of the church. Prophets are believed to receive revelations from God—in full they are called Prophet, Seer, and Revelator. These revelations direct church policy even today. Revelations include the move to Utah in the 1840s, the requirement to store a year's supply of food, and the 10-percent tithing.

PROSPECT IN NOUN FORM: (1) A likely spot for discovery of minerals, as in the term **PLACER** prospect. (2) The result of the first efforts to find minerals: Says Mark Twain in *Roughing It*, "A 'prospect' is what one finds in the first panful of dirt—and its value determines whether it is a good or bad prospect, and whether it is worth-while to tarry there or seek further."

IN VERB FORM: (1) To search for valuable minerals. (2) To examine dirt or rock in detail for minerals. A **LOCATION** is said to *prospect well* or *badly*.

COMBINATIONS: *prospect(ing) camp, prospect holder, prospect hole, prospect operation, prospect shaft, prospect tunnel, prospect work, prospecting diggings, prospecting pan, prospecting party, prospecting trip.*

PROSPECTOR A person who searches a particular region for gold or silver deposits (or sometimes for other minerals) with the intention of staking a **CLAIM**. In the myth of the West, he is usually a hard-bitten **ALKALI** or **SOURDOUGH**, often a little crazy, and operating with his **GRUB-STAKE** lashed onto his faithful **BURRO**.

PROVE (1) In mining, to take a sample of a vein of ore to evaluate it. (2) In mining and **HOMESTEADING**, to *prove up on a claim* is to comply with the requirements of the mining or homesteading laws to make your claim legal. The last formalities in this process are called the *final proof.*

PROWL To hunt cattle. Cows have a way of getting into draws, thickets, and other places where they're hard to find. When gathering them, the cowhand has to do some prowling.

Prospector.
[DRAWING BY E. L. REEDSTROM.]

PROXY Among **MORMONS**, a stand-in for ordinances performed in LDS temples on behalf of deceased persons. Ordinances can be for marriage sealing (marriage for eternity), sealings of children to parents for eternity, endowment, and baptism. The object is to link all members of the family together in paradise.

PUBLIC LAND Land owned by a government, usually state or federal. Various government agencies administer land owned in name by the public in the West, usually amid some controversy. In the days of the open range, the big cattle ranchers tried to use public land for grazing privately owned cows and to make sure no one else's cow ate the grass they regarded as theirs. Now the battles pit those who use public land for commercial purposes (grazing, logging, mining) and those who use it for purposes of enjoyment, recreation, and sometimes spiritual solace. Though national parks are mostly free from commercial exploitation, lands administered by the U. S. **FOREST SERVICE** and the **BUREAU OF LAND MANAGEMENT** are much quarreled over. (See also **WILDERNESS, RANGE WAR,** and **GRAZING PERMIT.**)

PUDDING FOOT   Cowboy talk for an awkward horse with big feet.

PUEBLO   (1) A village of stone or adobe buildings, often multistoried, where **PUEBLO** Indians lived or live. (2) Any small Southwestern town; in the nineteenth century, Los Angeles was called a pueblo. The word gives rise to the forms *puebloan* and *puebloism*.

PUEBLO   When capitalized, an Indian or tribe of Indians of the Pueblo culture of the Southwest. Pueblo culture had its origin around the time of Christ among the people now called the **BASKET MAKERS.** In the Classic Pueblo period a millennium later, the Puebloans of that day (often called the **ANASAZI**) had large population centers (for instance, at Chaco Canyon, Kayenta, and Mesa

Acoma Pueblo, New Mexico, 1879.
[PHOTOGRAPH BY JOHN K. HILLERS; COURTESY OF NATIONAL ARHIVES (391-JKH-3).]

Verde) with substantial agriculture and a complex ceremonial religion. Perhaps because of drought and pressure from enemies, they vanished from the area in the late thirteenth century. Contemporary Pueblo Indian culture contains many of the same components: an economy partly based on agriculture, living in multifamily communities, and the use of KIVAS in religious ceremonies.

The Pueblo rebellion occurred in 1680. Led by a San Juan Pueblo Indian named Pope, the Indians successfully repelled the Spanish colonizers, killing 400 Spanish. Pope, however, became a despotic ruler of the Pueblos, the alliance dissolved, and after his death the Spaniards reconquered New Mexico by 1692. (See also TEWA, ACOMA, HOPI, LAGUNA, TAOS, ZUNI, KACHINA, SHALAKO.)

PUKE A nickname of uncertain origin for a Missourian, usually unflattering. The MORMONS especially regarded the pukes as enemies because of the conflicts the two groups had when the Saints were in Missouri.

PULASKI A tool used by firefighters for both chopping and trenching, designed by E. C. Pulaski.

PULL BOG In cowboy talk, to haul cows out of bog holes with a rope.

PULQUE (POOL-kay) Among Southwestern Hispanics, a wine fermented from the AGAVE or MAGUEY. It was sold in a *pulqueria,* a tavern. Borrowed from Spanish. MESCAL and TEQUILA are distilled from the same plant.

PUMPKIN ROLLER (1) What a cowboy calls a complainer in a cow camp. Also called a *freak.* (2) What a cowboy calls an inexperienced hand. (See GREENER for similar names.)

PUNCH COWS To take care of cows; to drive them; to be a cowpuncher. *Puncher* is the shortened form of *cowpuncher.*

PUNCHE (PUNCH-ee) A light, mild tobacco grown, used, and traded by the Indians of the Southwest.

PUNCHEONS Rough timber split from a log and hewn on one side, the first step up from dirt. Originally said of flooring; now, portions of hiking trails that protect boggy areas.

PUNCTURE LADY What a cowboy called a gossip. What got punctured was someone's reputation.

PUNK In the post–Civil War West, a sliver of wood tipped with sulfur used to help build a fire. You touched the punk to glowing tinder, and it burst into flame. On the earlier frontier, punk was dry, powdery fuel (from rotten wood, BUFFALO CHIPS, etc.) used to help get a fire started.

PUREBLOOD An Indian whose bloodline is purely Indian, not mixed. (Animals of unmixed descent are called *purebred.*) The adjective form is *pure-blooded.* Same as full-blooded. A source of pride among many Indian people—thus this bumper sticker: I'M FBI/full-blooded Indian.

PUSH-UP A repetition of part of an Indian song, like a verse or chorus. At contemporary **POWWOWS**, when the master of ceremonies wants more choruses of the same song (which usually come in sets of two or four), he asks for another push-up. These segments usually start with a sharp and dramatic rise to a high pitch—thus the descriptive name. The term is also used as a verb—"Push it up again."

PUSSY-BACKING A gentle kind of bucking with an arched back. Also called *cat-backing*. (See also **BUCK**.)

PUSSYFOOT To move like a cat—softly, carefully, slyly. The word was evidently inspired by William E. Johnson, who got the nickname from the sly way he pursued fugitives in Indian Territory in the late nineteenth century.

PUT A SPOKE IN THE WHEEL To foul things up; to slow someone down or stop them.

PUT HIM TO BED WITH A PICK AND SHOVEL To bury someone. (See also LAND IN A SHALLOW GRAVE, MADE WOLF MEAT.)

PUT THE CALK TO HIM Among loggers, to beat someone up. The calks were studs on the bottoms of boots. (See also **CALK**.)

PUT UP A HERD To gather up a herd of cows for the trail. In legendary cases, herds were put together from various owners for the long drive from Texas to the railroad.

PUT UP OR SHUT UP Back up your words (with action, money, or whatever), The expression derives from **POKER**, where it is a demand to call, raise, or fold.

PUYALLUP (pew-AL-luhp, with the *u* as in *corral*) The name of a tribe of Salishan Indians, who still live on a reservation in Washington of the same name.

Q

QAGRI Among Alaskan Natives, a community house or men's house, sometimes used for ceremonies.

QANTAQ Among Alaskan Natives, a traditional wooden bowl; now often a souvenir.

QASPEQ In Alaska, a pullover, dress, or jersey. Originally, a hooded garment worn by Native people.

QUARANTINE LINE A north-south line drawn at various points in Kansas during the days of the great cattle drives from Texas. East of this, Texas cattle were not to go for fear of spreading **TEXAS FEVER**. Also called the *fever line*.

QUARTER HORSE The breed of the usual **STOCK HORSE**. Characteristically short-coupled and big-rumped, this breed has speed in the short distance (such as a quarter-mile) and the ability to make the sharp cuts needed in roping. Developed on Western ranges, it was known in its early days as a *short horse*.

QUARTZ MAN A gold miner. Quartz is a matrix that often contains **GOLD**, and in the 1930s, a quarter of an ounce of gold in a ton of quartz was enough to make milling profitable.

    COMBINATIONS: *quartz battery* (a stamp for pulverizing quartz ore), *quartz camp* (a camp of quartz men), *quartz claim* (a hard-rock gold claim), *quartz diggings* (a quartz mine), *quartz lead* (a vein of gold-bearing quartz), *quartz mill* or *crusher* (a machine or business establishment that pulverizes quartz ore), *quartz mine, miner,* and *mining, quartz on the brain* (gold fever), *quartz reefer* (a miner working a quartz vein or *reef*).

QUELITES (kay-LEE-tays) In the Southwest, wild herbs cooked and served like collard greens. Borrowed from Spanish.

QUERENCIA (kay-REN-see-uh) In the Southwest, your home place, the place you were born. Borrowed from Spanish (in which it means "haunt" or "favorite spot").

QUERIDA (kay-REE-duh) In the Southwest, darling, sweetheart, or a similar endearment. Borrowed from Spanish. The masculine form *querito* also occurs.

QUICK FREIGHTING Freighting done by trains of horses or mules, not oxen, which were slower.

QUICK-DRAW ARTIST A person skilled at getting his *six gun* out quickly. He might also be *quick on the trigger* or *quick to shoot it*. Recently, the term *quick-draw competition* means a competition of illustrators and artists rendering images of Western subjects rapidly.

QUIEN SABE? (kyen SAH-bay; keen SAH-bay) (1) In the Spanish of the Southwest, literally "Who knows?" A kind of philosophic shrug that sometimes suggests the unknowable. (2) What an impatient Texas cowboy says about an elaborate Mexican **BRAND** he can't read or something else incomprehensible.

QUILLWORK A technique among Indians of decorating clothing and other leather items. It preceded beadwork historically, and many beadwork customs and patterns are taken from older quillwork. Quillwork was done almost entirely by women and took geometrical rather than representational forms. The method is to soften porcupine quills with hot water; flatten them with the teeth, rocks, or metal quill flatteners; dye them with vegetable dyes; and lace them with a method like embroidery onto moccasins, shirts, pipe bags, and any number of other articles. As colored **BEADS** became more commonly available, beads often replaced quills, but quillwork is done even today. In full, *porcupine quillwork*.

QUIRLY Cowboy talk for a hand-rolled cigarette.

QUIRT A rider's whip, with a weighted handle about a foot long and several rawhide thongs. Most **PLAINS INDIANS** used quirts, often with antler handles. Cowboys sometimes made a fine craft of plaiting quirts. The weight in the handle makes the quirt effective for use as a **BLACKJACK** or to whack a rearing horse in the head. Adapted from the Spanish *cuarta*. It also occurs as a verb.

QUIT THE FLATS In cowboy talk, to leave the area.

QUYANA In Alaska, "thank you." From Native languages.

R

R. M. A **MORMONISM** meaning "Returned Missionary." (See also **MISSIONARY**.)

RABBIT DANCE A rarity, a social dance of many American Indian tribes in which men and women swing together. Adapted from Anglos.

RABBIT ROUNDUP The driving and killing of **JACK RABBITS** in areas where they create difficulties for farmers. A continuing but controversial practice.

RACK (1) An ambling gait of a horse. (See also **SINGLE-FOOT**.) (2) In cowboy talk, to ride.

RAFTER To lie under your blankets with your knees sticking up.

RAG CITY Originally, a mining camp of tents. Now a boomtown of trailers and campers.

RAG HOUSE Among loggers and soldiers, a tent. Also called a *rag bungalow*.

RAG OUT To dress up fancily.

RAIL To break sagebrush off at ground level by dragging an iron rail over it. Ranchers try to keep sagebrush down so more grass will grow, but the practice is less than effective. (See also **CHAIN**.)

RAILROAD BELT In Alaska, the area along the rail line between Anchorage and Fairbanks. Also called *rail belt*.

RAILROAD WITHOUT STEAM A logger's expression meaning "to go like hell."

RAIN FOLLOWS THE PLOW The slogan of the 1870s promoters of lands of the **GREAT PLAINS**, which were previously thought of as the Great American Desert. For commercial reasons, these folks (the railroads included) wanted Americans to homestead the Plains and farm them, so they propagated the idea that where man plowed, the good Lord would send rain. The notion was even given credence by the head of the U.S. Geographical and Geological Survey of the Territories. Even in a nation known for con artists, it was a considerable deception or self-delusion.

RAIN PRIESTHOOD A society of ZUNI Indians devoted to bringing abundant moisture through shamanic methods. Leaders of this society and the PRIESTHOOD OF THE BOW are generally civil leaders as well.

RAINBOW A term for what a bucking horse does when he arches his back and shakes his head.

RAINBOW TROUT One of two species of trout (*Salmo gairdneri*) native to the West. Since it is a good fish for sportfishing, the rainbow has been stocked in many Western creeks and rivers.

RAISE (1) To spot something far away, as in, "He raised buffalo near five miles off." (2) In POKER, to increase the stakes.

RAISE HAIR To take a SCALP; to kill someone. *Lift hair* is a similar expression; both come from the MOUNTAIN MEN. Sometimes the idea of the phrase was extended: "Raise horses" sometimes meant to steal horses. An old-time Anglo view of Indians was, "They never knew how to raise nothing but hell and hair."

RAKE In RODEO, for a bronc rider to scratch a horse with SPURS to make him buck. Also called BICYCLING.

RAKE UP THE PERSIMMON To win, to get the prize; particularly, to get the pot in POKER. The gambling phrase comes from Southern expressions that give high value to persimmons, such as "I wouldn't bet a huckleberry to a persimmon," which is like doughnuts to dollars. Also heard as *rake the persimmon* and *walk off with the persimmon*.

RAMADA In the Southwest, an arbor; a brush shelter. Borrowed from Spanish.

RAMROD The working boss of a ranch.

RANAHAN A top HAND; a good cowboy. Often shortened to *ranny*.

RANCH (1) An establishment where livestock is raised. In this most traditional sense, the word normally includes the land, building, critters—the whole OUTFIT. If this sort of ranch grows crops, they are usually feed for the livestock, not a cash crop. (2) The main building of a ranch, the main house, and the surrounding buildings. (3) As a verb, to raise livestock. From the Spanish *rancho*.

The word has taken on lots of meanings beyond these basics. In the old West, a way station for travelers could be called a *road ranch*; the word was eventually applied to every sort of establishment, even farms, leading to strange phrases like *dairy ranch* and *fruit ranch*.

COMBINATIONS: *ranch butter* and *ranch egg*, foods produced on the ranch and thus fresh, in contrast to a *States* egg, one shipped out from what was then called the States.

A Montana ranch with corrals and the main buildings, 1872.
[Photograph by William Henry Jackson; courtesy of National Archives (57 CS 16).]

Other terms for a ranch were *cap-and-ball layout, cocklebur outfit, cow outfit, good* **LAY,** *layout, one-horse outfit,* **SHIRTTAIL** *outfit, siwash outfit,* **SPREAD,** *three-up outfit,* and *tough lay.* A *rancho* (in American English) is a Mexican ranch, sometimes a large land grant operated as a ranch. A small outfit was sometimes called a *ranchito.*

RANCHER A ranch owner-operator, whether small outfit or large. To be a **CAT-TLEMAN** has always been a source of pride in the West. The rancher was also known as *big sugar, rawhider, suitcase rancher,* or a *white-collar rancher.*

A *ranch man* or *ranch hand* is a fellow who works on a ranch, not a rancher. When he's not called a cowboy or one of the various half-synonyms for that word, he may be known, depending on circumstance, as an *alfalfa desperado* (hay hand), **ARBUCKLE,** *fodder forker* (**HAY HAND**), *hay slayer* or *hay waddy* (again, a hay hand), *miller* or *mill roller* (hand who maintains windmills), *pitchfork gladiator* (hay hand), *stacker* (hand who works up top when stacking hay), *stiff man, two-buckle boy, windmiller* or *windmill monkey* (hand who maintains windmills), or *wood monkey* (supplier of firewood).

RANCHERIA (ranch-uh-REE-uh) In the Southwest, an Indian village or camp; occasionally, a ranch house. Borrowed from Spanish. A *ranchero* is usually a Hispanic ranch owner, sometimes a Hispanic ranch hand, and occasionally a ranch. *Ranchera* is an infrequently used word meaning "ranch woman."

RANGE An area of uncultivated grassland, suitable for grazing livestock or serving to graze livestock. The **OPEN RANGE** was such grassland before the days of fences and private property; the grass was free to all, or at least to the first comer. Cowmen spoke of "their" range—the country their cattle foraged— whether or not they owned it. Their proprietary attitudes about public land eventually led to a lot of trouble—what were called **RANGE WARS.**

COMBINATIONS: *home range* (where the buffalo no longer roam), *range boss* (a ranch manager, generally for an absentee ownership), *range bum* (an out-of-work hand riding from ranch to ranch looking for a job or a free meal; also known as a *chuckline rider*), *range cradle* (what a sheepherder calls his wagon), *range horse* (a horse raised entirely on grass and usually branded but not broke), *range rider* (a cowboy assigned to ride the outlying areas of a ranch, not just the lines or fences, and do whatever needs doing), *range rights* (in the days of the open range, entitlement to graze cattle on a range by virtue of past use, not ownership), *range saddle* (a stock saddle, one equipped with a horn for rope work), *range word* (a cowman's word of honor). To *be at range* is to be turned out on the grassland. To *cross over* (or *go over*) *the range* is to die (see also **CASH IN YOUR CHIPS**). To *range brand* was to brand calves where you found them, not at roundup. To *ride the range* is to look after cows out on the range. To *run on the same range* is to grow up together, hang out together, or the like. Early Westerners sometimes spoke of the customary country of an Indian tribe as its range.

RANGE WAR A conflict over grazing rights on the open range. These conflicts usually took place between cattlemen and sheepmen, or between large and small cattlemen. Either way, they could be violent. Among the most infamous of these were the Pleasant Valley War in Arizona, the Lincoln County War in New Mexico, and Wyoming's Johnson County War.

RANGER (1) Historically, one of a body of mounted men whose job is to protect a range against Indians. A member of the **TEXAS RANGERS**. A functionary of the Park Service or Forest Service. (2) An occasional term for a range-fed cow. (3) A cowman who range-feeds cattle.

RANK How a cowboy describes a vicious, hard-to-handle horse.

RATTLESNAKE WEED A low-growing spurge (*Euphorbia albormaginta*) with tiny white flowers and a milky sap. Once thought to cure rattlesnake bites, it is poisonous when ingested. Several roots used as a palliative for rattlesnake bites are called *rattlesnake root*. *Rattle weed* is another name for **LOCOWEED.**

RAVEN The large black bird called Raven looms large in Native mythology. Raven created the world (many tales say) by trickery, and is admired and feared as a trickster. He is also brother to the wolf. Because many tribes do not distinguish between the raven and the crow, it is probable that many stories spun about Crow are equally about Raven; the totem bird of the **GHOST DANCE,** for instance, could as well be said to be Raven as Crow.

RAW A cowboy's descriptive term for a green bronc; an unbroke horse.

RAWHIDE AS A NOUN: (1) Untanned, dehaired hide, usually of a cow or buffalo. (2) A whip made of rawhide. (3) A name given by cowboys of the Northern Plains to Texas cowboys.

Rawhide was used for everything on the frontier. Indians made drum heads, shield covers, and **PARFLECHES** from it. Anglos used it to repair gun stocks, wheel spokes, wagon tongues—anything. Trappers made **BULL BOATS** from it; cowboys made **REATAS** and hobbles; settlers made springs, door hinges, and even nails from it. It was so tough it became known as *Mexican iron* or *Mormon iron.*

AS A VERB: (1) To whip an animal (or a person). (2) To tease. (3) Among loggers, to roll logs down a skidway.

COMBINATIONS: *rawhide outfit* (a hard outfit to work for), *rawhide job* (a tough job), *rawhide lumber* (slabs with the bark left on), *rawhide Texan* (a tough **HOMBRE**). A *rawhider* was a small (**SHIRTTAIL**) cattleman or a Westerner who was always on the move. A *rawhiding* was a good whipping with a rawhide. A *rawhide artist* is a hand who's good with a branding iron.

RAWMANE In Alaska, a hide thong used for lashing. Also called *rummish* and *romaine.* Another term for this material, used by the **MOUNTAIN MEN** and still in use in Alaska, is **BABICHE.**

READERS Among gamblers, marked cards. Cards marked with indentations were called *reflectors.*

REAL (ray-AHL; ree-AHL) A Spanish coin, traditionally regarded as worth eight to a dollar. The Spanish **PESO** was a silver coin worth eight reales and was often cut into halves and quarters, giving rise to the expressions *two* **BITS** and *four bits* for a quarter and half dollar, respectively. A *quatrillo* (or *quartee*) was a quarter of the Mexican *real,* thus worth three cents. A *tlaco* (or *claco*) was one-eighth of a *real.* From Spanish (in which it means "royal").

REATA (ree-AH-tuh) A cowboy's rope of braided rawhide. (See also **LARIAT.**) Though the word is too often used to refer to any rope, the genuine reata was and is a special item. It was usually 40 to 80 feet long, and sometimes, according to old hand Jo Mora, *reatas largas* ran upwards of 100 feet; some **VAQUEROS** could make catches up to 60 feet away with them. Borrowed from Spanish. It is sometimes spelled *riata.* Says Jo Mora in *Trail Dust and Saddle Leather:*

> The rawhide reata was the original article, and through the Spanish and Mexican cow country, reateros grew up that were masters at the craft of braiding reatas and all other vaquero rawhide tools, many of which were

truly works of art. In our own country, California was where the making of reatas reached its highest peak. . . .

The finest reatas are made from the primest part only of several young heifer hides, well chosen, properly cured, and the strands cut by an expert. The braiding must also be done with that uniformity and even tension that only your true reatero knows. . . .

Reatas are braided in four, six, or eight strands. The latter two, especially the 8, if made by a top reatero, is a beautiful article and superb for light roping. For the average hard work on large stock, the 4-strand is the best. Diameters vary according to individual preference, but the ⅜-inch reata is the one most used. Naturally, a hand-made reata costs considerably more than a grass rope, yet, though it is vulnerable to certain accidents, with proper care and luck it should outlast a half dozen grass ones.

REBOZO (ruh-BOH-soh) In the Southwest, a shawl or long scarf Hispanic women wear over their heads and shoulders. A *ruana* is another Hispanic shawl. Borrowed from Spanish.

RECOMMEND Among **MORMONS,** a certificate issued by a bishop to identify persons as members of the church, and certify their worthiness to receive certain ordinances or blessings and eligibility to enter the temple. *Job recommends* are given to people in need, so that in exchange for work in one of the church's businesses, they may receive necessities for subsistence.

RED POWER The Indian equivalent of black power; a primary object of **AIM.** In the past three decades, Indian people have organized extensively and put aside old tribal rivalries in order to gain more of what they see as their birthright in this country. Battles have been fought and are being fought over water rights, mineral rights, hunting and fishing rights, rights to land, sovereignty, and the like—and Indians have won many battles in courts and in public opinion. At the same time, renewed interest in the old religions and cultures may be leading to a renaissance. These developments have led many Indians and Anglos to hope for a resurrection, a rejuvenation of spirit, among Indian people.

RED RIVER CART A freight cart used on the trade route along the Red River of the North in the mid-nineteenth century. It was cheap to make and was distinguished by huge, one-piece wheels cut from tree trunks. Since these wheels went ungreased, a cart train could be heard from a long distance. With wheels removed, the carts were paddled across lakes and rivers. The carts were pulled by oxen, and each carried up to 1,000 pounds of goods. The trade route went from the country of the **RED RIVER METIS**—its primary operators—to the area of St. Paul. (See also **CARRETA.**)

RED RIVER METIS An English, Scotch, or French-Cree mixed-blood of the settlements of the Red River of the North or the Saskatchewan River in Canada. The French-Cree **METIS**, often disliked and distrusted by early Americans, were very dark-skinned and noted for dressing entirely in black except for a multicolored sash around the waists of the men.

These three kinds of *metis,* products of liaisons between Canada's fur men and Indian women, ran the **RED RIVER CART** trade along the Red River between Canada and the United States. In 1869 when they were about to come under the jurisdiction of Canada, they formed a separatist movement under Louis Riel, but it failed. In 1884–85 they again attempted independence under Riel, who was tried for treason and hanged but remains a hero to his people. They are also known as the *Bois Brûlé* (the burnt-wood people), anglicized as the *Bob Ruly.*

RED ROAD In the tradition of the **LAKOTAS** and some other **PLAINS INDIANS**, a way of living that is good and fruitful; it runs north and south. (The Lakota word *sha* means both red and good.) The **BLACK ROAD**, by contrast, runs east west and means bristling with conflict and difficulty. Thus the Lakota seer Lame Deer reports that his grandfather used to say, "The earth is red, blood is red, the sun is red as it sets and rises, and our bodies are red. And we should be walking the Red Road, the good north-south road, which is the path of life."

A *road man* is a priest of the **NATIVE AMERICAN CHURCH** and gets his name because he shows worshippers how to stay on the good, red road. Red Road is now the name of an alcohol treatment program among the Lakota.

RED-EYED Cowboy talk for angry. *Red-rumped* can mean the same.

RED-LIGHT DISTRICT An area of brothels. The name is sometimes thought to have come from a sporting house called the Red Light in Dodge City, Kansas.

REDSKIN A term of Anglos for American Indian people, almost always derogatory and therefore offensive. Perhaps derived from the French and English contact with Newfoundland's Beothuk people, who painted their bodies and clothes red. The use of words indicating Indian people as nicknames of sports teams has become very controversial in recent years, and the Washington Redskins are often cited as the most objectionable instance.

REDWOOD A huge tree of California *(Sequoia sempervirens),* as tall as one hundred meters, regarded as a wonder of nature, and commercially important for timber.

RELOADING OUTFIT Cowboy talk for eating utensils.

RELOCATION CENTER A euphemistic term for the camps in which Japanese-Americans (primarily of California) were interned during World War II. The federal government established ten such camps, much like concentration camps, in the western United States. Decades later some of these Japanese-Americans and their descendants were awarded settlements for the government's actions.

REMINGTON Usually a rifle made by the Remington Arms Company. The Remington family of Ilion, New York, made guns—rifles, pistols, and shotguns—from 1816 forward. Remington was a major supplier of arms to the North during the Civil War. The armies of other nations adopted the Remington rifle as well. With **COLT** and **WINCHESTER**, Remington was a leading manufacturer of the firearms carried in the frontier West.

REMITTANCE MAN An Englishman, Irishman, or European, often a younger son of a titled family, who depended on remittances from home for his living. Many Westerners felt contempt for these fellows. Says a rancher in Steward Edward White's *Arizona Nights:*

> Now you're nothin' but a remittance man. Your money's nothin' to me, but the principle of the thing is. The country is plumb pestered with remittance men, doin' nothin', and I don't aim to run no home for incompetents. I had a son of a duke drivin' wagon for me; and he couldn't drive nails in a snow-bank. So don't you herd up with the idea that you can come on this ranch and loaf.

REMOVAL The relocation of Indian peoples from their historical lands in the East to lands then not wanted by white folks; especially, the relocation of the **FIVE CIVILIZED TRIBES** from the Southeast to Indian Territory (roughly what is now Oklahoma) in accordance with the Indian Removal Act of 1830. The most notorious of these removals, this time of the **CHEROKEES**, was the **TRAIL OF TEARS**. (See also **LONG WALK**.)

REMUDA (ruh-MOO-duh; occasionally ruh-MOO-thuh) A herd of saddle horses; a **CAVVY**. In the old West, every big outfit had a remuda, usually with scores of horses (geldings only), and each cowboy was assigned a string of a half dozen or more for his use. When not being ridden, the horses were herded by a *remudero* (**WRANGLER**) or kept in a *remudadero* (horse corral). In the Southwest, also called a *remonta*. Adapted from Spanish (in which it means "remount").

RENDEZVOUS The annual trade fair of the **MOUNTAIN MEN** during the heyday of the mountain **FUR TRADE**, held midsummer each year from 1825 through 1840. As many as several hundred trappers and several thousand Indians would gather at a pre-appointed spot (most often along the Green River) to meet the pack caravan from the settlements. The official business was exchanging beaver pelts (**PLEWS**) for **POWDER**, **LEAD**, tobacco, **BEADS**, maybe some clothing, maybe some traps or a new gun, and almost certainly some whiskey. The unofficial agenda was getting drunk, getting a woman, trading news, opening letters, gambling, indulging in competitions of horse, foot, knife, and gun, and joining up with someone to trap with during the autumn. Altogether the idea was to have a blowout.

Today's rendezvous is a hobby of people who re-create the ways of those old times, often under the sponsorship of the National Muzzle Loading Rifle

Association (NMLRA). Several thousand attend the larger rendezvous, wearing primitive dress and living in lean-tos and **TIPIS**, shooting muzzle-loading guns, and the like.

RENEGADE An outlaw cow or horse. A *renegade rider* was a cowboy who rode to outlying ranches to gather stock belonging to his outfit. (See also **REP**.)

REP A cowboy, usually a top **HAND**, representing his outfit at a **ROUNDUP**. His job was to gather his outfit's strays and a fair share of the **MAVERICKS** and trail them home. The cows and calves he claimed were known as the *rep's cut*. He was sometimes known as the *outside hand*.

REPRESA (ruh-PRAY-suh) A small earthen dam used in arid country to hold water from runoff. Often the resulting water holes are very small. Borrowed from Spanish. Also called a *presa*.

RE-RIDE (1) In **RODEO**, a second chance for a contestant to try an event when the horse fails to perform. When a calf or steer is used a second time for roping in the same go-round, it's called a *rerun*. (2) To ride an area of the range again to find cows missed on the first ride.

RESERVATION A tract of land held in trust for the use of one or more Native tribes as a nation within the United States, under tribal (and to some extent federal) jurisdiction but not always subject to the laws of the surrounding state. The legal history of reservations in this country is long, complex, and bloody.

These reservations at first were principally ways of controlling Indians and opening their former lands to passage or settlement by whites. Often the lands set aside for Indians were considered useless, making the subsequent attempts to teach the Indians to farm them hypocritical. In some cases, the lands set aside turned out to have great mineral value; then the whites often found ways of taking them back; sometimes the Indians got the mineral royalties and the last laugh.

The reservation system had dubious success from the start. Congress, **INDIAN AGENTS**, and even freighters constantly found ways to reduce (often by theft) the **ANNUITIES** the Indians had accepted as payment for settling on a reservation. Abraham Lincoln is said to have defined a reservation as where Indians live surrounded by thieves. Though the Indians were often hungry, they were not always permitted to leave the reservation to hunt. The old way of life had been taken away, and no new one provided. Starting in the late 1880s, federal policy was to end the Indians' communal ownership of their reservations, allot lands to individual Indians, and give the Indians what were considered the advantages of private property (and, not coincidentally, to open unalloted lands to white settlement). Through this policy, some two-thirds of Indian lands passed into white hands over the next fifty years.

The recent social history of reservations is little better. Many of them are centers of deep poverty, unemployment, alcoholism, high infant mortality, broken families, and other symptoms of troubled spirits. Perhaps the **RED POWER** movement, which is primarily political, and the resurgence of traditional religion and ways among Indians will heal some of these troubles. Many Indian peoples declare that such change must come not from the good will of white people but from within Indian communities.

COMBINATIONS: The slang of contemporary Indians and some Anglos for a reservation, sometimes lightly derisive, is *the rez*. The Canadian equivalent of reservation is *reserve*. To *be off the* (or *your*) *reservation* originally meant for Indians to be away from their assigned lands and (from the Anglo's point of view) likely causing trouble. It has come to mean to be crazy, to be going wild, sometimes to be committing infidelity. A non-Indian who either has a lot of time on the rez, cultural savvy, or both, is called a *rez rat*. To be *rezzed out* is to have had it up to here with rez life; to be up to your neck in **FRY BREAD**, your native language, and your people's ways.

RESERVATION HAT A tall, unblocked (uncreased), flat-brimmed, black hat originally issued by the federal government, associated primarily with **NAVAJOS** and **CROWS**.

RETABLO (ray-TAB-low) A painted or carved panel of religious iconography made by a *santero* (a person who carves religious images). From Spanish.

REVOLVER Usually a handgun (old-time Westerners did not say *pistol*) capable of shooting repeatedly because it had either several barrels or a multichambered cylinder with separate charges or cartridges. The first popular one was made by Samuel **COLT**.

RIB UP (1) In cowboy talk, to persuade. (2) To stiffen an **APAREJO** with sticks.

RIBBON SHIRT A shirt decorated with glossy ribbons, worn by Indians at **POW-WOWS** and other dress-up occasions. A *ribbon dress* is the equivalent for women and girls. The **NAVAJO** have a *ribbon dance*.

RICO (REE-coh) In the Southwest, a rich man. From Spanish. The rich are also known in the West as **BUMS ON THE PLUSH** or **PLUTES** and are said to be *in the chips* or *wallowing in velvet*.

RIDE Many combinations are formed with this word. In cowboy talk: *ride fence* (ride along an outfit's fences regularly to check their repair), *ride for a blind bridle* (work for farmers, whose horses wore blinders), *ride for a brand* (work for a cattle outfit), *ride herd* (keep watch on cows—or people—while riding in a circle around the herd, a person, or a situation), *ride line* (ride the understood boundaries of a ranch), *ride the chuck-line, grub line,* or *bag line* (see also **CHUCK**), *ride the rough string, ride sign* (check for sign that your cows have strayed). Cowboys also use these expressions: *ride herd on a woman* (court her), *ride into someone's dust* (follow them), *ride out a horse* (ride a horse until it quits bucking), *ride like a deputy sheriff* (ride recklessly), *ride slick* (ride a bucker without benefit of cheaters such as a bucking roll), *ride straight up* (ride erect in the saddle with the reins in one hand, as you should ride), *ride on your spurs* (hook your spurs into the cinch), *ride out of town with nothing but a head* (have a hangover), *ride over that trail again* (explain that better), *ride the bed wagon* (be laid up hurt or sick). The old phrase *a man to ride the river with* is a high compliment. A **TRAIL-DRIVE** expression, it means a fellow who will stick no matter how tough the going gets. Drives often had to cross rivers in the spring that were flooding and dangerous.

In **RODEO**, competitors *ride a beast with a belly full of bed springs* (ride a bucking horse) and *ride the shows* (compete on the rodeo circuit).

In reference to **BADMEN**: *ride the coulees* or *the high lines* (move along keeping one step ahead of the law), *ride the owl-hoot trail* (follow the outlaw life), *ride with an extra cinch ring* (improvise brands with cinch rings), *ride under a cottonwood limb* (get hanged).

Similar phrases among loggers: *ride Aunt Polly* or *board with Aunt Polly* (to be collecting pay while off work because of illness or injury), *ride her out* (what a logger had to do when a log jam gave way unexpectedly on a river drive), *ride shank's mare* (to walk), *ride the saw* (not to do your share on the crosscut saw, or generally be lazy).

RIDE BOG To ride through the boggy areas of a ranch looking for cows that are stuck and probably weak and pull them out with your rope. It's hard work. (See also **PULL BOG**.)

RIDE CIRCLE To search out the cows in a large area and drive them to the gathering spot, one of the principal chores of a **ROUNDUP**. It took on a metaphoric meaning: To *complete your circle* meant to finish your task, your earthly responsibilities, your life.

RIFFLE In **PLACER** mining, a slat or bar in the bottom of a **SLUICE** box. Riffles catch the particles of gold, which sink to the bottom as the water flows through. They're also called *riffle bars* and *riffle blocks*. Sluice boxes are sometimes called *riffle* (or *ripple*) *boxes*.

RIG (1) Cowboy talk for a saddle. Saddles are also said to be rigged in certain ways, meaning to have a certain arrangement of the cinch or cinches. The complete arrangement of cinch, rings, and other saddle leathers is known as its *rigging*. The Mexican saddle, father of all Western saddles, was *Spanish-rigged,* that is, the single cinch hung directly down from the forks. The Texas cowboys, wanting to rope big, wild cows in difficult terrain and *tie hard and fast* and never have the saddle slide, added another cinch farther back, creating what was called the **DOUBLE RIG**. That saddle would stay put, regardless.

On the other hand, the early Californians thought the cinch hanging from the forks tended to slip forward and chafe the horse. They moved the cinch back to the middle, creating the **CENTER-FIRE RIG** or *California saddle* (also known as the *California rig*). Later they experimented with moving it forward partway, giving us the five-eighths, three-fourths, and seven-eighths styles. But they stuck to a single cinch. Other rigging styles are the *Montana rig*, with the cinch just forward of the center-fire position; and RIM-FIRE, with a single cinch well forward.

Today all these rigs are used. The double rig is preferred by the Texas cowboys who tie hard and fast, the single by the cowboys who *dally*. The double-rig crowd says the single rig lets the saddle whump you in the ass when the horse bucks. The single-rig crowd says a horse with a single rig doesn't buck as much. (See also DOUBLE-RIG, SINGLE-RIG.)

(2) Almost any kind of vehicle, from a Plains-crossing wagon to a contemporary pickup truck, especially if the pickup is outfitted with a *stock rack* (animal pen) or other extra equipment. (3) In OIL DRILLING, the equipment for drilling a well.

RIGGING PECKER Among loggers, an IWW (Industrial Workers of the World) organizer.

RIGHT-HAND MAN Either a ranch foreman or his assistant: the straw boss; the key man.

RILDY Cowboy talk for a blanket or quilt.

RIMFIRE A way of describing a saddle rigged with a single cinch well forward. Such a saddle is also called a *Spanish rig* or a *rimmy*. (See also RIG, SINGLE-RIG.) To *rimfire a horse* is to put a burr under the blanket, a prank that is likely to get the next rider bucked off.

RIMROCK Steep rock on the rim of a canyon, channel, or basin. All over the West, rock has been left high and dry by water that may be hundreds or thousands of feet below or may have disappeared centuries ago. It makes climbing out of canyons difficult or impossible.

COMBINATIONS: To *get rimrocked* is to get penned in by rimrock. This has happened to most Westerners who've done much wandering on foot or horseback—even to the one-armed explorer John Wesley Powell climbing in the Grand Canyon. It can be dangerous. To *rimrock sheep* was to kill them by stampeding them over cliffs. A *rimrocker* is a horse surefooted enough for rimrock country.

RINCON (ring-KOHN) A protected spot, a valley or a nook, good as a location for a house or a settlement. Borrowed from Spanish.

RING BIT A CURB BIT with a ring that slips over the lower jaw. In careless hands, it's hard on the horse. Also called a *chileno*.

RING TOTER A RUSTLER; a man who carried an extra cinch ring so he could burn any brand he wanted.

RINGEY (1) Cowboy talk for riled up. (2) When referring to a woman, nervous, high strung; taken from the way a horse will wring its tail when nervous.

RIO In the Southwest, a river. It occurs mostly in proper names—Rio Grande, Rio Gavilan, and so on. Borrowed from Spanish.

RIPGUT A fence of **LATILLAS** erected side by side.

RIPPER A **GREAT BASIN** term for a big horse with plenty of **BOTTOM** (endurance). (See also **STOCK HORSE**.)

RISTRA (REES-truh) A string of dried red **CHILES** used decoratively and functionally in Southwestern kitchens. From Spanish.

RIVER MINING Mining done in a dry riverbed when the stream has been diverted.

RIVER RAT Among loggers, a *log driver* (or *river driver*), a man who floated logs from where they were cut downriver to the sawmill, a dangerous job because of log jams. Also a familiar denizen of rivers, parallel to a **DESERT RAT**.

RIVER SLUICING When done along a river, *hydraulic* mining (mining with powerful streams of water).

ROACH Among many Indian peoples, a spray of stiff hair put on top of a shaved head for ceremonies or other dress occasions. When a horse's mane is cut thus, it is said to be roached.

ROAD AGENT A highwayman, a stagecoach holdup man. It occasionally took the form *road agentry*. Road agents were sometimes called *roadsters* (this was the era before the automobile).

From this term came the phrase *road agent's spin,* or *Curly Bill spin,* said to have originated with Curly Bill Brocius (or Graham). It was a trick spin of a revolver into shooting position. Appearing to hand the gun over butt first and upside down, the road agent spun it on the trigger guard, cocking the hammer as it came under his thumb, and shot.

ROAD BRAND A brand put on Texas herds during **TRAIL DRIVES**. For a time, such a brand, high on the left side, was required by law for cows going north out of the state. Also used as a verb.

ROAD MAN A priest of the **NATIVE AMERICAN CHURCH**. He shows worshipers how to stay on the good, **RED ROAD**.

ROAD RANCH A name for an establishment providing supplies to travelers on a trail. Also called a **ROADHOUSE**.

ROAD RUNNER The chaparral cock (*Geococcyx californianus*) of the Southwestern deserts, which was legendary even before it hooked up with Wile E. Coyote. The name comes from its habit of running a trail ahead of riders or wagons. It is said to eat rats, mice, lizards, and snakes—including rattlesnakes, which may be why it's regarded as cuckoo; among its many names is *ground cuckoo*. Others are *chaparral bird, churrea, cock of the desert, lizard bird, paisano, runner bird, snake-killer,* and *snake-eater.* Josiah Gregg commented in 1840 that a road runner will perform all the vermin-eating duties of a cat.

ROAD STAKE Among loggers, the wages a man has saved up to take away to another job.

ROADHOUSE (1) A rustler's holding corral for stolen animals, usually in an out-of-way place. (2) More recently, and beyond the West, an establishment outside city limits for drinking. (See also **ROAD RANCH.**)

ROADOMETER A **MORMON** term for the mechanical means of measuring road distance that they worked out on their way to the Salt Lake in 1847, based on revolutions of a wagon wheel.

ROARING CAMP A mining camp that was wide open, with plenty of booze, gambling, and prostitutes. Both a common and proper noun, as in Bret Harte's "The Luck of Roaring Camp."

ROBBER'S ROOST A way of describing a place frequented by outlaws, as in such-and-such a place was "a real robber's roost." When capitalized, the hideout of the notorious gang the Wild Bunch in Utah's San Rafael Swell area, about forty miles from Hanksville.

ROBLE (ROH-buhl) In the Southwest, an oak (*Quercus lobata*). It is used principally in place names. Borrowed from Spanish.

ROCK WESTERN COMBINATIONS: *rock chuck* (another name for a **MARMOT**), *rock dog* or *rabbit* (another name for a *pika*), *rock wren* (any of several wrens of rimrock country).

ROCKER A primitive trough for separating gold from dirt. The miner shook gold-bearing dirt and water in the rocker (or *rocking cradle*) and retrieved gold from the **RIFFLE** bars in the rocker or the cloth below. Also called a *rocker sieve* or sometimes a *tom*. To use a rocker is to *rock*, or *rock out*, gold.

Cradling for gold near Virginia City, Montana, 1871.
[PHOTOGRAPH BY WILLIAM HENRY JACKSON; COURTESY OF NATIONAL ARCHIVES (57-HS-910).]

ROCKY MOUNTAIN COMBINATIONS: *Rocky Mountain canary* (a jocular name for a **BURRO**), *Rocky Mountain goat* (either a mountain goat or a bighorn sheep), *Rocky*

Mountain sheep (a bighorn sheep), *Rocky Mountain oyster* (a calf testicle), *Rocky Mountain pine* (the ponderosa or bull pine).

ROCKY MOUNTAIN COLLEGE The **MOUNTAIN-MAN** custom of reading during the winter, or learning to read; Shakespeare, Byron, Scott, Miss Jane Porter, and the Bible were favorites. In Osborne Russell's camp near Fort Hall, Idaho, books could be borrowed so the literate could teach the illiterate to read. Some contemporary **BUCKSKINNERS** use the phrase to mean the learning of wilderness skills, not the original meaning.

RODEO (roh-DAY-oh; ROH-dee-oh) (1) First, in the Southwest, a **ROUNDUP**, a gathering of cattle. (2) Later, a competition among cowboys of roping and riding skills that were originally developed from working cows. Still later, these competitions developed into today's rodeo circuit, a sequence of events sanctioned by the Professional Rodeo Cowboys Association (PRCA) with substantial prize money and official world championships. The five standard events are **BULL-DOGGING, CALF ROPING, SADDLE-BRONC RIDING, BAREBACK RIDING**, and **BULL RIDING**; *team roping* is also a recognized event.

In the first sense, which is obsolete, the word is pronounced roh-DAY-oh, in the second, ROH-dee-oh. Both stem from the Spanish *rodear* (to surround or encircle). Among **BUCKAROOS**, a *rodear* is a group of cattle that's been cut out.

COMBINATIONS: *rodeo clown* (a skilled rider dressed up as a clown; while entertaining the audience, he deliberately distracts the horses and bulls who have thrown their riders so the cowboys can hightail it), *rodeo chaps* (heavy chaps to protect against chutes and fences, they're often painted with resin to make the legs grip tightly), *rodeo cool* (a way of describing a beer that's cool enough to drink at a rodeo but not cold), *rodeo cowboy* (an athlete who works the arenas, not ranges), *rodeo arena, rodeo ground, rodeo producer*. Loggers sometimes called their log-rolling competitions *roleos* after the cowboy contests.

ROE ON KELP In Alaska, a food delicacy, herring eggs on seaweed. Also called *spawn on kelp*.

ROLL (1) An exhibition shooting trick. The shooter spins the gun on the trigger guard from and to the normal shooting position, cocking it with the thumb on the way around. In the *border roll*, the gun was spun the reverse direction of the usual roll, the butt going down first and the barrel up. (See also **ROAD AGENT, BORDER SHIFT**.) (2) A flip of the cowboy's rope that sends a corkscrewing wave along the string. It's often used to retrieve a rope from cows' heels. (3) A cowboy's name for his bedroll. (4) In **RODEO**, the bucking stock waiting to get into a chute.

COMBINATIONS: *rolling faro* (a **FARO** game played with a wheel, like roulette, instead of cards), *rolling mustang* (a gambling game), *roll in* (to go to bed or, depending on context, to arrive), among loggers, *roll them* (go to bed), *roll its tail* (what a cow will do with the near end of its tail just before it runs; also said of a man about to head out fast), *roll logs* (to float them downstream), *roll the cotton* (for a cowboy to roll up his bedroll and go), *roll the guff* (among loggers, to talk), *roll up* (when said of a horse, for it to take advantage of the saddle's coming off to roll on its back), *roll your own* (to make your own cigarette from tobacco and paper—and, figuratively, to make anything yourself instead of buying it), *roll your wheels* (to get going).

ROLLWAY A slope where logs were rolled into a river; the pile of logs to be rolled.

ROMAL (ruh-MAL, with the *a* as in *corral*) A whip or **QUIRT** braided from the end of reins, popular among the **CALIFORNIOS**. It often was about three feet long. Adapted from the Spanish *ramal* (which means "strand of rope").

ROMAN RIDING A **RODEO** stunt in which a rider stands on two horses' backs with a foot on each moving horse. Also known as a *hippodrome stand*.

ROOSTERED Cowboy talk for drunk. A drunk is called (in the Southwest) a *borracho*. He's a man who has *bottle fever*, **KEEPS THE DOUBLE DOORS SWINGING, CUTS HIS WOLF LOOSE, FREIGHTS HIS CROP, HEARS THE OWL HOOT,** *goes on a bender, goes on a high lonesome, goes on a jag, puts the rollers on,* or *ties on a bear.* When he's loaded up, he's a *walking whiskey vat* and often *somebody has stolen his rudder.*

ROPE In the West, this word usually doesn't mean just any sort of line but the string a cowboy uses on cows and horses, that is, a *catch rope,* **LARIAT, LASSO,** or **REATA,** usually made of **RAWHIDE, HAIR, HEMP, SISAL,** or cotton. He does everything with it—catches his horse in the morning, throws and holds cows, pulls critters out of bogs, hauls firewood, pickets mounts, and builds rope corrals. In the old days, he even administered what he thought of as justice with it.

All this proceeded historically from one necessity: The vaquero and his successor the cowhand needed to catch horses so they could ride them, and catch cows so they could brand them (or earmark them, doctor them, etc.). That led to the defining equipment of the Western rider, the saddle horn and the rope. Movies notwithstanding, most hands took far more pride in their riding and roping skills than in their competence with guns.

Some hands could and can do fancy tricks with ropes, but in the heyday of the open range, many hands could boggle the minds of greenhorns with rope skills needed for everyday work, like throwing the noose in a figure-eight throw so that the upper loop caught a calf's head and the lower loop its front feet. More rope throws are *backhand slip* (a rope throw over the calf behind the roper's horse), **BLOCKER LOOP,** *California twist* (a rope throw with no twirl), *cotton-patch* or *community loops* (large nooses in the rope), *forefooting* (a front-foot catch), **HEEL, HOOLIHAN,** *head catch* (catches the head rather than the feet or horns), *mangana* (an overhand throw), *overhand toss, peale* (a hind foot catch), *pitch* (an overhand rope throw with a horizontal loop), *roll* (a flip of the rope that starts a corkscrewing motion and frees it from a cow's heel), *rollup, slip* (an overhand with a vertical loop rope throw), *washerwoman's loop* (a big flat loop), and *underhand pitch*.

Some roping tricks are *body spin* (around the roper's own body), *complex spin* (two ropes simultaneously), *butterfly* (looks like a butterfly), *juggling* (a variation of the body spin), *rollover* (rolls the noose up and down his arm), *stargazing* (a body spin while lying down), *skipping* (jumping in and out of a vertical loop), and *setting spin* (jumping in and out of a vertical loop in a sitting position).

Other cowboy words for throwing ropes were CATGUT (when it was made of rawhide), *clothesline, coil, fling line, pass rope* (when of fiber), *gut line* (when of rawhide), HEMP (when of manila), LASS ROPE, *line*, MAGUEY (when of century-plant fiber), MANILA (when of that), *seago* (when of hemp), *skin string* (when of rawhide), *string, tom horn*, and *whale line*.

To rope a critter is to catch it with a rope. When applied to a man, it often means to entrap. A *roper* can mean either a man skilled with a rope or a horse trained to work with a rider in roping cattle. Such a horse has lots of smarts: It knows to catch up with a cow on the left side but not pass it, watch to see if the throw is accurate, face the catch straight on, and sit back hard on its hindquarters with the forefeet braced.

COMBINATIONS: *rope corral* (a pen improvised with lariats, or other ropes, to hold horses at a camp that has no corral), *rope shy* (a way of describing a critter that jumps away from a thrown rope), *smooth roper* (one who does his job without fancy tricks), *rope someone in* (to trick someone), *rope tosser* (a roper who ropes calves in a herd with the rope starting on the ground behind him, without swinging it above his head), *roping out* (catching the mounts in a corral).

ROSADERO (rohs-uh-DAIR-oh) The leather fender that goes underneath the saddle leathers, between the rider's knee and the horse, not to be confused with a *sudadero* (sweat pad on the underside of a saddle). Borrowed from Spanish.

ROSEBUD Cowboy talk for a knot in the DALLYING end of his rope. Other such names are *turk's head, crown knot,* and *Matthew Walker knot*.

ROSETTE A flower-shaped, decorative piece of leather on a saddle or bridle.

ROTTEN-LOGGING Cowboy talk for a couple's sitting on a log and necking.

ROUGH LOCK Historically, braking a wagon on a downslope by chaining wheels to prevent them from turning. In Alaska, chaining or roping dogsled runners so that the chain or rope bites the snow.

Rosettes were used to adorn saddles and other tack.

[FROM *Moseman's Illlustrated Guide for Purchasers of Horse Furnish Goods*, CA. 1892.]

ROUGH RIDER A hero-making name for a cowhand, perhaps first used in print by Teddy Roosevelt himself. It may have derived from **ROUGH-STRING** rider. Later, Roosevelt's Spanish-American War cavalry outfit, recruited from the Western cow country, was called the Rough Riders.

ROUGH STRING A cow outfit's bunch of half-broke or unbroke horses. On a big outfit, every hand was assigned a string, and there were usually some horses in the **CAVVY** that had never been ridden—the rough string. The hands who were paid extra to break these **CAYUSES** were known as *rough-string riders* and were thought to have more guts than brains. (See also **BREAK A HORSE**.)

COMBINATIONS: *rough-break a horse* (to stick with it two or three times, maybe get the kinks out, and call it broke), *rough gambler* (in the gold-rush days of Montana and Idaho, a thief or **ROAD AGENT**; the term also took the form *rough gambling*), *rough lock a wagon wheel* (to use a chain or other primitive device to brake it), *rough out a horse* (the same as to rough-break it).

ROUGHNECK A worker on an **OIL** drilling crew in an oil field, other than the driller.

ROUNDUP The gathering of cattle, usually to brand calves or to ship steers to market. Over the years, the Western roundup has varied considerably. In the early days, the Texans called it a *cow hunt,* procedures and rules were made up as folks went along, and beef wasn't shipped to market.

During the heyday of the open range, the couple of decades following the Civil War, it became the custom to round up the cows once in the spring for branding and again in the fall for shipping. The hands of the various cow out-fits of the region would meet at an appointed place and time (sometimes sev-eral successive places and times) under a **ROUNDUP BOSS** and an understood set of rules. The men would **RIDE CIRCLE** to gather the cows; then they'd **CUT** (separate) them by brand and make decisions about **MAVERICKS**; then they would do the jobs that needed to be done. (See also **BRANDING**.) Since this process wore out horses, each hand had his own string, with different mounts for circling, cutting, and roping.

These open-range roundups were huge enterprises. In *Cowboy Culture,* David Dary describes a big one in Texas in 1881: Eight or ten stockmen got together and rigged one **CHUCK WAGON** and headed for the roundup; altogether ten chuck wagons representing a total of ninety stock outfits showed up. The hands made dry camps overnight and then drove the cattle into one enormous herd. At the instruction of the roundup boss, the home outfit cut its cattle out and drove them back onto the range. Other outfits then took turns cutting while others held the herd. If disputes arose over unclear brands, the roundup boss settled them. The **REPS** were given their cuts. Mavericks were claimed by whoever had best title. Then each outfit proceeded to do its branding. And then each chuck wagon with its herd headed for the next roundup.

Roundup was a big social occasion. Hands got to socialize with seldom-seen friends and **JAWBONE** around the chuck wagon and campfire.

When the ranges were fenced, roundup changed. No longer were such vast areas to be ridden, and no longer were different brands mixed indiscriminately. But outfits (especially small outfits) continued to help each other. Today ranchers in a region often round up and brand on consecutive weekends at each other's places.

By metaphoric extension, *last roundup* came to mean the cowhand's final reward.

ROUNDUP BOSS The head honcho of a roundup. In the days of the open range, he had a huge job—coordinating the efforts of perhaps scores of outfits with chuck wagons, many cowboys to a wagon, and a string of horses for every cowboy. He sent men to ride circle on various parts of the range, oversaw the gathering, cutting, and branding, and kept the peace between rival outfits. Though he might not be an owner, here he was a monarch. Also called a *roundup captain.*

ROUTE Among loggers, the time of operation for a logging camp, or a logger's time on that job.

ROWEL The wheel of a **SPUR**, the business end, the part that scratches. Rowels come in a wide variety of styles and shapes, some with many small points and others with a few big, sharp points.

RUB OUT To kill. The expression dates at least to the **MOUNTAIN MEN**. Linguist J. L. Dillard suggests that it came from the **PLAINS INDIAN** sign meaning to kill, a rubbing motion. (See also **DRY-GULCH**.)

RUN (1) A stampede. (2) A land rush.

COMBINATIONS: *run cows* (to operate a cattle ranch or to work cattle), *run cows off* (to stampede them so you could steal them), *run buffalo* or *run meat* (to hunt them on horseback), *run mustangs* (to rope them from horseback), *run a rapid* or a stream as a whole (to navigate it in a boat), *run down his mainspring* (what a rider may let a runaway horse do: run unchecked until it decides to quit), *run like a Nueces steer* (to run fast and recklessly), *run a brand* (to draw it on a hide with a **RUNNING IRON**).

In **RODEO**, a *runaway bucker* is a kind of bucking horse; it runs like the devil for a distance before starting to buck, then gives a tremendous leap and comes down hard. Among Santa Fe Trail traders, a *runner* (sometimes called in French an *avant courier*) was a man sent ahead of a caravan to get provisions and send them back and make other necessary arrangements. *Running mate* is cowboy talk for partner or wife. A *running mount* is a jump onto the back of horse without benefit of stirrup. A *running W* is a **HOBBLE**.

RUNNING IRON A **BRANDING** iron without a stamp on the end. Using a plain rod or one with a little curl at the tip, the brander would draw his brand free-hand. Though the running iron had legitimate uses (for instance, applying a neighbor's brand when you didn't have one of his irons), it was the mark of the **RUSTLER**. If a man was caught with a running iron in his boot, he was often required to answer nasty questions from men ready to consider themselves judge, jury, and executioner. Running irons were outlawed in Texas in the 1870s.

RURALES The Mexican equivalent of Arizona Rangers—a paramilitary police force that operated in rural areas. During the Mexican Revolution of 1912, the enforcement corps consisted of killers and bandits released from prison that terrorized the *campesinos* of northern Mexico.

RUSHER A person who participates in a human stampede for gold or land. (See also **FORTY-NINER, RUN, SOONER.**)

RUSSIAN DRAG A method of trick riding, boot in a strap and head hanging off to the side of the horse.

RUSSIAN PIE In Alaska, a baked dish of rice, salmon, cabbage, spices, dough, and sometimes meat. Also called *pirok.*

RUST THE BOILER In cowboy talk, to drink **ALKALI** water.

RUSTLER (1) First, a hustler, an active enterprising fellow. (2) Later, a critter good at foraging (*rustling up* something to eat). (3) Later still, a horse **WRANGLER**, then a ranch cook.

(4) Finally and most memorably, a cow thief. Some authorities suggest that a fellow who was a hustler became a rustler when **MAVERICKING** (putting his brand on unbranded calves) lost acceptance. A rustler was also called a *brand artist, brand blotter, brand burner, brand botcher, Cattle Kate* (if a woman), *cow thief,* **CROSS BRANDER, HOODOO,** *mavericker,* **RING TOTER,** *rope and ring man,* and **TONGUE-SPLITTER.** He was a fellow said to be **CARELESS WITH HIS BRANDING IRON** or *handy with his running iron.* Similar expressions were *he doesn't keep his twine on the tree* (doesn't keep his rope coiled on the saddle horn), *he keeps his branding iron smooth* (not rusty), *he rides with an extra cinch ring* (for range branding), *he swings* (or *throws*) *a big loop, his calves don't suck the right cows, his cows have twins, he has a sticky rope, he packs a long rope, he's too handy with a rope, he works ahead of the roundup,* and *he works* (alters) *brands.*

One rustling technique was to change the brand. For instance, a lazy Y can easily be altered to a dumbbell. Another method was rebranding through a wet blanket. (See also **HAIR BRAND.**) One of the most common methods was *sleepering,* earmarking a calf without branding it in the hope that the real owner wouldn't notice the missing brand; when it was weaned and left its mother, the rustler would recrop the ear and put his own brand on it. Some authorities say that there's more rustling going on today, when trucks can move stock away quickly, than in the bad old days.

The verb form *to rustle* occurs with all the above meanings. **COMBINATIONS:** *rustler's pneumonia* (cold feet, fear) *rustle the pasture* (to bring in the horse herd).

SAB-CAT What a logger called a saboteur. It came from the black cat in an Industrial Workers of the World (IWW) emblem.

SABINO (suh-BEE-noh) A red roan with a white belly. A *sabina* is a cow with red and white spots. (See **BUCKSKIN** for other horse colors.) Borrowed from Spanish.

SACATONE (sah-kuh-TOHN) A popular forage grass of the Southwest (*Sporobolus wrightii*). Also called *sacate*, it is adapted from the Spanish *zacatón*.

SACK In logging, to trail after a drive and push grounded logs back into the water. It was laborious work. Also called *sacking the rear*. A man who did it was a *sacker*, and he was a member of the *sacking crew*.

SACK A HORSE When breaking a horse, **PEELERS (BRONC BUSTERS)** often rub a bronc with a sack or blanket and flip it at him to get him used to being touched and handled. Also called *sacking him out*.

SACRED ARROWS Among the **CHEYENNES**, the four arrows given to Sweet Medicine by the creator Maheo. Along with the Buffalo Hat, the central **MEDICINE** objects of the tribe.

SACRED HOOP In the world view (or religion) of the **LAKOTA** and other **PLAINS INDIANS**, a symbol of wholeness and completeness—the wholeness of the family, the tribe, even the species. Thus it is sacred, and when it is broken, the people are sundered, their health and spirit destroyed. The hoop is the particular gift, says Black Elk, of one of the cardinal points, the south, and in its center the tree will bloom.

SADDLE For Western saddles, see **STOCK SADDLE**. For names for English saddles, see **POSTAGE STAMP**. COMBINATIONS: *saddle slickers* and *saddle stiffs* (cowboys), *saddle bums* (cow-country drifters), *saddle tramps* (cowboys who spent their time riding the chuck line), *saddleman* (a man on horseback), *saddlebag doctor* (a doctor who rode to see his patients and took his medical implements in his saddlebags; see also **SAWBONES**), *saddle-blanket gambler* (a small-time gambler or a cowboy who gambled on a blanket), *saddle pockets* (another name for saddlebags), *saddle strings* (the leather strings used for tying gear on), *saddle gun* (a carbine—a short, light shoulder arm handy for use on horseback; it rides in a *saddle scabbard*), *saddle stand* (the wooden contraption, approximating the shape of a horse's back, for storing your saddle), *saddle mule* (the prairie-schooner mule ridden by the driver or a mule broke for riding, as opposed to a pack mule or mule broke to harness), *saddle-broke* (a term for a horse broke enough to tolerate a saddle on its back but no more), *saddle stock* (a ranch's saddle horses, its **CAVVY** or **REMUDA**).

In logging, a saddle is a transverse log shaped to guide other logs down a **SKID ROAD**.

Saddle-backed is an expression meaning sit across something like a saddle. The miners used to say that the Rockies are saddle-backed across the rangeland in Colorado.

SADDLE BLANKET (1) A pad or blanket that protects the horse's back against the chafing of the saddle. In the earliest days, an **APISHAMORE** (buffalo-calf hide) was used. For a long time, the *Navajo blanket* was the most popular. Recently the *cool pad* has been a favorite. Also called a *saddle mat.* (2) A griddle cake. (3) A dollar bill.

SADDLE TREE The frame of a saddle. Well-known trees have been California, Ellenburg, Frazier, and **VISALIA**. (See also **STRAINER**.)

SADDLE-BRONC RIDING One of the principal competitions of a **RODEO**. The rules specify that the rider must use an **ASSOCIATION SADDLE**, use just one rein, not touch anything with his free hand, and stay on the horse for eight seconds.

SAFETY In Alaska, a metal fitting that prevents a wood-stove pipe from getting a ceiling or wall too hot.

SAGE Sagebrush, the ubiquitous plant of the Plains and desert; an area covered with that plant, as in "they walked off into the sagebrush together arm in arm." The big sage (*Artemisia tridentata*) is more than head high, black sage (*Artemisia arbuscla*) grows at elevations below 5,800 feet, and *Artemisia nova* is only one to two feet high; all are members of the wormwood family rather than true sages (*Salvia* sp.). Sage is blue-gray-green and in thousands of places so thick and far-reaching, it looks like an ocean. It is beautiful. Westerners call sage *dogwood* (from its smell), *hickory, estafiata,* and *artemisia* (the latter two are Spanish names).

COMBINATIONS: Plants and animals with *sage* in their names are simply a version of the critter that lives in the sagebrush: *sage chipmunk, sage chicken,* **SAGE GROUSE,** *sage hare, sage quail, sage sparrow, sage thrush, sweet sage, sage willow.* The land is described as *sage country, sage desert, sage flat, sage hill, sage land, sage plain, sage prairie,* and *sage range.* Cowboys call people who live out in the boonies *sagebrushers,* and a *sage rat* is the equivalent of a **DESERT RAT**. *Sage hen* is used, fancifully, for girls and young women.

SAGE GROUSE A big grouse (*Centrocercus urophasianus*) that hangs out in the sagebrush. Also called a **FOOL HEN, SAGE HEN, SAGE COCK, PRAIRIE CHICKEN,** and *prairie turkey.* The sage grouse has a wonderful mating ritual, done in early spring. The males group together and strut, posture, show off their tail feathers, and *boom* (make plopping noises with their air sacs). The females and immature males watch, the females pretending to be uninterested. Birds slip off into the sage (not always excluding immature males) and before long there are chicks.

SAGEBRUSH PROCESS A method of attempting to amalgamate gold or silver from ore—with a tea brewed from sagebrush.

SAGEBRUSH REBELLION A political movement of the late 1970s and early 1980s. Some people in the Western states rebelled against the influence of the federal government in their states through control of public land. Usually the sagebrush rebel was a fellow who favored exploitation over preservation of public resources.

SAGEBRUSHER A sagebrusher is any inhabitant of the arid West, especially one in a remote area. He can be a person who camps out on his own (by implication, in the sagebrush) instead of staying at hotels. This meaning seems to have originated in Yellowstone National Park, where sagebrushers offended the proprietors of the great hotels and their tip-hungry staffs. The park developed its own lingo: Camp employees were *savages*, waitresses were *beavers*, bellmen were *puck ruts*, maids were *pillow punchers*, bus drivers were *gear jammers*, and couples billing and cooing were said to be **ROTTEN-LOGGING**.

SAGUARO (suh-WAR-oh) A huge cactus (*Carnegiea gigantea*) of the Southwest that grows in columns to the size and shape of a well-ordered tree, up to sixty feet high. The Native people and Anglos made (and make) syrup and wine from its fruit. Borrowed from Spanish, it's spelled variously, especially *sahuaro*. Also known as the *pillar cactus* or *pitahaya*.

SAHARA CLUB The mocking name some Westerners, especially Utahns, give the Sierra Club, which they see as opposing economic progress with its environmental crusades.

SAINT (1) A common name for one of the faithful of the Church of Jesus Christ of **LATTER-DAY SAINTS**, used both by **MORMONS** and gentiles and often capitalized. (2) *Winter saint* was a term of early Utah Mormons for a gentile **EMIGRANT** who spent the winter in Salt Lake instead of risking the crossing of the Great Basin and Sierra Nevada with cold weather approaching. (3) Without capitalization, a rustler's name for a cowboy who's honest.

SAKEY See **ACEQUIA**.

SALA (SAH-luh) In the Southwest, a big room; sometimes a big hall used for dancing. Borrowed from Spanish.

Cactus: yucca, saguaro, barrel, prickly pear.
[DRAWING BY E. L. REEDSTROM.]

SALADO (suh-LAH-doh) Said of a wind-broke horse. Borrowed from Spanish (in which it means "unlucky," "salty").

SALAL CHINOOK jargon for a small shrub of the Pacific Coast also called *shallon* (*Gaultheria shallon*) or its berry, valued as food. First mentioned in the journals of the Lewis and Clark Expedition.

SALE BRAND A brand burned over the original to show that the cow has changed hands. (See also **BRAND**.)

SALE RING Where the rancher goes to sell his cows at auction, mostly to buyers representing big meat-packing companies. Many times the sale ring tells the cattleman whether he's survived to ranch another year.

SALEA (suh-LAY-uh) A sheepskin used as a pad between a saddle and saddle blanket or beneath a pack saddle. Borrowed from the Spanish *zalea* (which means "sheepskin").

SALERATUS Baking soda. William A. Baillie-Grohman in *Camps in the Rockies* called saleratus "the grandest word in the trapper's very abridged dictionary." He meant the trapper of the later nineteenth century, for the early fur men had no baking soda, indeed no bread. A *saleratus lake* is an **ALKALINE** body of water, and *saleratus water* is alkaline.

SALINA (suh-LEE-nuh) A **SALT LICK**, salt pond, or the like. Borrowed from Spanish (in which it means "salt mine"). Likewise *salinera* is a salt pit.

SALISH A language family of the Northwest Pacific Coast and the interior plateau of Oregon, Washington, Idaho, and British Columbia. Among the tribes speaking these related languages are Flathead, Coeur d'Alene, Colville, and Kalispel (in the interior), and Bella Coola, Cowichan, Nisqually, **PUYALLUP**, Snohomish, and Tillamook (along the coast).

SALLIE A cowboy's name for the cook. (See also **COOKIE**.)

SALMON A principal food of the Native peoples of the Pacific Northwest, an important element in their cultures, and the focus of one of the main modern industries of the region. In *Western Lore and Language*, Thomas L. Clark describes five main kinds of salmon in this area: king, or chinook; red, or sockeye; silver, or coho; dog, or chum; and pink, or humpback. Each kind is edible, though the dog (chum) was originally used mostly as food for dogs or bait for other fish. Other common names for salmon include *Arctic trout, Columbia River salmon, fall chum, jack* (a male that returns a year or two early to the spawning ground), *kokanee* (a small, lake-dwelling sockeye), *spring salmon* (the first back to the spawning grounds), *summer chum,* and *tyee*.

Combinations formed using salmon as the first word include *salmon bake, belly, berry, cache, cannery, canning, chuck* (a stream thick with salmon), *house* (a shelter used by Native fishermen), *jerky, pirate, season, strips* (the flesh salted, smoked, and dried), *trout,* and *wheel* (a basket device for catching salmon).

For nearly a century white and red people had angry disputes over fishing rights in the state of Washington. Indians, who had used salmon as a principal food for centuries, fished surreptitiously and later even conducted fish-ins in defiance of the law. In 1974 the decision of Judge George H. Boldt brought revolution—the judge declared that the Indians have a right to half the harvestable salmon in their traditional waters. The Indians were delighted, much of the white community outraged. The United States Supreme Court upheld the decision.

The salmon population of the Lower 48 states, however, was diminishing sharply. Near the twenty-fifth anniversary of the Boldt decision, nine populations of salmon were officially listed as endangered species. A habitat diminished in quality and quantity keeps the fish far from its historic numbers in Oregon and Washington.

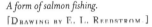

A form of salmon fishing.
[Drawing by E. L. Reedstrom.]

SALMON CHUCK In the Pacific Northwest, a stream full of salmon. (See also CHUCK.)

SALOONIST A Westernism for a saloon keeper. The word *saloon* appears to have been born in the South, even if it earned most of its bad reputation in COW TOWNS.

SALSA (SAHL-suh) A spicy sauce used in Mexican cuisine. A recent Westernism, it is borrowed from Spanish (in which it means "sauce"). Usually tomato-based, it can also have other ingredients; *salsa verde* is made from chiles and tomatillos.

SALT (1) Often a synonym for ALKALI in the West—thus terms like *salt flat* and *salt plain*. Gleaming white on the arid earth, alkali looks like salt, and *salts* can mean, instead of table salt, saline minerals such as alkali. A *salt desert* is a desert of alkaline soil, and a *salt flat* is an *alkali pan,* a flat stretch of alkaline soil. (2) To give livestock salt. (3) To put mineral into a mine to make it appear valuable. (The gold dust, precious stone, or other stashed mineral is itself called salt.) (4) In forestry, to spread salt and other minerals over a piece of country to get the animals redistributed; the country is then called *salt ground. Salt chuck* is CHINOOK jargon for the sea (see also CHUCK, SALMON CHUCK). *Salt horse* is a word for corned beef.

PLANT COMBINATIONS: *salt grasses* (such as *Distichlis spicata* and *Spartina* that grow on salt or alkali flats or marshes), *salt sage* (greasewood), *salt weed* (a variety of *Atriplex*), *salt bush* (shad scale), *salt wood* (*Purshia tridentata,* useful as forage in the winter).

SALT LICK A natural salt deposit used by animals, or a salt block set out for livestock.

SALTILLO BLANKET A blanket that often served as a poncho in Texas before hands had **SLICKERS**, according to Watts. It was made in Saltillo, Coahuila, Mexico.

SALTY DOG Anyone who's really good at his work. Also a tough fellow *(salty bacon* or *ham). Salty* means full of spirit and fight. When said of a hand, it's a compliment. But a horse that's salty may be mean.

SALVAGE CUTTING The harvesting of trees that are damaged, diseased, dying, or dead before they become worthless as timber.

SANCHO A lead goat.

SAND (1) Courage; grit; what a man has in his craw when he's brave. A fellow with sand is the sort you want to ride the river with. (2) Among loggers, a word for sugar.

COMBINATIONS: *sand flat* (an arid, sandy stretch of flat country, usually alkaline), *sand hills* (hills or dunes made of sand, as in the Sand Hills of Nebraska; the **BLACKFEET** speak of the dead as having gone to the sand hills), *sand storm* (a wind that blows sand up from the ground and into everything, particularly the eyes, nostrils, mouths, and ears of people, horses, and other critters, a nasty bit of work), *sand auger* (a little whirlwind of sand; a **DUST DEVIL**), *sand wagon* (a stagecoach especially built to cross rivers with quicksand; it had high clearance and wide tires and was also called a *sand liner,* as in ocean liner).

PLANTS: *sand bur* (the prickly part of any of several Western plants, very irksome), *sand cherry* (*Prunus besseyi), sand mat* (a euphorbia).

SAND CREEK Among those names that call mournfully to memory the atrocities committed by the U.S. government against Native peoples. The 3rd Colorado volunteers under John Chivington, a blood-and-thunder preacher, attacked a peaceful **CHEYENNE** village led by Black Kettle, at dawn on November 19, 1864, killed more than two hundred (mostly women and children), burned their belongings, and threw those who survied out onto the winter Plains destitute. (See also **WOUNDED KNEE, LONG WALK, TRAIL OF TEARS.**)

SAND PAINTING See **DRY PAINTING.**

SANDCAST Said of jewelry such as bracelets, rings, and bowguards made from molten silver (often from Mexican coins, in the old days) and poured into a two-part mold carved from soft tufa or pumice blocks wired together. These soft molds are usually only good for a few pours.

SANDHILL CRANE A huge, gangly gray bird *(Grus canadensis)* that inhabits marshes in the West. It sometimes congregates in large flocks and shares a similar habitat to the **WHOOPING CRANE**.

SANDIA (san-DEE-uh) A Southwesternism for watermelon. Borrowed from Spanish. When capitalized, it refers to the mountains on the east side of Albuquerque, New Mexico, or the pueblo just north of that city.

SANDLAPPER What old-timers in the Oregon desert called the homesteaders of the first two decades of this century. These newcomers plowed up the desert in hopes of raising crops, but the desert wasn't vanquished. (See also **NESTER**.)

SANTA ANA (SAN-tuh A-nuh; san-TA-nuh; the *a* as in *corral*) In California or the Southwest generally, a name for a hot wind that blows from the desert toward the west. Some old-timers say it's traditionally pronounced san-TA-nuh.

SANTA FE TRAIL A route of commerce between Missouri and the present capital of New Mexico, pioneered by William Becknell in 1821. It ran from Franklin or Independence, Missouri, to Council Grove and on to the Arkansas River. From the Arkansas in south-central Kansas, travelers followed one of two branches: The Cimarron Cutoff, starting with a dry **JORNADA** of 60 miles to the Cimarron River, or the Mountain Branch, past Bent's Fort and over Raton Pass. The 800-mile journey took two or three months for the freight-laden **CONESTOGA** wagons.

Josiah Gregg drew a firsthand and detailed picture of the traders, caravans, and life on the trail in *Commerce of the Prairies*, published in 1844. Since the Santa Fe Trail continued to function until superseded by the railroad in 1878, it endured longer than any of the **CATTLE TRAILS**.

COMBINATIONS: *Santa Fe tea* (tea made from the leaves of *Alstonia theaeformis*), *Santa Fe Expedition* (an effort by Texas in 1841 to lay claim to eastern New Mexico), *Santa Fe town* (any town in the part of New Mexico claimed by the Santa Fe Expedition), *Santa Fe trader*, *Santa Fe wagon* (one used on the Santa Fe Trail). (See also **CALIFORNIA TRAIL**, **OREGON TRAIL**.)

SANTA LUCIA FIR The bristlecone fir *(Abies venusta)* of the Santa Lucia Mountains in California.

SANTEE A group of the **DAKOTA** Indians, made of the Mdewakanton, Wahpekute, Wahpeton, and Sisseton tribes. In the nineteenth century, the Santee lived in southern Minnesota as farmers. In the rebellion of 1862, they killed more than 700 whites and suffered harsh reprisal. Now they live on the Santee Reservation in Nebraska, the Sisseton Reservation in South Dakota, and the Devil's Lake Reservation in North Dakota.

SANTERO (san-TAIR-oh) A Southwestern term for a person who carves religious images, especially *santos* (statues or images of saints). From Spanish.

SASQUATCH The legendary creature of the Pacific Northwest, since discovery of a huge set of prints in Canada in 1811; in northern California and southern Oregon it is called *Bigfoot*. A hairy, humanlike creature of monstrous size, it is brother in spirit to similar creatures all over the world, including the Yeti, the Abominable Snowman, and the Almas; in North America its kin are New Jersey's Jersey Devil, Missouri's Momo, and Arkansas's Fouke River Monster. Evidence for its existence (outside imagination and fear) consists partly of a set of remarkable footprints found in the state of Washington and a film clip made by a Californian; a Soviet scientist did in fact conclude that a remnant of Neanderthals still inhabits part of the world. Among scientists, however, doubters far outnumber believers.

SATEEN A satinlike fabric made of cotton; popular among the **NAVAJOS** (along with velveteen and silk plush) for clothing.

SAUK The Sac or Ousaukie Indians, an Algonquian woodlands tribe. They lived in what is now Michigan but were pushed west by the French and settled in Illinois and Iowa, allying with the Fox (properly Mesquakie) there. Under Black Hawk, they fought unsuccessfully against white encroachment in 1832; over the next two decades, they made a series of cessions of land to the United States. They now have Sauk-Fox communities in Iowa and Oklahoma.

SAVANERO (sa-vuh-NAIR-oh) A Santa Fe Trail expression for the fellow who guarded the mules at night to keep them from straying. From the Spanish *sabanero* and related to the English *savanna*.

SAVE To kill. Hunters sometimes spoke of saving deer, frontiersmen of saving Indians. After the Utah War in 1856, says Wallace Stegner in *The Gathering of Zion*, among Mormons "the phrase 'to save' a man came to have the precise meaning of our modern euphemism 'to liquidate.'" (See also **DRY-GULCH**.)

SAVE SADDLE LEATHER To ride standing up in the stirrups. The expression is often used with a smile, for it's a trick of inexperienced riders to save their bottoms.

SAVVY What a sensible man has—understanding. As a noun, it means knowledge, understanding. A wise man has savvy. Thus Jack London wrote in *Valley of the Moon:* "We ain't got the *sabe*, or the knack, or something or other." Also used as an adjective—"a beaver is a sabe critter." Cowboys are savvy about cows. As a verb, it means to understand—"Do you sabe?" A trapper savvies beaver. A common Western query was "Do you savvy?" (Do you get it?). Here the Spanish *sabe* was used interrrchangeably with savvy. The linguist J. L. Dillard, though, says savvy came to the West from the maritime lingua franca through Indian pidgin English, not directly from Spanish, as most authorities have believed.

SAWBONES A doctor, especially a surgeon. The expression likely arose because, in the days before sepsis was understood, wounds often required amputating limbs, which necessitated sawing through bones. Westerners also called a physician (according to Adams) *Epsom salts,* **GENUINE JIMMY,** *old pills, pill roller, Quinine Jimmy,* and *saddlebag doctor.*

SAWBUCK A name for a packsaddle. The usual packsaddle has ends that look like a sawbuck.

SAWDUST What a miner called dynamite. (See also **POWDER.**)

SAWYER (1) A log or tree caught in the riverbed, bobbing up and down in the stream and so a menace to boats. (See also **SNAG, STRAINER.**) (2) A bucker; a logger who cuts trees into logs; sometimes a fellow who both fells and saws them (see also **FALLER**). A log the right size for sawing is called a *saw log.*

SCAD In **PLACER** mining, the gold left in a pan after a washing.

SCAFFOLD Among many **PLAINS INDIAN** tribes, a platform for the dead, either on four poles or in the fork of a tree. Often weapons, food, and clothing were placed to accompany the dead on their journeys. The bodies were laid in a high place to be protected from scavengers, and once the flesh had decayed, some Indians made a ceremony of taking the scaffold down and placing the bones in a safe spot, such as a crevice in a rock or in the ground.

SCALAWAG A worthless cow, a likely **CULL.** The meaning with regard to people (a "rascal") is an Americanism but not a Westernism. The *scalawag bunch* is the band of horses useless for working cows (the **ROUGH STRING**).

SCALE (1) In logging, for logs to produce lumber, as in the phrase "the number of feet a tree will scale." (The lumber is measured in *board feet.*) (2) To calculate or estimate the amount of lumber in logs; the fellow who does this job is called a *scaler.*

Dakota Indians lifting a dead warrior onto the scaffold.
[DRAWING BY H. C. YARROW; COURTESY OF NATIONAL ARCHIVES (111-SC-87776).]

SCALLYHOOT To make tracks, to run off, to skedaddle.

SCALPING (1) The custom of cutting off part or all of the scalp of an enemy, not necessarily a dead one, was practiced in North America by most Indian tribes and some whites and Hispanics. Scalping was a venerable practice, performed not only in North America, but in Europe, Asia, and Africa. Often, as here, it stood for the taking of the entire head of an enemy as a ritual of war and as an insult to the fallen man and his tribe. It was widely performed by Native peoples (but not by all tribes), both before and after white contact. Among some peoples, into the nineteenth century, the taking of the entire head remained a more powerful act.

　　After white contact, the practice spread, partly because Anglo and Mexican governments offered bounties for the scalps of Native peoples who were causing difficulty. Some whites became *scalp hunters,* and other whites (for instance, mountain men) took scalps. The popular recent notion that white men corrupted the red man by teaching him to take scalps is a notable exaggeration.

　　Techniques of scalping varied. Sometimes the skin of the entire upper half of the head was taken, including the ears. Other times only a patch of skin (a *topknot*) with *scalp lock* was cut off. Among Indians, the deed was an act of MEDICINE, and the resulting trophy was an object of power. So scalps were kept, displayed, treasured, and sometimes traded. Among Anglos and Hispanics, a scalp was more often a symbol of vengeance and a hide that could be turned in for a bounty.

　　COMBINATIONS: *scalp dance* (a solemn Indian dance performed after fighting with the enemy), *scalp feast, scalping knife* (or *scalper*), *scalping party, scalp shirt* (a shirt decorated with scalps), *scalper* (a person who scalps or the knife he uses).

　　(2) In logging, to strip away turf.

SCATTERGUN A shotgun with a short barrel.

SCHMOEHAWK According to Carl Waldman in *Word Dance,* a word (apparently slang) among Indians for Anglos who pose as Indians for money.

SCHOOL SECTION From 1802, one section of land (a section is one square mile) out of every township was given by the federal government to the state governments for the support of public schools. It was often called the *sixteenth section* because it was the sixteenth in the thirty-six in each township surveyed. In the West, if not used for actual schools, these sections often have been leased to ranchers for grazing; left undeveloped, they are both producers of revenue and sanctuaries for wildlife.

SCHOOLMARM Logger's term for a forked tree that can't be used for timber.

SCISSORBILL A term of contempt generally; among COWBOYS it's a word for a shirker or incompetent. Among LOGGERS, it is a fellow of bourgeois values, one not of the true working class.

SCOOP A derogatory word for a **MORMON**, said to have been coined by canyon-country river runners. Also *double scoop*. It's nasty—it comes from the notion of brains having been scooped out.

SCOOT A single sled for dragging logs. Also known as a **GO-DEVIL** and a *lizard.*

SCORE In **RODEO**, the length of the head start given a **CALF** or **STEER** in a roping or wrestling event.

SCOTCH CAP On the **NORTHERN PLAINS**, a woolen cap with a short brim and a pillbox top, usually navy blue but sometimes a colorful plaid, worn by men who work outdoors, from carpenters to cowboys.

SCOTCH HOBBLE A hobble (fetter) that runs a rope from a horse's neck and lifts the hind leg off the ground several inches.

SCOURS A foul-smelling diarrhea that debilitates calves. These days it's treated with *scours pills* (antibiotics) the rancher gets from the vet.

SCOUT Scout itself, in the sense of a guide, a lookout, is not an Americanism. Historically, the army found itself half-helpless in the face of Western country, customs, and Indians, so it employed what it called an **INDIAN SCOUT** (either red or white) to find the way, find the water, and find the Natives; then to explain the Indians, interpret their languages, make promises to them, and, when deemed necessary, kill them. This fellow was usually a former **MOUNTAIN MAN** or fur trader, who didn't wear all the blinders of civilization, or an Indian of a tribe other than the one being sought. Scouts like Tom Fitzpatrick and Jim Bridger, who *beavered* around the mountains, were greatly valuable and tried to keep Indian-army encounters from being slaughters.

Later, another sort of fellow altogether called himself a scout, a show-off fellow in buckskin, fringes, beads, and long hair and full of lies. Says Bernard De Voto in *Across the Wide Missouri*, "The West has been fecund in the production of phonies: the Scout was one of the earliest and just about the most noisome." *On the scout* meant on the lam from the law.

SCRAPE A difficulty, a predicament, a fight. So a *shooting scrape* is a gun fight (with droll Western understatement), and a *water scrape* is a long ride or drive across a dry stretch of country.

SCRAPER (1) Among the **PLAINS INDIANS**, a tool for scraping flesh and fat off hides, usually made of elk antler; also called a **DUBBER**. (2) Among miners, a big blade like a hoe, dragged by a cable.

SCRATCH In **RODEO**, to keep your **SPURS** moving on the bucking animal you're trying to ride, to urge it to buck. The rules mandate scratching, and **SCREWING DOWN** is not permitted.

SCREW BEAN In the Southwest, the screw-pod **MESQUITE**.

SCREW DOWN In RODEO, when riding a bucking animal, to put your SPURS into the cinch instead of SCRATCHING. It's forbidden, because it helps the rider, and SCRATCHING is required.

SCRUB (1) Among cowboys, any critter of poor breeding; a runt. (2) Among loggers, brush or stunted trees that aren't salable.

SEAGO A rope woven from grass or hemp. Arizona cowboys called it a *yacht line*.

SEAGULL WIRELESS In Alaska, the equivalent of the MOCCASIN TELEGRAPH or MUKLUK WIRELESS.

SEAL HOOK In Alaska, a float with hooks used by Native fisherman to snag seals they have shot and haul them in.

SEALING An ordinance performed in MORMON temples in which a marriage union is sealed for time and eternity. The sealing ordinance and temple marriage are performed for newlyweds, and children born to that union are considered sealed to their parents, or "born under the covenant." Couples previously married in a civil ceremony can participate in the sealing ordinance, and have any children already born sealed to them. Sealings can be performed for widows, widowers, or deceased children; a PROXY stands in for the deceased.

SEALSKIN POKE In Alaska, an airtight, watertight bag made from a sealskin turned inside out.

SEARS ROEBUCK GUY What loggers called a novice. The equivalent among cowboys was an ARBUCKLE.

SECO In the old Southwest, the brass and aluminum tokens made by individual traders for use in place of silver coins. The silver coins were used in jewelry-making. Also in the Southwest, "dry," as in *arroyo seco*.

SECOND-GROWTH FOREST In logging, trees that have grown up since the cutting of the virgin forest. (See also OLD-GROWTH FOREST.)

SEE A MAN ABOUT A HORSE To urinate. A fellow drinking with his buddies will often excuse himself for a moment with the line (intended to fool nobody), "I've got to see a man about a horse."

SEE DAYLIGHT What the spectators do when a rider bounces high in the saddle of a bucking horse—they see it between bottom and saddle. It's considered poor form.

SEE THE ELEPHANT What you got to do at the climax of your journey—see whatever was there to be seen and do whatever there was to do. Often it had the implication of seeing enough and more than enough and heading home in disappointment. Gold-rushers said optimistically on the way west that they were going to see the elephant and said in disgust on the way back that they'd seen it. Trail hands spoke the same way about Kansas cattle towns.

SEED FOREST In logging, a forest primarily of trees grown from seed.

SEGO Also called *sego lily (Calochortus nuttallii)*, it is the state flower of Utah, growing thickly in beds on dry hillsides. The Indians and **MORMON** pioneers used the bulb for food.

SEGUNDO (suh-GOON-doh) The second in command; the assistant to the boss; the *straw boss.* Used particularly on **TRAIL DRIVES.** Borrowed from Spanish.

SEISMIC CREW A crew of workers hired by oil exploration companies to find oil and gas, especially during the 1970s and 1980s in the **OVERTHRUST BELT.** These workers (called *juggies*) set explosives on the surface of the earth, detonate them, record the resulting sound waves, and use computers to determine the rock structure.

SELECTIVE CUTTING In logging, a kind of cutting that harvests only trees of a certain size, value, or both, or trees that are diseased. (A forest that has been cut selectively is called a *culled forest.*) Controversy burns in the West today over **CLEAR-CUTTING** versus selective cutting. Many loggers argue that clear-cutting is more economical and efficient. Many environmentalists argue that selective cutting is more visually appealing and healthier for the forest.

SEÑOR (sayn-YOHR; seen-YOHR) A Hispanic man, especially a gentleman. Also an equivalent of Mister. Borrowed from Spanish. A *señora* is a lady, and a *señorita* a young girl.

SENT FOR SUPPLIES Among **SHEEPHERDERS,** an expression for crazy, driven around the bend by loneliness. Such a fellow was sent to town for supplies to get him back among folks. As grizzlies are fierce, coyotes skulky, and antelopes swift, sheepherders (Westerners do not say "shepherd") are legendary among cowboys for being crazy. Cowboys said they went crazy trying to determine which side of a square **SUGAN** (blanket) was the long side; cowboys also spoke of sheepherding as *trying to find the long end of a square quilt.* No doubt the sheepherders spend too much time by themselves; and probably most cowboys never get to know them.

Some Western expressions for "crazy" are **LOCO,** *crazy as a sheepherder, hunting for water,* and *short of hat size.*

SEQUOIA A genus of trees that includes two huge California conifers, the **RED-WOOD** *(Sequoia sempervirens)* and the sequoia or Big Tree of the Sierra Nevada. Also called a *Washington cedar,* it was named after Sequoyah, the Cherokee who devised a syllabary for his Native language.

SERAPE (suh-RAH-pay) A shawl or blanket worn as an outer garment, especially by Southwestern Hispanics. Borrowed from the Spanish *sarabe.* Sometimes spelled *sarape.*

SERVICEBERRY (SAR-vis-bear-ree) The dark blue fruit of the serviceberry shrub (*Amelanchier* sp.). The fruit is used as food by the Indians and Anglos. Sometimes spelled as two words or as *sarvisberry*; also called a *saskatoon* or a *juneberry*.

SET (1) A placement for a trap. (2) The ready position of the crewmen of a **KEEL-BOAT**, poles firm in the river bottom. The men then walked down the running board on each side of the craft from bow to stem, pushing the boat upriver. (3) Among cowboys, a short version of *settler*. (4) Among miners, according to Adams, a piece of ground worked by a **TRIBUTER**, a fellow who works a claim for wages.

> COMBINATIONS: *set close to the plaster* (for a rider to keep a tight seat in the saddle, not to show daylight), *set down* (to be fired, to be kicked off and set afoot), *set the buck* (to ride a bucking bronco successfully), *set the hair* (to ride a horse until he gentles a little), *set up* (to treat people, as in "Johnny set up the drinks"), *setdown* (what a friendly householder might give a bum—a chance to come in, wash, and "set" down to eat).

SETTLEMENT COMPANY A group of people who agreed to go to a certain place (often to cross the continent to the West Coast), to perform actions such as clearing the land together, and to take up their lives together there. It might have a bond, such as a religion or a utopian dream, or might simply be a practical assemblage. Thus *settlement duty, settlement road, settlement store*.

SEVEN CITIES Ancient cities of New Mexico, probably the **ZUNI** pueblos, whose mythical wealth drew the Spanish into that country. (See also **CIBOLA**.)

SEVEN COUNCIL FIRES The alliance of the **DAKOTA** Indians, commonly known as the Sioux. The seven groups are the Mdewakanton, Wahpekute, Wahpeton, Sisseton, Yankton, Yanktonai, and Teton.

SEVEN PERSONS A term among some **PLAINS INDIANS** for the Big Dipper. The **CHEROKEE** call them the *Six Pigs*.

SEVEN-UP The popular gambling card game also known as *all-fours*.

SEVENTY In the **MORMON** Church, one of the offices in the **MELCHIZEDEK** Priesthood. Seventies are elders with a special call and ordination to do **MISSIONARY** work. Members of the First and Second Quorums of the Seventy are General Authorities of the church, aid in the administration of church affairs, and act under the direction of the Council of the Twelve Apostles.

SEVERE Wild, headstrong. A horse was sometimes said to be severe. So was a fellow who "never killed a man who did not deserve killing."

SEWARD'S ICE BOX One of the early American names for Alaska, which was also called *Russian Alaska, Walrussia, Zero Island, Polaria, Icebargia,* and *American Siberia*.

SEWELLEL The so-called mountain beaver (*Aplodontia rufa*), a squirrel-like creature of the Pacific Northwest. The word was originally the **CHINOOK** jargon name for a robe made from the skin of these animals. Also called a *boomer* and a **SHOWT'L.**

SHABRACK A large piece of cloth, often ornamented, worn over the saddle pad to protect the rider from contact with a dirty and sweating horse. Also called a *chevrac.*

SHACK (1) A hut, a shanty. Mathews makes the case for it as a Westernism, indicating that the term came to English from the Aztec *xacalli* through the Spanish *xacal* (later *jacal*). COMBINATIONS: *claim shack, cook shack,* and, more recently in the West, *ski shack.* (2) A cowboy word for the bunkhouse. (3) To hole up for the winter. (4) To amble along.

SHAD SCALE A salty forage bush (*Atriplex canescens*) of the Southwestern deserts.

SHADE HOUSE In the Southwest, an arbor, a **RAMADA.** An essential shield from the sun, common in the yards of homes, and as freestanding roadside stands.

SHADING Resting. What a cowboy does when he finds a shady spot on the range, which is mostly treeless. Old hands in the desert advise that when you find shade, even the sliver made by a metal fencepost, you should stand in it.

SHADOW RIDER A rider who's so vain he goes along admiring his own shadow.

SHADOW-JUMPER Said of a horse that is skittish, apt to use any excuse to shy.

SHAG OUT A Texas expression meaning to run out on someone, to back out, as in, "His partner shagged out."

SHAGANAPPI (sha-guh-NAP-pee) Thongs of buffalo **RAWHIDE** used to bind or hold anything and everything; ubiquitous in the Northwest and sometimes called *Northwestern iron.* Originally a Cree word.

SHAKE HANDS WITH SAINT PETER Among cowboys, to die. For many similar expressions see **CASH IN YOUR CHIPS.**

SHALAKO The winter solstice ceremony of the **ZUNI** Indians.

SHANGHAI To spirit someone away, using force, drugs, or other means; especially, to recruit sailors for long voyages (such as to Shanghai) by force. Mathews says that the expression is believed to have originated in San Francisco about 1850.

SHANTY A frontier term for a rude cabin or **SHACK,** especially a shack in a lumber camp. Shanties, in the plural, often means a lumber camp.

COMBINATIONS: *shanty boy* or *man* (a logger), *shanty cake* (an unleavened bread), *shanty gang* (a timber crew), *shanty queen* (a logger's wife), *shanty team* (the same as a shanty gang), *shanty town* (a poor district full of shanties), *claim shanty, cook shanty, lumber shanty, timber shanty.*

SHAPELEEL (SHAP-uh-leel) In the Pacific Northwest, a **CHINOOK** jargon word for grain, or for an Indian. See **SIWASH.**

SHARPS Any of several models of firearms devised by Christian Sharps and produced by the Sharps Rifle Company until 1881. The firm was primarily known for its breechloading rifles, though it also made a **DERRINGER**. The most popular Sharps were Old Reliable, the cavalry carbine, and the heavy-caliber, single-shot buffalo-hunting rifle. Because of its low muzzle velocity, this monster was said to "fire today, kill tomorrow."

SHAVETAIL (1) A broke horse, in contrast to the **BROOMTAILS,** wild range horses (usually mares). In the days of the open range on the Northern Plains, it was customary to pluck the tails of horses as you broke them to make them easy to distinguish from the unbroke critters. (2) Among soldiers, a new, uneducated army mule. When new mules came on the scene, they weren't *bell-sharp,* that is, they didn't respond to bell commands. The soldiers shaved the tails of the new ones to identify them. Thus a shavetail was a mule that didn't know what it was doing. (3) A brand-new officer, a second lieutenant, so called precisely because he didn't know what he was doing.

SHE STUFF Female critters, whether women, girls, fillies, cows, or heifers. Fully grown cattle were called *grown stuff,* and cows and heifers, *she cattle.*

SHEARING FACTORY Sheepmen had elongated frame sheds where sheep were brought from up to fifty miles away to get sheared. David Lavender described the process as it took place in the 1930s in *One Man's West:*

> Generally the shearing is contracted to professionals who move from ranch to ranch. Piece payment, averaging twenty-five cents for a ewe, half a dollar for a big, husky ram. Their job folds on them with the season, and so they have developed astonishing skill. A good man can make twenty dollars a day.
>
> Inside the shed a gasoline motor drives an overhead shaft, powering a line of a dozen or so clippers, one man to a clipper. Behind each worker is a small pen, kept filled with sheep. He reaches into it, seizes an animal by the hind leg, drags it out, wrestles it into a sitting position, and kneels by its left side, using his left hand to hold its underjaw.
>
> The sheep lies helpless on the round of its rump, dumb terror in its yellow eyes. *Snip-snip-snip.* Along the neck and side from back to belly travel the shears. Sweat pours from the operator. This is work, holding a ninety-pound mutton with one hand while the other races against time. *Snip-snip-snip.* The fleece comes off in one unbroken greasy mass. The shearer—his hands are always debutante-soft from the lanolin in the wool—folds it with the clean hair inside and tosses it onto a conveyor belt running overhead. He pushes the shorn animal through a door in the outside wall, reaches back for another.

Sheepmen used to have shearing contests, men racing to get the most wool off in a set time. Ivan Doig describes one contest vividly in his fine novel *Dancing at the Rascal Fair.*

SHEEFISH In Alaska, a large whitefish sought by recreational fishermen.

SHEEP Sometimes a verb: A sheepman will *sheep* a cattleman, that is, claim he's obliged by circumstance to drive sheep across the cattleman's range. To *get sheeped,* in the days of the open range, was somewhere between annoying and infuriating.

A *sheep camp* is the moving home of the sheepherder, consisting mostly of a *sheep wagon,* a canvas-covered wagon where the sheepherder sleeps and stores his cookstove, bedding, and other gear. Range sheep require constant attendance, so the camps were and are supplied by camp tenders who drive out periodically from town. Sheep wagons were called *maniac dens* or *mansions* by cowboys and *cradles* by sheepherders.

A *sheep dipper* is a man who treats sheep with *dip* (a liquid disinfectant); a *sheep feeder* is a man who puts sheep into feed lots to fatten them for market; and a *sheep grower* or *sheepman* is the equivalent of a cattleman, the owner.

Sheep fever is the fervent desire to go into the wool-growing business, regarded by many cattlemen as a sickness. *Sheepherding* (Westerners do not say "shepherding"), *sheep meat* (for mutton), *sheep herd, sheep spread,* and *sheep range* are also Western coinages.

SHEEP DEADLINE A line marking sheep range from cow range. Such lines were strictly creations of cattlemen, who used to form associations and committees to declare such lines and order sheepmen to stay the hell out. In Jackson Hole, Wyoming, the cattlemen formed a "committee of safety" in 1897 and declared the area unblemished cow country. The object of cattlemen in Wyoming generally was to restrict sheep to the desert lands where cattle couldn't thrive anyway. The country overgrazed by sheep (or, in a cattleman's view, grazed at all by

A sheep wagon.
[COURTESY OF UTAH STATE HISTORICAL SOCIETY.]

sheep) was said to be *sheeped off*. The sheepmen wanted the grass—thus Wyoming's sheep wars.

The supposed destruction that sheep do to grazing lands was much exaggerated by cattlemen, and now many Wyoming stockmen raise both—cattle for respectability, as they like to say, and sheep for profit.

SHEEP-EATERS A branch of the **SHOSHONE** Indians who lived in high, remote country and hunted bighorn sheep instead of moving onto the Plains, employing the horse, and adopting the buffalo-hunting culture. Their name in their own language, *Tukuarika,* means sheep-eaters. They survived as a separate group, living on the Lemhi Reservation until 1912, when they joined other Shoshones on Fort Hall Reservation.

SHEEPHERDER The Westerner's word for the fellow who nursemaids sheep on the range, as cowboys might put it disparagingly. *Shepherd* (which Westerners do not use) is a much older word—*sheepherder* dates only from 1871—and shepherd probably sounded too pious to cowboys.

Western sheepherders are often Basques. Regardless of their ethnic origin, they have generally been regarded as about half crazy. When one gets strange from having spent too much time alone, he's **SENT FOR SUPPLIES**. Cowboys derogatorily call the sheepherder a *drop-band herder, jockey, lamb licker, mutton puncher, scab herder, snoozer, sheep puncher, social herder,* or *wagon herder.* He's also known more respectfully as a *campero,* **PASTOR,** or **PARTIDARIO.**

Sheep on Powder River.
[COURTESY OF THE AMERICAN HERITAGE CENTER, UNIVERSITY OF WYOMING.]

SHELTER CABIN In Alaska, a hut along a sled trail where **MUSHERS** can spend the night.

SHELTERWOOD In logging, a form of **SELECTIVE CUTTING**. It employs two or three cuttings so that the larger remaining trees provide shelter for young trees. The shelterwood approach preceded **CLEAR-CUTTING** as the usual technique; now it is making a comeback because it leaves a more attractive-looking forest than clear-cutting and one that's better for wildlife and recreational forest users.

SHENANIGAN A trick, a bit of nonsense or tomfoolery. The word appears to have been born in California in the 1850s but is of obscure origin; Webster speculates that it comes from an Irish verb that sounds similar and means "I play tricks."

SHEPHERD'S BIBLE What a cowboy called a mail-order catalog. Adams tells a funny story about a hand who ordered a dress from a catalog under the illusion that the girl who modeled it was part of the bargain. He then bragged that, since everything came postpaid, he didn't even have to pay a freight charge on her.

SHERIFF'S DEADLINE The equivalent of a **SHEEP DEADLINE** for sheriffs—outlaws in Texas, for example, called the Nueces River a line those law officers could not pass.

SHINDIG A dance, a party. The word's origin is unknown. Cowboys sometimes called a dance a *stomp*.

SHINE To do well, to stand out. This was a favorite verb of the **MOUNTAIN MAN**, as in, "You can't shine in this crowd." *Shining times* were stand out times, to be savored and remembered.

SHINER A reflective surface that a *card sharp* uses to see the faces of the cards as they're dealt. It might be anything—a ring, coin, etc. Also called a *glimmer*.

SHINING MOUNTAINS The name some early venturers used for the Rocky Mountains, perhaps because some of them are always snow covered.

SHINNERY The scrub oak (*Quercus gambelii, Q. undulata*) common in Texas, also called *shinnery oak* and *shin oak;* a thicket of scrub oak.

SHIP CLOSE A cattleman's term for sending every head of cattle halfway ready to market. Such cattle were held in a little pasture called a *shipping trap*.

SHIRTTAIL RANCH A small ranch, probably with too little grass, too few hands, too little land, and too little money. Also called a *rawhide outfit*, **GREASY SACK OUTFIT, ONE-HORSE OUTFIT,** *three-up outfit, two-by-four outfit, ranchito, cocklebur outfit, starve-out ranch,* and *stump farm* (when it's on newly cleared land).

SHITKICKER A redneck in high heels; a Western redneck.

SHIVAREE A noisy serenade, especially for a newly married couple. The verb form means to serenade them and perhaps annoy them. A *chivaree* was sometimes thrown to indicate community opinion that a couple ought to get married.

Unpopular people didn't get a shivaree. Also spelled *charivari* or *chaveree*. From the French *charivari*.

SHONGSASHA The bark of a red willow, mixed by **PLAINS INDIANS** with tobacco for smoking. (See also **KINNIKINNICK**.)

SHOOFLY A mine's passageway.

SHOOT (1) Among loggers, to *shoot a jam* is to dynamite a log jam to get it loose. (2) Among miners, *shooting* is getting oil or gas started flowing with a blast of dynamite. (3) A *shooting affair* is a gunfight, usually a duel between two men with pistols (also called a *shooting affray*), and to *shoot center* is to shoot accurately.

SHOOTING IRON A firearm, usually a handgun. The first use of this expression is evidently in 1787.

SHOOTIST A marksman with a gun. Glendon Swarthout wrote a fine novel called *The Shootist.*

SHOP-MADES Custom-made boots. Adams speaks of the cowman's scorn for ready-made boots. That's mostly a thing of the past, perhaps because profit in the cattle business may be a thing of the past.

SHORT A man who's past due to head somewhere else is short, as in "You're short in this town."

COMBINATIONS: *short bit* (a dime: since two bits make a quarter, one bit is twelve and one-half cents), *short staker* (among loggers, an itinerant worker; also known as a *boomer*), *short horse* (once a name for a **QUARTER HORSE,** *short yearling* (a calf just short of a year old), *short age* (a word for cattle under three years), *short of hat size* (what a cowboy called a **SHEEPHERDER** who was a little crazy), *short-trigger man* (a fellow who was quick on the trigger or with his temper, a gunman), *shorten his stake rope* (to get someone under control, cramp his style).

SHORTHORN (1) According to some Westerners, any cow of a breed other than **TEXAS LONGHORN,** the original Texas cattle; thus, any of various breeds that are imported and therefore foreigners, including the most common of contemporary range cattle, **HEREFORDS.** But other Westerners observe that the shorthorn is a distinct breed, imported later than the Hereford. (2) A **TENDERFOOT.** Perhaps this application to people is an extension of the notion that shorthorns are imported cows, not natives.

SHORTWOOD LOGGING The traditional method of logging, felling, and cross-cutting on the spot.

SHOSHONE (shoh-SHOH-nee; shoh-SHOHN) Native tribe of the Uto-Aztecan family. At the beginning of the eighteenth century, they lived in the Great Basin and along the Rocky Mountain front from what is now Alberta to Wyoming and in southern Idaho and northern Utah. Acquiring the horse at that time from the Spanish settlements through the Utes, the Idaho-Utah Shoshone began to adopt a buffalo-hunting culture and to supply their relatives on the east side of the Rockies with horses, which allowed them to hunt the buffalo more easily. (The desert Shoshone continued in the old ways.)

After smallpox and the **BLACKFEET** drove the Shoshone out of Montana and Alberta, they congregated into seven principal groups: the largest band, which hunted around what are now Idaho Falls and Pocatello; another buffalo-hunting band that lived along the Wind River in Wyoming; the Lemhi band, which lived along the Salmon River in Idaho and subsisted principally on salmon; a band along the Bear River in Idaho and Utah; and another salmon-eating band in southwestern Idaho. The Indians of the Great Basin that whites called **DIGGERS** were often a detached variety of Shoshones.

The Shoshone were mostly friendly to Anglos. The woman interpreter for the Lewis and Clark Expedition, Sacajawea, was a Shoshone. During the 1820s and 1830s, the **MOUNTAIN MEN** held most of their rendezvous in Shoshone country. Washakie, the great Shoshone chief, was an advocate of peace. The opening of the **OREGON TRAIL** through their country caused resentment, though, as did the establishment of **MORMON** colonies, and the Shoshone sometimes committed reprisals.

In 1863 Colonel Patrick Conner led California volunteers in a sneak attack on a village of Shoshone on Idaho's Bear River and killed several hundred Indians, mostly women and children, a massacre that is little known to the public. Treaties from 1868 created reservations in traditional Shoshone hunting grounds near Pocatello and along the Wind River, where they remain today.

Though most academics spell the tribal name *Shoshoni*, the press and the Indians themselves generally prefer Shoshone. An idiosyncracy is that when the word is used as an adjective among local people both red and white, the final *e* is often silent. They say, "I'm shoh-SHOH-nee" but speak of "the sho-SHOHN tribe."

Washakie, chief of the Shoshones, 1843-1900.
[COURTESY OF THE UNIVERSITY OF WYOMING.]

SHOT In mining, a packet of dynamite used for blasting. (See also **POWDER**.)

SHOT GOLD The pellet gold found in **PLACER** mining. Also known as *shotty gold*.

SHOTGUN (1) A smoothbore long arm that fires a load of shot instead of a single ball or bullet. Surprisingly, this term appears to be a frontierism, first recorded in the early days in Kentucky and acknowledged by James Fenimore Cooper as "the language of the west." It was also called a *two-shoot gun, two-scatter shotgun, scattergun, shot-scatter gun,* and so on.

Shotguns were relied on in the West by men who had to defend against groups; for instance, by lawmen and stage guards. Thus an *express messenger* was also called (though the references are of later date) a *shotgun messenger.* He had a difficult and demanding job, keeping him awake for days on end to guard the valuables on the stagecoach against road agents. The way shotguns scattered their pellets made it difficult to miss at short range, and if the barrel or barrels were sawed off, the shot scattered over an even greater area.

(2) *Shotgun* also became a description of any long, narrow, unelaborate shape: *Shotgun leg* was a term for **CHAPS** that followed the straight and narrow; *shotgun shack* meant a little house that went straight as a barrel from front room to bedroom to kitchen.

COMBINATIONS: *shotgun cavvy* (the bunch of saddle horses made by putting the mounts of several outfits at one roundup together; see **CAVVY**); *shotgun freighter* (a fellow who wasn't a regular trader but took trade goods to a gold field or other trading spot; farmers, for instance, might take eggs, butter, and other farm products); *shotgun pasture* (a homesteader's little pasture with a fence around it, protected against big trail herds with a shotgun), *shotgun wagon* (a wagon that didn't join the main roundup but worked independently).

SHOULDER SCABBARD A holster for a hidden pistol, out of sight under the clothing in the armpit. The cowboy turned **PINKERTON** detective Charlie Siringo tells us he owned such a holster for forty years. Also called a *shoulder holster*; the way you got the handgun out was a *shoulder draw.*

SHOVE-DOWN CREW A group of riders used to bring down cattle from the high country to lower ranges.

SHOW BUCKER In **RODEO**, a bucking horse that looks good but is easy to ride. This horse bucks straight away with his head between his front legs.

SHOWDOWN In **POKER**, what happens when the bet is called—the players have to show their cards, to **PUT UP OR SHUT UP**. By extension, any decisive confrontation, the legendary classic being a gunfight.

SHOWT'L See **SEWELLEL**.

SHUCK (1) A name for a cigarette or cigar made by rolling tobacco in a corn shuck, a particular custom of Hispanics. More fully called a *shuck cigar* or a *shuck cigarillo.* (2) An Anglo cowboy's word for a Hispanic because Mexicans liked shuck cigars. Like **GREASER**, it's a disparaging term. (3) As a verb, to take something off or get rid of it, as in shucking wet socks. (4) To get shucked out, though, is to get thrashed, as in a usage in Mark Twain's *The Celebrated Jumping Frog of Calaveras County, and Other Sketches.*

SI (SEE) One way of saying yes in the Southwest, often by playful Anglos. Borrowed from Spanish.

SIBLEY A tent often used by the U.S. Army in the West after the Civil War, said to have been designed by General Henry Hastings Sibley on the pattern of the **DAKOTA TIPI.** The *Sibley stove* was a small heating stove (also designed by Sibley) commonly used in the U.S. Army during the period of the Indian wars.

SIDE Among loggers, the crew and equipment needed to perform one task—the *high lead side, skidder side,* etc. The foreman of a side was called a *side push,* and the boss of the *yarding crew* a *side rod.* A *side ax* is an ax with both a beveled face and a flat face, for better hewing. A *side boom* is a barrier of logs along the side of a stream to keep floating logs from escaping.

SIDE RIDER A mounted man who accompanied a **STAGECOACH** through country suspected of harboring **ROAD AGENTS** (highwaymen).

SIDE-LINE To **HOBBLE** a horse by fixing a front leg and the hind leg on the same side together rather than two front legs. The horse is then said to be *side-hobbled* or *lined.* To side-line a steer is for a *buster* to tie a rope from its neck to its hind leg.

SIDEWINDER (1) A desert rattlesnake (*Crotalus cerastes*) that moves by looping itself along sideways, leaving a succession of discontinuous tracks. Also called a *side-liner, sidewiper,* and *horned snake,* it is regarded by many Westerners as especially dangerous. The principal Western rattlesnakes are the **PRAIRIE RATTLER,** several snakes of the prairies, and the **DIAMONDBACK** (*Crotalus adamanteus*) and *sidewinder,* which is mainly Southwestern. (2) A sneaky man, one who comes at things *sideways* or *left-handed.* (3) A tree knocked down by a falling tree; a tree that, while falling, hits another tree and is knocked from its path, thus veering out of the path of its fall and becoming dangerous.

SIERRA (see-AIR-ruh) In the Southwest, a range of hills or mountains. Borrowed from Spanish. Sometimes a common noun, it is more often a proper name, as in Sierra Nevada and Sierra Madre. In California it is usually short for Sierra Nevada and is used in various combinations with that sense: *Sierra bighorn, Sierra Big Tree, Sierra creeper,* and so on.

SIESTA (see-ES-tuh) In the Southwest (and now anywhere in the United States), a nap. Borrowed from Spanish.

SIFFLEUR A name given the **MARMOT** by the French-Canadian **VOYAGEURS,** meaning whistler. The French-Canadians used marmots as food.

SIGN CAMP Another name for a *line camp,* where **LINE RIDERS** (or *sign riders*) lived while working. This term traces its lineage at least back to Charlie Siringo's *A Texas Cow-Boy,* but has apparently fallen into disuse.

SIGN LANGUAGE The method of hand signaling that **PLAINS INDIANS**, and later Anglos conversant with it, used to communicate in the absence of a common tongue. Each tribe had its own identifying signals, and trades could be arranged with sign language alone. Normally the meaning of the term does not include gestures of communication intended to carry over substantial distances, such as waving a blanket, riding a horse in a circle, sending signals with smoke, and so on.

SILICON VALLEY An area in the Santa Clara Valley, on the peninsula south of San Francisco, that is a center for computer research and businesses. In the 1980s and 1990s, a synonym for the computer industry in the way that Wall Street is synonymous with finance.

SILK (1) The whip used by a driver of a stagecoach. Thus the driver is known as a *silk-popper* or *knight of the silk*. (2) Among cowboys, a word for **BARBWIRE**. (3) *Silk grass* is **BEAR GRASS** (*Yucca filamentosa*).

SILVER EXCHANGE A jocular name for a gambling hall.

SILVERTIP Another name for the **GRIZZLY BEAR**. The beast is called a silvertip because the ends of its hairs are sometimes silvery, as though frosted.

SIMPATICO (seem-PAH-tee-koh; sim-PAH-ti-koh) Congenial, even endearing. Borrowed from Spanish and used mostly in the Southwest.

SING (1) An Indian ceremony for healing, casting out evil spirits, divining, and the like through chants and other rites. Used principally to refer to ceremonies of the **NAVAJO**, it may also mean rituals of other Indians, even **PLAINS INDIANS**, especially in these days of pan-tribalism. Among the Navajo, a sing is given by a *singer* (shaman) elaborately trained for it—he will have memorized songs, chants, dances, dry paintings, and other religious gestures, or all of these, that go on sometimes for more than a week. Examples are the blessing way, the *hatal* (a curing ceremony), the mountain change, and the beauty way. The purpose is to restore harmony in the natural and spiritual worlds.

(2) The Navajo word *entah*, according to Smith, is also translated as "sing" but refers to an elaborate social get-together, with dancing, storytelling, games and contests, and general good times.

SINGING TO THEM A cowboy term for riding night guard on cows. The practice of singing while you rode was not a matter of lullabying the critters to sleep but of entertaining yourself and also letting them know you were nearby, so your approach wouldn't spook them and cause a **STAMPEDE**. One hand commented that the cowboy usually "has a voice like a burro with a bad cold, and the noise he calls singin'd drive all the coyotes out of the country."

SINGLE JACK In mining, a heavy hammer with a short handle used for hand drilling.

SINGLE RIG A saddle with just one cinch, which may be placed as far forward as the forks (the front end of the saddle) or as far back as the middle of the tree (saddle frame). Also known as *single-fire* or *single-barreled*. (See also **RIG**.)

SINGLE-FOOT A horse's fast, comfortable walk, also known as a **RACK**. A horse with such a gait is called *single-footed* or a *single-footer*. To move or ride at this pace is *to singlefoot*.

SINGLE-STEER TYING A **RODEO** competition that is not offered at most rodeos. As in **CALF ROPING**, the animal is roped and thrown and its feet tied with a **PIGGING STRING**. But in single-steer tying, the horse, not the cowboy, throws the roped animal—by running away from it. Also called *steer-roping*.

SINK (1) A depression in the land surface where water has no outlet and simply stands. The word is usually applied to dry lakebeds, where the evaporating water has left **ALKALI** and other mineral salts. The deserts of the **GREAT BASIN** are full of such lake beds. (2) By extension, from the notion of water disappearing, where a stream goes underground is a sink or sinks. Thus the spot above Lander, Wyoming, where the Popo Agie River goes beneath the surface (to reappear a half mile or so downstream) is known as The Sinks.

SINKER (1) A jocular word for a biscuit, which is also called a **HOT ROCK** and a *sourdough bullet*. In the twentieth century in many parts of the country, *sinker* has also come to mean dumplings, muffins, and especially doughnuts; a *soda sinker* is a doughnut made with soda. (2) Among loggers, a log too heavy to float.

A single-rig saddle has a single cinch.
[From *Moseman's Illustrated Guide for Purchasers of Horse Furnishing Goods*, CA. 1892.]

SIOUX (SOO) The Indians who call themselves **DAKOTA** or **LAKOTA**. Although this word is a shortened form of the **OJIBWAY** word for enemy, the Lakota now use it officially. The adjective form is *Siouan*.

SIPAPU (SEE-pah-poo) A hole in the earthen floor of a **PUEBLO** people's **KIVA**, symbolizing the entry to the spirit world, where the first human beings emerge, where the dead have gone, and through which legendary beings or semi-deities pass.

SISAL (SIH-sal) A Mexican-style rope made from the fiber of the leaves of the **AGAVE**. Like the **MAGUEY** and rawhide **LARIAT**, the sisal gave way to the more popular rope of manila hemp.

SISKADEE Name of the **MOUNTAIN MEN** for the Green River; it means "sage hen" and was borrowed from the **CROW**. The literature spells it with wonderful creativity—not only Siskadee but *Siskeedee, See-ka-cay, Seekeeder,* and so on. This river was heaven on earth for the mountain men, who found in its country beaver a-plenty, more sage hens than you could beat off with a stick, and friendly Indians, the **SHOSHONES**. Most of their rendezvous were held near or on the Siskadee. Early travelers called it *Spanish River.* With the Colorado, it forms **CANYON COUNTRY**, culminating in the Grand Canyon.

SISTERS A word among the early **MORMONS** for plural wives. Present-day Saints often refer to each other as sister and *brother.*

SITKA SLIPPERS Heavy-duty rubber boots worn by Southeast Alaskans. Sitka is from a **TLINGIT** word meaning by the sea. Also called *Alaska tennis shoes, Wrangell* or *Petersburg sneakers.*

SIWASH (1) In the Pacific Northwest, **CHINOOK** jargon for both a Native tribe and the lingua franca they developed for trade. As used by Anglos, it was often derogatory. Other Anglo words for Indians (mostly derogatory) were **FEATHER-DUSTER**, *gut-eater, hair-lifter, heap big chief,* **LO**, *Mr. John, redskin,* and *scalp lifter. Brave* and *buck* are mocking words for Indian men, **SQUAW** an often derogatory word for women.

(2) To bivouac, to camp in the open, without shelter. (3) To cook over an open fire with a stick. (4) As an adjective, Indian; often meant in an uncomplimentary way. For instance, the *siwash* side of a horse is the wrong side, a *siwash outfit* a poor ranch. (4) Among cowboys, to be *siwashed* is to be blackballed.

COMBINATIONS: *siwash tree* (among loggers, used to change the direction of a cable), *siwash coat* (a long, loose gown worn by Native women), *siwash dollar* (a cylindrical shell used for money among the Native peoples), *siwash onion* (an edible root of siwash country, known principally as **CAMAS**).

SIX-SHOOTER The most common generic term for a revolver in the West, though *five-shooters* and *four-shooters* were also around. The name got fixed when the Texas Rangers adopted the **COLT** version in 1847 and called it a six-shooter. **REMINGTON**, Starr, and **SMITH & WESSON** also were well-known manufacturers, and .44 was perhaps the most common caliber. (The so-called Navy revolvers were .36 caliber, since that was the official Navy bore.) In the years immediately after the Civil War, these weapons shot black powder and were set off by percussion caps; later they used self-contained cartridges, as modern weapons do. In *The Look of the Old West,* William Foster-Harris reminds us that hand weapons in those days were not called guns—that term was reserved for cannons.

Other names for the kinds of revolvers cowboys carried were called **BELLY GUN**, *black-eyed Susan, blue lightning, coffee mill, cutter, dewey, dragoon, equalizer, flame-thrower, forty-five, forty-four,* **HOGLEG**, *life preserver, lightning conductor,* **LEAD CHUCKER**, *old cedar, one-eyed scribe, parrot-bill,* **PEACEMAKER, PEPPERBOX, PERSUADER**, *plow handle,* **SLIP GUN**, *six gun, smoke pole, smoke wagon,* **TALKING IRON**, *thumb-buster,* and **WALKER**.

Six-shooter coffee is proper **COWBOY COFFEE**, strong enough to float a six-shooter, and *six-shooter law* is the law of the gun.

SIXTEEN-SHOOTER A rifle with a magazine holding sixteen shots. This term came to suggest some special kind of mean. Thus W. S. James in *Cow-Boy Life in Texas* in 1898 speaks of "some fiend incarnate tank[ed] up with 'sixteen shooting liquor.'"

SIX-WEEKS GRASS Any of various quick-growing grasses, especially in the Southwest. An example is *Poa annua*.

SIZE UP To take the measure of a man or situation; to estimate his or its nature and especially strength.

SKATE A lousy horse; a nag, a plug. (See also **CANNER**.)

SKID In logging, peeled poles laid so that logs can slide (be *skidded*) along them. In verb form, to do that skidding.
    COMBINATIONS: *skid greaser* (the man who oils the poles to facilitate the sliding), **SKID ROAD** (the prepared skidding route), *skidway* (poles on which logs are stacked). *Skidder* may mean a man who skids logs, a steam engine that does the same thing (with the help of what was called a *skid crew*), or the boss of a crew that builds skid roads.

SKID ROAD A district of derelicts and cheap bars, first called a *skidroad area*. According to linguist J. L. Dillard, "The big skidroad in Seattle first attracted men and money and then honkytonks and their usual accompaniments, thus becoming a bad area." *Skid road* gave rise to the misnomer *skid row*.

SKIDOO A snowmobile, especially a small one with just one front ski. Originally a brand name, it has now (like kleenex and scotch tape before it) become generic.

SKIJORING A form of recreation, being pulled along on skis behind a horse, motor vehicle, or snowmobile.

SKILLET OF SNAKES An Anglo cowboy's mocking description of the elaborate cattle **BRANDS** used by Mexicans. Other names for them were *fool brand* and *map of Mexico*.

SKIMMY A calf raised on skim milk.

SKIN (1) To *skin mules* is to drive them; thus the driver is a **MULESKINNER**. (2) To *skin your gun* is to draw it from a holster.

COMBINATIONS: *skin canoe* (an occasional name for a **BULL BOAT**), *skin lodge* (another word for a **TIPI**), *skin trade* (the **FUR TRADE**), *skin string* (an occasional term for any rope made of rawhide).

SKINNER (1) A skinning knife. (2) A workman with a buffalo-hunting crew whose job was to skin the beasts. Usually the skinners made some key cuts and the robe was pulled off using mules or horses. (3) In Texas, a hand employed to skin cattle after a **DIE-UP**. Winter was the skinning season. (4) Short for **MULESKINNER**. (5) Nowadays short for **BUCKSKINNER** (mountain-man hobbyist). (6) In logging, a *cat skinner* is the man who drives a Caterpillar.

SKINNY SKIS Contemporary slang for cross-country skis; so called because they are narrower than downhill skis.

SKINWALKER Among the **NAVAJOS**, a witch who goes about disguised in a wolf skin. He is said to have gotten his magical power by killing a relative.

SKIPPER Among loggers, a foreman. (See also **SUPREME BEING**.)

SKOOKUM (1) A noun from the **CHINOOK** trade jargon meaning a demon, evil spirit, or disease. (2) As an adjective, strong or powerful. (3) A *skookum house* is a jail on an Indian reservation.

SKUNK EGG An onion.

SKUNK WAGON A comical Wyoming and Montana name for an automobile. Adams says an old Indian named Black Coal in Lander, Wyoming, got a whiff of his first car and said, "Heap skunk wagon," and amused cattlemen picked it up. No one then could have known how prophetic Black Coal would turn out to be, for Yellowstone National Park now seems to many people to be skunk-wagon country.

SKY FARMER A farmer in arid country who plows and plants a piece of land that has no irrigation, hoping for manna from heaven. Sometimes there's a crop, and sometimes there isn't. (See also **DRY FARMING**, **RAIN FOLLOWS THE PLOW**.)

SKY PILOT One name cowboys used for a preacher. (See **BLACK ROBE** for other such names.)

SKYLINE LOGGING A technique of logging in which a heavy cable called a *skyline* (often two inches thick and more than 2,000 feet long) is stretched between two spar trees. A powered carriage, called a *sky hook*, travels along the cable, hauling logs. The **DONKEY** *engine* that provides the power is a *swing donkey*, and the cable that guides the loading boom is the *swing line*. Also called *cable logging*, *highline logging*, *aerial logging*, and *aerial skidding*.

SLAB (1) A person's rib. Cowboys called people with their ribs showing *slab-sided*. (2) A paved road. Mathews identifies it as a Westernism.

SLACK In today's overbooked **RODEOS**, a means of letting contestants compete outside the normal hours, usually in the day or after the paying crowd has gone home.

SLASH (1) In logging, the residue left on the ground after cutting—tops of trees, branches, stumps, twigs, bark, and leaves. The debris left by a wind storm is called *wind slash*. (2) An **EARMARK**—a diagonal slit.

SLAVE Among loggers, a man who works for wages. The *slave driver* is the foreman, especially a tough one. He's also called a *slave pusher* or *slave puncher*. A *slave market* is an employment office.

SLED DOG An Alaskan **HUSKY**; any dog used to pull a **DOGSLED**. Dogs are categorized into *lead dog* (the leader, the powerful, dominant dog at the front, accustomed to following commands), *team dog* (a dog between the lead and the wheel), and *wheel dog* (a powerful animal positioned immediately in front of the sled). The words originated with teams of horses pulling wagons, thus *wheel* on a vehicle that has none.

SLEEP In Indian pidgin English, a day, as "The big bend of the Wind River is seven sleeps away," thus a method of measuring distance. This frontier expression dates to early colonial times, so is not a Westernism. Likewise *moon* and *winter* mean month and year, respectively.

SLEEPER A calf in the midst of being cleverly rustled. Here's how it worked: New calves were **BRANDED** and **EARMARKED** to establish ownership. In the days of the open range, if a cowboy saw a **SLICK** (a calf that wasn't branded and earmarked) sucking at one of his outfit's cows, he would stop and do the job. The **RUSTLER**'s first task was to make it look like these matters had been taken care of when they hadn't. So he'd make a sleeper: He'd earmark the calf properly but brand it lightly or not at all, or pluck the hairs instead of burning them. Until weaning time, the calf would stick with its mother, and the cowboys would mostly just look at the ears, which stuck up conveniently, instead of making a hard examination of the brand. When the calf left its mother, the rustler would slap his own brand on, recut the earmark into a different shape, and declare himself the proud owner of the little critter. In those days, he didn't even have to take it away. He'd wait for **ROUNDUP**, and when the calves were sorted (cut) by brand, the sleepered calves would be herded in with his. This process was known as *sleepering*. A brand unknown on a particular range is a *sleeper brand*.

SLEEVE GUN A **HIDEOUT** gun (a small, concealed pistol) in a gambler's sleeve.

SLICK (1) A **MAVERICK**; an **OREJANO**; an unbranded calf, which is called a slick or *slick-ear* because it isn't **EARMARKED**. Unbranded horses are also known as slicks. A slick is sometimes called a *full-ear.* In the days of the open range, calves were sometimes missed in the spring ROUNDUP and turned up as slicks at the next roundup. Men who made a practice of branding slicks were considered enterprising in the early West and later on called RUSTLERS.

(2) Sometimes a fat cow, especially one with no calf. Since she's not giving suck, her hair is shiny and glossy-slick.

SLICK FORK Narrow shoulders on a saddle; the opposite of SWELL FORK, or fork with projections on each side of the horn. (See STOCK SADDLE illustration.)

SLICKENS The residue from hydraulic mining. This powdery soil washed downstream from the gold fields. It so degraded the water and the land downstream that legislatures enacted strict environmental standards.

SLICKENSIDES Among miners, the smooth, polished surface of the vein or its walls.

SLICKER An oilskin coat to ward off the rain, carried by many cowboys tied behind the cantle. Also called a *fish.* A cowboy's bedroll wrapped in his slicker is a *slicker roll.* Horses are sometimes *slicker-broke*—the slicker is dropped off the left side of the horse. When the horse learns not to kick at it, he'll also be less spooky in general, less of a SHADOW JUMPER.

SLICK-HEELED Among cowboys, a way of describing a man who's not wearing spurs.

SLICKROCK The red sandstone of the CANYON COUNTRY of the FOUR CORNERS, hundreds upon hundreds of miles of bare rock to walk upon, rise and fall with, wander through. It is the bones of the Earth exposed beneath the soft flesh of its soil, hard, sculpted over centuries by the ever-whispering wind, flowing, undulating, swelling, soaring, grand beyond human comprehension, speaking to us of time and eternity.

SLIDE (1) In logging, a chute for moving logs, usually a rough path down a mountainside. (2) In mining, a vertical displacement of a lode. (3) An occasional word for a BRANDING chute.

SLIDING LEATHER BLIND A leather strap that covers a horse's eyes, used on a horse by a BRONC BUSTER to immobilize the critter long enough to get the saddle on and get mounted. Then the rider slid the band up the headstall, and all hell broke loose.

According to Jim Bramlett in *Ride for the High Points,* the *peelers* (BRONC BUSTERS) in the old days were mostly breaking full-grown horses unaccustomed to human beings and soon learned that a shirt or bandanna tied over the beast's eyes gave the rider a little edge. Then they refined that into a three-inch-wide sliding leather band, which moved up to become a browband when not in use.

SLING In packing, a manila rope about thirty feet long used to tie the packs together on the mule's back. As a verb, it means to do such tying, as in *slinging the bed, cross-slinging, double-slinging,* and *double-cross-slinging.*

SLING HIS HEAD What a horse may do to object to pressure from the bit, which means he isn't *neck-reining* properly. Says Max Evans in his fine comic novel *The Rounders,* "If you have to turn a horse by force and pressure from the bits only, you are going to ruin his mouth. He will get high-headed and start slinging his head. That kind of horse is a disgrace to any cowboy."

SLING JOINT Among loggers, to work with your hands.

SLIP GUN A pistol fixed to fire when the thumb is slipped off the hammer. Usually the trigger was rendered nonfunctional, the spur on the hammer lowered, and the barrel sawed off so the pistol could fit in a pants pocket. *Slip shooting* is firing a gun by thumbing the hammer, which is more accurate than fanning. (See also FAN.)

SLIPPED HIS HOBBLES Said of a horse that has gotten out of its hobbles or a human being who has fallen from grace.

SLOPE In states on or near the Continental Divide, the terms *eastern slope* and *western slope* designate one side or the other of that high country. In Colorado, for instance, the folks on the western slope often complain that they don't get the consideration due them in state political matters because most of the population is on the eastern slope in cities such as Denver. Thus *eastern sloper, western sloper, Pacific sloper,* and so on. People who lived on the Pacific Coast were once called *slopers.*

SLOUCH HAT A wide-brimmed hat of soft felt, very common in the West in the decade after the Civil War, perhaps the most common hat of all. Also worn in the 1870s were the bowler, the homburg, the plug hat, and even the high silk hat. Social distinctions were naturally made according to the hat you wore, fur indicating high status and wool low, because wool was cheaper and held its shape poorly. (See also STETSON.)

SLOW ELK Beef from another man's cow, taken without his consent. It was said of many an old-time cattleman that he never tasted his own beef, unless it was at another man's table. Also known as *big antelope.*

SLUG (1) A nugget of gold or other precious metal. (2) A big gold coin issued privately in California around 1850.

SLUICE (1) In PLACER mining, a long, inclined trough or series of RIFFLE *boxes* for washing gold-bearing dirt. Gravel and sand were shoveled in at the top and washed down, cleats on the bottom catching the gold. (See also FLUME, LONG TOM.)

COMBINATIONS: *sluice box* (a riffle box), *sluicing claim* (a claim where sluice mining is done), *sluice fork* (a sluicing tool), *sluice head* (enough water to flush out a sluice), *sluice mine, sluice mining, sluice process, sluice robbing, sluice tailing* (a tailing of sluice dirt), *sluice trough* (a sluice), *sluiceway* (a sluice).

(2) In logging, a trough that floats logs downhill; also called a **FLUME, WATER SLIDE, AND** *wet slide.* The *sluicer* is the logger who helps push the logs through. As a verb, it means to do such washing down of dirt or logs. But to *get sluiced* is to be caught in a rush of logs out of control.

SLUMGULLION (1) Stew of meat and vegetables, especially potatoes and onions, also called *slum* and known for its mongrel vigor. Thus the fine Western essayist Edward Abbey called one of his collections *Slumgullion Stew.* Its quality is suggested by its origin, which is the next meaning. (2) The mud that comes out of the downhill end of **SLUICES.**

SMALL-LOOP MAN Among cowboys, a **ROPER** who used a small loop, as **BRUSH POPPERS** (brush-country cowboys) did.

SMART ALECK A know-it-all. Also spelled *smart Aleck.* The adjective form is *smart-alecky.*

SMART AS A WHIP Very clever; first used in Salt Lake City in 1860.

SMITH & WESSON A pistol invented by gunsmiths Horace Smith and Daniel B. Wesson and made in Springfield, Massachusetts, by the firm Smith & Wesson. Though the firm was innovative—it was the first (in 1857) in its field to use a metal cartridge—and the pistols were popular, they were never as much in demand with Westerners, or with the army, as the **COLT.** (For the many words the cowboy used for his pistol, see **SIX-SHOOTER.**)

SMOKE The smoke of the medicine pipe is often regarded among Indian peoples as carrying prayers up to the deities, or as similar to breath, which is a form of spirit. Smoke, steam, and fog are seen as similar or the same and sometimes represent human spirit in songs and prayers. Therefore several of these meanings related to Indians:

NOUNS: (1) Among the Indians generally, to have a council. (2) A smoke among Indians, **MOUNTAIN MEN,** or other Anglos could be a social occasion, time spent smoking pipes and talking. *Smoke the peace pipe* is an Anglo expression for making a treaty with Indians or just making up with a friend. (3) Among the **SAUK** and Fox Indians, to *smoke a horse* was a custom by which one acquired a horse via a ceremony. (4) Among the **CHEROKEES** and perhaps the other **FIVE CIVILIZED TRIBES,** to *smoke someone* means to use **MEDICINE** (usually smoking tobacco) against someone. (5) Among the **SALISH** people in the Pacific Northwest, a *smoke house* is a ceremonial building. (6) A *smoke flap* is the top of a **TIPI** cover, the **EARS,** above the crotch of poles. It can be moved to help draw smoke up or keep rain out. (7) Among **PLAINS INDIANS** the *smoke signal* was a means of long-distance communication. After the fire had attracted attention, the signaler would smother the smoke with a blanket and then let it out in the number of puffs wanted, spaced in order to send a message.

A *smoke pole* originally was a pistol; now, among **BUCKSKINNERS**, a muzzle-loading rifle. (See also **SIX-SHOOTER**.)

VERBS: (1) To subject something to smoke. Meat that was smoked would dry and take on a smoky flavor. Hide would harden, perhaps for a shield made of hide. (2) Among **COWBOYS**, to *take a smoke* came to mean not only to have a cigarette but to give yourself a short break, a period of relaxation spent smoking. (3) To *smoke out cattle* is to chase them out of brush or other hiding places by shooting. To *smoke up* is to shoot. (4) A horse that *smokes its pipe* has a torn lip where the bit sits. (5) To be *smoky* is to be shady, devious, snaky.

SMOOTH MOUTH A horse so aged that its teeth have worn down to little.

SMOOTH OUT THE HUMPS To take the rough edges off a horse, something a mount often needs in the spring after a winter of not being ridden. (See also **BREAK A HORSE**.) A *smooth horse* is an unshod one, and a *smooth-mouthed horse* is ten years old or older and has teeth worn down with age.

SMUDGE Among contemporary **PLAINS INDIANS**, to use **SMOKE** in a ceremonial manner, especially for purification. People are often smudged with cedar smoke, for instance; the **MEDICINE PIPE** is as well.

SNAFFLE BIT A bridle bit; like a *bar* (one-piece) *bit* but made of two pieces joined in the middle, so they flex.

SNAG (1) A tree or branch obstructing a river and dangerous to navigation; a **SAWYER**, preacher, planter, or **STRAINER**. (2) In logging, a standing dead tree consisting mostly of a trunk; if less than about twenty feet high, it's called a *stub*. (3) A **PLUG**, a **SKATE**, a *skin*—a worthless horse. (See also **CANNER**.) (4) As a verb, to cut away snags, whether in the water or on land. (5) To *get snagged* means to get caught on a snag in the river. (6) In current pan-Indian slang, a snag is a romantic date—"I have a snag after the powwow."

SNAKE (1) Another name for the **SHOSHONE** Indians, generally thought to have come from the sinuous sign-language gesture for that tribe. The gesture, which meant weaver, was misinterpreted to mean snake. (2) When not capitalized, a longhorn left in the brush after most have been gathered.

COMBINATIONS: *snake's alarm clock* (his rattles), *snake blood* (meanness), *snake eater* and *snake killer* (a **ROAD RUNNER**), *snake-headed* (a mean, ornery man), *snake hole* (in mining, a bore hole), *snake fence* (a zigzag fence of rails, built without posts), *snake a critter out* (to haul him out of the bog with a rope).

SNAKE DANCE A ceremony of the **HOPI** Indians performed for eight days in alternate years to bring rain. The handling of live rattlesnakes by dancers during the final day of the dance, followed by the release of the reptiles, has made it much remarked on by outsiders; but much of the ceremony takes place out of sight in the **KIVA**.

SNAKE-HEAD WHISKEY Rotgut whiskey, reputedly made with ingredients that included the heads of snakes; other reptilian words for whiskey are *snake juice, snake poison,* and *snake water.* (For many Western words for booze, see also **FIRE-WATER.**)

SNAKY A way of describing a man who's devious, shady, treacherous.

SNARE To catch something with a rope, especially a cow you've come on unexpectedly.

SNIPE (1) In logging, to trim the end of a log. The rounded end is referred to as *snipe-nosed.* (2) Among cowboys *snipe-gutted* was said of a horse or other critter that's slender in the barrel.

SNIRT A word for the mixture of snow and dirt you get on the **NORTHERN PLAINS** during the spring thaw—a nicely inventive coinage.

SNOOPER A cowboy who spotted another man's *hideout bottle* (hidden liquor bottle) at a dance and sneaked a snort or two.

SNOOSE Among loggers and sheepherders, a strong, moist variety of snuff introduced to the West by Scandinavian loggers; sometimes called *Scandihoovian dynamite, Swedish condition powder, rest powder,* or *heifer dust.*

SNORTY Said of a contrary or belligerent cow, of an irascible man, and of a high-spirited horse.

SNOW (1) A Red English term for year; a similar term is *winter*—an Indian would speak (or be translated as speaking) of something that happened four *snows* or *winters* ago. (See also **SLEEP.**) (2) What a miner calls a dusting from the roof that augurs a cave-in. (3) The West has various terms for forms and qualities of snow, which are of particular interest to skiers: *corn snow* (a heavy, granular spring snow), *hominy snow* (a term born in Kansas for a granular snow, like hominy grits), *powder snow* (a dry, fluffy snow adored by *powder hounds*), *sugar snow* (loose, unconsolidated snow). In Jackson Hole fresh powder brings people outside the way sunshine does in Seattle.

SNOW ANCHOR In Alaska, a hook on the end of a rope fixed to a **DOGSLED.** When the hook is anchored (in the snow, in ice, to a tree, etc.), the dogs can't move the parked sled. Also called an *ice anchor, ice hook,* or *snow hook.*

SNOW BERM In alpine country and the Northwest, the mound of snow made at the sides of roads by snowplows.

SNOW SHIRT In Alaska, a hooded pullover of cloth; worn over the parka to keep blowing snow off. Also called a *parka cover.*

SNOW SURVEYOR A government worker who measures the amount of snow in the mountains as a means of predicting how much water will fill the reservoirs (and be available for irrigation) the following summer. Thus the combinations *snow survey* and *snow surveying.*

SNOWBIRD (1) A Southwestern term for folks who desert cold climates for Arizona in the winter. *Sunbirds* make the reverse trip, leaving hot southern climes in the summer. (2) Originally, a soldier of the period of the Indian wars who enlisted for the winter for the sake of food, clothing, and shelter and deserted in the spring.

SNOWBOARDING A recent snow sport that uses equipment and skills like surfing, but on snow; originated on the slopes of Mount Baker in Washington.

SNOWMOBILE A machine for travel over snow, with runners in front and a *bogie wheel* in the rear. It travels well on unplowed roads and through trackless country. Though used mostly for recreation, snowmobiles are also used in the West for transportation to remote ranches and for work such as running trap lines. This word is not a native Westernism. Also called (especially in Alaska) a *snow machine*. A related word is **BILER**, short for snowmobiler.

The conflicts between snowmobilers and cross-country skiers are heated. In 2000 the National Park Service declared its intention to close Yellowstone Park to snowmobiling. In the interior of Alaska and some other isolated areas of the West, snowmobiles are the single practical means of transportation in the winter.

SNOWSHOE An early Western term for a ski. The verb *snowshoe* and noun *snowshoer* thus require caution—they sometimes meant to *ski* and *skier*. (The use of this word to mean a racketlike device lashed to the foot for traveling over snow in winter is as much Eastern as Western.)

COMBINATIONS: *snowshoe dance* (a ceremony of some Indians performed after the first snow of each winter), *snowshoe disease* or *snowshoe evil* (inflammation and swelling of tendons stressed by snowshoes), *snowshoe rabbit* (a Rocky Mountain hare, *Lepus bairdi*).

SNUB, SNUB UP (1) To tie an animal with a short rope to either a post or a saddle horn. You do this to a calf or cow you want to control and especially to a horse that's going to buck when you get on him. (2) To dehorn cattle. (3) In logging, to use a brake drum (a *snubber*) and a cable (a *snubbing line*) to keep a log being skidded downhill from getting out of control.

COMBINATIONS: *snubbing post* (a stout timber set in the ground in a corral to snub wild critters to), *snub horse* (in **RODEO**, the horse used for snubbing; the cowboy is the *snubber*).

SNUFFY A way of describing cattle or horses that are wild and spirited and likely to cause trouble.

SNY (rhymes with *cry*) A word of the Missouri and Mississippi Rivers signifying a narrow passage between the shore and an island. It derives from the French *chenal* (channel) through the French-Canadian *chenail* (which is pronounced shuh-NIGH).

SOAK Among cowboys, to rest, to loaf.

SOAPWEED Any one of several plants in the West and Southwest used by Indians and Anglo pioneers to make soap, especially **YUCCA**. *Soap apple* (also called *soap bulb*) was a California plant used for soap. Others, especially the *palmilla* of the Southwest, were called *soap plant*. *Soap wort* is another name for soapweed, and *soap ball* refers to the flowery head of yuccas.

SOBRECINCHA (soh-bray-SEEN-chah) See **SURCINGLE, CINCH, GIRTH**.

SOD CORN Indian corn, which needed little water; the whiskey made from that corn.

SOD HOUSE A **SODDY**. A *sod house claim* was claim of public land with a sod house on it. A *sod fence* was a wall on the Plains made of sod and dirt.

SODA (1) As an adjective, soda is often an equivalent of **ALKALINE**, or mineral-salt. Thus a *soda spring* is an alkaline spring, a *soda butte* a hill in alkali country, a *soda lake* a dry lake with a salt bed, and a *soda prairie* a prairie of mineral-salt soil. (2) In **FARO**, the first card, the one turned face up. The last card is called the *hock*, giving rise to the expression *from soda to hock*, meaning *all of it, from soup to nuts, from a to z.*

SODDY (1) A **SOD HOUSE**, a primitive Plains dwelling built from the turf itself. About half an acre was stripped of sod, which was cut in three-foot lengths and stacked like bricks. Some soddies were combined with **DUGOUTS**; that is, part of the house was dug into a hill. The inside was always a problem—the ceiling leaked water during rains and dropped dust when the sun was shining. Such were the first homes of many homesteaders. (2) A **HOMESTEADER** or **SOD-BUSTER**, because many of them lived in soddies. (See also **NESTER**.)

A *sod-soaker* was a good rain. (See also **GULLYWASHER**.)

SOD-PAWING MOOD A cowboy's expression for anger, because that's the way **SNORTY** bulls acted.

SOFKY Among the **CREEK** Indians, hominy, often flavored with wild meat. They prepared this dish during their time in the South and after the forced migration to Oklahoma; later replaced by grits. The **CHOCTAW** had and have a similar dish called *tahfula*. (See also **POSOLE**.)

SOFT Said of a horse that wears out easily, that has little endurance. *Soft-mouthed* is a term for a horse that's sensitive to the bit, just as *sweet-mouthed* is.

SOFT GRUB What a cowboy called fancy food; hotel food. (See also **CHOW, CHUCK**.)

SOLD HIS SADDLE Said of a cowman or cowboy who's hit bottom, who's lost his status. The bottom might be financial—he went belly-up; or personal—he went crazy; or moral—he sold us out. Philip A. Rollins told an apt story in *The Cowboy*: A school kid in Montana, asked by his teacher who Benedict Arnold was, answered, "'He was one of our generals and he sold his saddle.'"

A Nebraska family in front of their soddy.

SOLD TO HALTER An expression for a horse being sold with absolutely no guarantee.

SOLEDAD PINE The Torrey pine of California. Also called the *lone pine*. It grows singly or in small groups on highlands near the ocean.

SOMBRERO (sohm-BRAYR-roh; sahm-BRAYR-roh) A hat, especially a cowboy hat and more especially a Mexican style of hat that used to be common in the Southwest. It had a high-curved, wide brim; a sugar-loaf crown dented at the top; and a long, loose chin strap. Like cowboy hats generally, it kept off the sun and rain, fended off the branches, and served as a handy bucket or cup. Borrowed from Spanish.

SOME An adjective of admiration, especially among the **MOUNTAIN MEN**, as in "He was some hoss." Sometimes it was used as an emphatic positive, as in "That hoss could shoot some."

SON-OF-A-BITCH STEW A spicy stew of marrowgut from a freshly killed calf, said to have gotten started because calves couldn't keep up on trail drives and so were expendable. Adams says that the liver, tongue, kidneys, heart, sweetbreads, and brains were used, plus any vegetables that were handy. Jean Burroughs writes in *New Mexico* magazine that it "contained the 'hair, horns and holler.'" Of course, there were as many versions as there were **COOKIES** to cook it. The name varied. When female ears were present, it was *son-of-a-gun* *stew.* And after the jurisprudence system arrived and proved to be even more political than it is today, the dish naturally came to be called *district attorney stew.*

SON-OF-A-BITCH-IN-A-SACK Dough and dried fruit sewed into a sack and steamed. One authority suggests the name came from the difficulty of making it. Also called, of course, *son-of-a-gun-in-a-sack.*

SONORA A California expression for a winter rain that comes from the south, the direction of the Mexican state of Sonora.

SONORAN DESERT The hottest of the American deserts and the desert with the widest variety of plant life. Located in southern Arizona, California, and northern Mexico, it is home of the **SAGUARO**, the **OCOTILLO**, the **CHOLLA**, the **ORGANPIPE CACTUS**, and the **PALO VERDE**, among many plants.

SONORATOWN In the Southwest, a town's Mexican quarter. Neighborhoods of the disenfranchised went together; Chinatowns often grew up around Sonoratowns.

SONS OF DAN A vigilante organization of **MORMON** men and a scourge of the church's opponents and of apostates. The name alludes to Genesis 49:17— "Dan shall be a serpent by the way, an adder in the path. . . ." Members were also known as the *Danites, Big Fan, Shanpips, the Destroying Angels,* and *Daughters of Gideon.* Their job was sometimes to **SAVE** people, in that deft usage where to *save* means to *liquidate.* They were organized in the late 1830s in Missouri, in response to persecutions by non-Mormons there.

SOONER (1) Originally a person who jumped the gun, who got someplace too soon. The term applied particularly to people who claimed land in the **CHEROKEE STRIP** before it was legally open, or to premature claimants of any Oklahoma Indian land or any land reserved to Indians. That tendency came to be known as *soonerism.* Now any Oklahoman.

(2) Men who **BRANDED** ahead of the roundup. In the days of the open range, the cattlemen's associations would set dates for the roundup in each area, but some hustlers would work the cows ahead of the roundup to get any *mavericks* and *slicks* (unbranded calves) for themselves.

SOOPOLLALIE (soo-puh-LA-lee) In the Pacific Northwest, the buffalo berry, a shrub (*Shepherdia canadensis*) with an edible but bitter red berry. Comes from the **CHINOOK** jargon word *olallie.*

SOP What old-time Westerners called gravy. In a boardinghouse, says Libby Custer in *Following the Guidon,* "an Eastern man, a 'tenderfoot,' on one occasion asked some one to pass the gravy, whereupon the bouncer placed his pistol on the table and quietly remarked, 'Any man as calls sop gravy has got to eat dust or 'pologize.'" Cowboys called the **COOKIE** *sop and taters.* Loggers call sop *goozlam.*

SOPAIPILLA (soh-puh-PEE-yuh) A Mexican-American fritter, deep-fried in fat, like a *buñuelo.* Borrowed from Spanish.

SORREL A reddish brown horse with mane and tail of the same color; has the body color of a **BLOOD BAY**, which has a black mane and tail. (For other horse colors, see **BUCKSKIN**.)

SOTOL (soh-TOHL) A Southwestern plant similar in appearance to the yucca. The plant (*Dasylirion*) is long-leaved and was used (according to J. Frank Dobie) for torches and for fibers and food. Also a fermented drink of the poor, similar to **PULQUE**. Borrowed from Mexican Spanish (which in turn borrowed it from Aztec). Sometimes called the *desert spoon*.

SOURDOUGH From the original meaning, bread dough with active fermentation, came Western meanings and combinations: (1) An old hand, a fellow who's **ALKALIED** (adapted to the country), likely an old-timer, usually a prospector. In this sense, the word had its greatest currency in Alaska and the Northwest Territory. He got this name because he ate (perhaps essentially lived on) bread, pancakes, biscuits, etc. made from sourdough. (2) A bachelor. (3) Among cowboys, a cook, or simply a bachelor.

COMBINATIONS: *sourdough biscuit, sourdough bread, sourdough bullet* (a biscuit), *sourdough keg* (the container for sourdough), *sourdough pants* (blanket-lined pants for Northern Plains winters), *sourdough rolls, sourdough starter* (a piece of fermenting dough used to set a new batch of dough to fermenting).

SOUR-MOUTH What a cowboy calls a horse who worries at the bit. He ends up **HARD-MOUTHED**.

SOUVENIR An egg too old to be eaten, usually one shipped out from the United States proper, when the West was mostly territories. (See also *States eggs* under **STATES**.)

SOVEREIGN SQUATTER A settler in Kansas in the 1850s who thumbed his nose at Stephen A. Douglas's notion of "popular sovereignty," the doctrine that each new state should choose to be a free or slave state by popular vote. The *Sovereign Squats* held out for free-state status.

SOVIET OF WASHINGTON What the state was nicknamed after the Seattle General Strike in 1919.

SPADE BIT A long, wide bit that fills a horse's mouth. One of the great debates of Western horsemen is the **CURB BIT** versus the spade bit. Early-day cowboys of Texas and the Plains used the curb bit in breaking and riding their horses, rode them tight-reined, and regarded the spade bit as too hard on a horse. They also didn't spend much time breaking their horses. The **CALIFORNIOS** and the descendants of the **BUCKAROOS** took more time to break their horses, using **HACKAMORES**, riding them loose-reined, and graduating to a spade bit. Old hand Jo Mora, conceding that each way has its points, nevertheless wrote in *Trail Dust and Saddle Leather,* "On a horse that's been properly broken and reined with a hackamore, bitted by a good hand, and ridden by a loose-rein stockman who knows what it's all about, I consider the spade bit tops." Mora adds that the bit is cruel only in the hands of the unskilled. One cowboy name (surely derisive) for a spade bit was *stomach pump.*

SPANGLISH Mexican Spanish as spoken in the Southwest, mongrelized by grammatical and other elements from English; not the standard Spanish of the educated but what linguists call a bilingual dialect. Similar to these terms (which are sometimes used pejoratively) are *Tex-Mex, pocho,* and *border lingo.*

SPANISH DOLLAR A silver Spanish-American coin worth eight **REALES,** valued as hard currency.

SPANISH GRANT An award of land (often very large) from the government of Spain. Grant-holders once strode large upon the stage of the Southwest, especially California.

Spade bit.
[DRAWING BY E. L. REEDSTROM.]

SPANISH HORSE The Barb brought to the New World by the Spaniards. A big pony, it weighed on average 600 pounds, stood about thirteen **HANDS** high, and had one less vertebra than an American horse (one imported from the States). It was the horse of the **PLAINS INDIANS,** and they showed spectacularly what it could do. Though sometimes dismissed by Anglos as a runt and a mongrel (and associated with "those dirty Injuns"), it made a terrific reputation as a cowpony because it was tough and sturdy. It also was the ancestor of the **MUSTANG.** Says Jo Mora in *Trail Dust and Saddle Leather:* "The Spanish horse should have been called the American horse. He certainly rated that honor. He was the very first equine to set foot on American soil, and his get populated practically the entire hemisphere." (See also **CAYUSE.**)

OTHER COMBINATIONS USING "SPANISH": *Spanish bit* (a bit similar to a **SPADE BIT,** with a high port), *Spanish rig* (a saddle with the cinch hung straight down from the forks; see also **SINGLE-RIG**), *Spanish saddle* (a saddle from Mexico, usually heavy, elaborate, and decked out with silver), *Spanish spurs* (favored by many Hispanic riders, with a long shank and sharply pointed rowels), *Spanish trot* (an easy swinging trot), *Spanish cattle* (properly, the black cattle running wild in Texas at the beginning of American settlement; loosely, any cattle of Mexican origin), *Spanish fever* (another name for **TEXAS FEVER**, a cow disease caused by the cattle tick), *Spanish River* (the Green River or Siskadee), *Spanish brick* (**ADOBE**), *Spanish monte* (another name for the gambling game **MONTE**).

PLANTS: *Spanish bayonet* (one of several species of **YUCCA**, particularly *Yucca aloifolia*), *Spanish dagger* (a **YUCCA**), *Spanish needle* (porcupine grass, an irritant to the mouths of horses and cattle).

SPANISH TRAIL A name given to several Southwestern roads, principally the routes from Texas to New Orleans, Santa Fe to Los Angeles, and Salt Lake City to San Bernadino.

SPENCER A lever-action, repeating rifle (often a carbine) invented by C. M. Spencer, popular in the West in .52 and .56 calibers in the post–Civil War period.

SPICK A derogatory word for a Hispanic. Also spelled *spic* and *spik*. (For similar words, see **GREASER**.)

SPIDER (1) Among loggers, a little tool that checks the set of sawteeth. (2) A socket attached to the **CINCH** ring on the off side to serve as a rifle scabbard.

SPIDER WOMAN A culture hero of the great stories of many tribes, especially **PUEBLO** people and **NAVAJOS**; the bringer of weaving.

SPIKE Usually a young bull elk with spikelike, unbranched antlers. He's also called a *spike* (or *spiked*) *bull*. Also a deer, a young buck (also called a *spike buck*) with unbranched antlers. Historically, a young buffalo bull with short horns.

SPIKE A TREE To commit a contemporary form of **MONKEY WRENCHING** (sabotaging), driving spikes into trees that may be sold or have been sold for cutting. According to the head monkey wrencher himself, the late Edward Abbey, "one spike in a log can strip the teeth from a ten-thousand-dollar circular saw, put a crimp in profits, deter further logging, and thus preserve those living breathing respirating trees whose right to continued existence is at least as legitimate as that of any other creature including, but not limited to, the human." Others say that spiking trees is dangerous to the loggers who cut and meet metal unexpectedly.

SPIKE TEAM (1) A team of three draft animals hitched with one in front of the others. (2) Five draft animals pulling a stagecoach, hitched with the heaviest two at the rear and the lightest one alone in front.

SPIKE YOUR HORSE'S TAIL What a cowboy does when he brings his horse to such a sudden stop that it sits right down on its tail.

SPILLIONAIRE In Alaska, a joking name for people who made big bucks off the 1989 *Exxon Valdez* oil spill in Prince William Sound by renting their boats as part of the cleanup.

SPINNER Among **RODEO** cowboys, a horse with an inclination to buck in tight circles, which makes the rider dizzy and soon puts him in the dirt.

SPIRIT TRAIL In **NAVAJO** weaving, a line of contrasting yarn that runs from the center to the edge of the piece. Navajos in particular have a taboo against designs that form an unbroken border, whether in weaving, basket-making, or other crafts. The simple explanation is that the maker's soul might be trapped in the piece, so the spirit trail provided an escape.

Spider Woman gave the Navajo the art of weaving and its associated lore— hence the alternate term *spider trail.* In early times a small hole was often left in the center of a weaving or basket for similar reasons.

SPIRITUAL A synonym for **SEALED** one, a woman sealed to a **MORMON** man in celestial marriage. In full, *spiritual wife.* In practice, in the days of **PLURAL MARRIAGE,** it was used to mean a wife beyond the first. Mormon wives referred to each other as *sister.* In the nineteenth century some Mormon women were spiritual wives of past leaders such as Joseph Smith and Brigham Young. The custom of having spiritual wives is known as *spiritual wifery.*

SPIRITUAL WIDOWER A California expression meaning a married man who is away from home chasing gold. The woman he left behind was called a *California widow.*

SPIT Among miners, a lighted fuse. To light the fuses for the blast is to *spit a round.* Also *squip.*

SPLASH A head of water released suddenly to wash logs downstream. Previously it would have been held back by a *splash dam.*

SPLIT (1) An **EARMARK** consisting of a split in an animal's ear, reaching neither the tip nor the head. (2) In **RODEO**, for a pair of contestants to agree to pool their winnings and share equally.

SPLIT THE TAIL To cut a cow's tail lengthwise, a practice once believed to prevent **BLACKLEG**, usually a fatal disease.

SPOILED HERD Among cattlemen, a herd inclined to take any excuse to stampede.

SPOKANE A tribe of Salishan Indians that historically lived below the falls on the Spokane River in Washington. They subsisted primarily on salmon. After the Northwest Company established Spokane House at the mouth of the Little Spokane River, the chief's son, Spokane Garry, went to the Red River Settlements to learn Anglo culture. He later taught some of his people how to read, build log cabins, and grow some crops. During the gold rushes of the area in the 1850s, troubles arose between the Spokanes and the whites but passed without major incident. The Spokanes were assigned a reservation in their historical country, where they live today.

SPOOK To frighten horses, cattle, or other critters. They're then *spooky*—jumpy, nervous.

SPOOL YOUR BED Among cowboys, to get your bed rolled and ready to go.

SPOON (1) To turn over in your sleep. In the West, two men sometimes slept spoon-fashion in a small space. When one man wanted to turn over, he would tell the other to spoon. (2) Among miners, a rod for cleaning drill holes.

SPOTTED PUP Rice pudding; rice or tapioca cooked with raisins.

SPOTTER Among loggers, a man who spies for the company.

SPRADDLE HORNS Among cowboys, TEXAS LONGHORNS. For a cowboy to get *spraddled out* was for him to be dressed up in his Sunday-go-to-meeting clothes.

SPREAD A ranch—land, buildings, hands, and critters together. Used to identify a kind of ranch, as in *sheep spread,* or its owner, as in the *Chisum spread.*

SPREAD THE MUSTARD Among cowboys, to put on airs.

SPREADER DAM A dam of earth used to make surface runoff spread out rather than form a gully.

SPREE This word sometimes occurs in the West as a verb. Thus Owen Wister writes, "Hank bein' all trembly from spreein' it in town. . . ." For similar expressions, see **ROOSTERED**.

SPRING (1) Among cowmen, to be about to calve. A cow *springing heavy* is near her time, and a *springing heifer* is carrying her first calf. A *springer* is any cow carrying a calf.

(2) *Spring range* is the grazing ground for cows that's used before they're driven to their summer ranges. Cattle that are skinny from the winter are called *spring poor.* The *spring roundup,* also called the *calf roundup,* is primarily for branding new calves. The fall roundup is primarily for gathering cows for market or moving them to winter range.

(3) A *spring creek* is fed by a spring rather than runoff or snowmelt; often sought in the West as excellent for trout-fishing because it is clear all year-round.

(4) A *spring wagon* is a light wagon whose wheels were set individually on springs.

SPRINGFIELD A rifle made at Springfield, Massachusetts, by the United States Armory and used by the U.S. Army from the Civil War to World War I. The most common Springfield in the West was the Trap Door, a single-shot model adopted by the army in 1873.

SPUD (1) Among loggers, a hand tool for stripping bark from felled trees. (2) In oil drilling, to drill the first fifty or sixty feet of a hole with a drill attached to a rope and a drum. Such a rig is called a *spudder.* Nowadays, *spud* simply means starting the hole.

SPUR Though all spurs consist of a heel-band, a shank, and a **ROWEL,** the Western versions of these devices for giving the get-go to a horse are various. Historically, the main differences were between two styles—the Plains style, east of the Rockies, and the **CALIFORNIO** style, in California, the Southwest generally, and **BUCKAROO** country. In general, the California spur was bigger and fancier, the Plains spur smaller and simpler. Sometimes the old Californios wore spurs so curved they couldn't walk in them.

The *spur leather,* also called a *spur strap,* is the piece that goes over a rider's instep to hold it in place, and sometimes it's decoratively tooled, carved, or ornamented with conchas. The *spur chains,* usually two or three of them, go under the arch. People who don't ride sometimes assume that spurs are cruel,

Spur.

[FROM *Moseman's Illustrated Guide for Purchasers of Horse Furnishing Goods,* CA. 1892.]

especially big ones. In fact, they're only as severe as the man using them, and the ones with more points prick less. They're used as reminders and emergency starters.

Other words for spurs (sometimes indicating different types) are **BUZZ SAWS,** *California drag rowels, can openers,* **CARTWHEELS, CHIHUAHUAS, DIGGERS,** *gads, galves, goosenecks, grappling irons, gut hooks, gut lancers, gut wrenches, hell-rousers, hooks, Kelleys, pet-makers,* **PERSUADERS,** *rib wrenches, steel,* **STAR ROWEL,** *sunbursts, sunset rowels, tin bellies,* and *wagon-spoke rowels.*

SQUARE DEAL In card-playing, a fair game. The term arose from the dealer's using a pack of square-edged cards, which are harder to cheat with. By extension, any kind of fair arrangement. "A square deal" was Teddy Roosevelt's slogan in the 1904 campaign. When the term *square* is applied to a man, it is a compliment meaning that he's straightforward and trustworthy.

SQUATTER (1) A person who claimed land without legal rights; often a term meant and taken unkindly in the West because squatters accelerated the breaking up of the open range. The land you squatted on was your *squat.* A *squatteree* was a squatter's cabin. *Squatterism* meant the ways of squatters. *Squatterphobia* was antagonism to squatter sovereignty.

COMBINATIONS: *squatters' association* (an organization of squatters created to give credibility to the claims of squatters), *squatter's deed* (a claim to first right when an area was opened to settlement), *squatter law* (a structure of law made by squatters for their mutual protection), *squatter* or *squatter's right* (the legitimacy of a squatter's claim), *squatter sovereignty* (the right of squatters to govern themselves and their right to their claims).

(2) A **TEXAS LONGHORN** that hid out in the brush during the roundup.

SQUAW (1) An Indian woman. Used teasingly, it can also mean an Anglo woman. This word started life as an Algonquian term meaning female, then became part of the *lingua franca* developed by Eastern Indians for purposes of trading and was carried west by frontiersmen, according to linguist J. L. Dillard in *All-American English*. The Plains Indians saw it as a white man's word and found it objectionable, as most contemporary Indians do. The occasional assertion that it was a vulgar way of referring to female genitalia is false. See the book Introduction for a fuller discussion. (2) To *get squawed* was to marry an Indian woman; hence the expression *squaw man*.

COMBINATIONS: *squaw ax* (a small ax of the Indian trade, used mostly for splitting wood), *squaw blanket* (a trade blanket), *squaw camp* (a camp of Indian women and children while the men were out fighting or hunting), *squaw dance* (an Indian dance where the squaws chose their partners, or another name for the Navajo ceremony enemy way), *squaw fire* (a small fire), *squaw horse* (an Anglo word for a horse not worth having), *squaw medicine* (an Anglo word meaning Indian quackery), *squaw pony* (among U.S. soldiers, a horse fit only for carrying loads, not riders), *squaw saddle* (a blanket or quilt rigged out as saddle, after the fashion of Indian women's saddles), *squaw side* (the off side, the wrong side for getting on a horse; also called *Indian side*), *squaw talk* (women's talk), *squaw tits* (two leather pads that are tied on to the front forks of a saddle), *squaw wind* (a **CHINOOK**), *squaw winter* (a little winter preceding an Indian summer), *squaw wood* (light, easily gathered wood used for cooking).

PLANTS: *squaw carpet* (ceanothus, a shrub of the buckthorn family, common in the Sierra Nevada), *squaw corn* (soft-grained, multicolored Indian corn), *squaw currant* (*Ribes cereum*), *squaw grass* (**BEAR GRASS**, also known as *squaw lily*, *Xerophyllum terax*), *squaw root* (one of various plants believed to have worth as a medicine or a food, especially *Conopholis americana*), *squawweed* (one of several plants—a ragwort, *Senecio obovatus*, used medicinally; horseweed, *Erigeron canadensis*, or any of the squawberry), *squaw cabbage* (miner's cabbage, *Montia parviflora*, also called *Indian lettuce*; also the desert trumpet, *Eriogonum inflatum*), *squawberry* (a bewildering number of plants in the West: osoberry, *Osmaronia cerasiformis*; deerberry, *Vaccinium stamineum*; sumac, *Rhus aromatica* or *Rhus trifoliata*; *Mitchella repens*, a plant of the genus *Lyceum*, or its fruit), *squawbush* (one of several shrubs—Indian tobacco, *Cornus stolonifera*, *Cornus sericea*, or *Cornus canadenisis*; or a Western sumac, *Rhus trilobata*).

SQUAW CANDY In Alaska, long pieces of salmon that has been dried, salted, and smoked. Also called *Alaska candy*, *Eskimo candy*, *fish strips*, *salmon strips*, *siwash candy*, and *Yukon candy*.

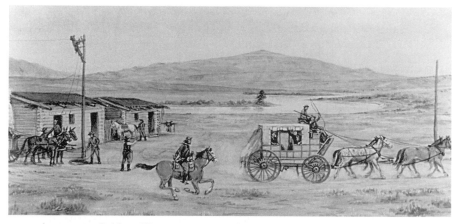

A stage station, Red Butte, Wyoming.
[Painting by Wiullliam Henry Jackson; courtesy of American Heritage Center, University of Wyoming.]

SQUEEZE CHUTE A narrow chute to hold cattle for **BRANDING**. Also called a *squeezer, snapping turtle,* or a *branding chute.*

SQUEEZE SPINDLE A hidden device used for cheating by the operators of gambling wheels such as roulette wheels. The squeeze spindle, also called a *squeeze wheel,* stops the wheel where the operator wants.

SQUEEZE THEM DOWN In driving a tail herd, for the cowboys to reduce the width of the line of cows, perhaps to herd them across a river. This was also called *narrowing the string.*

SQUIRREL CAN A big can used by the camp cook for scraps.

STACKWAD A lazy cowboy who looks for the easy jobs.

STAG (1) When said of cattle, an animal not castrated until it reached maturity. (2) In the sense of a social event for men, as in a *stag dance* or *stag party,* it appears also to be an expression of the frontier, when men were often without women. (3) Among loggers, to cut off your pants at calf level.

STAGE STATION Where the **STAGECOACH** stopped en route to give the passengers a break as well as to change horses. The passengers might have found some soap, something to eat and drink, perhaps a bunk, and surely a handy deck of cards. The larger stations (often called *home stations*) were usually homes to the station masters, their families, and other stage line employees. Small communities often grew up around them. They were usually about fifty miles apart on the line. The smaller stations, placed closer together and often called *swing stations,* provided only a change of livestock. Stage stations were also called *stage stands.*

STAGECOACH A wheeled, enclosed, horse-drawn vehicle of public transportation; a principal object of desire for *road agents* (highwaymen); a principal locale of Western adventure stories. Also called simply a *stage*. Though the West made stagecoaches famous among modern Americans, they were not native sons—they'd been used to move the public, its mail, and its valuables for two centuries before they became common on the Western frontier. The best-known stagecoaches in the nineteenth century were the **CONCORD** coaches, made in Concord, New Hampshire, from the 1820s. These were luxury vehicles, built for comfort, with three seats holding three passengers each comfortably, elaborately sprung and cushioned; the middle seat could be shifted into a bed. Two boots for luggage were provided, one under the driver's box and the other in back. The coaches were pulled by two or three pairs of horses.

The stagecoaches scratched their ways to almost all the population centers of the West, from the edge of the prairies at St. Louis to the edge of the continent at San Francisco. This journey took about $200 and twenty-five days. You traveled night and day at the rate of four or five miles an hour, on the average, changing horses at relay stations, eating, cleaning up, and sometimes sleeping at **STAGE STATIONS** or **ROAD RANCHES**. It was a rugged trip—modern readers wanting to enjoy the experience vicariously need only to turn to Mark

Stagecoaches were used for tourists in the early years of Yellowstone Park.
[COURTESY OF TETON COUNTY HISTORICAL SOCIETY.]

Twain's *Roughing It*. They'll have a lot more laughs than did Sam Clemens, or any other traveler of the time.

COMBINATIONS: *stage barn, stage connection, stage holdup, stage line* (a stagecoach system), *stage station, stage house, stage post,* or *stage ranch* (all terms for a stopping point on a stage line). A *stage* was also a section of road between stage stations.

STAKE VERB COMBINATIONS: *stake a claim* (literally, to mark it with stakes or in any way to make a mineral claim; figuratively, one could stake a claim to anything, including a pretty girl), *stake a person* (to supply someone with the means for a project such as prospecting; to *grubstake* someone), *make* or *raise a stake* (to earn some money, perhaps enough to start a business or otherwise get started in life), *move stakes* (change where you live), *staked to a fill* (have your stomach full).

NOUNS: (1) In the **MORMON** Church, a district, according to Wallace Stegner in *Mormon Country*, "roughly equivalent to the dioceses of the Catholic Church." Stakes are subdivided into smaller units called **WARDS**. COMBINATIONS: *stake house* (an assembly building), *Stake of* (or in) *Zion* (a stake in the "tent of Zion").

(2) In mining, a *staker* is an itinerant worker, and a *stake notice* is a declaration of a mining claim posted on a stake.

(3) Among loggers, *stakey* describes someone with enough money to be itchy to get to town, and *stake-bound* is being well-off enough to quit your job.

COMBINATIONS: *stake horse* (a horse tethered by a stake); *stake-broke* (a horse accustomed to being staked); *stake pin* (a picket pin for a horse); *stake rope* (what a Texan calls a *picket rope*); *staking ground* (what teamsters called the space near a wagon where horses were staked).

STAKED PLAIN A wide treeless plain, perhaps so barren that you had to mark the trail across it with stakes; sometimes called a *staked prairie*. The celebrated Staked Plain was the Llano Estacado of Texas and New Mexico, 40,000 square miles of barrenness and even larger in the tales told about crossing it.

STAMP AX Among loggers, an ax for *log-branding*. Also called a *branding ax*.

STAMP IRON Any **BRANDING IRON** with a brand forged at the business end, as opposed to a **RUNNING IRON**, which is adaptable for writing any brand whatever.

STAMPEDE NOUNS: (1) What every open-range cowman feared, especially on a trail drive—a blind, lurching, crashing takeoff of cattle (or, for that matter, horses or buffalo). It was always serious trouble and sometimes disaster. The animals would run until they were worn out, which damaged their condition for the trail drive and seriously reduced their weight and thus their value for market. They also got broken bones, got trampled, got lost, and got drowned.

Anything could and did start a stampede, 1,000-pound critters being afraid not only of jackrabbits but nearly anything that moved. The most frequent causes were storms. It happened suddenly: "The remarkable thing about it," said the veteran cattleman Charles Goodnight, "was that the whole herd started instantly, jarring the earth like an earthquake." The hands tried to keep them from getting clear to hell and gone by getting alongside the leaders and turning them into a circle, using up their furious energy running around and around on safe ground, instead of having them end up in the river or off the top of a mesa. Some cowboys, though, believed that the best strategy was to get in front of them, make yourself the leader, and gradually slow down. Riding hell for leather to catch the leaders or in front of them, often at night, was risky business and killed many a hand.

The stampedes of buffalo were formidable—5,000 and 10,000 beasts half again the size of cows on the rampage, utterly unstoppable, a force of nature.

Now that cattle are tended by people from birth, not allowed to get wild and **SNORTY** off by themselves and mostly kept within fences, the stampede is primarily a danger of the past.

(2) A charge of gold miners to new *diggings* was called a stampede. Such stampedes were a subject of much hilarity, even among the miners themselves. This joke comes down to us:

"A miner came to the pearly gates and asked for permission to enter. But St. Peter said heaven couldn't stand another miner. Why, just the week before the critters were breaking up the pavement of the gold streets with picks and assaying their harps.

"So the miner proposed a bargain: If he would get rid of these trouble-makers, would St. Peter let him stay in heaven? Agreed.

"By the end of the day came a stampede of miners, lickety-split, for the lower place. At its end came the miner who made the bargain with St. Peter, his gear packed and headed out. St. Peter asked in amazement how the fellow managed to get all the miners to leave voluntarily. The fellow said he'd just started a rumor that someone had struck color in hell. St. Peter chuckled, but went on to ask why the miner himself was packed up and headed south. 'Well,' drawled the fellow, 'you never know.'"

(3) Stampede is one of the early words for **RODEO**, as in Calgary Stampede.

(4) A *stampeder* may be an animal prone to start stampedes, a horse inclined to run off blindly, a man who causes a stampede or who simply takes part in one, or a miner who rushes into a new mineral area.

VERBS: (6) To set off on a flight, whether you're a critter or a person; to cause a stampede, a common technique of horse thieves both Indian and Anglo; to rush into anything, as to *stampede into marriage*. (6) To *stampede to the wild bunch* meant to go on the dodge, to cast your lot with outlaws.

Often pronounced stom-PEDE by old-timers, the word comes from the Spanish *estampida*. Early forms of the word in American English were *stampedo*, *stampido*, and *stampado*.

STAND (1) What **BUFFALO RUNNERS** called an episode of shooting into a herd. Interested only in quantity of kill, the runners would approach and shoot undetected from downwind. Some authorities say the leaders were killed first. Often the beasts would not pay attention to the disturbance and would stand until the hunter had felled as many as twenty or thirty animals. Some stands are said to have run into the hundreds. And thus were the great herds decimated.

(2) A stallion's breeding efforts; the place where he is available for breeding. In verb form, such a stallion is said to be *standing at stud*. Not a Westernism but now most common in the West.

STAND HITCHED This is what a well-trained horse will do when the reins are dropped—stand as if hitched to the ground. (See also **GROUND-HITCHED**.) Also, how you should act when a gun is pointed at you.

STAND PAT In **POKER**, to accept your hand the way it was dealt the first time. What you keep is called a *pat hand*. Figuratively, to stick where you are or with what you've got.

STANDARD EVENT The Professional Rodeo Cowboy's Association recognizes five standard events: **BAREBACK RIDING, BULLDOGGING, BULL RIDING, CALF ROPING,** and **SADDLE-BRONC RIDING**.

STANDING FEED What a cowman calls grass and hay still growing.

STANDOFF A situation in which neither side has the upper hand. The term comes from card gambling.

STAPLE A device used to nail **BARBWIRE** to a fence post, U-shaped and sturdy. in Texas, it's called a *steeple*.

STAR A patch of white on a horse's forehead. Stars, blazes, and stockings are among the markings most commonly used to identify horses. Also a term for a **FOUR DIRECTIONS** wheel of the Indians.

STAR CANDLE A candle of stearine, an army-issue candle when George Armstrong Custer was on the Plains. Also called an *adamantine candle*.

STAR ROWEL A **ROWEL** made of just five or six points and thus likely to be rough on the horse.

STARGAZER Said of a horse that goes around with his head high in the air, and not said kindly. Often the result of the trainer being rough with the bit.

STAR-GAZING Among the **NAVAJOS**, divining or diagnosing sicknesses by studying the celestial bodies. Similar practices are **HAND-TREMBLING** and *crystal-gazing*.

STAR-PITCH To bivouac, to sleep outside without a tent or other covering.

START A BRONC To **BREAK A HORSE**; to give an unbroke horse its first ride, often a hair-raising experience for mount and rider.

STARTER (1) A batch of **SOURDOUGH** used to set new dough fermenting. (2) A logger who gets logs started downstream on the first spring rise. (3) *For a starter* or *as a starter* means as a beginning, as in "He gave me twenty bucks for a starter." The first uses of these expressions are Western.

STAR-TOTER An officer of the law, so called from his badge.

STARVED RAT A small hare *(Ochotona princeps)* of the Rocky Mountains; also called a *pika, coney,* or *rock rabbit.*

STARVE-OUT A horse pasture without water and grass. Hands used to pen horses there overnight to make them easy to catch in the morning. Perhaps this word gave birth to the term *starve-out ranch* in Elmer Kelton's novel *The Man Who Rode Midnight,* meaning a ranch short on water and grass.

STATES Short for the United States. In the early West, it meant the settled half of the country as opposed to the unsettled West. The settled areas were divided into states, but most of the West hadn't even been made into territories. Until 1846, the Southwest was Mexico, and the Northwest was disputed with Britain. Thus a trapper in the Rockies or a fur trader on the Pacific shore would speak of heading back to the States.

COMBINATIONS: *States blood* (genes from the eastern United States introduced into the **MUSTANG** line), *States cattle* (also called *pilgrims* and *barnyard stock;* cows from the eastern United States as opposed to the native longhorns), *States eggs* (eggs from the eastern United States; in early frontier days, chickens were few, and eggs had to be shipped out from the settled areas), *States fruit* (also called *hen fruit;* the same as States eggs).

STATION (1) A **STAGE STATION.** (2) In the latter eighteenth century on the frontier of Kentucky, Tennessee, and the Old Northwest, a residence (usually of several families) fortified against Indians. (3) In mining, a landing place at different levels of a mine.

COMBINATIONS: *station agent* (the fellow in charge of a stage station), *station drink* (the drink, evidently free, a stage driver was entitled to at each station), *station house* (a stage station), *station keeper* (on the Oregon Trail, a station agent).

STEAL (1) For a ewe to give birth to a lamb out of season. Her offspring is called a *stolen lamb.* (2) In **POKER,** to *steal a pot* is to bluff a player with a better hand into folding. (3) To *steal a start,* in the old days, meant for a cowboy to get enough **MAVERICKS** (or otherwise pilfer enough calves) to start his own herd and become a cowman.

STEAMER DAY In San Francisco, from the 1850s, people called the day before the next steamship sailed for the States *steamer day,* a big day for merchants, bankers, and other businessmen to settle bills. Later, in Virginia City, Nevada, it was extended to mean any Monday, when businessmen were supposed to make good on their contracts.

STEELHEAD A large, ocean-going trout (*Salmo gairdneri* or *S. irideus*) of the Pacific Coast. Some say the name comes from its color, others from the hardness of its head.

STEER A male bovine that's been castrated. Not a Westernism but a term whose significance seems mostly lost outside cattle country. Steers are what you raise for beef. Cutting (castrating) them rechannels their energy away from fighting and fornicating, making them easier to handle and their meat more flavorful. A *feeder steer,* in cow business lingo, is one raised for beef and sold to a feedlot man for fattening for slaughter; a *blackjack steer* is a skinny critter from timber country ; a *bulling steer* is a castrated animal that nevertheless has some sexual odor and draws other steers; a *lead steer* was the one who got at the head of a trail drive and led 'em out; a *rough steer* is a runt with a poor bloodline.

Steer busting is roping and throwing steers singlehandedly. You ride up on the left side of the beast, rope its horns, loop your rope around its right hip and around its hind end, and then ride off sharply to the left, jerking the critter off its feet. There are many **RODEO** events featuring steers: *steer roping* or *single steer tying* (the horse throws the steer and the cowboy ties its feet with a *pigging string*), *steer wrestling* (**BULLDOGGING**), *steer decorating* (a gentler form of bulldogging, usually a ladies event, in which a ribbon is grabbed off of the steer's back).

STELLER'S DUCK In Alaska, an eider duck. COMBINATIONS: *Steller's jay, Steller's eider, Steller's sea cow,* and *Steller's sea lion,* all Alaskan.

STETSON The most popular brand of broad-brimmed hat in the West—so popular that, like Colt and Winchester for handguns and rifles, it became a generic name for *hat.* What someone called a Stetson might be another brand. Now the principal alternatives to the Stetson brand are American Hat, Bailey, and Resistol.

Official Stetsons, familiarly called John B.s or J.B.s, were made by John B. Stetson of Philadelphia from 1865 onward. The model most popular with cowboys in the early days was the Carlsbad; the first Western style was the Boss, another the high and wide Buckeye. A Stetson cowboy model cost almost as much as boots, ten to twenty bucks or more. (When you consider that in those days a hand probably made thirty dollars a month, the price of head cover was substantial.) But you needed a hat: It kept the sun out of your eyes and off your neck. It was an umbrella. It gave you a bucket (the crown) to water your horse and a cup (the brim) to water yourself. It made a hell of a fan, which you need sometimes for a fire but more often to shunt cows this direction or that.

Stetsons (and Western hats generally) were and are made of felt, which is in turn made from wool or animal fur, especially beaver fur. Stetsons are made from beaver, rabbit, and hare fur. The more beaver in it, the more durable and resistant to weather the hat is. Stetson indicates the amount of beaver with *Xs*—100 percent beaver being 20X. Stetsons now range from $70 to ten times that much. They're supposed to stand up to a terrific beating—they're not even broken in until they've been trampled in the mud and manure by horses—and should last halfway to forever.

Of course, Western hats were and are sometimes for show (for example, Dallas stockbrokers wear them to work). In that case they're likely to be decorated with a band of some sort, woven horsehair, snakeskin, concha-studded leather, BEADWORK, QUILLWORK, or whatever, even fancy concoctions from pheasant feathers.

An important consideration for show is the shape. Old-timers used to be able to tell where a hand was from by the shape of his hat. These days the most popular is the *rancher* or *cattleman crease*, dented straight down the middle and on both sides, the crease flat from front to back. Newly popular is the *Gus crease* or *Montana slope*, named after the one worn by the character Gus in the television miniseries *Lonesome Dove*. It's a modification of the *Montana peak*, in which the crown stands high and is creased sharply from the top toward the front brim. Many hands like the *rodeo crease, the bullrider's crease* (which used to be called the *RCA crease*, for Rodeo Cowboys of America), the *quarter horse crease* and the *tycoon*, with a pinched front.

But you can be a cowboy without a cowboy hat. A popular joke tells of a cowboy and a tourist in Jackson Hole. The tourist saw some hands moving cows along a highway and noticed one was wearing a baseball cap. Curious, this greenhorn pulled up alongside the rider and asked why he wasn't wearing a cowboy hat. The cowboy tugged at his cap brim and, perhaps thinking of pheasant feathers, replied, "Don' wanna look like a goddam truck driver."

Not all broad-brimmed, Western hats were or are cowboy hats: see also BEAVER, KOSSUTH HAT, RESERVATION HAT, SLOUCH HAT.

STICK EARS Cowboy talk for cows that have been EARMARKED.

STICK HORSE A horse that doesn't want to work and has to be forced.

STICK LIKE A POSTAGE STAMP What a good BRONC RIDER does on a bucking horse.

STICKY ROPE What a cowboy calls a RUSTLER, because his rope has a way of sticking to other men's cows.

STIFF (1) A corpse. (2) A *stiff man*—a fellow who burned carcasses on the range. (3) An important person, especially a self-important person, a MUCKAMUCK; also spelled *mucky-muck*. Perhaps this usage stems from the stiffness of the fronts of their BOILED SHIRTS. (4) Among loggers, a word for a white-collar worker. (5) A laboring man. Thus *hard rock stiff* (a miner), a *shovel stiff* (a laborer with a shovel), *saddle stiff* (a cowboy), *lumber stiff* and BINDLE STIFF (both terms for a logger). This word sometimes appears to mean simply "person," as in *working stiff* (any worker). It is also a hobo's word for hobo, and a *mission stiff* is, wonderfully, a bum who goes to a mission and pretends to get religion in order to get food and a bed.

STINGER (1) A Johnson bar, the back, handheld bar of a **FRESNO** (a wheel-barrow-like device for building earth dams). When it kicks, it stings like hell. (2) What loggers call the part of a logging truck that sticks out behind the trailer's wheels.

STINKY HEAD In Alaska, an **ESKIMO** food made by putting salmon heads into a pit about two feet deep, covering them with mud, and letting them age from ten days to two weeks.

STIRRUP The support for the rider's foot that hangs from the saddle tree. Though stirrup is a very old word in English, elements of the Western stirrup were distinctive: the stirrups of the early range were big affairs carved from a single piece of wood; they were called **OXBOWS** or sometimes **DOGHOUSE STIRRUPS**. Later the wooden bar that went beneath the instep was wrapped in rawhide and still later was made of steel. Western-ers often wore and wear their stir-rups with **TAPADEROS**, covers for the front part of the boot, open at the back.

Dog-house stirrups.
[FROM *Moseman's Illustrated Guide for Purchasers of Horse Furnishing Goods*, CA. 1892.]

COMBINATIONS: **DROP STIRRUP** (a leather loop dropped below the stirrup for short riders to use to get a leg up); **HOBBLED STIRRUPS** (stirrups linked beneath the horse's belly with a strap; though they make it easier to stay on a bucking horse, they're dangerous, and good riders are scornful of them); *stirrup hood* (a *tapadero*); *stirrup iron* (the part of the stirrup that goes beneath the foot and supports it; in the early West it wasn't made of metal see above), *stirrup leather* (also called by the Spanish word **ACION**, the leather straps that hang from the saddle framework and support the stirrup iron).

STOCK Short for *livestock,* which in the West usually means cows, sheep, or horses rather than other critters raised for market.

COMBINATIONS: *stock buyer* (at one time a man who bought draft animals for stage lines; now a cattle buyer for the big packing houses); *stock car* (a railway car for shipping cows and other livestock to market, which became a huge business on the Great Plains in the decades after the Civil War); *stock corral* (a pen for horses, cows, or sheep); *stock country* (any land more fit for grazing than tilling, especially the grasslands of the Great Plains); *stock inspector* (a person who checks brands to make sure stock is being transported or sold legally, also called a **BRAND INSPECTOR**); *stock law* (the body of law governing the stock-raising industry);

stocker (a calf being raised for slaughter, not yet a *feeder*); *stockman, stockraiser, stock grower,* or *stock rancher* (the raisers and breeders of cattle, horses, or sheep, not farmers or dairymen), *stock tank* (a big container on the range for water for the stock to drink, usually supplied by a well), *stock train* (a railroad train of stock cars); *stock water* (water for the stock to drink, in the West often in stock tanks or reservoirs, in contrast with irrigation water), *stockyard* (a pen where cows are held for shipping or for slaughter).

STOCK CONTRACTOR A person who provides the stock for a **RODEO**—bucking horses, calves for roping, bulls to ride, and steers to bulldog. He may also be the rodeo producer.

STOCK GROWERS' ASSOCIATION An organization of cattlemen formed to protect what they saw and see as their rights. Such associations began to spring up after the first great trail drives after the Civil War. They sought to keep "their" range for themselves, to fight against **RUSTLERS**, to coordinate **ROUNDUPS**, to get recognition of their **BRANDS**, in some areas to keep **TEXAS FEVER** out, and to face other common problems. Eventually they hired brand inspectors and stock detectives. Tom Horn was a *stock detective* for the Wyoming Stock Growers' Association when he was convicted and hanged in 1903 for the bushwhacking of Willie Nickell, the teenage son of a sheepman.

In the days of the open range, the associations often fought against what homesteaders and small ranchers saw as their rights. One result of such conflict was the Johnson County War, in which the powerful Wyoming Stock Growers' Association in 1892 went against the small ranchers of Johnson County, thought to be **MAVERICKERS**.

Because stockmen continue to have common interests and problems, their associations still exist. Sometimes they're called *cattlemen's associations, stockmen's associations,* or *stock grazers' associations.*

STOCK HORSE A cow pony, one trained for the chores on a ranch. In cow country, a horse traditionally is not only any equine but in particular a grown male horse. Females are designated *mare* or *filly*; a *colt* is a young male. Mares were generally unwelcome on the range as saddle horses in the early days because they might be in heat.

DESCRIPTIVE TERMS FOR HORSES: *barn sour* (one in a hurry to get back to the barn), *camp staller* (one resistant to starting out), **CINCH BINDER** (a bucking horse that rears up on its hind legs and falls over backward), **CLEAR-FOOTED** (agile of foot), **CLOUD HUNTER** (a horse that rears and paws), *cloud watcher* (a horse that holds its head too high), *cold collar* (a balky horse), *cold-blooded* (not pure-bred), *cold-jawed* (a horse with a hard or insensitive mouth), *cold-shouldered* (one that is newly harnessed and balky), **COON-FOOTED** (one whose rear feet aren't straight; long and low-pastered), **CRIBBER** (a horse in the habit of sucking on wood), **CROW BAIT** (a worthless horse), **DEAD-MOUTHED** or **HARD-MOUTHED** (insensitive to the bit), *halter puller* (a horse in the habit of pulling back on the halter rope), *halter-shy, man-killer* (a vicious horse), **OUTLAW,** *pie biter* (one that snoops in the chuck wagon), *puller* (one that pulls eagerly on the bit), **RIPPER** (a big horse with plenty of endurance), *second saddle* (a bronc buster's name for a horse that has been ridden twice), **SHADOW JUMPER** (a skittish horse), **SKATE** (a lousy horse), *snorter* (an excitable horse), **SNORTY** (a high-spirited horse), **SUGAR EATER** (a pampered horse), **SWITCH TAIL** (a nervous horse), **WATERMELON UNDER THE SADDLE** (one that arches its back a lot), **WIDOW MAKER** (an outlaw horse), **WRINGTAIL** (a nervous horse).

OTHER TERMS FOR PHYSICAL CHARACTERISTICS OF HORSES: **CALF-LEGS** (a short-legged horse), **CHAPO** (a short-coupled horse), *close-coupled* (short-bodied), *cow-hocked* (with legs nearly touching at the hocks), *ewe-necked* (with a bowed neck), *fiddle-foot* (with dancing or nervous feet), *fiddle-headed* (with an ugly head), **LIGHT IN THE TIMBER** (light-boned in the lower legs), **GOTCH EAR** (with a drooping ear), **MOON-EYED** (glassy white eye), *mule-footed* (round-hoofed), *mule-hipped* (with hips sloping too much), *nigger-heeled* (the opposite of pigeon-toed in front), *parrot-mouth* (with buck teeth), **PUDDING FOOT** (big-footed, clumsy), *rat-tailed* (with a thin tail), *snipe-gutted* (with a slender barrel), *tender* (saddle-sore or sore-footed), **WHEY-BELLY** (big-gutted).

TERMS FOR HORSES THAT DO JOBS: *brush horse* (good in the brush), **BUFFALO RUNNER,** *calf horse* (a roper), *circle horse* (one used to ride circle), **DINK** (a horse poor for roping or bulldogging), **GUT TWISTER** (a good bucking horse), *night horse* (one good for night use), *peg pony* or *pegger* (a horse with unusual ability to change directions), *rimrocker* (one surefooted in rough rimrock), *roper* or *rope horse, snub horse* (a horse used to snub buckers at a rodeo), **SUNDAY HORSE** (one for show), *swimming horse* (a horse to cross rivers on), *whittler* (a good cutter), *winter horse* (one kept at the main ranch for winter riding), *wrangle horse* (a horse for bringing up the cavvy).

(See also **CUTTING HORSE, MUSTANG, SHAVETAIL.** For horse colors, see **BUCKSKIN.** For terms for unfit horses, see **CANNER.** For names for saddle horses, see **COW HORSE.**)

STOCK SADDLE The Western stock saddle is different from the English riding saddle, which Western riders used to refer to derisively as a **POSTAGE STAMP.** The principal difference is the high **HORN,** which the cowboy uses for *dallying* or *tying hard and fast* when he ropes. Bruce Grant, in *How to Make Cowboy Horse Gear,* lists the parts of the Western saddle as a *tree* (frame), the seat, the **CANTLE,** the horn, the swell and gullet, the front jockey and back jockey, skirt, fender (or **ROSADERO**), **STIRRUPS,** stirrup-leathers, **CINCH** rings, **LATIGO,** conchas, and tie-strings.

Stock saddles were and are usually named for the maker or the shape of the tree. Common Western saddles are the **ASSOCIATION**, California, **CHARRO**, Conestoga, eight-string (an ordinary work saddle, whose leathers are secured with eight sets of strings), Great Plains (or Texas Trail), McClellan, Mother Hubbard, Pony Express, Santa Fe (a mountain-man saddle), and Spanish. For rigging, see **SINGLE-RIG**. In the old days you could tell where a rider hailed from by the way his saddle was rigged.

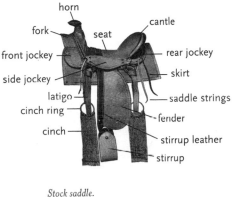

Stock saddle.

[FROM *Moseman's Illustrated Guide for Purchasers of Horse Furnishing Goods,* CA. 1892.]

STOGIE (1) A cheap cigar. The people from Lancaster County, Pennsylvania, rolled the local tobacco into cigars, and some smokers drove **CONESTOGA** wagons. Thus the cigar got called a *Conestogie,* which was shortened to *stogie.*

(2) What cowboys used to call cheap boots. Both are also spelled *stogy* and *stoga.*

STONE ON THE CHEST A miner's name for tuberculosis, the disease he fears.

STONE-BOILING Among Indian peoples, heating stones in a fire and dropping them into food in a hide container as a method of cooking.

STOOL PIGEON Among gamblers, a **CAPPER** for a **FARO** bank; any shill or gambler's decoy.

STOOL-AND-BUCKET COW What a cowboy may call a cooperative milk cow.

STORE TOBACCO In the middle period of the Far West, many items available from merchants were referred to as *store this* and *store that,* as opposed to home-made—*store boots, store candy, store cheese, store dress, store goods, store medicine, store pants, store sugar, store teeth,* and so on. Tobacco in the earlier days was **KINNIKINNICK** or came from traders, either in *twists* (long pieces thicker than a thumb twisted around themselves) or *plugs* (bricklike hunks).

STORM CELLAR The south-central Plains and prairies, northern Texas, Oklahoma, parts of Kansas, and Arkansas are **TWISTER** (tornado) country, and many houses are outfitted with outside cellars with doors low to the ground for protection against such storms. Also called a *fraidy hole,* which could also be a cave.

STORM PORCH In Alaska, a small porch shielding the front door of a house; also called an *arctic entrance* or a *storm shed.*

STORM THE PUNCHEONS One of the old-time cowboy's figures of speech for dancing. In pioneer days, many floors were made of **PUNCHEONS**, and the cowboy's style of dancing was often vigorous to a fault. (See also **SHINDIG**.)

STOVE UP Beaten up, worn out, banged up, damaged. Often said of an old cowboy who has **PEELED** (broke) too many **BRONCS** in the rough, old way, which makes old men out of young ones in a hurry.

STRADDLE BUG Three boards put up in tripod form to mark a land or mining **CLAIM**.

STRAIGHT BUCK A horse's buck that's straight ahead, without twists, turns, or curlicues. A horse that does this is said to be *bucking straight away,* and however vigorous he may be, he's comparatively easy to ride.

STRAIGHT GOODS The truth. The usage seems to appear in print first in a story by Western novelist Owen Wister—"I'm givin' yu' straight goods, yu' see."

STRAIGHT-COLORED HORSE A solid-colored horse like a **BUCKSKIN** or **SORREL**, traditionally the preference of the cowboy. This preference is quite possibly ethnocentric; such horses were what Westerners called **AMERICAN HORSES**, brought out from the East. Multicolored horses, such as **PAINTS**, **PINTOS**, and **APPALOOSAS**, are descendants of **MUSTANGS** (ultimately of the Spanish Barb) and bear a negative association with Indians.

STRAINER (1) A tree, often a fir, whose position on the riverbank was so undercut it fell into the river and floated downstream; also called a *sifter*. Such trees constitute a significant hazard to boatmen on western rivers, whether the tree is still floating or has run aground somewhere, often on a sandbar. In the Pacific Northwest such a tree still clinging with its roots to the bank is called a *sweeper*. (See also **SAWYER, PLANTER**.)

(2) Also the part of the **SADDLE TREE** (the framework of a saddle) that supports the middle, where the rider sits. It is galvanized iron and is covered with leather.

STRANGITE A follower of J. J. Strang, who laid claim to leadership of the **LATTER-DAY SAINTS** church after Joseph Smith died in Illinois. Strang led his group to Beaver Island in Lake Michigan. Their beliefs were called *Strangism*.

STRANGLER A **VIGILANTE**, so named because he enforced his opinions with ropes around the neck. That made the victim do what was called the *strangulation jig*. Some vigilance committees were even named the Stranglers. (See also **STRING PARTY**.)

STRAPPED ON HIS HORSE TOES DOWN Sent home dead. Adams points out that since a loose horse would usually find its way home, it could be used in a range war to send a message, the body of its rider. (See also **DRY-GULCH**.)

STRAW BOSS A ranch foreman who works under the superintendent; any boss who's second dog to the top boss.

STRAY A cow that has wandered from its range. (Wandering horses were called *stray horses*, not just strays.) Such critters were sought out by *reps*, *stray hands*, or *stray men*, riders assigned to visit ranges or especially roundups outside their outfit's usual territory and bring back strays.

STRETCH OUT (1) An expression used by traders and freighters meaning to get the caravan going. (2) To stretch a critter out is for two cowhands to rope it by the horns and hind feet and stretch its legs out. It's now standard practice in team roping in **RODEO**. (3) To *stretch the blanket* is to **STUFF DUDES**, tell a windy, spin a tall tale or **YARN**.

STRETCHING FRAME A square of wooden poles devised by trappers to hold buffalo skins while hair was scraped from them.

STRIKE (1) A sudden discovery of valuable ore or oil. (2) In verb form, to come upon a vein, to hit oil or pay dirt. This use appears to have originated during the California gold rush, as did the expression *strike it rich*, meaning to get great wealth suddenly. (3) The expression to *strike camp*, meaning to take down and pack the camping gear, also appears to be originally Western.

STRING (1) The group of horses assigned to a cowboy by his outfit. A cowboy's *string* was essential. Typically it comprised four to six mounts or more—a *circle horse*, **CUTTING HORSE**, *roping horse*, and *night horse* plus one or two **BRONCOS** who were learners. The string belonged completely to the cowboy it was assigned to—he was responsible for it, and it was hands off to everyone else. Outfits kept strings together from each rider to his successor. The new cowboy was never told anything about the horses in the string—the assumption was that he rode well enough to need no advice. If a cowboy *broke his string* by losing a horse or getting one hurt, that was a bad omen. For the boss to break the string by assigning one of the horses to someone else was the same as telling the cowboy to find another job.

(2) A cowboy's rope (called a *skin string* when made of rawhide). (3) A leather tie on a saddle. (4) Among loggers, a group of logs floated downstream together. (5) Among miners, a fuse. (6) Among trappers, twelve traps, the usual number one man would tend.

COMBINATIONS: to *string a greener* is to play a joke on a **DUDE**; to *string a whizzer* is to **STUFF DUDES**, tell a *windy*, a *stringer*, spin a tall tale ; to *string them out* on a trail drive is to get the cattle off the **BED GROUND** and onto the trail.

STRING PARTY A hanging. Other expressions for this fate: *to be guest of honor at a string* (or *necktie*) *party, be a cottonwood blossom, decorate a cottonwood, die in a horse's nightcap, die with throat trouble, gurgle on a rope, do a midair dance, do a strangulation jig, get exalted, get dressed in a hemp four-in-hand, get hemp fever, get used to trim a tree, gone up, gurgle on a rope,* *look through cottonwood leaves,* **LOOK UP A LIMB,** *ride under a cottonwood limb, telegraph him home, do a Texas cakewalk, stretch hemp, string up.*

STRINGHALT A disorder of horses' nerves that makes their hocks swell and leaves them with an awkward, pigeonlike walk.

STRIPPER (1) A person who skins the hides from buffalo or cattle. (2) A dry cow or a heifer. (3) People trying to get land in the Cherokee Strip were also called strippers. (4) In **FARO** or **POKER,** strippers are cards trimmed for cheating.

STRONGER THAN THE NUTS An expression for a gambling game tilted excessively in favor of the dealer or house. The nuts meant the shell of the old shell game, so the implication is, less honest even than the shell game.

STROUD A wool cloth common as a trade item in the **FUR TRADE** and known for its bright colors. It was named for Stroud, Gloucester, where it was made. Also called *strouding.*

STUB In logging, the trunk of a tree broken off to about twenty feet or less, standing bare of leaves and branches. (See also **SNAG.**)

STUB-HORN An old bull of many fights whose horns are now chipped down. Also said of battle-scarred men.

STUD A stud horse, a stallion, a male horse kept for breeding, so not **CUT** (castrated). Now his owner gets a stud fee for his *covering* (copulating with) a mare. Western Indians are said to have preferred studs as war horses because they had lots of aggressiveness. Because studs are a nuisance to mares and to their riders, Anglos usually prefer to ride geldings. The term is applied by extension to young, virile men.

STUDEBAKER A well-known freight wagon of the Plains first built by the Studebaker Brothers in 1852. (See also **MURPHY, CONESTOGA.**)

STUFFED SHIRT A man of pompous, overformal manner, which in the West included most Easterners. *Stuffed-shirtism* meant the tendency to such qualities.

STUFFING DUDES The time-honored practice of having a little fun with **GREENERS** by telling them tall tales. It comes naturally in the West, where half of what's real is so crazy or spectacular that **DUDES** can hardly believe what they're seeing. So the old-timers **STRING** them along with stories like this one from David Lavender's fine memoir *One Man's West:*

> When a greenhorn ventured that it was cold, often a safe conversational opening, an old hand replied, "I wouldn't say so. Now when it gets so that a man rides along whistlin' to himself and the whistle don't make any noise on account of freezing solid and fallin' to the ground as fast as it comes out, then it is cold. You'll notice it in the spring," he said. "The woods sound like a steam calliope loose and the stops tied down—all them frozen whistles thawin' out and poppin' off. It spooks the mules considerable and the first few days. For a fact," he said, solemn as an owl.

A tall tale is also called a **YARN**, *windy,* **STRINGER,** *corral dust,* and in the Pacific Northwest a **NORTHWESTER.** To tell one is to *string a whizzer, stretch the blanket, load,* and among loggers *build a high line.*

STUMP SUCKER See **CRIBBER.**

STUMPAGE In logging, standing timber; the value of standing timber; the right to cut it. Such wood is said to be *worth so much at* or *in the stump,* meaning as it stands, unfelled. A *stump detective* is a person who calculates the amount of waste in standing timber.

SUBLETTE'S CUTOFF A shortcut on the **OREGON TRAIL** from the west side of Wyoming's South Pass to Bear River and the Fort Bridger–Fort Hall trail. Though it saved more than fifty miles, some emigrants avoided it because thirty of them were waterless. Also called the *Sublette Road* and *Greenwood's Cutoff. Sublette's Lake* was the trappers' name for Yellowstone Lake, discovered by William Sublette in 1826.

SUBSISTENCE FISHING In Alaska, fishing for food for consumption rather than for sale. An equivalent is *subsistence hunting,* a contrast, *commercial fishing.*

SUCK LICK A **SALT LICK** that's liquid enough to drink, which some Western licks were in wet weather. Also called simply a *suck.*

SUCKLEY'S SALMON TROUT A fish first found in the Coeur d'Alene range, named after American surgeon Dr. George Suckley. Also *Suckley's gull,* found in Puget Sound.

SUDADERO (soo-duh-DAIR-roh) The leather lining of a **SADDLE**'s skirt. It's not the same as a **ROSADERO,** which is attached to the stirrup leathers, though the sudadero is sometimes used that way. Borrowed from Spanish (in which it means "sweat cloth").

SUGAN (SOO-guhn) A heavy blanket or comforter homemade from patchwork materials; the mainstay of the cowboy's bedroll. Also spelled *soogan, soogin, suggan, sugin,* and *sougan.* Evidently adapted from an Irish term.

SUGAR PINE A pine of the Pacific Coast (*Pinus lambertiana*) whose gum is said to taste like sugar mixed with turpentine.

SUICIDE GUN A pistol hardly big enough to irritate a man, such as a .32-caliber. A rancher considering carrying such a gun once is said to have asked his foreman what would happen if the rancher shot the foreman with the little thing. The hand answered that, if he noticed it, he'd up and whup his boss.

SUICIDE HORSE What a cowboy calls a horse that goes crazy when anyone tries to ride it, that bucks in any direction and into anything. So called because it's likely to kill itself.

SUITCASE RANCHER A man who owns a ranch but lives elsewhere and only visits. Suitcase ranchers have been in the West as long as ranching has. Many owners of ranches on the Great Plains in the 1870s and 1880s were Britons and Scots looking for big profits. The winter of '87, with its huge DIE-UPS, inhibited their adventuring. In the 1960s and 1970s, some suitcase ranchers were stars of the entertainment industry who bought cattle ranches as tax hedges. In the 1980s and '90s the source of resentment was ranchers from Japan.

Local people see suitcase ranchers as involved in ranching mainly for reasons of finance, not reasons of emotion, lifestyle, and sense of connection with the land, so lacking in motive to be conservators and stewards.

SULL To act sullen. It is said especially of a cow that, regardless of a cowboy's cajoling, pleading, or provocation, absolutely refuses to move. This, and not cattleman-sheepman conflicts, may be what should be called a *range war*.

SUMMER RANGE Grazing land for cattle or sheep that is appropriate for use in the summer. It's likely to be in country that's deep in snow during the winter and a long trail drive or truck ride from the main ranch.

SUMMER TENT A summer shelter of TIPI-dwelling Indians. When these Indians found their tipis cumbersome in the summer, they would use temporary shelters of branches and poles set in a semicircle and covered with hides or blankets. (See also RAMADA.)

SUN DANCE A central religious ceremony of about two dozen tribes of PLAINS INDIANS, especially the DAKOTA, CHEYENNE, and ARAPAHO. The name *Sun Dance* is Anglo, though most Indians now keeping the practice use it. The Dakota originally called it the *sun-gazing dance;* the Cheyenne, the *medicine lodge ceremony;* and other tribes, the *thirsting dance* because participants did not drink during the actual four days of dancing.

The entire ceremony lasts about a week. It is held during the summer months, usually in July. The goal is to put the tribe in harmony with itself and with the spiritual powers (the dancers are not worshiping the sun).

Generally the ceremony follows this form: A tree is chosen, cut down (symbolically attacked), trimmed, and erected (with religious emblems attached) as the center pole of an arbor. An altar is made, featuring a buffalo skull and facing east. At the proper time, the men and women who have pledged themselves begin their four days of dancing, neither eating nor drinking, intermittently blowing eagle-bone whistles, and singing. A BERDACHE, or half man—half woman, may have a key role in preparation. The ceremony was historically understood as an act of the whole tribe, an expression of their oneness as a people. The dancers are expressing their awareness of the paramount importance of the common good.

Different tribes perform the ceremony in different ways. It is famous for one gesture of self-scourging: Some dancers permit skewers to be passed under the skin of the chest (or the back), then are tied by leather thongs to a pole, and rip out the skewers by leaning back against the thongs. Not all tribes accepted this *piercing* historically—it principally belonged to the Oglala Lakota—and some forbade it. Early missionaries and Indian agents were horrified by it and had the ceremony itself officially banned for a long time. Today the Sun Dance is practiced among many Western tribes, and piercing continues among the LAKOTAS, CROWS, and some others.

SUN DOG A pale, rainbowlike spot in the winter sky, caused by sunlight illuminating ice crystals. Sun dogs are often a sign of impending weather change. James Willard Schultz indicates in *My Life as an Indian* that the BLACKFEET understood sun dogs to be warnings of approaching danger.

SUNDAY HORSE The horse a cowboy rides for dress-up or festive occasions. It likely has some style and some looks but may not be worth a damn for work. A counterpart of Sunday-go-to-meeting clothes (which is not a Westernism).

SUNDAY SCHOOL Among loggers, a poker game. They worked six days and played cards on Sunday.

SUNDOWN A way of describing the Pacific Coast country, as in reference to Oregon as a *sundown land*. It sometimes simply meant further west. To emigrate to the West was sometimes expressed as to *seek a home beyond sundown*. A *sundowner* was a man headed west to stay ahead of the law.

SUNFISH A way of BUCKING. The horse throws its middle violently to one side, then the other, so that it seems its shoulder may touch the ground and the critter *sun its belly*. Such a horse is called a *sunfisher*.

SUNSET TRAIL A figure of speech for the death of an individual or a group. The Indians of the West, being pushed aside by Anglos, were sometimes said to be on the sunset trail, headed for extinction. (For other Western words and phrases for death, see CASH IN YOUR CHIPS.)

SUPREME BEING What loggers called their superintendent, no doubt behind his back. Also known as *brass nuts, big bull, big savage, bigwig, enemy, gaffer, governor, grandpa, skipper, uncle,* and *walking boss*.

SURCINGLE A strap that goes around a horse's belly. Used as an added precaution to hold a saddle on or for riding with stirrups but no saddle. The term did not originate in the West. (See also CINCH.)

SURE AS SHOOTING Damn sure, as in, "That bear is sure as shooting going to make dinner out of us."

SURE CURE A remedy that won't fail. Often used in a jocular way, as a cowboy might say that getting your teeth punched out is a sure cure for cavities. Mathews shows the first appearance of the phrase in print in the *Oregon State Journal* of Eugene, Oregon, in 1881.

SURF BUMP A deposit of calcium under the kneecap, from time spent kneeling on a surf board. See SURFING.

SURFACE COAL What a cowboy calls **BUFFALO CHIPS** or cow chips for the fire. Also called *surface fuel, prairie coal,* and *Babcock coal.*

SURFACE DIGGINGS In mining, diggings at or near the surface of the Earth. COMBINATIONS: *surface dirt* (ore-bearing dirt near the surface), *surface lead* (a vein of ore near the surface, with the implication that it doesn't go far into the Earth), *surface placer.*

SURFACE FIRE Among **FIREFIGHTERS**, a fire that moves along the forest floor, burning the *duff,* other surface litter, and small vegetation. Same as a **GROUND FIRE**. Its opposite is a **CROWN** fire.

SURFING Riding ocean waves on a rigid board, a recreation developed on the West Coast in the 1950s. It became hugely popular, developed worldwide competitions, and became an industry. COMBINATIONS: *surf bum, surf bunnie, surf dude, surf nazi, surf rebel; surf bumps* (a form of housemaid's knee); also *surf bird, surf clam, surf smelt, surf perch, surf whiting.*

SURROUND A way of hunting herds of game used primarily by Indians. The hunters encircled the animals, often antelope or buffalo, and herded them over a cliff or drove them into a hidden pen or other trap and shot them. Much Indian hunting was a way of getting a large quantity of meat for a large number of people as surely and efficiently as possible.

SUSTAINABLE A term describing an activity that can be continued indefinitely without destroying the resource. *Sustainable timber harvests* are thought to be of the size that will permit the forest to thrive and logging to continue indefinitely.

SUTLER A civilian who traded goods to soldiers on or near a military post. This was the fellow who sold necessities of life such as cloth, buttons, knives, and tobacco, plus whiskey, of course, and was licensed or otherwise approved by the commander, as opposed to the unlicensed fellow who sold whiskey and women at the **HOG RANCH**. The word "fell into disuse" in the mid-1800s, says memoirist Martha Summerhayes in *Vanished Arizona,* apparently in favor of *post trader.* And sometime later the sutler's store became the *post exchange.* The word *sutler* was not originally a Westernism.

SWAINSON'S HAWK A hawk (*Buteo swainsoni*) seen especially on the **GREAT PLAINS**, with a dark breast-band and white coloring underneath. William Swainson's name (he was a British naturalist) was also given to the Western (or Swainson's) warbling vireo (*Vireoslyva gilva swainsoni*).

SWALLOW ITS HEAD For a bucking horse to put its head and tail way down and arch the devil out of its back. (See also **BUCK**.)

SWAMP In logging, to clear underbrush away, make a place for a **SKID ROAD** and get trees out of the woods. A *swamper* is a worker who's low on the totem pole. In logging, he clears underbrush or trims trees for the **SAWYERS**. On a freighting team, he's the assistant to the **SKINNER**. In a cow camp, he helps

Sutler's store in Round Valley, California, 1876.
[COURTESY OF NATIONAL ARCHIVES (75-IP-2-7).]

the cook. On a river-rafting trip, he takes care of the camp. In a saloon, he does a little of everything.

SWAP ENDS What a bucking horse is said to do when he makes a quick half-circle, putting his hind end where his front was an instant ago. (See also **BUCK.**)

SWEAR OFF A promise to abstain, as in "This new year's resolution is going to be the big swear-off" (of booze).

SWEAT LODGE Among Western Indians, a low hut for a ritual of purification and to cure illness. In the nineteenth century the huts were framed of willow branches and were generally covered with hides, with exterior and interior fire pits and a low entrance facing east. Now they are covered with tarpaulins, rugs, and the like. The ritual varies from tribe to tribe and leader (known as a **POURER**) to leader. Usually water is thrown onto fire-heated rocks to create very hot steam, prayers are offered, and songs are sung. Normally the ritual takes place in several sessions, called *rounds,* with a short break between each. To lead such a ritual is called *to pour* because the leader pours the water on the rocks. Historically, the sweat lodge was also sometimes called a *sweat house* or *sweat tipi.*

SWEDE FIDDLE (1) What a cowboy calls an accordion. (2) What a logger calls a crosscut saw.

SWEENEY A trophy of a horse's shoulder muscles; a horse with that condition is said to be *sweenied.*

SWEET SAGE Among contemporary **PLAINS INDIANS**, a common plant of the Northern Plains (*Artemisia cana*) used for ceremonial purposes. For instance, the dirt floor of the sweat lodge is often covered with sweet sage.

SWEETGRASS A grass (*Torresia ordorata*) of the **NORTHERN PLAINS** often burned in rituals for purification or as a welcoming of the spirits. Wallace Black Elk writes in his book *Black Elk,* "Sweetgrass is Mother Earth's hair. It is a perfume. When my grandma's spirit comes she carries that smell, that perfume, and you can smell it. That's why we use the sweetgrass as a prayer at the altar."

SWEET-MOUTHED Said of a horse that's sensitive to the **BIT**; the same as *soft-mouthed* and opposite of *hard-mouthed* or *dead-mouthed.*

SWELL FORK On a **STOCK SADDLE**, projections on either side of the horn that a rider can press his knees under when the horse bucks; the opposite of a **SLICK FORK**.

SWIM THE HERD On a **TRAIL DRIVE**, to get the herd across a river. They could be ornery about going into rivers. Sometimes they went freely. Sometimes they'd follow the horse herd or a *swimming horse* (a horse chosen for its swimming ability) across. Sometimes they'd **SULL** and balk for days.

SWING Part of a trail herd, checked by the *swing riders.* Swing riders minded the trail herd from a position about a third of the way back from the **POINT** riders and in front of the **FLANK** riders.

SWING STATION A place on a stage line where the draft animals were changed. These stations were about ten or twelve miles apart and offered no services. Principal **STAGE STATIONS**, also called *home stations,* were usually about 50 miles apart.

SWINGDINGLE Among loggers, a kind of **CHUCK WAGON** on runners that brought the workers a hot lunch.

SWITCH MAN Among some **PLAINS INDIANS**, a man chosen to keep people dancing at a ceremony; also called a *whipman.* He used (and uses) a horsewhip and switches people's legs. But if he drew blood, he had to pay one horse.

SWITCHBACK A reversal in the direction of a trail as it angles up or down a hill or mountain. It also takes a verb form, as in, "We switchbacked up the ridge."

SWITCH-TAIL A nervous horse. Also called a *switcher.* (See also **STOCK HORSE**, **WRING-TAIL**.)

SYCAMORE INDIAN White on the outside, red on the inside; the opposite of an **APPLE**.

SYDNEY BIRD A California gold-rusher from Australia, often a convict and regarded as a ruffian or worse. These men were also called *Sydney ducks* and *clipped ears* because such convicts' ears had been cut as a punishment.

T

TABLITA (tab-LEE-tuh) A ceremonial headdress of **PUEBLO** people, made of flat wood and carved and painted.

TACO From the Southwest and now used throughout the United States, a Mexican-American food, usually meat, cheese, lettuce, tomato, and salsa stuffed into a folded, hard tortilla called a *taco shell*.

TAIGA The moist coniferous forest of interior Alaska; from Russian for "land of little sticks."

TAIL A verb. The **VAQUEROS** made a spsort of *tailing* cattle, or *tailing them down*. The rider came alongside a cow on the left and grabbed the tail and twisted it until the critter went down hard. Sometimes other moves are ascribed to the rider.

Anglos developed a similar method of *tailing* for branding—throwing a calf by twisting its tail so you could slap a brand on it. Cowboys also *tail cows up*—get them onto their feet by twisting their tails. It is used, for instance, to get cows out of bog holes.

Tail rider was another name for **DRAG** rider. To *roll your tail* or to *tail out* is to head out in a hurry.

TAILINGS (1) The refuse of the mining process. They're taken away suspended in water (called *tail water*) in a *tail race*. Uranium tailings now litter the canyon country, and sometimes these are called *tailings dumps* or the *tail end*. A *tail sluice* is the end sluice. (2) The stragglers of a cattle herd.

TAKU In Juneau, Alaska, a hard, cold wind that blows from the valley of the Taku River. The *Matanuska, Stikine,* and *Knik* are Alaskan winds named for their regions, but the Knik is a warm wind. (See also **CHINOOK, SANTA ANA.**)

TALKING Westerners have lots of expressions for talking, too much talking, and people who won't shut up. A *talking load* is enough whiskey to make a hand talkative. To *talk like a Texan*, naturally, is to brag. Other expressions include: *chew the fat* or *cud, coyote around the rim, dally your tongue, diarrhea of the* **JAWBONE,** *flannel mouth, giggle talk,* **LEAKY MOUTH,** *medicine tongue, more lip than a muley cow, powwow, slack in the jaw, talking talent, tongue oil,* and *wag your chin.* What stockmen do most is *talk cows* or maybe *talk horses.* For their next favorite, telling big stories, see **STUFFING DUDES.**

TALKING STICK Among many Indian peoples, an ornamented staff held by each speaker during council.

TALL TIMBER Wilderness, especially deep wilderness. To *head for tall timber* is to skedaddle to where people can't find you.

TALLOW FACTORY A business establishment where cow carcasses were boiled for tallow. This practice was common in Texas until markets developed for beef and the days of the great cattle drives began. *Tallowweed* is a forage *(Tetraneus linearifolia)* of southern and western Texas known for putting fat on cows.

TALLY HAND The fellow who kept count of the calves at **BRANDING**, often a hand too old, too young, or too **STOVE UP** to wrestle calves. Sometimes he used knots on a string or pebbles to keep track of every ten calves. The result was called the *tally* and was kept in the *tally book* (or on the *tally sheet*). Counting cows was called *tally branding*.

The **SHEEP** world has a different language—the fellow who weighs the wool after shearing is a *tallier*.

TAMALE (tuh-MAH-lee) A Mexican entree, minced meat rolled in **MASA** dough and (originally) steamed in a corn shuck. Now sometimes prepared in the form of a pie. The *real tamale* means "the real McCoy." Borrowed from Nahuatl by way of the Spanish.

TAMARISK A shrublike tree *(Tamarix chinensis)* introduced to the Southwest at the beginning of the twentieth century. Too successful in many people's view, it now proliferates abundantly, especially along watercourses, choking out native plants. Called *tammy* for short; also called *salt cedar*.

TAME INDIAN A friendly Indian, as opposed to a **HOSTILE**; more accurately, a member of a tribe that has accepted a reservation by treaty, rather than an indication of personal attitude. All members of the bands of Crazy Horse and Sitting Bull were known as hostiles until they came in to the reservation, friendlies thereafter.

TANK In the Southwest, a hollow in the ground (often in sandstone) that holds water during the rainy season; sometimes a reservoir made by damming runoff water. Later a *stock tank* (metal tank for watering stock). (See also **TINAJA**.)

TANNER CRAB In Alaska, two species of crabs of commercial value (genus *bairdi* and *opilio*); also called a *snow crab*.

TAOS A **TEWAN** people of the northern Rio Grande, their pueblo, and the adjacent town. The name, derived from Tewa, means red willow place. The people are now sometimes called Taoseños or Taosans.

Taos became the site of an early mission and then of a settlement well known to **MOUNTAIN MEN** and traders. In 1847 the Taos pueblo was the center of an unsuccessful revolt against the Americans who were occupying New Mexico during the Mexican-American War.

In the twentieth century, the town became a colony for artists, home to the painters of the Taos Society of Artists and others, including Woody Crumbo, and writers such as D. H. Lawrence and Max Evans.

Taos lightning was a fierce variety of **FIREWATER** popular among the mountain men.

Taos Pueblo, New Mexico, 1941.
[Photograph by Ansel Adams; courtesy of National Archives (79-AAQ-2).]

TAPADERO (ta-puh-DAIR-roh) A leather covering for the **STIRRUP**, open at the rear; valued in brush country as protection and in general to keep the boot from slipping too far forward in the stirrup, which could cause a rider to be dragged by the stirrup. Adapted from Spanish.

Tapaderos with conchos on the toe are called *hognose taps*. Tapaderos are also called *taps*, **BULLDOGS**, **EAGLE BILLS**, and *monkey noses*.

TAPAJO (tah-PAH-hoh) A blind for a horse or mule, usually attached to the headstall. It's often used to help with mounting an unbroke horse or to keep a mule still for loading. Adapted from Spanish. Sometimes spelled *tapaojos*.

A tapadero, the leather stirrup covering.
[From *Moseman's Illustrated Guide for Purchasers of Horse Furnishing Goods*, ca. 1892.]

TARRABEE (TAIR-ruh-bee) In the Southwest, a wooden hand tool used to spin the threads for making CINCHES. Adapted from the Spanish *taraba* or *tarabilla*.

TASAJO (tuh-SAH-hoh) (1) In the Southwest, JERKY (dried meat). Borrowed from Spanish. A *tasajero* was a building where meat was dried. (2) A CACTUS of the genus *Opuntia,* which looks like strips of jerky.

TEAM ROPING A standard RODEO event. Two ropers, a HEELER and a HEADER (who rope the critter by the heels and head, respectively), lasso a steer and tie it, against time. After the steer's head and two hind feet are tied, the header faces his horse to the steer. A winning time is five to six seconds, although four seconds is sometimes seen.

TECOLOTE (teh-kuh-LOH-tee) A small burrowing owl of the Southwest. Borrowed from Nahuatl by way of Spanish.

TEETH IN THE SADDLE Among cowboys, a way of describing a saddle that rubs a horse's back raw.

TEJANO A Texan. From the Spanish name of that state, Tejas, which came from the name given to an Indian tribe by early explorers.

TELLY Nickname for a telemark skier or telemark skiing. Though telemark skiing did not originate in the West, it's very popular there.

TEMESCAL In the Southwest, originally a hot springs where Indians took baths, then a SWEAT LODGE. This temescal was made of branches caulked with mud. Red-hot stones were put inside and water poured over the stones to make steam.

TENDERFOOT A newcomer, an inexperienced person, a greenhorn, a PILGRIM, a PORK-EATER. First applied to imported cattle (which were tender-footed), then used by miners for ignorant males of the human variety. The tenderfoot has been an object of a good deal of teasing in the West, much of it unkind. A nice trick played on the innocents was the one that the Wyoming writer Struthers Burt used on the Easterners who came to his DUDE ranch each summer. In those early days, visitors had to travel to Jackson Hole by stagecoach from Idaho. Burt had his dude wranglers mask themselves and rob the stagecoach on Teton Pass—pick the guests completely clean, money, luggage, the lot. When they got to the ranch, the dudes were amazed and hugely grateful to find their belongings in their rooms and even laid out in their drawers.

TEN-GALLON HAT An oversize stockman's hat, one with an extra-high crown and an extra-wide brim. Named, says Thomas Clark, not after any quantity of liquid it might hold but after the number of braids (Spanish *galóns*) used as a hat band.

TEPARY In the Southwest, a bean (*Phaseolus acutifolius*) that is particularly resistant to drought.

TEPEE See TIPI.

TEQUILA (tuh-KEE-luh) An alcoholic drink made from the MAGUEY plant. The first stage of fermentation produces PULQUE, the next MESCAL, and tequila is distilled from mescal. The name came from the town of Tequila, Mexico, which made and makes the distilled spirit from the maguey. Old-timers call it *cactus juice.*

TESQUITE (tes-KEE-tay) An ALKALI of commercial value that oozes from the earth around Southwestern bodies of water.

TETON (1) A mountain, when its shape suggests a breast. Used in place names such as the Teton Range and the Grand Teton. From the French word for breast. (2) The largest and most powerful branch of the Dakota Indians. From an Indian word meaning "prairie dwellers." (See also DAKOTA.)

TEWA (1) A family of PUEBLO peoples living in villages of the upper Rio Grande of northern New Mexico (Nambe, Pojoaque, San Ildefonso, San Juan, Santa Clara, and Tesuque Pueblos) and at the HOPI Reservation in Arizona (Hano Pueblo). (2) Also the ankle-high moccasins originally made by these people and worn by many Indians, Hispanics, and Anglos of the pioneer and modern Southwest. The name is the Keresan word for "moccasin" and is also spelled *Tegua.* There's a good story about the Tewa and Hopi and their defenses against Navajo raiders:

A long time ago, the Hopis sat down and talked about a problem. It was bad medicine for a Hopi to fight, and they sure weren't going to bring bad medicine on themselves. On the other hand, because they wouldn't fight, the Navajos regularly came and took food or women or whatever they wanted. The Hopis talked it over and decided to invite some Tewa people to come live with them. Tewas were fighters, and if it brought bad medicine on them—hey, that was their problem, not the Hopis'.

The Tewas came and built Hano Village, the first of the villages on Third Mesa, right where you find them today. The next summer the Navajos came raiding, thirty-two of them. The Tewas gave them a fierce battle, and captured three.

The Hopis, still not worried about anyone else's bad medicine, said eagerly, "Hey, kill those three."

The Tewas, not bloodthirsty, said, "No, we need to keep them alive, go back where they came from and tell what happened, that we Tewas are here now and things will be different from now on."

"Then kill two of them," said the Hopis.

The Tewas said no.

"Well, kill one," said the Hopis.

"No," said the Tewas, "if three go home and tell the story, the other Navajos will believe it."

But the Hopis laughed heartily and cried, "Too late for that—everyone knows it takes four Navajos to tell the truth."

A complementary (joking) custom is that if you want a straight answer from a Navajo, you must ask the question four times.

Modern Navajos still get a chuckle out of both of these sayings.

TEXAN Both a person and a cow. The cows called Texans were **TEXAS LONG-HORNS,** half-wild and in need of considerable taming, like some of the people. Texas people are also known as *beef heads, rawhiders,* **TEJANOS,** *Texians,* and *Texicans.* The lore of the state is called *Texana* (the equivalent of *Americana*). The language is also called *Texan,* and its characteristic expressions are *Texanisms.* The Texan Republic was the sovereign state founded by Texans after independence from Mexico and before admission to the Union, lasting from 1836 to 1845.

COMBINATIONS: *Texas butter* (gravy made from rendered animal fat, flour, and water), *Texas cakewalk* (a hanging), *Texas gate* (a gate made of three strands of barbed wire and wide-spaced poles, ubiquitous in ranch country), *Texas house* (two log cabins with a covered dog trot in between; also called a *double log cabin* or a *saddlebag house*), *Texas itch* (a skin disease of cattle also known as scabies), *Texas Panhandle* (the northern piece of the state that extends between Oklahoma and New Mexico, famous for its barren plains; sometimes referred to as *down in the skillet*), *Texas leg* (a way of describing **SHOTGUN CHAPS** that go all the way around the leg), *Texas rig* (any **DOUBLE-RIGGED** saddle), *Texas saddle* (the Texas adaptation of the old vaquero **STOCK SADDLE,** with small, high horn, high cantle, square skirt, and two cinches—a double rig), *Texas skirt* (a square saddle-skirt such as was the rule in Texas until the late nineteenth century), *Texas tie* (the tying of the catch rope to the saddle horn, the way **TIE-HARD-AND-FAST MEN** do it), *Texas tree* (the **SADDLE TREE** of a Texas rig), *Texas yell* (a ferocious holler bellowed in combat, intimidating the foe, perhaps adapted from the **COMANCHE** or **CREEK** Indians).

TEXAS FEVER (1) A parasitic fever that made Texas cattle sick and killed other cows. From the mid-1850s, Kansans, Missourians, and Indians of the **FIVE CIVILIZED TRIBES** tried to keep Texas cattle from coming into their country. In the 1860s, laws were passed against the importation of Texas cows, and all through the era of the great **CATTLE DRIVES, QUARANTINE LINES** kept these cows west of certain points in Kansas. The **JAYHAWKERS** also used the fever as an excuse to steal cows. Later, Texas fever was discovered to be caused by a tick the Texas cows carried. Texas fever was also called *Spanish fever, southern fever, splenic fever,* and *Texas murrain.*

(2) A powerful desire to go to Texas, felt especially by people in trouble with their creditors or the law. The cure was sometimes symbolized by the initials **G.T.T.—GONE TO TEXAS.**

TEXAS LONGHORN The wild cow of Texas, known for its wide span of horns. Descended from the mission cattle of old Mexico, these cattle thrived on their own until the time of the settlement of Texas, and during their years of independence developed considerable hardiness, not to mention wildness, cantankerousness, and even nastiness. The longhorn can forage on barren lands that more delicate cattle starve on. Its hardiness led cattlemen to drive the longhorns in the 1870s and 1880s from Texas to the great ranges of the Northern Plains. But there the longhorn gave way to various shorthorn breeds because these cattle produce more beef, as well as more tender beef, and don't have the nuisance of long horns, which make shipping difficult. After near extinction at the beginning of the twentieth century, the longhorn has made a modest comeback. Also called *broadhorns, coasters, sea lions, cactus boomers, horned jackrabbits, Indian cattle, mossy horns* or *backs, Texas cattle, Spanish cattle,* and *twisthorns.* The classic book about these critters is J. Frank Dobie's *The Longhorns.*

Longhorn can also mean a person—a Texan or any old-timer.

TEXAS RANGERS A fabled group of Indian fighters, soldiers, and mounted police in Texas. They were first organized while Texas was still part of Mexico to protect settlers against Indians. They operated in military units in the war against Mexico, and by the 1870s were an important police force, though not bound by formalities such as uniforms.

TEX-MEX The blend of Mexican and Texas cultures distinctive to Texas. Tex-Mex cooking, for instance, is significantly different from **NORTEÑO** cooking.

THERE GOES HOSS AND BEAVER Mountain-man talk for "We just lost everything," which they too often did, to raiding Indians, raging waters, and so on.

THERE'S A ONE-EYED MAN IN THE GAME In gambling, a warning that someone's cheating. Adams says it came from a superstition that one-eyed gamblers gave other players bad luck forever.

THOMPSON SEEDLESS A raisin grape of California, from the 1890s.

THREE SADDLES A professional **BRONC BUSTER**'s expression for a horse that he's broke. In the nineteenth century, a horse ridden three times was considered broke, which was some distance yet from trained or gentled. (See also **BREAK A HORSE**.)

THREE-SEVEN-SEVENTY-SEVEN At Virginia City, Montana, in the 1860s, a code name for the Vigilance Committee. Says Berry, a stand-in for the actual trader Joseph Kipp in James Willard Schultz's *My Life as an Indian,* "You don't know who they are, but you may be sure that they are representative men who stand for law and order: they are more feared by criminals than are the courts and prisons of the East, for they always hang a murderer or robber." The code name often appeared as 3-7-77, and may have meant the number of days, hours, and minutes offered to get out of town. (See also **VIGILANTE**.)

THROUGH HERD A herd of cows being driven or shipped through to a further point. Through herds were a problem to local stockmen during the days of the great **TRAIL DRIVES**, for local people didn't want to provide free grass and bed grounds to those passing by.

THROW A HITCH To tie a knot, a hitch, which in the West is not tied but thrown (or throwed).

THUMB THE HAMMER To fire a revolver by pulling the hammer back with the second joint of the thumb and letting the hammer slide forward from the thumb's web area. A man who used the hammer this way, instead of a trigger, was called a *thumber*. The older revolvers, with stiff hammers, were called *thumb busters*. (See also **FAN**.)

THUNDERBIRD One version of what many Native peoples call *thunder beings,* spirits of power associated with the west, with lightning, thunder, and rain. The thunderbird is an icon particularly in the religious art (and all of their art is religious) of Southwestern Indians; it causes the thunderstorm by fighting with a giant serpent. In **LAKOTA** lore the terrible strife of a thunderstorm results from the ancient enmity of Thundercloud, the bringer of rain, and Wind Storm, the illegitimate son of Earth's waters.

TIE COMBINATIONS: *tied to the ground* (a way of describing a horse trained to stand still with the reins dropped to earth, as secure as if he were tied, **GROUND-HITCHED**), *tie down a steer* (to rope it and hog-tie it, as in a **RODEO**), *tie-down man* (a gunman with his holster tied to his leg to facilitate his draw), *tie on the bear* (to become inebriated), *tie rail* (a hitching rail), *tie rope* (either a **MECATE** or a **PIGGING STRING**), *tie strings* (leather strings on a saddle, usually through a rosette, used to tie on a bedroll or other gear). To *tie on to something* means to rope it. *Tie one to that!* is an invitation to top a good story.

TIE HACK A man who cut railroad ties. These men often lived in a *tie camp* and hewed the lumber into the ties on site, sometimes as many as forty a day. Wyoming, with its stands of timber, had many tie camps. Once the ties were made, they were driven down the river in the spring runoff.

TIE-HARD-AND-FAST MAN A roper who ties his rope to the saddle horn instead of taking dallies to stop the critter he's roped. This style has been most popular in Texas and on the Great Plains generally. This fellow is also known as a *tie man* or *tie peeler*. (See also **DALLY**.)

TIGER The game **FARO**, because of the tiger conventionally painted on the faro box. Thus to play faro was to **BUCK** (or *twist*) **THE TIGER**.

TIGHT-LEGGING Riding a horse with the legs pressed right against it. The rules in **RODEO** require the competitor to be scratching, not tight-legging.

TILIKUM (TIL-uh-kuhm) **CHINOOK** jargon for a friend; *tilikums* may also mean plain folks. Also spelled *tillicum*.

TIMBER *Timber beast, timber head, timberjack* (*lumberjack* is little used in the West), *timber savage*, and *timber wolf* are all names for a logger. OTHER COMBINATIONS: *timber claim* (a section of public land with a claim filed for its timber), *timber marking* (blazing, painting, or otherwise marking trees for timbering), *timber cattle* (cows that range in timber), *timber fall* (an area of *blowdown*), *timberline* (in mountain country, the elevation where trees give way to shrubs and grasses; also called *tree line*).

TIMBER CRUISER A person who finds choice tracts of timber for cutting. Such locations were once much prized business secrets. Also called a *timber looker* or *tree looker*.

TIN DOGS A string of tin cans rattled by a **SHEEPHERDER** to get the sheep to move along.

TIN PANTS Heavy, woolen, water-resistant trousers such as loggers and other outdoorsmen of the North Woods use. A *tin coat* is made of similar material.

TINAJA (tih-NAH-hah) An earthen jar for water, associated with the **PUEBLO** peoples. Historically, a natural water hole in rock, or such a hole dug by Indians; a **TANK**. Adapted from Spanish, where it means a big, earthern jar.

TINHORN A gambler of the flashy sort.

TIPI The **LODGE** of the Indians of the **GREAT PLAINS**, a dwelling shaped like an upside-down cone. Typically, it was made from buffalo hides (later of canvas) stretched over a frame of poles of peeled lodgepole pine. From the **DAKOTA** *tipi*, meaning "used to live in," it is also spelled *teepee* and *tepee*.

Tipi recede and the Tipis were as small as twelve feet in diameter for a small traveling family and could be very large when intended for councils. Women made them, women owned them, and only women erected them. A center fire kept the lodge warm in winter, and lifting the lodge skin from the bottom allowed a breeze in the summer. The entrance faced east, a gesture of acknowledgment of the spirit powers. Modern Indians and interested Anglos still use tipis, especially at **POW-WOWS** and **RENDEZVOUS**. Much lore of the tipi and practical instructions for putting one up are found in Reginald and Gladys Laubin's *The Indian Tipi*.

Tipi.
[DRAWING BY E. L. REEDSTROM.]

Tipi rings are circles of stone used to hold down the cover of a hide tipi. They are still found, half in the ground, at popular Indian camping sites on the Plains.

TISWIN (tis-WEEN) A sweet **APACHE** drink made from corn, says Smith, but usually confused with its fermented form, **TULAPAI**, a kind of beer. Tulapai was used religiously but was also known for getting Apaches drunk and troublesome. Tiswin is adapted from the Spanish *tesgüino;* it's also spelled *tizwin.* This bit of doggerel (quoted by Smith) by Charles Poston, called the father of Arizona, sets the story straight:

> *The Tizauin drink is much enjoyed,*
> *to make it, Indian corn's employed.*
> *They bury the corn until it sprouts,*
> *destroying food for drinking bouts.*
> *They grind it in a kind of tray,*
> *they boil it strong for one long day,*
> *strain off the juice in willow-sieve*
> *and in the sun to ferment, leave.*
> *Fermented juice is then Tulpai*
> *on which Apache chiefs get high.*

TLINGIT A Native tribe of the Pacific Coast in the Alaskan panhandle and northern British Columbia. They speak the Nadene language, previously called *Koluschan;* the Russian name for them is *Kolusch.*

TOBACCO According to the old stories of various Indian tribes, the first plant given to the people by the Creator. Smoked, burned, and spread on the ground ceremonially; a significant gift; used in healing—a major element of most American Indian cultures. See **PIPE.**

TOBACCO ROOT In the Pacific Northwest, a tuber once eaten by Indians, now sometimes made into a bread. Said to smell like tobacco when cooked.

TOBACCO TIE Among **PLAINS INDIANS,** a prayer symbol made of a small square of cloth around a pinch of tobacco, closed and tied onto a string. Originally these ties were made of dyed buckskin; after traders made cloth available, the custom changed. Also called a *tobacco-tie garland* or a *prayer tie.*

TOBIANO A **PINTO** horse whose white color is on top, on the back and the hindquarters, and extends downward.

TOGGLE A piece of wood or chain fixed to the front foot of a horse or cow so that the critter can walk but will step on the toggle if it tries to run. That way it can graze but not flee. (See also **HOBBLE.**)

TOM In **PLACER** mining, to wash gold-bearing gravel in a **LONG TOM**. A sheet of perforated iron put over the **RIFFLE** box to strain out the larger stones was called a *tom iron*.

TOMATILLO (toh-muh-TEE-yoh) A vinelike plant *(Physallis ixocarpa)* that produces tart, green, tomato-like fruits that are an important ingredient in Mexican sauces.

TOMBE (tohm-BAY) In the Southwest, an Indian drum made from a hollow log with a piece of hide stretched over one end, said to produce a far-carrying sound. The word is of obscure origin.

TONG An American-Chinese word for a fraternal organization among Chinese in the United States, especially in San Francisco, often used to control gambling interests. San Francisco's *tong wars* over gambling began about 1899.

TONGUE-SPLITTING A practice of **RUSTLERS**. When they cut a calf's tongue, it couldn't suck and would stop following its mother, and so would become a **MAVERICK** and belong to the first claimant. Thieves who did this were called *tongue-splitters*.

TOO MUCH MUSTARD Descriptive cowboy talk for a prickly fellow or a braggart.

TOO THICK TO DRINK, TOO THIN TO PLOW An eloquent description of Powder River or the Platte or many another Western river with everything but enough water to get a decent drink from. (See also **POWDER RIVER, LET 'ER BUCK!**)

TOOL NIPPER Miner's talk for the worker who distributed the tools in a mine; also called an *abajador*. The *toolpusher* is the superintendent of an oil rig.

TOOTHPICK TIMBER Among loggers, a mocking term for little trees.

TOP COMBINATIONS: *topknot* (a scalp), *top out* or *top off a bronc* (to *take the kinks* out of it), *top-railer* (a person who sits on the top rail of the corral and gives advice), *top screw* (to both cowboys and loggers, a foreman).

TOP HAND (1) A first-rate cowhand. Also called a *top* **WADDY**. In cowboy talk, top was and is added to a number of other nouns to indicate superiority—thus *top man, top roper, top cutter,* and so on. (2) Among miners, a recruit off the farm.

TORNILLO (tohr-NEE-yoh) In the Southwest, the screwpod **MESQUITE** *(Prosopis pubescens)* or its bean, which cows and horses feed on. Borrowed from Spanish.

TORO An occasional name for jerked buffalo meat, from the Spanish word meaning "bull." Also, in the circumspect nineteenth century, a euphemism for the common name for the male bovine (bull), which wasn't mentioned in front of ladies. Later, a general U.S. word for bull, often used jocularly.

TORREON (toh-ray-OHN) In the Southwest, a lookout spot, such as a hill. Borrowed from Spanish (in which it means "big tower").

TORTILLA (tor-TEE-yuh) A flat, round, unleavened bread, originally of Mexican-American and **PUEBLO** peoples, made either of wheat flour or cornmeal, used to wrap meats and vegetables in various Mexican dishes. Originally tortillas were baked on a slab of hot stone, later on hot iron. Now mass-produced and widely available. Borrowed from Spanish.

TOSTADO (tohs-TAH-doh) An open-faced tortilla covered with beans and cheese.

TOTEM POLE Among Indian peoples of the Pacific Northwest (and some Eastern Indians), a pole of carved, painted totems that tells the mythic history of the people and the genealogy of the family. Sometimes it is part of a building, sometimes it stands alone.

TOUCH HIM UP In cowboy talk, to **SPUR** a horse.

TOURON Contemporary and derogatory slang for a tourist. It derives from the combination of *tourist* and *moron.*

TOWLINE In Alaska, the main rope from the **SLED DOGS** to the sled. Also called a *gangline.*

TOWNSEND'S FOX SPARROW A western bird named for naturalist J. K. Townsend; other western birds bearing Townsend's name are *Townsend's solitaire, Townsend's sparrow,* and *Townsend's warbler.*

TRACE A track made by animals, wagons, and so on—*buffalo trace, wagon trace, Comanche trace*—also, a trail or road, such as the Natchez Trace.

TRADE BLANKET A heavy woollen blanket made for trade to the Indians. Blankets were from the beginning a staple of the **INDIAN TRADE**. Probably the best-known brand was the Hudson's Bay Company's; others were the Witney and Northwest blankets (Hudson and Witney are still made today). They became so closely associated with Indian ways that the expression for a red man's returning to his tribal traditions became **BACK TO THE BLANKET**.

The blankets were graded by size, shown by stripes woven into the fabric; a four-point (-stripe) blanket cost four beaver skins (**PLEWS**), a six-point six skins, and so on.

Coats, leggings, and other items of clothing were also made from the blankets. (See also **CAPOTE**.) From the reservation period (about 1870) forward, the most popular brand has been Pendleton, made in the Oregon town of that name.

TRADING POST The commercial establishment of an Anglo trader for trade with the Indians and for supply of trappers roaming the country for beaver. Though goods were exchanged with Indians from the time of earliest white contact, the term wasn't used until 1796, and then was applied mostly to the West. The great trading posts, from Fort Vancouver to Fort Leavenworth, were situated beside the great rivers—the Missouri, Platte, Arkansas, Snake, Columbia, and Yellowstone. The traders in charge of these posts usually became expert in Indian ways and languages; some later became **INDIAN AGENTS**; others even became white (or black) Indians.

The INDIAN TRADE was the basis of Western economies from the beginning of colonization of this continent. The FUR TRADE of Canada and the United States, in fact, was the motivation for exploration. At the heart of this activity were trading goods such as blankets, hatchets, knives, guns, beads, and whiskey for beaver plews.

The prices of these items were high enough to make the greedy gleeful—or so the Anglos thought. The Indians probably saw four beaver hides for a blanket or a gun as trading the common for the rare, and wondered at the whites who would do it. So both sides profited at the time, though Indian dependence on trade goods contributed significantly to their subjugation.

Some such American posts were operated by the big fur companies, Hudson's Bay Company and American Fur. Others, like Bent's Fort and Fort Laramie, were built by independent traders. As the West changed, so did these outposts. Laramie was typical: It started as a fur post, became a center for the emigrant trade, and finally endured as a military post. Later the federal government licensed trading posts on the reservations. David Lavender's *Bent's Fort* gives a marvelous picture of life at a major trading post.

TRAIL (1) To drive cattle from one place to another, not necessarily on a trail. The great CATTLE TRAILS ran from Texas north, at first to the Kansas railroad towns, later to the grasslands of Colorado, Wyoming, and Montana.

(2) A more or less permanent track beaten by human use (possibly a Westernism, it first occurred in the journal of Patrick Gass on the Lewis and Clark Expedition). Also called a *single track*. (See also TRACE.) After rivers, trails were the first major roads of the West. The great emigrant trails chiefly ran from the Missouri settlements to the West—the SANTA FE TRAIL to New Mexico, the OREGON TRAIL to the Pacific Northwest, and so on. One trail of legend was a forced emigrant trail: The TRAIL OF TEARS was the route of the U.S. government removal of the CHEROKEE people to INDIAN TERRITORY (present-day Oklahoma), a journey of great suffering.

COMBINATIONS: *trail blazer* (one who finds the way and marks it), *trail boss* (the man in charge of a cattle drive, especially responsible for finding good water, good grass, and good bed grounds and for handling the trail crew), *trail-broke* (a way of describing cows accustomed to the cattle trail and therefore manageable), *trail crossing* (a place where a cattle trail fords a river, sometimes remembered for the deaths that took place there), *trail cutter* (an inspector responsible for checking passing cattle herds for cows that didn't belong in them; what he did was called *trimming the herd*), *trail hand* (a trail driver, a cowboy engaged in taking cows up the trail, which was one of the ambitions of most Texas cowboys), *trail ride* (a dude activity on most guest ranches, horseback riding on a trail to a pleasant spot—not anything to do with a cattle drive).

VERBS: *take the trail somewhere* (to set out for that destination), *camp on someone's trail* (to follow someone), *cut someone's trail* (to come upon his track; to block his trail while you inspect his herd), *hit the trail* (to leave), *break trail* (to make a way through obstacles, especially through deep snow).

TRAIL DRIVE See CATTLE TRAIL.

TRAIL OF BROKEN PROMISES Contemporary Indian talk for the pattern of treaties that, from the Indian point of view, were either violated or misrepresented by the whites.

TRAIL OF TEARS The mass march of CHEROKEES from their Appalachian homeland eight hundred miles to Indian Territory (roughly what is now Oklahoma) in the fall of 1838 and winter of 1839, forced and supervised by U.S. soldiers. Because of cold, lack of food, and other difficult conditions, about four thousand of the sixteen thousand Indians removed died on the trail (which Cherokees sometimes call the Trail Where They Cried). For some years Anglos living around the Cherokees, especially in Georgia, which passed flagrantly discriminatory laws, harassed them, and made their lives hard. The Cherokees who managed to avoid the removal hid in the mountains of North Carolina, and now have a reservation there. REMOVALS took place throughout the 1830s, subsequent to Congress passing the Indian Removal Act. (See also WOUNDED KNEE, SAND CREEK, LONG WALK.)

TRAVEL WITH THE GRASS In the days of the great TRAIL DRIVES, to trail cows north as the grass comes green, starting in Texas early in the spring and getting to the northern ranges as the snow clears and the grass comes.

TRAVOIS A vehicle for hauling belongings; the horse Indians' equivalent of a wagon. A travois was made by taking a pair of LODGEPOLES (which you already had for the TIPI), crisscrossing the small ends on a horse's back, letting the butt ends drag behind, slinging skins (or straps of skin) in between, and tying gear on. Small children and old folks might be put on, also. Before Indians had the horse to drag big travois, they hitched small ones onto their dogs. Adapted from the French-Canadian *travail;* also spelled *travée.*

An Indian village on the move was carrying everything it owned, most of it on travois. It was slow, it lacked mobility, and the butts of the poles, dragging on the ground, left a big trail, called a *travois trail.* Such a village was vulnerable and needed defending, which was provided by the young men.

Since they were in roadless country and had no wheels, MOUNTAIN MEN often adopted the travois. Later, loggers used travois to transport logs and developed the transitive verb *to travois.*

TREASURE BOX A STAGECOACH's strongbox, the main object of the ROAD AGENT's desire. A stagecoach carrying gold away from diggings and designed for defense against road agents was called a *treasure coach.*

TREATY INDIAN An Indian whose tribe had come to a peace agreement with the federal government and was therefore "pacified." This notion caused a lot of

Travois were the Indians' way of transporting their villages; the travois poles doubled as tipi poles.
[DRAWING BY CHARLES M. RUSSELL; COURTESY OF NATIONAL ARCHIVES (111-SC-825310.]

misunderstanding in the West, partly because Anglos didn't understand the nature of Indian leadership. The whites were always designating one Indian as head of a band or a tribe, often because he was cooperative. But that fellow might not have had any real leadership, and his people might not have felt obliged to respect any agreements he made. Also, the Indians regarded by whites as chiefs often were only leaders in war. The U.S. government made this mistake in coming to terms with Red Cloud but not the real leaders of the Oglala Lakota in 1868 at Fort Laramie.

Another important matter about Indian leadership: Indians acknowledged the rights of individuals to do what they thought right (often to do what their MEDICINE indicated), regardless of what the group did. This might include making war when peace was promised. Altogether, a treaty Indian might have been warlike, in his view, without violating any promises.

From early colonial times, *treaty* referred not only to an agreement with Indians but to the conference at which the agreement was reached.

TREE A TOWN An expression of trail-drive cowboys. When they strutted and drank and shot their guns until they had a whole town scared and **BUF-FALOED**, including its law officers, they said they *had it treed.* They also spoke of *treeing the marshal.* It's all an extension of the notion (from the Eastern frontier) of making an animal you're hunting take refuge in a tree.

TRIBAL GOVERNMENT Native tribes recognized by the federal government (not all are) have governments, generally with elected officials, that deal with the Bureau of Indian Affairs and in some ways govern the tribe. However, in many tribes this is still viewed as a white-man way, so there is a shadow government that may be as powerful, the traditional leaders of the tribe, men and women who have earned respect and leadership by the demonstration of traditional virtues, **MEDICINE MEN,** etc. *Tribal headquarters* is where the tribal government meets and administers programs.

TRIBUTER A miner who works a claim, taking mineral as wages, without rights as owner or leaser.

TRICKS Especially in Texas, belongings, personal possessions, what the **MOUNTAIN MAN** called **POSSIBLES.**

TRIGGER IS DELICATE Cowboy talk for a man with a quick temper or maybe literally quick on the trigger. This latter fellow is said to have *trigger itch* and to be **EASY ON THE TRIGGER.**

TRIGUEÑO (tree-GAYN-yoh; truh-GAYN-yoh) In the Southwest, a way of describing a brown horse. Borrowed from Spanish (in which it means "dark," "swarthy"). (For horse colors, see **BUCKSKIN.**)

TRIP ROPE A rope tied to the front foot of a difficult horse when it's being trained and used to jerk it off its feet as a lesson.

TRIPAS (TREE-puhs) In the Southwest of the nineteenth century, a socially acceptable word for guts. Borrowed from Spanish.

TRIPPING In **OIL DRILLING,** pulling all the pipe out of a drill hole in order to replace the drill bit.

TROMPER During **SHEARING,** the worker who stands in the wool sacks and compresses the fleece with his feet. Usually the job is given to a boy or an apprentice.

TROUBLE WAGON A wagon used to transport the cowboy who looked after the windmill, pipes, and water troughs, and to haul salt.

TULAPAI An Apache beer made from corn. (See **TISWIN.**)

TULE (TOO-lee) In the Southwest and on the Pacific Coast, either of two bulrushes of the genus *Scirpus,* often used by Indians to thatch huts. Borrowed from Spanish.

    COMBINATIONS: *tule balsa* (a raft of tules), *tule boat* (a boat somewhat like a **KEELBOAT** made of tules), *tule elk* (the small California elk), *tule fog* (in California, a fog on the Sacramento or San Joaquin River), *tule root* or *potato* (the tuber of the tule, used for food in California by Indians, Chinese, and some Anglos), *tule wren* (the California marsh wren).

To *pull freight for* (or *take to*) *the tules* meant to go on the dodge, to run from the law. To *be in the deep tules* means to be in trouble. *Tulares* are areas overgrown with tules; they were also a band of Indians living on San Francisco Bay.

TUMBLEWEED Any of several globe-shaped plants, for instance the Russian thistle *(Salsola australis)*, which break off at the roots, blow and roll all over the country, and often end up caught on fences. Tumbleweed was accidentally introduced to South Dakota in 1877, and rapidly spread over the West. It grows in disturbed and agricultural areas, causes the destruction of rangeland, and is dangerous to motorists and livestock. Also called *saltwort, Russian cactus, and wind witch.*

A *tumbleweed wagon* was a jail on wheels that took prisoners to more permanent **CALABOOSES**.

The tumbleweed has become a symbol of a footloose, roving Western fellow, liable to drift in any direction and stay nowhere long.

TUM-TUM In **CHINOOK** jargon, the heart, the mind, or the will. The word imitates the beating of the heart.

TURISTAS Traveler's diarrhea, often the result of contaminated water, or simply of different water. From the Mexican-Spanish word for "tourist."

TURKEY (1) A bedroll. (2) Among loggers, a bag to carry tools in. *Turkey season* is tourist season; surely an extension from the common derogatory slang term *turkey.*

TURN ON A DIME AND GIVE YOU BACK FIVE CENTS CHANGE What a first-rate **CUTTING HORSE** can do. A horse that makes quick cuts is also said to have *turned through itself.*

TURRON (too-ROHN) A dessert blended of almonds and honey, a favorite of Hispanics in Arizona a century ago. Borrowed from Spanish.

TURTLE A **RODEO COWBOY**; a member of the Cowboy's Turtle Association, the ancestor of the current Professional Rodeo Cowboy's Association. One story about how the first rodeo rider's union got named is that someone called the rodeo cowboys turtles because they were practically the last working men to organize.

TURTLE ISLAND Among many Indians, this continent or the Western hemisphere; by extension, this world we live in. From the Algonquian legend that the Earth rests on the back of a turtle.

TUS (TOOS) A jug-shaped basket of the **APACHES**. Other tribes have similar baskets, now sometimes called by the same name, some saturated with pitch so they hold water.

TUSKER A person who takes the canine teeth (tusks) of elk for sale as souvenirs, charms, and decorations. (See also **ELK TOOTH**.) Such men poached thousands of elk in Jackson Hole and the Yellowstone country, but in 1906 vigilante action in Jackson put a stop to the *tusking.*

TWELVE APOSTLES In the **MORMON** church, the members of the Council of Twelve, often referred to simply as the Twelve. The principal ruling body of the church under the first Presidency. Members of the Council of Twelve are also set apart as "prophets, seers, and revelators." (See also **PROPHET**.)

TWENTY-ONE See **BLACKJACK**.

TWIST A rope of tobacco; one of the two chief forms in which chewing and smoking tobacco were traded and sold in the old West, the other being **PLUG**. It was seasoned with such flavorings as licorice, molasses, sugar, fruit juices, and so on and was sold in substantial hunks. For mountain-man hobbyists, tobacco is still available in twist form.

TWIST DOWN For a bulldogger to force a steer down by twisting its neck. To *twist a horse,* or *twist it down* is to break it. (See also **BREAK A HORSE**.)

TWISTER (1) Slang for a tornado. Tornados are common on the **SOUTHERN** and **CENTRAL PLAINS**. (2) A **BRONC BUSTER**. (3) A cord put around the lip of a difficult horse and twisted with a stick to inflict pain and teach a lesson; perhaps this is the source of the term *bronc twister.* (4) A nail on the end of the pole of a railroad **COWPUNCHER**, used to catch in the tail of a troublesome critter and twist.

TWO BITS A quarter of a dollar—originally of a Spanish or Spanish colonial dollar. These dollars were called *pieces of eight,* eight *reales* to a dollar, and the frontiersmen called the *reales* bits. Prices were high in the old West: two bits for a shot of rotgut, four bits or a dollar for a meal at a stage station, compared to a *short bit* (dime) for a full meal in many St. Louis restaurants, coffee and pie included. (See also **REAL**.)

TWO WHOOPS AND A HOLLER Cowboy talk for a short distance. But *two jumps ahead of the sheriff,* meaning "on the lam," was never far enough.

TWO-GUN MAN A gunman who wore two pistols and shot with both hands, a rarity in the West and a dubious advantage.

TWO-TRACK A crude road, not graded but merely two tracks made by the passage of tires; the common road of ranch country. The automotive explorer who hasn't explored the West via two-tracks hasn't begun to explore. Also called *double-track.*

TYEE In **CHINOOK** jargon, a chief or other person of special consequence.

U

ULU Among **ESKIMO** people, a woman's knife, crescent-shaped, with a bone, ivory, or wood handle.

UMIAK Among **INUITS** (**ESKIMOS**), a large, open boat of hides stretched over a framework of wood. As much as thirty feet long, it can transport many people or lots of freight. (See also **KAYAK**.)

UNCLE TOMAHAWK The Indian equivalent of an Uncle Tom, a red man who is overaccommodating or subservient to whites. The Indian equivalent of what blacks call an Oreo (black outside and white inside) is an *apple*.

UNCORK A HORSE To take the edges off a **BRONC**, the beginning of breaking it; to ride a bucking horse into submission. Also said as *unrooster*.

UNITED ORDER The United Order of Enoch, an economic utopian concept of Joseph Smith's. He proposed that all worldly goods be shared communally by **MORMONS**. They experimented with it in Ohio and Missouri but failed; in the 1870s, they made an effort at Brigham City and Orderville, Utah, but it didn't last. Though polygamous factions experimented with this style of cooperative living even in the twentieth century, the orthodox church no longer advocates it.

UNSHUCKED Cowboy talk for naked. An unshucked gun is one that's out of the holster.

UNTRACK A HORSE To lead a horse forward a little before mounting. If the horse is in a mood to blow up, he's likely to show it at that point. Old hands don't get on a horse without untracking it.

UP AND DOWN AS A COW'S TAIL Cowboy talk for honest, straightforward.

UP TO TRAP Said by **MOUNTAIN MEN** of an experienced trapper, a man who knew what he was doing. Another expression with the same meaning is *up to beaver*. The opposite is **DON'T KNOW WHAT WAY THE STICK FLOATS**.

URANIUM ON THE CRANIUM Utah slang for the mental state of uranium **PROSPECTORS** in canyon country.

UTE A Uto-Aztecan people who lived, from the time of white contact, in western Colorado and eastern Utah. The name of the tribe, meaning "high up" or "land of the sun," is also rendered as *Utah, Utaw,* and *Eutaw*. The Indians called *Ute Diggers* were **PAIUTES**. In the nineteenth century, Anglos called them *Goshutes, Grasshopper Indians,* and *Land Pitches*.

When the Utes, primarily hunter-gathers, acquired the horse in the late 1600s, they adopted a nomadic life similar to that of the **PLAINS INDIANS**, yet they rarely hunted buffalo. In the nineteenth century, they developed a formidable reputation as horse thieves, venturing as far as California on raids. Their custom of stealing Navajo children bred an enmity that still endures.

Through the leadership of Chief Ouray, the Utes received a large reservation in western Colorado by treaty in 1863, but after their killing of Indian agent Nathan Meeker in 1879, the government reduced their lands greatly. In the late 1940s the Utes won a large judgment against the federal government as reimbursement for their Colorado reservation, and they presently have reservations in eastern Utah and southwest Colorado.

VACA (VAH-kuh) The Spanish word for cow, used commonly in the Southwest, sometimes jocularly. A *vacada* is a herd of cows.

VACIERO (vah-SYAYR-oh) In the Southwest, the fellow who brought supplies to the camps of the **SHEEPHERDERS**, who couldn't leave their herds. From Spanish.

VALGAME DIOS! (VAL-gah-may DEE-ohs) In the Southwest, an exclamation, literally "God help me," and the approximate equivalent of "for heaven's sakes." Borrowed from Spanish.

VALLEY TAN In Mormondom, a derisive term for anything homemade. First it was applied to a second-rate leather made in Salt Lake, then generalized to anything made at home. It particularly applied to a potent brand of whiskey, which was also called **LEOPARD SWEAT**.

VAMOOSE (vah-MOOS; va-MOOS) "Let's go, let's get a move on, let's get out of here." Adapted from the Spanish verb *ir*, which in first-person plural is *vamos* (VAH-mohs). The term started in the Southwest and has spread all over the United States. American practice widened the term to looser usages, such as the infinitive (to *vamoose*), the gerund (*vamoosing*), and even the transitive verb—thus Libby Custer writes, "They vamoosed the ranch."

VAQUERO (vah-KAYR-oh) A cowboy, especially a Hispanic cowboy, or an Anglo hand of the border country or California. Borrowed from Spanish; also spelled *vacquero* and *baquero*.

The vaqueros of New Spain and Mexico discovered and refined much of the gear, technique, and lore that became the standard equipment of American cowboys. Early Texans learned it from vaqueros and sent it north to the Great Plains with the great trail herds. David Dary's excellent *Cowboy Culture* shows how cowboy learning developed and was disseminated.

VARA (VAHR-uh) A Spanish yard, thirty-three inches. Borrowed from Spanish.

VARRUGA (vah-ROO-guh) Historically in the Southwest, a cut in the jaw or wattle that made a strip of flesh hang down (a mark of ownership like the **EARMARK**). Borrowed from Spanish. (See also **DEWLAP, JUG HANDLE, WATTLE.**)

VENT BRAND A **SALE BRAND**; a brand replacing the original brand of ownership and indicating that the cow has been sold. To *vent a brand* was to put on such a brand and perhaps burn a slash through the old brand. Derived from the Spanish *venta* (a sale).

VERDAD (vayr-DAHD) Sometimes used in the modern Southwest to mean really, truly, for sure. From Spanish.

VIGA (VEE-guh) Among Mexican-Americans and **PUEBLO** peoples historically, a horizontal peeled log supporting the roof of a building and often projecting a foot or two beyond the walls into the exterior. It is often associated with **ADOBE** buildings; when used with **LATILLAS**, it is called *viga and latilla construction.* Traditionally, vigas were erected as supports, latillas laid across them (sometimes in herringbone patterns), straw spread over the latillas, and the whole covered with mud. These elements are now in widespread use by all peoples in the Southwest. Borrowed from Spanish (in which it means "rafter").

VIGILANTE A member of a vigilance committee. Citizens banded together in the West as vigilance committees, without legal sanction and usually in the absence of effective law enforcement, to take action against men viewed as threats to life and property. The usual pattern of vigilance committees (also called *hemp committees, committees of vigilance,* or *associations of vigilance*) was to grab the "bad" guys, stage a sort of trial, and hang their enemies. Others of their enemies then were likely to see discretion as the better part of valor and **VAMOOSE.**

Vaquero.
[DRAWING BY E. L. REEDSTROM.]

These committees started not in the West but the South, where they arose to intimidate blacks and abolitionists. In the West, they usually claimed to set out to make life safe for ordinary citizens. In the Virginia City, Montana, gold rush, they were respected men and probably acted from commendable motives. But other vigilantes may have been motivated by religious or racial intolerance or a desire for power, and were afflicted with blood lust after they got started. Most areas of the West saw some vigilantism.

The committees sometimes signed themselves V.C., so that a traveler might see a grave with a marker bearing a name and the ominous inscription "died by the hands of the V.C."

The first uses of *vigilante*, which was also called a *regulator, vigilant,* or *vigy,* date from Colorado and Montana in the 1860s, in both cases in newspapers during times of vigilance committee activity. The form *vigilantism* was used in California in the 1850s. (See also THREE-SEVEN-SEVENTY-SEVEN.)

VILLAGE In Alaska, a community of Native people, as opposed to a community of white people, which is called a *town.*

VINEGARROON (vin-uh-guh-ROON) In the Southwest, the whip scorpion, which also has been called a *vinagrillo.* The name comes from the vinegarish stink of the critter when disturbed. Adapted from the Spanish *vinagrón,* which suggests a strong vinegar smell.

VISALIA A popular SADDLE TREE that gave its name to the saddle; *visa* for short.

VISION QUEST A traditional form of seeking among Indian men and sometimes women, very widespread. Typically, during adolescence the quester purifies himself in a SWEAT LODGE, isolates himself for four days, does not eat or drink during that time, and seeks MEDICINE, which is most likely to be revealed in the form of a dream. He may repeat the quest several times during his life, or many times.

This custom, once common to many Native peoples and still vital among Indians, is now spreading in a modest way to Anglos, who seek not medicine specifically but life-guiding wisdom. See the excellent *The Book of the Vision Quest* by Steven Foster and Meredith Little for this new form of an ancient rite.

VOLANTE (voh-LAHN-tay) (1) In the Southwest, a light, two-wheeled vehicle drawn by horses or mules. (2) A veil-like woman's head covering. Adapted from Spanish (in which it means "flying").

VOLUNTEER A RODEO hand who sets calves and steers free from the competitors' ropes and pigging strings.

VOMITO (VAH-mi-toh) A virulent form of yellow fever, often accompanied by black vomit. Borrowed from Spanish.

VOUCHER In Texas and perhaps more broadly through the Southwest, a SCALP taken for bounty.

VOYAGEUR (vwa-yah-JHER) A French-Canadian boatman. He was a hired laborer with a canoe paddle. For an appreciation of him, see Peter Newman's *Caesars of the Wilderness.* Borrowed from Canadian French.

WADDY One of the words for a cowboy, especially a cowboy who drifted from ranch to ranch and helped out in busy times. Adams and Jo Mora, in *Trail Dust and Saddle Leather*, both suggest that the word derived from *wad*, something used to fill in, but this notion isn't widely accepted. Neither is the suggestion that it comes from a wad of chewing tobacco. To add to the mystery, waddy meant "rustler" before it indicated "cowboy." Also spelled *waddie*.

WAGH! An interjection of the **MOUNTAIN MEN**, indicating vigorous assent, amazement, or the like. Some authorities speculate that it may have derived from the grunt of an Indian or of a grizzly bear. A more likely suggestion is that it came from an exclamation of Santa Fe Trail men, *Hua!*, meaning "Get along," which in turn comes from the Spanish exclamation *Gua!*, meaning something like "Gracious!" Many mountain men first came west on the Sante Fe Trail in the 1820s and 1830s, and the first recorded use among the mountain men is by Lieutenant George Frederick Ruxton in the late 1840s, in *Life in the Far West*.

WAGON BOSS The wagon master, the leader of a train of freight, often reported to be an absolute monarch on the trail, in charge of finding grass and water, choosing places for nooning and camping, security against Indians, and so on. Also a name for the **ROUNDUP BOSS**.

WAGON TRAIN A group of wagons bearing emigrants west, or sometimes bearing freight. (Trains of freight wagons were more likely to be called **BULL TRAINS**, **GRASS TRAINS**, and so on.) The emigrant train has been one of the yeasty myths of the West, giving birth to tales of epic adventure, heroism, cowardice, villainy, and the like. Emerson Hough's *The Covered Wagon*, a hugely popular novel and movie, and A. B. Guthrie Jr.'s *The Way West*, which won a Pulitzer Prize, describe the experience.

Mormon emigrants going through Echo Canyon.

[COURTESY OF AMERICAN HERITAGE CENTER, UNIVERSITY OF WYOMING.]

The wagon of legend and history was the **PRAIRIE SCHOONER**. For the Oregon Trail, the principal emigrant trail, and the Santa Fe Trail, these wagons generally assembled at Westport, Missouri, and started in the spring when the grass was good. They bunched up in trains big enough to offer protection against Indians, which the emigrants imagined to be the biggest danger, though they weren't. Thunderstorms, dust storms, high rivers, lack of water, scarcity of game, steep grades, and disgruntled companions all took their toll on the emigrants. The Plains Indians, perhaps after being placated with some gifts, most years simply let the wayfarers pass. The most celebrated disaster to an emigrant train came from starvation—when the Donner party got stuck in the Sierras in 1846 and had to winter there. Most emigrants passed without disaster to Oregon, California, the kingdom of Deseret, or wherever they were going and set up a new life or even a hoped-for utopia.

WAKAN (wah-KAHN) Among contemporary **PLAINS INDIANS** of various tribes, sacred, spiritual. Borrowed from the **DAKOTA** language. One Dakota word for deity, or the great mystery, is *wakantanka*.

WALKAHEAP Red English for an infantryman, who walked rather than rode. Also *heap-walk-man*.

WALK-DOWN A technique of catching wild horses. The hunters ride slowly along behind the animals, at a distance, careful not to spook them, and finally exhaust them. This has even been accomplished on foot.

WALKER A .44-caliber, six-shooting **COLT** produced by Samuel Colt and Eli Whitney Jr. from 1847 into the 1860s. It was named after Texas Ranger Sam Walker.

WALLA WALLA A Shahaptin-speaking tribe of southeastern Washington. With Umatilla and Cayuse Indians, they share the Umatilla Reservation. The *Walla Walla chinook* is a cold, easterly wind (though a *chinook* is normally a warm wind). The *Walla Walla sweet* is a much-sought onion, actually sweet to the tongue, grown in that area.

WALLET A saddle sack for a cowboy to carry his food and personal gear in. It was tied behind the saddle.

WALL-EYE A big-eyed surf fish of the Pacific Coast.

WALRUSSIA An early name for Alaska. Before the **ALEUT** word *Alaska* was accepted for the territory purchased from Russia, many names were suggested, such as American Siberia, Zero Island, Polaria, and Icebargia.

WAMPUS CAT An imaginary critter loggers attribute night sounds to.

WANNIGAN (1) What a **SHEEPHERDER** called his supply wagon or even his sheep wagon. (2) Among loggers, a box for storing small items; a chest for storing clothes. (3) The logging camp office where loggers got paid. (4) A boat carrying the men and equipment of a woods logging camp. (5) A shelter loggers lived in. It is from an Abenaki word and variously spelled.

WAPATOO In the Pacific Northwest, one of several edible roots, particularly of the two species arrowhead.

WAPITI The American elk, which the British call a *stag*. The name (sometimes occurring as *wapiti deer* and variously spelled) comes from a **SHAWNEE** word meaning "white rump"; the Cree have a similar word. For a study of these creatures and part of the country they inhabit, see Margaret and Olaus Murie's *Wapiti Wilderness* (1966), which views the animals both scientifically and from personal experience.

WAR COMBINATIONS: *war budget* (a sack containing an Indian's war medicine and trophies), *war chief* (a leader in war, who would suggest military missions and methods), *war dance* (an Indian ceremony, including dancing, held as a preparation for war to solicit the help of the spirit powers; an Anglo imitation of the dancing, often done in jest), *war eagle* (the golden eagle, whose feathers represent prowess in fighting), *war paint* (paint applied by a warrior to his face or body or both in a design revealed to him to offer protection against injury, and perhaps offer enhanced fighting prowess; also, a mixture of soot and grease cowboys put on their faces as a protection against the glare of the snow), *war party* (a group of Indians on a mission of war and, by extension, a bunch of whites out for blood), *war path* or *trail* (first, a trail used to go to war; later, a military expedition or the way or mode of war generally, first applied to Indians, then sometimes jokingly to white soldiers and even to housewives), *war shield* (a shield made of heat-treated **PARFLECHE** and made powerful by **MEDICINE**), *war tent* (Red English for the Sibley tent used by soldiers on the Great Plains), *war whoop* (an Indian war cry, understood by whites to be a joyous and bloodthirsty outburst, but these whites usually didn't understand the words; also occurred in verb form).

WAR BAG A cowboy's bag for his personal possessions, often canvas but sometimes just a flour or grain sack. In the days of the open range, a snoop probably would have found some town clothing, the makings (for cigarettes), cartridges, and maybe some letters from home in it. The word has survived to today, and the contents have changed with the times. It's also called a *war sack*, a *tucker bag*, and a *possible sack*.

WAR BONNET Among the **PLAINS INDIANS**, and many other Indians, Red English for a hat of **MEDICINE**, worn in war or on ceremonial occasions or both. The medicine typically protected the warrior against injury or death and usually required certain behaviors on his part.

In popular imagination this hat has become a full-length eagle-feather headdress worn by the Plains Indians like the **SIOUX** (**DAKOTA**) and **CHEYENNE**. Actual war bonnets were made of many materials, especially the skin of the buffalo, and often included horns. The full eagle-feather version was also real, mentioned by John C. Frémont as early as 1845.

George Bird Grinnell (*The Cheyenne Indians*) was fortunate enough to get the story of a famous war bonnet, the one worn by the Cheyenne warrior Roman Nose, directly from the man who made the bonnet, White Bull. Discovering that White Bull had seen protection against lightning in a dream, Roman Nose asked him to make a war bonnet like the one dreamed. To make paints, White Bull pulverized stones and animal bones, and he gathered minerals and clay and charcoal.

> In the front of the war-bonnet, close to the brow-band, and over the warrior's forehead, stood a single buffalo-horn. Immediately behind this horn, on top of the bonnet, was the skin of a kingfisher, tied to the hair. At the right side of the head was tied a hawk-skin. This hawk represented the person who in White Bull's vision had held in its claws [a] gun and saber. From the headpiece, on either side, two tails of eagle-feathers ran down toward the ground, the feathers on the right side being red, and those on the left side white. At the back of the head, part way down on the war-bonnet, was the skin of a barnswallow, while to the right side of the war-bonnet, where the feathers were red, was tied a bat, so that the warrior might safely fight in the night, for a bat flies at night and cannot be caught.

White Bull goes on to explain that when an enemy shoots at the man on horseback, the real person will be the bat, above, or the barn swallow flying close to the ground. The kingfisher was to close holes in the body made by bullets, as the water closes over the kingfisher when it dives.

WAR BRIDLE A painful halter used to lead unruly horses, made of a noose hitched onto a horse's mouth and around its head.

WAR KNOT A knot in the tail or mane of a horse, tied by **BUCKAROOS** and **CALIFORNIOS** to keep the long hair out of the way when working.

WARD A congregation in the **MORMON** church, headed by an executive known as a *bishop*; similar to the Catholic parish. The local church building, often referred to as the *ward house,* is the center of a Mormon family's religious and social life. (See also **STAKE.**)

WARRIOR SOCIETY Among the **PLAINS INDIANS,** a kind of club or association that men belonged to and fought with. Admission to such a society was an important mark of standing for a young man. These societies had varying functions within the tribes. Most typical were policelike duties, maintaining order on the march and on the buffalo hunt, and protecting the rear of the people during retreat or flight. The position of chief of a warrior society was considered a heavy responsibility, and a man who accepted the position had to be prepared to die at all times. Also called an **AKICITA.**

Many tribes had the same societies—the kit fox men, for instance, was a society in various tribes. George Bird Grinnell (in *The Cheyenne Indians*) reports seven soldier societies of the **CHEYENNE**—the *kit foxes, elk soldiers, dog soldiers, red shields, crazy dogs, bowstrings,* and *chief soldiers,* the latter band consisting of the forty-four chiefs of the tribe.

WASH (1) A ravine; a dry, flat-bottomed gully with steep walls created by occasional runoff. (2) A way of describing gold-bearing earth and gravel, as in the usages *wash dirt* or *washing stuff;* also occurs in the noun form—the *wash,* meaning the wash dirt. (3) A bear den; a hole dug in the bank of a stream by a beaver.

COMBINATIONS: *wash gold* (gold found in **PLACER** diggings rather than in veins in rock), *wash pan* or *washer* (an implement—pan—for panning gold).

WASHINANGO In the Southwest, a person of mixed Indian and Black blood. Also called a *Zambo.* In Louisiana and East Texas, a person of red, black, and white blood is a *redbone.*

WASHINGTON COMBINATIONS: *Washington navel* (the principal navel orange of California), *Washington cedar* (sequoia), *Washington clam* (a butter clam), *Washington lily* (Lilium washingtonianum, common on the Pacific Coast), *Washington palm* (the California fan palm).

WASHOE (WAH-shoh) A name for the territory that became the state of Nevada, after Indians of that name who lived on the Truckee River. A *Washoeite* was a person who came to the great silver mines of the Comstock lode (Sam Clemens was one) and, later, any Nevadan. Also spelled *Washo.*

Washoe canary is a name for a **BURRO.** The *Washoe process* was a method of treating silver ore by grinding and adding mercury, blue vitriol, and salt. In Nevada a *Washoe zephyr* (Western drollery) is a strong west wind.

WATAP (wa-TAHP, with the first *a* as in *corral*) The roots of the spruce or pine used for weaving or sewing. Indians in fir country from Montreal to the Pacific Coast pounded the roots and separated the fibers to make the threads and could weave a bowl tight enough to hold water. From Canadian French.

WATER COMBINATIONS: *water hole* (a spot naturally containing water—a **TANK,** a wallow, a water pocket—where you can water stock), *water master* (a supervisor of an irrigation system), *water-shy* (descriptive, among cowboys, of a person who doesn't bathe often enough), *water wally* (a batamote, the seep-willow tree), *water trap* (a corral at a water hole, with a gate that closes when the horses are in), *water at night* (to be on the dodge), *water a herd* (in the days of the open range, to drive the cattle into and out of the river in such a way that all cows got clean water, got enough water, and didn't stampede—it was a tricky job).

WATER DOG One of several salamanders; also called a *mud puppy, hell-bender, ground puppy,* and *water puppy.*

WATER SCRAPE A waterless stretch of country to cross. (See also **JORNADA.**) Smith says the origin was that, if water was to be found, it had to be scraped for. A good many of the great stories of the West come from crossings of water scrapes, with stock half-mad from thirst.

WATERBELLY An affliction of steers, the blocking of the urinary canal with stones, often leading to death.

WATERMELON UNDER THE SADDLE Among cowboys, a way of describing a horse that arches its back a lot. (See also STOCK HORSE.)

WATTLE A mark of ownership, like a brand or an earmark, consisting of a flap of skin cut from the jaw or neck of livestock so that it hangs. (See also JUG HANDLE, VARRUGA.)

WAVE AROUND Especially in the days of the open range, to wave your hat in a signal for someone to ride around and not come toward you; a not-welcome sign.

WAWA (WAH-wah) CHINOOK jargon for talk, speech. Also used as a verb meaning "to speak." A council was a *hyas* (big) *wawa,* and one newspaper even put *wawa* in its name.

WEANER A newly weaned calf; a calf ready to wean. Calves are often weaned in a *weaning corral.* By extension among cowmen, a human infant.

WEAR THE BUSTLE WRONG To be pregnant. Good cowboy humor, based on a mental picture.

WEAVER A horse that bucks with a weaving motion rather than straight away, a hard horse to stay on. Also a term of BUCKAROO country for a horse that continually sways in the stall.

WEAVER'S PATHWAY See PATHWAY.

WEBFOOT A resident of western Oregon, because of the wet weather.

WEDDING JAR Among PUEBLO peoples, a tall, double-necked work of pottery with two spouts, joined by a handle, representing husband and wife. Made by the HOPIS, was never part of a traditional marriage ceremony. Also called *wedding vase.*

WELL-HEELED Well off, depending on context, for either money or firearms.

WELSH INDIAN One of the will-o'-the-wisps of the West. Reports of Welsh-speaking Indians with fair skin, beards, and blue eyes led to efforts by a good many explorers to find this "lost tribe" and to various accounts of its discovery. Reports of twelfth-century colonies established in America by Welshmen led by Madoc inflamed the speculation. The Mormons were especially keen to find this tribe as confirmation of declarations in *The Book of Mormon,* and they sometimes thought they spotted Welsh words in the language of the Hopi. Others found Welsh words in the Mandan language

WEST Geographically, it is the region of the United States between the 100th meridian and the Pacific Ocean, including Alaska and some western parts of

Canada and Mexico, an area where the land is mostly high and dry. Economically, a region where the Native ways of living on the land have been supplanted by explorers, fur traders, emigrants, miners, loggers, and ranchers—should we add movie makers, skiers, surfers, and computer hot-shots? Culturally, a place where the ways of living in the East, South, and Midwest blended somehow with the ways of buffalo-hunting Indians, pueblo peoples, fish-eating Indians, **ESKIMOS**, **ALEUTS**, and other Native peoples, and with those of French-Canadians, Mexicans, Mormons, Russians, and others, into a melange that is elusively indescribable but delectable. A place where races clashed, some prevailed, and others suffered. Mythologically, a place where our national dream was played out, and continues to be; an Eden where people sought new beginnings; a place where enterprise and grit told the story, or one story; and much, much more. It is a place ever-changing and ever-fascinating, to the keen eye always distinct from the rest of the nation. Some of us believe that, even as the monopolies change, American Fur Company giving way to Microsoft, and the people change, free trappers supplanted by surfers, growers of corn and beans replaced by growers of mari-juana, the older West is perpetually reborn in the new, and that a vigorous spirit continually informs and invigorates life in our homeland.

Western, meaning of or pertaining to the West, occurs in a large number of names of plants and animals. *Westerner* means a person born in, raised in, living in, or otherwise strongly associated with the West. A *westernism* is a word, phrase, or saying associated with the West.

WEST COAST The states along the Pacific Ocean—California, Oregon, and Washington. In most usage the term seems not to include Alaska.

WET STOCK Livestock stolen in Mexico and forced to swim the Rio Grande. Thus *wet horse* and *wet cow.*

WETBACK A derogatory term for a Mexican who gains illegal entry to the United States by swimming a border river. Such a person is also called *mojado* (from the Spanish word for wet), *alambrista* (fence climber), *illegal alien,* and *undocumented worker.*

WHALE In Alaska, a huge halibut, weighing more than eighty pounds; one under ten pounds is called a *chicken.*

WHANG A leather **STRING** such as hung from deerskin hunting shirts and still hangs from saddles. Such hide strips were used to repair almost anything, as baling wire is used in the West today. On saddles, they're used to tie things on.

WHAT I KNOW ABOUT THAT YOU COULD PUT IN ONE EYE "I don't know a damn thing about that." A nice example of self-deprecatory cowboy humor. It also occurs in an even better form: "What I know about that you could put between your eye and your eyelid and it wouldn't scratch."

WHAT IN THE SAM HILL . . . Phrase meaning "what in the world," named after the eccentric who built a museum on the Columbia Gorge, the son of railroad tycoon James J. Hill.

WHEEL Cowboy slang for the cylinder of a pistol. **NO BEANS IN THE WHEEL** means "an empty gun."

WHEN COWS CLIMB TREES! A cowboy expression for when he'll do what he doesn't mean to do—never.

WHEY-BELLY Cowboy talk for a *potgutted* (second-rate) horse. (See also **CANNER**.)

WHILE THE GATE'S OPEN Rancher talk meaning while the opportunity is there.

WHISKERINO A beard-growing contest, usually associated with a celebration such as pioneer days. The prizes may be for the longest, ugliest, etc.

WHISKEY See **AGUARDIENTE**, **FIREWATER**.

WHISKEY TRADER A fellow who traded whiskey to the Indians for hides, which was illegal but profitable and gave these small traders an advantage over the government's trading posts and forts. A *whiskey Indian* was one who was fond of booze. (See also **INDIAN WHISKEY**.) Westerners of the nineteenth century called places that sold whiskey *whiskey holes, joints, mills,* and *ranches.*

WHISPERING BELLS California yellow bells (*Emmenanthe peduliflora*). They dry on the stem and in a breeze make a rustling sound.

WHISTLE Cowboy talk for a young 'un, a **BUTTON**. Whistle was also a nineteenth-century word for the call of the bull elk in mating season; it's now called *bugling.* A *whistler* (or *whistle pig*) may be either a **MARMOT** (because of its cry) or a horse that wheezes because it's **WIND-BROKE**.

WHISTLE JUDGE In **RODEO**, the official who signaled you had stayed on the horse or bull long enough to qualify. These days a Pro Rodeo official called the timer *blows* an airhorn up in the crow's nest; the judges in the arena have stop watches.

WHISTLEBERRY A cowboy's name for a bean. He also called them *strawberries* (Arkansas, Mexican, or prairie) and *ribstickers.*

WHITE A way of describing a fair, decent, right sort of man. Though this usage may be pre-Western, most of the early citations are from the West, like this one: "Although your color is cinnamon, and you may have Spanish, Navajo, or even Apache blood in your veins, you treat me white all the same," wrote John Cook in *The Border and the Buffalo.* A similar phrase was "That's mighty white of you." Normally the notion of who was white included only northern Europeans and Americans of that descent; sometimes even Irish, Germans, and the Spanish were left out. (It's good to remember how strong racism was.)

COMBINATIONS: *white Cherokee* or *Choctaw* (a member of one of those tribes with considerable white blood), *white doctor* (a physician who practiced scientific medicine—was not a medicine man—even if an Indian), *white flesh* (white people, considered collectively), *white heart* (a red bead with a white center made popular in the Indian trade by the French, who called it a *coeur blanc*), *white house* (one of the cowboy's names for the main ranch house), *white-water man* (a logger's name for a log driver).

ANIMALS: *white bear* (the grizzly), *whiteface* (a Hereford cow, red with a white face), *white horse* (a notice to a logger that he's fired and is to get his pay and leave— go to town on a white horse), *white mule* (what a logger called cheap whiskey), *white weasel* (among old Northwest traders, an ermine), *white brant* (western name for the snow goose).

WHITE BUFFALO A buffalo that is cream-colored or even spotted dark and white. These creatures were sacred objects to nearly all the PLAINS tribes. When a hunter found and killed one, its hide was tanned especially well and made a gift to the sun. This act brought blessings not only to him but his entire tribe. Though it is often assumed that white buffalo were albinos, WHITE INDIAN James Willard Schultz says their eyes were of normal color.

WHITE BUFFALO WOMAN A principal culture hero of the LAKOTA, who brought the MEDICINE PIPE to the people. Also called White Buffalo Calf Woman.

WHITE INDIAN Either a member of a tribe noted for light skin, or a white man who adopted an Indian way of life. The term was applied to people who joined the tribes voluntarily rather than captives. Many white people did choose an Indian way of life for at least a few years, especially men. MOUNTAIN MEN still in the mountains after the heyday of the fur trade passed sometimes joined their wives' people. Sam Houston was for a time a white Indian.

WHITE SAGE A plant of the Northern Plains and northern Rockies (*Salva apiana*) sacred to the tribes of that region, used for cleansing and purifying, and used medicinally. Though it smells like sagebrush, it is not woody and grows in a single, slender stem with whitish leaves.

WHITTLE WHANGING Cowboy talk for quarreling.

WHOOPING CRANE The tallest bird (*Grus americana*) in North America and one of the rarest. Almost brought to extinction by hunting and habitat pressures, but small populations are making a comeback. The largest flock winters in the Aransas National Wildlife Refuge in Texas; there is an experimental population at Grays Lake National Wildlife Refuge in Idaho.

WHOOP-UP An establishment that traded whiskey to Indians; an Indian who liked to drink. Adams says that the term comes from a bar called Fort Whoop-up on the Canadian-American border. The border literally ran through the building, and the proprietors sold whiskey to Indians.

WICKIUP (WIH-kee-up) A brush hut used by Western Indians, principally those who were not tipi dwellers, and especially Indians of the desert Southwest. Often woven from willow branches, reeds, ocotillo stalks, and the like, and covered with brush, hides, or blankets. Probably from a Sauk, Fox, and Kickapoo word for dwelling. Sometimes Anglos applied this word jocularly to their own houses.

WIDOW-MAKER (1) Among cowboys, an outlaw horse. (2) Among loggers, a falling tree or a branch apt to fall. (3) Among miners, an excavating drill. (4) Uncommonly, a revolver.

WILD BUNCH (1) A gang of OUTLAWS, such as the one usually called the Wild Bunch, which was led by Robert Leroy Parker, best known as Butch Cassidy. (2) A bunch of horses not accustomed to being handled.

WILD CELERY In Alaska, one of two celery-like plants, cow parsnip (*Heracleum lanatum*) or seacoast angelica (*Angelica lucida*). They grow to more than five feet and more than three feet, respectively, and are edible. Also called *puchki* (from Russian). COMBINATIONS: *wild hyacinth* (another name for camas), *wild onion* (a name for the death camas), *wild parsley* (in Alaska, the edible coastal plant *Ligusticum scotium*, also called *beach lovage, sea parsley,* or *petruski*).

WILD COW MILKING A RODEO event in which a pair of cowboys rope a wild cow, milk her, and hoof it to the judge's stand with some milk.

A Kickapoo wickiup, Oklahoma Territory, 1880.
[COURTESY OF NATIONAL ARCHIVES (75-IP-3-4).]

WILD HORSE RACE A RODEO event in which a trio of cowboys catch and saddle a wild horse and ride it across the finish line.

WILD RICE Not rice but an aquatic grass (*Zizania aquatica*) that grows in northern Minnesota and Wisconsin. Difficult to cultivate, it is mostly harvested from the wild by the OJIBWAY Indians and today is a major source of revenue for them.

WILD WEST SHOW An outdoor entertainment showing "characteristic" scenes from the days of the "Wild West." Buffalo Bill Cody, though not the first entrepreneur of a Wild West show, created the best-known in *Buffalo Bill's Wild West*, which started in Omaha in 1883. Cody staged for his audiences exhibitions of shooting, riding bucking broncos, roping, an attack on a stagecoach, Pony Express–style riding, and so on. Annie Oakley and Sitting Bull were among the performers. The show even toured Europe and was a direct ancestor of the RODEO. Also called a *Bill show*.

WILDCAT In California from the 1860s, a mine of dubious value. Later, an oil well dug in a new oil area. Men who dug such wells or sold such mines, where deposits are unproven, were called *wildcatters*. *Wildcatting* meant to engage in dangerous or highly speculative activities.

COMBINATIONS: *wildcat claim* (a mining claim in an established area that's half-fraudulent, or all fraudulent, but much touted by the owner and sold to the unwary), *wildcat mine* (one of doubtful value, perhaps *salted* to make it look good) *wildcat oil company*, etc.

WILDERNESS Land protected by the 1964 Wilderness Act and managed to preserve its natural condition. Each wilderness area is usually 5,000 acres or greater and reserved for travel by foot or animal. Hiking, grazing, and hunting have been deemed compatible uses; in most instances, drilling and logging are not permitted, and no permanent improvements for human habitation are made.

Buffalo Bill and Sitting Bull, participants in the most famous Wild West show.
[COURTESY OF AMERICAN HERITAGE CENTER, UNIVERSITY OF WYOMING.]

Primitive area is a former name for wild areas designated by government agencies rather than by Congress; these areas are now incorporated into wilderness areas or are sometimes called *wilderness study areas*.

WILLIWAW A cold, violent wind gusting suddenly onto the sea from coastal mountains. Though not originally a westernism, it is strongly associated with Alaska.

WILLOW BACKREST The chair of the **PLAINS INDIANS**. The user sat on the floor and leaned against it. It was made of strips of willow peeled and laced together and was hung from a tripod to give support for the back. Many were beautifully decorated with pieces of blanket and buckskin or beads, and only a poor **TIPI** was without at least one. Indians and hobbyists still use them, primarily at **POWWOWS** and at **RENDEZVOUS**.

WILLOW GROUSE In Alaska and northwestern Canada, a grouse (*Lagopus lagopus*) also known as the *ruffed grouse, willow ptarmigan,* or *sharp-tailed grouse.*

WILSON'S PETREL The common stormy petrel (*Oceanites oceanicus*) of the Pacific Coast, named after the Scottish-born American ornithologist Alexander Wilson. *Wilson's phalarope* is a large phalarope of the West.

WIN YOUR SPURS To earn your place or standing, as a cowboy or in any endeavor. Thus novelist Owen Wister, talking about a favorable review, wrote, "They say I've already 'won my spurs,' and if not 'spoiled by undue literary petting' I shall probably etc., etc. I don't think I've won my spurs, though I propose to. But I'm glad they think so, and as many other friendly critics as possible."

WINCHESTER A repeating rifle. As Colt came to mean any pistol and Stetson any hat, Winchester came also to mean any repeating rifle. The company that made it, the Winchester Repeating Arms Company, was a reorganized form of the New Haven Arms Company, which made the **HENRY** rifle. Winchester's Model 1873, a .44-caliber, center-fire, fifteen-shot rifle, became "the rifle that won the West." In the twentieth century the .30-.30 Winchester became hugely popular.

Other Western names for rifles: **BIG FIFTY**, *buffalo gun,* **FUSIL,** **HAWKEN,** *Henry, lightning stock, long tom, meat in the pot, needle gun, reliable, saddle gun, smoke pole, trade gun, Worcestershire, Yager.*

Left: Winchester 1873; right: Sharps "Buffalo" gun.
[DRAWING BY E. L. REEDSTROM.]

WIND-BROKE A way of describing a horse with partially paralyzed vocal cords. Because of its wheezing, it's called a *whistler;* of this critter it's said, "He can't keep a secret." (See also **CANNER**.)

WINDMILLER A hand hired (on ranches big enough for one) to keep the windmills in repair. Also called a *windmill monkey.*

WINDSURFING A recent sport that combines surfing and sailing; originated in the Columbia Gorge.

WINDY A cow hard to drive from the canyons onto the flats; Adams says this use comes from the fact that such work exhausts the cowboys. Also a tall tale—see **STUFFING DUDES**.

WINTER (1) In Red English, a year. Thus an Indian toddler was two winters old, and the Plains Indian calendar was called a **WINTER COUNT**. (2) To winter was to spend the winter in the Western wilderness, among trappers a mark of an experienced man. (See also **HIVERNANT**.)

COMBINATIONS: *winter horse* (a horse not turned out for the winter but grained and kept ready for work), *winter kill* (cattle killed by cold weather; sometimes wild animals such as elk killed by cold weather), *Winter Quarters* (the temporary home of the Mormons on the west side of the Missouri River on their great 1846–47 migration from Nauvoo, Illinois, to the valley of the Salt Lake in Utah), *winter Saint* (an emigrant who spent a winter among the Mormons at Salt Lake instead of attempting to cross the remaining deserts and mountains to the West Coast late in the season).

WINTER COUNT An Indian history book, a pictographic record of past years painted on hide by **PLAINS INDIANS**. Each pictograph indicated what happened in one year, such as the year Crazy Woman Creek flooded, the year of the big prairie fire, the year the three kit fox men got killed, and so on. Winter counts are now important both as art objects and as historical records.

WINTER ROAD In Alaska, a road for use in winter, when freezing makes wet areas solid; also called a *winter trail,* which in turn sometimes becomes an established trail for **DOGSLEDS**.

WIPE OUT Among surfers, for your board to throw you as a bronc throws a rider. Among skiers, to fall down in a big way. Also takes noun form, a *wipeout.* The meaning, to crash, has been extended to other contexts.

WIRE ROAD A trail (or road) following a telegraph line.

WIRECUTTERS (1) A combination of pliers, cutters, and small hammer carried by Westerners who ride the range these days on horseback or in pickups. Along with the wire stretcher, wirecutters are one of the essential tools of the modern cowboy. (2) Over a century ago a wirecutter was a person who cut a fence in a range war or started a range war.

WISH BOOK A mail-order catalog, a chief source of news on the latest developments for remote ranches.

WOBBLY A member of Industrial Workers of the World(IWW). This labor union was founded in 1905 by labor groups that believed the American Federation of Labor was stodgy because it accepted capitalism. It sought to achieve its ends by more radical means such as general strikes, boycotts, and sabotage. Its strongest influence was in the Pacific Northwest, among miners and loggers. The term is spelled both upper and lower case. Said by some to stand for "I Won't Work."

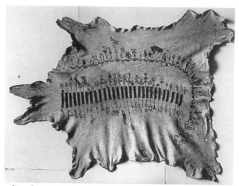

Winter count, a calendar of 37 months, 1889–92, kept by Anko, a Kiowa man. [COURTESY OF NATIONAL ARCHIVES (1895-106-JN-79).]

WOHAW A term of Red English for cattle. It spread to cattlemen as well and also occurred in the form *wohaw John.* The source of the word has been attributed to the cries of the bullwhackers to draft animals: *whoa, gee,* and *haw.* Though a recent lexicographer doubts this, it appears to be confirmed by Lieutenant George Frederick Ruxton, who in the 1840s called the wagon driver's talk to his oxen *wohaws.* It has also been suggested that wohaw is an Indian adaptation of the Spanish word for cow, *vaca.*

WOKAS The seed of the great yellow water lily (*Nuphar polysepalum*), dried and roasted by Oregon Indians for food.

WOLF Like the buffalo, elk, grizzly bear, and coyote, the wolf is a major character on the stage of Western imagination, beloved as a symbol of things wild, despised as a predator upon livestock, the hero or villain of thousands of stories and myths. *Canis lupus,* mostly wiped out in Lower 48 states, is now making a controversial comeback in the Greater Yellowstone area and central Idaho, sponsored by federal programs. Some persist in northern Minnesota, northern Idaho, northern Montana, Louisiana, and near the Mexican border. Canada and Alaska have wolves in abundance.

The *timber wolf,* also known as the *gray wolf* and the *lobo,* may grow to more than three feet at the shoulders and weigh as much as 175 pounds. (The red wolf of the Deep South is smaller.) They are social, and live and hunt as families. Except for an incident involving single rabid beasts, attacks on human beings are unknown.

WOLF EEL On the coast of California, an elongated fish that looks like an eel; sources disagree about whether it is *Anarhichthis felis* or *A. ocellatus.*

WOLFER A man who hunted wolves for money, using traps or poison. Often he was paid by ranchers and also collected a bounty from the government. Wolves were a threat to livestock in the older West, but references to them in diaries and journals are to be handled with care—often the coyote (*prairie wolf*) was meant, not the wolf. *Wolfing* is wolf hunting.

WOOD HAWK A man who cut wood along a river for steamboats, which he stacked at *wooding stations.*

WOOD RANCH An area (particularly in treeless country) where wood was available.

WOODEN OVERCOAT (1) A coffin. See, for instance, Paul St. Pierre's wonderful story "Antoine's Wooden Overcoat." (2) Also, in the army, a barrel worn as a punishment. (See also **BARREL-JACKET PUNISHMENT.**)

WOOLLY (1) A sheep. Sheep are subject to all kinds of derisive names: *Ba-ah, grass shavers, hoofed locusts, maggots, stinkers, stubble jumper, underwears,* and *wool locusts.* (2) As an adjective, a way of describing a wild place or person. (3) *Woollies* are angora **CHAPS** with the hair on.

WOOLSEY A second-rate cowboy hat, probably one made entirely of wool felt rather than beaver or a beaver-wool blend.

WORK A BRAND OVER To change a brand, once a cause for lynching if unauthorized.

COMBINATIONS: To *work cows* is to handle them—round them up, drive them, cut them, and so on. To *work a horse* is to train it. To *work ahead of the roundup* was to get there early and claim the **MAVERICKS.** To *work the bed ground* was for a sheepherder to help the ewes and their lambs get together. To *work like a beaver* was to work hard, an expression perhaps made common by the **MOUNTAIN MEN.**

WORM The most menial worker on an oil rig. The name comes from the 1920s when an imported weevil (worm) started putting Western farmers out of business. The farmers headed for the oil patches of Oklahoma and Texas, where they got the lowest jobs and were called the worms.

WOUNDED KNEE A creek and a village on the Pine Ridge Reservation in South Dakota, Wounded Knee has given its name to two major events in the history of red-white relations, the Wounded Knee Massacre (1890) and Wounded Knee II (1973).

On December 29, 1890, Big Foot's Mniconjou **LAKOTAS** came to the Wounded Knee under supervision of the Seventh Cavalry. Big Foot was on the way to Pine Ridge on a peaceful mission, but the government feared that the dash south signified an outbreak, and ordered the soldiers to disarm Big Foot's people and escort them back to their home. The next morning, while the soldiers were taking away rifles against protests and in much tension, fighting broke out between warriors and soldiers. Quickly, the soldiers began firing their Hotchkiss guns into the village of women and children, as well as attacking the men (now mostly unarmed) at the council. The people fled in terror and chaos to a nearby ravine, and fighting continued there for some time. The outcome was the slaughter of two to three hundred Indians, mostly women and children. Because the Indians were mostly unarmed, and attacks were made deliberately against women and children, it is rightly termed a massacre.

In 1973, to protest the trail of broken treaties, **AMERICAN INDIAN MOVEMENT (AIM)** members put on a protest at Wounded Knee. The episode ended only after long negotiations, much gunfire, many accusations of bad faith on both sides, and the deaths of two Indians. Some Lakota and other Indian people point to this event as a particular inspiration for the struggles for rights soon to come. (See also **RED POWER**.)

WRANGLER Once, the hand who took care of the horses; now any cowboy, especially one who leads dudes on rides. Historically, taking care of the horse herd (*cavvy*) at the ranch or on the trail was a beginner's job. Ironically, the word has come to imply experience and expertise. The top literary awards of the National Cowboy Hall of Fame each year are called Wranglers. The word is an American version of the Spanish *caballerango*; it also occurs in the form *caverango* and in the verb form *to wrangle*.

A wrangler was also called a *cavvy man*, *dew wrangler* (one who has the early morning shift), *horse pestler*, *horse rustler* (in Texas), *jingler*, *wrangating*, or *wrango*. The saddle horse he kept at hand to bring in the horses was the *wrangle horse*. The hand who minded the horse herd (*remuda*) while the sun was up was the *day wrangler*. At night, the *nighthawk* did it.

WRECK PAN The tub for dirty dishes at the **CHUCK WAGON**. Also called the *wreck tub*.

WRING-TAIL A horse that is nervous or overtired, because it then wrings its tail as it runs.

WRINKLE-HORN An old steer with wrinkled, scaly horns; a wise, experienced person. Also called *mossy horn*.

YAH-TAY The **NAVAJO** equivalent of hello, which has come into use among some Anglos in the **FOUR CORNERS** country. This spelling comes by ear from the Anglo pronunciation.

YAKAMA A tribe of Shahaptian Indians that lived and live along the Columbia and Yakima Rivers in Washington. After they got the horse in the 1730s, they became skilled horsemen and added to their salmon fishing the custom of crossing the mountains and hunting buffalo; they also incorporated some elements of Plains Indian culture.

The Yakama had difficult relationships with the early fur traders, but when Washington became a territory, they agreed to accept a reservation and permit whites to use trails across their lands in exchange for annuities. Disagreements about this treaty led to the Yakima War of 1855–56. In the 1860s, many Yakama became involved in the **DREAMER CULT**. In the twentieth century, the dams on the Columbia River have destroyed many of their traditional salmon-fishing areas, and the federal government has paid them millions of dollars in reparations.

Since the Yakama were well-known horse traders, *Yakima* also became a word meaning "horse," in the way that *cayuse* derived from the Cayuse Indians, a neighboring tribe.

YAMPA One of two herbs (genus *Atenia*) with an edible, potato-like tuber. Also spelled *yamp*.

YANNIGAN BAG A logger's equivalent of a cowboy's **WAR BAG** or a trapper's **POSSIBLE** sack—what he carried his personal gear in.

YARB WOMAN In the Southwest, a Hispanic woman who knows how to use herbs medicinally. It derives from the Spanish word for herb, *hierba*.

YARD LIGHT The mercury vapor lamp kept on through the night in most ranch yards today.

YARD THE GRUB In logger talk, to eat.

YARN To tell a tale, probably an adventure, and probably a tall tale. It has a noun form—the tale is a yarn. Yarning is an old Western custom, a campfire entertainment, and an occasional way of **STUFFING DUDES**. (The custom is hardly exclusively Western—the East had its own tall tales in the Pennsylvany hurricane and the Caroliny swamper.) Some greenhorns mistook yarning for prevaricating: A Montana newspaper editor missed an international scoop by refusing to report the existence of the fabulous Yellowstone region—he didn't want to get caught printing old Jim Bridger's lies. The yarn was first and most tellingly associated with the **MOUNTAIN MAN**. Black Harris's tale of the "putrefied" forest is a classic, and Bridger told encyclopedias of them. Here's one from David Lavender's *One Man's West* that shows that the later West kept the tradition alive and well:

> Why, these mosquitoes ain't nothin'. You ought to see 'em in Greasewood. They put scouts along the trails, an' when a man shows up you can hear 'em holler, 'Here comes meat!' They fly over in droves that shade the sun. They sound like a millrace. Oncet I thought to fool 'em by takin' along a copper wash boiler. When I saw 'em headin' my way I crawled underneath it. But do you think that stopped 'em? No sir! They lit on it an' began to bore like woodpeckers. *Rat-a-tat-tat*—it near broke

my eardrums. I picked up a rock an' when they drilled through I clinched their beaks over like you would a nail. It weren't no use. They reared back, picked up the boiler with their beaks, an' flew off with it. The rest really did go for me then. If a forest fire hadn't come up an' smudged 'em off, I never would of got away.

YEDRA (YAYD-ruh) In the Southwest, poison ivy or poison oak. Adapted from the Spanish *hiedra,* which means "ivy."

YEIBICHAI (YAY-buh-chay) The Night Chant, an important ceremony of the **NAVAJOS,** held over nine days in the winter, when neither snakes nor lightning is active. Masked Yeibichai play the *yei,* deities who are **GRANDFATHER** to monsters and to Female Divinity.

YELLOW BELLY (1) A denigrating term for a Mexican. (2) A Mexican breed of cow.

YELLOW LEG A name for the cavalryman of the post—Civil War period, from the yellow stripe down the seam of his britches. Likewise, an artilleryman was a red leg.

YELLOW-BACKED ROCKFISH A rockfish of the Pacific Coast (*Pteropodus maliger*). COMBINATIONS: *yellow-bellied marmot* (found on the eastern slopes of the Rockies), *yellow-billed magpie* (*Pica nuttalli,* a magpie of coastal California and the valleys of the Sacramento and San Joaquin Rivers).

A cavalryman, also called a yellow leg.
[DRAWING BY E. L. REEDSTROM.]

YELLOWCAKE Uranium oxide, the fissionable material in *carnotite* ore; highly valuable.
The hunt for yellowcake tore up a good deal of the **FOUR CORNERS** country during the uranium-rush days of the 1950s and 1960s.

YELLOWDOG In oil drilling, a water pump.

YERBA BUENA (YAYR-buh BWAY-nuh) (1) One of several kinds of mint used medicinally by the California Indians, especially *Satureja douglasii.* (2) An early name of what is now the city of San Francisco. (3) Another name for Goat Island in San Francisco Bay. Adapted from the Spanish *hierba buena* (which literally means "good herb").
　　Other medicinal herbs are *yerba de vibora,* used by California Indians to alleviate the effects of snakebite (*vibora* being Spanish for viper); *yerba santa* (sacred herb, *Eriodictyon californinum*), used by California Indians to treat respiratory and stomach problems; *yerba del manso* (*Anemopsis californica*), used by the **PIMAS** to treat syphilis.

YO Sheepherder talk for a ewe.

YOSEMITE A valley formed by glacial action, having a flat floor and steep walls, such as Yosemite Valley in what is now the national park of the same name. It also forms the adjective *yosemitic*. The original Native (Miwok) word, which *yosemite* is a re-creation of, means "grizzly bear."

YOSEMITE DECIMAL SYSTEM The rating system used to indicate the difficulty of a rock climb, consisting of arabic numerals 1 through 5; decimal points are used with Class 5 ratings, up to 5.18; letters are used with Class 5.10 and up to indicate increasing difficulty, for example, 5.10a up to 5.10d, etc. Originated with climbers who scaled the big walls in the Yosemite Valley in the 1950s and '60s.

YOUNKER A kid, a youngster (though in the East, a man of position).

YUCCA A genus of arid-land plants of the lily family, sometimes treelike and bearing white blossoms. The yucca of the Southwest has creamy flowers, its root was used by Indians and Hispanics to make soap, and it is also called *soap-weed, palmilla, Spanish bayonet* or *Our Lord's Candle*. Southwestern Indians used yucca fiber for weaving. *Yucca palm* is another name for the JOSHUA TREE.

YUKON BOAT In the Yukon, a square-ended boat for floating downstream, often cheaply made from scavenged boards.

YUKON SLED In Alaska, a DOGSLED used for freighting, with broad runners and no basket, railing, or stanchion, to allow for unwieldy loads.

YUMA An Indian tribe of the lower Colorado River more properly known as the Quechan. Their Yuman-speaking relatives (such as the Cocopa, Halchidhoma, Havasupai, Maricopa, MOJAVE, Walapai, and Yavapai) live along the Colorado, Salt, and Gila Rivers in Arizona. Traditionally, the Yuma have been an agricultural people, known for their baskets, beadwork, and pottery.

In historic times, they controlled the crossing of the Colorado near the mouth of the Gila. The Spanish built a settlement there, but the Yuma attacked and killed the settlers. In the 1840s, Americans began heavy use of this crossing. The Yuma charged to raft people across the river until subdued by the army. From 1884 they have lived on the Fort Yuma Reservation.

Z

ZACATE (sah-KAH-tay) In the Southwest, forage. Borrowed from Spanish.

ZAGUAN (sah-WHAN) In the Southwest, a gate, entrance, vestibule. Borrowed from Spanish.

ZANJA (SAHN-hah) An irrigation ditch. The main ditch was called a *zanja madre* (mother ditch) and the man who dug ditches was a *zanjero*. Borrowed from Spanish. (See also **ACEQUIA**.)

ZAPATO (suh-PAH-toh) A boot or shoe. Borrowed from Spanish.

ZCMI Zion's Cooperative Mercantile Institution, the first department store in the United States. It was founded in 1868 by the **MORMON** church to compete with the gentile merchants in Utah Territory, and its stock was sold only to faithful Saints. This large chain of department stores throughout Mormon country was bought in 2000 by Myer and Frank.

ZEBRA DUN A dun horse with a dorsal stripe and sometimes zebralike stripes on the legs. (See also **BUCKSKIN**.)

ZINFANDEL A red table wine, claret-like, made in California from a grape that was possibly Hungarian.

ZION (1) In **LATTER-DAY SAINT** thought, the name given by the Lord to the future home of the Saints; thus Joseph Smith counseled the Saints to move west and "build Zion in the tops of the mountains," a goal realized in Salt Lake City. (2) In **MORMON** scripture, the Lord's chosen people, "because they were of one heart and one mind, and dwelt in righteousness." (3) Now the name of a national park in southwestern Utah, in which large rock formations have been given religious names like Isaac, the Patriarchs, etc.

ZOPILOTE (soh-pee-LOH-tay; zoh-pi-LOH-tee) In the Southwest, a turkey vulture, a buzzard. From Spanish (which got it from an Aztec word). Sometimes spelled *sopilote.*

ZORRILLA A line-backed **TEXAS LONGHORN**, often speckled white on the flanks and belly.

ZUNI (ZOO-nee) A pueblo of western New Mexico; also the pueblo's people. The Zuni have a ceremonial religion like the other Pueblo tribes and a unique language. Their central religious ceremony is **SHALAKO**, near the winter solstice each year. Their economy historically was agricultural.

Coronado sought Zuni as one of the fabled **SEVEN CITIES** of Cibola, and the Spanish established a mission there in 1629. Relations between Zunis and Americans were generally peaceful in the nineteenth century, and they still inhabit their original territory. Today the Zunis are primarily known for their fine silversmithing and jewelry-making.

The name *Zuni* is a Spanish version of a Keresan word whose meaning is lost. Though occasionally spelled Zuñi, it is pronounced without the tilde (ñ).

A Guide to Further Reading

THIS LIST IS NOT A FORMAL BIBLIOGRAPHY OF SOURCES FOR THE
DICTIONARY BUT A GUIDE TO FURTHER STUDY FOR THE INTERESTED READER.

THE SERIOUS STUDENT SHOULD NOT VENTURE FORTH WITHOUT THESE ESSENTIAL
REFERENCE BOOKS WITHIN REACH:

Cassidy, Frederic G., and Joan H. Hall, eds. *Dictionary of American Regional English*.
Cambridge: Harvard University Press, from 1985. Three volumes (through
the letter O) have been published to date. This dictionary is authoritative. It
is on historical principles, which means the reader can see the order in which
meanings of a given word came into the language, and read quotations that
illustrate its use.

Lamar, Howard R., ed. *The New Encyclopedia of the American West*. New Haven: Yale University
Press, 1998. A cornucopia of information, presented in a form reflecting recent
thinking about Western history.

Mathews, Mitford M., ed. *A Dictionary of Americanisms on Historical Principles*. Chicago:
University of Chicago Press, 1951. Because of the quotations from early sources, an
indispensable book.

Adams, Ramon F. *Western Words: A Dictionary of the American West*. Norman, OK: University
of Oklahoma Press, 1968. Excellent on cows and horses; primarily a Texas and cattle-
history point of view.

Murray, James A. H., ed., *Oxford English Dictionary* and *Supplement*. Oxford: Oxford University
Press, 1972. The master dictionary of English, on historical principles.

Tabbert, Russell. *Dictionary of Alaskan English*. Juneau: Denali Press, 1991. Superb on Alaska.

One should also have a good dictionary of English and one of Spanish. I've used
Webster's Ninth New Collegiate Dictionary, because it lists the date of the first appearance
of the first meaning.

ON A NEARBY SHELF SHOULD BE THESE BOOKS:

Clark, Thomas L. *Western Lore and Language: A Dictionary for Enthusiasts of the American West*. Salt
Lake: University of Utah Press, 1996. Excellent on contemporary language, the Pacific
Coast, and Alaska.

Foster-Harris, William. *The Look of the Old West*. New York: Viking, 1955. Good for sketches
of clothes, tools, and the like, plus descriptions of how things worked.

Smith, Cornelius Cole. *A Southwestern Vocabulary*. Burbank: A. H. Clark, 1985. The historical language of the Southwest.

Watts, Peter. *A Dictionary of the Old West*. New York: Alfred A. Knopf, 1977. A sound book,
limited to the second half of the nineteenth century.

THESE BOOKS ARE NEEDED LESS OFTEN, AND SO MIGHT BE USED AT THE LIBRARY:

LANGUAGE REFERENCES:

Dillard, J. L. *All-American English*. New York: Random House, 1975. Good on pidgin English and frontier speech.

——. *American Talk: Where Our Words Came From*. New York: Random House, 1976. Good sections on cowboys, mountain men, and gamblers.

Mencken, H. L. *The American Language*. New York: Alfred A. Knopf, 1986. Valuable for understanding the development of American English.

Wentworth, Harold, and Stuart Berg Flexner. *Dictionary of American Slang*. New York: Thomas Y. Crowell Company, 1975. Second supplemented edition.

Weseen, Maurice. *A Dictionary of American Slang*. New York: Thomas Y. Crowell Company, 1934.

Chapman, Robert L. *New Dictionary of American Slang*. New York: Harper & Row, 1986.

Adams, Ramon F. *The Cowman Says It Salty*. Tucson: University of Arizona Press, 1971.

——. *Cowboy Lingo*. Boston: Houghton Mifflin, 1936.

McCullough, Walter F. *Woods Words: A Comprehensive Dictionary of Loggers Terms*. Portland: Oregon Historical Society, 1958.

McDermott, John Francis. *A Glossary of Mississippi Valley French, 1673-1850*. St. Louis: Washington University Press, 1941.

Morrow, Baker H. *Dictionary of Landscape Architecture*. Albuquerque: University of New Mexico Press, 1987. Useful for definitions of landscape forms in the Southwest.

Ford-Robertson, F. C., ed. *Terminology of Forest Science, Technology, Practice and Products*. Washington, D. C.: Society of American Foresters, 1971.

Potter, Edgar. *Cowboy Slang*. Seattle: Hangman Press, Superior Publishing Co., 1971.

REFERENCE ABOUT INDIAN PEOPLES:

Sturtevant, William C., and Alfonso Ortiz. *Handbook of North American Indians*. Washington, D. C.: Smithsonian Institution, 1983. A remarkable and authoritative resource.

Hodge, Frederick W. *Handbook of Indians North of Mexico*. Washington, D. C.: Bureau of American Ethnology, 1912. Two volumes. (Available currently in several reprints.)

REFERENCES ON LAND FORMS AND PLANTS:

Audubon Society. *Deserts*. New York: Alfred A. Knopf, 1985.

Craighead, John J., Frank C. Craighead, Jr., and Ray J. Davis. *A Field Guide to Rocky Mountain Flowers*. Boston: Houghton Mifflin Company, 1963.

FURTHER EXPLORATION OF THE LIBRARY: THE READER SHOULD ROAM THROUGH FIRST-RATE HISTORIES OF THE WEST BY WESTERNERS. THESE BRIEF RECOMMENDATIONS ARE MEANT ONLY AS STARTING POINTS:

On cowboys: of many, many works, particularly helpful are David Dary's *Cowboy Culture* and Jo Mora's *Trail Dust and Saddle Leather*.

On Indians: of many, many works, start with George Bird Grinnell's *The Cheyenne Indians,* Robert Lowie's *Indians of the Plains,* Clyde Kluckhohn and Dorothea Leighton's *The Navajo,* and Dee Brown's *Bury My Heart at Wounded Knee.*

On mountain men: Bernard De Voto's *Across the Wide Missouri,* David Lavender's *Bent's Fort,* and Winfred Blevins's *Give Your Heart to the Hawks.*

On Mormons: Wallace Stegner's *The Gathering of Zion* and *Mormon Country.*

On Texas and the Southwest: the works of J. Frank Dobie.

On gamblers: Herbert Asbury's *The Sucker's Progress.*

On growing up Western in the first half of the twentieth century: David Lavender's *One Man's West.*

THE JOURNALS, MEMOIRS, AND AS-TOLD-TO BIOGRAPHIES OF WESTERNERS ARE A TREASURE TROVE. EXAMPLES:

On the lives of women in the West, see works by Frances Anne Mullen Boyd, Elizabeth Custer, Martha Farnsworth, Alice Kirk Grierson, Martha Summerhayes, and Teresa Griffin Viclé.

On the lives of Indians, see the narratives of Black Elk, Plenty Coups, Pretty Shield, Son of Old Man Hat, Don Talayesva, and Two Leggings.

On cowboys and trail drives, look for the recollections of Teddy Blue Abott, Charlie Siringo, Andy Adams, and Charlie Russell.

On mountain men, see works by James Clyman, Warren Angus Ferris, Josiah Gregg, Joe Meek, James Ohio Pattie, and Osborne Russell.

Various Mormons, Indian traders, travelers on the Oregon Trail, miners, and others have also left their recollections and much of their language; the opportunities for rambling are vast.

In addition, the better works of fiction are worthwhile, particularly those by A. B. Guthrie, Jr., Vardis Fisher, Will Henry, Oliver La Farge, Frederick Manfred, Jack Schaefer, James Willard Schultz, Wallace Stegner, and, for the modern Southwest, Edward Abbey.

THROUGHOUT THE TEXT I'VE REFERRED TO A FEW WRITERS BY NAME OR LAST NAME ONLY, WITHOUT TITLE.

Adams is Ramon F. Adams (*Cowboy Lingo* and *Western Words*); **Clark** is Thomas L. Clark (*Western Lore and Language*); **Mathews** is Mitford M. Mathews (*A Dictionary of Americanisms*); Smith is Cornelius Cole Smith (*A Southwestern Vocabulary*); and **Watts** is Peter Watts (*A Dictionary of the Old West*).